THE GREATEST STORIES OF THE BIBLE

Devotional Writings
by Dr. Philip Patterson

New Century Version

NCV
NEW CENTURY VERSION®

THOMAS NELSON
Since 1798

NASHVILLE DALLAS MEXICO CITY RIO DE JANEIRO BEIJING

www.thomasnelson.com

TABLE OF CONTENTS

OLD TESTAMENT

1. Genesis 1:1–13 ....Living in the Light 1
2. Genesis 1:14–31 ....In His Image 3
3. Genesis 2:4–22 ....Powerful and Present...........................5
4. Genesis 3:1–13, 22–24 ....Know Your Enemy 7
5. Genesis 4:1–16 ....Giving Our Best 9
6. Genesis 6:1–22 ....Perfect Timing....................................11
7. Genesis 7:1–24 ....The Great Escape 13
8. Genesis 8:1–21 ....Living Sacrifices..................................15
9. Genesis 8:21—9:2, 8–17.............The God of Promises 17
10. Genesis 11:1–9 ....One Voice...19
11. Genesis 12:1–9 ....Just Visiting 21
12. Genesis 13:1–18 ....Living Near Sodom 23
13. Genesis 14:8–24 ....Designed for a Purpose 25
14. Genesis 15:1–21 ....Living by Faith 27
15. Genesis 16:1–6; 21:1–3, 9–18 ....Color-Blind 29
16. Genesis 18:1–16 ....Pray First 31
17. Genesis 18:16–33 ....Taking Part in God's Plan 33
18. Genesis 19:1–3, 12–25...............Look Forward to His Coming..............35
19. Genesis 20:1–18 ....Forgetting God's Promises...................37
20. Genesis 21:1–21 ....A Bigger Problem Later......................39
21. Genesis 22:1–19 ....Giving up Everything..........................41
22. Genesis 23:1–20 ....Earning Respect...................................43
23. Genesis 24:1–4, 9–27.................Where's Your Umbrella? 45
24. Genesis 24:28–40, 50–58...........Clearly from the LORD 47
25. Genesis 25:19–34 ....God Is Enough.....................................49
26. Genesis 26:1–18 ....More Powerful Than Words................51
27. Genesis 27:1–24 ....Questionable Motives..........................53
28. Genesis 27:25–41 ....Blessing the Next Generation..............55

29. Genesis 27:42—28:5 ....Our Permanent Home 57

30. Genesis 28:10–22 ....Finding His Presence.................................59

31. Genesis 29:1–14 ....Trusting God's Provision 61

32. Genesis 28:1–5; 29:16–30...........Persistent Love...63

33. Genesis 29:31—30:13, 17–24 ....A New Name 65

34. Genesis 30:25–43 ....In God's Hands 67

35. Genesis 31:1–18 ....God's Family 69

36. Genesis 31:22–29, 43–50............Living in Harmony 71

37. Genesis 32:1–20 ....Praying Boldly...73

38. Genesis 32:22–32 ....Wrestling with God..................................75

39. Genesis 33:1–20 ....Making Things Right................................77

40. Genesis 35:1–15 ....Who Moved?...79

41. Genesis 37:1–17 ....Following God's Dreams 81

42. Genesis 37:18–36; 39:1–2...........A Step in the Right Direction 83

43. Genesis 39:3–23 ....Tough Lessons...85

44. Genesis 40:1–23 ....Forgotten Kindness 87

45. Genesis 41:1–16 ....Solvable Problems.....................................89

46. Genesis 41:17–36 ....Feed the World..91

47. Genesis 41:39–57 ....The Lure of Prosperity 93

48. Genesis 42:1–22 ....Desperate Measures..................................95

49. Genesis 42:23–38 ....Appreciating What You Earn 97

50. Genesis 43:1–17 ....The Pain of Separation..............................99

51. Genesis 43:18–34 ....The Importance of Patience....................101

52. Genesis 44:1–18, 30–34..............Looking into the Heart 103

53. Genesis 45:1–11 ...."Why Am I Here?" 105

54. Genesis 45:16—46:7 ....Daring Faith...107

55. Genesis 46:26—47:12.................Droughts and Showers 109

56. Genesis 47:13–26 ....Use Your Time for God's Work.................111

57. Genesis 47:27—48:5,
    7–14, 17–19 ....Last Request 113

58. Genesis 49:28—50:11.................The Right Blessing....................................115

59. Genesis 50:12–26 ....Turning Evil into Good.............................117

60. Exodus 1:1–21 .... Resolved Witnesses for God 119

61. Exodus 1:8–10, 22—2:10 .... Finding Our Mission 121

62. Exodus 2:11–25 .... Forgive and Forget 123

63. Exodus 3:1–15 .... Holy Ground 125

64. Exodus 4:1–16 .... Bring Your Strengths *and* Weaknesses 127

65. Exodus 5:1–21 .... Choose Straw or Worship 129

66. Genesis 5:22—6:13 .... He Looks for the Moldable 131

67. Exodus 6:26—7:13 .... Representing God 133

68. Exodus 7:14–25 .... Ignoring God's Miracles 135

69. Exodus 8:1–15 .... Stubbornness Wins 137

70. Exodus 8:16–32 .... Even the Tiniest of Beings 139

71. Exodus 9:1–12 .... Learning from Suffering 141

72. Exodus 9:13–35 .... The Supreme God 143

73. Exodus 10:1–11 .... A Hardened Heart 145

74. Exodus 10:12–29 .... Momentary Repentance 147

75. Exodus 11:1–10 .... No One Is Innocent 149

76. Exodus 12:1–5, 11–15, 21–30 .... In Remembrance 151

77. Exodus 12:31–42; 13:17–22 .... Short Notice 153

78. Exodus 13:1–16 .... God's Firstborn 155

79. Exodus 14:1–14 .... Fast Horses 157

80. Exodus 14:15–31 .... Lessons of the Desert 159

81. Exodus 15:22–27; 17:1–7 .... The LORD Is with Us 161

82. Exodus 16:1–18, 31 .... Daily Provisions 163

83. Exodus 17:8–16 .... Working Together 165

84. Exodus 18:1, 5–9, 13–26 .... Learning to Delegate 167

85. Exodus 19:1–9, 14–22 .... His Own Possession 169

86. Exodus 20:1–20 .... Marginalizing God's Law 171

87. Exodus 24:1–18 .... Symbolic Blood 173

88. Exodus 32:1–16 .... A God Who Changes His Mind? 175

89. Exodus 33:11–23; 34:29–35 .... Ever Greater Glory 177

90. Exodus 34:1–14 .... God Is Faithful 179

91. Exodus 35:4–9, 20–24; 36:3–7 ... Sacrificial Giving 181

92. Exodus 40:1–17, 34–38 ....God's Dwelling Place 183

93. Leviticus 8:1–4, 14–21 ....Sweet-Smelling..................................185

94. Leviticus 10:1–7 ....True Worship 187

95. Numbers 11:4–13, 18–23,
    31–32....................................Accepting God's Answers 189

96. Numbers 12:1–15.......................Handling Criticism 191

97. Numbers 13:1–2, 17–33 ....Giants in the Land 193

98. Numbers 14:1–10, 26–35 ....Wishing for Slavery 195

99. Numbers 15:27–36 ....A Time of Renewal....................................197

100. Numbers 16:1–5, 12–14,
     20–33...................................A Life of Submission 199

101. Numbers 16:41—17:11 ....Fruit-Bearing Followers 201

102. Numbers 20:1–13; 27:12–14;
     Deuteronomy 34:1–5 ....Honor the Holiness of God 203

103. Numbers 20:22–29 ....Second Fiddle 205

104. Numbers 21:1–9.........................Victory over Death....................................207

105. Numbers 22:1–19........................Selling Out 209

106. Numbers 22:20–35.....................Unexpected Messengers............................211

107. Numbers 22:36—23:12 ....A Nonnegotiable Message 213

108. Numbers 25:1–18........................Sin's Destructive Power............................215

109. Numbers 27:12–23;
     Deuteronomy 34:1–9 ....Leadership Qualities................................217

110. Numbers 31:1–12, 48–54 ....Gifts from God 219

111. Numbers 32:1–24.......................Faithful to the End....................................221

112. Joshua 1:1–11, 16–18 ....Nothing to Fear..223

113. Joshua 2:1–14 ....The Red Cord of Salvation 225

114. Joshua 3:1–17 ....Tomorrow Holds Hope............................227

115. Joshua 4:1–24 ....Monuments to God's Faithfulness............229

116. Joshua 5:1–15 ....God's Mark on Us....................................231

117. Joshua 6:1–21 ....Victory Comes from God 233

118. Joshua 7:1–15 ....Throw Away Sin..235

119. Joshua 7:16—8:2........................The Same Inside and Out........................237

120. Joshua 8:3–22 ....By Their Own Might 239

121. Joshua 9:3–23 ....Depend on God 241

122. Joshua 10:1–15 ....Powerful Prayer 243

123. Joshua 10:28–43 ....Our God Will Fight for Us 245

124. Joshua 14:6–15 ....Hill Country 247

125. Joshua 24:14–29 ....Salvation Only through God 249

126. Judges 2:6–22 ....Teach Your Children 251

127. Judges 3:12–30 ....Condemned to Repeat It 253

128. Judges 6:11–24 ....Not Our Own Strength 255

129. Judges 6:25–40 ....Knowing What God Wants 257

130. Judges 7:1–15 ....The True Source of Victories 259

131. Judges 7:16—8:3 ....Ongoing Idolatry 261

132. Judges 8:22–35 ....Satan's Earrings 263

133. Judges 11:1–9, 29–39 ....No Deals Required 265

134. Judges 15:1–15 ....Righteous Anger 267

135. Judges 16:4–20 ....Reckless with God's Gifts 269

136. Judges 16:21–31 ....Your "Esther Moment" 271

137. Ruth 1:1–17 ....Love That Knows No Borders 273

138. Ruth 2:1–12 ....Paid in Full 275

139. Ruth 3:1–18 ....Ruth's Redeemer 277

140. Ruth 4:1–17 ....From Bitterness to Joy 279

141. 1 Samuel 1:2–3, 9–20, 24–28 .....No Hesitation 281

142. 1 Samuel 3:1–21 ....A Message from God 283

143. 1 Samuel 4:1–18 ....Decisions and Consequences 285

144. 1 Samuel 7:2–17 ....Ebenezer Stones 287

145. 1 Samuel 8:1–22 ....Our Only King 289

146. 1 Samuel 9:17–21; 10:1–7 ....Humble Beginnings 291

147. 1 Samuel 10:9–27 ....Changed Hearts 293

148. 1 Samuel 15:1–3, 7–10, 13–22 ...God Prefers Obedience 295

149. 1 Samuel 16:1–13 ....Idols of Flesh and Blood 297

150. 1 Samuel 17:1–24 ....Defeat through Discouragement 299

151. 1 Samuel 17:32–51 ....The Right "Armor" 301

152. 1 Samuel 18:1–16, 28–30 ....Consumed with Envy 303

153. 1 Samuel 20:1–17......................Be a "Jonathan" 305

154. 1 Samuel 26:7–24......................Rewarded for Loyalty 307

155. 1 Samuel 31:1–10......................Crowding Out God's Presence.................309

156. 2 Samuel 2:8–12, 17—3:1..........Seeking Unity..311

157. 2 Samuel 6:1–8..........................Brain Freeze...313

158. 2 Samuel 7:1–17........................Be Content with Your Part........................315

159. 2 Samuel 9:1–13........................Debts of Gratitude 317

160. 2 Samuel 11:1–17......................"Nicked Up" Individuals...........................319

161. 2 Samuel 12:1–18......................An Eternal Solution...................................321

162. 2 Samuel 18:1–17......................Deadly Trees..323

163. 2 Samuel 24:1–16......................Not by Might...325

164. 1 Kings 1:5–25 ....Keeping God on Your Guest List.............327

165. 1 Kings 1:28–35, 49–53; 2:1–4...Our Faithful God..329

166. 1 Kings 3:4–9, 16–27.................Losing Sight of What Is Precious 331

167. 1 Kings 6:1–6, 11–14.................A Temple for God.......................................333

168. 1 Kings 11:1–13 ....Trading Convictions for Compromises.....335

169. 1 Kings 11:27–40 ....The Right Frame of Mind 337

170. 1 Kings 11:42—12:15.................Who Do You Run With? 339

171. 1 Kings 12:20–33 ....Not My People..341

172. 1 Kings 17:1–22 ....Give What You Have 343

173. 1 Kings 18:1–21 ....Deciding between Two Choices 345

174. 1 Kings 18:22–40 ....Chasing False Gods....................................347

175. 1 Kings 19:1–14 ....Don't Give Up...349

176. 1 Kings 21:1–19 ....Life–Destroying Lies 351

177. 1 Kings 22:1–9, 13–17................Hearing What We Want to Hear 353

178. 1 Kings 22:18–38 ....Gambling with the Truth 355

179. 2 Kings 2:1–15 ....Taking up the Cloak 357

180. 2 Kings 2:11–22 ....Those Who Have Gone Before.................359

181. 2 Kings 4:1–7 ....God Will Provide 361

182. 2 Kings 4:18–37 ....God's Power over Death............................363

183. 2 Kings 4:38–44; 6:1–6...............Preaching without Words..........................365

184. 2 Kings 5:1–14 ....The Message That Sounds Foolish............367

185. 2 Kings 5:15–27 ....Restored in the End 369

186. 2 Kings 6:8–23 ....Right There with Us..................................371

187. 2 Kings 6:24–31; 7:1–9.............Don't Remain Silent! 373

188. 2 Kings 9:1–10, 30–37...............Justice in the End......................................375

189. 2 Kings 10:17–33 ....Diminished by Sin 377

190. 2 Chronicles 26:3–10, 16–21......Just a Man..379

191. 2 Kings 17:1–18 ....Becoming Useless 381

192. 2 Chronicles 31:20—32:8,
     20–22....................................Three Steps...383

193. 2 Kings 20:1–11 ....Our True Home 385

194. 2 Kings 22:1–11; 23:1–3............A Temple Not Built by Human Hands.....387

195. 2 Kings 22:1–13 ....Preserve That Which Is Precious 389

196. 2 Kings 23:4–7, 21–30...............The Price of Sin 391

197. 2 Kings 24:18—25:12.................When Did the Love Go Out? 393

198. Ezra 2:64—3:6, 10–13 ....Finding the "New Normal".......................395

199. Nehemiah 2:1–7, 11–17.............Walls for Spiritual Protection 397

200. Nehemiah 4:1–20 ....Fighting for What's Right..........................399

201. Nehemiah 6:15–16; 7:1–3;
     8:1–3, 9–14 ....Spiritual Erosion......................................401

202. Esther 1:1–15 ....A Life That Demands an Explanation.......403

203. Esther 3:1–14 ....Come Humbly or Not at All.....................405

204. Esther 4:1–14 ....For Just Such a Time................................407

205. Esther 4:15—5:8; 7:1–6.............The Path of Bravery 409

206. Job 1:1–12 ....More Than Fair 411

207. Job 2:1–10 ....Bless God to the End 413

208. Job 38:1–7, 12–18.....................Remember Who God Is............................415

209. Job 42:1–6, 10–16.....................Waiting on God 417

210. Isaiah 6:1–11 ...."Here I am…Send Me!" 419

211. Jeremiah 38:1–13 ....Bitter or Better?.......................................421

212. Ezekiel 37:1–14 ....New Life..423

213. Daniel 1:1–16...........................Your Body Is a Temple 425

214. Daniel 2:1–12, 24......................God Is Near..427

215. Daniel 3:1–18 ....But Even If... 429

216. Daniel 3:19–30 ....There beside You 431

217. Daniel 5:1–7, 13–17, 23–31 ....Measured and Weighed 433

218. Daniel 6:1–12 ....Obeying God's Laws 435

219. Daniel 6:13–26 ....Only Pure Worship 437

220. Hosea 1:1–9; 3:1–5 ....Harvest the Storm 439

221. Joel 1:1–4, 10–11; 2:12–14 ....Blessings or Locusts? 441

222. Jonah 1:1–17 ....Running from God's Will 443

223. Jonah 3:3–10; 4:5–11 ....Priorities on a Lifeboat 445

224. Micah 6:6–8 ....Our Offering to God 447

New Testament

225. Luke 1:5–25 ....Too Difficult for God? 449

226. Luke 1:26–45 ....Take God at His Word 451

227. Luke 1:39–66 ....Big Promises 453

228. Matthew 1:16–25 ....Unquestioning Faith 455

229. Luke 2:1–21 ....Opportunities or Obstacles? 457

230. Luke 2:22–40 ....Waiting for the Messiah 459

231. Matthew 2:1–15 ....Give God Your Best 461

232. Matthew 2:1–16 ....Saved by His Blood 463

233. Luke 2:41–52 ....In My Father's House 465

234. Mark 1:1–15 ....Preparing for Another's Success 467

235. Matthew 4:1–11 ....Don't Play the Enemy's Game 469

236. Matthew 5:1–16 ....The Sacrifice Seems Lighter 471

237. Luke 5:1–11, 27–32 ....Welcome at His Table 473

238. John 1:35–51 ....The Humble Messiah 475

239. John 2:1–11 ....In His Name 477

240. Matthew 21:12–17;
     John 2:12–17 ....Instructive Discipline 479

241. John 3:1–21 ....Simple Wisdom 481

242. John 4:5–26 ....In Spirit and in Truth 483

243. John 4:27–42 .... Seeing the Harvest 485

244. Luke 4:14–30 .... Peace or a Sword 487

245. John 4:43–54 .... Believing Jesus' Words 489

246. Matthew 7:18–29 .... Built to Withstand the Storms 491

247. Matthew 8:1–4 .... Retying Loose Ends 493

248. Luke 7:1–10 .... Physical and Spiritual Healing 495

249. Mark 4:30–41 .... Mustard Seed Faith 497

250. Mark 5:1–20 .... His Power Is Greater 499

251. Matthew 8:28–34 .... Potential Beauty 501

252. Mark 2:1–17 .... The Opportunity Gate 503

253. Luke 5:17–26 .... Your Sins Are Forgiven 505

254. John 5:1–18 .... A Healthy Faith 507

255. Mark 2:23—3:6 .... The God of the Sabbath 509

256. Luke 7:11–17 .... A God Who Helps 511

257. Luke 7:36–50 .... Forgiven of Much 513

258. Matthew 13:1–13, 18–23 .... Rocky Ground 515

259. Matthew 13:24–30, 36–43 .... A Good Harvest 517

260. Mark 5:21–42 .... Nothing to Lose 519

261. Matthew 9:27–38 .... Workers to Gather His Harvest 521

262. Matthew 10:1–22 .... Search for the Lost 523

263. Matthew 14:1–12 .... Truth and Consequences 525

264. John 6:1–15 .... Small but Significant 527

265. Matthew 14:22–36 .... Keep Looking Forward 529

266. Matthew 15:21–31 .... Overcoming Prejudice 531

267. Mark 7:24–37 .... Intentional Obscurity 533

268. Mark 8:1–21 .... No Reason to Worry 535

269. Mark 8:22–33 .... May God Open Our Eyes 537

270. Matthew 16:13–23 .... "Who Do You Say I Am?" 539

271. Luke 9:23–36 .... Taking Jesus Seriously 541

272. Mark 9:14–29 .... Only by Prayer 543

273. Matthew 17:24–27 .... A Room Prepared for Me 545

274. Luke 17:11–19 .... A Higher Calling 547

275. John 8:1–11 ....Throwing Stones 549

276. John 9:1–15 ....Who Sinned? 551

277. John 9:18–41 ....Now I See 553

278. Mark 9:33–42 ....Come as a Child 555

279. Matthew 19:16–30 ....A Hole in Your Swing 557

280. Luke 10:1–20 ....Culture Shock 559

281. Luke 10:25–37 ....Limitation of Liability 561

282. Luke 11:1–13 ....Approaching God Boldly 563

283. Mark 10:35–45 ....Drinking the Cup God Offers 565

284. Mark 10:46–52 ...."I Can't See My Sins" 567

285. Luke 10:38—11:13 ....A Prayer Away 569

286. John 11:1–7, 20–28, 33–44 ...."Where Are You, God?" 571

287. Luke 12:13–34 ....Lasting Treasures 573

288. Luke 13:6–21 ....Human Rules vs. True Goodness 575

289. Luke 14:7–24 ....A Seat at the Table 577

290. Luke 15:1–10 ....Rare and Valuable 579

291. Luke 15:11–25, 28–32 ....A Second Chance 581

292. Luke 16:19—17:4 ....Heaven's Currency 583

293. Matthew 18:21–35 ....Patient and Forgiving 585

294. Luke 18:1–14 ....Persistence and God's Timetable 587

295. Luke 18:9–17 ....Being Genuine with God 589

296. Luke 18:35—19:10 ....Jesus' Invitation 591

297. Mark 11:1–11, 15–19 ....Teachable Moments 593

298. Matthew 20:1–16 ....The Early Workers 595

299. Matthew 21:33–46 ....Plotting against God 597

300. Matthew 22:1–14 ....Wedding Clothes 599

301. Matthew 22:15–33 ....An Agreement Stronger than Death 601

302. Mark 12:28–40 ....Obedience First, Then Sacrifice 603

303. Matthew 25:1–13 ....Closed Doors 605

304. Matthew 25:14–30 ....Two-Bag People 607

305. Matthew 25:31–46 ....Faithful Repetition 609

306. Mark 12:35–44 ....Press Releases 611

307. Luke 22:1–6..............................What's Your Price?.....................................613

308. Luke 22:7–13............................The Passover Lamb 615

309. John 13:1–20.............................Leading with a Servant's Heart.................617

310. Matthew 26:26–30; Acts 20:7;
     1 Corinthians 11:23–26 ....A Ritual of Remembrance........................619

311. John 13:21–38...........................Denying Our Lord....................................621

312. John 14:1–24.............................Final Instructions 623

313. Mark 14:32–42..........................A Spirit/Body Problem............................625

314. Luke 22:1–6, 14–23, 47–51........The Betrayal..627

315. John 18:1–11;
     Matthew 26:52–56......................Ignoring the Miraculous...........................629

316. Matthew 26:31–35, 57–58,
     69–75..Stages of Denial...631

317. Matthew 26:47–50; 27:1–10 ......A Legacy of a Traitor 633

318. Luke 22:63—23:12 ....The Most Important Question 635

319. Matthew 27:11–31 ....Washing Our Hands 637

320. Mark 15:16–24;
     Matthew 27:50–54......................Decision Time..639

321. Mark 15:21–39...........................Freed from Slavery 641

322. Mark 15:40–47;
     Matthew 27:62–66......................Waiting for the Kingdom.........................643

323. John 20:1–18 ....The Only Empty Tomb 645

324. Mark 15:40—16:8......................The Best Ending 647

325. Matthew 28:1–15 ....The Evidence of Faith 649

326. John 20:19–31 ....Believing without Seeing..........................651

327. Luke 24:13–35...........................Seeing Jesus 653

328. John 20:26—21:14......................Gone Fishing...655

329. John 21:20–22 ...."Follow Me"..657

330. Luke 24:45–53;
     Acts 1:1–3, 6–11.........................Taken up to Heaven..................................659

331. Acts 2:43–47; 4:32–37; 6:1–7.....Sharing Everything...................................661

332. Acts 3:1–16...............................Newfound Boldness 663

333. Acts 4:1–22...............................Daily Miracles 665

334. Acts 4:32—5:11............................Real Generosity 667

335. Acts 5:12–30 ....Faith and Adversity 669

336. Acts 5:27–42 ....Living Proof 671

337. Acts 6:8—7:1, 51–60 ....Martyr or Fraud? 673

338. Acts 8:5–25 ....Casual Christianity............................675

339. Acts 8:26–40 ....Immediate Responses 677

340. Acts 9:1–19 ....Finding the Will of God 679

341. Acts 9:19–31 ....Finding Acceptance 681

342. Acts 9:32–43 ....Called to Be Different 683

343. Acts 10:1–23 ....The Prayer of a Sinner 685

344. Acts 10:24–36..............................Jesus, the Lord of *All* People............687

345. Acts 11:1–18 ....Evidence of Conversion.....................689

346. Acts 12:1–23 ....Praying Hard 691

347. Acts 14:8–28 ....Suffering with Christ.........................693

348. Acts 15:1–11, 30–31; 16:1–5......Insignificant Distinctions 695

349. Acts 16:16–39..............................The Source of All Joy 697

350. Acts 17:16–34..............................The Unknown God 699

351. Acts 19:23–41..............................Bad for Business 701

352. Acts 20:1–12 ....Carefully Examine the Truth.............703

353. Acts 20:13–17; 21:1–16 ....Undeterred by Consequences....................705

354. Acts 21:27–40; 22:22–29 ....Giving up Freedom 707

355. Acts 23:12–35..............................The Right Man for the Job 709

356. Acts 24:1–16, 22–25 ....No Time for the Truth 711

357. Acts 24:27—25:12 ....Every Circumstance Is Useful...................713

358. Acts 25:13—26:8..........................Always Ready 715

359. Acts 26:9–32................................Stop Resisting....................................717

360. Acts 27:1, 4–26............................Storms of Life 719

361. Acts 27:27–44..............................Working within God's Providence.............721

362. Acts 28:1–16, 30–31 ....The Purpose behind Our Trials................723

363. Colossians 4:5–18........................Spiritual Ancestors............................725

364. Philemon 1:1–21 ....From Slavery to Freedom 727

365. Revelation 20:11—21:5 ....No More Tears 729

INTRODUCTION

AT ITS HEART, THE BIBLE IS A STORY—but not just any story. The Bible is the great love story of an almighty God's desire to have a relationship with men and women, people he made in his own image. At the start of the story, he has that relationship with Adam and Eve in the perfect setting of the Garden of Eden. Then the relationship is severed. By the end of the story, God has restored the hope of a relationship with men and women once again, but this opportunity for reconciliation has come at unimaginable cost to God.

This book is meant to tell that story in 365 parts, one a day for the next year. As a journalist by training, I read the Bible with an editor's eye for a good story. The soul of good writing is a good story, and the Bible is full of plots and subplots, all leading to the grand reconciliation, played out by real characters, many of whom never even realized their roles in the story.

Teachers of writing tell their students that all of the great stories have at their core a central question that is answered only after the complicating factors are worked through. Will Dorothy get home to Kansas? Will Ahab land his whale? Will Alice escape Wonderland? Will Peter Pan have to grow up? Will King Arthur see a peaceful Camelot? Good stories are timeless because the questions are timeless. All of us are Dorothy, longing for home and all it means. All of us are Ahab, trying to land that one spectacular accomplishment that will define a lifetime of toil.

Like any good story, the Bible has a central question. The burning question of the entire Bible story is this: *Can fallen humans make their way back to God?* Or, stated another way: *Can the sons and daughters of Adam and Eve ever live in the new garden?*

Like any good story, the Bible has plot twists and suspense and plenty of interesting characters. The story begins when sin separates humans from God. Even as the Garden of Eden is emptied of its occupants, God puts into motion the opportunity for us to join him in a new garden called heaven. But much has to happen before this glorious reunion between God and his creation can occur.

Those of us who grew up in Sunday school heard the stories—Noah and the Ark, Jonah and the Whale, the Wise Men, etc. However, I think some of us need to be reminded why they were divinely included in the text of the Bible.

But more than that, I think we've failed to see The Story…the overall narrative of the Bible beginning in the Garden of Eden and continuing through the Cross, the Resurrection, and the attempts of the first-century followers of Jesus to keep the message of the risen Christ alive for you and me today.

These 365 stories contain that journey from Eden to heaven and answer the Bible's central question in a way that gives hope even for those of us who get stuck in the laws or the genealogies when reading the Bible.

You know the end of the story, but you need to be reminded of the journey. You need to watch as God helps prostitutes, adulterers, and murderers to rise above their weaknesses and fulfill their roles in moving the story forward. You need to be reminded that the Son of God not only spent most of his brief time on earth with unlearned disciples and unwashed masses—he was comfortable with them. Even in the home of a rich man, he praised the chaste hospitality of the interloping prostitute over the actions of his wealthy host.

But most importantly, you need to be told that The Story is not over. It's repeated every day when a man or a woman leaves his or her life of sin and turns to the One who called himself the way, the truth and the life and who claimed that "the only way to the Father is through me" (John 15:6). The same path he offered the sinners in these stories is still available to you today.

Can you enjoy a story even when you know the ending? I think so. I'm a sucker for "The Wizard of Oz" every time it's shown on television. I've read *To Kill a Mockingbird* four times. I like the first for the journey and the second for the strong characters.

Even if you think you know The Story, please read the stories again. Acquaint yourself with some of the most interesting characters in the history of literature. See what God can do with Moses the stutterer when he needs a leader for his people. See Rahab the harlot risk her life and then turn it around so dramatically that she joins the lineage of Christ. See God both punish David for his sin and then call him "beloved." See the irony of Paul—a killer of Christians—becoming the writer of most of the letters to the churches.

Discovering the subplots will bring new joy to this journey through the Bible. See God distribute responsibility for the survival of humanity between eight people on a giant boat. See God put the future deliverance of his chosen people in the hands of a baby floating down the Nile in a basket. See God place the hope for the salvation of all humanity in a manger in a stable surrounded by livestock.

So let's make 365 appointments to read the stories that make up The Story. The parts are truly as important as the whole. The New Testament tells us that the stories are there to be our "hope" (Romans 15:4), our "example" (1 Corinthians 10:11), and our "guardian" (Galatians 3:24). As we read them together, they will lead us to "have great wisdom and understanding in spiritual things so that you will live the kind of life that honors and pleases the Lord in every way" (Colossians 1:9–10).

My prayer is that by reacquainting you with The Story, you will discover its Author and his purpose for your life.

PERHAPS I WAS THE ONLY CUSTOMER who saw the irony in the sign at the bookstore: "Self-Improvement, Bargain Priced," it said in bold letters. Below were dozens of forgettable books on getting thinner, getting richer, living longer, becoming a better parent, a better negotiator (perhaps parents needed that one even more than the prior) and getting out of debt…just to name a few of the ways one might "self-improve." Most of the books cost less than $10.

It was the last business day of the year, and an entire new cadre of self-improvement books by the latest gurus were already on the shelves just in time for the season of New Year's resolutions, so the old books with their old ideas had to go. Now it was time for "new ideas" on how to be younger, wealthier, and happier. Next year, these books will undoubtedly move over to "Self-Improvement, Bargain Priced."

But one "self-improvement" book has never gone out of style. In fact, it's never gone out of print. No book has ever rivaled it in sales or popularity. And the good news is that you're holding it (in part): it's the Bible—God's instruction book on how we can become transformed into his children! In it, you can learn how to be happy from Solomon, how to be patient from Job, how to overcome disappointment with yourself from David. In truth, the Bible isn't merely another "self-improvement" book at all. Instead, this Book reveals God's ability and desire to improve us with his infinite love and power.

Instead of reading another book about improving yourself, try reading the Book that tells the story of how God can improve you. If you'd like to make the reading of this story a daily habit, I applaud you. It will change your life. And if you're thinking about using this book for that purpose, let me tell you a little about it.

As one who has failed over and over to read the entire Bible in a calendar year, I decided that perhaps folks like me could read a story a day with a short application. So I set out to find a Bible story for every day of the year—no genealogies, no Jewish laws, no letters—just stories. And there were plenty, each of them a piece in the overall puzzle of how sinful humans can reunite with a holy God.

A word about the way the book is put together. Not all of the stories are of equal length. But to keep our time together of equal length each day, I will quote the heart of the story and refer you to the original text for further reading. Some stories will last more than one day; others are omitted as repetitive of stories already included in the book. Each story will have an application, often a modern day analogy that applies the ancient story to modern living. The day ends with one or two thoughts to ponder, followed by a prayer. If you keep a diary, perhaps the thoughts to ponder will be a starting point for your daily entries.

But let me leave you with a warning: true improvement is never "bargain priced." When Jesus said, "Follow me," he didn't allow his followers to look back. The road ahead promised to be hard, but the destination would be worth the journey, just like an exhilarating hike to an awesome scenic view—only this hike lasts a lifetime and the view is for all eternity.

Philip Patterson
December 31, 2005

LIVING IN THE LIGHT

GENESIS 1:1–13

1 In the beginning God created the sky and the earth. ²The earth was empty and had no form. Darkness covered the ocean, and God's Spirit was moving over the water.

³Then God said, "Let there be light," and there was light. ⁴God saw that the light was good, so he divided the light from the darkness. ⁵God named the light "day" and the darkness "night." Evening passed, and morning came. This was the first day.

⁶Then God said, "Let there be something to divide the water in two." ⁷So God made the air and placed some of the water above the air and some below it. ⁸God named the air "sky." Evening passed, and morning came. This was the second day.

⁹Then God said, "Let the water under the sky be gathered together so the dry land will appear." And it happened. ¹⁰God named the dry land "earth" and the water that was gathered together "seas." God saw that this was good.

¹¹Then God said, "Let the earth produce plants—some to make grain for seeds and others to make fruits with seeds in them. Every seed will produce more of its own kind of plant." And it happened. ¹²The earth produced plants with grain for seeds and trees that made fruits with seeds in them. Each seed grew its own kind of plant. God saw that all this was good. ¹³Evening passed, and morning came. This was the third day.

DEVOTION

PERHAPS YOU'RE READING this story on the first day of a New Year. Whether or not that's the case, think for a moment about this event in time—the original New Year's Day. "In the beginning God . . ." Four of the most powerful words in all of history. In fact, history begins with those words.

I think there's a great deal of symbolism in the fact that the first act of creation was the separation of light from dark. In a literal sense, it means God created day and night. But I see a symbolic reading in that first act of creation. You see, God has always been about dividing the darkness from the light.

Jesus, in a conversation with Nicodemus recorded in John 3:19, says his coming is like a light illuminating a dark world. Speaking of himself, he says, "The Light has come into the world, but they did not want light. They wanted darkness, because they were doing evil things."

Light chases out darkness. Every sunrise since creation has chased away the night. Turn on a light in the darkest room in your house and the darkness leaves immediately. That's why Jesus says to his followers, "You are the light that gives light to the world," followed with the admonition, "You should be a light for other people. Live so that they will see the good things you do and will praise your Father in heaven" (Matthew 5:14, 16).

Jesus compared his followers to a light that would illuminate the entire house, or a city set high on a hill—it simply cannot be hidden. John describes the Christian life as living "in the light, as God is in the light" (1 John 1:7).

Perhaps you've forgotten that. Perhaps you've walked in darkness even after God has welcomed you into his light. This day would be a good day to change. It's the first day of your journey through the great stories of the Bible . . . what better way to begin than welcoming the regenerative light of creation into your life?

Since this is a day of beginning, let me give you a maxim for the year we'll spend in this book together. It comes from the apostle Paul, a man who had quite a dark past before God literally hit him with a blinding light to bring him into the kingdom (see Acts 9 for this story). Later he would write to the church in Philippi: "Forgetting the past and straining toward what is ahead, I keep trying to reach the goal" (Philippians 3:13–14). Like Paul, I have a lot to forget. But I also have a lot of goals I want to achieve; this instruction, coming from a man like Paul, gives me hope.

Want to reach your goals for the next year? Take this hint from Paul: don't drag your past with you as you run toward your goals—it only adds to the strain. So for now, forget the dark days and head toward the Light that can make your tomorrows better than your yesterdays.

And live brave. In the words of David "The LORD is my light and the one who saves me. So why should I fear anyone?" (Psalm 27:1).

THOUGHTS TO PONDER

What does it mean for followers of Jesus to be "the light of the world"? Why did Jesus choose that quality to describe his followers?

PRAYER

God, we know you are light and that in you there is no darkness at all. Help us walk in the light all the days of our lives. Amen.

In His Image

GENESIS 1:14–31

¹⁴Then God said, "Let there be lights in the sky to separate day from night. These lights will be used for signs, seasons, days, and years. ¹⁵They will be in the sky to give light to the earth." And it happened.

¹⁶So God made the two large lights. He made the brighter light to rule the day and made the smaller light to rule the night. He also made the stars. ¹⁷God put all these in the sky to shine on the earth, ¹⁸to rule over the day and over the night, and to separate the light from the darkness. God saw that all these things were good. ¹⁹Evening passed, and morning came. This was the fourth day.

²⁰Then God said, "Let the water be filled with living things, and let birds fly in the air above the earth."

²¹So God created the large sea animals and every living thing that moves in the sea. The sea is filled with these living things, with each one producing more of its own kind. He also made every bird that flies, and each bird produced more of its own kind. God saw that this was good. ²²God blessed them and said, "Have many young ones so that you may grow in number. Fill the water of the seas, and let the birds grow in number on the earth." ²³Evening passed, and morning came. This was the fifth day.

²⁴Then God said, "Let the earth be filled with animals, each producing more of its own kind. Let there be tame animals and small crawling animals and wild animals, and let each produce more of its kind." And it happened.

²⁵So God made the wild animals, the tame animals, and all the small crawling animals to produce more of their own kind. God saw that this was good.

²⁶Then God said, "Let us make human beings in our image and likeness. And let them rule over the fish in the sea and the birds in the sky, over the tame animals, over all the earth, and over all the small crawling animals on the earth."

²⁷So God created human beings in his image. In the image of God he created them. He created them male and female. ²⁸God blessed them and said, "Have many children and grow in number. Fill the earth and be its master. Rule over the fish in the sea and over the birds in the sky and over every living thing that moves on the earth."

²⁹God said, "Look, I have given you all the plants that have grain for seeds and all the trees whose fruits have seeds in them. They will be food for you. ³⁰I have given all the green plants as food for every wild animal, every bird of the air, and every small crawling animal." And it happened. ³¹God looked at everything he had made, and it was very good. Evening passed, and morning came. This was the sixth day.

DEVOTION

AT THE END of every day of creation we read a phrase like this: God saw that it was good. Then man and woman are created on the sixth day and we read this phrase: "God looked at everything he had made, and it was very good." Think about this for a moment: you are the crowning achievement of creation. Even on your worst day, you are "very good" in the eyes of God.

The key to why this is true is found in verse 26. You and I are made in the image of God. Want to see God? Look no further than those around you. But here's the really good part. Our earthly body is temporary. Someday we'll take on the image of Christ. I read about this in Paul's first letter to the church at Corinth when he writes about Adam and Christ:

> "There is a physical body, and there is also a spiritual body. It is written in the Scriptures: 'The first man, Adam, became a living person.' But the last Adam became a spirit that gives life. Just as we were made like the man of earth, so we will also be made like the man of heaven. I tell you this, brothers and sisters: Flesh and blood cannot have a part in the kingdom of God. Something that will ruin cannot have a part in something that never ruins. But look! I tell you this secret: We will not all sleep in death, but we will all be changed. It will take only a second— as quickly as an eye blinks—when the last trumpet sounds. The trumpet will sound, and those who have died will be raised to live forever, and we will all be changed." (1 Corinthians 15:44–46, 49–52)

The Christian gets two bodies. The first will last a lifetime; the second will last an eternity. And both are "very good."

THOUGHTS TO PONDER

What do you think it means to be made in the image of God? What roles did God give the man and the woman in the story above?

PRAYER

God, we pray that we will see your image in everyone around us and that we will treat everyone with the knowledge that they were created "very good." Amen.

POWERFUL AND PRESENT

GENESIS 2:4–22

⁴This is the story of the creation of the sky and the earth. When the LORD God first made the earth and the sky, ⁵there were still no plants on the earth. Nothing was growing in the fields because the LORD God had not yet made it rain on the land. And there was no person to care for the ground, ⁶but a mist would rise up from the earth and water all the ground.

⁷Then the LORD God took dust from the ground and formed a man from it. He breathed the breath of life into the man's nose, and the man became a living person. ⁸Then the LORD God planted a garden in the east, in a place called Eden, and put the man he had formed into it. ⁹The LORD God caused every beautiful tree and every tree that was good for food to grow out of the ground. In the middle of the garden, God put the tree that gives life and also the tree that gives the knowledge of good and evil.

¹⁰A river flowed through Eden and watered the garden. From there the river branched out to become four rivers. ¹¹The first river, named Pishon, flows around the whole land of Havilah, where there is gold. ¹²The gold of that land is excellent. Bdellium and onyx are also found there. ¹³The second river, named Gihon, flows around the whole land of Cush. ¹⁴The third river, named Tigris, flows out of Assyria toward the east. The fourth river is the Euphrates.

¹⁵The LORD God put the man in the garden of Eden to care for it and work it. ¹⁶The LORD God commanded him, "You may eat the fruit from any tree in the garden, ¹⁷but you must not eat the fruit from the tree which gives the knowledge of good and evil. If you ever eat fruit from that tree, you will die!"

¹⁸Then the LORD God said, "It is not good for the man to be alone. I will make a helper who is right for him."

¹⁹From the ground God formed every wild animal and every bird in the sky, and he brought them to the man so the man could name them. Whatever the man called each living thing, that became its name. ²⁰The man gave names to all the tame animals, to the birds in the sky, and to all the wild animals. But Adam did not find a helper that was right for him. ²¹So the LORD God caused the man to sleep very deeply, and while he was asleep, God removed one of the man's ribs. Then God closed up the man's skin at the place where he took the rib. ²²The LORD God used the rib from the man to make a woman, and then he brought the woman to the man.

DEVOTION

DO YOU HAVE a favorite name for your spouse or any of your children that only you use? A name that is special only within your family? In the passage above, God tells us his personal name, because he wants a relationship with his latest and best creation—humans.

There are two Hebrew words primarily used to denote deity throughout the Old Testament, and it's important to note the difference here. In the first chapter of Genesis, God is referred to as *Elohim*, translated "God." It's a name that denotes his power and distinctiveness.

At the beginning of chapter two, however, the Hebrew text calls him *Yahweh*, which is his personal name. This name is always translated "LORD" in our English texts and pronounced "Jehovah" by us today. However, the Orthodox Jews never even said this name aloud and substituted the word "Lord" in public readings. *Yahweh* is a form of the verb "to be." But it goes far beyond mere existence. It denotes God's active presence among his people. That is why he calls himself "I AM WHO I AM" when he reveals himself to Moses (Exodus 3:14). By telling his people his name, God is revealing his true desire to be actively present in our lives.

Why does God ask Adam to name all the birds and the animals? He wants Adam to feel connected to them. Why does God reveal his personal name to Adam? He wants a relationship with him as well.

If you recall, after each of the first five days of creation, God looks over his work and pronounces it to be "good." On the sixth day—the day he creates man—God looks over everything and proclaims it to be "very good." But now, there is one thing that is not good: the fact that the man is alone. So God fashions a woman for him out of a rib. Now, the one thing in all of creation that was not good is corrected.

THOUGHTS TO PONDER

What significance do you see in the two names of God? What does it tell you about God that he has a name that denotes his power and a name that denotes his relationship to us?

PRAYER

God, we know you are all-powerful, but we also know that you are loving. We thank you for revealing your nature to us and for wanting a relationship with us. Amen.

KNOW YOUR ENEMY

GENESIS 3:1–13, 22–24

3 Now the snake was the most clever of all the wild animals the LORD God had made. One day the snake said to the woman, "Did God really say that you must not eat fruit from any tree in the garden?"

²The woman answered the snake, "We may eat fruit from the trees in the garden. ³But God told us, 'You must not eat fruit from the tree that is in the middle of the garden. You must not even touch it, or you will die.' "

⁴But the snake said to the woman, "You will not die. ⁵God knows that if you eat the fruit from that tree, you will learn about good and evil and you will be like God!"

⁶The woman saw that the tree was beautiful, that its fruit was good to eat, and that it would make her wise. So she took some of its fruit and ate it. She also gave some of the fruit to her husband who was with her, and he ate it.

⁷Then, it was as if their eyes were opened. They realized they were naked, so they sewed fig leaves together and made something to cover themselves.

⁸Then they heard the LORD God walking in the garden during the cool part of the day, and the man and his wife hid from the LORD God among the trees in the garden. ⁹But the LORD God called to the man and said, "Where are you?"

¹⁰The man answered, "I heard you walking in the garden, and I was afraid because I was naked, so I hid."

¹¹God asked, "Who told you that you were naked? Did you eat fruit from the tree from which I commanded you not to eat?"

¹²The man said, "You gave this woman to me and she gave me fruit from the tree, so I ate it."

¹³Then the LORD God said to the woman, "How could you have done such a thing?"

She answered, "The snake tricked me, so I ate the fruit."

²²Then the LORD God said, "Humans have become like one of us; they know good and evil. We must keep them from eating some of the fruit from the tree of life, or they will live forever." ²³So the LORD God forced Adam out of the garden of Eden to work the ground from which he was taken. ²⁴After God forced humans out of the garden, he placed angels and a sword of fire that flashed around in every direction on its eastern border. This kept people from getting to the tree of life.

DEVOTION

DURING THE SECOND World War, the military issued playing cards to the enlisted men to help them pass the time. However, these cards, now collector's items, had a secondary purpose.

On the playing surface of each card was the image of an enemy ship, vehicle, or aircraft. The more the GI's played cards, the more they learned to recognize the armory of the enemy.

Recognize your enemy. It's advice my wife's dad passed on to his children repeatedly from the time they were young, because Satan will take many forms—far more than just the fifty-two enemy vehicles on those playing cards. When he came as a serpent, Eve failed to recognize him and fell for his story.

If only he would come as a serpent today. We'd do exactly what God said when he cursed Satan as Adam and Eve left the garden . . . we'd step on his head, suffering only a bruised heel in the process, thanks to the redemptive work of Christ.

But Satan is too smart for that. He has no intention of being crushed. In fact, Peter compared him to "a roaring lion"—the ultimate predator. But he's not even going to come as a lion. He's too wily for that as well.

Know your enemy and his ammunition. He'll come in the form of unjust criticism from someone you thought was a friend. He'll come in the form of good works in the name of the Lord that yield no visible results. He'll make you think that, like Elijah hiding in the cave, you are the only one living right.

A good friend of mine involved in full-time ministry said once in a devotional, "Don't ever be surprised who Satan will use to discourage you." If that's true (and I believe it is), then encouragers must be sent from God. Seek them out, stay in their company, and imitate them.

THOUGHTS TO PONDER

What do you picture Satan looking like? Why? What are some of the likely directions from which he'll attack you? What is an unexpected way for him to test you? Are you ready?

PRAYER

Father, we're mindful of the power of Satan in this world, but we're equally mindful that you have utterly defeated him. Help us resist his temptations and claim the victory in you. Amen.

GIVING OUR BEST

GENESIS 4:1–16

4 Adam had sexual relations with his wife Eve, and she became pregnant and gave birth to Cain. Eve said, "With the LORD's help, I have given birth to a man." ²After that, Eve gave birth to Cain's brother Abel. Abel took care of flocks, and Cain became a farmer.

³Later, Cain brought some food from the ground as a gift to God. ⁴Abel brought the best parts from some of the firstborn of his flock. The LORD accepted Abel and his gift, ⁵but he did not accept Cain and his gift. So Cain became very angry and felt rejected.

⁶The LORD asked Cain, "Why are you angry? Why do you look so unhappy? ⁷If you do things well, I will accept you, but if you do not do them well, sin is ready to attack you. Sin wants you, but you must rule over it."

⁸Cain said to his brother Abel, "Let's go out into the field." While they were out in the field, Cain attacked his brother Abel and killed him.

⁹Later, the LORD said to Cain, "Where is your brother Abel?"

Cain answered, "I don't know. Is it my job to take care of my brother?"

¹⁰Then the LORD said, "What have you done? Your brother's blood is crying out to me from the ground. ¹¹And now you will be cursed in your work with the ground, the same ground where your brother's blood fell and where your hands killed him. ¹²You will work the ground, but it will not grow good crops for you anymore, and you will wander around on the earth."

¹³Then Cain said to the LORD, "This punishment is more than I can stand! ¹⁴Today you have forced me to stop working the ground, and now I must hide from you. I must wander around on the earth, and anyone who meets me can kill me."

¹⁵The LORD said to Cain, "No! If anyone kills you, I will punish that person seven times more." Then the LORD put a mark on Cain warning anyone who met him not to kill him.

¹⁶So Cain went away from the LORD and lived in the land of Nod, east of Eden.

DEVOTION

THERE WAS A WOMAN who discovered a turkey that had been frozen in the back of her freezer for at least a decade. She called the local farm extension agent to see if it would be advisable to cook it. The agent replied that while it probably wouldn't have any bacteria, it probably wouldn't have any taste either. Her solution: she brought it to her church for inclusion in a holiday basket for a low-income family in the community.

Can you imagine the family's dismay on Christmas day when they slowly thawed, basted, and cooked that decade-old turkey only to be rewarded with tasteless, chewy meat for the holiday meal?

The Bible repeatedly talks about God wanting the firstfruits of our labor (see Leviticus 23:10 and Numbers 18:12 for examples). In the story above, Cain simply selects "some food from the ground" while Abel selects "the best parts from some of the firstborn of his flock" (Genesis 4:3–4). Not just any sheep, but a firstborn sheep, and not just any part of the sheep, but the best parts. Abel went above and beyond Cain's nominal sacrifice. His sincerity and humility made his gift acceptable.

In one of the most poignant parables in the Gospels, Jesus gives us a glimpse of what Judgment Day will be like (Matthew 25:31–46). God will separate all of the people of the earth on his right hand and his left. The ones on his right—those who pleased God, like Abel—are the ones who visited the sick and imprisoned, gave the hungry something to eat, gave the thirsty water to drink. The ones on his left—who, like Cain, displeased God—did none of these acts of charity.

And here is the interesting part—neither side knew they were being tested. God does not place a heavenly halo over the head of the homeless person, pointing the way for our charity. But he does say, "I tell you the truth, anything you did for even the least of my people here, you also did for me" (Matthew 25:40).

God is not some divine waiter to be "tipped" for his good service to us. God is the owner of everything we have. When we give our gifts to him, we are simply giving back to him what is already his. In his gospel account, John tells us that God loved us so much that he gave us the gift of his Son (John 3:16). Shouldn't our gifts to him reflect the depth of our love as well? Which will it be: some of your bounty like Cain, or the best like Abel?

THOUGHTS TO PONDER

What are some of the best gifts you've ever received for Christmas or for a birthday? How did those gifts make you feel? What are some of the best gifts God has given you? How did you thank him?

PRAYER

God, we know that every good and perfect gift comes from you, and we pray that in our lives we will be models of generosity as well. Amen.

PERFECT TIMING

GENESIS 6:1–22

6The number of people on earth began to grow, and daughters were born to them. ²When the sons of God saw that these girls were beautiful, they married any of them they chose. ³The LORD said, "My Spirit will not remain in human beings forever, because they are flesh. They will live only 120 years."

⁴The Nephilim were on the earth in those days and also later. That was when the sons of God had sexual relations with the daughters of human beings. These women gave birth to children, who became famous and were the mighty warriors of long ago.

⁵The LORD saw that the human beings on the earth were very wicked and that everything they thought about was evil. ⁶He was sorry he had made human beings on the earth, and his heart was filled with pain. ⁷So the LORD said, "I will destroy all human beings that I made on the earth. And I will destroy every animal and everything that crawls on the earth and the birds of the air, because I am sorry I have made them." ⁸But Noah pleased the LORD.

⁹This is the family history of Noah. Noah was a good man, the most innocent man of his time, and he walked with God. ¹⁰He had three sons: Shem, Ham, and Japheth.

¹¹People on earth did what God said was evil, and violence was everywhere. ¹²When God saw that everyone on the earth did only evil, ¹³he said to Noah, "Because people have made the earth full of violence, I will destroy all of them from the earth. ¹⁴Build a boat of cypress wood for yourself. Make rooms in it and cover it inside and outside with tar. ¹⁵This is how big I want you to build the boat: four hundred fifty feet long, seventy-five feet wide, and forty-five feet high. ¹⁶Make an opening around the top of the boat that is eighteen inches high from the edge of the roof down. Put a door in the side of the boat. Make an upper, middle, and lower deck in it. ¹⁷I will bring a flood of water on the earth to destroy all living things that live under the sky, including everything that has the breath of life. Everything on the earth will die. ¹⁸But I will make an agreement with you—you, your sons, your wife, and your sons' wives will all go into the boat. ¹⁹Also, you must bring into the boat two of every living thing, male and female. Keep them alive with you. ²⁰Two of every kind of bird, animal, and crawling thing will come to you to be kept alive. ²¹Also gather some of every kind of food and store it on the boat as food for you and the animals."

²²Noah did everything that God commanded him.

DEVOTION

GREGOR MENDEL, an obscure monk toiling in the monastery gardens, made groundbreaking discoveries in the nineteenth century about the workings of genetics by observing the characteristics of peas. But because of his inability to publicize his findings, he never got credit in his lifetime.

Galileo claimed that the earth revolved around the sun. But all the scientific evidence he could muster to prove his claim couldn't save him from the religious leaders who claimed the earth was the center of the universe. He was put to death years before other scientists would prove him right.

Chester Carlson unsuccessfully shopped his idea for a machine that could copy documents to several U.S. companies, including IBM, before finally finding a small little company named Xerox that believed in the idea. He died without seeing his invention revolutionize the business world of the latter twentieth century.

Now consider Noah. Using God's instructions, he built an enormous ship on dry land when no one had any concept of a flood. The writer of Hebrews lists him among the heroes of faith for what must have been years of ridicule he endured for the huge folly he was creating by hand, board by board. Didn't he have doubts when he put his tired body to bed at night? Wasn't he afraid the quality of his handiwork might not be up to par as the animals began to board and the rain began to fall?

Think of this: whatever God has called you to do may not even be fully accomplished in your lifetime. Or like Noah, it may take years to see the results. Our schedule is rarely God's schedule, whether it's healing from a disease or discovering his will in our lives. But this much is true: God's timing is always right. As Scripture tells us, Christ came "at just the right time" to save us from our sins (Hebrews 9:26).

THOUGHTS TO PONDER

What has God asked you to do that required a great amount of faith? How do you develop and maintain a focus on the voice of God when he wants to get your attention?

PRAYER

God, we know you control everything. Help us have the faith of Noah to follow your lead, even if we don't clearly see the end result from where we are now. Help us to be faithful to the end. Amen.

The Great Escape

GENESIS 7:1–24

7 Then the LORD said to Noah, "I have seen that you are the best person among the people of this time, so you and your family can go into the boat. ²Take with you seven pairs, each male with its female, of every kind of clean animal, and take one pair, each male with its female, of every kind of unclean animal. ³Take seven pairs of all the birds of the sky, each male with its female. This will allow all these animals to continue living on the earth after the flood. ⁴Seven days from now I will send rain on the earth. It will rain forty days and forty nights, and I will wipe off from the earth every living thing that I have made."

⁵Noah did everything the LORD commanded him.

⁶Noah was six hundred years old when the flood came. ⁷He and his wife and his sons and their wives went into the boat to escape the waters of the flood. ⁸The clean animals, the unclean animals, the birds, and everything that crawls on the ground ⁹came to Noah. They went into the boat in groups of two, male and female, just as God had commanded Noah. ¹⁰Seven days later the flood started.

¹¹When Noah was six hundred years old, the flood started. On the seventeenth day of the second month of that year the underground springs split open, and the clouds in the sky poured out rain. ¹²The rain fell on the earth for forty days and forty nights.

¹³On that same day Noah and his wife, his sons Shem, Ham, and Japheth, and their wives went into the boat. ¹⁴They had every kind of wild and tame animal, every kind of animal that crawls on the earth, and every kind of bird. ¹⁵Every creature that had the breath of life came to Noah in the boat in groups of two. ¹⁶One male and one female of every living thing came, just as God had commanded Noah. Then the LORD closed the door behind them.

¹⁷Water flooded the earth for forty days, and as it rose it lifted the boat off the ground. ¹⁸The water continued to rise, and the boat floated on it above the earth. ¹⁹The water rose so much that even the highest mountains under the sky were covered by it. ²⁰It continued to rise until it was more than twenty feet above the mountains.

²¹All living things that moved on the earth died. This included all the birds, tame animals, wild animals, and creatures that swarm on the earth, as well as all human beings. ²²So everything on dry land that had the breath of life in it died. ²³God destroyed from the earth every living thing that was on the land—every man, animal, crawling thing, and bird of the sky. All that was left was Noah and what was with him in the boat. ²⁴And the waters continued to cover the earth for one hundred fifty days.

DEVOTION

IMAGINE BEING THE only faithful person on earth. Imagine being the only human pleasing to God. That was the situation Noah found himself in, and because of his faithfulness, God offered him a way to escape from the imminent destruction of the world by flood.

The escape was elaborate. Noah built a boat as long and wide as one and a half football fields and nearly as high as a five-story building. Only the largest football stadium today could hold the boat that Noah, more than five hundred years old, built without modern tools. But because he was faithful, God saved him and his family.

Now I want you to imagine that the opposite is true. Imagine you are the only sinful person on earth. Not the worst sinner—the only sinner. Guess what? God would offer even you a way of escape through his Son. He doesn't wait for us to be good; he doesn't wait for us to earn it (we can't). He simply extends to us salvation through his only Son because of his love for us (John 3:16).

In the New Testament, Peter, speaking of our salvation, compares it to the saving of the eight members of Noah's family when he writes: "Only a few people—eight in all—were saved by water. And that water is like baptism that now saves you—not the washing of dirt from the body, but the promise made to God from a good conscience. And this is because Jesus Christ was raised from the dead" (1 Peter 3:20–21).

Being rescued from drowning in our own sins doesn't depend on our goodness. Salvation is a free gift. What good works we do are a faith response to the wonderful gift of salvation offered through Jesus to us.

THOUGHTS TO PONDER

Out of all the possible natural disasters, why would God use a flood to destroy the earth? What traits do you see in Noah so far that might have garnered God's favor?

PRAYER

God, we pray that you will find good in us like you found in Noah. But God, we know our goodness is not the source of our salvation, so we ask for your mercy and grace as well. Amen.

LIVING SACRIFICES

GENESIS 8:1–21

8 But God remembered Noah and all the wild and tame animals with him in the boat. He made a wind blow over the earth, and the water went down. ²The underground springs stopped flowing, and the clouds in the sky stopped pouring down rain. ³⁻⁴The water that covered the earth began to go down. After one hundred fifty days it had gone down so much that the boat touched land again. It came to rest on one of the mountains of Ararat on the seventeenth day of the seventh month. ⁵The water continued to go down so that by the first day of the tenth month the tops of the mountains could be seen.

⁶Forty days later Noah opened the window he had made in the boat, and ⁷he sent out a raven. It flew here and there until the water had dried up from the earth. ⁸Then Noah sent out a dove to find out if the water had dried up from the ground. ⁹The dove could not find a place to land because water still covered the earth, so it came back to the boat. Noah reached out his hand and took the bird and brought it back into the boat.

¹⁰After seven days Noah again sent out the dove from the boat, ¹¹and that evening it came back to him with a fresh olive leaf in its mouth. Then Noah knew that the ground was almost dry. ¹²Seven days later he sent the dove out again, but this time it did not come back.

¹³When Noah was six hundred and one years old, in the first day of the first month of that year, the water was dried up from the land. Noah removed the covering of the boat and saw that the land was dry. ¹⁴By the twenty-seventh day of the second month the land was completely dry.

¹⁵Then God said to Noah, ¹⁶"You and your wife, your sons, and their wives should go out of the boat. ¹⁷Bring every animal out of the boat with you—the birds, animals, and everything that crawls on the earth. Let them have many young ones so that they might grow in number."

¹⁸So Noah went out with his sons, his wife, and his sons' wives. ¹⁹Every animal, everything that crawls on the earth, and every bird went out of the boat by families.

²⁰Then Noah built an altar to the LORD. He took some of all the clean birds and animals, and he burned them on the altar as offerings to God. ²¹The LORD was pleased with these sacrifices and said to himself, "I will never again curse the ground because of human beings. Their thoughts are evil even when they are young, but I will never again destroy every living thing on the earth as I did this time."

DEVOTION

OUR FIRST ACCOUNT of the great religious tradition of building altars begins in this story when Noah emerges from the boat and builds an altar to God. Altars permeate the Old Testament account as the primary form of communion between God and his people. Altars ranged from crude piles of stones to the elaborately constructed altar in the Temple, but all were designed to perform the sacrifices to make sinful humans acceptable in the eyes of God.

After building the altar, Noah takes one of each of the clean birds and animals and sacrifices them to God. You might remember that he was commanded to take seven pairs of these clean animals into the boat, probably for food and for sacrifices. The aroma of the sacrifices reaches God and pleases him.

Altars and sacrifices became an integral part of the worship practices of God's people from this moment forward. The blood of the animals, shed for the sins of humans. The priests and Levites eventually took on the role of offering these sacrifices on behalf of God's people.

But the blood of animals would never be a permanent remedy for sin. Centuries after this sacrifice of Noah's, Jesus came to the earth to be the perfect sacrifice for sins. His blood was the last blood shed for the forgiveness of sin…the perfect sacrifice, once and for all, for your sins and mine.

Then comes our part. Paul tells the believers in Rome that "since God has shown us great mercy, I beg you to offer your lives as a living sacrifice to him. Your offering must be *only* for God and pleasing to him, which is the spiritual way for you to worship" (Romans 12:1, emphasis added).

How do I respond to the great sacrifice of Jesus? Live a "sacrificed" life. Let the aroma of my thoughts and actions rise to heaven and please God.

THOUGHTS TO PONDER

What do you think is meant by a "living sacrifice"? How do we know when our lives are pleasing as a sacrifice to God?

PRAYER

God, we thank you for saving us from our sins, just like you saved Noah from the flood. We pray that our sacrifice to you will be acceptable each day. Amen.

THE GOD OF PROMISES

GENESIS 8:21—9:2, 8—17

²¹The LORD was pleased with these sacrifices and said to himself, "I will never again curse the ground because of human beings. Their thoughts are evil even when they are young, but I will never again destroy every living thing on the earth as I did this time.

²²"As long as the earth continues,
planting and harvest,
cold and hot,
summer and winter,
day and night
will not stop."

9 Then God blessed Noah and his sons and said to them, "Have many children; grow in number and fill the earth. ²Every animal on earth, every bird in the sky, every animal that crawls on the ground, and every fish in the sea will respect and fear you. I have given them to you."

Editor's note: God makes various laws for Noah and his descendants to follow here.

⁸Then God said to Noah and his sons, ⁹"Now I am making my agreement with you and your people who will live after you, ¹⁰and with every living thing that is with you—the birds, the tame and the wild animals, and with everything that came out of the boat with you—with every living thing on earth. ¹¹I make this agreement with you: I will never again destroy all living things by a flood. A flood will never again destroy the earth."

¹²And God said, "This is the sign of the agreement between me and you and every living creature that is with you. ¹³I am putting my rainbow in the clouds as the sign of the agreement between me and the earth. ¹⁴When I bring clouds over the earth and a rainbow appears in them, ¹⁵I will remember my agreement between me and you and every living thing. Floods will never again destroy all life on the earth. ¹⁶When the rainbow appears in the clouds, I will see it and I will remember the agreement that continues forever between me and every living thing on the earth."

¹⁷So God said to Noah, "The rainbow is a sign of the agreement that I made with all living things on earth."

DEVOTION

IN THE VALLEY below our summer cabin in New Mexico, it is not uncommon for a rainbow to appear after the frequent summer rains. And unlike rainbows I see in the city, these rainbows touch the earth at both ends, a phenomenal arc of color with the mountains as a backdrop. My wife and I often hike to the road below to get a better view of this marvel; it never gets old. And, on rare occasions, we are rewarded for our trek with a double rainbow, something I saw for the first time just a few years ago.

God's promise to Noah was actually an agreement between God and humans, lasting all the way until today—a promise that he would never again destroy the earth with a flood. The Hebrew word for "rainbow" is also the word for "war-bow," signifying that God metaphorically lowered his bow to earth, showing that his wrath was over.

We have other agreements. Marriage is an agreement between a husband and a wife, and we seal it with a ring. The marriage agreement is far more sacred and binding than the mere contract the state requires, and should never be broken lightly. God, too, takes his agreement seriously. The rainbow is God's "ring" for his agreement with us. It tells us that even in our sinful state we are safe from his ultimate wrath on this earth. And even though he chastises and punishes his chosen people (the Israelites) throughout their history, he never destroys them.

We will see as we continue to read through Scripture that God makes several more agreements with his people. He promises them an earthly home. He promises to make their numbers greater than the stars in the sky. He promises to never forsake them. And finally, he promises to redeem them from their sins. That's what I remember when I enjoy a summer rainbow.

THOUGHTS TO PONDER

Why would God choose the rainbow to seal his agreement with Noah? Other than marriage, what are some of the agreements in your life? What promises have you made that are more binding than contracts? Why did you make them?

PRAYER

God, we thank you for your patience with us and for leaving us with the rainbow as your promise of patience and love. Amen.

ONE VOICE

GENESIS 11:1–9

11 At this time the whole world spoke one language, and everyone used the same words. ²As people moved from the east, they found a plain in the land of Babylonia and settled there.

³They said to each other, "Let's make bricks and bake them to make them hard." So they used bricks instead of stones, and tar instead of mortar. ⁴Then they said to each other, "Let's build a city and a tower for ourselves, whose top will reach high into the sky. We will become famous. Then we will not be scattered over all the earth."

⁵The LORD came down to see the city and the tower that the people had built. ⁶The LORD said, "Now, these people are united, all speaking the same language. This is only the beginning of what they will do. They will be able to do anything they want. ⁷Come, let us go down and confuse their language so they will not be able to understand each other."

⁸So the LORD scattered them from there over all the earth, and they stopped building the city. ⁹The place is called Babel since that is where the LORD confused the language of the whole world. So the LORD caused them to spread out from there over the whole world.

DEVOTION

WE ARRIVED AT the train station in Vienna about 6 P.M., my family of five and the thirty-five university students we were sponsoring for a semester in Europe. We were boarding a train for an overnight trip to Florence, where we would begin a tour of Italy.

The tickets had been purchased months earlier, and each student was to have a sleeping berth. Each of us had a pass to board the train, and I held the manifest to show that we had upgraded to the sleeping cars. The plan was to sit in the general seating area in second class, then switch to the sleeping berths about midnight when we stopped for the passport checks to enter Italy.

But when a new crew boarded the train at the border, there was a problem. The conductor of the first-class sleeping cars had no record of our 45 reservations and he dismissed my manifest as irrelevant. Worse, passengers with reservations now needed our second-class seats. It looked as if we'd spend the nights in the overflow seating in the aisles.

I continued to plead. But the conductor was in no mood to argue in English. Did I speak Italian, he wanted to know? No, I answered. He waved me off—typical American, coming to the continent and expecting everyone to know English.

I gave it one last try: "Sprechen sie Deutsch?" I wanted to know. Do you speak German? "Yah," was the reply.

So we proceeded to talk out our problem—me in my barely acquired second language and he in his third language. No one had the "home field" advantage of speaking in a native tongue. Using simple grade-school vocabulary, we agreed to put the group in the sleeping cars and check with the railroad in the morning to see if we owed any money before we disembarked. The rest of the trip went smoothly and the paperwork was in Florence when we arrived.

I won the conductor over when I proved I had made some effort to learn a European language. Why? Because it's very hard to overcome a language barrier, and many people never even try. Language barriers are stronger than any borders, walls, or checkpoints ever devised by politicians. We are quite literally separated, or united, by language.

As a professor of communication, I'm fascinated by the implications of the story above: if the people speak a common language, they will be able to do anything they want. What does that mean for us today?

The reason God scrambled the languages of the people at Babel (which literally means "confused") is that the people were going to use that power for vain, human purposes. Is it possible that if we try to speak with a common language today—and if we use that common language for good—that God will bless the effort?

The common language I'm referring to is not our daily conversational language; it's our witness to the world. Jesus prayed that his followers would be one as he and his Father were one (John 17:11), yet today we're so religiously divided, we can scarcely witness to the world.

Christians must find a way to speak with one voice, finding our common language in the Good News—the life, death, and resurrection of Jesus. And when we do that, no one will be able to stop us.

THOUGHTS TO PONDER

When we have a "failure to communicate" with someone, even though there is no language barrier, what has happened? What makes for good communication in a family? A church?

PRAYER

Father, we pray that our communication will always speak volumes to the world about what we believe and who you are. Amen.

JUST VISITING

GENESIS 12:1–9

12 The LORD said to Abram, "Leave your country, your relatives, and your father's family, and go to the land I will show you.

²I will make you a great nation,
  and I will bless you.
I will make you famous,
  and you will be a blessing to others.
³I will bless those who bless you,
  and I will place a curse on those who harm you.
And all the people on earth
  will be blessed through you."

⁴So Abram left Haran as the LORD had told him, and Lot went with him. At this time Abram was 75 years old. ⁵He took his wife Sarai, his nephew Lot, and everything they owned, as well as all the servants they had gotten in Haran. They set out from Haran, planning to go to the land of Canaan, and in time they arrived there.

⁶Abram traveled through that land as far as the great tree of Moreh at Shechem. The Canaanites were living in the land at that time. ⁷The LORD appeared to Abram and said, "I will give this land to your descendants." So Abram built an altar there to the LORD, who had appeared to him. ⁸Then he traveled from Shechem to the mountain east of Bethel and set up his tent there. Bethel was to the west, and Ai was to the east. There Abram built another altar to the LORD and worshiped him. ⁹After this, he traveled on toward southern Canaan.

DEVOTION

IN THE BOOK of Hebrews, the great heroes of faith are listed along with their accomplishments. One after another, the brave men and women of the Old Testament are praised for having the faith to do God's will whether or not they fully understood it.

But the longest praise goes to Abraham (the name God later gave to Abram) for the act of faith in this story:

⁸It was by faith Abraham obeyed God's call to go to another place God promised to give him. He left his own country, not knowing where he was to go. ⁹It was by faith that he lived like a foreigner in the country God promised to give him. He lived in tents with Isaac and Jacob, who had received that same promise from God. ¹⁰Abraham was waiting

for the city that has real foundations—the city planned and built by God. [11]He was too old to have children, and Sarah could not have children. It was by faith that Abraham was made able to become a father, because he trusted God to do what he had promised. (Hebrews 11:8–11)

Why did Abraham make the journey that God asked him to make? The Hebrew writer gives us a clue in the very next verse: "All these great people died in faith. They did not get the things that God promised his people, but they saw them coming far in the future and were glad. They said they were like visitors and strangers on earth" (Hebrews 11:13).

Want to follow God's will in your life like Abraham did? The formula is simple—start living like a foreigner. Quit staking yourself so deeply in your possessions, quit drowning yourself in debt to accumulate more, and start living in a spiritual "tent," ready to act on God's will for your life.

John, speaking of Jesus, tells us "The Word became a human and lived among us" (John 1:14). The Greek word John uses for "lived" literally means "pitched a tent." Jesus didn't come to stay. He came to live the life he was called to live, to die for our sins, and then return to the Father. He lived like Abraham—like a stranger on the earth.

Can you live like a visitor on earth, ready to go wherever God wills you to go? Can you believe him, as Abraham did, even when you think his promises are as implausible as having children in your old age? When we can answer these questions affirmatively and wholeheartedly, we are ready for the journey that leads to the place God has promised us.

THOUGHTS TO PONDER

What thoughts do you think Abram had when he first heard the call of God? How can we be certain that what we are hearing is God's call and not our own selfish will?

PRAYER

God, we pray that you will lead us to a land you are preparing for us and that we will follow you in faith to reach that final destination. Amen.

LIVING NEAR SODOM

13 So Abram, his wife, and Lot left Egypt, taking everything they owned, and traveled to southern Canaan. ²Abram was very rich in cattle, silver, and gold.

³He left southern Canaan and went back to Bethel where he had camped before, between Bethel and Ai, ⁴and where he had built an altar. So he worshiped the LORD there.

⁵During this time Lot was traveling with Abram, and Lot also had flocks, herds, and tents. ⁶Abram and Lot had so many animals that the land could not support both of them together, ⁷so Abram's herdsmen and Lot's herdsmen began to argue. The Canaanites and the Perizzites were living in the land at this time.

⁸Abram said to Lot, "There should be no arguing between you and me, or between your herdsmen and mine, because we are brothers. ⁹We should separate. The whole land is there in front of you. If you go to the left, I will go to the right. If you go to the right, I will go to the left."

¹⁰Lot looked all around and saw the whole Jordan Valley and that there was much water there. It was like the LORD's garden, like the land of Egypt in the direction of Zoar. (This was before the LORD destroyed Sodom and Gomorrah.) ¹¹So Lot chose to move east and live in the Jordan Valley. In this way Abram and Lot separated. ¹²Abram lived in the land of Canaan, but Lot lived among the cities in the Jordan Valley, very near to Sodom. ¹³Now the people of Sodom were very evil and were always sinning against the LORD.

¹⁴After Lot left, the LORD said to Abram, "Look all around you—to the north and south and east and west. ¹⁵All this land that you see I will give to you and your descendants forever. ¹⁶I will make your descendants as many as the dust of the earth. If anyone could count the dust on the earth, he could count your people. ¹⁷Get up! Walk through all this land because I am now giving it to you."

¹⁸So Abram moved his tents and went to live near the great trees of Mamre at the city of Hebron. There he built an altar to the LORD.

DEVOTION

HOW CLOSE TO Sodom do you camp? By that I mean, how close to evil do you try to get without becoming a part of it?

When Lot chose the Jordan Valley, he was taking the best for himself. It's a testament to the character of Abram that he didn't choose the better part for himself. In the culture of the day, it would have been right for the younger Lot to defer to the elder Abram. But Abram let Lot choose first, and Lot chose to live close to Sodom.

The decision would prove to be tragic for Lot. He would eventually move into the wicked city, where every manner of evil imaginable was tolerated. In a story we find in Genesis 19, Lot escapes God's wrath only because God intervenes with his angels and saves him. He leaves with nothing, losing his wife in the process.

I think this is the way temptation works. First we decide to get close to it. But pretty soon, we're drawn inside. And eventually, there's scarcely a way to get out.

Notice the opposite reaction of Abram. He moves away from the sinful valley to the plains. And once there, he builds an altar to God. It's no wonder he is blessed by God, while Lot only sees trouble for his choice.

Now the question comes to us. Where are you going to live your life? Are you going to live as close to temptation as possible, or are you going to opt to live in the presence of the altar?

The problems of sin begin so innocently. We may call it flirting. We may call it social drinking. But before long it may be called adultery and alcoholism.

Few people plan to live inside of Sodom. We simply want a good view. We want close proximity for the occasional foray inside. But then comes the entrapment of sin, followed eventually by the wrath of God.

How close to Sodom will you camp? The choice is yours.

THOUGHTS TO PONDER

Who do you know that became caught in sin after getting too close? Were there warning signs? What sins attract you? What steps do you take to stay away from them?

PRAYER

God, we pray that we will stay far away from temptation. Give us the strength to walk in your ways. Amen.

DESIGNED FOR A PURPOSE

GENESIS 14:8–24

[8]At that time the kings of Sodom, Gomorrah, Admah, Zeboiim, and Bela went out to fight in the Valley of Siddim. (Bela is called Zoar.) [9]They fought against Kedorlaomer king of Elam, Tidal king of Goiim, Amraphel king of Babylonia, and Arioch king of Ellasar—four kings fighting against five. [10]There were many tar pits in the Valley of Siddim. When the kings of Sodom and Gomorrah and their armies ran away, some of the soldiers fell into the tar pits, but the others ran away to the mountains.

[11]Now Kedorlaomer and his armies took everything the people of Sodom and Gomorrah owned, including their food. [12]They took Lot, Abram's nephew who was living in Sodom, and everything he owned. Then they left. [13]One of the men who was not captured went to Abram, the Hebrew, and told him what had happened. At that time Abram was camped near the great trees of Mamre the Amorite. Mamre was a brother of Eshcol and Aner, and they had all made an agreement to help Abram.

[14]When Abram learned that Lot had been captured, he called out his 318 trained men who had been born in his camp. He led the men and chased the enemy all the way to the town of Dan. [15]That night he divided his men into groups, and they made a surprise attack against the enemy. They chased them all the way to Hobah, north of Damascus. [16]Then Abram brought back everything the enemy had stolen, the women and the other people, and Lot, and everything Lot owned.

[17]After defeating Kedorlaomer and the kings who were with him, Abram went home. As he was returning, the king of Sodom came out to meet him in the Valley of Shaveh (now called King's Valley).

[18]Melchizedek king of Salem brought out bread and wine. He was a priest for God Most High [19]and blessed Abram, saying,

"Abram, may you be blessed by God Most High,
the God who made heaven and earth.
[20]And we praise God Most High,
who has helped you to defeat your enemies."

Then Abram gave Melchizedek a tenth of everything he had brought back from the battle.

[21]The king of Sodom said to Abram, "You may keep all these things for yourself. Just give me my people who were captured."

[22]But Abram said to the king of Sodom, "I make a promise to the LORD, the God Most High, who made heaven and earth. [23]I promise that I will not keep anything that is yours. I will not keep even a thread or a sandal strap so that you cannot say, 'I made Abram rich.' [24]I will keep nothing but the food my young men have eaten. But give Aner, Eshcol, and Mamre their share of what we won, because they went with me into battle."

DEVOTION

IN THIS STORY we get a look at some of the characteristics of Abram that will serve him well as the father of the nation God will call his own.

First, Abram is caring. A lesser man might have turned his back on Lot. After all, he had taken the best land. He had chosen to live in the city. Abram could have just turned away the messenger and let Lot and his family remain in captivity.

But Abram cared about Lot. He mustered all his men and chased the army across the plain, south to Dan. By raising his own private army, Abram put himself and his fortune at risk and chased the four kings who had ransacked Sodom.

Second, Abram is generous. When he defeated the four kings, Abram turned toward home. He didn't wish to occupy their cities. He didn't want any of the spoils of war, even though that has always been the privilege of the victor. And when the priest Melchizedek comes to give him a blessing, Abram tithes to him from the riches of the battle. The rest he gives to the men who joined him. He takes nothing for himself.

Melchizedek has an unusual place in biblical history. Nobody seems to know where he came from or where he went after this. He is referred to once in the Psalms and that verse is quoted again in Hebrews. David writes: "The LORD has made a promise and will not change his mind. He said, 'You are a priest forever, a priest like Melchizedek'" (Psalm 110:4).

But it's the next verse that contains a statement Abram already knew: "The Lord is beside you to help you. When he becomes angry, he will crush kings" (Psalm 110:5).

THOUGHTS TO PONDER

How would the traits of Abram seen in this story be important to the role God would have for him? What traits has he given you in order to do his will?

PRAYER

God, we pray that we will be caring and generous toward others and that we will be the people you have designed us to be. Amen.

LIVING BY FAITH

GENESIS 15:1–21

15 After these things happened, the LORD spoke his word to Abram in a vision: "Abram, don't be afraid. I will defend you, and I will give you a great reward."

²But Abram said, "Lord GOD, what can you give me? I have no son, so my slave Eliezer from Damascus will get everything I own after I die." ³Abram said, "Look, you have given me no son, so a slave born in my house will inherit everything I have."

⁴Then the LORD spoke his word to Abram: "He will not be the one to inherit what you have. You will have a son of your own who will inherit what you have."

⁵Then God led Abram outside and said, "Look at the sky. There are so many stars you cannot count them. Your descendants also will be too many to count."

⁶Abram believed the LORD. And the LORD accepted Abram's faith, and that faith made him right with God.

⁷God said to Abram, "I am the LORD who led you out of Ur of Babylonia so that I could give you this land to own."

⁸But Abram said, "Lord GOD, how can I be sure that I will own this land?"

⁹The LORD said to Abram, "Bring me a three-year-old cow, a three-year-old goat, a three-year-old male sheep, a dove, and a young pigeon."

¹⁰Abram brought them all to God. Then Abram killed the animals and cut each of them into two pieces, laying each half opposite the other half. But he did not cut the birds in half. ¹¹Later, large birds flew down to eat the animals, but Abram chased them away.

¹²As the sun was going down, Abram fell into a deep sleep. While he was asleep, a very terrible darkness came. ¹³Then the LORD said to Abram, "You can be sure that your descendants will be strangers and travel in a land they don't own. The people there will make them slaves and be cruel to them for four hundred years. ¹⁴But I will punish the nation where they are slaves. Then your descendants will leave that land, taking great wealth with them. ¹⁵And you, Abram, will die in peace and will be buried at an old age. ¹⁶After your great-great-grandchildren are born, your people will come to this land again. It will take that long, because I am not yet going to punish the Amorites for their evil behavior."

¹⁷After the sun went down, it was very dark. Suddenly a smoking firepot and a blazing torch passed between the halves of the dead animals. ¹⁸So on that day the LORD made an agreement with Abram and said, "I will give to your descendants the land between the river of Egypt and the great river Euphrates. ¹⁹This is the land of the Kenites, Kenizzites, Kadmonites, ²⁰Hittites, Perizzites, Rephaites, ²¹Amorites, Canaanites, Girgashites, and Jebusites."

DEVOTION

ABRAM BELIEVED GOD, and because he did, God accepted his faith. I like this statement: "The LORD accepted Abram's faith, and that faith made him right with God." Sometimes, faith is all I have to offer God, because I can't see where he's leading me. But I've been promised that if I follow in faith, that faith will make me right with God.

But here's the really unusual thing about the story above. Right after Abram is complimented for having believed, he asks for proof. What a bold question! "Lord GOD, how can I be sure that I will own this land?" It's as if Abram is saying, "God, I know you made the promise, but can you actually deliver?"

Now here's the amazing thing: God doesn't get angry. He could have destroyed Abram and begun looking for another man to father his nation. He could have punished Abram for his questioning. He could have lectured Abram like he lectured Job for his doubt (see Job chapters 38—41).

But God is greater than my doubts. In fact, God can work with my doubts to create even greater faith. God was patient with Abram, revealing to him everything that would happen to his descendants before they returned to this land. Later, God was patient with Gideon when he asked for first one miraculous sign and then another to be sure that God would bless the Israelites in battle against their enemy (see Judges 6 for this story).

Sometimes, like Abram, I have faith in the promise that God has made to me of an eternal home with him. But other days, the promise looks so far away—so impossible to reach. Those are the days I want to say to God, "Prove it.". And on those days, the life of Abram and the "great cloud of people whose lives tell us what faith means" (Hebrews 12:1) remind me that others have lived their lives by faith and so can I.

THOUGHTS TO PONDER

What made the promise of God hard for Abram to believe? What is it about God's promises to us that is challenging?

PRAYER

God, we know you are able to keep your promises to us. Please give us the strength to claim the victory over sin you have won for us. Amen.

COLOR-BLIND

GENESIS 16:1−6; 21:1−3, 9−18

16Sarai, Abram's wife, had no children, but she had a slave girl from Egypt named Hagar. ²Sarai said to Abram, "Look, the LORD has not allowed me to have children, so have sexual relations with my slave girl. If she has a child, maybe I can have my own family through her."

Abram did what Sarai said. ³It was after he had lived ten years in Canaan that Sarai gave Hagar to her husband Abram. (Hagar was her slave girl from Egypt.)

⁴Abram had sexual relations with Hagar, and she became pregnant. When Hagar learned she was pregnant, she began to treat her mistress Sarai badly. ⁵Then Sarai said to Abram, "This is your fault. I gave my slave girl to you, and when she became pregnant, she began to treat me badly. Let the LORD decide who is right—you or me."

⁶But Abram said to Sarai, "You are Hagar's mistress. Do anything you want to her." Then Sarai was hard on Hagar, and Hagar ran away.

21The LORD cared for Sarah as he had said and did for her what he had promised. ²Sarah became pregnant and gave birth to a son for Abraham in his old age. Everything happened at the time God had said it would. ³Abraham named his son Isaac, the son Sarah gave birth to.

⁹But Sarah saw Ishmael making fun of Isaac. (Ishmael was the son of Abraham by Hagar, Sarah's Egyptian slave.) ¹⁰So Sarah said to Abraham, "Throw out this slave woman and her son. Her son should not inherit anything; my son Isaac should receive it all."

¹¹This troubled Abraham very much because Ishmael was also his son. ¹²But God said to Abraham, "Don't be troubled about the boy and the slave woman. Do whatever Sarah tells you. The descendants I promised you will be from Isaac. ¹³I will also make the descendants of Ishmael into a great nation because he is your son, too."

¹⁴Early the next morning Abraham took some food and a leather bag full of water. He gave them to Hagar and sent her away. Carrying these things and her son, Hagar went and wandered in the desert of Beersheba.

¹⁵Later, when all the water was gone from the bag, Hagar put her son under a bush. ¹⁶Then she went away a short distance and sat down. She thought, "My son will die, and I cannot watch this happen." She sat there and began to cry.

¹⁷God heard the boy crying, and God's angel called to Hagar from heaven. He said, "What is wrong, Hagar? Don't be afraid! God has heard the boy crying there. ¹⁸Help him up and take him by the hand. I will make his descendants into a great nation."

DEVOTION

KENNY WAS ONE of the best players on our team, a member of the varsity since his freshman year. Kenny handled the ball with ease, got it to the right player or took the shot when needed.

I saw Kenny as a good friend and teammate. It never really occurred to me that he was the only African-American student in our school.

One night the locals in a small Texas town decided to harass Kenny. I wanted to go into the stands and convince them what a great guy Kenny was. Or fight them—whichever worked.

I grew up naïve about racism. During college, when I was a camp counselor and went to town to do laundry, I thought the handwritten "whites only" sign meant I couldn't wash my blue jeans there. I couldn't agree that some people should endure discrimination just because they happened to be African-American.

When Sarah offered Hagar to Abraham to help him begin the nation God promised, it seemed like a rational idea. But now Sarah had conceived Isaac, and the illegitimate son, Ishmael, threatened the inheritance of Isaac. Hagar and Ishmael had to go. But God saw her plight in the desert and promised he would make a great nation through Ishmael.

Same father, two nations. But they would never see eye to eye. And as their customs, languages, and deities began to differ, enmity between the sons of Isaac and the sons of Ishmael became inevitable.

I'm glad God doesn't see me for the color I am. "Though your sins are like scarlet, they can be as white as snow" (Isaiah 1:18). We need to be "color-blind" people in our churches, not judging the scarlet colors of others, but sharing the grace of God that can cleanse the deepest scarlet and make us truly "color-blind" ourselves.

THOUGHTS TO PONDER

Have you ever had a family situation where people you love dearly don't get along? How did you handle it? Why do you think God allowed a great nation to come from Ishmael rather than letting him die under the bush? What does that say about God?

PRAYER

God, help us see through the superficial differences that divide people and see the unity that comes in you. May the nations of the world, who all spring from you, find peace in this world. Amen.

PRAY FIRST

GENESIS 18:1–16

18 Later, the LORD again appeared to Abraham near the great trees of Mamre. Abraham was sitting at the entrance of his tent during the hottest part of the day. [2]He looked up and saw three men standing near him. When Abraham saw them, he ran from his tent to meet them. He bowed facedown on the ground before them [3]and said, "Sir, if you think well of me, please stay awhile with me, your servant. [4]I will bring some water so all of you can wash your feet. You may rest under the tree, [5]and I will get some bread for you so you can regain your strength. Then you may continue your journey."

The three men said, "That is fine. Do as you said."

[6]Abraham hurried to the tent where Sarah was and said to her, "Hurry, prepare twenty quarts of fine flour, and make it into loaves of bread." [7]Then Abraham ran to his herd and took one of his best calves. He gave it to a servant, who hurried to kill it and to prepare it for food. [8]Abraham gave the three men the calf that had been cooked and milk curds and milk. While they ate, he stood under the tree near them.

[9]The men asked Abraham, "Where is your wife Sarah?"

"There, in the tent," said Abraham.

[10]Then the LORD said, "I will certainly return to you about this time a year from now. At that time your wife Sarah will have a son."

Sarah was listening at the entrance of the tent which was behind him. [11]Abraham and Sarah were very old. Since Sarah was past the age when women normally have children, [12]she laughed to herself, "My husband and I are too old to have a baby."

[13]Then the LORD said to Abraham, "Why did Sarah laugh? Why did she say, 'I am too old to have a baby'? [14]Is anything too hard for the LORD? No! I will return to you at the right time a year from now, and Sarah will have a son."

[15]Sarah was afraid, so she lied and said, "I didn't laugh."

But the LORD said, "No. You did laugh."

[16]Then the men got up to leave and started out toward Sodom. Abraham walked along with them a short time to send them on their way.

DEVOTION

WHAT IS THE hardest thing you've ever gone through? The death of a loved one, perhaps? A debilitating illness? A financial reversal? Dealing with rebellious children? Adversity touches us all; it's a fact of living in a fallen world.

Abraham and Sarah were living their heartbreak on a daily basis. Far away from home, they were living in a land that God had said would be populated with their descendants, yet they had no children. And with Sarah's advancing age, the window of opportunity for seizing that promise was now closed. All the moving and living in tents now looked to be in vain. Had the promise been an illusion?

I've been there. Perhaps you have too. I've been so overwhelmed by the circumstances of the present that the promises of God seem to be as distant and unlikely as the prospect of children seemed to Sarah.

Is anything too hard for the LORD? What an intriguing question. *No,* my mind says. *Yes,* my actions and my anxiety seem to say. I'll just work and worry my way to a solution, just in case this problem is too hard for God.

Then I found someone in the New Testament just like me. In Mark 9, a man brings his child to the disciples to be healed, but they are unable to help. The boy has been possessed by a spirit which has robbed him of speech and repeatedly thrown him to the ground, foaming at the mouth through clenched teeth.

After the disciples' failed attempts to help, the man takes his child to Jesus. At that point we read this conversation, paraphrased from Mark 9:21–24:

Jesus: How long has he been like this?

Father: Since birth. But if you can do anything, take pity and help us.

Jesus: *If* I can? All things are possible for those who believe!

Father: I do believe! Help me to believe more!

I think Sarah wanted to believe the visitors in the story from Genesis 18, but her doubt got the better of her. I know I want to believe that all things are possible with God, but my doubt creeps in and gets in the way.

What's the solution? It's found later in Mark when the disciples are alone with Jesus. They ask him why they failed to cast the demon out of the boy while Jesus was successful. Jesus answers: "That kind of spirit can only be forced out by prayer" (Mark 9:29).

No matter what adversity you're facing, try prayer first.

Thoughts to ponder

Do you take your problems to God? What is our role in working out the problems we take to him? What is the role of faith?

Prayer

God, we pray we will turn to you with our needs because we know you are always there. Amen.

Taking Part in God's Plan

GENESIS 18:16–33

¹⁶Then the men got up to leave and started out toward Sodom. Abraham walked along with them a short time to send them on their way.

¹⁷The LORD said, "Should I tell Abraham what I am going to do now? ¹⁸Abraham's children will certainly become a great and powerful nation, and all nations on earth will be blessed through him. ¹⁹I have chosen him so he would command his children and his descendants to live the way the LORD wants them to, to live right and be fair. Then I, the LORD, will give Abraham what I promised him."

²⁰Then the LORD said, "I have heard many complaints against the people of Sodom and Gomorrah. They are very evil. ²¹I will go down and see if they are as bad as I have heard. If not, I will know."

²²So the men turned and went toward Sodom, but Abraham stood there before the LORD. ²³Then Abraham approached him and asked, "Do you plan to destroy the good people along with the evil ones? ²⁴What if there are fifty good people in that city? Will you still destroy it? Surely you will save the city for the fifty good people living there. ²⁵Surely you will not destroy the good people along with the evil ones; then they would be treated the same. You are the judge of all the earth. Won't you do what is right?"

²⁶The LORD said, "If I find fifty good people in the city of Sodom, I will save the whole city because of them."

²⁷Then Abraham said, "Though I am only dust and ashes, I have been brave to speak to the Lord. ²⁸What if there are only forty-five good people in the city? Will you destroy the whole city for the lack of five good people?"

The LORD said, "If I find forty-five there, I will not destroy the city."

²⁹Again Abraham said to him, "If you find only forty good people there, will you destroy the city?"

The LORD said, "If I find forty, I will not destroy it."

³⁰Then Abraham said, "Lord, please don't be angry with me, but let me ask you this. If you find only thirty good people in the city, will you destroy it?"

He said, "If I find thirty good people there, I will not destroy the city."

³¹Then Abraham said, "I have been brave to speak to the Lord. But what if there are twenty good people in the city?"

He answered, "If I find twenty there, I will not destroy the city."

³²Then Abraham said, "Lord, please don't be angry with me, but let me bother you this one last time. What if you find ten there?"

He said, "If I find ten there, I will not destroy it."

[33]When the LORD finished speaking to Abraham, he left, and Abraham returned home.

DEVOTION

SIN CRIES OUT. Ever since the blood of Abel cried out to God and indicted Cain (Genesis 4:10) God has heard the noise of sin in our lives. And in Sodom and Gomorrah, the sin of the people was so great that the outcry of the iniquity even preceded God's knowledge of the details.

There are two qualities of God we see in this story. First, we see God's willingness to share his plan with us. "Should I tell Abraham what I am going to do now?" God asks (Genesis 18:17). He has always wanted his children to know his plan. In fact, John tells us that the signs and miracles recorded in his Gospel are put there so that we might believe (John 20:31). God has always wanted us to know his plan.

Second, God is willing to work in our circumstances if we ask in prayer. Sin can be erased. Diseases can be healed. Relationships can be restored. Even the cities of Sodom and Gomorrah, with all their wickedness, could have been saved from the wrath of God for a mere ten righteous men.

Even though my sins cry out, the blood of Jesus speaks even louder. And because God is willing to show me grace, my eternal destiny has been changed.

THOUGHTS TO PONDER

Why did Abraham care so deeply for Sodom and Gomorrah? What does God's willingness to bargain with Abraham tell us about his nature? Is there a lesson for today from this story? What is it?

PRAYER

God, thank you for overlooking my sins, even when they cry out to you. God, bless this nation; let there always be a righteous remnant and help us to be the salt and light you have called us to be. Amen.

LOOK FORWARD TO HIS COMING

GENESIS 19:1–3, 12–25

19 The two angels came to Sodom in the evening as Lot was sitting near the city gate. When he saw them, he got up and went to them and bowed facedown on the ground. ²Lot said, "Sirs, please come to my house and spend the night. There you can wash your feet, and then tomorrow you may continue your journey."

The angels answered, "No, we will spend the night in the city's public square."

³But Lot begged them to come, so they agreed and went to his house. Then Lot prepared a meal for them. He baked bread without yeast, and they ate it.

¹²The two men said to Lot, "Do you have any other relatives in this city? Do you have any sons-in-law, sons, daughters, or any other relatives? If you do, tell them to leave now, ¹³because we are about to destroy this city. The LORD has heard of all the evil that is here, so he has sent us to destroy it."

¹⁴So Lot went out and said to his future sons-in-law who were pledged to marry his daughters, "Hurry and leave this city! The LORD is about to destroy it!" But they thought Lot was joking.

¹⁵At dawn the next morning, the angels begged Lot to hurry. They said, "Go! Take your wife and your two daughters with you so you will not be destroyed when the city is punished."

¹⁶But Lot delayed. So the two men took the hands of Lot, his wife, and his two daughters and led them safely out of the city. So the LORD was merciful to Lot and his family. ¹⁷After they brought them out of the city, one of the men said, "Run for your lives! Don't look back or stop anywhere in the valley. Run to the mountains, or you will be destroyed."

¹⁸But Lot said to one of them, "Sir, please don't force me to go so far! ¹⁹You have been merciful and kind to me and have saved my life. But I can't run to the mountains. The disaster will catch me, and I will die. ²⁰Look, that little town over there is not too far away. Let me run there. It's really just a little town, and I'll be safe there."

²¹The angel said to Lot, "Very well, I will allow you to do this also. I will not destroy that town. ²²But run there fast, because I cannot destroy Sodom until you are safely in that town." (That town is named Zoar, because it is little.)

²³The sun had already come up when Lot entered Zoar. ²⁴The LORD sent a rain of burning sulfur down from the sky on Sodom and Gomorrah ²⁵and destroyed those cities. He also destroyed the whole Jordan Valley, everyone living in the cities, and even all the plants.

DEVOTION

THE CHARACTERS IN this story that interest me the most are the two future sons-in-law who had an opportunity to be saved but passed it up, thinking that Lot was joking. I wonder how much time they had from when the first sulfurous balls of fire rained down on Sodom to ponder their choices before they died.

The Bible teaches that there will be a time when the entire earth will be destroyed by fire. But unlike Lot and his family, those on earth at the time will have no warning of the pending destruction. In fact, the event is compared to the coming of a thief in the night. Like the thief who sneaks up on his victims, the fiery end—called the Day of the Lord by many Bible writers—will sneak up on the world, as Peter tells his readers. He writes: "But the day of the Lord will come like a thief. The skies will disappear with a loud noise. Everything in them will be destroyed by fire, and the earth and everything in it will be exposed. In that way everything will be destroyed" (2 Peter 3:10–11).

After he reminds them of how the world will end, Peter asks his readers this question: "So what kind of people should you be?" He answers his own question: "You should live holy lives and serve God, as you wait for and look forward to the coming of the day of God" (2 Peter 3:11–12).

Since you know how the end of world will happen, Peter tells his readers, it should affect the way you live every day. Don't you think Lot's future sons-in-law would have lived differently if they had known the fire was coming? Shouldn't we?

THOUGHTS TO PONDER

What do you think a "holy life" looks like? Who do you know who most fits the description of the type of life Peter says we should live? What changes do you need to make to live a more holy life?

PRAYER

God, we pray that we will be ready for your coming and that you will come quickly. Amen.

Forgetting God's Promises

GENESIS 20:1–18

20 Abraham left Hebron and traveled to southern Canaan where he stayed awhile between Kadesh and Shur. When he moved to Gerar, ²he told people that his wife Sarah was his sister. Abimelech king of Gerar heard this, so he sent some servants to take her. ³But one night God spoke to Abimelech in a dream and said, "You will die. The woman you took is married."

⁴But Abimelech had not gone near Sarah, so he said, "Lord, would you destroy an innocent nation? ⁵Abraham himself told me, 'This woman is my sister,' and she also said, 'He is my brother.' I am innocent. I did not know I was doing anything wrong."

⁶Then God said to Abimelech in the dream, "Yes, I know you did not realize what you were doing. So I did not allow you to sin against me and touch her. ⁷Give Abraham his wife back. He is a prophet. He will pray for you, and you will not die. But if you do not give Sarah back, you and all your family will surely die."

⁸So early the next morning, Abimelech called all his officers and told them everything that had happened in the dream. They were very afraid. ⁹Then Abimelech called Abraham to him and said, "What have you done to us? What wrong did I do against you? Why did you bring this trouble to my kingdom? You should not have done these things to me. ¹⁰What were you thinking that caused you to do this?"

¹¹Then Abraham answered, "I thought no one in this place respected God and that someone would kill me to get Sarah. ¹²And it is true that she is my sister. She is the daughter of my father, but she is not the daughter of my mother. ¹³When God told me to leave my father's house and wander in many different places, I told Sarah, 'You must do a special favor for me. Everywhere we go tell people I am your brother.'"

¹⁴Then Abimelech gave Abraham some sheep, cattle, and male and female slaves. He also gave Sarah, Abraham's wife, back to him ¹⁵and said, "Look around you at my land. You may live anywhere you want."

¹⁶Abimelech said to Sarah, "I gave your brother Abraham twenty-five pounds of silver to make up for any wrong that people may think about you. I want everyone to know that you are innocent."

¹⁷Then Abraham prayed to God, and God healed Abimelech, his wife, and his servant girls so they could have children. ¹⁸The LORD had kept all the women in Abimelech's house from having children as a punishment on Abimelech for taking Abraham's wife Sarah.

DEVOTION

THIS IS ACTUALLY the second time that Abraham tries this ruse. Earlier, in a story recorded in Genesis 12:10–20, when Abraham takes Sarah and goes to Egypt to escape a famine, he also tells the king of Egypt that his beautiful wife is actually his sister. In that case, God strikes the king and his household with a "terrible disease" for taking Sarah (called Sarai at the time) into his household.

In this story, we learn there was a little truth to Abraham's ruse—Sarah was his half-sister—but in both cases Abraham fails to identify her as his wife for fear that he will be killed. There is no evidence that either the king or Abimelech slept with Sarah, but in both cases, God was angered by the action.

The lesson I get from this story is that good people can make bad decisions. Abraham lied not once, but twice, to save himself from potential harm even after he had heard the promise of God that he would make a great nation of him. Since he had no male heir at this point, wouldn't it make sense that God would preserve his life in Egypt and then again in Gerar in order to honor that promise? By running scared and asking Sarah to pose as his sister, Abraham was showing a lack of faith in the agreement.

Do we ever have the same failing? God has promised to take care of my needs and has commanded me to not worry. Jesus said, "So I tell you, don't worry about the food or drink you need to live, or about the clothes you need for your body. Life is more than food, and the body is more than clothes. . . . You cannot add any time to your life by worrying about it" (Matthew 6:25, 27).

Sometimes I fail to believe this agreement God has made with me, just like Abraham temporarily forgot his agreement. *Follow me, unburdened by worries about tomorrow*, God asks me. A reassuring promise, but easy to forget, just like Abraham temporarily forgot his promise. The more I mature as a Christian, the more I must learn to take God at his word.

THOUGHTS TO PONDER

Have you ever been scared like Abraham? Have you ever doubted that God would protect you? How do you handle your doubts?

PRAYER

God, we pray that wherever we go, you will watch over us and that we will take you at your word when you promise to provide for us. Amen.

A Bigger Problem Later

GENESIS 21:1–21

21 The LORD cared for Sarah as he had said and did for her what he had promised. ²Sarah became pregnant and gave birth to a son for Abraham in his old age. Everything happened at the time God had said it would. ³Abraham named his son Isaac, the son Sarah gave birth to. ⁴He circumcised Isaac when he was eight days old as God had commanded.

⁵Abraham was one hundred years old when his son Isaac was born. ⁶And Sarah said, "God has made me laugh. Everyone who hears about this will laugh with me. ⁷No one thought that I would be able to have Abraham's child, but even though Abraham is old I have given him a son."

⁸Isaac grew, and when he became old enough to eat food, Abraham gave a great feast. ⁹But Sarah saw Ishmael making fun of Isaac. (Ishmael was the son of Abraham by Hagar, Sarah's Egyptian slave.) ¹⁰So Sarah said to Abraham, "Throw out this slave woman and her son. Her son should not inherit anything; my son Isaac should receive it all."

¹¹This troubled Abraham very much because Ishmael was also his son. ¹²But God said to Abraham, "Don't be troubled about the boy and the slave woman. Do whatever Sarah tells you. The descendants I promised you will be from Isaac. ¹³I will also make the descendants of Ishmael into a great nation because he is your son, too."

¹⁴Early the next morning Abraham took some food and a leather bag full of water. He gave them to Hagar and sent her away. Carrying these things and her son, Hagar went and wandered in the desert of Beersheba.

¹⁵Later, when all the water was gone from the bag, Hagar put her son under a bush. ¹⁶Then she went away a short distance and sat down. She thought, "My son will die, and I cannot watch this happen." She sat there and began to cry.

¹⁷God heard the boy crying, and God's angel called to Hagar from heaven. He said, "What is wrong, Hagar? Don't be afraid! God has heard the boy crying there. ¹⁸Help him up and take him by the hand. I will make his descendants into a great nation."

¹⁹Then God showed Hagar a well of water. So she went to the well and filled her bag with water and gave the boy a drink.

²⁰God was with the boy as he grew up. Ishmael lived in the desert and became an archer. ²¹He lived in the Desert of Paran, and his mother found a wife for him in Egypt.

DEVOTION

THE BIRTH OF ISAAC was a cause for joy in the household of Abraham and Sarah. There was the fulfillment of the promise that God made to Abraham that he would make a great nation from his descendants. There was the personal fulfillment that Sarah felt at finally having a son, giving Abraham the joy of his old age. God had brought such joy to Sarah that she named the boy "Isaac" which sounds like the Hebrew word for "laugh." You might recall that Sarah did, indeed, laugh at the prospect of having a child so late in life when Abraham had entertained the three heavenly visitors near Mamre in Genesis 18:1–16.

The lesson of the birth of Isaac is that God will find a way for his will to be done. When Abraham tried to work his way around the promise of God, considering it unlikely that Sarah would bear a child, he created the problem of Ishmael. Born of Sarah's Egyptian slave, Hagar, Ishmael was now growing up and he and his mother could no longer peacefully coexist with the rest of the household anymore. So Abraham sent them away.

I don't think Abraham expected either of them to survive. There is no evidence that he gave them any means of transportation or even enough food and water to survive more than a day. Perhaps he wanted to put his problems out of sight and hope that they simply would go away.

Do we ever do the same thing? Do we sweep the problems we have created out of our sight and hope that no one else finds them? Do we fail to pay proper attention to a problem only to have it become a bigger problem later?

Because Abraham failed to address the problem he created with Ishmael, the descendants of his two sons would contend with one another for generations to come. The angel of God appeared to Hagar and assured her that Ishmael's descendants would be a great nation as well.

THOUGHTS TO PONDER

Why did God not allow Ishmael to die under the bush in the desert? If God wanted to save Ishmael, why not have him raised in Abraham's camp? What scenario was God creating by blessing these boys separately?

PRAYER

God, we know you choose people for your own purposes. Thank you for choosing us as your spiritual nation. Amen.

GIVING UP EVERYTHING

GENESIS 22:1–19

22 After these things God tested Abraham's faith. God said to him, "Abraham!"

And he answered, "Here I am."

2Then God said, "Take your only son, Isaac, the son you love, and go to the land of Moriah. Kill him there and offer him as a whole burnt offering on one of the mountains I will tell you about."

3Abraham got up early in the morning and saddled his donkey. He took Isaac and two servants with him. After he cut the wood for the sacrifice, they went to the place God had told them to go. 4On the third day Abraham looked up and saw the place in the distance. 5He said to his servants, "Stay here with the donkey. My son and I will go over there and worship, and then we will come back to you."

6Abraham took the wood for the sacrifice and gave it to his son to carry, but he himself took the knife and the fire. So he and his son went on together.

7Isaac said to his father Abraham, "Father!"

Abraham answered, "Yes, my son."

Isaac said, "We have the fire and the wood, but where is the lamb we will burn as a sacrifice?"

8Abraham answered, "God will give us the lamb for the sacrifice, my son."

So Abraham and his son went on together 9and came to the place God had told him about. Abraham built an altar there. He laid the wood on it and then tied up his son Isaac and laid him on the wood on the altar. 10Then Abraham took his knife and was about to kill his son.

11But the angel of the LORD called to him from heaven and said, "Abraham! Abraham!"

Abraham answered, "Yes."

12The angel said, "Don't kill your son or hurt him in any way. Now I can see that you trust God and that you have not kept your son, your only son, from me."

13Then Abraham looked up and saw a male sheep caught in a bush by its horns. So Abraham went and took the sheep and killed it. He offered it as a whole burnt offering to God, and his son was saved. 14So Abraham named that place The LORD Provides. Even today people say, "On the mountain of the LORD it will be provided."

15The angel of the LORD called to Abraham from heaven a second time 16and said, "The LORD says, 'Because you did not keep back your son, your only son, from me, I make you this promise by my own name: 17I will surely bless you and give you many descendants. They will be as many as the stars in the sky and the sand on the seashore, and they will capture the cities of their enemies. [18]Through your descendants all the nations on the earth will be blessed, because you obeyed me.'"

[19]Then Abraham returned to his servants. They all traveled back to Beersheba, and Abraham stayed there.

DEVOTION

THE ORDER CAME to the missionaries late at night. Although they had been in China with their families through much of the 1930s and 1940s, change was in the air and they would have to be ready to be deported in the morning. Between the families, they could take 250 pounds of possessions.

All night long they agonized. China had been their home. They had furniture; it would stay. Ditto on the heavy books. The children would need a change of clothes. It didn't take long to exceed the 250 pound limit and the rest of the night was spent deciding what to take and what to leave behind.

By the morning, a pile of possessions stood in the living room carefully weighed on the bathroom scale. The families were preparing for a last look around when the soldiers knocked on their door. Entering the room, they looked at the pile of possessions and asked, "Have you weighed your children yet?"

Suddenly, the pile of stuff in the living room became exactly that—stuff. Mere possessions. Not nearly as precious as even one child. Without so much as a look back at the pile, the couples gathered their children and headed out into the pre-dawn morning, never to see China again.

Abraham was being asked to do the unthinkable. "Abraham, have you weighed Isaac for the altar of sacrifice?" God seemed to say. And without hesitation, Abraham did it. But because of Abraham's faith, Isaac was spared.

A few hundred years later, God himself would give up a Son as a sacrifice, only this time, there would be no last minute reprieve. What are you willing to give up in response?

THOUGHTS TO PONDER

What thoughts must have been going through Abraham's mind as he climbed the mountain? What must Isaac have been thinking? Why would God put Abraham to such a severe test?

PRAYER

God, we pray that when we are asked to make our greatest sacrifice, we will do it with gladness and never lose faith in you. Amen.

Earning Respect

GENESIS 23:1–20

23 Sarah lived to be one hundred twenty-seven years old. ²She died in Kiriath Arba (that is, Hebron) in the land of Canaan. Abraham was very sad and cried because of her. ³After a while he got up from the side of his wife's body and went to talk to the Hittites. He said, ⁴"I am only a stranger and a foreigner here. Sell me some of your land so that I can bury my dead wife."

⁵The Hittites answered Abraham, ⁶"Sir, you are a great leader among us. You may have the best place we have to bury your dead. You may have any of our burying places that you want, and none of us will stop you from burying your dead wife."

⁷Abraham rose and bowed to the people of the land, the Hittites. ⁸He said to them, "If you truly want to help me bury my dead wife here, speak to Ephron, the son of Zohar for me. ⁹Ask him to sell me the cave of Machpelah at the edge of his field. I will pay him the full price. You can be the witnesses that I am buying it as a burial place."

¹⁰Ephron was sitting among the Hittites at the city gate. He answered Abraham, ¹¹"No, sir. I will give you the land and the cave that is in it, with these people as witnesses. Bury your dead wife."

¹²Then Abraham bowed down before the Hittites. ¹³He said to Ephron before all the people, "Please let me pay you the full price for the field. Accept my money, and I will bury my dead there."

¹⁴Ephron answered Abraham, ¹⁵"Sir, the land is worth ten pounds of silver, but I won't argue with you over the price. Take the land, and bury your dead wife."

¹⁶Abraham agreed and paid Ephron in front of the Hittite witnesses. He weighed out the full price, ten pounds of silver, and they counted the weight as the traders normally did.

¹⁷⁻¹⁸So Ephron's field in Machpelah, east of Mamre, was sold. Abraham became the owner of the field, the cave in it, and all the trees that were in the field. The sale was made at the city gate, with the Hittites as witnesses. ¹⁹After this, Abraham buried his wife Sarah in the cave in the field of Machpelah, near Mamre. (Mamre was later called Hebron in the land of Canaan.) ²⁰So Abraham bought the field and the cave in it from the Hittites to use as a burying place.

DEVOTION

MY DAD WAS a rarity in the business world—he was a highly regarded, honest used car dealer. Everyone knew him as a hard worker and everyone knew that he would never lie about the merits of a car. I've heard him tell more than one person, "You don't want that car" when they asked. I've seen him make no money on a deal so that a ministerial student could have a car to drive. I've watched the entire community of Christians rally around him when, late in his life, his business burned to the ground.

Love and respect like that don't just happen for a used car dealer—they have to be earned. I joked with my dad when I decided to be a journalist that we held the two lowest rungs in the ladder of public respect, but the old used car dealer clichés didn't really hold true with my dad, and thousands of his customers would attest to that.

One of the indicators of Abraham's good character is the respect he commanded as he conducted his business. A couple of chapters earlier, we read of Abimelech visiting Abraham to make a treaty saying, "God is with you in everything you do. So make a promise to me here before God that you will be fair with me and my children and my descendants. Be kind to me and to this land where you have lived as a stranger—as kind as I have been to you" (Genesis 21:22–23). And because Abraham had been both fair and kind to Abimelech and to the Hittites, he enjoyed a great reputation among the foreigners with which he cohabitated.

So the story above is not surprising. Abraham, grieving for his beloved Sarah, wants the best burial spot for her—the cave of Machpelah. And because of his excellent reputation, the owner of the cave was immediately willing to let him have it, but reluctant to take any money.

Why would the owner of the cave make such an offer? Respect.

What do people in the community think of the way you do your work? Is God glorified by the way we act in our business dealings? Abraham, a very wealthy man for his day, had earned the respect of strangers around him. Can the same be said of us?

THOUGHTS TO PONDER

What do you think Abraham did to earn the respect of the Hittite people? What does the reaction of Ephron above tell you about Abraham? What do you want your reputation to be in your community? What are you doing to earn that reputation?

PRAYER

God, we pray that in all of our dealings we will honor you and the world will know we belong to you. Amen.

WHERE'S YOUR UMBRELLA?

GENESIS 24:1–4, 9–27

24 Abraham was now very old, and the LORD had blessed him in every way. [2]Abraham said to his oldest servant, who was in charge of everything he owned, "Put your hand under my leg. [3]Make a promise to me before the LORD, the God of heaven and earth. Don't get a wife for my son from the Canaanite girls who live around here. [4]Instead, go back to my country, to the land of my relatives, and get a wife for my son Isaac."

[9]So the servant put his hand under his master's leg and made a promise to Abraham about this.

[10]The servant took ten of Abraham's camels and left, carrying with him many different kinds of beautiful gifts. He went to Northwest Mesopotamia to Nahor's city. [11]In the evening, when the women come out to get water, he made the camels kneel down at the well outside the city.

[12]The servant said, "LORD, God of my master Abraham, allow me to find a wife for his son today. Please show this kindness to my master Abraham. [13]Here I am, standing by the spring, and the girls from the city are coming out to get water. [14]I will say to one of them, 'Please put your jar down so I can drink.' Then let her say, 'Drink, and I will also give water to your camels.' If that happens, I will know she is the right one for your servant Isaac and that you have shown kindness to my master."

[15]Before the servant had finished praying, Rebekah, the daughter of Bethuel, came out of the city. (Bethuel was the son of Milcah and Nahor, Abraham's brother.) Rebekah was carrying her water jar on her shoulder. [16]She was very pretty, a virgin; she had never had sexual relations with a man. She went down to the spring and filled her jar, then came back up. [17]The servant ran to her and said, "Please give me a little water from your jar."

[18]Rebekah said, "Drink, sir." She quickly lowered the jar from her shoulder and gave him a drink. [19]After he finished drinking, Rebekah said, "I will also pour some water for your camels." [20]So she quickly poured all the water from her jar into the drinking trough for the camels. Then she kept running to the well until she had given all the camels enough to drink.

[21]The servant quietly watched her. He wanted to be sure the LORD had made his trip successful. [22]After the camels had finished drinking, he gave Rebekah a gold ring weighing one-fifth of an ounce and two gold arm bracelets weighing about four ounces each. [23]He asked, "Who is your father? Is there a place in his house for me and my men to spend the night?"

[24]Rebekah answered, "My father is Bethuel, the son of Milcah and Nahor." [25]Then she said, "And, yes, we have straw for your camels and a place for you to spend the night."

[26]The servant bowed and worshiped the LORD [27]and said, "Blessed is the LORD, the God of my master Abraham. The LORD has been kind and truthful to him and has led me to my master's relatives."

DEVOTION

"THE LORD PROVIDES." It was the name that Abraham gave the mountain of sacrifice after God prevented him from killing Isaac and provided a ram instead for the altar. And the text tells us that the Israelites continued long afterward with a saying: "On the mountain of the LORD it will be provided" (Genesis 22:14). It's still true today: God does, indeed, provide for us.

Do you pray in faith? I mean do you *really* pray in faith? As I write this, my home state of Texas and my adopted state of Oklahoma are being ravaged by drought and wildfires, and I'm reminded of an old story from the "Dust Bowl" days about a church that gathered on a special night to pray for rain. The circuit-riding preacher got up and asked the crowd on this hot, cloudless night, "Where are your umbrellas?"

Perhaps we're too sophisticated to carry our umbrellas when we pray for rain in this day of relatively accurate forecasts. But I think we often forget our spiritual "umbrellas" when we pray for God's blessings. We often don't even recognize the spiritual shower of blessings when it rains down on us. We pray for healing, then credit only the doctors and the medicine when a cure comes. We pray for better employment, then simply credit networking and a good résumé when our prayer is answered.

When you pray, expect an answer! And when you get the answer, do as Abraham's servant did: give God the praise and credit he deserves.

THOUGHTS TO PONDER

What specific things have you prayed for that later came to pass? Could you see the hand of God in the process? Did you give thanks? What are you still praying for today?

PRAYER

Father, we thank you that we can bring our petitions to you in prayer and that you listen to us. We pray that we will hear your answer and that we will accept it and praise you for it. Amen.

CLEARLY FROM THE LORD

GENESIS 24:28–40, 50–58

²⁸Then Rebekah ran and told her mother's family about all these things. ²⁹She had a brother named Laban, who ran out to Abraham's servant, who was still at the spring. ³⁰Laban had heard what she had said and had seen the ring and the bracelets on his sister's arms. So he ran out to the well, and there was the man standing by the camels at the spring. ³¹Laban said, "Sir, you are welcome to come in; you don't have to stand outside. I have prepared the house for you and also a place for your camels."

³²So Abraham's servant went into the house. After Laban unloaded the camels and gave them straw and food, he gave water to Abraham's servant so he and the men with him could wash their feet. ³³Then Laban gave the servant food, but the servant said, "I will not eat until I have told you why I came."

So Laban said, "Then tell us."

³⁴He said, "I am Abraham's servant. ³⁵The LORD has greatly blessed my master in everything, and he has become a rich man. The LORD has given him many flocks of sheep, herds of cattle, silver and gold, male and female servants, camels, and horses. ³⁶Sarah, my master's wife, gave birth to a son when she was old, and my master has given everything he owns to that son. ³⁷My master had me make a promise to him and said, 'Don't get a wife for my son from the Canaanite girls who live around here. ³⁸Instead, you must go to my father's people and to my family. There you must get a wife for my son.' ³⁹I said to my master, 'What if the woman will not come back with me?' ⁴⁰But he said, 'I serve the LORD, who will send his angel with you and will help you. You will get a wife for my son from my family and my father's people.'"

⁵⁰Laban and Bethuel answered, "This is clearly from the LORD, and we cannot change what must happen. ⁵¹Rebekah is yours. Take her and go. Let her marry your master's son as the LORD has commanded."

⁵²When Abraham's servant heard these words, he bowed facedown on the ground before the LORD. ⁵³Then he gave Rebekah gold and silver jewelry and clothes. He also gave expensive gifts to her brother and mother. ⁵⁴The servant and the men with him ate and drank and spent the night there. When they got up the next morning, the servant said, "Now let me go back to my master."

⁵⁵Rebekah's mother and her brother said, "Let Rebekah stay with us at least ten days. After that she may go."

⁵⁶But the servant said to them, "Do not make me wait, because the LORD has made my trip successful. Now let me go back to my master."

⁵⁷Rebekah's brother and mother said, "We will call Rebekah and ask her what she wants to do." ⁵⁸They called her and asked her, "Do you want to go with this man now?"

She said, "Yes, I do."

DEVOTION

"THIS IS CLEARLY from the LORD, and we cannot change what must happen," Laban says. And with that pronouncement, Rebekah is headed for Canaan to be the wife of Isaac.

I think it's sometimes easy to think of these as simpler times where people made such commitments casually because they had no other options anyway. So when Jesus says that you have to leave behind everything to follow him, we somehow think that command was easier for folks who didn't have a two-story house with a three-car garage. So we dismiss it.

Do you think it was easy for Abraham to leave the familiarity of his home and family in Ur and travel to a land he had never seen, his only map the angel of God? Do you think it was easy for Hannah to take her only boy—the boy she cried out to God to be able to conceive—and give him over to the service of the Temple? Do you think it was easy for Peter—a family man—to leave his nets and his boats and follow the Teacher from Galilee?

We do these folks a disservice to think it was somehow easier then. Rebekah has no way of knowing if she will ever see her family again. She has no personal knowledge of the man she is to marry. But because it appears to be the will of God, she agrees to go.

I pray to God to find out what his will is for my life. But what if the answer is something very hard? What if it's out of my "comfort zone"? To quote Laban, if it is "clearly from the LORD," then you cannot change what must happen.

THOUGHTS TO PONDER

How does God convey his will to us today? What task has he put on your heart to do for him?

PRAYER

God, we pray that when you call, we will hear, and that we will not simply hear, but that we will obey as Rebekah did, with clarity and without question. Amen.

GOD IS ENOUGH

GENESIS 25:19–34

[19]This is the family history of Isaac. Abraham had a son named Isaac. [20]When Isaac was forty years old, he married Rebekah, who came from Northwest Mesopotamia. She was Bethuel's daughter and the sister of Laban the Aramean. [21]Isaac's wife could not have children, so Isaac prayed to the LORD for her. The LORD heard Isaac's prayer, and Rebekah became pregnant.

[22]While she was pregnant, the babies struggled inside her. She asked, "Why is this happening to me?" Then she went to get an answer from the LORD.

[23]The LORD said to her,

"Two nations are in your body,
   and two groups of people will be taken from you.
One group will be stronger than the other,
   and the older will serve the younger."

[24]When the time came, Rebekah gave birth to twins. [25]The first baby was born red. Since his skin was like a hairy robe, he was named Esau. [26]When the second baby was born, he was holding on to Esau's heel, so that baby was named Jacob. Isaac was sixty years old when they were born.

[27]When the boys grew up, Esau became a skilled hunter. He loved to be out in the fields. But Jacob was a quiet man and stayed among the tents. [28]Isaac loved Esau because he hunted the wild animals that Isaac enjoyed eating. But Rebekah loved Jacob.

[29]One day Jacob was boiling a pot of vegetable soup. Esau came in from hunting in the fields, weak from hunger. [30]So Esau said to Jacob, "Let me eat some of that red soup, because I am weak with hunger." (That is why people call him Edom.)

[31]But Jacob said, "You must sell me your rights as the firstborn son."

[32]Esau said, "I am almost dead from hunger. If I die, all of my father's wealth will not help me."

[33]But Jacob said, "First, promise me that you will give it to me." So Esau made a promise to Jacob and sold his part of their father's wealth to Jacob. [34]Then Jacob gave Esau bread and vegetable soup, and he ate and drank, and then left. So Esau showed how little he cared about his rights as the firstborn son.

DEVOTION

IT'S INTERESTING HOW little idiom—those phrases we use which stand for something else—has changed over the centuries. In the days of Isaac, to "grab the heel" was to try to deceive someone. Centuries later we have a similar term when we speak of trying to "trip someone up" with questions or wrong information.

After struggling with his brother in the womb, Jacob emerges holding on to the heel of his older twin brother. Because of his actions on the day he was born, Jacob gets a name which sounds like the word for heel and implies a devious nature. And before long, Jacob is indeed involved in devious behavior, first in this story and later in the story where he steals the birthright from Esau by tricking his aging father.

It's fascinating to see the way God's will plays out through human personality. Even though Esau was the oldest, and therefore heir to the worldly household of Isaac, he was not suited to be the heir to the spiritual promise made first to Abraham and later to Isaac. Jacob's life was spent among the tents, soaking up the stories of their promise and God's plan. Esau's life was spent in the fields. God was planning to build a great nation, and that nation would come from Jacob— later named Israel—and not Esau.

Next comes one of the most famous stories in the Bible: Esau sells his birthright for a bowl of soup. What folly! A lifetime heritage thrown away for the temporary satisfaction of a meal.

But haven't we all seen people turn their backs on their special relationships as children of God for something no more lasting than a bowl of soup? Haven't we seen people turn their lives upside down, caught in an extramarital affair? Or caught cheating at work? Don't we all sometimes drink from the "bowl" of gossip and slander, even when Scripture warns us repeatedly about idle talk?

In his Letter to the Galatians, Paul reminds us that God wants to treat us like sons who are due a blessing. He writes: "Since you are God's children, God sent the Spirit of his Son into your hearts, and the Spirit cries out, 'Father.' So now you are not a slave; you are God's child, and God will give you the blessing he promised, because you are his child" (Galatians 4:6–7). And because we enjoy that special relationship with God, we pass up all the tempting "bowls of soup" the world offers us that ultimately fail to bring satisfaction or fulfillment.

THOUGHTS TO PONDER

How do we recognize the "bowls of soup" the world offers that look so tempting? How do we avoid them?

PRAYER

God, we know we are your sons and daughters, and therefore your heirs…help us to live that way. Amen.

MORE POWERFUL
THAN WORDS

GENESIS 26:1–18

26 Now there was a time of hunger in the land, besides the time of hunger that happened during Abraham's life. So Isaac went to the town of Gerar to see Abimelech king of the Philistines. ²The LORD appeared to Isaac and said, "Don't go down to Egypt, but live in the land where I tell you to live. ³Stay in this land, and I will be with you and bless you. I will give you and your descendants all these lands, and I will keep the oath I made to Abraham your father. ⁴I will give you many descendants, as hard to count as the stars in the sky, and I will give them all these lands. Through your descendants all the nations on the earth will be blessed. ⁵I will do this because your father Abraham obeyed me. He did what I said and obeyed my commands, my teachings, and my rules."

⁶So Isaac stayed in Gerar. ⁷His wife Rebekah was very beautiful, and the men of that place asked Isaac about her. Isaac said, "She is my sister," because he was afraid to tell them she was his wife. He thought they might kill him so they could have her.

⁸Isaac lived there a long time. One day as Abimelech king of the Philistines looked out his window, he saw Isaac holding his wife Rebekah tenderly. ⁹Abimelech called for Isaac and said, "This woman is your wife. Why did you say she was your sister?"

Isaac said to him, "I was afraid you would kill me so you could have her."

¹⁰Abimelech said, "What have you done to us? One of our men might have had sexual relations with your wife. Then we would have been guilty of a great sin."

¹¹So Abimelech warned everyone, "Anyone who touches this man or his wife will be put to death."

¹²Isaac planted seed in that land, and that year he gathered a great harvest. The LORD blessed him very much, ¹³and he became rich. He gathered more wealth until he became a very rich man. ¹⁴He had so many slaves and flocks and herds that the Philistines envied him. ¹⁵So they stopped up all the wells the servants of Isaac's father Abraham had dug. (They had dug them when Abraham was alive.) The Philistines filled those wells with dirt. ¹⁶And Abimelech said to Isaac, "Leave our country because you have become much more powerful than we are."

¹⁷So Isaac left that place and camped in the Valley of Gerar and lived there. ¹⁸Long before this time Abraham had dug many wells, but after he died, the Philistines filled them with dirt. So Isaac dug those wells again and gave them the same names his father had given them.

DEVOTION

MY SON SMILES like I smile, which is not particularly a good thing since broad smiles are not what I do best. But he adopted my smile anyway. I see other mannerisms in each of my children and I realize they have become like their parents in many ways.

The lie that Isaac tells Abimelech in this story is the same lie that his father, Abraham, told Abimelech in Genesis 20. In both cases, they put their fears ahead of their honesty, even putting their wives, Sarah and Rebekah, at risk in the process.

What have you passed along to your children? Are we guilty of talking to them about honesty at school and then cheating on our taxes? Do we stress abstinence from drugs, then fail to model moderation or abstinence in our own drinking or eating habits?

Children learn not only from what is "taught" but also from what is "caught." And the latter is often more convincing than the former.

There is no evidence that Isaac ever heard the story of how Abraham fooled Abimelech into thinking that Sarah was his sister, a deception so convincing that Abimelech actually took Sarah for one of his wives. Isaac certainly wasn't around at the time.

But somehow, like that habit or that smile you don't even teach your child, he picked up the trait: when in trouble, lie. The trait began with Abraham and continued with Isaac.

It's easy to remember the things you've taught your children. After all, the words come out of your mouth. But we don't always know the things they've "caught" from us while we weren't intending to teach. Those actions can be much more powerful than words.

THOUGHTS TO PONDER

What are your traits you want to pass on to your children? What are your traits that you hope your children don't adopt? How can we change our lives so we are teaching the right lessons?

PRAYER

Father, we pray that we will always model our lives after you, so that the lives we lead before our children and before the world will reflect only you. Amen.

QUESTIONABLE MOTIVES

GENESIS 27:1–24

27 When Isaac was old, his eyesight was poor, so he could not see clearly. One day he called his older son Esau to him and said, "Son."

Esau answered, "Here I am."

²Isaac said, "I am old and don't know when I might die. ³So take your bow and arrows and go hunting in the field for an animal for me to eat. ⁴When you prepare the tasty food that I love, bring it to me, and I will eat. Then I will bless you before I die." ⁵So Esau went out in the field to hunt.

Rebekah was listening as Isaac said this to his son Esau. ⁶She said to her son Jacob, "Listen, I heard your father saying to your brother Esau, ⁷'Kill an animal and prepare some tasty food for me to eat. Then I will bless you in the presence of the LORD before I die.' ⁸So obey me, my son, and do what I tell you. ⁹Go out to our goats and bring me two of the best young ones. I will prepare them just the way your father likes them. ¹⁰Then you will take the food to your father, and he will bless you before he dies."

¹¹But Jacob said to his mother Rebekah, "My brother Esau is a hairy man, and I am smooth! ¹²If my father touches me, he will know I am not Esau. Then he will not bless me but will place a curse on me because I tried to trick him."

¹³So Rebekah said to him, "If your father puts a curse on you, I will accept the blame. Just do what I said. Go get the goats for me."

¹⁴So Jacob went out and got two goats and brought them to his mother, and she cooked them in the special way Isaac enjoyed. ¹⁵She took the best clothes of her older son Esau that were in the house and put them on the younger son Jacob. ¹⁶She also took the skins of the goats and put them on Jacob's hands and neck. ¹⁷Then she gave Jacob the tasty food and the bread she had made.

¹⁸Jacob went in to his father and said, "Father."

And his father said, "Yes, my son. Who are you?"

¹⁹Jacob said to him, "I am Esau, your first son. I have done what you told me. Now sit up and eat some meat of the animal I hunted for you. Then bless me."

²⁰But Isaac asked his son, "How did you find and kill the animal so quickly?"

Jacob answered, "Because the LORD your God helped me to find it."

²¹Then Isaac said to Jacob, "Come near so I can touch you, my son. Then I will know if you are really my son Esau."

²²So Jacob came near to Isaac his father. Isaac touched him and said, "Your voice sounds like Jacob's voice, but your hands are hairy like the hands of Esau." ²³Isaac did not know it was Jacob, because his hands were hairy like Esau's hands, so Isaac blessed him. ²⁴Isaac asked, "Are you really my son Esau?"

Jacob answered, "Yes, I am."

DEVOTION

REBEKAH HAD BEEN told that her boys will represent two nations and that the older will serve the younger. Now Isaac is dying and one of his sons will receive the blessing of the father and the larger share of the inheritance that went with it. It is time for Rebekah to act.

There's an interesting question posed by this story: Does God's plan ever require my devious behavior in order for it to come to fruition? Does the end result of Jacob getting the blessing justify lying to Isaac and stealing the blessing from Esau?

Jacob is God's man. Within days, he will receive a vision to confirm that he is a part of the promise of his grandfather Abraham and his father Isaac. He will be the father of the twelve tribes of Israel. It's all in God's plan.

But did it require the trickery of Rebekah to come about?

This is an important question. A severe misinterpretation of this can lead to all kinds of terrible things, from "holy wars" to bombings of abortion clinics in the name of God's will. Just look at the behavior of Saul in the New Testament before he became the apostle named Paul. No activity, including murder, was too extreme in furthering the cause of radical Judaism.

While we know that God is fully capable of accomplishing his plan, it is difficult to judge Rebekah from afar. She saw the blessing of Isaac as important and irreversible and she did what she thought was right to secure that blessing for Jacob. But while it's difficult to judge Rebekah, we can judge our own actions in the light of Scripture and question our own motivations.

THOUGHTS TO PONDER

Are you ever tempted to do something wrong in order to achieve something good? Is it ever justified?

PRAYER

Father, we ask that you will help us to always choose right as we try to discern how to do your will in this world. Amen.

Blessing the Next Generation

GENESIS 27:25–41

²⁵Then Isaac said, "Bring me the food, and I will eat it and bless you." So Jacob gave him the food, and he ate. Jacob gave him wine, and he drank. ²⁶Then Isaac said to him, "My son, come near and kiss me." ²⁷So Jacob went to his father and kissed him. When Isaac smelled Esau's clothes, he blessed him . . .

Editor's note: Isaac blesses Jacob, still thinking he's blessing Esau.

³⁰Isaac finished blessing Jacob. Then, just as Jacob left his father Isaac, Esau came in from hunting. ³¹He also prepared some tasty food and brought it to his father. He said, "Father, rise and eat the food that your son killed for you and then bless me."

³²Isaac asked, "Who are you?"

He answered, "I am your son—your firstborn son—Esau."

³³Then Isaac trembled greatly and said, "Then who was it that hunted the animals and brought me food before you came? I ate it, and I blessed him, and it is too late now to take back my blessing."

³⁴When Esau heard the words of his father, he let out a loud and bitter cry. He said to his father, "Bless me—me, too, my father!"

³⁵But Isaac said, "Your brother came and tricked me. He has taken your blessing."

³⁶Esau said, "Jacob is the right name for him. He has tricked me these two times. He took away my share of everything you own, and now he has taken away my blessing." Then Esau asked, "Haven't you saved a blessing for me?"

³⁷Isaac answered, "I gave Jacob the power to be master over you, and all his brothers will be his servants. And I kept him strong with grain and new wine. There is nothing left to give you, my son."

³⁸But Esau continued, "Do you have only one blessing, Father? Bless me, too, Father!" Then Esau began to cry out loud.

³⁹Isaac said to him,

"You will live far away from the best land,
    far from the rain.
⁴⁰You will live by using your sword,
    and you will be a slave to your brother.
But when you struggle,
    you will break free from him."

⁴¹After that Esau hated Jacob because of the blessing from Isaac. He thought to himself, "My father will soon die, and I will be sad for him. Then I will kill Jacob."

DEVOTION

IN HEBREW CULTURE, the blessing was irrevocable. It was also thought to be prophetic of things to come. And it always went to the oldest son, the rightful heir of the father.

It's interesting that sibling rivalry dates back thousands of years. Think Cain and Abel. And now, Jacob and Esau. These twins had been fighting since birth. Esau was born first, but Jacob came out of the womb grasping the heel of his brother. With his knowledge of the outdoors, Esau became a favorite of his father, while Jacob stayed around the tents and became a favorite of his mother.

Now the failing health of Isaac brought the rivalry to a climax: who will get the blessing?

This story reinforces the power of invoking God's blessing. Note that Isaac can't take it back; he gets no second chance. Jacob will inherit the land and rule over his brother. The power of God has been invoked, and it's not something to be trivialized or reversed.

I think there's something to be said for formally blessing our children today. In the New Testament, we're told about the power of prayer, yet all too often, we shy away from invoking a blessing on our children. But I think they need to hear it. They need to know their expected role in carrying on the heritage of our faith. And the beauty of it is that under the new agreement, made possible by the blood of Christ, there's a blessing for every child of God.

We should have blessings for newborns, blessings for engagements and marriages, blessings for the sick and dying. Just as Isaac did, it's the responsibility of each generation to invoke the Lord's comfort, guidance, grace, and mercy on the next generation.

THOUGHTS TO PONDER

Have you ever prayed a blessing over someone? Have you had a blessing prayed over you? How might a prayer of blessing differ from our traditional prayers to God? How might it be the same?

PRAYER

God, we know you have blessed us with every good gift we have, and we pray that you will bless the ones we love as long as life lasts. Amen.

Our Permanent Home

GENESIS 27:42—28:5

⁴²Rebekah heard about Esau's plan to kill Jacob. So she sent for Jacob and said to him, "Listen, your brother Esau is comforting himself by planning to kill you. ⁴³So, my son, do what I say. My brother Laban is living in Haran. Go to him at once! ⁴⁴Stay with him for a while, until your brother is not so angry. ⁴⁵In time, your brother will not be angry, and he will forget what you did to him. Then I will send a servant to bring you back. I don't want to lose both of my sons on the same day."

⁴⁶Then Rebekah said to Isaac, "I am tired of Hittite women. If Jacob marries one of these Hittite women here in this land, I want to die."

28 Isaac called Jacob and blessed him and commanded him, "You must not marry a Canaanite woman. ²Go to the house of Bethuel, your mother's father, in Northwest Mesopotamia. Laban, your mother's brother, lives there. Marry one of his daughters. ³May God Almighty bless you and give you many children, and may you become a group of many peoples. ⁴May he give you and your descendants the blessing of Abraham so that you may own the land where you are now living as a stranger, the land God gave to Abraham." ⁵So Isaac sent Jacob to Northwest Mesopotamia, to Laban the brother of Rebekah. Bethuel the Aramean was the father of Laban and Rebekah, and Rebekah was the mother of Jacob and Esau.

Devotion

THERE'S A SHORT PHRASE that I find intriguing in the blessing Isaac gives his son before he leaves on his journey. After Isaac asks God to bless Jacob with many children, he asks God to bring the blessing of Abraham to Jacob so that "you may own the land where you are now living as a stranger" (Genesis 28:4).

Have you ever been a visitor or resident in a foreign land? Have you ever felt the discomfort of not knowing the language or not being able to read the signs? How did it make you feel? What if you lived that way for a lifetime?

Did you know that Christians are strangers on this earth? The writer of Hebrews recounts how Abraham and Isaac lived by faith as foreigners or aliens, not considering the world their permanent home: "They said they were like visitors and strangers on earth. When people say such things, they show they are looking for a country that will be their own. If they had been thinking about the country they had left, they could have gone back. But they were waiting for a better country—a heavenly country. So God is not ashamed to be called their God, because he has prepared a city for them" (Hebrews 11:13–16).

A grandfather, a son, and now a grandson. Three generations living by faith like aliens in a land that their descendants would someday own, and they're praised for their faith. So the question for us is this: are we living for this world or are we looking ahead, by faith, for our permanent home?

THOUGHTS TO PONDER

What does it mean to be an alien? How do we as Christians live differently in this world, knowing that heaven is our home? Are we willing, like Jacob did with Isaac, to go where our heavenly Father leads us?

PRAYER

God, we pray we will go where you lead, for we know there is more to life than this current place. Amen.

FINDING HIS PRESENCE

GENESIS 28:10–22

¹⁰Jacob left Beersheba and set out for Haran. ¹¹When he came to a place, he spent the night there because the sun had set. He found a stone and laid his head on it to go to sleep. ¹²Jacob dreamed that there was a ladder resting on the earth and reaching up into heaven, and he saw angels of God going up and coming down the ladder. ¹³Then Jacob saw the LORD standing above the ladder, and he said, "I am the LORD, the God of Abraham your grandfather, and the God of Isaac. I will give you and your descendants the land on which you are now sleeping. ¹⁴Your descendants will be as many as the dust of the earth. They will spread west and east, north and south, and all the families of the earth will be blessed through you and your descendants. ¹⁵I am with you and will protect you everywhere you go and will bring you back to this land. I will not leave you until I have done what I have promised you."

¹⁶Then Jacob woke from his sleep and said, "Surely the LORD is in this place, but I did not know it." ¹⁷He was afraid and said, "This place frightens me! It is surely the house of God and the gate of heaven."

¹⁸Jacob rose early in the morning and took the stone he had slept on and set it up on its end. Then he poured olive oil on the top of it. ¹⁹At first, the name of that city was Luz, but Jacob named it Bethel.

²⁰Then Jacob made a promise. He said, "I want God to be with me and to protect me on this journey. I want him to give me food to eat and clothes to wear ²¹so I will be able to return in peace to my father's house. If the LORD does these things, he will be my God. ²²This stone which I have set up on its end will be the house of God. And I will give God one-tenth of all he gives me."

DEVOTION

WHERE DO YOU go to feel the presence of God more closely? Do you prefer the mountains? Or the ocean? Do you have a special place in your home? A favorite time of day?

Do you have to be still to feel the presence of God? Or do you want to jump on a bicycle or take a hike to draw near to God?

Jacob was on the run. In just a few short days, he had gone from being his mother's favorite child who stayed among the tents while his older brother hunted game to being a man without a home. Unable to return because of his brother's wrath, he was on his way to a foreign land known as Paddan Aram to meet an uncle he didn't know and to take a wife from among women he had never met.

When I think of times that I've felt God come near (or, more accurately, that I've moved near to him) I've always equated it with being at peace. Perhaps it was while enjoying a blazing campfire at church camp. Or watching the sun rise over the mountains. Or watching the sun set over the ocean.

But Jacob didn't have the luxury of peace. He was on the run. And even though he was a stranger in a foreign land, with only a stone for a pillow, Jacob is ushered into the presence of God. He's assured that his trip will be safe and that he and his descendants will someday return to this land and inhabit it. Jacob names the place Bethel, meaning "house of God."

What does this story tell us?

It tells us that God can come close to me and comfort me even when I am in the worst of circumstances. I can feel the presence of God anywhere, anytime. I thank God for mountaintop experiences, but I'll also welcome his presence in the middle of a hectic day at the office or in the midst of a traffic jam at rush hour.

The lesson of Jacob and the stone is this: seek your Bethel where you can find it, and when you do, God will come and dwell in it.

Years later, Jacob was rich. He was the father of twelve sons. He had settled his differences with Esau. Then God commanded him to return to Bethel (Genesis 35:1).

Why? God wanted Jacob to return to Bethel, literally and spiritually, for Jacob had foreign gods in his household—gods he had to purge before traveling to that holy place. The "house of God" calls us back, no matter how far we've traveled.

THOUGHTS TO PONDER

Where are the Bethel stones in your life? Where are the reminders that God keeps his promises to those who are faithful to him? How closely do we feel the daily presence of God?

PRAYER

God, you come to us in so many ways—in prayer, in nature, in the loving spirit of one of your followers. Help us see you and hear you, that we may know your direction for our lives. Amen.

TRUSTING GOD'S PROVISION

GENESIS 29:1–14

29 Then Jacob continued his journey and came to the land of the people of the East. ²He looked and saw a well in the field and three flocks of sheep lying nearby, because they drank water from this well. A large stone covered the mouth of the well. ³When all the flocks would gather there, the shepherds would roll the stone away from the well and water the sheep. Then they would put the stone back in its place.

⁴Jacob said to the shepherds there, "My brothers, where are you from?"

They answered, "We are from Haran."

⁵Then Jacob asked, "Do you know Laban, grandson of Nahor?"

They answered, "We know him."

⁶Then Jacob asked, "How is he?"

They answered, "He is well. Look, his daughter Rachel is coming now with his sheep."

⁷Jacob said, "But look, it is still the middle of the day. It is not time for the sheep to be gathered for the night, so give them water and let them go back into the pasture."

⁸But they said, "We cannot do that until all the flocks are gathered. Then we will roll away the stone from the mouth of the well and water the sheep."

⁹While Jacob was talking with the shepherds, Rachel came with her father's sheep, because it was her job to care for the sheep. ¹⁰When Jacob saw Laban's daughter Rachel and Laban's sheep, he went to the well and rolled the stone from its mouth and watered Laban's sheep. Now Laban was the brother of Rebekah, Jacob's mother. ¹¹Then Jacob kissed Rachel and cried. ¹²He told her that he was from her father's family and that he was the son of Rebekah. So Rachel ran home and told her father.

¹³When Laban heard the news about his sister's son Jacob, he ran to meet him. Laban hugged him and kissed him and brought him to his house, where Jacob told Laban everything that had happened.

¹⁴Then Laban said, "You are my own flesh and blood."

DEVOTION

FOLLOWING HIS FATHER'S orders to take a wife from his mother's side of the family, Jacob continues his journey east to the land known as Paddan Aram. Isaac knew that Jacob's uncle, Laban, had a large family and that there would be a suitable bride for Jacob there. Together, they would have heirs to secure the eventual possession of the land promised to them. It was important that Jacob find a proper bride.

The providence of God is clear in this story. No sooner does Jacob arrive in the land than he meets Rachel, tending her father's sheep.

Jacob breaks with protocol in rolling away the stone in the middle of the day to water the sheep that Rachel was tending for her father, Laban. Perhaps he did this so they could go home and tell Laban of his arrival. Jacob had found the love he had left home to find, and in his joy and relief he kissed her and cried. His long journey was over. He was home with his mother's relatives.

What has God provided for you at the end of a long journey? Perhaps he restored you or a loved one to good health. Perhaps you asked his help in finding a better job or getting a promotion at your current job. Or, maybe, like Jacob, you turned over the search for a mate to the hand of God.

We need to take a cue from Jacob. While he depended on the providence of God, he headed east. He walked in the direction of his future bride, all the while trusting God to provide. When we take the first steps of faith, God will meet us along the way.

I don't know where the providence of God is going to take me. But I do know that I am more likely to find his will for me if I'm going in his direction. Jacob's life, and indeed Jewish history, would have been different had he decided to forego the arduous journey and marry a local woman of Canaan like his brother Esau did to spite his father, Isaac (Genesis 28:8–9). By listening to his earthly father and his heavenly Father, Jacob found his destiny, setting a good example for all of us.

THOUGHTS TO PONDER

What are you currently depending on God to provide in your life? What are some of the things you've turned over to his providence? Are you trying to direct too many of the major decisions in your life without turning them over to him?

PRAYER

God, we know that the outcomes of all our current problems are in your hands. Help us, like Jacob, to turn to you for direction in the major and minor decisions of our lives. Amen.

PERSISTENT LOVE

GENESIS 28:1–5; 29:16–30

28 Isaac called Jacob and blessed him and commanded him, "You must not marry a Canaanite woman. ²Go to the house of Bethuel, your mother's father, in Northwest Mesopotamia. Laban, your mother's brother, lives there. Marry one of his daughters. ³May God Almighty bless you and give you many children, and may you become a group of many peoples. ⁴May he give you and your descendants the blessing of Abraham so that you may own the land where you are now living as a stranger, the land God gave to Abraham." ⁵So Isaac sent Jacob to Northwest Mesopotamia, to Laban the brother of Rebekah. Bethuel the Aramean was the father of Laban and Rebekah, and Rebekah was the mother of Jacob and Esau.

¹⁶Now Laban had two daughters. The older was Leah, and the younger was Rachel. ¹⁷Leah had weak eyes, but Rachel was very beautiful. ¹⁸Jacob loved Rachel, so he said to Laban, "Let me marry your younger daughter Rachel. If you will, I will work seven years for you."

¹⁹Laban said, "It would be better for her to marry you than someone else, so stay here with me." ²⁰So Jacob worked for Laban seven years so he could marry Rachel. But they seemed like just a few days to him because he loved Rachel very much.

²¹After seven years Jacob said to Laban, "Give me Rachel so that I may marry her. The time I promised to work for you is over."

²²So Laban gave a feast for all the people there. ²³That evening he brought his daughter Leah to Jacob, and they had sexual relations. ²⁴(Laban gave his slave girl Zilpah to his daughter to be her servant.) ²⁵In the morning when Jacob saw that he had had sexual relations with Leah, he said to Laban, "What have you done to me? I worked hard for you so that I could marry Rachel! Why did you trick me?"

²⁶Laban said, "In our country we do not allow the younger daughter to marry before the older daughter. ²⁷But complete the full week of the marriage ceremony with Leah, and I will give you Rachel to marry also. But you must serve me another seven years."

²⁸So Jacob did this, and when he had completed the week with Leah, Laban gave him his daughter Rachel as a wife. ²⁹(Laban gave his slave girl Bilhah to his daughter Rachel to be her servant.) ³⁰So Jacob had sexual relations with Rachel also, and Jacob loved Rachel more than Leah. Jacob worked for Laban for another seven years.

Devotion

SOMETIMES YOU READ a Bible story and you simply can't relate. This is one of those passages for me.

It always amazes my college students when I tell them I dated my wife for two weeks and proposed to her. Five months later we were married. That means I dated my wife one day for every year that Jacob labored to marry Rachel.

I don't know any modern courtships of fourteen years hard labor, but I have seen this love story play out in reverse. I've seen a husband push his wife in a wheelchair for years. I've seen a wife change the IV drip and the bedpan of her dying husband for months. I've seen the Jacob and Rachel story in "rewind mode," over and over in the lives of good people.

I tell my college students that when they say "for better or worse" they had better be thinking, "for better and then probably worse." Because if the marriage agreement is unbroken, one of them will someday be burying the love of his or her youth.

My wife was 19 when we married, young and healthy and so was I. Today she has MS and I have degenerative disc disease. But quitting or trading in for a "newer model" has never been an option for either of us.

Jacob was fooled by Laban, but he was not deterred. He worked the years and earned his wife. Years later they would meet to form a peace pact when their herds had become too large for them to coexist. Laban asked Jacob to not take any other wives but his daughters. He must have been pleased with Jacob. I'm married to a daughter of God and he's asked me to keep my agreement with her all the days of my life even if the really hard work is yet to come.

Thoughts to Ponder

How is the agreement that God has with his people like the agreement of marriage? What does that say about our relationship to him? What does it say about our relationship to our spouse?

Prayer

Father, you made us man and woman and made us attractive to one another. We pray that our commitments to one another will be an honor to you and to the agreement you have with each of us. Amen.

A New Name

GENESIS 29:31—30:13, 17—24

³¹When the LORD saw that Jacob loved Rachel more than Leah, he made it possible for Leah to have children, but not Rachel. ³²Leah became pregnant and gave birth to a son. She named him Reuben, because she said, "The LORD has seen my troubles. Surely now my husband will love me."

³³Leah became pregnant again and gave birth to another son. She named him Simeon and said, "The LORD has heard that I am not loved, so he has given me this son."

³⁴Leah became pregnant again and gave birth to another son. She named him Levi and said, "Now, surely my husband will be close to me, because I have given him three sons."

³⁵Then Leah gave birth to another son. She named him Judah, because she said, "Now I will praise the LORD." Then Leah stopped having children.

30 When Rachel saw that she was not having children for Jacob, she envied her sister Leah. She said to Jacob, "Give me children, or I'll die!" ²Jacob became angry with her and said, "Can I do what only God can do? He is the one who has kept you from having children."

³Then Rachel said, "Here is my slave girl Bilhah. Have sexual relations with her so she can give birth to a child for me. Then I can have my own family through her."

⁴So Rachel gave Bilhah, her slave girl, to Jacob as a wife, and he had sexual relations with her. ⁵She became pregnant and gave Jacob a son. ⁶Rachel said, "God has judged me innocent. He has listened to my prayer and has given me a son," so she named him Dan.

⁷Bilhah became pregnant again and gave Jacob a second son. ⁸Rachel said, "I have struggled hard with my sister, and I have won." So she named that son Naphtali.

⁹Leah saw that she had stopped having children, so she gave her slave girl Zilpah to Jacob as a wife. ¹⁰When Zilpah had a son, ¹¹Leah said, "I am lucky," so she named him Gad. ¹²Zilpah gave birth to another son, ¹³and Leah said, "I am very happy! Now women will call me happy," so she named him Asher.

¹⁷Then God answered Leah's prayer, and she became pregnant again. She gave birth to a fifth son ¹⁸and said, "God has given me what I paid for, because I gave my slave girl to my husband." So Leah named her son Issachar.

¹⁹Leah became pregnant again and gave birth to a sixth son. ²⁰She said, "God has given me a fine gift. Now surely Jacob will honor me, because I have given him six sons," so she named him Zebulun. ²¹Later Leah gave birth to a daughter and named her Dinah.

²²Then God remembered Rachel and answered her prayer, making it possible for her to have children. ²³When she became pregnant and gave birth to a son, she said, "God has taken away my shame," ²⁴and she named him Joseph.

DEVOTION

IN THE DAYS of Jacob, names had meaning. For instance, Reuben, the oldest child had a Hebrew name which meant "he has seen my troubles." It was appropriate for Leah, who feared that her husband didn't love her, but hoped that a male heir might change that. Simeon means "he has heard" because God heard Leah's prayers for another son.

And on it goes with each son: Levi, Judah, Dan, Naphtali, Gad, Asher, Issachar, Zebulun, and finally Joseph.

Names have meaning today. We tell our children that something is expected of them because they are carrying our name and the name of their grandparents through many generations. We want our name to mean something in the communities—work, neighborhood, church, etc.—in which we live.

We carry the name of Christ today. We're called Christians.

Peter tells his readers to expect a certain amount of suffering for being a follower of Christ. Then, he once and for all validates the name "Christian" when he writes, "But if you suffer because you are a Christian, do not be ashamed. Praise God because you wear that name" (1 Peter 4:16).

But another name awaits us. John, in his Revelation, writes, "I will also give to each one who wins the victory a white stone with a new name written on it. No one knows this new name except the one who receives it" (Revelation 2:17). Those of us who wear the name of Christ in this world will wear a new name forever with God in heaven.

THOUGHTS TO PONDER

Looking at the story, how does God use the rivalry between Rachel and Leah to fulfill his purpose? What factors did, or would, you consider when naming your children?

PRAYER

Father, we are so proud to be called your children and to wear the name of Christ every day. Help us to walk in a manner worthy of the name. Amen.

In God's Hands

GENESIS 30:25–43

²⁵After the birth of Joseph, Jacob said to Laban, "Now let me go to my own home and country. ²⁶Give me my wives and my children and let me go. I have earned them by working for you, and you know that I have served you well."

²⁷Laban said to him, "If I have pleased you, please stay. I know the LORD has blessed me because of you. ²⁸Tell me what I should pay you, and I will give it to you."

²⁹Jacob answered, "You know that I have worked hard for you, and your flocks have grown while I cared for them. ³⁰When I came, you had little, but now you have much. Every time I did something for you, the LORD blessed you. But when will I be able to do something for my own family?"

³¹Laban asked, "Then what should I give you?"

Jacob answered, "I don't want you to give me anything. Just do this one thing, and I will come back and take care of your flocks. ³²Today let me go through all your flocks. I will take every speckled or spotted sheep, every black lamb, and every spotted or speckled goat. That will be my pay. ³³In the future you can easily see if I am honest. When you come to look at my flocks, if I have any goat that isn't speckled or spotted or any lamb that isn't black, you will know I stole it."

³⁴Laban answered, "Agreed! We will do what you ask." ³⁵But that day Laban took away all the male goats that had streaks or spots, all the speckled and spotted female goats (all those that had white on them), and all the black sheep. He told his sons to watch over them. ³⁶Then he took these animals to a place that was three days' journey away from Jacob. Jacob took care of all the flocks that were left.

³⁷So Jacob cut green branches from poplar, almond, and plane trees and peeled off some of the bark so that the branches had white stripes on them. ³⁸He put the branches in front of the flocks at the watering places. When the animals came to drink, they also mated there, ³⁹so the flocks mated in front of the branches. Then the young that were born were streaked, speckled, or spotted. ⁴⁰Jacob separated the young animals from the others, and he made them face the streaked and dark animals in Laban's flock. Jacob kept his animals separate from Laban's. ⁴¹When the stronger animals in the flock were mating, Jacob put the branches before their eyes so they would mate near the branches. ⁴²But when the weaker animals mated, Jacob did not put the branches there. So the animals born from the weaker animals were Laban's, and those born from the stronger animals were Jacob's. ⁴³In this way Jacob became very rich. He had large flocks, many male and female servants, camels, and donkeys.

DEVOTION

JACOB OBTAINED HIS birthright by tricking his aged father, Isaac. Now he's had the unpleasant experience of being on the receiving end of deception. First, Laban fooled Jacob into working an extra seven years by tricking him into first marrying Leah rather than the beautiful Rachel. And now, even when they appear to have worked out a fair arrangement for Jacob to get the speckled and spotted goats and the black sheep for his own, Laban first purges the flock of animals with those traits to make it less likely that Jacob's herd will flourish.

Jacob's methods for overcoming Laban's attempt to defraud him ranged from mere superstition to good genetics. Apparently, he believed that if the flock mated in front of mottled sticks, that the resulting newborns would be mottled. Stripping the bark off the sticks was probably a custom he learned from the shepherds of Canaan who prized livestock of motley color. But it was God's divine favor on Jacob that produced a number of spotted animals and black sheep. Once he had his stock, Jacob mated the strong animals so he eventually became the owner of a large flock of healthy animals.

Here's what I like about this story: God overruled Jacob's ignorance of genetics and blessed the increase of his flocks anyway. I wonder how often I've tried to control my own destiny with the modern-day equivalent of striped sticks when God had my best interests in mind all along. The writer of Proverbs reminds us that God is in control of our destiny when he writes: "Trust the LORD with all your heart, and don't depend on your own understanding. Remember the LORD in all you do, and he will give you success" (Proverbs 3:5–6).

I might not understand God's plan for me any more than Jacob understood genetics, but I can understand that my future is in God's hands.

THOUGHTS TO PONDER

Why do you think it is hard to trust God for our future success instead of trying to do it all by ourselves? Does God want to be involved in our everyday lives or is he just looking at his creation from a distance today? What proof do you have?

PRAYER

God, we pray that we will always turn to you when we make our plans, and that our plans will always be in accordance with your will. Amen.

GOD'S FAMILY

GENESIS 31:1–18

31 One day Jacob heard Laban's sons talking. They said, "Jacob has taken everything our father owned, and in this way he has become rich." ²Then Jacob noticed that Laban was not as friendly as he had been before. ³The LORD said to Jacob, "Go back to the land where your ancestors lived, and I will be with you."

⁴So Jacob told Rachel and Leah to meet him in the field where he kept his flocks. ⁵He said to them, "I have seen that your father is not as friendly with me as he used to be, but the God of my father has been with me. ⁶You both know that I have worked as hard as I could for your father, ⁷but he cheated me and changed my pay ten times. But God has not allowed your father to harm me. ⁸When Laban said, 'You can have all the speckled animals as your pay,' all the animals gave birth to speckled young ones. But when he said, 'You can have all the streaked animals as your pay,' all the flocks gave birth to streaked babies. ⁹So God has taken the animals away from your father and has given them to me.

¹⁰"I had a dream during the season when the flocks were mating. I saw that the only male goats who were mating were streaked, speckled, or spotted. ¹¹The angel of God spoke to me in that dream and said, 'Jacob!' I answered, 'Yes!' ¹²The angel said, 'Look! Only the streaked, speckled, or spotted male goats are mating. I have seen all the wrong things Laban has been doing to you. ¹³I am the God who appeared to you at Bethel, where you poured olive oil on the stone you set up on end and where you made a promise to me. Now I want you to leave here and go back to the land where you were born.'"

¹⁴Rachel and Leah answered Jacob, "Our father has nothing to give us when he dies. ¹⁵He has treated us like strangers. He sold us to you, and then he spent all of the money you paid for us. ¹⁶God took all this wealth from our father, and now it belongs to us and our children. So do whatever God has told you to do."

¹⁷So Jacob put his children and his wives on camels, ¹⁸and they began their journey back to Isaac, his father, in the land of Canaan. All the flocks of animals that Jacob owned walked ahead of them. He carried everything with him that he had gotten while he lived in Northwest Mesopotamia.

DEVOTION

HAVE YOU EVER outgrown your current situation? Perhaps you were getting too old to live with your mother and father. Then later, maybe you tired of having roommates and wanted a place of your own. Or maybe that first job or starter home that looked so wonderful when you were young suddenly isn't a good fit anymore.

Time changes us all. Sometimes we control the situations that propel us to make changes. Sometimes circumstances control us. Reuniting with my old high school friends recently, we were all amazed to discover that virtually none of us were doing what we thought we would be doing at this stage of our lives. But even more amazing was seeing how God's hand was so clearly at work in each of our lives, taking us from graduation from that Christian high school so many years ago, and leading us to the places we are today.

Moving on is not only healthy . . . it is God-ordained. As soon as God created woman, Adam recognized her as something special. In Genesis we read, "The LORD God used the rib from the man to make a woman, and then he brought the woman to the man. And the man said, 'Now, this is someone whose bones came from my bones, whose body came from my body. I will call her "woman," because she was taken out of man.' So a man will leave his father and mother and be united with his wife, and the two will become one body" (Genesis 2:22–24).

Marketers say most of us will be the product of two families—the family into which we are born and the family that we make with someone else. Mentally healthy individuals take the best of both families and blend them into a unit.

But Christians are also members of the family of God. A family whose home is not on this earth (Hebrews 11:13–16). Like Jacob, we're just strangers in this world, on the way to our true home. Because of that, this world will never be a perfect fit.

THOUGHTS TO PONDER

What situations have you outgrown in your life? How did you handle them? What goals are you moving toward? How do you hope to achieve them?

PRAYER

God, we pray that you will guide us through all the journeys of our lives and guide our paths to the ultimate home you have prepared. Amen.

LIVING IN HARMONY

GENESIS 31:22–29, 43–50

²²Three days later Laban learned that Jacob had run away, ²³so he gathered his relatives and began to chase him. After seven days Laban found him in the mountains of Gilead. ²⁴That night God came to Laban the Aramean in a dream and said, "Be careful! Do not say anything to Jacob, good or bad."

²⁵So Laban caught up with Jacob. Now Jacob had made his camp in the mountains, so Laban and his relatives set up their camp in the mountains of Gilead. ²⁶Laban said to Jacob, "What have you done? You cheated me and took my daughters as if you had captured them in a war. ²⁷Why did you run away secretly and trick me? Why didn't you tell me? Then I could have sent you away with joy and singing and with the music of tambourines and harps. ²⁸You did not even let me kiss my grandchildren and my daughters good-bye. You were very foolish to do this! ²⁹I have the power to harm you, but last night the God of your father spoke to me and warned me not to say anything to you, good or bad."

⁴³Laban said to Jacob, "These girls are my daughters. Their children belong to me, and these flocks are mine. Everything you see here belongs to me, but I can do nothing to keep my daughters and their children. ⁴⁴Let us make an agreement, and let us set up a pile of stones to remind us of it."

⁴⁵So Jacob took a large rock and set it up on its end. ⁴⁶He told his relatives to gather rocks, so they took the rocks and piled them up; then they ate beside the pile. ⁴⁷Laban named that place in his language A Pile to Remind Us, and Jacob gave the place the same name in Hebrew.

⁴⁸Laban said to Jacob, "This pile of rocks will remind us of the agreement between us." That is why the place was called A Pile to Remind Us. ⁴⁹It was also called Mizpah, because Laban said, "Let the LORD watch over us while we are separated from each other. ⁵⁰Remember that God is our witness even if no one else is around us. He will know if you harm my daughters or marry other women."

DEVOTION

GOD IS HONORED when his people learn to live in harmony. With Jacob and Laban, that harmony was accomplished with the boundary stone. Today, we have to find some mechanism to allow us to live together. I might not like every decision made at my local congregation, but God is honored when Christians find a way to get along. I might not get my way at home as often as I want, but God is honored when couples work out their differences together and learn to find common ground.

Like the compromise made by Jacob and Laban, life between those of us who profess to be Christians includes learning to get along, or if we disagree, learning to do it without being disagreeable. Perhaps the best example of this from the New Testament is that of Paul and Barnabas agreeing to go their separate ways when they could no longer agree over whether John Mark should accompany them on their next missionary journey. After the young John Mark had deserted them on the first trip, Paul felt that Mark was not up for the rigors of the next journey. Barnabas felt otherwise. In fact, Luke says this "serious argument" caused them to part company (Acts 15:39).

But God worked through the separation, creating two missionary groups where there had been one. And late in his life, Paul came full circle on the issue of John Mark. In fact, John Mark was with Paul during his time in prison to comfort him and assist him in his advanced age.

The stones of Jacob and Laban teach us that boundaries do not have to divide. Paul and Barnabas teach us that disagreements do not have to be ultimately divisive.

Why is harmony so important? Because the world is watching, and because God is our witness.

When we fail to work out our differences, when we split our churches in half like a bad marriage, we send an unmistakable signal to the world that threatens to drown out our witness. When we live side by side despite our differences, like Jacob and Laban or Paul and Barnabas, we send a message that proclaims that our love for God is greater than any of our minor differences.

THOUGHTS TO PONDER

When have you been forced to make a compromise in order to keep the peace? How did you feel about it? Was the sacrifice worth the peace? Would you do it again?

PRAYER

God, we pray that we will be a people of peace and that our harmony will be a testimony to the world of our dedication to you. Amen.

PRAYING BOLDLY

GENESIS 32:1–20

32 When Jacob also went his way, the angels of God met him. ²When he saw them, he said, "This is the camp of God!" So he named that place Mahanaim.

³Jacob's brother Esau was living in the area called Seir in the country of Edom. Jacob sent messengers to Esau, ⁴telling them, "Give this message to my master Esau: 'This is what Jacob, your servant, says: I have lived with Laban and have remained there until now. ⁵I have cattle, donkeys, flocks, and male and female servants. I send this message to you and ask you to accept us.'"

⁶The messengers returned to Jacob and said, "We went to your brother Esau. He is coming to meet you and has four hundred men with him."

⁷Then Jacob was very afraid and worried. He divided the people who were with him and all the flocks, herds, and camels into two camps. ⁸Jacob thought, "Esau might come and destroy one camp, but the other camp can run away and be saved."

⁹Then Jacob said, "God of my father Abraham! God of my father Isaac! LORD, you told me to return to my country and my family. You said that you would treat me well. ¹⁰I am not worthy of the kindness and continual goodness you have shown me. The first time I traveled across the Jordan River, I had only my walking stick, but now I own enough to have two camps. ¹¹Please save me from my brother Esau. I am afraid he will come and kill all of us, even the mothers with the children. ¹²You said to me, 'I will treat you well and will make your children as many as the sand of the seashore. There will be too many to count.'"

¹³Jacob stayed there for the night and prepared a gift for Esau from what he had with him: ¹⁴two hundred female goats and twenty male goats, two hundred female sheep and twenty male sheep, ¹⁵thirty female camels and their young, forty cows and ten bulls, twenty female donkeys, and ten male donkeys. ¹⁶Jacob gave each separate flock of animals to one of his servants and said to them, "Go ahead of me and keep some space between each herd." ¹⁷Jacob gave them their orders. To the servant with the first group of animals he said, "My brother Esau will come to you and ask, 'Whose servant are you? Where are you going and whose animals are these?' ¹⁸Then you will answer, 'They belong to your servant Jacob. He sent them as a gift to you, my master Esau, and he also is coming behind us.'"

¹⁹Jacob ordered the second servant, the third servant, and all the other servants to do the same thing. He said, "Say the same thing to Esau when you meet him. ²⁰Say, 'Your servant Jacob is coming behind us.'" Jacob thought, "If I send these gifts ahead of me, maybe Esau will forgive me. Then when I see him, perhaps he will accept me."

DEVOTION

WHEN YOU THINK about it, the prayer of Jacob is pretty bold. He thanks God for the many blessings he's received. But Jacob also reminds God of the promise that God made to him: your children will be as numerous as the sand on the seashore. Now was the time, Jacob prays, for God to keep his promise and protect him and his children.

Even though it had been many years, Esau still had reason to be angry with Jacob, his younger twin brother. First, Jacob "sold" a famished Esau a bowl of soup in exchange for Esau's birthright (Genesis 25:29–34). Later, Jacob and his mother, Rebekah, conspired to trick Isaac into giving Jacob the blessing reserved for the oldest son (Genesis 27). Esau, if still angry, was potentially dangerous to Jacob, having vowed to kill him (Genesis 27:41). By the time of the New Testament, Esau's life was a cautionary tale: "Be careful that no one takes part in sexual sin or is like Esau and never thinks about God" (Hebrews 12:16).

Jacob's prayer gives me hope; it gives me boldness to ask God to remember the promises he has made. Jesus made this promise to his disciples shortly before his death: "There are many rooms in my Father's house; I would not tell you this if it were not true. I am going there to prepare a place for you. After I go and prepare a place for you, I will come back and take you to be with me so that you may be where I am" (John 14:2–3).

Like Jacob, I can boldly ask God to remember this promise. In turn, I should remain faithful in my promises to him.

THOUGHTS TO PONDER

What promises of God are especially meaningful to you? What does God expect of us, the recipients of his promises?

PRAYER

God, we know you are faithful to keep your promises to us. Please help us remain faithful all the days of our lives. Thank you for your promise of eternal life with you. Amen.

Wrestling with God

GENESIS 32:22–32

²²During the night Jacob rose and crossed the Jabbok River at the crossing, taking with him his two wives, his two slave girls, and his eleven sons. ²³He sent his family and everything he had across the river. ²⁴So Jacob was alone, and a man came and wrestled with him until the sun came up. ²⁵When the man saw he could not defeat Jacob, he struck Jacob's hip and put it out of joint. ²⁶Then he said to Jacob, "Let me go. The sun is coming up."

But Jacob said, "I will let you go if you will bless me."

²⁷The man said to him, "What is your name?"

And he answered, "Jacob."

²⁸Then the man said, "Your name will no longer be Jacob. Your name will now be Israel, because you have wrestled with God and with people, and you have won."

²⁹Then Jacob asked him, "Please tell me your name."

But the man said, "Why do you ask my name?" Then he blessed Jacob there.

³⁰So Jacob named that place Peniel, saying, "I have seen God face to face, but my life was saved." ³¹Then the sun rose as he was leaving that place, and Jacob was limping because of his leg. ³²So even today the people of Israel do not eat the muscle that is on the hip joint of animals, because Jacob was touched there.

Devotion

THERE WAS A TIME when angels visited earth in the form of men. Abraham received three such heavenly visitors in Genesis 18, and in the course of entertaining them he discovered that even in his old age he was going to have a son.

But Jacob, sleeping alone by the river crossing, was in no entertaining mood. Having sent his family and possessions ahead, Jacob was no doubt worrying about his upcoming meeting with his brother, Esau. Years earlier, he had tricked their father into giving him the blessing that would have normally gone to Esau as the oldest son. After the deception, Jacob fled to Haran where he had prospered with wives and sons and flocks. He hadn't seen his brother in years. His hope was that some of the wounds had healed and that Esau's vow to kill him was no longer valid.

It couldn't have been a night conducive to sleep. And then comes this man— no doubt sent from God—who evidently frightens Jacob. They begin to wrestle. In fact, they wrestle all night long. Jacob is eventually left with a limp, but he is also left with a blessing from God and a new name. From that time on he's known as Israel, meaning "he wrestles with God." From that great name will come the name of his descendants—the Israelites.

I take an important point away from this short story: it's okay to wrestle with God.

I've wrestled with God many times. I've wrestled with him over a wife who copes with multiple sclerosis, a son who is dependent on insulin for his diabetes, and a daughter who struggles with arthritis. I wrestle with God over a classmate who contracted an aggressive form of cancer at far too young an age. And I've wrestled mightily with God over one of my students called up to active duty and killed in the war on terror.

But I serve a God who allows us to wrestle with him. The prophets did it. Even Jesus cried out on the cross: "My God, why have you abandoned me?" (Matthew 27:46).

When Jesus arrived in Bethany a couple of days after his beloved friend Lazarus died, both of the dead man's sisters came to him and said, in essence, "Where in the world were you?" Each one—Mary and Martha—came to Jesus as soon as he arrived and told him if he had only been there that their brother would not have died. They wrestled with why Jesus waited when he first heard that Lazarus was sick rather than coming immediately. They wrestled with why their brother had died when Jesus had the power to heal all manner of diseases (John 11:1–37).

I sometimes do the same thing. I think God is a little slow doing what I want him to do. Like Jacob, I want a blessing. I want good health for my family and friends. I want loving spouses and good jobs for my children. And like Jacob, I especially don't want to cross the river to face my Esau, whatever form that challenge takes.

But I must, and so must you. And for that, we, like Jacob, will be blessed.

THOUGHTS TO PONDER

What have you wrestled with in your life? How has God responded?

PRAYER

God, we know you allow us to beseech you, even wrestle with you when we don't understand your ways. Be patient with us as our understanding is made complete. Amen.

MAKING THINGS RIGHT

GENESIS 33:1–20

33 Jacob looked up and saw Esau coming, and with him were four hundred men. So Jacob divided his children among Leah, Rachel, and the two slave girls. ²Jacob put the slave girls with their children first, then Leah and her children behind them, and Rachel and Joseph last. ³Jacob himself went out in front of them and bowed down flat on the ground seven times as he was walking toward his brother.

⁴But Esau ran to meet Jacob and put his arms around him and hugged him. Then Esau kissed him, and they both cried. ⁵When Esau looked up and saw the women and children, he asked, "Who are these people with you?"

Jacob answered, "These are the children God has given me. God has been good to me, your servant."

⁶Then the two slave girls and their children came up to Esau and bowed down flat on the earth before him. ⁷Leah and her children also came up to Esau and also bowed down flat on the earth. Last of all, Joseph and Rachel came up to Esau, and they, too, bowed down flat before him.

⁸Esau said, "I saw many herds as I was coming here. Why did you bring them?"

Jacob answered, "They were to please you, my master."

⁹But Esau said, "I already have enough, my brother. Keep what you have."

¹⁰Jacob said, "No! Please! If I have pleased you, then accept the gift I give you. I am very happy to see your face again. It is like seeing the face of God, because you have accepted me. ¹¹So I beg you to accept the gift I give you. God has been very good to me, and I have more than I need." And because Jacob begged, Esau accepted the gift.

¹²Then Esau said, "Let us be going. I will travel with you."

¹³But Jacob said to him, "My master, you know that the children are weak. And I must be careful with my flocks and their young ones. If I force them to go too far in one day, all the animals will die. ¹⁴So, my master, you go on ahead of me, your servant. I will follow you slowly and let the animals and the children set the speed at which we travel. I will meet you, my master, in Edom."

¹⁵So Esau said, "Then let me leave some of my people with you."

"No, thank you," said Jacob. "I only want to please you, my master." ¹⁶So that day Esau started back to Edom. ¹⁷But Jacob went to Succoth, where he built a house for himself and shelters for his animals. That is why the place was named Succoth.

¹⁸Jacob left Northwest Mesopotamia and arrived safely at the city of Shechem in the land of Canaan. There he camped east of the city. ¹⁹He bought a part of the field where he had camped from the sons of Hamor father of Shechem for one hundred pieces of silver. ²⁰He built an altar there and named it after God, the God of Israel.

DEVOTION

SETTING THINGS RIGHT is never easy, but it's often not as bad as we dread it will be. I remember vividly needing to make a belated apology for a relationship I had messed up rather badly many years ago. The reply came back to me: "That's alright. God worked everything out!"

Jacob wronged Esau, conspiring with their mother to steal the all-important blessing that was due Esau as the oldest child. Now it was time to apologize. Taking the blessing had presumably harmed Esau financially. Jacob's generous offer of the herds was to make restitution for his deception, much like a court would award financial damages today in a civil lawsuit.

But Esau had also been blessed—in fact his name was synonymous with the land of Edom where he lived and where he invited Jacob to join him. Esau was equally gracious to Jacob, hugging and kissing his brother when he first saw him, and initially declining his gifts.

Perhaps the example of "Uncle Esau" was passed on as part of the lore of Jacob's family; years later, Joseph's brothers owed a huge apology to him for the wicked deed they had done in selling him into slavery. But like Esau, Joseph had been blessed after the mistreatment and he was willing to forgive. He told his brothers, each of them no doubt as fearful as their father Jacob had been on that day so long ago, "Now don't be worried or angry with yourselves because you sold me here. God sent me here ahead of you to save people's lives" (Genesis 45:5).

After burying their father, the two brothers would never meet again. But isn't it an awesome God who can take our wrongs and turn them into blessings for others?

THOUGHTS TO PONDER

What is the hardest apology you've ever had to make? What is the hardest apology you've ever had to accept? Which was more difficult to do? Why?

PRAYER

God, we know we disappoint you and we know that we sometimes disappoint those around us as well. Help us make things right as quickly as we can so that our actions honor you. Amen.

WHO MOVED?

GENESIS 35:1–15

35 God said to Jacob, "Go to the city of Bethel and live there. Make an altar to the God who appeared to you there when you were running away from your brother Esau."

²So Jacob said to his family and to all who were with him, "Put away the foreign gods you have, and make yourselves clean, and change your clothes. ³We will leave here and go to Bethel. There I will build an altar to God, who has helped me during my time of trouble. He has been with me everywhere I have gone." ⁴So they gave Jacob all the foreign gods they had, and the earrings they were wearing, and he hid them under the great tree near the town of Shechem. ⁵Then Jacob and his sons left there. But God caused the people in the nearby cities to be afraid, so they did not follow them. ⁶And Jacob and all the people who were with him went to Luz, which is now called Bethel, in the land of Canaan. ⁷There Jacob built an altar and named the place Bethel, after God, because God had appeared to him there when he was running from his brother.

⁸Deborah, Rebekah's nurse, died and was buried under the oak tree at Bethel, so they named that place Oak of Crying.

⁹When Jacob came back from Northwest Mesopotamia, God appeared to him again and blessed him. ¹⁰God said to him, "Your name is Jacob, but you will not be called Jacob any longer. Your new name will be Israel." So he called him Israel. ¹¹God said to him, "I am God Almighty. Have many children and grow in number as a nation. You will be the ancestor of many nations and kings. ¹²The same land I gave to Abraham and Isaac I will give to you and your descendants." ¹³Then God left him. ¹⁴Jacob set up a stone on edge in that place where God had talked to him, and he poured a drink offering and olive oil on it to make it special for God. ¹⁵And Jacob named the place Bethel.

DEVOTION

HAVE YOU EVER wandered away from where you once were in your walk with God? Have you ever felt like your prayers were going no higher than the ceiling? If you have, ask yourself this: "Who moved . . . me or God?"

Some people appear to move away from God all at once, and we've seen it happen. Maybe they get caught up in an affair and leave their family behind. Maybe it's alcohol or drugs. We've heard of or know people who seem to be faithful one day and then abandon home, church, or a job for something or someone else.

But those are the rare, dramatic cases. Most often, the drift away from God is slow, perhaps even glacial, in pace. So slow, in fact, that it's possible for us to fool ourselves that no movement has occurred at all. We do our job, we stay with our families, we worship our God. But perhaps not with the zest we once did. Perhaps we find it harder to control our tongue, to give our offering, to find the time to do good works.

And then God calls us back to Bethel.

As you may recall from Genesis 28, Jacob was not unfamiliar with this place. It was here that Jacob—a young man fleeing the wrath of this brother—received a vision from God. God promised him protection for his journey and, eventually, possession of the very land on which he slept. In commemoration of the event, Jacob erected a stone, poured oil over it, and made a vow to God to tithe from God's generosity.

He called the place "Bethel," meaning "house of God."

Years passed. Foreign idols crept into his household. His children wore earrings, symbols of the pagan culture around them. There was baggage to bury before Jacob and his household could get back to Bethel. And once there, Jacob is reminded of his new name—Israel—and the great nation God will one day make of his descendants.

Years have passed since I gave my life to God. The idols of the world—money, possessions, power, etc.—always call. The desire to be like the culture around me is always there. And like Jacob, if I am to get back to my Bethel—my intimate relationship with God—there are some things I need to bury.

Then God will remind me once again of my new name—Christian—and the great eternal nation of which I am a part.

THOUGHTS TO PONDER

When you feel close to God, what factors cause that feeling? When you feel far from God, what factors cause that feeling? What can we do to draw nearer to God?

PRAYER

God, we know you call us to yourself and that you promise to be there for us. We pray that when we seek you, we will find you. Amen.

Following God's Dreams

GENESIS 37:1–17

37 Jacob lived in the land of Canaan, where his father had lived. ²This is the family history of Jacob:

Joseph was a young man, seventeen years old. He and his brothers, the sons of Bilhah and Zilpah, his father's wives, cared for the flocks. Joseph gave his father bad reports about his brothers. ³Since Joseph was born when his father Israel was old, Israel loved him more than his other sons. He made Joseph a special robe with long sleeves. ⁴When Joseph's brothers saw that their father loved him more than he loved them, they hated their brother and could not speak to him politely.

⁵One time Joseph had a dream, and when he told his brothers about it, they hated him even more. ⁶Joseph said, "Listen to the dream I had. ⁷We were in the field tying bundles of wheat together. My bundle stood up, and your bundles of wheat gathered around it and bowed down to it."

⁸His brothers said, "Do you really think you will be king over us? Do you truly think you will rule over us?" His brothers hated him even more because of his dreams and what he had said.

⁹Then Joseph had another dream, and he told his brothers about it also. He said, "Listen, I had another dream. I saw the sun, moon, and eleven stars bowing down to me."

¹⁰Joseph also told his father about this dream, but his father scolded him, saying, "What kind of dream is this? Do you really believe that your mother, your brothers, and I will bow down to you?" ¹¹Joseph's brothers were jealous of him, but his father thought about what all these things could mean.

¹²One day Joseph's brothers went to Shechem to graze their father's flocks. ¹³Israel said to Joseph, "Go to Shechem where your brothers are grazing the flocks."

Joseph answered, "I will go."

¹⁴His father said, "Go and see if your brothers and the flocks are all right. Then come back and tell me." So Joseph's father sent him from the Valley of Hebron.

When Joseph came to Shechem, ¹⁵a man found him wandering in the field and asked him, "What are you looking for?"

¹⁶Joseph answered, "I am looking for my brothers. Can you tell me where they are grazing the flocks?"

¹⁷The man said, "They have already gone. I heard them say they were going to Dothan." So Joseph went to look for his brothers and found them in Dothan.

DEVOTION

PERHAPS YOU'VE HEARD this story. Perhaps you heard about "Joseph and his coat of many colors." It was a good story, this tale of the remarkable, vivid coat created by Jacob and hated by the brothers. The coat that the brothers would spot coming from a long way off.

But it's only a story. Later scholarship shows that the remarkable thing about this robe was that it had long sleeves. Unlike the one-piece, tunic-style robes worn by his brothers, this robe would have required tailoring. And this robe would have protected the arms of the wearer from sun or from blowing sand. It would be warmer at night with no gaping holes for bare arms to stick out. Rather than a gaudy coat of many colors, this was a thoughtful, protective coat, and it spoke volumes to Jacob's other sons.

Then there were the dreams. Dreams are a privilege of the young. How dreary would life be if we couldn't dream, and if in our dreams we couldn't be better than we are? Inventors, poets, artists . . . all of them are dreamers at heart, I think. And Joseph's dreams were a sign of the creativity and resourcefulness he would have all his life.

But his brothers weren't dreamers. They were down-to-earth grown men who took offense at the teenage boy and his dreams. They knew their role: to tend the family's flocks. And who was this kid to think he'd be any better than them?

The dreams would someday come true. But the cost would be very high—for Joseph, for his brothers, and for their father.

What if you could achieve your dreams, but along the way you'd suffer treachery, estrangement, and separation from your family? Even if you were promised a happy ending, would you pursue your dreams at that great a cost?

When he left home that morning, following the orders of his father, Joseph had no way of knowing that he would never see home again, or that he would begin the journey to see his dreams fulfilled.

THOUGHTS TO PONDER

Do you have dreams you keep to yourself? Why do you not share them? Why do you think Joseph shared his dreams with his family? Does God use dreams to send messages today?

PRAYER

Father, we thank you that we can dream and enjoy the hope that comes with dreams. But we thank you most of all for the hope that comes through your Son. Amen.

A Step in the Right Direction

GENESIS 37:18–36; 39:1–2

¹⁸Joseph's brothers saw him coming from far away. Before he reached them, they made a plan to kill him. ¹⁹They said to each other, "Here comes that dreamer. ²⁰Let's kill him and throw his body into one of the wells. We can tell our father that a wild animal killed him. Then we will see what will become of his dreams."

²¹But Reuben heard their plan and saved Joseph, saying, "Let's not kill him. ²²Don't spill any blood. Throw him into this well here in the desert, but don't hurt him!" Reuben planned to save Joseph later and send him back to his father. ²³So when Joseph came to his brothers, they pulled off his robe with long sleeves ²⁴and threw him into the well. It was empty, and there was no water in it.

²⁵While Joseph was in the well, the brothers sat down to eat. When they looked up, they saw a group of Ishmaelites traveling from Gilead to Egypt. Their camels were carrying spices, balm, and myrrh.

²⁶Then Judah said to his brothers, "What will we gain if we kill our brother and hide his death? ²⁷Let's sell him to these Ishmaelites. Then we will not be guilty of killing our own brother. After all, he is our brother, our own flesh and blood." And the other brothers agreed. ²⁸So when the Midianite traders came by, the brothers took Joseph out of the well and sold him to the Ishmaelites for eight ounces of silver. And the Ishmaelites took him to Egypt.

²⁹When Reuben came back to the well and Joseph was not there, he tore his clothes to show he was upset. ³⁰Then he went back to his brothers and said, "The boy is not there! What shall I do?" ³¹The brothers killed a goat and dipped Joseph's robe in its blood. ³²Then they brought the long-sleeved robe to their father and said, "We found this robe. Look it over carefully and see if it is your son's robe."

³³Jacob looked it over and said, "It is my son's robe! Some savage animal has eaten him. My son Joseph has been torn to pieces!" ³⁴Then Jacob tore his clothes and put on rough cloth to show that he was upset, and he continued to be sad about his son for a long time. ³⁵All of his sons and daughters tried to comfort him, but he could not be comforted. He said, "I will be sad about my son until the day I die." So Jacob cried for his son Joseph.

³⁶Meanwhile the Midianites who had bought Joseph had taken him to Egypt. There they sold him to Potiphar, an officer to the king of Egypt and captain of the palace guard.

39 Now Joseph had been taken down to Egypt. An Egyptian named Potiphar was an officer to the king of Egypt and the captain of the palace guard. He bought Joseph from the Ishmaelites who had brought him down there. ²The

LORD was with Joseph, and he became a successful man. He lived in the house of his master, Potiphar the Egyptian.

DEVOTION

THE MOST FAMOUS cases of sibling rivalry occur in the Bible. Cain and Abel. Joseph and his brothers. It seems that human nature hasn't changed much.

As you can tell from this story, clothing made a statement in these times, perhaps not unlike today. Joseph's robe with sleeves was a sign of status and a source of envy among his brothers. When Reuben's plan to privately save Joseph was foiled by his brother's actions, he tore his robe—an ancient sign of mourning. And Jacob, in his grief, goes one step further: he tears his clothes and puts on rough, irritant clothing to compound his grief. Just as we might wear black to a funeral today, the ancient mourners were recognized by their torn clothes, often adorned with ashes as well.

The number of parallels between the last days of Jesus and the treatment of Joseph in this story are both remarkable and interesting. Like Jesus, Joseph was sold for a small amount of silver. Joseph was lowered into a well and later raised by his brothers; Jesus went into the tomb and was raised by his Father. Joseph's robe was dipped in blood; soldiers gambled at the foot of the cross for the robe of Jesus. Joseph was mourned by his father; Jesus was mourned by his mother. The brothers betrayed Joseph; the apostles abandoned Jesus.

The second chapter of Joseph's life was about to begin. It was a long way from the dream, but—unknown to Joseph—it was a step in the right direction. Isn't that the way life is?

THOUGHTS TO PONDER

Looking back on your life, has the path to your dream taken any detours? What do you think was the purpose of those delays? Why might God be delaying our dreams?

PRAYER

Father, we see your hand in the life of Joseph. Help us acknowledge your hand in our lives, even when we tug in a different direction. Amen.

Tough Lessons

GENESIS 39:3–23

[3]Potiphar saw that the LORD was with Joseph and that the LORD made Joseph successful in everything he did. [4]So Potiphar was very happy with Joseph and allowed him to be his personal servant. He put Joseph in charge of the house, trusting him with everything he owned. [5]When Joseph was put in charge of the house and everything Potiphar owned, the LORD blessed the people in Potiphar's house because of Joseph. And the LORD blessed everything that belonged to Potiphar, both in the house and in the field. [6]So Potiphar left Joseph in charge of everything he owned and was not concerned about anything except the food he ate. Now Joseph was well built and handsome. [7]After some time the wife of Joseph's master began to desire Joseph, and one day she said to him, "Have sexual relations with me."

[8]But Joseph refused and said to her, "My master trusts me with everything in his house. He has put me in charge of everything he owns. [9]There is no one in his house greater than I. He has not kept anything from me except you, because you are his wife. How can I do such an evil thing? It is a sin against God."

[10]The woman talked to Joseph every day, but he refused to have sexual relations with her or even spend time with her.

[11]One day Joseph went into the house to do his work as usual and was the only man in the house at that time. [12]His master's wife grabbed his coat and said to him, "Come and have sexual relations with me." But Joseph left his coat in her hand and ran out of the house.

[13]When she saw that Joseph had left his coat in her hands and had run outside, [14]she called to the servants in her house and said, "Look! This Hebrew slave was brought here to shame us. He came in and tried to have sexual relations with me, but I screamed. [15]My scream scared him and he ran away, but he left his coat with me." [16]She kept his coat until her husband came home, [17]and she told him the same story. She said, "This Hebrew slave you brought here came in to shame me! [18]When he came near me, I screamed. He ran away, but he left his coat."

[19]When Joseph's master heard what his wife said Joseph had done, he became very angry. [20]So Potiphar arrested Joseph and put him into the prison where the king's prisoners were put. And Joseph stayed there in the prison.

[21]But the LORD was with Joseph and showed him kindness and caused the prison warden to like Joseph. [22]The prison warden chose Joseph to take care of all the prisoners, and he was responsible for whatever was done in the prison. [23]The warden paid no attention to anything that was in Joseph's care because the LORD was with Joseph and made him successful in everything he did.

DEVOTION

JOSEPH ROSE TO the top in any situation. As a slave in Potiphar's house, he was trusted with everything his master owned. As a prisoner, he ascended to the role of trustee over the other inmates. So you have to ask yourself, if Joseph is so trustworthy, why is he in jail? If God is with him, overseeing his success, why isn't Joseph's life going somewhere?

The only answer I can come up with that makes any sense is this: for Joseph to do all the great things that God had in mind for him, he needed to learn the lessons of jail. He needed to feel firsthand the betrayal of not only his brothers but also of Potiphar's lustful wife. Joseph's plight in this chapter reminds me of Martin Luther King's manifesto, "Letters from a Birmingham Jail," where from the seclusion of jail he set out his plans for social and justice reform through nonviolence.

If you feel trapped right now, if you feel surrounded by walls as real as Joseph's prison cell, ask yourself: "What is the lesson here? Is God trying to teach me something now that will make me a more capable servant in the future?"

I now see some of the hardest times in my life as the most instructive. Hard times get your attention. And sadly, good times often make us forget.

Joseph is a pupil, learning God's hard lessons to better prepare him for the important duties he'll face in the future. What does God have in store for you?

THOUGHTS TO PONDER

What were some of the hardest times in your life? What did you learn from those times?

PRAYER

Father, we pray that in the hour of adversity, we will look to you, and that we will learn your way for our lives. Amen.

Forgotten Kindness

GENESIS 40:1–23

40 After these things happened, two of the king's officers displeased the king—the man who served wine to the king and the king's baker. ²The king became angry with his officer who served him wine and his baker, ³so he put them in the prison of the captain of the guard, the same prison where Joseph was kept. ⁴The captain of the guard put the two prisoners in Joseph's care, and they stayed in prison for some time.

⁵One night both the king's officer who served him wine and the baker had a dream. Each had his own dream with its own meaning. ⁶When Joseph came to them the next morning, he saw they were worried. ⁷He asked the king's officers who were with him, "Why do you look so unhappy today?"

⁸The two men answered, "We both had dreams last night, but no one can explain their meaning to us."

Joseph said to them, "God is the only One who can explain the meaning of dreams. Tell me your dreams."

⁹So the man who served wine to the king told Joseph his dream. He said, "I dreamed I saw a vine, and ¹⁰on the vine were three branches. I watched the branches bud and blossom, and then the grapes ripened. ¹¹I was holding the king's cup, so I took the grapes and squeezed the juice into the cup. Then I gave it to the king."

¹²Then Joseph said, "I will explain the dream to you. The three branches stand for three days. ¹³Before the end of three days the king will free you, and he will allow you to return to your work. You will serve the king his wine just as you did before. ¹⁴But when you are free, remember me. Be kind to me, and tell the king about me so I can get out of this prison. ¹⁵I was taken by force from the land of the Hebrews, and I have done nothing here to deserve being put in prison."

¹⁶The baker saw that Joseph's explanation of the dream was good, so he said to him, "I also had a dream. I dreamed there were three bread baskets on my head. ¹⁷In the top basket were all kinds of baked food for the king, but the birds were eating this food out of the basket on my head."

¹⁸Joseph answered, "I will tell you what the dream means. The three baskets stand for three days. ¹⁹Before the end of three days, the king will cut off your head! He will hang your body on a pole, and the birds will eat your flesh."

²⁰Three days later, on his birthday, the king gave a feast for all his officers. In front of his officers, he released from prison the chief officer who served his wine and the chief baker. ²¹The king gave his chief officer who served wine his old position, and once again he put the king's cup of wine into the king's hand. ²²But the king hanged the baker on a pole. Everything happened just as Joseph had said it would, ²³but the officer who served wine did not remember Joseph. He forgot all about him.

DEVOTION

NO ONE KNOWS the crimes that landed the king's baker and cupbearer in jail. All we know is that they displeased the king. And in an absolute monarchy, that's a sure road to a disastrous end. The Egyptian king could act as judge and executioner for those he didn't like, and there was no concept of due process to protect the innocent. So the cupbearer and the baker had reason to be afraid. Their destiny was in the hands of a powerful king who was displeased with them.

Each man had a separate dream, and each one had a separate outcome. The king's actions at the feast for his officers were similar to what occurred hundreds of years later when Herod threw a feast and ended up executing John the Baptist for the pleasure of his wife (Matthew 14:1–12). Public hangings and beheadings at events such as these served as a not-so-subtle reminder that treachery would be dealt with severely.

There's a certain logic to the king's selection of who to kill and who to set free. As the server of wine to the king, the cupbearer would be expected to taste the wines for poison. He had to be above suspicion, and finding someone who would not be subject to bribes or treachery was a major concern of royalty. Evidently, the king became convinced that his cupbearer was trustworthy, and returned him to the position. We know from the next story that the cupbearer lasted at least two more years in the role.

But, alas, he forgot his promise to Joseph, joining a long list of disappointments in Joseph's life of betrayal and imprisonment.

THOUGHTS TO PONDER

Have you ever done a good deed for someone and then been forgotten? How did it feel? Are we as gracious to those who have done us a favor as we should be?

PRAYER

God, we're thankful that you never break your promises to us. One of your promises is that you will never forsake us; we thank you for that assurance. Amen.

SOLVABLE PROBLEMS

GENESIS 41:1–16

41 Two years later the king dreamed he was standing on the bank of the Nile River. ²He saw seven fat and beautiful cows come up out of the river, and they stood there, eating the grass. ³Then seven more cows came up out of the river, but they were thin and ugly. They stood beside the seven beautiful cows on the bank of the Nile. ⁴The seven thin and ugly cows ate the seven beautiful fat cows. Then the king woke up. ⁵The king slept again and dreamed a second time. In his dream he saw seven full and good heads of grain growing on one stalk. ⁶After that, seven more heads of grain sprang up, but they were thin and burned by the hot east wind. ⁷The thin heads of grain ate the seven full and good heads. Then the king woke up again, and he realized it was only a dream. ⁸The next morning the king was troubled about these dreams, so he sent for all the magicians and wise men of Egypt. The king told them his dreams, but no one could explain their meaning to him.

⁹Then the chief officer who served wine to the king said to him, "Now I remember something I promised to do, but I forgot about it. ¹⁰There was a time when you were angry with the baker and me, and you put us in prison in the house of the captain of the guard. ¹¹In prison we each had a dream on the same night, and each dream had a different meaning. ¹²A young Hebrew man, a servant of the captain of the guard, was in the prison with us. When we told him our dreams, he explained their meanings to us. He told each man the meaning of his dream, and ¹³things happened exactly as he said they would: I was given back my old position, and the baker was hanged."

¹⁴So the king called for Joseph. The guards quickly brought him out of the prison, and he shaved, put on clean clothes, and went before the king.

¹⁵The king said to Joseph, "I have had a dream, but no one can explain its meaning to me. I have heard that you can explain a dream when someone tells it to you."

¹⁶Joseph answered the king, "I am not able to explain the meaning of dreams, but God will do this for the king."

DEVOTION

THERE'S A BEAUTIFUL principle at work here in Joseph's story: when life threatens to imprison us, God provides us with the tools for escape.

By this point, Joseph has suffered many injustices—sold into slavery by his jealous brothers, falsely accused by Potiphar's adulterous wife, and forgotten by the king's cupbearer. That last injustice resulted in two additional years of needless imprisonment.

It was his uncanny ability to interpret dreams that would ultimately free Joseph from the prison walls. But face-to-face with the most powerful man in Egypt, Joseph refused to take the credit for what he was about to do, giving the glory to God instead.

God is not the author of the bad things that happen in life. Satan seems to have a lot of room to roam in this world and we'll never understand all the reasons for disease and crime and disasters until we meet God in eternity.

But God is the one who supplies me with the way out. In the New Testament we're told that we're always provided a means of escape from any temptation that comes our way (1 Corinthians 10:13). God gave Joseph the means to escape the prison walls that held him in. But God has also given you and me the means to escape from our problems if we only ask and then listen.

Addiction. Marital discord. Temptation. All of these situations are solvable problems in God's hands.

Left to our own devices, Satan becomes our jailer. In God's hands, however, we find the keys to freedom.

Following a nine-hour spinal fusion, the pain that drove me to surgery in the first place remained. I became dependent on pain medication to get through the day. My life revolved around medication. I decided to find a way out, and I did. It wasn't easy; in fact it was quite hard, but the further I went, the more I felt God's power running through my body rather than painkilling drugs. Within a short time, I was out of the prison of prescription medications.

What has you in jail? Is it debt? Worry? Addiction? Lust? God has the key to all these prisons and he will give it to you if you only ask.

THOUGHTS TO PONDER

What do you think sustained Joseph as the two years passed and the cupbearer continued to forget his promise to tell the king? What sustains you when an injustice is done to you?

PRAYER

God, we pray that we will look to you for the way out when Satan tries to box us in. Amen.

FEED THE WORLD

GENESIS 41:17–36

¹⁷Then the king said to Joseph, "In my dream I was standing on the bank of the Nile River. ¹⁸I saw seven fat and beautiful cows that came up out of the river and ate the grass. ¹⁹Then I saw seven more cows come out of the river that were thin and lean and ugly—the worst looking cows I have seen in all the land of Egypt. ²⁰And these thin and ugly cows ate the first seven fat cows, ²¹but after they had eaten the seven cows, no one could tell they had eaten them. They looked just as thin and ugly as they did in the beginning. Then I woke up.

²²"I had another dream. I saw seven full and good heads of grain growing on one stalk. ²³Then seven more heads of grain sprang up after them, but these heads were thin and ugly and were burned by the hot east wind. ²⁴Then the thin heads ate the seven good heads. I told this dream to the magicians, but no one could explain its meaning to me."

²⁵Then Joseph said to the king, "Both of these dreams mean the same thing. God is telling you what he is about to do. ²⁶The seven good cows stand for seven years, and the seven good heads of grain stand for seven years. Both dreams mean the same thing. ²⁷The seven thin and ugly cows stand for seven years, and the seven thin heads of grain burned by the hot east wind stand for seven years of hunger. ²⁸This will happen as I told you. God is showing the king what he is about to do. ²⁹You will have seven years of good crops and plenty to eat in all the land of Egypt. ³⁰But after those seven years, there will come seven years of hunger, and all the food that grew in the land of Egypt will be forgotten. The time of hunger will eat up the land. ³¹People will forget what it was like to have plenty of food, because the hunger that follows will be so great. ³²You had two dreams which mean the same thing. This shows that God has firmly decided that this will happen, and he will make it happen soon.

³³"So let the king choose a man who is very wise and understanding and set him over the land of Egypt. ³⁴And let the king also appoint officers over the land, who should take one-fifth of all the food that is grown during the seven good years. ³⁵They should gather all the food that is produced during the good years that are coming, and under the king's authority they should store the grain in the cities and guard it. ³⁶That food should be saved to use during the seven years of hunger that will come on the land of Egypt. Then the people in Egypt will not die during the seven years of hunger."

DEVOTION

IN A DAY before the global reach of all-news channels on television, in a time before the Internet, most Americans got their news from one of the three established television networks each evening. It was in the early 1980s that a news anchor looked into the camera and reported that disturbing footage had just come in showing starvation in Africa. The footage was so recent that the network producers scarcely had time to package it as a story, but it was so important that it was rushed to air anyway.

There in the living rooms and kitchens of America—right over our plentiful dinner hour—were the first visuals of starvation in Ethiopia. Babies with bellies swollen by malnutrition. Children with heads oversized for their emaciated bodies. Nursing mothers with no milk to give their infants. The images, which we've now seen many times in the years since, were startling to us on that evening. It was hard to imagine that anyone in this world could suffer such extreme hunger.

U.S. aid followed. The largest rock concert in history raised money for the starving. "Feed the World" became a slogan and a song.

The interesting thing about this famine that touched the world is that it was the result of two years with no rainy season. Two years. Now imagine Egypt after seven years. No rain. No swelling of the Nile River to enrich the soil. No crops and no food.

But Joseph had a plan. His idea would not only save Egypt . . . it would also save his own family, as we shall see. God was providing Egypt with a means of escape from her problems while at the same time elevating Joseph to a position where he could help his family through the crisis.

THOUGHTS TO PONDER

How can God work though natural disasters like tornadoes and hurricanes? Why would God give the king a preview of the impending disaster?

PRAYER

God, we pray that we will see your hand in both the good times and the lean, and that we will never allow our faith to be dependent on our fortune. Amen.

THE LURE OF PROSPERITY

GENESIS 41:39–57

³⁹So the king said to Joseph, "God has shown you all this. There is no one as wise and understanding as you are, so ⁴⁰I will put you in charge of my palace. All the people will obey your orders, and only I will be greater than you."

⁴¹Then the king said to Joseph, "Look! I have put you in charge of all the land of Egypt." ⁴²Then the king took off from his own finger his ring with the royal seal on it, and he put it on Joseph's finger. He gave Joseph fine linen clothes to wear, and he put a gold chain around Joseph's neck. ⁴³The king had Joseph ride in the second royal chariot, and people walked ahead of his chariot calling, "Bow down!" By doing these things, the king put Joseph in charge of all of Egypt.

⁴⁴The king said to him, "I am the king, and I say that no one in all the land of Egypt may lift a hand or a foot without your permission." ⁴⁵The king gave Joseph the name Zaphenath-Paneah. He also gave Joseph a wife named Asenath, who was the daughter of Potiphera, priest of On. So Joseph traveled through all the land of Egypt.

⁴⁶Joseph was thirty years old when he began serving the king of Egypt. And he left the king's court and traveled through all the land of Egypt. ⁴⁷During the seven good years, the crops in the land grew well. ⁴⁸And Joseph gathered all the food produced in Egypt during those seven years of good crops and stored the food in the cities. In every city he stored grain that had been grown in the fields around that city. ⁴⁹Joseph stored much grain, as much as the sand of the seashore—so much that he could not measure it.

⁵⁰Joseph's wife was Asenath daughter of Potiphera, the priest of On. Before the years of hunger came, Joseph and Asenath had two sons. ⁵¹Joseph named the first son Manasseh and said, "God has made me forget all the troubles I have had and all my father's family." ⁵²Joseph named the second son Ephraim and said, "God has given me children in the land of my troubles."

⁵³The seven years of good crops came to an end in the land of Egypt. ⁵⁴Then the seven years of hunger began, just as Joseph had said. In all the lands people had nothing to eat, but in Egypt there was food. ⁵⁵The time of hunger became terrible in all of Egypt, and the people cried to the king for food. He said to all the Egyptians, "Go to Joseph and do whatever he tells you."

⁵⁶The hunger was everywhere in that part of the world. And Joseph opened the storehouses and sold grain to the people of Egypt, because the time of hunger became terrible in Egypt. ⁵⁷And all the people in that part of the world came to Joseph in Egypt to buy grain because the hunger was terrible everywhere in that part of the world.

DEVOTION

FIRST THERE WAS the test of being sold into slavery. Then there was the treachery of Potiphar's wife. Then the broken promise of the king's cupbearer. Joseph had been tested time and again by the actions of others.

Now we read of perhaps the greatest test of Joseph's life: the temptation of prosperity. The king's ring on his finger. The king's clothes to wear. A chariot with criers running in front of it commanding people to bow down.

This prosperity poses some serious temptations for Joseph. Perhaps he could use his power to exact revenge on those who have wronged him, or use his position to increase his personal wealth. In many ways, this is Joseph's greatest temptation . . . not the temptation to despair in the midst of false imprisonment or treachery, but the temptation to misuse the abundant blessings of God.

In one of the stories of Jesus, we read of a farmer who was blessed with a great crop (Luke 12:16–21). In fact, the crop was so good that his barn wouldn't hold it. Rather than using his bounty to enrich others, he ordered bigger barns to be built and then said to himself that he'd live the easy life now.

Joseph could have done the same, but he didn't. He worked hard at the job he was given so that when the seven years of plenty were finished, the supply of grain was more than sufficient. Joseph was the same man in the king's chariot that he was in the king's prison. Paul tells us that riches can be a "trap." He adds that money can "ruin and destroy people" (1 Timothy 6:9–10). So can power . . . and Joseph had both money and power. But he refused to fall into the trap, thus dodging the greatest temptation of all.

THOUGHTS TO PONDER

Why do people turn to God in times of trouble? Conversely, why do people tend to forget God when things are going well? How can we keep from falling into the lure of prosperity?

PRAYER

God, we pray that we remember you in good times and in bad. Bless us to the extent that we can remain faithful to you. Amen.

DESPERATE MEASURES

GENESIS 42:1–22

42Jacob learned that there was grain in Egypt, so he said to his sons, "Why are you just sitting here looking at one another? ²I have heard that there is grain in Egypt. Go down there and buy grain for us to eat, so that we will live and not die."

³So ten of Joseph's brothers went down to buy grain from Egypt. ⁴But Jacob did not send Benjamin, Joseph's brother, with them, because he was afraid that something terrible might happen to him. ⁵Along with many other people, the sons of Israel went to Egypt to buy grain, because the people in the land of Canaan were also hungry.

⁶Now Joseph was governor over Egypt. He was the one who sold the grain to people who came to buy it. So Joseph's brothers came to him and bowed face-down on the ground before him. ⁷When Joseph saw his brothers, he knew who they were, but he acted as if he didn't know them. He asked unkindly, "Where do you come from?"

They answered, "We have come from the land of Canaan to buy food."

⁸Joseph knew they were his brothers, but they did not know who he was. ⁹And Joseph remembered his dreams about his brothers bowing to him. He said to them, "You are spies! You came to learn where the nation is weak!"

¹⁰But his brothers said to him, "No, my master. We come as your servants just to buy food. ¹¹We are all sons of the same father. We are honest men, not spies."

¹²Then Joseph said to them, "No! You have come to learn where this nation is weak!"

¹³And they said, "We are ten of twelve brothers, sons of the same father, and we live in the land of Canaan. Our youngest brother is there with our father right now, and our other brother is gone."

¹⁴But Joseph said to them, "I can see I was right! You are spies! ¹⁵But I will give you a way to prove you are telling the truth. As surely as the king lives, you will not leave this place until your youngest brother comes here. ¹⁶One of you must go and get your brother. The rest of you will stay here in prison. We will see if you are telling the truth. If not, as surely as the king lives, you are spies." ¹⁷Then Joseph put them all in prison for three days.

¹⁸On the third day Joseph said to them, "I am a God-fearing man. Do this and I will let you live: ¹⁹If you are honest men, let one of your brothers stay here in prison while the rest of you go and carry grain back to feed your hungry families. ²⁰Then bring your youngest brother back here to me. If you do this, I will know you are telling the truth, and you will not die."

The brothers agreed to this. ²¹They said to each other, "We are being punished for what we did to our brother. We saw his trouble, and he begged us to save him, but we refused to listen. That is why we are in this trouble now."

[22]Then Reuben said to them, "I told you not to harm the boy, but you refused to listen to me. So now we are being punished for what we did to him."

DEVOTION

DOESN'T IT OFTEN seem in life that there is "grain in Egypt"? By that I mean, doesn't it seem that what we need is just out of our reach and if we are to get it, we have to do something extraordinary to obtain it?

I've known people who have traveled all over the country in search of a qualified specialist for a rare disease, spending small fortunes trying to get relief from their affliction. I've watched people spend fortunes on experimental treatments, often outside of the United States, once they exhausted every option modern American medicine had to offer.

When your life is at stake, you'll do almost anything for the "grain in Egypt." Borrow against the home equity; cash in the insurance policies. None of these things matter if you don't think you'll live to see next Christmas.

I thank God I've never been in that situation, but I've seen enough families who have been to understand the combination of panic and desperation that causes someone to find their hope somewhere far off. And I've seen the best plans go awry as the savings are exhausted and the disease wins.

The brothers didn't know how difficult their task would be when they started. They only knew that they were starving and that there was food in Egypt. I'm sure they were almost giddy with optimism when they left. Imagine how they felt upon realizing that not all of them would be going home.

THOUGHTS TO PONDER

Have you ever felt the desperation of the brothers in this story? Have you known anyone who has? What would you do if you had to make an expensive trip far away in order to survive?

PRAYER

God, we thank you for the sustenance you give us every day and thank you for the safety of home. Amen.

Appreciating What You Earn

GENESIS 42:23–38

[23]When Joseph talked to his brothers, he used an interpreter, so they did not know that Joseph understood what they were saying. [24]Then Joseph left them and cried. After a short time he went back and spoke to them. He took Simeon and tied him up while the other brothers watched. [25]Joseph told his servants to fill his brothers' bags with grain and to put the money the brothers had paid for the grain back in their bags. The servants were also to give them what they would need for their trip back home. And the servants did this.

[26]So the brothers put the grain on their donkeys and left. [27]When they stopped for the night, one of the brothers opened his sack to get food for his donkey. Then he saw his money in the top of the sack. [28]He said to the other brothers, "The money I paid for the grain has been put back. Here it is in my sack!"

The brothers were very frightened. They said to each other, "What has God done to us?"

[29]The brothers went to their father Jacob in the land of Canaan and told him everything that had happened. [30]They said, "The master of that land spoke unkindly to us. He accused us of spying on his country, [31]but we told him that we were honest men, not spies. [32]We told him that we were ten of twelve brothers—sons of one father. We said that one of our brothers was gone and that our youngest brother was with our father in Canaan.

[33]"Then the master of the land said to us, 'Here is a way I can know you are honest men: Leave one of your brothers with me, and take grain to feed your hungry families, and go. [34]And bring your youngest brother to me so I will know you are not spies but honest men. Then I will give you back your brother whom you leave with me, and you can move about freely in our land.'"

[35]As the brothers emptied their sacks, each of them found his money in his sack. When they and their father saw it, they were afraid.

[36]Their father Jacob said to them, "You are robbing me of all my children. Joseph is gone, Simeon is gone, and now you want to take Benjamin away, too. Everything is against me."

[37]Then Reuben said to his father, "You may put my two sons to death if I don't bring Benjamin back to you. Trust him to my care, and I will bring him back to you."

[38]But Jacob said, "I will not allow Benjamin to go with you. His brother is dead, and he is the only son left from my wife Rachel. I am afraid something terrible might happen to him during the trip to Egypt. Then I would be sad until the day I die."

DEVOTION

TO THE BROTHERS, the man was Zaphenath-Paneah, the number-two man in all of Egypt . . . the man who held their fate in his hands. But to Joseph, these men were not just more of the Canaanite hordes who were coming to Egypt in pursuit of grain—these were his brothers. And the enormity of that fact, coupled with the news that his brother and father were still alive, was more than Joseph could handle, so he went into another room and cried.

Joseph could have chosen to reveal himself to them at any point in this elaborate charade, yet he kept playing them. He had never before exhibited a spirit of revenge. Even when he rose to be the second-in-command in the land of Egypt, there is no indication that he settled scores with Potiphar's wife who lied about him or the lazy cupbearer who forgot about him.

So why does he make things hard on his brothers now? Maybe it's to test their resolve. Maybe it's to make them sorry once again for what they put him through. Maybe Joseph has to be politically cautious before he moves his large extended family to Egypt, where the locals would not even eat with Hebrews.

But there's something else at work here. Joseph offers his brothers a way of escape from their plight, but he wants them to appreciate it. Given early and given freely, perhaps the invitation to Egypt would not have seemed so sweet.

Isn't that the way things are in life? In our house, my boys paid for their first cars after I made the down payment. They watched in amazement as their friends who were given cars abused them. I think we're just like that: what we don't earn, we're likely to not appreciate.

THOUGHTS TO PONDER

What is something you worked very hard to achieve or obtain? A degree? A better home? A new job? How did you overcome obstacles along the way? How did you feel when you finally achieved your goal?

PRAYER

God, help us to be grateful for the gifts you give and help us to never overlook them. Father, help us to overcome any obstacles between us and our promised destination. Amen.

The Pain of Separation

GENESIS 43:1–17

43 Still no food grew in the land of Canaan. ²When Jacob's family had eaten all the grain they had brought from Egypt, Jacob said to them, "Go to Egypt again and buy a little more grain for us to eat."

³But Judah said to Jacob, "The governor of that country strongly warned us, 'If you don't bring your brother back with you, you will not be allowed to see me.' ⁴If you will send Benjamin with us, we will go down and buy food for you. ⁵But if you refuse to send Benjamin, we will not go. The governor of that country warned us that we would not see him if we didn't bring Benjamin with us."

⁶Israel said, "Why did you tell the man you had another brother? You have caused me a lot of trouble."

⁷The brothers answered, "He questioned us carefully about ourselves and our family. He asked us, 'Is your father still alive? Do you have another brother?' We just answered his questions. How could we know he would ask us to bring our other brother to him?"

⁸Then Judah said to his father Jacob, "Send Benjamin with me, and we will go at once so that we, you, and our children may live and not die. ⁹I will guarantee you that he will be safe, and I will be personally responsible for him. If I don't bring him back to you, you can blame me all my life. ¹⁰If we had not wasted all this time, we could have already made two trips."

¹¹Then their father Jacob said to them, "If it has to be that way, then do this: Take some of the best foods in our land in your packs. Give them to the man as a gift: some balm, some honey, spices, myrrh, pistachio nuts, and almonds. ¹²Take twice as much money with you this time, and take back the money that was returned to you in your sacks last time. Maybe it was a mistake. ¹³And take Benjamin with you. Now leave and go to the man. ¹⁴I pray that God Almighty will cause the governor to be merciful to you and that he will allow Simeon and Benjamin to come back with you. If I am robbed of my children, then I am robbed of them!"

¹⁵So the brothers took the gifts. They also took twice as much money as they had taken the first time, and they took Benjamin. They hurried down to Egypt and stood before Joseph.

¹⁶When Joseph saw Benjamin with them, he said to the servant in charge of his house, "Bring those men into my house. Kill an animal and prepare a meal. Those men will eat with me today at noon." ¹⁷The servant did as Joseph told him and brought the men to Joseph's house.

DEVOTION

THE FIRST TRIP must have been hard on Jacob—watching his ten sons ride across the parched land toward the west, he knew that he might not see them again. Anything could happen on the road; they were carrying a lot of money. The Egyptian authorities might refuse to help them, making them return home empty-handed. His mind must have raced as he watched that caravan wind its way in the direction of Egypt.

But however he felt the first time, the stakes were even higher the second time around. The only remaining son of his beloved wife Rachel was being summoned to Egypt. Rachel was the one he had worked fourteen years for after Laban had tricked him into marrying Leah first. Rachel had given him Joseph and Benjamin. Jacob believed Joseph had been killed by a wild animal years ago—he still kept the bloody coat Joseph wore that day—and now there was a chance he could lose Benjamin. And with that, all ties to his beloved Rachel would be gone.

If you've ever lost a loved one, you know they don't leave all at once. Their smell is still on the pillow, perhaps; their clothes in the closet. That kind of tea that only he or she would drink is still in the cabinet.

But one by one, the reminders go away. And with each piece that leaves, a lingering part of that person begins to go away, too.

Benjamin was the remnant of Rachel. He was the reminder of Joseph. He held a special place in the heart of Jacob. If something happened to Benjamin, Jacob's heart would finally break under the strain.

But the family needed the food. So Jacob once again watched a caravan travel into the western horizon—only this time, it carried away a very large piece of this heart.

THOUGHTS TO PONDER

Have you ever been separated from a loved one for a long time? Have you ever said goodbye to someone, not knowing if you would ever see him or her again? What thoughts ran through your mind?

PRAYER

God we know that with life comes separation, but we also know that because of you, death brings reunion and we love you and praise you for that. Amen.

THE IMPORTANCE
OF PATIENCE

GENESIS 43:18–34

¹⁸The brothers were afraid when they were brought to Joseph's house and thought, "We were brought here because of the money that was put in our sacks on the first trip. He wants to attack us, make us slaves, and take our donkeys." ¹⁹So the brothers went to the servant in charge of Joseph's house and spoke to him at the door of the house. ²⁰They said, "Master, we came here once before to buy food. ²¹While we were going home, we stopped for the night and when we opened our sacks each of us found all his money in his sack. We brought that money with us to give it back to you. ²²And we have brought more money to pay for the food we want to buy this time. We don't know who put that money in our sacks."

²³But the servant answered, "It's all right. Don't be afraid. Your God, the God of your father, must have put the money in your sacks. I got the money you paid me for the grain last time." Then the servant brought Simeon out to them.

²⁴The servant led the men into Joseph's house and gave them water, and they washed their feet. Then he gave their donkeys food to eat. ²⁵The men prepared their gift to give to Joseph when he arrived at noon, because they had heard they were going to eat with him there.

²⁶When Joseph came home, the brothers gave him the gift they had brought into the house and bowed down to the ground in front of him. ²⁷Joseph asked them how they were doing. He said, "How is your aged father you told me about? Is he still alive?"

²⁸The brothers answered, "Your servant, our father, is well. He is still alive." And they bowed low before Joseph to show him respect.

²⁹When Joseph saw his brother Benjamin, who had the same mother as he, Joseph asked, "Is this your youngest brother you told me about?" Then he said to Benjamin, "God be good to you, my son!" ³⁰Then Joseph hurried off because he had to hold back the tears when he saw his brother Benjamin. So Joseph went into his room and cried there. ³¹Then he washed his face and came out. He controlled himself and said, "Serve the meal."

³²So they served Joseph at one table, his brothers at another table, and the Egyptians who ate with him at another table. This was because Egyptians did not like Hebrews and never ate with them. ³³Joseph's brothers were seated in front of him in order of their ages, from oldest to youngest. They looked at each other because they were so amazed. ³⁴Food from Joseph's table was taken to them, but Benjamin was given five times more food than the others. Joseph's brothers ate and drank freely with him.

DEVOTION

IN THE STORY ABOVE, note how the tables have completely turned. Joseph, the brother sold into slavery by his brothers, now has total control over his brothers' destinies. Joseph, once a servant in Potiphar's house, now has servants in his own home. God has been good to Joseph. But even in his position of power, revenge and gloating are not on Joseph's agenda.

Notice how Joseph makes sure that the immediate needs of his brothers are met. Their donkeys are fed. Their feet, dirty from a long journey in sandals, have been washed. The food is prepared.

So what is the lesson for us?

Just this: when I reach one of those times that I'm so righteously correct that I can't wait to verbally fly into someone, I need to pause and pray. Maybe it's a student whose work is less than stellar. Or a child who disappoints me yet again. I can't wait to be right, to make them understand my good arguments.

But in nearly three decades of teaching and parenting, I've discovered something that psychologists will bear out. Until you remove the fear from the situation, and until you lower the intense emotions in the situation, none of your best logical arguments will make any difference. Brains are not ready to comprehend rational arguments when they are dealing with irrational fear.

Until a student in my office knows it to be a safe place—even when he or she might be in trouble—none of my arguments about the need for attendance or the importance of deadlines will be heard. Until a child knows we love him or her unconditionally, none of our best advice on how they should change will register.

Joseph wants his brothers to trust him so that his future advice would be heard. Do we have the patience to do the same with those who have harmed us?

THOUGHTS TO PONDER

When someone has hurt you, how do you approach them? What should be the ultimate goal when we must rebuke or discipline someone?

PRAYER

Father, we thank you for the example of Joseph, who still loved those who wronged him. Help us have the courage to do the same. Amen.

LOOKING INTO THE HEART

GENESIS 44:1–18, 30–34

44 Then Joseph gave a command to the servant in charge of his house. He said, "Fill the men's sacks with as much grain as they can carry, and put each man's money into his sack with the grain. ²Put my silver cup in the sack of the youngest brother, along with his money for the grain." The servant did what Joseph told him.

³At dawn the brothers were sent away with their donkeys. ⁴They were not far from the city when Joseph said to the servant in charge of his house, "Go after the men. When you catch up with them, say, 'Why have you paid back evil for good? ⁵The cup you have stolen is the one my master uses for drinking and for explaining dreams. You have done a very wicked thing!'"

⁶So the servant caught up with the brothers and said to them what Joseph had told him to say.

⁷But the brothers said to the servant, "Why do you say these things? We would not do anything like that! ⁸We brought back to you from the land of Canaan the money we found in our sacks. So surely we would not steal silver or gold from your master's house. ⁹If you find that silver cup in the sack of one of us, then let him die, and we will be your slaves."

¹⁰The servant said, "We will do as you say, but only the man who has taken the cup will become my slave. The rest of you may go free."

¹¹Then every brother quickly lowered his sack to the ground and opened it. ¹²The servant searched the sacks, going from the oldest brother to the youngest, and found the cup in Benjamin's sack. ¹³The brothers tore their clothes to show they were afraid. Then they put their sacks back on the donkeys and returned to the city.

¹⁴When Judah and his brothers went back to Joseph's house, Joseph was still there, so the brothers bowed facedown on the ground before him. ¹⁵Joseph said to them, "What have you done? Didn't you know that a man like me can learn things by signs and dreams?"

¹⁶Judah said, "Master, what can we say? And how can we show we are not guilty? God has uncovered our guilt, so all of us will be your slaves, not just Benjamin."

¹⁷But Joseph said, "I will not make you all slaves! Only the man who stole the cup will be my slave. The rest of you may go back safely to your father."

¹⁸Then Judah went to Joseph and said, "Master, please let me speak plainly to you, and please don't be angry with me. I know that you are as powerful as the king of Egypt himself."

³⁰"Now what will happen if we go home to our father without our youngest brother? He is so important in our father's life that ³¹when our father sees the young boy is not with us, he will die. And it will be our fault. We will cause the great sorrow that kills our father.

[32]"I gave my father a guarantee that the young boy would be safe. I said to my father, 'If I don't bring him back to you, you can blame me all my life.' [33]So now, please allow me to stay here and be your slave, and let the young boy go back home with his brothers. [34]I cannot go back to my father if the boy is not with me. I couldn't stand to see my father that sad.'"

DEVOTION

JOSEPH REMEMBERS THE reason he was sold into slavery. His brothers were jealous of him because of the great love his father Jacob showed him. And it is possible that this final test, before Joseph reveals his true identity to his unknowing brothers, is to determine whether his younger brother, Benjamin, is suffering the same type of abuse Joseph had experienced so many years before. Would the brothers protect Benjamin or would they leave him as a slave in Egypt the same way they left Joseph so many years before? It was the last test of their character.

Many years ago, a well-known journalist ended a nationally televised interview with a declared candidate for president with an almost throw-away question, asking, "Sir, why do you want to be president?" The candidate stumbled badly. None of his scripted answers prepared him for the simple question of why he wanted the job.

I've instructed my journalism students to have questions ready even while the cords are being wrapped up. You never know when the real person will emerge.

Joseph had seen the scripted honesty of the brothers, but he is looking for the candid truth: are they capable of more treachery? If they pass this last test, Joseph will be satisfied.

THOUGHTS TO PONDER

How have the brothers changed in the years since they sold Joseph into slavery? What factors do you think entered into the changes?

PRAYER

God, we pray that when you look into our hearts you will find us pure. Forgive us of our past sins. Amen.

"Why Am I Here?"

GENESIS 45:1–11

45 Joseph could not control himself in front of his servants any longer, so he cried out, "Have everyone leave me." When only the brothers were left with Joseph, he told them who he was. ²Joseph cried so loudly that the Egyptians heard him, and the people in the king's palace heard about it. ³He said to his brothers, "I am Joseph. Is my father still alive?" But the brothers could not answer him, because they were very afraid of him.

⁴So Joseph said to them, "Come close to me." When the brothers came close to him, he said to them, "I am your brother Joseph, whom you sold as a slave to go to Egypt. ⁵Now don't be worried or angry with yourselves because you sold me here. God sent me here ahead of you to save people's lives. ⁶No food has grown on the land for two years now, and there will be five more years without planting or harvest. ⁷So God sent me here ahead of you to make sure you have some descendants left on earth and to keep you alive in an amazing way. ⁸So it was not you who sent me here, but God. God has made me the highest officer of the king of Egypt. I am in charge of his palace, and I am the master of all the land of Egypt.

⁹"So leave quickly and go to my father. Tell him, 'Your son Joseph says: God has made me master over all Egypt. Come down to me quickly. ¹⁰Live in the land of Goshen where you will be near me. Your children, your grandchildren, your flocks and herds, and all that you have will also be near me. ¹¹I will care for you during the next five years of hunger so that you and your family and all that you have will not starve.'"

DEVOTION

WHY AM I HERE? It's one of life's biggest questions and one of the most perplexing. In my role as a professor, I see college students wrestling with this question all the time. For that matter, I see adults who are searching just as desperately for the answer to that question.

Repeatedly, Joseph tells his brothers that he knows why he was put on earth. God placed him in a position to save the lives of people who would have otherwise perished in the seven brutal years of famine, including his own family.

I can't tell you why you're here, but I think I've found a formula to help you find out. It's from the writing of the apostle Paul, to the Christians in Rome. In Romans 12:1–2, he writes:

> "So brothers and sisters, since God has shown us great mercy, I beg you to offer your lives as a living sacrifice to him. Your offering must be

only for God and pleasing to him, which is the spiritual way for you to worship. Do not be shaped by this world; instead be changed within by a new way of thinking. Then you will be able to decide what God wants for you; you will know what is good and pleasing to him and what is perfect."

Note the progression here. First, get off the throne of your life and climb on to the altar of sacrifice. Second, quit thinking like the rest of the world; quit allowing the world to shape you. When you've accomplished these two steps—no small feat for most of us—you'll find the promise: you will be able to know what God wants for you . . . his good and perfect will for your life.

Here's the formula: sacrifice and transformation must precede revelation. But here's the downside. I think God's will is hidden from people too busy to receive it. I think God's will isn't revealed to folks who selfishly pursue money or fame or anything else the world holds valuable. You may even know a few good folks who have never heard God's will for their lives because they haven't put themselves in the right posture to hear it. God does not shout his will for my life at me, He whispers it to me when I have humbled myself.

Joseph knew life on the altar of sacrifice. Joseph knew what it meant to be transformed. He was never merely a servant in Potiphar's house or an inmate in the king's prison—he was different. So he was ready when God revealed his will to Joseph.

The times in my life when I've been the least selfish with my time and talents are the times that God's voice has been the clearest. And the times when I've been selfishly absorbed in my own interests, he has been silent.

Joseph knew that God put him in Egypt for a reason. Do you know why you're here?

THOUGHTS TO PONDER

What purpose do you think God has for your life? How can you be sure? What are you doing to ensure that God's will is played out in your life?

PRAYER

Father, show us your good and perfect will for our lives and give us the courage to follow it. Amen.

DARING FAITH

GENESIS 45:16—46:7

¹⁶When the king of Egypt and his officers learned that Joseph's brothers had come, they were very happy. ¹⁷So the king said to Joseph, "Tell your brothers to load their animals and go back to the land of Canaan ¹⁸and bring their father and their families back here to me. I will give them the best land in Egypt, and they will eat the best food we have here. ¹⁹Tell them to take some wagons from Egypt for their children and their wives and to bring their father back also. ²⁰Tell them not to worry about bringing any of their things with them, because we will give them the best of what we have in Egypt."

²¹So the sons of Israel did this. Joseph gave them wagons as the king had ordered and food for their trip. ²²He gave each brother a change of clothes, but he gave Benjamin five changes of clothes and about seven and one-half pounds of silver. ²³Joseph also sent his father ten donkeys loaded with the best things from Egypt and ten female donkeys loaded with grain, bread, and other food for his father on his trip back. ²⁴Then Joseph told his brothers to go. As they were leaving, he said to them, "Don't quarrel on the way home."

²⁵So the brothers left Egypt and went to their father Jacob in the land of Canaan. ²⁶They told him, "Joseph is still alive and is the ruler over all the land of Egypt." Their father was shocked and did not believe them. ²⁷But when the brothers told him everything Joseph had said, and when Jacob saw the wagons Joseph had sent to carry him back to Egypt, he felt better. ²⁸Israel said, "Now I believe you. My son Joseph is still alive, and I will go and see him before I die."

46 So Israel took all he had and started his trip. He went to Beersheba, where he offered sacrifices to the God of his father Isaac. ²During the night God spoke to Israel in a vision and said, "Jacob, Jacob."

And Jacob answered, "Here I am."

³Then God said, "I am God, the God of your father. Don't be afraid to go to Egypt, because I will make your descendants a great nation there. ⁴I will go to Egypt with you, and I will bring you out of Egypt again. Joseph's own hands will close your eyes when you die."

⁵Then Jacob left Beersheba. The sons of Israel loaded their father, their children, and their wives in the wagons the king of Egypt had sent. ⁶They also took their farm animals and everything they had gotten in Canaan. So Jacob went to Egypt with all his descendants— ⁷his sons and grandsons, his daughters and granddaughters. He took all his family to Egypt with him.

DEVOTION

LIFE IS SOMETIMES like the Indiana Jones movie where he has to pass a test in order to reach the room where the Holy Grail lies. The test is to step out in faith, and Indiana literally walks off the face of a cliff when no step is there. Suddenly, the step appears and keeps him from falling. And then another appears, and another, until an entire path opens itself up where only air had been.

Jacob did something as daring as that in this story. An old man, he left the comfort of the only land he had ever known. There was no guarantee he would be hearty enough to make the trip, but he longed to see his long lost son. It was a risk he was willing to take.

Along the way, he stops to worship God. God responds to the act of worship by revealing himself to Jacob in a dream, confirming that Jacob will indeed make it to Egypt and see his beloved Joseph. Plus, he's assured that his sons will prosper there. Notice that it's after Jacob begins his journey that God appears to him.

Are you wondering about the direction God wants you to go? Start out in faith, and pray. Then see if the answer comes.

Stuck on the top of Mount Everest overnight, Dr. Beck Weathers was assumed to be dead by his fellow climbers. But the next day, he awoke from the frigid night, the only person to ever survive a night alone on top of Everest. He knew he had to try to reach base camp. No one was coming to rescue him. But blinding snow obscured the way. Although completely disoriented, he knew he had to choose to walk in one direction or he would die. He safely arrived at the camp, unharmed except for the effects of frostbite.

So many choices in life . . . which one to take? Follow the example of Jacob: start the journey and pray.

THOUGHTS TO PONDER

What "leap of faith" have you been asked to make in your life? How do you know where God wants you to go? How often do you ask him?

PRAYER

God, we pray that we will take the journey you have planned for us and that we will always be willing to follow your lead. Amen.

DROUGHTS AND SHOWERS

GENESIS 46:26—47:12

²⁶So the total number of Jacob's direct descendants who went to Egypt was sixty-six, not counting the wives of Jacob's sons. ²⁷Joseph had two sons born in Egypt, so the total number in the family of Jacob in Egypt was seventy.

²⁸Jacob sent Judah ahead of him to see Joseph in Goshen. When Jacob and his people came into the land of Goshen, ²⁹Joseph prepared his chariot and went to meet his father Israel in Goshen. As soon as Joseph saw his father, he hugged him, and cried there for a long time.

³⁰Then Israel said to Joseph, "Now I am ready to die, because I have seen your face and I know you are still alive."

³¹Joseph said to his brothers and his father's family, "I will go and tell the king you are here. I will say, 'My brothers and my father's family have left the land of Canaan and have come here to me. ³²They are shepherds and take care of farm animals, and they have brought their flocks and their herds and everything they own with them.' ³³When the king calls you, he will ask, 'What work do you do?' ³⁴This is what you should tell him: 'We, your servants, have taken care of farm animals all our lives. Our ancestors did the same thing.' Then the king will allow you to settle in the land of Goshen, away from the Egyptians, because they don't like to be near shepherds."

47 Joseph went in to the king and said, "My father and my brothers have arrived from Canaan with their flocks and herds and everything they own. They are now in the land of Goshen." ²Joseph chose five of his brothers to introduce to the king.

³The king said to the brothers, "What work do you do?"

And they said to him, "We, your servants, are shepherds, just as our ancestors were." ⁴They said to the king, "We have come to live in this land, because there is no grass in the land of Canaan for our animals to eat, and the hunger is terrible there. So please allow us to live in the land of Goshen."

⁵Then the king said to Joseph, "Your father and your brothers have come to you, ⁶and you may choose any place in Egypt for them to live. Give your father and your brothers the best land; let them live in the land of Goshen. And if any of them are skilled shepherds, put them in charge of my sheep and cattle."

⁷Then Joseph brought in his father Jacob and introduced him to the king, and Jacob blessed the king.

⁸Then the king said to Jacob, "How old are you?"

⁹Jacob said to him, "My life has been spent wandering from place to place. It has been short and filled with trouble—only one hundred thirty years. My ancestors lived much longer than I." ¹⁰Then Jacob blessed the king and left.

¹¹Joseph obeyed the king and gave his father and brothers the best land in Egypt, near the city of Rameses. ¹²And Joseph gave his father, his brothers, and everyone who lived with them the food they needed.

DEVOTION

THE LAND OF GOSHEN was fertile territory (during times of rain) in eastern Egypt, separated from the main population center of Egypt by the Nile River. Immediately upon settling there, the brothers of Joseph were given the task of keeping the royal herds.

In normal times, this region experienced three seasons. The rainy season from about mid-July to November caused the Nile River to overflow its banks. From mid-November to mid-March was the season known as "coming forth," a time when the land emerged from the water and seeds began to grow. Finally, there was the annual drought that lasted until the rains came again in July.

Rather than being a square geo-political block we see on the map today, ancient Egypt was a six-hundred-mile ribbon of civilization dwelling close to the Nile, living and dying by its flood patterns. Because of the Nile, there were times when food was available in Egypt and not in Palestine, which depended on the Mediterranean rains for crops (see Genesis 12:10). So food exports were a significant part of the Egyptian economy.

The land of Goshen was valuable for grazing, with its predictable weather patterns, lush growth, and ready water supply. We have no way of knowing how many years the children of Israel spent in this fertile lowland, but it was a very generous provision indeed for Jacob and his sons, and a sign of how highly regarded Joseph was in the eyes of the king.

THOUGHTS TO PONDER

Why would Jacob say, "Now I am ready to die"? What events in his life was he referring to when he said it had been "short and filled with trouble"?

PRAYER

God, we know you bring the rains and that you shower us with blessings every day. Help us to see past the temporary droughts in our lives to the showers yet to come. Amen.

USE YOUR TIME
FOR GOD'S WORK

GENESIS 47:13–26

¹³The hunger became worse, and since there was no food anywhere in the land, Egypt and Canaan became very poor. ¹⁴Joseph collected all the money that was to be found in Egypt and Canaan. People paid for the grain they were buying, and he brought that money to the king's palace. ¹⁵After some time, when the people in Egypt and Canaan had no money left, they went to Joseph and said, "Please give us food. Our money is gone, and if we don't eat, we will die here in front of you."

¹⁶Joseph answered, "Since you have no money, give me your farm animals, and I will give you food in return." ¹⁷So people brought their farm animals to Joseph, and he gave them food in exchange for their horses, sheep, goats, cattle, and donkeys. And he kept them alive by trading food for their farm animals that year.

¹⁸The next year the people came to Joseph and said, "You know we have no money left, and all our animals belong to you. We have nothing left except our bodies and our land. ¹⁹Surely both we and our land will die here in front of you. Buy us and our land in exchange for food, and we will be slaves to the king, together with our land. Give us seed to plant so that we will live and not die, and the land will not become a desert."

²⁰So Joseph bought all the land in Egypt for the king. Every Egyptian sold Joseph his field, because the hunger was very great. So the land became the king's, ²¹and Joseph made the people slaves from one end of Egypt to the other. ²²The only land he did not buy was the land the priests owned. They did not need to sell their land because the king paid them for their work. So they had money to buy food.

²³Joseph said to the people, "Now I have bought you and your land for the king, so I will give you seed and you can plant your fields. ²⁴At harvest time you must give one-fifth to the king. You may keep four-fifths for yourselves to use as seed for the field and as food for yourselves, your families, and your children."

²⁵The people said, "You have saved our lives. If you like, we will become slaves of the king."

²⁶So Joseph made a law in Egypt, which continues today: One-fifth of everything from the land belongs to the king. The only land the king did not get was the priests' land.

DEVOTION

IN THIS PASSAGE we see Joseph's skills as a politician. Knowing the number of years remaining in the devastating famine because of his revelation from the Lord, Joseph conceives a plan that simultaneously preserves the peace, saves the people from starvation, and establishes the wealth of the king.

Egypt is probably in the sixth year of famine when the people come to Joseph, willing to barter their farm animals for food. Their money—probably obtained from selling their excess grain during the years of plenty—is now gone. They are desperate and their desperation presents a political problem for the king. If the people die, he has few subjects and his kingdom is vulnerable to invasion. If they riot, their numbers are probably too great for his guard, who might very well turn on him too.

So Joseph devises a plan; in the final year he gives the people not only food to eat, but seeds to plant. Eventually, the rains will come, the Nile will swell again, and the fertile overflow will enrich the soil for crops to grow. Joseph knows all this, and his leadership keeps the peace in the final, brutal years of the famine.

Meanwhile, his people live down in the land called Goshen. Undoubtedly, they are commissioned to tend many of the animals given to the king. And as those flocks increased, so did the wealth and the political power of these Canaanites who had found the favor of the king through their brother, Joseph. But in their good fortune, we can see the seeds of a problem that eventually came to fruition four hundred years later, in the days of Moses, when the children of Israel were slaves to the Egyptians.

Joseph used his time to do God's work. He kept the ancient world from starvation during the worst famine in history. He made a law ensuring that the king of Egypt and his successors will be the wealthiest men on earth. He stands ready to exit the stage.

God used one man, Noah, to save the world from flooding, and he used one man, Joseph, to save the world from starvation. And he sent his Son—fully God and fully man—to save the world from sin.

THOUGHTS TO PONDER

What do you rank as your greatest accomplishment? Why do you say that? What do you hope to accomplish in the future? Have you prayed about your goals?

PRAYER

God, we see in Joseph what can happen when someone listens to your voice. Help us to follow his example. Amen.

LAST REQUEST

GENESIS 47:27–48:5, 7–14, 17–19

²⁷The Israelites continued to live in the land of Goshen in Egypt. There they got possessions and had many children and grew in number.

²⁸Jacob lived in Egypt seventeen years, so he lived to be one hundred forty-seven years old. ²⁹When Israel knew he soon would die, he called his son Joseph to him and said to him, "If you love me, put your hand under my leg. Promise me you will not bury me in Egypt. ³⁰When I die, carry me out of Egypt, and bury me where my ancestors are buried."

Joseph answered, "I will do as you say."

³¹Then Jacob said, "Promise me." And Joseph promised him that he would do this. Then Israel worshiped as he leaned on the top of his walking stick.

48 Some time later Joseph learned that his father was very sick, so he took his two sons Manasseh and Ephraim and went to his father. ²When Joseph arrived, someone told Jacob, "Your son Joseph has come to see you." Jacob was weak, so he used all his strength and sat up on his bed.

³Then Jacob said to Joseph, "God Almighty appeared to me at Luz in the land of Canaan and blessed me there. ⁴He said to me, 'I will give you many children. I will make you the father of many peoples, and I will give your descendants this land forever.' ⁵Your two sons, who were born here in Egypt before I came, will be counted as my own sons. Ephraim and Manasseh will be my sons just as Reuben and Simeon are my sons."

⁷"When I came from Northwest Mesopotamia, Rachel died in the land of Canaan, as we were traveling toward Ephrath. This made me very sad, and I buried her there beside the road to Ephrath." (Today Ephrath is Bethlehem.)

⁸Then Israel saw Joseph's sons and said, "Who are these boys?"

⁹Joseph said to his father, "They are my sons that God has given me here in Egypt."

Israel said, "Bring your sons to me so I may bless them."

¹⁰At this time Israel's eyesight was bad because he was old. So Joseph brought the boys close to him, and Israel kissed the boys and put his arms around them. ¹¹He said to Joseph, "I thought I would never see you alive again, and now God has let me see you and also your children." ¹²Then Joseph moved his sons off Israel's lap and bowed facedown to the ground. ¹³He put Ephraim on his right side and Manasseh on his left. (So Ephraim was near Israel's left hand, and Manasseh was near Israel's right hand.) Joseph brought the boys close to Israel. ¹⁴But Israel crossed his arms and put his right hand on the head of Ephraim, who was younger. He put his left hand on the head of Manasseh, the firstborn son.

[17]When Joseph saw that his father put his right hand on Ephraim's head, he didn't like it. So he took hold of his father's hand, wanting to move it from Ephraim's head to Manasseh's head. [18]Joseph said to his father, "You are doing it wrong, Father. Manasseh is the firstborn son. Put your right hand on his head."

[19]But his father refused and said, "I know, my son, I know. Manasseh will be great and have many descendants. But his younger brother will be greater, and his descendants will be enough to make a nation."

DEVOTION

WHAT WOULD YOUR last request be? In this story, we get a glimpse of Jacob's two true loves—the land of Canaan and his beloved wife Rachel.

If a dying wish says anything about someone—and it no doubt does—then we learn how deeply Jacob loved his homeland and his wife. Jacob had lived in Canaan 130 years before coming to Egypt, and God had personally promised him that the land would eventually belong to his descendants. His wife was buried there. So he had many reasons for calling Joseph to his side and requesting that he be buried in Canaan. But he also had another reason: he had buried Rachel in Canaan and he wanted to return to be buried with her.

It says volumes about how much Jacob loved Joseph, the first son of Rachel, that he would spend his last seventeen years in a foreign land to be near him. But Jacob's love for Rachel was even stronger, stretching a century beyond her death. It's one of the amazing love stories of all time.

Consider the facts: To love someone so much that you would work fourteen years to gain her hand in marriage. To love someone so much that being close to her sons meant more than life itself. To love someone so much that a century after her death, your last wish is to be buried near her.

That's real love.

THOUGHTS TO PONDER

What would your last request be? Why is it important to you?

PRAYER

Father, our fervent hope is that when we die, we will be with you in heaven. Amen.

The Right Blessing

GENESIS 49:28—50:11

²⁸These are the twelve tribes of Israel, and this is what their father said to them. He gave each son the blessing that was right for him. ²⁹Then Israel gave them a command and said, "I am about to die. Bury me with my ancestors in the cave in the field of Ephron the Hittite. ³⁰That cave is in the field of Machpelah east of Mamre in the land of Canaan. Abraham bought the field and cave from Ephron the Hittite for a burying place. ³¹Abraham and Sarah his wife are buried there. Isaac and Rebekah his wife are buried there, and I buried my wife Leah there. ³²The field and the cave in it were bought from the Hittite people." ³³After Jacob finished talking to his sons, he lay down. He put his feet back on the bed, took his last breath, and died.

50When Jacob died, Joseph hugged his father and cried over him and kissed him. ²He commanded the doctors who served him to prepare his father's body, so the doctors prepared Jacob's body to be buried. ³It took the doctors forty days to prepare his body (the usual time it took). And the Egyptians had a time of sorrow for Jacob that lasted seventy days.

⁴When this time of sorrow had ended, Joseph spoke to the king's officers and said, "If you think well of me, please tell this to the king: ⁵'When my father was near death, I made a promise to him that I would bury him in a cave in the land of Canaan, in a burial place that he cut out for himself. So please let me go and bury my father, and then I will return.'"

⁶The king answered, "Keep your promise. Go and bury your father."

⁷So Joseph went to bury his father. All the king's officers, the elders of his court, and all the elders of Egypt went with Joseph. ⁸Everyone who lived with Joseph and his brothers went with him, as well as everyone who lived with his father. They left only their children, their flocks, and their herds in the land of Goshen. ⁹They went with Joseph in chariots and on horses. It was a very large group.

¹⁰When they came to the threshing floor of Atad, near the Jordan River, they cried loudly and bitterly for his father. Joseph's time of sorrow continued for seven days. ¹¹The people that lived in Canaan saw the sadness at the threshing floor of Atad and said, "Those Egyptians are showing great sorrow!" So now that place is named Sorrow of the Egyptians.

DEVOTION

IN THE PRECEDING VERSES, Jacob blesses each of his sons, telling each of them the fate of the nations that will come from their tribes. The diverse personalities of the men come out in the various blessings of Jacob.

Then we read a verse that I love: "He gave each son the blessing that was right for him" (Genesis 49:28). That's what good earthly fathers still do today. And it most certainly is what our heavenly Father does for each of us.

When I was young, no older than Joseph when he first had his dreams, I dreamed of nothing but sports. I wanted to be taller. I wanted to be more athletically talented. I wanted to play sports not only in high school, but in college and even beyond.

But that wasn't the blessing I received. So I reacted poorly: I resented God for it. And while I was wasting that time, I was ignoring the blessing he had given me. For better or worse, I was a writer. I wasn't blessed to be an athlete. God had given me the blessing that was right for me.

As parents, it's sometimes difficult to watch our children seek their way in life. But part of our role as parents is to remind our children that God has given them a blessing, and whatever that blessing is, it is right for them.

Jesus told a story about three men who were given a gift and how they used it. Two men took the gifts of the master and did wonderful things, earning great returns. One man, afraid of the wrath of his master, took the gift and hid it. On his return, the master blessed the first man and the second one as well. But the third man incurred the very wrath that had paralyzed him from using the blessing to begin with (Matthew 25:14–30).

The lesson then (and the lesson now) is this: your blessing is right for you, and you ignore it at your own peril.

THOUGHTS TO PONDER

What is your blessing from God? How have you used that blessing? How can we help our children find their blessing?

PRAYER

God, we know we are given gifts by you. Please let our gift to you to be the way we use those gifts in the service of others. Amen.

TURNING EVIL INTO GOOD

GENESIS 50:12–26

¹²So Jacob's sons did as their father commanded. ¹³They carried his body to the land of Canaan and buried it in the cave in the field of Machpelah near Mamre. Abraham had bought this cave and field from Ephron the Hittite to use as a burial place. ¹⁴After Joseph buried his father, he returned to Egypt, along with his brothers and everyone who had gone with him to bury his father.

¹⁵After Jacob died, Joseph's brothers said, "What if Joseph is still angry with us? We did many wrong things to him. What if he plans to pay us back?" ¹⁶So they sent a message to Joseph that said, "Your father gave this command before he died. ¹⁷He said to us, 'You have done wrong and have sinned and done evil to Joseph. Tell Joseph to forgive you, his brothers.' So now, Joseph, we beg you to forgive our wrong. We are the servants of the God of your father." When Joseph received the message, he cried.

¹⁸And his brothers went to him and bowed low before him and said, "We are your slaves."

¹⁹Then Joseph said to them, "Don't be afraid. Can I do what only God can do? ²⁰You meant to hurt me, but God turned your evil into good to save the lives of many people, which is being done. ²¹So don't be afraid. I will take care of you and your children." So Joseph comforted his brothers and spoke kind words to them.

²²Joseph continued to live in Egypt with all his father's family. He died when he was one hundred ten years old. ²³During Joseph's life Ephraim had children and grandchildren, and Joseph's son Manasseh had a son named Makir. Joseph accepted Makir's children as his own.

²⁴Joseph said to his brothers, "I am about to die, but God will take care of you. He will lead you out of this land to the land he promised to Abraham, Isaac, and Jacob." ²⁵Then Joseph had the sons of Israel make a promise. He said, "Promise me that you will carry my bones with you out of Egypt."

²⁶Joseph died when he was one hundred ten years old. Doctors prepared his body for burial, and then they put him in a coffin in Egypt.

DEVOTION

DAVE DRAVECKY WAS on top of the world. He'd not only reached his dream—pitching in the major leagues with the San Francisco Giants—he was one of the best in the world at what he did.

But in his seventh year in Major League Baseball, Dave developed a cancerous tumor in his pitching arm. Despite years of surgery and treatments, he eventually lost his arm to cancer in order to save his life. But while he lost his arm—and admittedly suffered serious depression over it—he didn't lose faith.

In 1991, in response to the thousands of requests from hurting people everywhere, Dave and his wife, Jan, founded Outreach of Hope ministry. The mission of the ministry, according to his Web site, is to "offer comfort, encouragement and hope through Jesus Christ to those who suffer" from cancer or any serious illness.

Dravecky describes his experience with cancer as a chance for God to show his mercy and comfort; the encouragement he's now able to offer to others is worth far more than a career as a professional ballplayer—a triumph rather than a tragedy.

"God turned your evil into good," Joseph told his brothers. What an amazing feat!

Only God can transform the wickedness of the brothers selling Joseph into slavery into the triumph of saving the known world from starvation. Only God can turn the tragedy of a young man's experience with cancer at the peak of his career into the triumph of a story that has inspired millions to not only battle the cancer in their bodies, but the cancer of sin in their lives as well.

Could I be as forgiving as Joseph? I can't imagine it. For that matter, could I even be as upbeat as Dave Dravecky? Again, I think not. Not on my own, anyway. But with Christ in me, I begin to see the bad things that happen in this life through a different lens.

Does that make the pain go away immediately? No. But with the new lens, the pain gets focused into the bigger picture of what God is doing in my life: he's turning evil into good.

THOUGHTS TO PONDER

What is the greatest hardship you've ever had to endure? What lessons did you learn from it? What is God trying to teach you even now with the challenges in your life?

PRAYER

God, we pray that adversity will not be wasted in our lives. We pray it will be the opportunity that you intend, drawing us closer to you. Amen.

Resolved Witnesses
for God

EXODUS 1:1–21

1 When Jacob went to Egypt, he took his sons, and each son took his own family with him. These are the names of the sons of Israel: ²Reuben, Simeon, Levi, Judah, ³Issachar, Zebulun, Benjamin, ⁴Dan, Naphtali, Gad, and Asher. ⁵There was a total of seventy people who were descendants of Jacob. Jacob's son Joseph was already in Egypt.

⁶Some time later, Joseph and his brothers died, along with all the people who had lived at that same time. ⁷But the people of Israel had many children, and their number grew greatly. They became very strong, and the country of Egypt was filled with them.

⁸Then a new king began to rule Egypt, who did not know who Joseph was. ⁹This king said to his people, "Look! The people of Israel are too many and too strong for us to handle! ¹⁰If we don't make plans against them, the number of their people will grow even more. Then if there is a war, they might join our enemies and fight us and escape from the country!"

¹¹So the Egyptians made life hard for the Israelites. They put slave masters over them, who forced the Israelites to build the cities Pithom and Rameses as supply centers for the king. ¹²But the harder the Egyptians forced the Israelites to work, the more the Israelites grew in number and spread out. So the Egyptians became very afraid of them ¹³and demanded even more of them. ¹⁴They made their lives bitter. They forced the Israelites to work hard to make bricks and mortar and to do all kinds of work in the fields. The Egyptians were not merciful to them in all their painful work.

¹⁵Two Hebrew nurses, named Shiphrah and Puah, helped the Israelite women give birth to their babies. The king of Egypt said to the nurses, ¹⁶"When you are helping the Hebrew women give birth to their babies, watch! If the baby is a girl, let her live, but if it is a boy, kill him!" ¹⁷But the nurses feared God, so they did not do as the king told them; they let all the boy babies live. ¹⁸Then the king of Egypt sent for the nurses and said, "Why did you do this? Why did you let the boys live?"

¹⁹The nurses said to him, "The Hebrew women are much stronger than the Egyptian women. They give birth to their babies before we can get there." ²⁰God was good to the nurses. And the Hebrew people continued to grow in number, so they became even stronger. ²¹Because the nurses feared God, he gave them families of their own.

DEVOTION

THE CHILDREN OF ISRAEL lived in Egypt approximately four hundred years. At the time of this story, the memory of what Joseph had done to save the nation of Egypt had been long forgotten. But the nation continued to grow. From the original seventy who arrived from Canaan until the time of this story, approximately 350 years, the nation had grown exponentially. Scholars' estimates range from two hundred fifty thousand to 1.2 million. So it's easy to see why the Hebrews were considered a threat by the Egyptians.

At some point during their stay, the Hebrews lost their status as welcome guests of the king, becoming slaves used to build the great cities of Egypt. But God blessed his people, and still they thrived, growing stronger in numbers each day, despite the efforts of the king.

The reason for all this injustice is found in this phrase: a new king began to rule who did not know Joseph.

We live in a nation where open prayer is no longer allowed in any public school classroom or at any school event. We live in a time when nativity displays are being banned from public property in municipalities everywhere. We live in a society where the Ten Commandments, the basis for our legal system, are banned from public display in courtrooms where justice is allegedly dispensed. Words like "Thanksgiving" and "Christmas" are being weeded out of the public square.

While there are two sides to all these issues and the debates are highly politicized, it is undeniable that we live in a nation where God is becoming marginalized at best and forgotten at worst.

But here's the good news: Christians can prosper in this environment just like the Hebrews thrived even during their time of intense persecution. The current challenges can make us more resolved than ever to be witnesses for God.

THOUGHTS TO PONDER

In what ways is it hard to be a Christian today? How do you feel about the attempts to eliminate religion from the public square in America?

PRAYER

God, we know you make people and nations great. We pray that we'll always find favor in your sight and acknowledge you at every opportunity. Amen.

FINDING OUR MISSION

EXODUS 1:8–10, 22—2:10

⁸Then a new king began to rule Egypt, who did not know who Joseph was. ⁹This king said to his people, "Look! The people of Israel are too many and too strong for us to handle! ¹⁰If we don't make plans against them, the number of their people will grow even more. Then if there is a war, they might join our enemies and fight us and escape from the country!"

²²So the king commanded all his people, "Every time a boy is born to the Hebrews, you must throw him into the Nile River, but let all the girl babies live."

2 Now a man from the family of Levi married a woman who was also from the family of Levi. ²She became pregnant and gave birth to a son. When she saw how wonderful the baby was, she hid him for three months. ³But after three months she was not able to hide the baby any longer, so she got a basket made of reeds and covered it with tar so that it would float. She put the baby in the basket. Then she put the basket among the tall stalks of grass at the edge of the Nile River. ⁴The baby's sister stood a short distance away to see what would happen to him.

⁵Then the daughter of the king of Egypt came to the river to take a bath, and her servant girls were walking beside the river. When she saw the basket in the tall grass, she sent her slave girl to get it. ⁶The king's daughter opened the basket and saw the baby boy. He was crying, so she felt sorry for him and said, "This is one of the Hebrew babies."

⁷Then the baby's sister asked the king's daughter, "Would you like me to go and find a Hebrew woman to nurse the baby for you?"

⁸The king's daughter said, "Go!" So the girl went and got the baby's own mother.

⁹The king's daughter said to the woman, "Take this baby and nurse him for me, and I will pay you." So the woman took her baby and nursed him. ¹⁰When the child grew older, the woman took him to the king's daughter, and she adopted the baby as her own son. The king's daughter named him Moses, because she had pulled him out of the water.

DEVOTION

AT THE END of the musical, *Camelot*, the dream of King Arthur has shattered. His round table where differences could be settled peacefully is no more. His vision of a land has come unraveled. The nation is quickly returning to the old system where the sword rules.

Arthur has been betrayed by everyone close to him—his wife, his best friend, his son—and civil war is only minutes away. Arthur knows he won't survive the battle, and given the betrayals, he doesn't care.

In the pre-dawn moments before the battle that will end the dream of Camelot, Arthur encounters a young boy. He's no larger than the bow he carries, obviously too young to help fight. Arthur stops the boy and asks him why he's there. He's there to fight, he replies.

But Arthur sees a higher purpose for this young man than losing his life in battle. He tells him to run behind the lines and go home. Then later, Arthur says, he is to tell everyone about the glorious days of Camelot when problems were solved in a civil manner and countries didn't fight over meaningless differences.

It was a huge task for a young boy. The entire legacy of Camelot entrusted to one person.

Risky? Possibly. But God did it as well. Not once, but on several occasions.

He put the future of the human race in the hands of Noah before he destroyed the world with a flood. He put Joseph in charge of saving the world from famine. In this story, he put the future deliverance of his nation from Egyptian slavery in a basket containing a little baby, floating down the Nile.

God uses people like you and me as his ambassadors on earth. Our role is to find our mission and accept it.

THOUGHTS TO PONDER

What has God entrusted to you and only you? Who can you best help in this world? What wrong are you best positioned to right? What legacy are you leaving?

PRAYER

God, you've done great things over and over through individuals like Moses. Help me see what great thing you have planned for my life. Amen.

FORGIVE AND FORGET

EXODUS 2:11–25

¹¹Moses grew and became a man. One day he visited his people and saw that they were forced to work very hard. He saw an Egyptian beating a Hebrew man, one of Moses' own people. ¹²Moses looked all around and saw that no one was watching, so he killed the Egyptian and hid his body in the sand.

¹³The next day Moses returned and saw two Hebrew men fighting each other. He said to the one that was in the wrong, "Why are you hitting one of your own people?"

¹⁴The man answered, "Who made you our ruler and judge? Are you going to kill me as you killed the Egyptian?"

Moses was afraid and thought, "Now everyone knows what I did."

¹⁵When the king heard what Moses had done, he tried to kill him. But Moses ran away from the king and went to live in the land of Midian. There he sat down near a well.

¹⁶There was a priest in Midian who had seven daughters. His daughters went to that well to get water to fill the water troughs for their father's flock. ¹⁷Some shepherds came and chased the girls away, but Moses defended the girls and watered their flock.

¹⁸When they went back to their father Reuel, he asked them, "Why have you come home early today?"

¹⁹The girls answered, "The shepherds chased us away, but an Egyptian defended us. He got water for us and watered our flock."

²⁰He asked his daughters, "Where is this man? Why did you leave him? Invite him to eat with us."

²¹Moses agreed to stay with Jethro, and he gave his daughter Zipporah to Moses to be his wife. ²²Zipporah gave birth to a son. Moses named him Gershom, because Moses was a stranger in a land that was not his own.

²³After a long time, the king of Egypt died. The people of Israel groaned, because they were forced to work very hard. When they cried for help, God heard them. ²⁴God heard their cries, and he remembered the agreement he had made with Abraham, Isaac, and Jacob. ²⁵He saw the troubles of the people of Israel, and he was concerned about them.

DEVOTION

HAVE YOU EVER tried to hide a sin and found out that you couldn't? Have you ever tried to solve a problem by running away? If the answer to either question is "yes," then you have good company as we see in this story. Moses, in a fit of anger, killed an Egyptian, and even though the body was hidden in the sand, the sin was not.

Because his problem didn't remain hidden long, Moses was forced to live life on the run. Moses eventually discovered what the prophet Jonah later discovered: you can't run from God and his will in your life. But he would also discover what King David, the apostle Paul, and countless others have found: your sin is not greater than God's grace.

David slept with a woman who was not his wife, and when she became pregnant, he saw to it that her warrior husband would be killed in battle. Yet David eventually felt the forgiveness of God and wrote: "God, be merciful to me because you are loving. Because you are always ready to be merciful, wipe out all my wrongs. Wash away all my guilt and make me clean again" (Psalm 51:1–2).

Paul, before he became a Christian, persecuted Christians. He cast them into prisons, and a few were even killed. Later he wrote: "What I say is true, and you should fully accept it: Christ Jesus came into the world to save sinners, of whom I am the worst. But I was given mercy so that in me, the worst of all sinners, Christ Jesus could show that he has patience without limit" (1 Timothy 1:15–16).

Here's the good news: God forgives sins and God loves sinners. But here's a word of caution: God doesn't forgive hidden sins—he forgives confessed sins. Hide your sin in the sand and run away from it, and you'll likely be on the run for a long time. Get your sins out in the open before God—and remember he knows your sin anyway—and the Bible says he is quick to forgive.

Here's the wonderful thing about God's forgiveness: when God forgives, he forgets. The psalmist says that God will remove our sins "as far as the east is from west" (Psalm 103:12). In a vision to the prophet Isaiah, God says, "Though your sins are like scarlet, they can be as white as snow" (Isaiah 1:18). So take your sins out of the sand and offer them to God.

THOUGHTS TO PONDER

Why do you think we try to hide our sins from God? What are the spiritual benefits of confessing our sins, even though God already knows them?

PRAYER

God, we know you forgive our sins when we ask, and we know that you also use people who have been bruised by sin for your purposes. Thank you for using us even with our weaknesses. Amen.

HOLY GROUND

EXODUS 3:1–15

3 One day Moses was taking care of Jethro's flock. (Jethro was the priest of Midian and also Moses' father-in-law.) When Moses led the flock to the west side of the desert, he came to Sinai, the mountain of God. ²There the angel of the LORD appeared to him in flames of fire coming out of a bush. Moses saw that the bush was on fire, but it was not burning up. ³So he said, "I will go closer to this strange thing. How can a bush continue burning without burning up?"

⁴When the LORD saw Moses was coming to look at the bush, God called to him from the bush, "Moses, Moses!"

And Moses said, "Here I am."

⁵Then God said, "Do not come any closer. Take off your sandals, because you are standing on holy ground. ⁶I am the God of your ancestors—the God of Abraham, the God of Isaac, and the God of Jacob." Moses covered his face because he was afraid to look at God.

⁷The LORD said, "I have seen the troubles my people have suffered in Egypt, and I have heard their cries when the Egyptian slave masters hurt them. I am concerned about their pain, ⁸and I have come down to save them from the Egyptians. I will bring them out of that land and lead them to a good land with lots of room—a fertile land. It is the land of the Canaanites, Hittites, Amorites, Perizzites, Hivites, and Jebusites. ⁹I have heard the cries of the people of Israel, and I have seen the way the Egyptians have made life hard for them. ¹⁰So now I am sending you to the king of Egypt. Go! Bring my people, the Israelites, out of Egypt!"

¹¹But Moses said to God, "I am not a great man! How can I go to the king and lead the Israelites out of Egypt?"

¹²God said, "I will be with you. This will be the proof that I am sending you: After you lead the people out of Egypt, all of you will worship me on this mountain."

¹³Moses said to God, "When I go to the Israelites, I will say to them, 'The God of your ancestors sent me to you.' What if the people say, 'What is his name?' What should I tell them?"

¹⁴Then God said to Moses, "I AM WHO I AM. When you go to the people of Israel, tell them, 'I AM sent me to you.'"

¹⁵God also said to Moses, "This is what you should tell the people: 'The LORD is the God of your ancestors—the God of Abraham, the God of Isaac, and the God of Jacob. He sent me to you.' This will always be my name, by which people from now on will know me."

DEVOTION

WHERE DO YOU go to find "holy ground?" Psalms contains the command, "Be still and know that I am God" (Psalm 46:10). Where do you go to be still? Where do you find holy ground?

Before God revealed his plan to Moses, he instructed Moses to take off his shoes and come no closer because the ground was holy. Only when Moses got in the proper location and in the right demeanor was he allowed to hear the will of God for his life.

I'm afraid we don't have enough holy ground in our lives. I can sometimes find it within the confines of my home church on Sunday mornings, but only if I can crowd out all the distractions Satan tries to pack in my mind during worship time. I can sometimes find it in the hills behind my cabin, but I get there only a few days a year and the endless chores of keeping up a cabin and the surrounding forest sometimes replace the devotional time.

So I've looked for holy ground in other places, and here's an inventory of my findings.

I've found holy ground by working my body clock to be an early riser so I can watch the sun rise, the dew melt, or the fog lift—a sight as miraculous to me as the burning bush must have been to Moses.

I've found holy ground in my car on the way to work when I listen to Christian music and on the way home when I decide to turn off the radio and just enjoy the silence.

I've found holy ground in my office between appointments when I remember to breathe deeply and read from my daily Bible or when I listen to the problems of one of my students and end the session with a prayer.

THOUGHTS TO PONDER

Where will you find holy ground? Where will you get physically and spiritually ready to hear the voice of God? Will you follow that voice as Moses did?

PRAYER

God, help us find holy ground in your presence daily through the avenue of prayer and the path of your Word. Amen.

BRING YOUR STRENGTHS
AND WEAKNESSES

EXODUS 4:1–16

4 Then Moses answered, "What if the people of Israel do not believe me or listen to me? What if they say, 'The LORD did not appear to you'?"

²The LORD said to him, "What is that in your hand?"

Moses answered, "It is my walking stick."

³The LORD said, "Throw it on the ground."

So Moses threw it on the ground, and it became a snake. Moses ran from the snake, ⁴but the LORD said to him, "Reach out and grab the snake by its tail." When Moses reached out and took hold of the snake, it again became a stick in his hand. ⁵The LORD said, "This is so that the Israelites will believe that the LORD appeared to you. I am the God of their ancestors, the God of Abraham, the God of Isaac, and the God of Jacob."

⁶Then the LORD said to Moses, "Put your hand inside your coat." So Moses put his hand inside his coat. When he took it out, it was white with a skin disease.

⁷Then he said, "Now put your hand inside your coat again." So Moses put his hand inside his coat again. When he took it out, his hand was healthy again, like the rest of his skin.

⁸Then the LORD said, "If the people do not believe you or pay attention to the first miracle, they may believe you when you show them this second miracle. ⁹After these two miracles, if they still do not believe or listen to you, take some water from the Nile River and pour it on the dry ground. The water will become blood when it touches the ground."

¹⁰But Moses said to the LORD, "Please, Lord, I have never been a skilled speaker. Even now, after talking to you, I cannot speak well. I speak slowly and can't find the best words."

¹¹Then the LORD said to him, "Who made a person's mouth? And who makes someone deaf or not able to speak? Or who gives a person sight or blindness? It is I, the LORD. ¹²Now go! I will help you speak, and I will teach you what to say."

¹³But Moses said, "Please, Lord, send someone else."

¹⁴The LORD became angry with Moses and said, "Your brother Aaron, from the family of Levi, is a skilled speaker. He is already coming to meet you, and he will be happy when he sees you. ¹⁵You will speak to Aaron and tell him what to say. I will help both of you to speak and will teach you what to do. ¹⁶Aaron will speak to the people for you. You will tell him what God says, and he will speak for you."

DEVOTION

HERE'S A CONFESSION for you. If I'd known I was going to be a writer, I would have learned to type. All those days I spent goofing off in high school typing class—long before the days of computers—and all those times I bribed (and even dated) girls in college to get my papers typed have now officially come back to haunt me. My self-taught system of typing stinks.

Now that's quite a confession from a former working journalist, a current professor of journalism, and a person who has written quite a few books, but it's true. I type worse than anyone I know. It's fast—I can type up a blur—but it's riddled with errors. That means that writing tasks take me longer than they should because I'm forced to deal with my "handicap" on a daily basis.

If I let my typing skill determine whether or not I would be a writer, then I would never write. But I consider my writing to be a ministry, and I can't tell you how many times in this project that God has intervened with just the right story at just the right time. And even though I don't seem to have acquired a knack for typing even after publishing millions of words, I am not going to call it quits.

Moses didn't think he could speak. He was so convinced of it he begged God to pick someone else to be the leader of his people. Yet, aided by Aaron, some of the great statements of the Bible come from his mouth.

It's so easy to dwell on what we can't do. I'm not comfortable talking with strangers, and I'll do almost anything to avoid it. That probably means that I'm not as well equipped as others to do foreign missions or one-on-one evangelism, but it doesn't mean that I'm worthless in the kingdom of God. I prefer speaking in public—the number one fear of Americans—but even if you don't, that doesn't mean you can't find your own role in proclaiming the Good News.

So get prepared to discover the same thing Moses did: God can work with both your strengths and your weaknesses if you only give yourself over to his purposes.

THOUGHTS TO PONDER

What are some of the gifts you have been given by God? What are some of your weaknesses? What ministry can you find that utilizes your strengths? What help can God provide for your weaknesses?

PRAYER

Father, we pray that we will always use our gifts for you and not worry about our shortcomings. Amen.

CHOOSE STRAW
OR WORSHIP

EXODUS 5:1–21

5 After Moses and Aaron talked to the people, they went to the king of Egypt and said, "This is what the LORD, the God of Israel, says: 'Let my people go so they may hold a feast for me in the desert.'"

²But the king of Egypt said, "Who is the LORD? Why should I obey him and let Israel go? I do not know the LORD, and I will not let Israel go."

³Then Aaron and Moses said, "The God of the Hebrews has met with us. Now let us travel three days into the desert to offer sacrifices to the LORD our God. If we don't do this, he may kill us with a disease or in war."

⁴But the king said to them, "Moses and Aaron, why are you taking the people away from their work? Go back to your jobs! ⁵There are very many Hebrews, and now you want them to quit working!"

⁶That same day the king gave a command to the slave masters and foremen. ⁷He said, "Don't give the people straw to make bricks as you used to do. Let them gather their own straw. ⁸But they must still make the same number of bricks as they did before. Do not accept fewer. They have become lazy, and that is why they are asking me, 'Let us go to offer sacrifices to our God.' ⁹Make these people work harder and keep them busy; then they will not have time to listen to the lies of Moses."

¹⁰So the slave masters and foremen went to the Israelites and said, "This is what the king says: I will no longer give you straw. ¹¹Go and get your own straw wherever you can find it. But you must make as many bricks as you made before." ¹²So the people went everywhere in Egypt looking for dry stalks to use for straw. ¹³The slave masters kept forcing the people to work harder. They said, "You must make just as many bricks as you did when you were given straw." ¹⁴The king's slave masters had made the Israelite foremen responsible for the work the people did. The Egyptian slave masters beat these men and asked them, "Why aren't you making as many bricks as you made in the past?"

¹⁵Then the Israelite foremen went to the king and complained, "Why are you treating us, your servants, this way? ¹⁶You give us no straw, but we are commanded to make bricks. Our slave masters beat us, but it is your own people's fault."

¹⁷The king answered, "You are lazy! You don't want to work! That is why you ask to leave here and make sacrifices to the LORD. ¹⁸Now, go back to work! We will not give you any straw, but you must make just as many bricks as you did before."

¹⁹The Israelite foremen knew they were in trouble, because the king had told

129

them, "You must make just as many bricks each day as you did before." [20]As they were leaving the meeting with the king, they met Moses and Aaron, who were waiting for them. [21]So they said to Moses and Aaron, "May the LORD punish you. You caused the king and his officers to hate us. You have given them an excuse to kill us."

DEVOTION

"BRICKS WITHOUT STRAW" has become a metaphor over time for unreasonable expectations of any employer for his workers, a dilemma now faced by the Israelites. Straw was the "binder" for the bricks, keeping them from shattering easily. But the straw was grown far away from the fertile Nile region where important crops were grown. So the trek to the straw would add to the length of the workday, especially if there was no corresponding decrease in the expectation of output.

How many of us have seen additional duties heaped on us at work with no new resources or time to complete them? How many of us have become slaves to the technology that was supposed to free us? Tied to the office on weekends and vacations. Afraid to take a day off for the scores of messages that will be awaiting our return. It's a helpless, trapped feeling.

The king of Egypt made the decision in order to drive a wedge between the Israelites and Moses. Blame your leader, he told the foremen. If you have time to worship, you have time to gather straw.

I think Satan wants to make us face the same bargain today. I think he wants us to choose straw or worship. I think he's delighted when our days start earlier and our evenings last longer, because he knows that devotion time is one of the first things that gets squeezed out in the rush to make more bricks than ever before.

It was a clever tactic by the king; don't let Satan get away with it, too.

THOUGHTS TO PONDER

In what ways has your life "sped up" in recent years? What steps have you taken to protect your spiritual life?

PRAYER

God, we pray that in our pursuit of our goals and objectives that we will never marginalize our time with you. Amen.

HE LOOKS
FOR THE MOLDABLE

GENESIS 5:22—6:13

²²Then Moses returned to the LORD and said, "Lord, why have you brought this trouble on your people? Is this why you sent me here? ²³I went to the king and said what you told me to say, but ever since that time he has made the people suffer. And you have done nothing to save them."

6Then the LORD said to Moses, "Now you will see what I will do to the king of Egypt. I will use my great power against him, and he will let my people go. Because of my power, he will force them out of his country."

²Then God said to Moses, "I am the LORD. ³I appeared to Abraham, Isaac, and Jacob by the name God Almighty, but they did not know me by my name, the LORD. ⁴I also made my agreement with them to give them the land of Canaan. They lived in that land, but it was not their own. ⁵Now I have heard the cries of the Israelites, whom the Egyptians are treating as slaves, and I remember my agreement. ⁶So tell the people of Israel that I say to them, 'I am the LORD. I will save you from the hard work the Egyptians force you to do. I will make you free, so you will not be slaves to the Egyptians. I will free you by my great power, and I will punish the Egyptians terribly. ⁷I will make you my own people, and I will be your God. You will know that I am the LORD your God, the One who saves you from the hard work the Egyptians force you to do. ⁸I will lead you to the land that I promised to Abraham, Isaac, and Jacob, and I will give you that land to own. I am the LORD.'"

⁹So Moses told this to the Israelites, but they would not listen to him. They were discouraged, and their slavery was hard.

¹⁰Then the LORD said to Moses, ¹¹"Go tell the king of Egypt that he must let the Israelites leave his land."

¹²But Moses answered, "The Israelites will not listen to me, so surely the king will not listen to me either. I am not a good speaker."

¹³But the LORD spoke to Moses and Aaron and gave them orders about the Israelites and the king of Egypt. He commanded them to lead the Israelites out of Egypt.

DEVOTION

ACCORDING TO THE best historians, Thomas Jefferson had a poor speaking voice. It was rather high-pitched and contained the nasal twang of his native Virginia. Considering the amount of time he spent in his career as an ambassador in

Europe, Jefferson's tinny rendition of the American tongue must have been an irritant to those accustomed to hearing the King's English. Yet he is numbered among our nation's great statesmen.

I think it was his shortcoming as a speaker that made Jefferson such a prolific writer. If you think about it, none of the major documents that make Jefferson one of our most important founders are transcripts of speeches he gave. They were meant to be writings, and not just any writings—they proved to be words that would last for ages. It's as if he was gifted beyond his peers with his ability to turn a phrase in compensation for his inability to mesmerize a crowd with the spoken word. Interestingly, he became president in an era when it was considered unseemly to campaign, so most Americans of the time probably never heard Jefferson give a speech.

Moses was another leader who wasn't a particularly impressive speaker. He would never rally the people with his eloquence or his tone. But God still wanted him to lead, and when he calls us, I think he empowers us.

But the emotions Moses felt in this story are quite natural. When things aren't going well, we all have a tendency to doubt ourselves. At various times I've doubted my abilities as a father, a spouse, a professor, a writer. Doubt creeps in on each of us, and it's one of Satan's most effective tools.

But God has never depended on our abilities to do his work; he depends on our willingness. Would God rather have an eloquent but insubordinate Moses? Of course not. The lack of eloquence could be overcome; a lack of submission could not.

God looks for moldable individuals to craft for his work. Our talents will always be too few for the work ahead, but God is not looking at talents . . . he's looking at hearts.

THOUGHTS TO PONDER

What shortcomings do you have as a Christian? What strengths do you have? How can you emphasize your strengths for the maximum benefit of God's kingdom?

PRAYER

God, we know you have endowed us with talents, and we pray that we when examine ourselves we will see our God-given abilities and not our flaws. Amen.

REPRESENTING GOD

EXODUS 6:26—7:13

²⁶This was the Aaron and Moses to whom the LORD said, "Lead the people of Israel out of Egypt by their divisions." ²⁷Aaron and Moses are the ones who talked to the king of Egypt and told him to let the Israelites leave Egypt.

²⁸The LORD spoke to Moses in the land of Egypt ²⁹and said, "I am the LORD. Tell the king of Egypt everything I tell you."

³⁰But Moses answered, "I am not a good speaker. The king will not listen to me."

7 The LORD said to Moses, "I have made you like God to the king of Egypt, and your brother Aaron will be like a prophet for you. ²Tell Aaron your brother everything that I command you, and let him tell the king of Egypt to let the Israelites leave his country. ³But I will make the king stubborn. I will do many miracles in Egypt, ⁴but he will still refuse to listen. So then I will punish Egypt terribly, and I will lead my divisions, my people the Israelites, out of that land. ⁵I will punish Egypt with my power, and I will bring the Israelites out of that land. Then they will know I am the LORD."

⁶Moses and Aaron did just as the LORD had commanded them. ⁷Moses was eighty years old and Aaron was eighty-three when they spoke to the king.

⁸The LORD said to Moses and Aaron, ⁹"Moses, when the king asks you to do a miracle, tell Aaron to throw his walking stick down in front of the king, and it will become a snake."

¹⁰So Moses and Aaron went to the king as the LORD had commanded. Aaron threw his walking stick down in front of the king and his officers, and it became a snake.

¹¹So the king called in his wise men and his magicians, and with their tricks the Egyptian magicians were able to do the same thing. ¹²They threw their walking sticks on the ground, and their sticks became snakes. But Aaron's stick swallowed theirs. ¹³Still the king was stubborn and refused to listen to Moses and Aaron, just as the LORD had said.

DEVOTION

"I HAVE MADE you like God to the king of Egypt" (Exodus 7:1). God is essentially designating Moses as his representative, an ambassador for God. What an awesome responsibility! Note the next statement: Moses will not be successful at first. But God commands him to try anyway.

Do you represent God to anyone today? Those of us who are Christians must be as noticeable in this world as light in the darkness, salt in bland food, a

city set up high on a hill that can't be missed (Matthew 5:13–14). It is imperative that Christians be "like God" to the world; we have no choice. Light is not
to be hidden. Salt without flavor is useless.

But the same problem that plagued Moses is at work in the world today . . .
the hearers might be stubborn.

God has not asked us to be speakers for him only when the world wants to
listen. God does not judge the success of our ministry by our conversions, but by
our faithfulness. In fact, in the story of the farmer, Jesus predicted that the Word
would be scattered among many people who would never take it to heart and
grow spiritual fruit (Matthew 13:1–23). But nowhere is the farmer allowed to
quit planting seeds just because a large percentage of his effort resulted in no
yield.

So Moses goes into the court of the king, his brother, Aaron, acting as his
spokesman. But when it comes time to perform the miracle that should convince
the king of their power, the magicians of the day produce the same trick. I remember distinctly how this disturbed me as a child. How was it possible that the
other sticks turned into snakes?

My answer today: I still don't know. But as I've matured in my Christianity,
I've seen that Satan has certain powers in this world, and his powers can appear
every bit as mesmerizing as those of God. We'll have occasional victories where
the right overcomes the evil—Aaron's snake did swallow the other snakes—but
we'll have other times when it appears that Satan holds the upper hand.

But we're only told to be "like God" in this world and trust him for the victories. Our job is not to defeat Satan—Jesus took care of that on the cross—our
role is to proclaim the victory offered in Jesus.

THOUGHTS TO PONDER

To whom have you been called to represent God? Is it easy? Do you
ever feel like quitting? Where do you get the courage to be "like
God" in your community or workplace?

PRAYER

God, we pray that we will be like you in every situation you place
us in, and that we will be found faithful in our calling. Amen.

Ignoring God's Miracles

EXODUS 7:14–25

[14]Then the LORD said to Moses, "The king is being stubborn and refuses to let the people go. [15]In the morning the king will go out to the Nile River. Go meet him by the edge of the river, and take with you the walking stick that became a snake. [16]Tell him: The LORD, the God of the Hebrews, sent me to you. He said, 'Let my people go worship me in the desert.' Until now you have not listened. [17]This is what the LORD says: 'This is how you will know that I am the LORD. I will strike the water of the Nile River with this stick in my hand, and the water will change into blood. [18]Then the fish in the Nile will die, and the river will begin to stink. The Egyptians will not be able to drink the water from the Nile.'"

[19]The LORD said to Moses, "Tell Aaron: 'Take the walking stick in your hand and stretch your hand over the rivers, canals, ponds, and pools in Egypt.' The water will become blood everywhere in Egypt, both in wooden buckets and in stone jars."

[20]So Moses and Aaron did just as the LORD had commanded. In front of the king and his officers, Aaron raised his walking stick and struck the water in the Nile River. So all the water in the Nile changed into blood. [21]The fish in the Nile died, and the river began to stink, so the Egyptians could not drink water from it. Blood was everywhere in the land of Egypt.

[22]Using their tricks, the magicians of Egypt did the same thing. So the king was stubborn and refused to listen to Moses and Aaron, just as the LORD had said. [23]The king turned and went into his palace and ignored what Moses and Aaron had done. [24]The Egyptians could not drink the water from the Nile, so all of them dug along the bank of the river, looking for water to drink. [25]Seven days passed after the LORD changed the Nile River.

Devotion

THE FIRST OF the plagues that God rained down on Egypt struck the very heart of the country—the Nile River. The vast majority of the nation of Egypt was desert, inhabited only by nomadic people. Almost all agriculture and commerce was dependent on the Nile, and the nation lived by its seasons—periods of rain and flooding followed by dry months.

The Nile brought life to the land. Its floods made the land fertile by bringing rich soil to the fields adjacent to the river. Its waters gave the people plenty to drink without the bother and expense of digging deep wells in the desert sand. So when Aaron stretched out his hand and turned the water into blood, he devastated the only lifeline of the country. And the devastation was not limited to

135

the Nile. The water in the tributaries, pools, ponds, and even the buckets in people's houses also turned to blood.

The act struck at the heart of the religion of the Egyptians who worshiped the great river, perhaps the reason why the king was on its banks in the morning. "Hapi," the Nile God, was considered to be self-created, the equivalent of God who told Moses to tell the people that "I AM" sent him (Exodus 3:14). The holy waters were now defiled by blood.

One of the myths told about the Nile was that it had once flowed with honey for a period of eleven days, bringing prosperity to the land. Now Jehovah God was writing a new Nile story, and this one was no myth. The river was flowing blood, and the stink could be smelled across the country.

It's unclear how the people survived for seven days, particularly since the water in the homes was instantly affected as well. The only hint is found in the mention that the Egyptians began to dig along the bank of the river in search of fresh water. Perhaps God was merciful to them in this way.

Nowhere in the story is there any mention of the Israelites who were presumably spared from the plague of the blood at least in their private stores of water. In later miracles, the text is specific that the Israelites are exempt, so we can be assured that they were not the targets or unintended victims of God's wrath on the Egyptians.

Just like they did with the snakes, the king's magicians duplicated the feat of turning water to "blood," probably using a dye, although it's unclear where they got fresh water for their demonstration. Perhaps this entered into the king's decision to not grant the request of Moses and Aaron to let the Israelites go into the desert in order to worship. As the story ends, the king leaves the bank of the Nile and returns to the palace, his heart still hard and unrepentant.

THOUGHTS TO PONDER

What is the symbolism of blood as the first plague visited on Egypt? How could the king ignore the request of Moses after he saw the miracle?

PRAYER

God, we see your awesome power in your ability to control nature for your purposes. We praise you for your hand in delivering your children from bondage. Amen.

STUBBORNNESS WINS

EXODUS 8:1–15

8 Then the LORD told Moses, "Go to the king of Egypt and tell him, 'This is what the LORD says: Let my people go to worship me. [2]If you refuse, I will punish Egypt with frogs. [3]The Nile River will be filled with frogs. They will come up into your palace, into your bedroom, on your bed, into the houses of your officers, and onto your people. They will come into your ovens and into your baking pans. [4]The frogs will jump all over you, your people, and your officers.'"

[5]Then the LORD said to Moses, "Tell Aaron to hold his walking stick in his hand over the rivers, canals, and ponds. Make frogs come up out of the water onto the land of Egypt."

[6]So Aaron held his hand over all the waters of Egypt, and the frogs came up out of the water and covered the land of Egypt. [7]The magicians used their tricks to do the same thing, so even more frogs came up onto the land of Egypt.

[8]The king called for Moses and Aaron and said, "Pray to the LORD to take the frogs away from me and my people. I will let your people go to offer sacrifices to the LORD."

[9]Moses said to the king, "Please set the time when I should pray for you, your people, and your officers. Then the frogs will leave you and your houses and will remain only in the Nile."

[10]The king answered, "Tomorrow."

Moses said, "What you want will happen. By this you will know that there is no one like the LORD our God. [11]The frogs will leave you, your houses, your officers, and your people. They will remain only in the Nile."

[12]After Moses and Aaron left the king, Moses asked the LORD about the frogs he had sent to the king. [13]And the LORD did as Moses asked. The frogs died in the houses, in the yards, and in the fields. [14]The Egyptians put them in piles, and the whole country began to stink. [15]But when the king saw that they were free of the frogs, he became stubborn again. He did not listen to Moses and Aaron, just as the LORD had said.

DEVOTION

THIS SECOND PLAGUE had a religious component as well. Among the gods of Egypt was a frog-headed goddess named "Heka," and frogs were considered sacred animals. So the plague served two purposes. First, it inflicted pain on the Egyptian people whose king refused to let the Israelites go into the desert to worship. Second, the plague disparaged one of their sacred symbols—the frog.

The perversity of this miracle is that the Egyptians were not only afflicted with the frogs created by Aaron as he held out his walking stick over the waters, they were pummeled with an extra dose of the frogs when the magicians used their sorcery to produce even more frogs, according to the text. You can almost see the joy of God in allowing these pseudo-magicians to compound the problem in an attempt to impress the king.

Making matters worse was the fact that the Egyptians were prohibited by their religion from killing their tormentors. Frogs were everywhere—in bedrooms, kitchens, on clothing and bodies—yet they were considered holy, and therefore protected.

Perhaps this is why the king turns to Moses and Aaron for relief, asking them to pray to their God to take the frogs away. For the first time, he promises to let the people go to offer sacrifices to God if the frogs are taken away.

Notice that God doesn't make the frogs disappear or go off to live in the Nile, although some do survive there. Instead, God allows them to die all over the nation, once again causing a great stink. I think God intended for the people to have to sweep up this amphibian they worshiped and see it in its most disgusting, finite state—piled up in a stinking, rotting heap.

But with the crisis over, the king did what people still do today—he turned his back on his promise to God. There would be no worship time for the Israelites.

Haven't you seen that attitude before? "God, let this illness pass . . . help me find a good job . . . help me get over this crisis in our family . . . and I'll turn to you." But when times get better, the promise is forgotten. Stubbornness wins; good intentions lose.

THOUGHTS TO PONDER

Who do you know who is like the king? Who do you know that lets stubbornness rule their better judgment in making decisions? How can we resist that problem in our own lives?

PRAYER

God, we pray that we will keep our promises to you and keep our own stubborn will in subjection to your will. Amen.

Even the Tiniest of Beings

EXODUS 8:16–32

[16]Then the LORD said to Moses, "Tell Aaron to raise his walking stick and strike the dust on the ground. Then everywhere in Egypt the dust will change into gnats." [17]They did this, and when Aaron raised the walking stick that was in his hand and struck the dust on the ground, everywhere in Egypt the dust changed into gnats. The gnats got on the people and animals. [18]Using their tricks, the magicians tried to do the same thing, but they could not make the dust change into gnats. The gnats remained on the people and animals. [19]So the magicians told the king that the power of God had done this. But the king was stubborn and refused to listen to them, just as the LORD had said.

[20]The LORD told Moses, "Get up early in the morning, and meet the king of Egypt as he goes out to the river. Tell him, 'This is what the LORD says: Let my people go so they can worship me. [21]If you don't let them go, I will send swarms of flies into your houses. The flies will be on you, your officers, and your people. The houses of Egypt will be full of flies, and they will be all over the ground, too. [22]But I will not treat the Israelites the same as the Egyptian people. There will not be any flies in the land of Goshen, where my people live. By this you will know that I, the LORD, am in this land. [23]I will treat my people differently from your people. This miracle will happen tomorrow.'"

[24]So the LORD did as he had said, and great swarms of flies came into the king's palace and his officers' houses. All over Egypt flies were ruining the land. [25]The king called for Moses and Aaron and told them, "Offer sacrifices to your God here in this country."

[26]But Moses said, "It wouldn't be right to do that, because the Egyptians hate the sacrifices we offer to the LORD our God. If they see us offering sacrifices they hate, they will throw stones at us and kill us. [27]Let us make a three-day journey into the desert. We must offer sacrifices to the LORD our God there, as the LORD told us to do."

[28]The king said, "I will let you go so that you may offer sacrifices to the LORD your God in the desert, but you must not go very far away. Now go and pray for me."

[29]Moses said, "I will leave and pray to the LORD, and he will take the flies away from you, your officers, and your people tomorrow. But do not try to trick us again. Do not stop the people from going to offer sacrifices to the LORD."

[30]So Moses left the king and prayed to the LORD, [31]and the LORD did as he asked. He removed the flies from the king, his officers, and his people so that not one fly was left. [32]But the king became stubborn again and did not let the people go.

DEVOTION

THE COMMON MESSAGE of these two plagues is that God can use even the tiniest of beings. As large as the first two plagues had been—the entire Nile turned to blood and frogs so thick one could not even walk without crunching them beneath his or her feet—these two plagues were relatively small, but pervasive.

The word *kinnim* in Hebrew, translated "gnats" above, has also been translated "lice" or "mosquitoes" in various translations. There is no single agreed upon translation for the word. But it is known that the area is prone to infestations of tiny insects during the rainy season. Similarly, the word *'arob* translated "flies" above, cannot be pinned to a specific species—such as the housefly—but could be any of a number of swarming insects. It is likely that the flies were tiny beetles, since they apparently ruined the land in addition to bothering the people in their homes.

In this story we are told for the first time of the special protection that the Israelites enjoyed from the plagues, for no gnats or flies were to be found in the land of Goshen where they lived.

Apparently, the king's first signs of relenting are not due to the discomfort, but rather to the fact that his magicians have given up on using trickery to "replicate" the miracles of God. After failing to turn the dust into gnats, they tell the king that he's dealing with the power of God. Afterward, you can see the king relent in stages. Offer sacrifices here in this country, he says first. Then he retreats a little more: you can go into the desert but not very far.

But in the end, the king returns to his stubbornness, setting the stage for more encounters with God.

THOUGHTS TO PONDER

Why is it fair for all the people of Egypt to suffer because of the stubbornness of the king? What do you see in the story above that tells you something about the nature of the Egyptians?

PRAYER

God, we thank you that you are persistent in wanting your people to be free. Help us to be free from sin and its clutches today. Amen.

LEARNING FROM SUFFERING

EXODUS 9:1–12

9 Then the LORD told Moses, "Go to the king of Egypt and tell him, 'This is what the LORD, the God of the Hebrews, says: Let my people go to worship me. ²If you refuse to let them go and continue to hold them, ³the LORD will punish you. He will send a terrible disease on your farm animals that are in the fields. He will cause your horses, donkeys, camels, cattle, goats, and sheep to become sick. ⁴But the LORD will treat Israel's animals differently from the animals of Egypt. None of the animals that belong to the Israelites will die. ⁵The LORD has set tomorrow as the time he will do this in the land.'" ⁶The next day the LORD did as he promised. All the farm animals in Egypt died, but none of the animals belonging to Israelites died. ⁷The king sent people to see what had happened to the animals of Israel, and they found that not one of them had died. But the king was still stubborn and did not let the people go.

⁸The LORD said to Moses and Aaron, "Fill your hands with ashes from a furnace. Moses, throw the ashes into the air in front of the king of Egypt. ⁹The ashes will spread like dust through all the land of Egypt. They will cause boils to break out and become sores on the skin of people and animals everywhere in the land."

¹⁰So Moses and Aaron took ashes from a furnace and went and stood before the king. Moses threw ashes into the air, which caused boils to break out and become sores on people and animals. ¹¹The magicians could not stand before Moses, because all the Egyptians had boils, even the magicians. ¹²But the LORD made the king stubborn, so he refused to listen to Moses and Aaron, just as the LORD had said.

DEVOTION

IN RECENT YEARS we've seen instances of entire poultry populations numbering in the thousands being destroyed because of the fear of "bird flu." We've also seen cattle populations quarantined or destroyed when yet another panic over "mad cow disease" ripples through the country. In every case, the economic fallout is great, but the threat to humans necessitates the actions.

The earlier plagues affected the human population greatly. And while the lack of water and the infestations of insects and frogs might have had some effect on the livestock population, this fifth plague was a direct attack on the economy of the nation. A nation such as Egypt depended on the animals for milk, for meat, for plowing, and bearing burdens. Their skins, hair, and wool were used for clothing. Their ability to carry goods made trading with other nations possible. The swiftness of the horses was a factor in battle (Isaiah 30:16).

So a nation without farm animals was hungry, economically depressed, and militarily weak. The text tells us that every farm animal died, but again the animals of the Israelites were protected. The fallout from this plague would have lasted for a very long time. Although we don't know how long the plagues lasted, most scholars think they took a year or more to play out, possibly longer. It would take even longer to restore things to normal.

When the Israelites were allowed to go into the desert, the king changed his mind and pursued them with horses and chariots. Evidently, those animals were spared from this fate—the story refers to the losses as being limited to farm animals—so that God could make a much more dramatic point at the Red Sea, a story we will read in a few days.

The boils represent a return to the plagues of personal discomfort—this time on people and on animals. Although we don't know the exact malady that is described here, it was severe enough that the magicians—who had been beside the king since the day Moses arrived—were unable to stand at court because of their afflictions.

The plague was severe enough that God brought it to the people's memory again in Deuteronomy 28:27. In a message designed to warn those who might disobey his commandments, God promises that he will punish them "with boils like those the Egyptians had. You will have bad growths, sores, and itches that can't be cured." Evidently, the boils manifested different ways in different people, but the effect was memorable enough for God to use it as an example months later to his people.

But one more interesting fact remains here. For the first time, the text says that God made the king stubborn, a phrase that will be repeated in several of the remaining plagues. Did the king still have free will in the matter? It's a much discussed question we'll look at in another plague.

THOUGHTS TO PONDER

Have you ever suffered from a skin disease? What do you think the nation was like as the entire population suffered the symptoms above?

PRAYER

God, we know you give us health and welfare. We see the awesome power you have to take those blessings away. Please help us to be ever grateful for your blessings and obedient to your will. Amen.

THE SUPREME GOD

EXODUS 9:13–35

[13]Then the LORD said to Moses, "Get up early in the morning and go to the king of Egypt. Tell him, 'This is what the LORD, the God of the Hebrews, says: Let my people go to worship me. [14]If you don't, this time I will punish you, your officers, and your people, with all my power. Then you will know there is no one in the whole land like me. [15]By now I could have used my power and caused a terrible disease that would have destroyed you and your people from the earth. [16]But I have let you live for this reason: to show you my power so that my name will be talked about in all the earth. [17]You are still against my people and do not want to let them go. [18]So at this time tomorrow, I will send a terrible hailstorm, the worst in Egypt since it became a nation. [19]Now send for your animals and whatever you have in the fields, and bring them into a safe place. The hail will fall on every person or animal that is still in the fields. If they have not been brought in, they will die.'" [20]Some of the king's officers respected the word of the LORD and hurried to bring their slaves and animals inside. [21]But others ignored the LORD's message and left their slaves and animals in the fields.

[22]The LORD told Moses, "Raise your hand toward the sky. Then the hail will start falling in all the land of Egypt. It will fall on people, animals, and on everything that grows in the fields of Egypt." [23]When Moses raised his walking stick toward the sky, the LORD sent thunder and hail, and lightning flashed down to the earth. So he caused hail to fall upon the land of Egypt. [24]There was hail, and lightning flashed as it hailed—the worst hailstorm in Egypt since it had become a nation. [25]The hail destroyed all the people and animals that were in the fields in all the land of Egypt. It also destroyed everything that grew in the fields and broke all the trees in the fields. [26]The only place it did not hail was in the land of Goshen, where the Israelites lived.

[27]The king sent for Moses and Aaron and told them, "This time I have sinned. The LORD is in the right, and I and my people are in the wrong. [28]Pray to the LORD. We have had enough of God's thunder and hail. I will let you go; you do not have to stay here any longer."

[29]Moses told the king, "When I leave the city, I will raise my hands to the LORD in prayer, and the thunder and hail will stop. Then you will know that the earth belongs to the LORD. [30]But I know that you and your officers do not yet fear the LORD God."

[31]The flax was in bloom, and the barley had ripened, so these crops were destroyed. [32]But both wheat crops ripen later, so they were not destroyed.

[33]Moses left the king and went outside the city. He raised his hands to the LORD, and the thunder and hail stopped. The rain also stopped falling to the ground. [34]When the king saw that the rain, hail, and thunder had stopped,

he sinned again, and he and his officers became stubborn. [35]So the king became stubborn and refused to let the Israelites go, just as the LORD had said through Moses.

DEVOTION

THE WORST HAILSTORM I've witnessed hit one night more than twenty-five years ago. We were at a prayer service at the church building adjacent to the university campus where I teach. As residents of "tornado alley," we'd seen severe storms before, but this one was different.

The sky turned sickly gray, and the temperature rapidly dropped fifteen degrees. Hail stones, some as large as baseballs, began to fall. Hardly a car was left unscathed. Windshields were cracked. Fist-sized dents pocked the hoods and roofs of vehicles. Every skylight on campus was broken. Newly planted flowerbeds were ruined. Virtually every roof in the area was destroyed. The damage was more widespread than any of the three tornadoes I've witnessed.

Hail is an amazing feat of nature. I've seen large hail destroy a community. I've seen small hail in the mountains pile up a foot deep within minutes. In either case, one can only sit back in awe of God's power as the hailstones fall.

This plague was not designed for maximum destruction—notice the warning to the Egyptians. It was designed to send an unmistakable message that the God whom the king was ignoring was the supreme God. Even the king seems to acknowledge this, saying, "We have had enough of God's thunder and hail."

We serve a God who brings us the spring rains that allow the crops to grow. But he also creates the forces that allow droughts, blizzards, and the occasional hurricane. All of nature—mild and severe—proclaims the power of God.

THOUGHTS TO PONDER

When have you seen God's power in nature? Why do you think that power can result in both beauty and destruction?

PRAYER

God, the universe is your handiwork. It proclaims your majesty. Help us become a part of that chorus of praise as well. Amen.

A HARDENED HEART

EXODUS 10:1–11

10 The LORD said to Moses, "Go to the king of Egypt. I have made him and his officers stubborn so I could show them my powerful miracles. ²I also did this so you could tell your children and your grandchildren how I was hard on the Egyptians. Tell them about the miracles I did among them so that all of you will know that I am the LORD."

³So Moses and Aaron went to the king and told him, "This is what the LORD, the God of the Hebrews, says: 'How long will you refuse to be sorry for what you have done? Let my people go to worship me. ⁴If you refuse to let my people go, tomorrow I will bring locusts into your country. ⁵They will cover the land so that no one will be able to see the ground. They will eat anything that was left from the hailstorm and the leaves from every tree growing in the field. ⁶They will fill your palaces and all your officers' houses, as well as the houses of all the Egyptians. There will be more locusts than your fathers or ancestors have ever seen—more than there have been since people began living in Egypt.'" Then Moses turned and walked away from the king.

⁷The king's officers asked him, "How long will this man make trouble for us? Let the Israelites go to worship the LORD their God. Don't you know that Egypt is ruined?"

⁸So Moses and Aaron were brought back to the king. He said to them, "Go and worship the LORD your God. But tell me, just who is going?"

⁹Moses answered, "We will go with our young and old people, our sons and daughters, and our flocks and herds, because we are going to have a feast to honor the LORD."

¹⁰The king said to them, "The LORD will really have to be with you if ever I let you and all of your children leave Egypt. See, you are planning something evil! ¹¹No! Only the men may go and worship the LORD, which is what you have been asking for." Then the king forced Moses and Aaron out of his palace.

DEVOTION

BEFORE LOOKING at the devastation of the final three plagues, let's examine the stubbornness of the king of Egypt and his declining state of mind.

Looking back over the earlier plagues, we are told that the king is the source of his own stubbornness (Exodus 7:14; 8:15, 32; 9:7, 35). But we also see evidence that God is aiding the stubbornness of the king. It begins during the plague of the boils (Exodus 9:12) and is specifically stated here just prior to the plague of the locusts. Older readers might remember versions of the Bible that spoke of the king's heart being "hardened" by God during this time.

The Hebrew word here can mean "to make obtuse." The king of Egypt is losing the ability to make rational judgments. Even his own officers now recognize that this is a battle they cannot win, and they urge the king to let the Israelites go worship in the desert before the plague of locusts can descend on them. The nation already lies in ruin from the earlier plagues and another is on the horizon, yet the king is being obtuse.

The concept of a hard heart or stubborn will is discussed frequently in scripture. The writer of Proverbs uses the term in this passage reminiscent of the king of Egypt: "Whoever is stubborn after being corrected many times will suddenly be hurt beyond cure" (Proverbs 29:1). Jesus speaks of hearts being hardened by God when he explains why some people will never come to him, despite the many wonders he performed in their midst. Quoting from Isaiah, he says: "He has blinded their eyes, and he has closed their minds. Otherwise they would see with their eyes and understand *in* their minds and come back to me and be healed" (John 12:40, emphasis added).

I think there is a direct parallel here. The king saw the awesome power of God in the plagues and refused to believe. The Pharisees of Jesus' time saw the awesome power of God displayed in miracles; they, too, refused to believe. God then allows Satan to complete the hardening process that has already been begun by stubborn men.

We have stubborn men and women today, and their hearts are being hardened by Satan. They see design in the world, but refuse to admit the existence of a Designer. They see charity in the world and refuse to acknowledge a God who is the source of all love.

Why? Because if we admit to the existence of God, we must submit to him. And for some, like the king, that is impossible to do.

THOUGHTS TO PONDER

What is required before God allows a heart to be hardened? What are the signs of a hardened heart? How can we protect ourselves against it?

PRAYER

God, we know you protect the hearts of those who bend to your will. We pray we will always be open to your will. Amen.

MOMENTARY REPENTANCE

EXODUS 10:12–29

[12]The LORD told Moses, "Raise your hand over the land of Egypt, and the locusts will come. They will spread all over the land of Egypt and will eat all the plants the hail did not destroy."

[13]So Moses raised his walking stick over the land of Egypt, and the LORD caused a strong wind to blow from the east. It blew across the land all that day and night, and when morning came, the east wind had brought the locusts. [14]Swarms of locusts covered all the land of Egypt and settled everywhere. There were more locusts than ever before or after, [15]and they covered the whole land so that it was black. They ate everything that was left after the hail—every plant in the field and all the fruit on the trees. Nothing green was left on any tree or plant anywhere in Egypt.

[16]The king quickly called for Moses and Aaron. He said, "I have sinned against the LORD your God and against you. [17]Now forgive my sin this time. Pray to the LORD your God, and ask him to stop this punishment that kills."

[18]Moses left the king and prayed to the LORD. [19]So the LORD changed the wind. He made a very strong wind blow from the west, and it blew the locusts away into the Red Sea. Not one locust was left anywhere in Egypt. [20]But the LORD caused the king to be stubborn again, and he did not let the Israelites go.

[21]Then the LORD told Moses, "Raise your hand toward the sky, and darkness will cover the land of Egypt. It will be so dark you will be able to feel it." [22]Moses raised his hand toward the sky, and total darkness was everywhere in Egypt for three days. [23]No one could see anyone else, and no one could go anywhere for three days. But the Israelites had light where they lived.

[24]Again the king of Egypt called for Moses. He said, "All of you may go and worship the LORD. You may take your women and children with you, but you must leave your flocks and herds here."

[25]Moses said, "You must let us have animals to use as sacrifices and burnt offerings, because we have to offer them to the LORD our God. [26]So we must take our animals with us; not a hoof will be left behind. We have to use some of the animals to worship the LORD our God. We won't know exactly what we will need to worship the LORD until we get there."

[27]But the LORD made the king stubborn again, so he refused to let them go. [28]Then he told Moses, "Get out of here, and don't come again! The next time you see me, you will die."

[29]Then Moses told the king, "I'll do what you say. I will not come to see you again."

DEVOTION

At the bottom of Carlsbad Caverns, a national park in New Mexico, the tour guide will turn out the lights for a few seconds to give the tourists a feel for the complete darkness of the cave when the man-made lighting is removed. The darkness is so thick and so complete that it's hard to even process images in your brain. Even the "mind's eye" goes temporarily dark in the absence of any input. Perhaps you've experienced something similar.

Now imagine that feeling for three days when the plague of darkness came on unannounced. Imagine being trapped in total darkness, perhaps caught away from home, out in the fields. Children separated from their parents. Livestock unable to move. No way to cook or gather water from the Nile. I think the effect would be a form of darkness-induced insanity.

By blotting out the sun, God was once again striking at one of the deities of the Egyptians, who worshiped Re, the sun god. But another spiritual point is being made here. The children of darkness—the Egyptians—are in darkness while the children of light—the Israelites—are in the light.

The eighth plague, which came just before the darkness, was the infestation of locusts. To understand the ferocity of a plague of locusts, read the Book of Joel, the prophet who warned Israel that God would send a swarm of locusts to punish them for their disobedience.

Like the frogs and gnats before them, the locusts were pervasive and destroyed everything the hail had not found. The pace of these verses indicates that these three plagues—hail, locust, and darkness—might have happened almost consecutively with no relief for the Egyptians, who by this time were tiring of their own king's stubbornness. Even the king seems for a moment to realize his folly ("I have sinned") only to change his mind when the locusts are cast into the sea, setting the stage for his final showdown with God.

THOUGHTS TO PONDER

Have you known anyone like the king who repents primarily to avoid the consequences of sin? Are we ever guilty of the same thing?

PRAYER

Father, we know you know our motives and we pray that when we ask your forgiveness it will be from a pure motivation and a strong desire to change. Amen.

No One Is Innocent

EXODUS 11:1–10

11 Now the LORD had told Moses, "I have one more way to punish the king and the people of Egypt. After this, the king will send all of you away from Egypt. When he does, he will force you to leave completely. ²Tell the men and women of Israel to ask their neighbors for things made of silver and gold." ³The LORD had caused the Egyptians to respect the Israelites, and both the king's officers and the Egyptian people considered Moses to be a great man.

⁴So Moses said to the king, "This is what the LORD says: 'About midnight tonight I will go through all Egypt. ⁵Every firstborn son in the land of Egypt will die—from the firstborn son of the king, who sits on his throne, to the firstborn of the slave girl grinding grain. Also the firstborn farm animals will die. ⁶There will be loud outcries everywhere in Egypt, worse than any time before or after this. ⁷But not even a dog will bark at the Israelites or their animals.' Then you will know that the LORD treats Israel differently from Egypt. ⁸All your officers will come to me. They will bow facedown to the ground before me and say, 'Leave and take all your people with you.' After that, I will leave." Then Moses very angrily left the king.

⁹The LORD had told Moses, "The king will not listen to you and Aaron so that I may do many miracles in the land of Egypt." ¹⁰Moses and Aaron did all these great miracles in front of the king. But the LORD made him stubborn, and the king would not let the Israelites leave his country.

Devotion

ON APRIL 19, 1995, I heard the boom at 9:02 A.M. in my office in far north Oklahoma City and I felt a slight jolt in my chair. Within an hour, I was downtown, where I smelled the smoke and tasted the ashes from the blast that destroyed the Alfred Murrah Federal Office Building, taking the lives of 168 people.

As a professor of journalism and a part-time reporter, I stayed at the site the rest of the day and into the night. Lights were brought in. Rescue teams from across the state, and, eventually, from across the nation poured into Oklahoma City. We stood in a roped off media area about a block from the site, getting only the official information we were given.

We thought on that first night that it was still a rescue operation. We were wrong. With one exception, they were all gone. The casualties included several children—babies, actually—who were in the first floor daycare center just feet away from the blast.

It was the death of those innocent children that shook me and the rest of the community more than anything else. I left Oklahoma City about eight days after the blast to fulfill a speaking appointment on the West Coast. It was my first day away from the bombing site. I got off the plane, rented my car, and made my way to the ocean where I sat and cried and prayed for a long time. And it was the children I asked God about most. "Why the babies?" I wanted to know.

There's something particularly tragic about the death of a child. I've seen it happen to friends. Perhaps you have too. "No father should bury his son," a friend told me as he laid to rest his son killed in Afghanistan. It's true.

But all across Egypt, fathers and mothers awakened to see firstborn children dead in their beds. It would be the final and the most severe of the plagues. The entire country paid the ultimate price for the stubbornness of the king.

"Why the children?" we might ask today.

I don't think it's too impertinent a question to ask, and I don't pretend to know the answer. But perhaps it's the wrong question. I think we could just as easily ask this question: "Why not all of us?"

I've stubbornly resisted God's offers. I've wanted the benefits of following Jesus without having to carry my own personal cross as he commanded (Matthew 10:38). I've continued to sin even after tasting the grace of God, despite the warnings (Romans 6:1–2). Each of us has a measure of the stubbornness of the king of Egypt inside us as we struggle to decide how much control of our lives to yield to God even after he has purchased us with the blood of Jesus, his Son.

I'm still perplexed by the death of the "innocents," but I stand amazed at the continued sustenance of the "guilty," of which I am one.

THOUGHTS TO PONDER

How would you answer the question about why the children had to die in order for Israel to be freed from Egyptian bondage? How do you control your own stubborn nature and give God control?

PRAYER

God, we pray that you will continue to love us and protect us in your care even when we disappoint you. Amen.

IN REMEMBRANCE

EXODUS 12:1–5, 11–15, 21–30

12 The LORD spoke to Moses and Aaron in the land of Egypt: ²"This month will be the beginning of months, the first month of the year for you. ³Tell the whole community of Israel that on the tenth day of this month each man must get one lamb for the people in his house. ⁴If there are not enough people in his house to eat a whole lamb, he must share it with his closest neighbor, considering the number of people. There must be enough lamb for everyone to eat. ⁵The lamb must be a one-year-old male that has nothing wrong with it. This animal can be either a young sheep or a young goat."

¹¹"This is the way you must eat it: You must be fully dressed as if you were going on a trip. You must have your sandals on and your walking stick in your hand. You must eat it in a hurry; this is the LORD's Passover.

¹²"That night I will go through the land of Egypt and kill all the firstborn animals and people in the land of Egypt. I will also punish all the gods of Egypt. I am the LORD. ¹³But the blood will be a sign on the houses where you are. When I see the blood, I will pass over you. Nothing terrible will hurt you when I punish the land of Egypt.

¹⁴"You are always to remember this day and celebrate it with a feast to the LORD. Your descendants are to honor the LORD with this feast from now on. ¹⁵For this feast you must eat bread made without yeast for seven days."

²¹Then Moses called all the elders of Israel together and told them, "Get the animals for your families and kill the lamb for the Passover. ²²Take a branch of the hyssop plant, dip it into the bowl filled with blood, and then wipe the blood on the sides and tops of the doorframes. No one may leave that house until morning. ²³When the LORD goes through Egypt to kill the Egyptians, he will see the blood on the sides and tops of the doorframes, and he will pass over that house. He will not let the one who brings death come into your houses and kill you.

²⁴"You must keep this command as a law for you and your descendants from now on. ²⁵Do this when you go to the land the LORD has promised to give you. ²⁶When your children ask you, 'Why are we doing these things?' ²⁷you will say, 'This is the Passover sacrifice to honor the LORD. When we were in Egypt, the LORD passed over the houses of Israel, and when he killed the Egyptians, he saved our homes.'" Then the people bowed down and worshiped the LORD. ²⁸They did just as the LORD commanded Moses and Aaron.

²⁹At midnight the LORD killed all the firstborn sons in the land of Egypt— from the firstborn of the king who sat on the throne to the firstborn of the

prisoner in jail. Also, all the firstborn farm animals died. [30]The king, his officers, and all the Egyptians got up during the night because someone had died in every house. So there was a loud outcry everywhere in Egypt.

DEVOTION

THIS MOST SACRED Jewish feast was born out of necessity. The Israelites were about to travel, so God gave them several practical instructions to follow. Eat all of the lamb. Don't wait for the bread to rise. Wear your traveling clothes and eat with your walking stick in hand.

But one command was more unusual than the rest: place the blood of the lamb on the sides and tops of the doorframes of the house. This will be the sign for God to pass over the house when he brings death to the firstborn in every house. At that point, the nation should be ready to move because the king of Egypt would finally relent and let them go.

God likes ceremony because ceremonies help us remember. For thousands of years, the Jewish nation has kept the Passover, remembering each year that God delivered his people from Egyptian bondage. For centuries, Christians have celebrated the communion, remembering each time the breaking of the body of Jesus and the shedding of his blood for our sins. By keeping the ceremonies, God tells Moses, we are bearing witness to the next generation.

God has saved his people repeatedly, and it is important that we remember. In the oral tradition, it was the stories that kept the memory alive. And even today, with our ready access to the Scriptures, we still need the ceremonies to help us vividly remember the most important message of the Bible: God has saved his people from the bondage of slavery and sin.

THOUGHTS TO PONDER

Do you think the people fully understood the instructions of Moses? Why do you think God chose the symbolic painting of the doorframes as a means of salvation for his people?

PRAYER

God, we pray that we will always obey you in faith, and that in our obedience, we will be saved. Amen.

SHORT NOTICE

EXODUS 12:31-42; 13:17-22

³¹During the night the king called for Moses and Aaron and said, "Get up and leave my people. You and your people may do as you have asked; go and worship the LORD. ³²Take all of your flocks and herds as you have asked, and go. And also bless me." ³³The Egyptians also asked the Israelites to hurry and leave, saying, "If you don't leave, we will all die!"

³⁴So the people took their dough before the yeast was added. They wrapped the bowls for making dough in clothing and carried them on their shoulders. ³⁵The Israelites did what Moses told them to do and asked their Egyptian neighbors for things made of silver and gold and for clothing. ³⁶The LORD caused the Egyptians to think well of them, and the Egyptians gave the people everything they asked for. So the Israelites took rich gifts from them.

³⁷The Israelites traveled from Rameses to Succoth. There were about six hundred thousand men walking, not including the women and children. ³⁸Many other people who were not Israelites went with them, as well as a large number of sheep, goats, and cattle. ³⁹The Israelites used the dough they had brought out of Egypt to bake loaves of bread without yeast. The dough had no yeast in it, because they had been rushed out of Egypt and had no time to get food ready for their trip.

⁴⁰The people of Israel had lived in Egypt for four hundred thirty years; ⁴¹on the very day the four hundred thirty years ended, the LORD's divisions of people left Egypt. ⁴²That night the LORD kept watch to bring them out of Egypt, and so on this same night the Israelites are to keep watch to honor the LORD from now on.

¹⁷When the king sent the people out of Egypt, God did not lead them on the road through the Philistine country, though that was the shortest way. God said, "If they have to fight, they might change their minds and go back to Egypt." ¹⁸So God led them through the desert toward the Red Sea. The Israelites were dressed for fighting when they left the land of Egypt.

¹⁹Moses carried the bones of Joseph with him, because before Joseph died, he had made the Israelites promise to do this. He had said, "When God saves you, remember to carry my bones with you out of Egypt."

²⁰The Israelites left Succoth and camped at Etham, on the edge of the desert. ²¹The LORD showed them the way; during the day he went ahead of them in a pillar of cloud, and during the night he was in a pillar of fire to give them light. In this way they could travel during the day or night. ²²The pillar of cloud was always with them during the day, and the pillar of fire was always with them at night.

DEVOTION

ESTIMATES OF HOW many people left Egypt that night range from 1.2 million to more than two million. We know that only the men are counted in the number above, and we know that some Egyptians chose to go with the Israelites as well. Never in human history had such a massive group of people been mobilized. Great portions of the Pentateuch—the first five books of the Old Testament—are devoted to regulations necessary to maintain health and sanitation for this large group of people who suddenly became nomadic after more than four centuries of existence in Egypt.

The long Egyptian odyssey was coming to an end. It began with Jacob (also known as Israel) and his family of seventy-five moving to Egypt to escape the famine in Canaan. It ended 435 years later when Moses led the six hundred thousand males and their families out into the desert. The exodus, as it is called, was the fulfillment of a promise God made to Jacob long ago when he said, "I will go to Egypt with you, and I will bring you out of Egypt again" (Genesis 46:4).

The unleavened bread which the Jews took into the desert in their haste to leave Egypt became an important symbol in their faith; eventually, it was incorporated into the Christian religion by Jesus during his last supper with his followers (Matthew 26:26–29). The night of the Passover would be celebrated with unleavened bread for centuries to come.

God even made financial provisions for his nation, causing the Egyptians to give them gifts of value before they left. Some of these gifts, no doubt, ended up as ornamentation for the Temple. The gifts also supplied the Israelites with valuable items to barter during their travels and settlement of their new home.

THOUGHTS TO PONDER

What is the shortest notice you've ever had for a major trip? What kind of preparations were you able to make? What type of adjustments did you make? What would Israel need for their journey?

PRAYER

God, we pray that when you call us to action that we will be ready to go like the ancient Jews who followed you into the desert so many years ago. Amen.

God's Firstborn

EXODUS 13:1–16

13 Then the LORD said to Moses, ²"Give every firstborn male to me. Every firstborn male among the Israelites belongs to me, whether human or animal."

³Moses said to the people, "Remember this day, the day you left Egypt. You were slaves in that land, but the LORD with his great power brought you out of it. You must not eat bread made with yeast. ⁴Today, in the month of Abib, you are leaving Egypt. ⁵The LORD will lead you to the land of the Canaanites, Hittites, Amorites, Hivites, and Jebusites. This is the land he promised your ancestors he would give you, a fertile land. There you must celebrate this feast during the first month of every year. ⁶For seven days you must eat bread made without yeast, and on the seventh day there will be a feast to honor the LORD. ⁷So for seven days you must not eat any bread made with yeast. There must be no bread made with yeast anywhere in your land. ⁸On that day you should tell your son: 'We are having this feast because of what the LORD did for me when I came out of Egypt.' ⁹This feast will help you remember, like a mark on your hand or a reminder on your forehead. This feast will remind you to speak the LORD's teachings, because the LORD used his great power to bring you out of Egypt. ¹⁰So celebrate this feast every year at the right time.

¹¹"And when the LORD takes you into the land of the Canaanites, the land he promised to give you and your ancestors, ¹²you must give him every firstborn male. Also every firstborn male animal must be given to the LORD. ¹³Buy back every firstborn donkey by offering a lamb. But if you don't want to buy the donkey back, then break its neck. You must buy back from the LORD every firstborn of your sons.

¹⁴"From now on when your son asks you, 'What does this mean?' you will answer, 'With his great power, the LORD brought us out from Egypt, the land where we were slaves. ¹⁵The king of Egypt was stubborn and refused to let us leave. But the LORD killed every firstborn male in Egypt, both human and animal. That is why I sacrifice every firstborn male animal to the LORD, and that is why I buy back each of my firstborn sons from the LORD.' ¹⁶This feast is like a mark on your hand and a reminder on your forehead to help you remember that the LORD brought us out of Egypt with his great power."

DEVOTION

IN THE DAYS of Moses, the firstborn male held a special place in the household. He received the greater inheritance. He carried on the family name (see 1 Chronicles 7:1–4 for an example). In all the genealogical lists, we see the firstborn son listed first, even if there was an older daughter (see 1 Samuel 14:49 for an example).

It was the death of the firstborn male that was the greatest of the plagues in Egypt and the one that broke the strong will of the king of Egypt, who was no doubt affected as well. As a remembrance of God's delivery of the Israelites from slavery, he asks that they dedicate all firstborn—human or animal—to him as well.

The law of the firstborn remained in force until replaced by a subsequent command we find in Numbers (3:5–6, 12–13) where we read: "The LORD said to Moses, 'Bring the tribe of Levi and present them to Aaron the priest to help him. I am choosing the Levites from all the Israelites to take the place of all the firstborn children of Israel. The Levites will be mine, because the firstborn are mine. When you were in Egypt, I killed all the firstborn children of the Egyptians and took all the firstborn of Israel to be mine, both animals and children. They are mine. I am the LORD.' "

What does this request tell us about God? That he asks for and expects the very best from us. And why does he deserve such a lavish offering? Because he sent his own "firstborn" to save us from our sins.

The term "firstborn" is applied to Jesus in the New Testament in a variety of ways. He is called the "first son of Mary" (Luke 2:7), the "first one raised from the dead" (Colossians 1:18; Revelation 1:5), and the "firstborn of many brothers and sisters" (Romans 8:29). And in the most famous variation of the term, John calls Jesus God's "one and only Son" sent into the world so we could have eternal life (John 3:16).

When God looked for a gift for all humans, he sent his firstborn. What possible response can we have to that gift?

THOUGHTS TO PONDER

> If you have children, how did you feel the day your first child was born? How would you feel if you had to give up that child? Why would God place such an emphasis on the firstborn in the family?

PRAYER

> God, we know that Jesus is with you now at your right hand where he has been since creation. We thank you for the life he lived on earth so that we might some day be united with you. Amen.

FAST HORSES

EXODUS 14:1–14

14 Then the LORD said to Moses, ²"Tell the Israelites to turn back to Pi Hahiroth and to camp between Migdol and the Red Sea. Camp across from Baal Zephon, on the shore of the sea. ³The king will think, 'The Israelites are lost, trapped by the desert.' ⁴I will make the king stubborn again so he will chase after them, but I will defeat the king and his army. This will bring honor to me, and the Egyptians will know that I am the LORD." The Israelites did just as they were told.

⁵When the king of Egypt was told that the Israelites had left, he and his officers changed their minds about them. They said, "What have we done? We have let the Israelites leave. We have lost our slaves!" ⁶So the king prepared his war chariot and took his army with him. ⁷He took six hundred of his best chariots, together with all the other chariots of Egypt, each with an officer in it. ⁸The LORD made the king of Egypt stubborn, so he chased the Israelites, who were leaving victoriously. ⁹The Egyptians—with all the king's horses, chariot drivers, and army—chased the Israelites. They caught up with them while they were camped by the Red Sea, near Pi Hahiroth and Baal Zephon.

¹⁰When the Israelites saw the king and his army coming after them, they were very frightened and cried to the LORD for help. ¹¹They said to Moses, "What have you done to us? Why did you bring us out of Egypt to die in the desert? There were plenty of graves for us in Egypt. ¹²We told you in Egypt, 'Let us alone; we will stay and serve the Egyptians.' Now we will die in the desert."

¹³But Moses answered, "Don't be afraid! Stand still and you will see the LORD save you today. You will never see these Egyptians again after today. ¹⁴You only need to remain calm; the LORD will fight for you."

DEVOTION

THE SIGHT OF the chariots must have been awesome. Hundreds of them, with sword-wielding officers at the reins, bearing down on the Israelites. The same fierce army that had kept them in captivity for so many years was now coming to recapture them, and the Israelites weren't even armed. They would be slaughtered in the desert.

Notice the instructions of God. He doesn't tell them to dig in and fortify themselves, he tells them to "stand still." Why? Because God would do the fighting on this day. It's a lesson he wants the Israelites to learn.

Years later, the nation of Israel drifted away from God, and he raised up an enemy that surrounded the Israelites. Faced with this overwhelming enemy, the people prayed for the way out in an episode found in the book of the prophet Isaiah (30:15–16): "This is what the Lord GOD, the Holy One of Israel, says: 'If you come back to me and trust me, you will be saved. If you will be calm and trust me, you will be strong.' But you don't want to do that. You say, 'No, we need horses to run away on.' So you will run away on horses. You say, 'We will ride away on fast horses.' So those who chase you will be fast."

Want a way out, God asks? "Be calm and trust me," he tells them. Instead of girding for war, make yourselves the most vulnerable you can in the presence of your enemies and trust me for the rest.

What was Israel's response? Forget the offer of help—we'll mount up on swift horses and ride away. And God's response to that? He provided fast horses for the enemies. The nation of Israel trusted those fast horses and paid the price when God had left them with a formula for strength: be calm and trust me. I will save you. It's the same message he gave the nation those many years ago on the banks of the Red Sea.

Today, sin is our enemy, and God chose the Cross as our way out. Paul told the Corinthians that the idea was so simple that it would confound the wise (1 Corinthians 1:18–19). It's too easy. Surely one death—in the manner of a common criminal no less—couldn't actually defeat sin for all time. So people still reach for something else today. Like the Israelites running to their fast horses, we run to legalism, to mysticism, to humanism—and try to ride away from sin. But sin always catches up until we accept the Cross as God's divine solution.

THOUGHTS TO PONDER

Why do you think God wanted the Israelites vulnerable on this day against the Egyptians? Why not a military victory? Why is it our nature to worry about battles that God has already promised to fight for us?

PRAYER

God, we pray that we will always trust you for the victory over sin in our lives and that we will live victoriously. Amen.

LESSONS OF THE DESERT

EXODUS 14:15–31

¹⁵Then the LORD said to Moses, "Why are you crying out to me? Command the Israelites to start moving. ¹⁶Raise your walking stick and hold it over the sea so that the sea will split and the people can cross it on dry land. ¹⁷I will make the Egyptians stubborn so they will chase the Israelites, but I will be honored when I defeat the king and all of his chariot drivers and chariots. ¹⁸When I defeat the king, his chariot drivers, and chariots, the Egyptians will know that I am the LORD."

¹⁹Now the angel of God that usually traveled in front of Israel's army moved behind them. Also, the pillar of cloud moved from in front of the people and stood behind them. ²⁰So the cloud came between the Egyptians and the Israelites. This made it dark for the Egyptians but gave light to the Israelites. So the cloud kept the two armies apart all night.

²¹Then Moses held his hand over the sea. All that night the LORD drove back the sea with a strong east wind, making the sea become dry ground. The water was split, ²²and the Israelites went through the sea on dry land, with a wall of water on their right and on their left.

²³Then all the king's horses, chariots, and chariot drivers followed them into the sea. ²⁴When morning came, the LORD looked down from the pillar of cloud and fire at the Egyptian army and made them panic. ²⁵He kept the wheels of the chariots from turning, making it hard to drive the chariots. The Egyptians shouted, "Let's get away from the Israelites! The LORD is fighting for them and against Egypt."

²⁶Then the LORD told Moses, "Hold your hand over the sea so that the water will come back over the Egyptians, their chariots, and chariot drivers." ²⁷So Moses raised his hand over the sea, and at dawn the sea returned to its place. The Egyptians tried to run from it, but the LORD swept them away into the sea. ²⁸The water returned, covering the chariots, chariot drivers, and all the king's army that had followed the Israelites into the sea. Not one of them survived.

²⁹But the Israelites crossed the sea on dry land, with a wall of water on their right and on their left. ³⁰So that day the LORD saved the Israelites from the Egyptians, and the Israelites saw the Egyptians lying dead on the seashore. ³¹When the Israelites saw the great power the LORD had used against the Egyptians, they feared the LORD, and they trusted him and his servant Moses.

DEVOTION

WHEN STUDENTS OF the Old Testament see a map of the ancient world, it becomes obvious that the route the Israelites took to the Promised Land is not the most direct one. It would have been far shorter for the group, perhaps more than a million strong, to have taken a route that stayed closer to the Mediterranean Sea. It was a route preferred by traders and is possibly the route taken by the brothers of Joseph twice during the period of famine. Instead, the Israelites headed south from Goshen, a much longer route to their eventual destination.

I think there are at least two reasons for this. First, the most obvious reason is that the shorter route would have taken the Israelites into the land of the Amalekites, a ruthless nation of warriors. Without military experience, the nation of Israel could have been slaughtered on this route.

But I think there is a greater reason for the route God gave Moses. God wanted his people to learn the lessons of the desert, and the first lesson was that he would protect them if they only trusted him. In a display of power that would be remembered by everyone present, God held back the waters of the Red Sea, allowing the Israelites to escape. Perhaps you already know that only two of the adults who passed through the waters on that day—Joshua and Caleb—would get to enter the Promised Land. But God created a display of power so great that even the children would remember the day they walked on dry land though the Red Sea and watched it close up again on the approaching Egyptian army.

There would be other lessons to be learned in the desert as well. The nation would learn to depend on God for their daily food and drinking water. They would learn reverence for God at the foot of Mount Sinai as Moses stayed on the mountain for forty days, receiving the Law from God. They would learn patience as God punished their doubts with years of wandering in the desert.

Why is our route to heaven so circuitous? Why am I faced with the drudgery of day-to-day life? Why not snatch us away from the moment of our salvation into eternal glory? Perhaps it's because we, like the Israelites, still have lessons to learn along the way.

THOUGHTS TO PONDER

What symbolism do you see in the way that God saved the Israelites? How does he protect us today on our journey toward our Promised Land?

PRAYER

God, we pray that you will deliver us safely to our home with you. Defeat our enemy. Protect us from the evil one. Amen.

The Lord Is with Us

EXODUS 15:22–27; 17:1–7

²²Moses led the Israelites away from the Red Sea into the Desert of Shur. They traveled for three days in the desert but found no water. ²³Then they came to Marah, where there was water, but they could not drink it because it was too bitter. (That is why the place was named Marah.) ²⁴The people grumbled to Moses and asked, "What will we drink?"

²⁵So Moses cried out to the LORD, and the LORD showed him a tree. When Moses threw the tree into the water, the water became good to drink.

There the LORD gave the people a rule and a law to live by, and there he tested their loyalty to him. ²⁶He said, "You must obey the LORD your God and do what he says is right. If you obey all his commands and keep his rules, I will not bring on you any of the sicknesses I brought on the Egyptians. I am the LORD who heals you."

²⁷Then the people traveled to Elim, where there were twelve springs of water and seventy palm trees. So the people camped there near the water.

17 The whole Israelite community left the Desert of Sin and traveled from place to place, as the LORD commanded. They camped at Rephidim, but there was no water there for the people to drink. ²So they quarreled with Moses and said, "Give us water to drink."

Moses said to them, "Why do you quarrel with me? Why are you testing the LORD?"

³But the people were very thirsty for water, so they grumbled against Moses. They said, "Why did you bring us out of Egypt? Was it to kill us, our children, and our farm animals with thirst?"

⁴So Moses cried to the LORD, "What can I do with these people? They are almost ready to stone me to death."

⁵The LORD said to Moses, "Go ahead of the people, and take some of the elders of Israel with you. Carry with you the walking stick that you used to strike the Nile River. Now go! ⁶I will stand in front of you on a rock at Mount Sinai. Hit that rock with the stick, and water will come out of it so that the people can drink." Moses did these things as the elders of Israel watched. ⁷He named that place Massah, because the Israelites tested the LORD when they asked, "Is the LORD with us or not?" He also named it Meribah, because they quarreled.

DEVOTION

IS THE LORD *with us or not?* The people wanted to know. On the surface, it looks like an absurd question. They had been protected from the fury of the ten plagues even as the Egyptians had suffered greatly. They had been delivered from slavery in Egypt. They had watched God part the Red Sea to let the Israelites pass and close it back to swallow up their Egyptian pursuers. Now they ask, "Is God with us or not?"

But they were thirsty, and because they were in the middle of a desert, far from the reliable source of water they had in the land of Goshen, they were afraid. Had God led them out there to die?

I think their question is similar to one Peter asked of Jesus. After seeing a rich young man leave sadly because he was unwilling to sell his possessions to follow Jesus, the people were dismayed. They wondered if anyone could be saved. Then Peter spoke up (Matthew 19:27) and asked Jesus: "Look, we have left everything and followed you. So what will we have?"

I don't get the idea that this was a polite question. I think it was more confrontational. "Look Jesus, we've laid a lot on the line here. What's in it for us?" It's reminiscent of, "Look, Moses, we may have been slaves in Egypt, but we *did* have food and water. Is God with us on this journey or not?"

But God is so great that he allows our questioning without punishing us. He provided the water that the children of Israel needed to survive, and Jesus provided the answer that Peter needed. In Matthew 19:29 we read: "And all those who have left houses, brothers, sisters, father, mother, children, or farms to follow me will get much more than they left, and they will have life forever."

Sometimes I'm like those Israelites—griping because I can't see the providence of God at work in my life. Other times I'm like Peter—wondering if following Christ holds anything for me. The fact that God can handle my questions and even my gripes is just one more manifestation of his greatness and his love for us.

THOUGHTS TO PONDER

Why were the Israelites so quick to question God even after seeing the miracles? Are we ever like that today?

PRAYER

God, we pray that we will see your many blessings that shower on us every day and be grateful for each one. Amen.

DAILY PROVISIONS

EXODUS 16:1–18, 31
Read the entire story at Exodus 16:1–36.

16 The whole Israelite community left Elim and came to the Desert of Sin, which was between Elim and Sinai; they arrived there on the fifteenth day of the second month after they had left Egypt. ²Then the whole Israelite community grumbled to Moses and Aaron in the desert. ³They said to them, "It would have been better if the LORD had killed us in the land of Egypt. There we had meat to eat and all the food we wanted. But you have brought us into this desert to starve us to death."

⁴Then the LORD said to Moses, "I will cause food to fall like rain from the sky for all of you. Every day the people must go out and gather what they need for that day. I want to see if the people will do what I teach them. ⁵On the sixth day of each week, they are to gather twice as much as they gather on other days. Then they are to prepare it."

⁶So Moses and Aaron said to all the Israelites: "This evening you will know that the LORD is the one who brought you out of Egypt. ⁷Tomorrow morning you will see the glory of the LORD, because he has heard you grumble against him. We are nothing, so you are not grumbling against us, but against the LORD." ⁸And Moses said, "Each evening the LORD will give you meat to eat, and every morning he will give you all the bread you want, because he has heard you grumble against him. You are not grumbling against Aaron and me, because we are nothing; you are grumbling against the LORD."

⁹Then Moses said to Aaron, "Speak to the whole community of the Israelites, and say to them, 'Meet together in the presence of the LORD, because he has heard your grumblings.'"

¹⁰While Aaron was speaking to the whole community of the Israelites, they looked toward the desert. There the glory of the LORD appeared in a cloud.

¹¹The LORD said to Moses, ¹²"I have heard the grumblings of the people of Israel. So tell them, 'At twilight you will eat meat, and every morning you will eat all the bread you want. Then you will know I am the LORD your God.'"

¹³That evening quail came and covered the camp, and in the morning dew lay around the camp. ¹⁴When the dew was gone, thin flakes like frost were on the desert ground. ¹⁵When the Israelites saw it, they asked each other, "What is it?" because they did not know what it was.

So Moses told them, "This is the bread the LORD has given you to eat. ¹⁶The LORD has commanded, 'Each one of you must gather what he needs, about two quarts for every person in your family.'"

¹⁷So the people of Israel did this; some people gathered much, and some gathered little. ¹⁸Then they measured it. The person who gathered more did not have too much, nor did the person who gathered less have too little. Each person gathered just as much as he needed.

[31]The people of Israel called the food manna. It was like small white seeds and tasted like wafers made with honey.

DEVOTION

GOD HAS ALWAYS provided for his people. When there was a need for physical food in the desert, he sent the fine, sweet manna from heaven each evening. Over the next forty years, it was eaten just as it was gathered or made into cakes (see Numbers 11:7–8), and God's people never went hungry as long as they gathered the manna. But the food could not be hoarded. The account in Exodus 16 tells of some people who gathered more than they needed only to find worms in the manna jars the next day.

God still provides for his people. When there was a need for spiritual "food" for his children, he sent Jesus. In the Gospel of John (6:30–35) we read this exchange:

So the people asked, "What miracle will you do? If we see a miracle, we will believe you. What will you do? [31]Our ancestors ate the manna in the desert. This is written in the Scriptures: 'He gave them bread from heaven to eat.'"

[32]Jesus said, "I tell you the truth, it was not Moses who gave you bread from heaven; it is my Father who is giving you the true bread from heaven. [33]God's bread is the One who comes down from heaven and gives life to the world."

[34]The people said, "Sir, give us this bread always."

[35]Then Jesus said, "I am the bread that gives life. Whoever comes to me will never be hungry, and whoever believes in me will never be thirsty."

Just as the manna gave life to those Israelites who had the faith to gather it in, Jesus gives eternal life to those who will partake of him.

THOUGHTS TO PONDER

Why would God want the people to gather manna six days a week, rather than all at once for a week or month? Why would Jesus compare himself to the manna of the Israelites?

PRAYER

Father, we know you provide for our physical and spiritual needs and we pray that we will accept Jesus as the source of eternal life. Amen.

WORKING TOGETHER

EXODUS 17:8–16

[8]At Rephidim the Amalekites came and fought the Israelites. [9]So Moses said to Joshua, "Choose some men and go and fight the Amalekites. Tomorrow I will stand on the top of the hill, holding the walking stick of God in my hands."

[10]Joshua obeyed Moses and went to fight the Amalekites, while Moses, Aaron, and Hur went to the top of the hill. [11]As long as Moses held his hands up, the Israelites would win the fight, but when Moses put his hands down, the Amalekites would win. [12]Later, when Moses' arms became tired, the men put a large rock under him, and he sat on it. Then Aaron and Hur held up Moses' hands—Aaron on one side and Hur on the other. They kept his hands steady until the sun went down. [13]So Joshua defeated the Amalekites in this battle.

[14]Then the LORD said to Moses, "Write about this battle in a book so people will remember. And be sure to tell Joshua, because I will completely destroy the Amalekites from the earth."

[15]Then Moses built an altar and named it The LORD Is My Banner. [16]Moses said, "I lifted my hands toward the LORD's throne. The LORD will fight against the Amalekites forever."

DEVOTION

WHO HOLDS UP your hands? In the story above, God planned a great victory for Israel over the Amalekites in this first battle fought by the Israelites on their way to the Promised Land. In order for the people to know God was fighting for them, Moses stood high on a hill, clearly visible to the armies below. As long as he held his hands high—walking stick probably in one of them—the battle proceeded in favor of the Israelites. When he grew tired and put his hands down, the Amalekites began to get the upper hand.

So the plan to hold up the hands of Moses was executed by Aaron and Hur, the two men who had climbed the hill with Moses. Together, they held up his hands until the sun went down and the enemy was defeated.

All of us who try to do the work of God sometimes grow weary. There's a term called "donor fatigue" used to describe what happens when too many natural or man-made disasters happen in rapid succession and the same pool of people are asked to give time and money to the recovery efforts. I'm sure there's a comparable malady for overworked volunteers. From prison ministries to food pantries to free health clinics, the world is full of good works we can plunge ourselves into, but it's always possible to tire out even when we're doing good. The solution of Moses is a sound one: get someone to help you in your good works.

The Book of Ecclesiastes contains the wisdom of King Solomon, a man who was given his choice of any gift from God and asked for wisdom as his gift. His writings are contained in what some scholars call the "wisdom literature" of the Old Testament. In Ecclesiastes 4:9–12 we read:

"Two people are better than one,
    because they get more done by working together.
[10]If one falls down,
    the other can help him up.
But it is bad for the person who is alone and falls,
    because no one is there to help.
[11]If two lie down together, they will be warm,
    but a person alone will not be warm.
[12]An enemy might defeat one person,
    but two people together can defend themselves;
a rope that is woven of three strings is hard to break."

When you choose your good work, choose your companions, Solomon would say. Then you have a greater chance of going the distance as Moses did with his two helpers. It's important because we are placed here to help others. To the church in Galatia the apostle Paul wrote: "We must not become tired of doing good. We will receive our harvest of eternal life at the right time if we do not give up. When we have the opportunity to help anyone, we should do it. But we should give special attention to those who are in the family of believers" (Galatians 6:9–10).

THOUGHTS TO PONDER

How do you stay energized to do good works? Whose encourager are you? Who are your encouragers?

PRAYER

Father, we pray that we will not grow tired of doing good, and that we will take every opportunity to show the world the difference you have made in us through helping others. Amen.

Learning to Delegate

EXODUS 18:1, 5–9, 13–26

18 Jethro, Moses' father-in-law, was the priest of Midian. He heard about everything that God had done for Moses and his people, the Israelites, and how the LORD had led the Israelites out of Egypt.

⁵So Jethro, Moses' father-in-law, took Moses' wife and his two sons and went to Moses. He was camped in the desert near the mountain of God. ⁶Jethro had sent a message ahead to Moses that said, "I, Jethro, your father-in-law, am coming to you with your wife and her two sons."

⁷So Moses went out to meet his father-in-law and bowed down and kissed him. After the two men asked about each other's health, they went into Moses' tent. ⁸Moses told his father-in-law everything the LORD had done to the king and the Egyptians to help Israel. He told about all the problems they had faced along the way and how the LORD had saved them.

⁹Jethro was very happy to hear all the good things the LORD had done for Israel when he had saved them from the Egyptians.

¹³The next day Moses solved disagreements among the people, and the people stood around him from morning until night. ¹⁴When Moses' father-in-law saw all that Moses was doing for the people, he asked, "What is all this you are doing for the people? Why are you the only one to solve disagreements? All the people are standing around you from morning until night!"

¹⁵Then Moses said to his father-in-law, "It is because the people come to me for God's help in solving their disagreements. ¹⁶When people have a disagreement, they come to me, and I decide who is right. I tell them God's laws and teachings."

¹⁷Moses' father-in-law said to him, "You are not doing this right. ¹⁸You and the people who come to you will get too tired. This is too much work for you; you can't do it by yourself. ¹⁹Now listen to me, and I will give you some advice. I want God to be with you. You must speak to God for the people and tell him about their disagreements. ²⁰Warn them about the laws and teachings, and teach them the right way to live and what they should do. ²¹But choose some capable men from among the people—men who respect God, who can be trusted, and who will not change their decisions for money. Make these men officers over the people, to rule over groups of thousands, hundreds, fifties, and tens. ²²Let these officers solve the disagreements among the people all the time. They can bring the hard cases to you, but they can decide the simple cases themselves. That will make it easier for you, because they will share the work with you. ²³If you do this as God commands you, then you will be able to do your job, and all the people will go home with their disagreements solved."

[24]So Moses listened to his father-in-law and did everything he said. [25]He chose capable men from all the Israelites and made them leaders over the people; they were officers over groups of thousands, hundreds, fifties, and tens. [26]These officers solved disagreements among the people all the time. They brought the hard cases to Moses, but they decided the simple cases themselves.

DEVOTION

I AM NOT THE best judge of my schedule; my wife is. And even though I have written entire books on the spiritual benefits of a "rightsized" life, I don't always practice it. So it didn't come as a great shock on the first day of this year when my wife, only a little playfully, suggested I read my own book . . . but it still "stung."

Moses was becoming increasingly busy as the political, military, and judicial leader of Israel. Only the spiritual duties had been delegated to Aaron. Everything else fell at the feet of Moses. It was an unsustainable situation, as Jethro—a priest himself—quickly surmised. His counsel to Moses: delegate all but the thorniest of the problems and decide only the hard cases yourself. By the end of the chapter, the system is in place and working.

It has been said: "If the devil can't make us bad, he'll just make us busy." What does that mean? You see, the two can have the same effect. Both sin and excessive busyness cause me to turn my attention away from God—the former out of shame and the latter out of hurriedness. One of the devil's tricks is to convince me that no one can do what I do. Moses didn't need to hear every case; some could be delegated. And if the people were taught to live right, many could be avoided altogether.

THOUGHTS TO PONDER

What does your daily schedule say about you? How does your daily routine differ from someone who is not a follower of God? How do you ensure that you do "first things first?"

PRAYER

God, we pray that we will be good stewards of our time and talents and that our lives will reflect our desire to be more dedicated to you. Amen.

His Own Possession

EXODUS 19:1–9, 14–22

19 Exactly three months after the Israelites had left Egypt, they reached the Desert of Sinai. ²When they left Rephidim, they came to the Desert of Sinai and camped in the desert in front of the mountain. ³Then Moses went up on the mountain to God. The LORD called to him from the mountain and said, "Say this to the family of Jacob, and tell the people of Israel: ⁴'Every one of you has seen what I did to the people of Egypt. You saw how I carried you out of Egypt, as if on eagle's wings. And I brought you here to me. ⁵So now if you obey me and keep my agreement, you will be my own possession, chosen from all nations. Even though the whole earth is mine, ⁶you will be my kingdom of priests and a holy nation.' You must tell the Israelites these words."

⁷So Moses went down and called the elders of the people together. He told them all the words the LORD had commanded him to say. ⁸All the people answered together, "We will do everything he has said." Then Moses took their answer back to the LORD.

⁹And the LORD said to Moses, "I will come to you in a thick cloud and speak to you. The people will hear me speaking with you and will always trust you." Then Moses told the LORD what the people had said.

¹⁴After Moses went down from the mountain to the people, he made them prepare themselves for service to God, and they washed their clothes. ¹⁵Then Moses said to the people, "Be ready in three days. Do not have sexual relations during this time."

¹⁶On the morning of the third day, there was thunder and lightning with a thick cloud on the mountain. There was a very loud blast from a trumpet, and all the people in the camp trembled. ¹⁷Then Moses led the people out of the camp to meet God, and they stood at the foot of the mountain. ¹⁸Mount Sinai was covered with smoke, because the LORD came down on it in fire. The smoke rose from the mountain like smoke from a furnace, and the whole mountain shook wildly. ¹⁹The sound from the trumpet became louder. Then Moses spoke, and the voice of God answered him.

²⁰When the LORD came down on top of Mount Sinai, he called Moses to come up to the top of the mountain, and Moses went up. ²¹The LORD said to Moses, "Go down and warn the people that they must not force their way through to see me. If they do, many of them will die. ²²Even the priests, who may come near me, must first prepare themselves. If they don't, I, the LORD, will punish them."

DEVOTION

NINETY DAYS AFTER they had been carried out of Egypt "as if on eagle's wings," it is time for the Israelites to meet God. He is making them an incredible offer: "If you obey me and keep my agreement, you will be my own possession, chosen from all nations" (Exodus 19:5). The people quickly affirm that they will be God's chosen people.

But sadly, they would break their promise to God repeatedly during their history. Eventually, the prophet Hosea would be instructed to name his third child "Lo-Ammi" which in Hebrew means "not my people." It's a symbolic gesture to all of Israel as we see in the words of God to Hosea: "Name him Lo-Ammi, because you are not my people, and I am not your God" (Hosea 1:9).

How does a nation go from being favored by God to being shunned by him? In a word: disobedience. The troubles begin when the nation refuses to believe that God will deliver the Promised Land to them. The difficulties continue when they begin to worship the gods of the nations around them. Eventually, even the Book of the Agreement, containing their covenant with God, will be lost. Destruction and captivity lie ahead. And even when God's own Son comes to earth, the opposition to his claims come from the religious leaders of the nation of Israel.

But God is still jealous to have a people of his own. So he makes the same offer to us that he made long ago to Israel. John writes in the Book of Revelation that we have a chance to live in the new Jerusalem. He writes: "And I heard a loud voice from the throne, saying, 'Now God's presence is with people, and he will live with them, and they will be his people. God himself will be with them and will be their God'" (Revelation 21:3).

Now, you and I have the chance to make the choice that Israel rejected so many years ago: obey God, and he will make us his own possession.

THOUGHTS TO PONDER

Why does our human nature compel us to forget so quickly the good things that God does for us? Who are God's people today? What does he expect of his people?

PRAYER

God, we pray that we will accept your offer to be your people so that we can someday live with you in the new Jerusalem. Amen.

Marginalizing God's Law

EXODUS 20:1–20

20 Then God spoke all these words:

²"I am the LORD your God, who brought you out of the land of Egypt where you were slaves.

³"You must not have any other gods except me.

⁴"You must not make for yourselves an idol that looks like anything in the sky above or on the earth below or in the water below the land. ⁵You must not worship or serve any idol, because I, the LORD your God, am a jealous God. If you hate me, I will punish your children, and even your grandchildren and great-grandchildren. ⁶But I show kindness to thousands who love me and obey my commands.

⁷"You must not use the name of the LORD your God thoughtlessly; the LORD will punish anyone who misuses his name.

⁸"Remember to keep the Sabbath holy. ⁹Work and get everything done during six days each week, ¹⁰but the seventh day is a day of rest to honor the LORD your God. On that day no one may do any work: not you, your son or daughter, your male or female slaves, your animals, or the foreigners living in your cities. ¹¹The reason is that in six days the LORD made everything—the sky, the earth, the sea, and everything in them. On the seventh day he rested. So the LORD blessed the Sabbath day and made it holy.

¹²"Honor your father and your mother so that you will live a long time in the land that the LORD your God is going to give you.

¹³"You must not murder anyone.

¹⁴"You must not be guilty of adultery.

¹⁵"You must not steal.

¹⁶"You must not tell lies about your neighbor.

¹⁷"You must not want to take your neighbor's house. You must not want his wife or his male or female slaves, or his ox or his donkey, or anything that belongs to your neighbor."

¹⁸When the people heard the thunder and the trumpet, and when they saw the lightning and the smoke rising from the mountain, they shook with fear and stood far away from the mountain. ¹⁹Then they said to Moses, "Speak to us yourself, and we will listen. But don't let God speak to us, or we will die."

²⁰Then Moses said to the people, "Don't be afraid, because God has come to test you. He wants you to respect him so you will not sin."

Devotion

THE WORDS ABOVE are evidently the most frightening ones ever written. They're so frightening that public schools can't post them on the walls. Courthouses can't place them in the lobby. If the actions of American officials are any indication, these are words to be feared. If placed near a government structure, great and irreparable damage will be done to some invisible "wall of separation" between church and state.

The term "separation of church and state" doesn't appear in the Constitution of the United States. It doesn't appear in the Declaration of Independence. The term actually appears first in a writing of Thomas Jefferson, and its premise goes largely unchallenged today.

But the writer of Proverbs tells us that "doing what is right makes a nation great, but sin will bring disgrace to any people" (Proverbs 14:34). Repeatedly in the Old Testament, God tells his people that they will continue to be blessed as long as they live within the agreement relationship he set for them. To God, there was no separation between the political life of the people and their religious life.

As a professor of First Amendment law for more than twenty-five years, I know all the arguments for both freedom *of* religion and freedom *from* religion. As a Christian for many more years, I know the arguments for a nation living inside the will of God in the hopes of preserving and securing his blessings. And I have to say, in my mind the latter argument outweighs the former. There is far more potential harm to be done in divorcing God from public life than allowing him into our public institutions.

Moses told the people: "Don't be afraid, because God has come to test you." Perhaps he's testing us today. Perhaps he's saying, "These are my laws. Will you write them on your hearts? Will you post them in your public places? Will you honor me by putting me in the center of your public life, not marginalized to an hour a week?" Because if we do, his blessings await us. If we decide to compartmentalize God, will he continue to bless us?

God doesn't bully his way into our hearts, our classrooms, or our courtrooms. He gives us the freedom to choose or reject him. But as a nation, we reject him at our own peril.

Thoughts to Ponder

Where do you stand on religion in public life? How do you act on your convictions?

Prayer

God, we ask your forgiveness that our collective wisdom has been foolish and that we have separated ourselves from you in large areas of our lives. Please forgive us. Amen.

Symbolic Blood

EXODUS 24:1–18

24 The LORD told Moses, "You, Aaron, Nadab, Abihu, and seventy of the elders of Israel must come up to me and worship me from a distance. ²Then Moses alone must come near me; the others must not come near. The rest of the people must not come up the mountain with Moses."

³Moses told the people all the LORD's words and laws for living. Then all of the people answered out loud together, "We will do all the things the LORD has said." ⁴So Moses wrote down all the words of the LORD. And he got up early the next morning and built an altar near the bottom of the mountain. He set up twelve stones, one stone for each of the twelve tribes of Israel. ⁵Then Moses sent young Israelite men to offer whole burnt offerings and to sacrifice young bulls as fellowship offerings to the LORD. ⁶Moses put half of the blood of these animals in bowls, and he sprinkled the other half of the blood on the altar. ⁷Then he took the Book of the Agreement and read it so the people could hear him. And they said, "We will do everything that the LORD has said; we will obey."

⁸Then Moses took the blood from the bowls and sprinkled it on the people, saying, "This is the blood that begins the Agreement, the Agreement which the LORD has made with you about all these words."

⁹Moses, Aaron, Nadab, Abihu, and seventy of the elders of Israel went up the mountain ¹⁰and saw the God of Israel. Under his feet was a surface that looked as if it were paved with blue sapphire stones, and it was as clear as the sky! ¹¹These leaders of the Israelites saw God, but God did not destroy them. Then they ate and drank together.

¹²The LORD said to Moses, "Come up the mountain to me. Wait there, and I will give you two stone tablets. On these are the teachings and the commands I have written to instruct the people."

¹³So Moses and his helper Joshua set out, and Moses went up to Sinai, the mountain of God. ¹⁴Moses said to the elders, "Wait here for us until we come back to you. Aaron and Hur are with you, and anyone who has a disagreement with others can take it to them."

¹⁵When Moses went up on the mountain, the cloud covered it. ¹⁶The glory of the LORD came down on Mount Sinai, and the cloud covered it for six days. On the seventh day the LORD called to Moses from inside the cloud. ¹⁷To the Israelites the glory of the LORD looked like a fire burning on top of the mountain. ¹⁸Then Moses went into the cloud and went higher up the mountain. He was on the mountain for forty days and forty nights.

DEVOTION

THE VISUAL SYMBOLISM of the system of sacrifices was unmistakable. The priest slaughtered the bull in the presence of the people. Imagine all the sights and smells and sounds that ritual must have evoked. Imagine the sight of the blood as it was drained. Surely it wasn't a job for the squeamish.

Now imagine being in the audience when Moses walked through, sprinkling fresh blood from the young bulls on the people. It wouldn't be something you would forget very quickly.

Blood is highly symbolic in Scripture, and special rules were made about it. The Israelites were to avoid consuming it (Leviticus 17:10). They were to avoid coming in contact with it (Leviticus 15:19). They were to avoid "spilling" it in murder (Genesis 4:10). Blood was both sacred and purifying to the Jews. The handling of blood in the ritual of sacrifice was carefully detailed in the laws of the Israelites.

The use of blood as a sacrifice for sins continued until the time of Jesus. In his Letter to the Romans, Paul writes of Jesus: "God sent him to die in our place to take away our sins. We receive forgiveness through faith in the blood of Jesus' death" (Romans 3:25). The blood of Jesus—shed on the cross—became the perfect sacrifice for all time. Speaking of Jesus, the writer of Hebrews says: "With one sacrifice he made perfect forever those who are being made holy. Now when these have been forgiven, there is no more need for a sacrifice for sins. So, brothers and sisters, we are completely free to enter the Most Holy Place without fear because of the blood of Jesus' death" (Hebrews 10:14, 18–19).

Because of the blood of Jesus, we can walk boldly where even the leading priest did not dare to go—the very throne room of God. Just as in the time of Moses, there is power in blood today.

THOUGHTS TO PONDER

Why would God want the sacrifices to be done in full view of the people? What message would the sprinkled blood send to those on whom it fell? How do we come in contact with the blood of Jesus today?

PRAYER

God, we are thankful that you forgive sins and we marvel that in your great wisdom you have arranged the perfect sacrifice for our sins. Amen.

A God Who Changes
His Mind?

EXODUS 32:1–16

32 The people saw that a long time had passed and Moses had not come down from the mountain. So they gathered around Aaron and said, "Moses led us out of Egypt, but we don't know what has happened to him. Make us gods who will lead us."

²Aaron said to the people, "Take off the gold earrings that your wives, sons, and daughters are wearing, and bring them to me." ³So all the people took their gold earrings and brought them to Aaron. ⁴He took the gold from the people and formed it with a tool and made a statue of a calf. Then the people said, "Israel, these are your gods who brought you out of the land of Egypt!"

⁵When Aaron saw all this, he built an altar before the calf and announced, "Tomorrow there will be a special feast to honor the LORD." ⁶The people got up early the next morning and offered whole burnt offerings and fellowship offerings. They sat down to eat and drink, and then they got up and sinned sexually.

⁷Then the LORD said to Moses, "Go down from this mountain, because your people, the people you brought out of the land of Egypt, have ruined themselves. ⁸They have quickly turned away from the things I commanded them to do. They have made for themselves a calf covered with gold, and they have worshiped it and offered sacrifices to it. They have said, 'Israel, these are your gods who brought you out of Egypt.'"

⁹The LORD said to Moses, "I have seen these people, and I know that they are very stubborn. ¹⁰So now do not stop me. I am so angry with them that I am going to destroy them. Then I will make you and your descendants a great nation."

¹¹But Moses begged the LORD his God and said, "LORD, don't let your anger destroy your people, whom you brought out of Egypt with your great power and strength. ¹²Don't let the people of Egypt say, 'The LORD brought the Israelites out of Egypt for an evil purpose. He planned to kill them in the mountains and destroy them from the earth.' So stop being angry, and don't destroy your people. ¹³Remember the men who served you—Abraham, Isaac, and Israel. You promised with an oath to them and said, 'I will make your descendants as many as the stars in the sky. I will give your descendants all this land that I have promised them, and it will be theirs forever.'" ¹⁴So the LORD changed his mind and did not destroy the people as he had said he might.

¹⁵Then Moses went down the mountain, and in his hands he had the two stone tablets with the Agreement on them. The commands were written on both sides of each stone, front and back. ¹⁶God himself had made the tablets, and God himself had written the commands on the tablets.

DEVOTION

THE MOST REMARKABLE part of the story above is not the sin of the nation of Israel. Even though they had seen the plagues, the parting of the Red Sea, the manna, the pillar of fire, they still wanted a god they could see and touch, and the golden calf served that purpose well. But turning from God, even in light of everything he had done, is not all that remarkable because I've done it and I suppose you've done it too.

To me, the most remarkable part of this story is that God chose to change his mind. What an unbelievable statement! God heard the pleas of Moses and changed his mind about destroying the Israelite nation. Would there be a penalty for their behavior? Yes. About three thousand of the men would be killed by the Levites for their behavior on that day. More punishments were to come, according to God, but the nation would not be totally destroyed on this day.

I'm glad I serve a God who is capable of changing his mind, because I need him to change his mind about me. Paul told the Christians in Rome that "God shows his great love for us in this way: Christ died for us while we were still sinners" (Romans 5:8). God didn't wait for us to be good in order to love us. He didn't wait until we were living right in order to send his Son as a solution for my sins. He met me at the foot of the mountain, worshiping the gods of success, wealth, lust, and pride, and he changed his mind about destroying me.

I'm glad I serve a God who chooses to change his mind.

THOUGHTS TO PONDER

Why do you think the people preferred the god of gold to the unseen Jehovah? Why do you think God spared the nation? What does that say about God today?

PRAYER

God, we are thankful for the second chances you give us in life. We pray that our actions will bring honor to you. Amen.

Ever Greater Glory

EXODUS 33:11–23; 34:29–35

[11]The LORD spoke to Moses face to face as a man speaks with his friend. Then Moses would return to the camp, but Moses' young helper, Joshua son of Nun, did not leave the Tent.

[12]Moses said to the LORD, "You have told me to lead these people, but you did not say whom you would send with me. You have said to me, 'I know you very well, and I am pleased with you.' [13]If I have truly pleased you, show me your plans so that I may know you and continue to please you. Remember that this nation is your people."

[14]The LORD answered, "I myself will go with you, and I will give you victory."

[15]Then Moses said to him, "If you yourself don't go with us, then don't send us away from this place. [16]If you don't go with us, no one will know that you are pleased with me and with your people. These people and I will be no different from any other people on earth."

[17]Then the LORD said to Moses, "I will do what you ask, because I know you very well, and I am pleased with you."

[18]Then Moses said, "Now, please show me your glory."

[19]The LORD answered, "I will cause all my goodness to pass in front of you, and I will announce my name, the LORD, so you can hear it. I will show kindness to anyone to whom I want to show kindness, and I will show mercy to anyone to whom I want to show mercy. [20]But you cannot see my face, because no one can see me and live.

[21]"There is a place near me where you may stand on a rock. [22]When my glory passes that place, I will put you in a large crack in the rock and cover you with my hand until I have passed by. [23]Then I will take away my hand, and you will see my back. But my face must not be seen."

[29]Then Moses came down from Mount Sinai, carrying the two stone tablets of the Agreement in his hands. But he did not know that his face was shining because he had talked with the LORD. [30]When Aaron and all the people of Israel saw that Moses' face was shining, they were afraid to go near him. [31]But Moses called to them, so Aaron and all the leaders of the people returned to Moses, and he talked with them. [32]After that, all the people of Israel came near him, and he gave them all the commands that the LORD had given him on Mount Sinai.

[33]When Moses finished speaking to the people, he put a covering over his face. [34]Anytime Moses went before the LORD to speak with him, Moses took off the covering until he came out. Then Moses would come out and tell the Israelites what the LORD had commanded. [35]They would see that Moses' face was shining. So he would cover his face again until the next time he went in to speak with the LORD.

DEVOTION

WHEN YOU'VE BEEN in the presence of God, you change. Whether that change is a face so bright that Moses had to cover it from the people or the confident glow of someone at peace with God, when we commune with God it should show on our faces.

In writing about this incident to the church in Corinth, Paul says this:

> "We have this hope, so we are very bold. [13]We are not like Moses, who put a covering over his face so the Israelites would not see it. The glory was disappearing, and Moses did not want them to see it end. [14]But their minds were closed, and even today that same covering hides the meaning when they read the old agreement. That covering is taken away only through Christ. [15]Even today, when they read the law of Moses, there is a covering over their minds. [16]But when a person changes and follows the Lord, that covering is taken away. [17]The Lord is the Spirit, and where the Spirit of the Lord is, there is freedom. [18]Our faces, then, are not covered. We all show the Lord's glory, and we are being changed to be like him. This change in us brings ever greater glory, which comes from the Lord, who is the Spirit." (2 Corinthians 3:12–18)

Want to look like God? Then change and follow Christ. Soon you'll reflect God's glory and be "changed to be like him." And it's cyclical: the more we change, the more he changes us, on to "ever greater glory." The glow on the face of Moses eventually faded, Paul tells his readers (2 Corinthians 3:7). But the glow we get from trying to do God's will never fades. It just gets brighter and brighter as we invite the Spirit into our lives.

THOUGHTS TO PONDER

Who do you know whose face best reflects the Lord's glory? What is it about them that is different from others? How can we become people who show the Lord's glory?

PRAYER

God, we pray that even today others may look at us and see you, just as the Israelites saw the evidence of God's presence on Moses' face. Amen.

God Is Faithful

EXODUS 34:1–14

34 The LORD said to Moses, "Cut two more stone tablets like the first two, and I will write the same words on them that were on the first two stones which you broke. ²Be ready tomorrow morning, and then come up on Mount Sinai. Stand before me there on the top of the mountain. ³No one may come with you or even be seen any place on the mountain. Not even the flocks or herds may eat grass near that mountain."

⁴So Moses cut two stone tablets like the first ones. Then early the next morning he went up Mount Sinai, just as the LORD had commanded him, carrying the two stone tablets with him. ⁵Then the LORD came down in the cloud and stood there with Moses, and the LORD called out his name: the LORD.

⁶The LORD passed in front of Moses and said, "I am the LORD. The LORD is a God who shows mercy, who is kind, who doesn't become angry quickly, who has great love and faithfulness ⁷and is kind to thousands of people. The LORD forgives people for evil, for sin, and for turning against him, but he does not forget to punish guilty people. He will punish not only the guilty people, but also their children, their grandchildren, their great-grandchildren, and their great-great-grandchildren."

⁸Then Moses quickly bowed to the ground and worshiped. ⁹He said, "Lord, if you are pleased with me, please go with us. I know that these are stubborn people, but forgive our evil and our sin. Take us as your own people."

¹⁰Then the LORD said, "I am making this agreement with you. I will do miracles in front of all your people—things that have never before been done for any other nation on earth—and the people with you will see my work. I, the LORD, will do wonderful things for you. ¹¹Obey the things I command you today, and I will force out the Amorites, Canaanites, Hittites, Perizzites, Hivites, and Jebusites ahead of you. ¹²Be careful that you don't make an agreement with the people who live in the land where you are going, because it will bring you trouble. ¹³Destroy their altars, break their stone pillars, and cut down their Asherah idols. ¹⁴Don't worship any other god, because I, the LORD, the Jealous One, am a jealous God."

DEVOTION

HOW CAN GOD claim to be a "God who shows mercy, who is kind, who doesn't become angry quickly" when he has just allowed—even commanded—the men of Levi to go through the camp killing three thousand men (see Exodus 32:27–29 for this story) for their part in worshiping the golden calf? I think we find the answer in the very next verse. We read: "The LORD forgives people for evil, for sin, and for turning against him, but he does not forget to punish guilty people" (Exodus 34:7).

The nature of God is a combination of both justice and mercy, and both traits are wrapped up in his infinite capacity for love. If it was his nature to be angered quickly, the entire nation would have been destroyed at the foot of Mount Sinai as they danced around the golden calf. Aaron would have been killed for his role in the idolatry.

But God is "faithful," the text tells us—a word we usually associate with our response to him. He is faithful to his promises to us, and one of his promises was made to Abraham and Isaac. He promised that he would make a great nation of their descendants and that they would inhabit the land given to Abraham so long ago. By not totally destroying the Israelite nation on the plains below Sinai, God was being faithful to his centuries-old promise first made to Abraham.

Now he makes another agreement: "I, the LORD, will do wonderful things for you." If you allow me, Israel, I will show you things that no other nation on earth has ever seen. And the cost to you, God says, is this: *obey me and stay away from the gods of other nations. Why? Because I am a jealous God.*

God is the same today as he was then. He has made promises to us—salvation through Jesus, his Son, an eternal home in heaven with him—and he has made demands as well. In his Revelation, John hears the angel say to the church in Smyrna, "Be faithful even if you have to die, and I will give you the crown of life" (Revelation 2:10). God is faithful and he requires us to be faithful as well. It's been written in stone since the days of Moses.

THOUGHTS TO PONDER

What do you think it means for God to be "faithful?" What does it mean that he describes himself as a "jealous" God? How does that differ from our human jealousy?

PRAYER

God, we know you are unchanging even as we are fickle, and that you are anxious for us to return to you. Help this to be the day that we resolve to walk closer to you. Amen.

SACRIFICIAL GIVING

EXODUS 35:4–9, 20–24; 36:3–7

⁴Moses said to all the Israelites, "This is what the LORD has commanded: ⁵From what you have, take an offering for the LORD. Let everyone who is willing bring this offering to the LORD: gold, silver, bronze, ⁶blue, purple and red thread, and fine linen, goat hair ⁷and male sheepskins that are colored red. They may also bring fine leather, acacia wood, ⁸olive oil for the lamps, spices for the special olive oil used for appointing priests and for the sweet-smelling incense, ⁹onyx stones, and other jewels to be put on the holy vest and chest covering of the priests."

²⁰Then all the people of Israel went away from Moses. ²¹Everyone who wanted to give came and brought a gift to the LORD for making the Meeting Tent, all the things in the Tent, and the special clothes. ²²All the men and women who wanted to give brought gold jewelry of all kinds—pins, earrings, rings, and bracelets. They all presented their gold to the LORD. ²³Everyone who had blue, purple, and red thread, and fine linen, and anyone who had goat hair or male sheepskins colored red or fine leather brought them to the LORD. ²⁴Everyone who could give silver or bronze brought that as a gift to the LORD, and everyone who had acacia wood to be used in the work brought it.

³The people continued to bring gifts each morning because they wanted to. ⁴So all the skilled workers left the work they were doing on the Holy Tent, ⁵and they said to Moses, "The people are bringing more than we need to do the work the LORD commanded."

⁶Then Moses sent this command throughout the camp: "No man or woman should make anything else as a gift for the Holy Tent." So the people were kept from giving more, ⁷because what they had was already more than enough to do all the work.

DEVOTION

THE HOMELESS MAN sat in the back booth of the McDonald's, just in front of the restrooms. We were a church youth group from Texas on our way to a ski trip in Colorado. He was out of options. He had lost his job and headed west looking for better weather and a stronger economy. The plan was working until his beat-up car hit the unforgiving passes through the Rocky Mountains and his transmission failed.

He was stranded—living in the defunct car parked at the back of a huge lot that held more than a hundred trucks nightly. The self-contained world of the truck stop with its restaurant, convenience store, and fast food outlet was all he had known for several days.

He was homeless in his own car; we were traveling through—a bunch of teens on our way to a weekend of skiing and renewal. But now he was the equivalent of the man in the parable of the Good Samaritan. We had to pass by him on our way to a weekend of communing with nature and with God. Would we ignore him or help him?

A girl in the group offered him her fries. "I didn't touch them," she stammered, a little intimidated by his deep-set eyes.

"Thanks," he said. "But I can't eat after other people. Made me sick last week and I haven't done it since. I'd rather starve." His surprisingly soft voice trailed off at the end.

"Besides, I'm not hungry. I just need money to get on my way," he added. No anger. No begging. Just a matter of fact statement.

Since when does an unshaven guy living in his car, and nursing a cup of coffee in a McDonald's restaurant so he can have a booth, turn down a perfectly good bag of fries? Can't he just play the role of the grateful beggar and let us get on our way to our weekend of worship and recreation?

In the story above, the Israelites gave so much, the ones making the Meeting Tent told Moses to halt the giving. They couldn't handle any more gifts and still get the work done. Yet when given the opportunity today, I think we often give our fries to God, or at least the equivalent of it. Haven't we all cleaned out our outdated clothes from our bulging closets to give them to the poor? Or given a sofa or mattress to the poor because it was cheaper than hauling it to the local dump? How often do we follow the example of the children of Israel above and give sacrificially?

I've thought about that man a few times over the thirty-plus years since we met him that night. Did he make it to the West Coast? Did he find work? Did we make any impression on him with the money we hurriedly raised or the prayer we said with him before we left?

But the most important question is this: when the opportunity to help comes again, will I give fries or will I give from my riches?

THOUGHTS TO PONDER

What do you think explains the generosity of Israelites in the story above? How does it feel when you give a generous gift?

PRAYER

God, we know all our wealth comes from you. We pray that when we are asked to share, we will do so willingly and glorify you in our giving. Amen.

GOD'S DWELLING PLACE

EXODUS 40:1–17, 34–38

40 Then the LORD said to Moses: [2]"On the first day of the first month, set up the Holy Tent, which is the Meeting Tent. [3]Put the Ark of the Agreement in it and hang the curtain in front of the Ark. [4]Bring in the table and arrange everything on the table that should be there. Then bring in the lampstand and set up its lamps. [5]Put the gold altar for burning incense in front of the Ark of the Agreement, and put the curtain at the entrance to the Holy Tent.

[6]"Put the altar of burnt offerings in front of the entrance of the Holy Tent, the Meeting Tent. [7]Put the bowl between the Meeting Tent and the altar, and put water in it. [8]Set up the courtyard around the Holy Tent, and put the curtain at the entry to the courtyard.

[9]"Use the special olive oil and pour it on the Holy Tent and everything in it, in order to give the Tent and all that is in it for service to the LORD. They will be holy. [10]Pour the special oil on the altar for burnt offerings and on all its tools. Give the altar for service to God, and it will be very holy. [11]Then pour the special olive oil on the bowl and the base under it so that they will be given for service to God.

[12]"Bring Aaron and his sons to the entrance of the Meeting Tent, and wash them with water. [13]Then put the holy clothes on Aaron. Pour the special oil on him, and give him for service to God so that he may serve me as a priest. [14]Bring Aaron's sons and put the inner robes on them. [15]Pour the special oil on them in the same way that you appointed their father as priest so that they may also serve me as priests. Pouring oil on them will make them a family of priests, they and their descendants from now on." [16]Moses did everything that the LORD commanded him.

[17]So the Holy Tent was set up on the first day of the first month during the second year after they left Egypt.

[34]Then the cloud covered the Meeting Tent, and the glory of the LORD filled the Holy Tent. [35]Moses could not enter the Meeting Tent, because the cloud had settled on it, and the glory of the LORD filled the Holy Tent.

[36]When the cloud rose from the Holy Tent, the Israelites would begin to travel, [37]but as long as the cloud stayed on the Holy Tent, they did not travel. They stayed in that place until the cloud rose. [38]So the cloud of the LORD was over the Holy Tent during the day, and there was a fire in the cloud at night. So all the Israelites could see the cloud while they traveled.

DEVOTION

WHERE DOES GOD LIVE? It's been an interesting question throughout human existence. For two years the Israelites had seen the manifestations of God—miraculous appearances of food and water, for instance—but there had been no place for him to dwell among them. The completion of the Meeting Tent was an important milestone in the history of the Israelite nation. Now there was a religious center to their camp, a physical manifestation of the glory of God.

But does God really live in our buildings?

When Jesus visited with a Samaritan woman, she asked about the place to worship. Her people worshiped in a nearby mountain, banished from the Temple in Jerusalem because of their nationality. Jesus replied, "The time is coming when neither in Jerusalem nor on this mountain will you actually worship the Father" (John 4:21). He went on to talk about true worship being found in spirit and in truth, not in location. When Paul addressed the Athenians in Acts, he proclaimed, "The God who made the whole world and everything in it is the Lord of the land and the sky. He does not live in temples built by human hands" (Acts 17:24).

God's presence covered the Meeting Tent because the Israelites needed the visible symbol. Today, the church—the *ecclesia* in Greek—is not the building, it is the people. The word literally means "the called out." To the *ecclesia,* God has given the gift of the Holy Spirit. Like that light of God that shone in that Meeting Tent, the light of God is in us today (Matthew 5:14).

So we know where God lives: he lives in us. But we also know where God will live for all eternity, and we know that we have been offered an invitation to live with him there, as John tells us in his Revelation: "And I heard a loud voice from the throne, saying, "Now God's presence is with people, and he will live with them, and they will be his people. God himself will be with them and will be their God" (Revelation 21:3).

THOUGHTS TO PONDER

How do you know the Holy Spirit dwells in you? Why do you think God chose to dwell in us rather than in a physical place today?

PRAYER

Father, we thank you for the Holy Spirit that lights our path to you and shines to all the world. Help us make our hearts a worthy dwelling place for you. Amen.

SWEET-SMELLING

LEVITICUS 8:1–4, 14–21

8 The LORD said to Moses, [2]"Bring Aaron and his sons and their clothes, the special olive oil used in appointing people and things to the service of the LORD, the bull of the sin offering and the two male sheep, and the basket of bread made without yeast. [3]Then gather the people together at the entrance to the Meeting Tent." [4]Moses did as the LORD commanded him, and the people met together at the entrance to the Meeting Tent.

[14]Then Moses brought the bull for the sin offering, and Aaron and his sons put their hands on its head. [15]Moses killed the bull, took the blood, and with his finger put some of it on all the corners of the altar, to make it pure. Then he poured out the rest of the blood at the bottom of the altar. In this way he made it holy and ready for service to God. [16]Moses took all the fat from the inner organs of the bull, the best part of the liver, and both kidneys with the fat that is on them, and he burned them on the altar. [17]But he took the bull's skin, its meat, and its intestines and burned them in a fire outside the camp, as the LORD had commanded him.

[18]Next Moses brought the male sheep of the burnt offering, and Aaron and his sons put their hands on its head. [19]Then Moses killed it and sprinkled the blood on all sides of the altar. [20]He cut the male sheep into pieces and burned the head, the pieces, and the fat. [21]He washed the inner organs and legs with water and burned the whole sheep on the altar as a burnt offering made by fire to the LORD; its smell was pleasing to the LORD.

DEVOTION

HOW DO YOU SMELL? I'm not asking if you need a bath. I'm asking how you smell to God. You see, we serve a God who smells our sacrifice and is pleased by it. The story above ends by telling us that the sacrifice that Moses offered on behalf of Aaron and his sons was pleasing to God.

As early as the days of Noah, we read that God notices our sacrifices and is pleased (Genesis 8:20–21). Repeatedly in the Old Testament we read of sacrifices giving off a pleasing odor to God, as in Exodus 29:18 where we read about the offerings made at the consecration of the priests: "Burn the whole sheep on the altar; it is a burnt offering made by fire to the LORD. Its smell is pleasing to the LORD." So as Moses carefully follows the instructions of God in the consecration of Aaron and his sons, the result is once again pleasing to God.

By the time Paul wrote his letters, the sacrifice God wanted to smell was not a bull or a ram or a goat. God desires his people to become living sacrifices. To the Romans Paul wrote, "So brothers and sisters, since God has shown us great mercy, I beg you to offer your lives as a living sacrifice to him. Your offering must be only for God and pleasing to him, which is the spiritual way for you to worship" (Romans 12:1). Then, when he wrote to the Corinthians, he informed them that their self-sacrifice gave off a sweet aroma to God. He wrote, "Our offering to God is this: We are the sweet smell of Christ among those who are being saved and among those who are being lost" (2 Corinthians 2:15).

When Moses did exactly as God asked, the result was a sweet smell to God. When we give up trying to be the kings or queens of our own lives and instead turn our lives over to God, something beautiful happens. We begin to have a sweet smell—to God, to our brothers and sisters in Christ, and to those who don't yet know our Savior.

I've known a lot of sweet-smelling people in my life. There were the sweet-smelling ladies who encouraged me when I made my first abbreviated attempts as a young boy to offer a lesson at our small church in Texas. There was the sweet-smelling preacher who gave me a concordance—the first book in my Bible library and still a treasure of mine today—when I was in the fourth grade.

All along the way, I've been blessed and shaped by sweet-smelling people who have made Jesus the Lord of their lives, and I suspect you have too. Now it is our turn to be a sweet smell to others whose lives we can bless. And the wonderful part of it is this: as we attempt to be the sweet smell of Christ to those around us, the aroma will reach all the way to the throne of God.

THOUGHTS TO PONDER

What does it mean to be a "living sacrifice"? What are some of the things we can do that would be a sweet-smelling offering to God?

PRAYER

God, we pray that our sacrifices to you will be acceptable and sweet-smelling throughout each day we live. Amen.

TRUE WORSHIP

LEVITICUS 10:1–7

10 Aaron's sons Nadab and Abihu took their pans for burning incense, put fire in them, and added incense; but they did not use the special fire Moses had commanded them to use in the presence of the LORD. ²So fire came down from the LORD and destroyed Nadab and Abihu, and they died in front of the LORD. ³Then Moses said to Aaron, "This is what the LORD was speaking about when he said,

'I must be respected as holy
by those who come near me;
before all the people
I must be given honor.'"

So Aaron did not say anything about the death of his sons.

⁴Aaron's uncle Uzziel had two sons named Mishael and Elzaphan. Moses said to them, "Come here and pick up your cousins' bodies. Carry them outside the camp away from the front of the Holy Place." ⁵So Mishael and Elzaphan obeyed Moses and carried the bodies of Nadab and Abihu, still clothed in the special priest's inner robes, outside the camp.

⁶Then Moses said to Aaron and his other sons, Eleazar and Ithamar, "Don't show sadness by tearing your clothes or leaving your hair uncombed. If you do, you will die, and the LORD will be angry with all the people. All the people of Israel, your relatives, may cry loudly about the LORD burning Nadab and Abihu, ⁷but you must not even leave the Meeting Tent. If you go out of the entrance, you will die, because the LORD has appointed you to his service." So Aaron, Eleazar, and Ithamar obeyed Moses.

DEVOTION

WHEN WE FIRST read of Nadab and Abihu, they are among a group of seventy of the elders of Israel who were allowed to go up Mount Sinai as Moses went to communicate with God. The account in Exodus tells us: "Moses, Aaron, Nadab, Abihu, and seventy of the elders of Israel went up the mountain and saw the God of Israel. Under his feet was a surface that looked as if it were paved with blue sapphire stones, and it was as clear as the sky! These leaders of the Israelites saw God, but God did not destroy them" (Exodus 24:9–11).

Imagine the sight! These two sons of Aaron were allowed to see God from afar and lived to tell about it. It had to be a life-changing experience. Soon after, they were appointed to serve as priests with their father.

It was on the eighth day of the ceremonies to consecrate the temple that the story above occurs. God had instructed that the fire offered to him should come from a special fire. Instead, they did the convenient thing and simply used fire from their own censers in the presence of God—fire that older versions of the Bible text translate as "profane fire" in a later recounting found in Numbers 3:2–4.

Notice what God says after he consumes Nadab and Abihu: "I must be respected as holy by those who come near me" (Leviticus 10:3). They had come near enough to God to see his glory on Mount Sinai, yet they failed to respect his instructions. Somehow, the holiness of God had not made a permanent impact on their role in leading the nation in worship.

I think there is a lesson to learn here today: God's holiness limits his tolerance. He cannot and will not accept just any worship from his people, then or now. In the Bible, we are told repeatedly to enter his presence with reverence, yet all too often our modern worship reflects our typical American preferences—casual in dress, late to start, and as entertaining as possible. The command of the prophet Habakkuk is relevant today when he writes, "The LORD is in his Holy Temple; all the earth should be silent in his presence" (Habakkuk 2:20). When's the last time your local worship service devoted any significant amount of time to silence?

When Jesus was talking with the Samaritan woman by the well in the Gospel of John, they have an exchange about where to worship. In response to her questions, Jesus answers, "The time is coming when the true worshipers will worship the Father in spirit and truth, and that time is here already. You see, the Father too is actively seeking such people to worship him. God is spirit, and those who worship him must worship in spirit and truth" (John 4:23–24).

Is our worship in the right spirit? Is our worship true? Or does our worship seem like "profane fire" to God?

THOUGHTS TO PONDER

> What does it mean to worship both in spirit and in truth? What does such worship require of us if we are to know that our offering is acceptable? What is some of the "profane fire" you've seen offered to God?

PRAYER

> God, we know you are holy. We pray that we will enter our worship time with you with the deep reverence and awe you deserve. Amen.

Accepting God's Answers

NUMBERS 11:4–13, 18–23, 31–32

⁴Some troublemakers among them wanted better food, and soon all the Israelites began complaining. They said, "We want meat! ⁵We remember the fish we ate for free in Egypt. We also had cucumbers, melons, leeks, onions, and garlic. ⁶But now we have lost our appetite; we never see anything but this manna!"

⁷The manna was like small white seeds. ⁸The people would go to gather it, and then grind it in handmills, or crush it between stones. After they cooked it in a pot or made cakes with it, it tasted like bread baked with olive oil. ⁹When the dew fell on the camp each night, so did the manna.

¹⁰Moses heard every family crying as they stood in the entrances of their tents. Then the LORD became very angry, and Moses got upset. ¹¹He asked the LORD, "Why have you brought me, your servant, this trouble? What have I done wrong that you made me responsible for all these people? ¹²I am not the father of all these people, and I didn't give birth to them. So why do you make me carry them to the land you promised to our ancestors? Must I carry them in my arms as a nurse carries a baby? ¹³Where can I get meat for all these people?"

¹⁸"Tell the people this: 'Make yourselves holy for tomorrow, and you will eat meat. You cried to the LORD, "We want meat! We were better off in Egypt!" So now the LORD will give you meat to eat. ¹⁹You will eat it not for just one, two, five, ten, or even twenty days, ²⁰but you will eat that meat for a whole month. You will eat it until it comes out your nose, and you will grow to hate it. This is because you have rejected the LORD, who is with you. You have cried to him, saying, "Why did we ever leave Egypt?"'"

²¹Moses said, "LORD, here are six hundred thousand people standing around me, and you say, 'I will give them enough meat to eat for a month!' ²²If we killed all the flocks and herds, that would not be enough. If we caught all the fish in the sea, that would not be enough."

²³But the LORD said to Moses, "Do you think I'm weak? Now you will see if I can do what I say."

³¹The LORD sent a strong wind from the sea, and it blew quail into the area all around the camp. The quail were about three feet deep on the ground, and there were quail a day's walk in any direction. ³²The people went out and gathered quail all that day, that night, and the next day. Everyone gathered at least sixty bushels, and they spread them around the camp.

DEVOTION

"DO YOU THINK I'm weak?" God asks Moses. Do you not think I can do what I say I can do? Stand back and watch, he says to Moses, and before long the meat that the children of Israel wanted is stacked up as far as the eye can see.

It was an object lesson that Moses needed to be reminded of and a lesson that the nation of Israel needed to see again. Come to think of it, it's a lesson for all of us.

Right now I'm wrestling with why the tumors in the brain of the five-year-old son of my next-door colleague at the university reappeared on the MRI yesterday, even in the middle of aggressive chemotherapy treatment. Are you weak, God? I want to ask, but the blasphemy of the words frightens me. Can't you see he's a little boy? What are a couple of golf-ball sized tumors to the Creator of the universe?

Too often we misinterpret God's silence, assuming it's a sign that he doesn't care or can't help. Job made the same mistake when he was severely tested, and for four chapters God asks Job questions like these found in Job 38:4–7: "Where were you when I made the earth's foundation? Tell me, if you understand. Who marked off how big it should be? Surely you know! Who stretched a ruler across it? What were the earth's foundations set on, or who put its cornerstone in place while the morning stars sang together and all the angels shouted with joy?"

My timetable is not yours, God says. Try as you might, you will never understand my ways. It's a tough lesson to learn, and one that comes into focus only through the prism of faith.

THOUGHTS TO PONDER

Why do you think God reacted as he did to the request of the people? How do you think he reacts to our requests today?

PRAYER

Father, we know you hear us when we pray earnestly to you. Help us accept your answers to our sincere requests. Amen.

HANDLING CRITICISM

NUMBERS 12:1–15

12 Miriam and Aaron began to talk against Moses because of his Cushite wife (he had married a Cushite). ²They said, "Is Moses the only one the LORD speaks through? Doesn't he also speak through us?" And the LORD heard this.

³(Now Moses was very humble. He was the least proud person on earth.)

⁴So the LORD suddenly spoke to Moses, Aaron, and Miriam and said, "All three of you come to the Meeting Tent." So they went. ⁵The LORD came down in a pillar of cloud and stood at the entrance to the Tent. He called to Aaron and Miriam, and they both came near. ⁶He said, "Listen to my words:

When prophets are among you,
I, the LORD, will show myself to them in visions;
I will speak to them in dreams.
⁷But this is not true with my servant Moses.
I trust him to lead all my people.
⁸I speak face to face with him—
clearly, not with hidden meanings.
He has even seen the form of the LORD.
You should be afraid
to speak against my servant Moses."

⁹The LORD was very angry with them, and he left.

¹⁰When the cloud lifted from the Tent and Aaron turned toward Miriam, she was as white as snow; she had a skin disease. ¹¹Aaron said to Moses, "Please, my master, forgive us for our foolish sin. ¹²Don't let her be like a baby who is born dead. (Sometimes a baby is born with half of its flesh eaten away.)"

¹³So Moses cried out to the LORD, "God, please heal her!"

¹⁴The LORD answered Moses, "If her father had spit in her face, she would have been shamed for seven days, so put her outside the camp for seven days. After that, she may come back." ¹⁵So Miriam was put outside of the camp for seven days, and the people did not move on until she came back.

DEVOTION

DON'T KID YOURSELF. It hurts to be criticized. No matter how much good we do—no matter how convinced we are that we are doing what's right and that our motives are pure—someone is going to criticize. And the closer your critics are to your inner circle, the more it stings.

So Moses had to be hurt by the events of this chapter. Miriam was likely the one who had helped save the life of her brother Moses at a time when the king of Egypt was killing all the Hebrew male babies in an effort to control the growth of the Israelite population. It was Miriam who led the female chorus in celebration of the Israelites salvation from the Egyptians at the Red Sea (Exodus 15:20–21). Aaron had been the mouthpiece for Moses when they went before the king demanding that he let the Israelites go into the desert to worship. He had stood beside Moses and made the announcements at considerable risk to himself as God rained down ten plagues on Egypt.

I'm sure that both of them had been confidantes of Moses on the trip. Aaron was now his leading priest, the spiritual leader of the nation. Both of them had been beside Moses every step of the way since Egypt. Now they were complaining to the people about Moses and undermining his leadership.

The pair was contesting the supremacy of Moses as the leader of the Israelites on two grounds. First, they raised issues about his marriage to a Cushite woman, probably jealous of the informal influence she would have over her husband. Second, they contended that their own powers of prophesy were equal to the revelations of Moses.

God's settlement of the matter was swift: he upheld Moses as the supreme leader of the Israelites and inflicted a skin disease on Miriam that made her unclean. But we get a glimpse of the magnanimous nature of Moses when he begs God, "Please heal her!" and when he has the people remain camped for the entire seven days of her purification ritual.

It is much more important in life to learn how to handle criticism than it is to learn how to avoid it, and the example of Moses is a valid one even today. When criticized, take the matter to God who knows the hearts of all the parties involved.

THOUGHTS TO PONDER

How well do you handle criticism? Do you ever think to take the criticisms to God in prayer? What lessons can we learn from Moses in this story?

PRAYER

Father, we pray that we will not let critics or criticism stop us from doing the good that we can do today. Amen.

GIANTS IN THE LAND

NUMBERS 13:1–2, 17–33

13 The LORD said to Moses, ²"Send men to explore the land of Canaan, which I will give to the Israelites. Send one leader from each tribe."

¹⁷Moses sent them to explore Canaan and said, "Go through southern Canaan and then into the mountains. ¹⁸See what the land looks like. Are the people who live there strong or weak? Are there a few or many? ¹⁹What kind of land do they live in? Is it good or bad? What about the towns they live in—are they open like camps, or do they have walls? ²⁰What about the soil? Is it fertile or poor? Are there trees there? Try to bring back some of the fruit from that land." (It was the season for the first grapes.)

²¹So they went up and explored the land, from the Desert of Zin all the way to Rehob by Lebo Hamath. ²²They went through the southern area to Hebron, where Ahiman, Sheshai, and Talmai, the descendants of Anak lived. (The city of Hebron had been built seven years before Zoan in Egypt.) ²³In the Valley of Eshcol, they cut off a branch of a grapevine that had one bunch of grapes on it and carried that branch on a pole between two of them. They also got some pomegranates and figs. ²⁴That place was called the Valley of Eshcol, because the Israelites cut off the bunch of grapes there. ²⁵After forty days of exploring the land, the men returned to the camp.

²⁶They came back to Moses and Aaron and all the Israelites at Kadesh, in the Desert of Paran. The men reported to them and showed everybody the fruit from the land. ²⁷They told Moses, "We went to the land where you sent us, and it is a fertile land! Here is some of its fruit. ²⁸But the people who live there are strong. Their cities are walled and very large. We even saw some Anakites there. ²⁹The Amalekites live in the southern area; the Hittites, Jebusites, and Amorites live in the mountains; and the Canaanites live near the sea and along the Jordan River."

³⁰Then Caleb told the people near Moses to be quiet, and he said, "We should certainly go up and take the land for ourselves. We can certainly do it."

³¹But the men who had gone with him said, "We can't attack those people; they are stronger than we are." ³²And those men gave the Israelites a bad report about the land they explored, saying, "The land that we explored is too large to conquer. All the people we saw are very tall. ³³We saw the Nephilim people there. (The Anakites come from the Nephilim people.) We felt like grasshoppers, and we looked like grasshoppers to them."

DEVOTION

THE LARGEST HUMANS I've ever seen were twins, each of them seven feet tall, and they were at the other end of the court warming up. This was high school basketball in the 1970s—small high schools at that—where a "tall" team might include a couple of players over six feet tall. We had seen nothing like these guys.

But once the game started, all of our fears about the twins disappeared. They were slow and a little clumsy. Neither could dribble without one of us taking the ball away. They were not in good physical condition, so one would rest on the bench while the other played. Dunking was outlawed in basketball during those days, and neither had a good shot.

We actually won that day, despite the "giants" on the other team. It occurred to me shortly after tip-off that the main benefit of the twins to their team was in their presence during warm-ups before the game . . . they got into our heads and made us feel small. Once the game started, however, that advantage evaporated.

Caleb, speaking for himself and Joshua, saw the same gigantic warriors and the same fortified cities as the other ten spies, yet the two faithful spies are confident in the ability of God to deliver the land into their hands. "Just get us into the battle and give God a chance to work," Joshua and Caleb are begging.

In the decades since that day on the court, I've looked at the future and seen other "giants"; perhaps you have, too. Chronic pain. Debt. Layoffs. Doubt. These are some of the giants I've experienced or watched others experience.

When faced with a giant, the question becomes this: are you going to get in the game and do battle or will you stay on the sidelines and give up without a fight? The choice is yours.

THOUGHTS TO PONDER

What are some of the "giants" you have had to face in your life? How did you handle the challenge? What giants are you still facing today?

PRAYER

Father, we pray that when we are faced with impossible tasks we will turn to you for our help and our salvation. Amen.

WISHING FOR SLAVERY

NUMBERS 14:1–10, 26–35

14 That night all the people in the camp began crying loudly. ²All the Israelites complained against Moses and Aaron, and all the people said to them, "We wish we had died in Egypt or in this desert. ³Why is the LORD bringing us to this land to be killed with swords? Our wives and children will be taken away. We would be better off going back to Egypt." ⁴They said to each other, "Let's choose a leader and go back to Egypt."

⁵Then Moses and Aaron bowed facedown in front of all the Israelites gathered there. ⁶Joshua son of Nun and Caleb son of Jephunneh, who had explored the land, tore their clothes. ⁷They said to all of the Israelites, "The land we explored is very good. ⁸If the LORD is pleased with us, he will lead us into that land and give us that fertile land. ⁹Don't turn against the LORD! Don't be afraid of the people in that land! We will chew them up. They have no protection, but the LORD is with us. So don't be afraid of them."

¹⁰Then all the people talked about killing them with stones. But the glory of the LORD appeared at the Meeting Tent to all the Israelites.

²⁶The LORD said to Moses and Aaron, ²⁷"How long will these evil people complain about me? I have heard the grumbling and complaining of these Israelites. ²⁸So tell them, 'This is what the LORD says. I heard what you said, and as surely as I live, I will do those very things to you: ²⁹You will die in this desert. Every one of you who is twenty years old or older and who was counted with the people—all of you who complained against me—will die. ³⁰Not one of you will enter the land where I promised you would live; only Caleb son of Jephunneh and Joshua son of Nun will go in. ³¹You said that your children would be taken away, but I will bring them into the land to enjoy what you refused. ³²As for you, you will die in this desert. ³³Your children will be shepherds here for forty years. Because you were not loyal, they will suffer until you lie dead in the desert. ³⁴For forty years you will suffer for your sins—a year for each of the forty days you explored the land. You will know me as your enemy.' ³⁵I, the LORD, have spoken, and I will certainly do these things to all these evil people who have come together against me. So they will all die here in this desert."

DEVOTION

CAN YOU IMAGINE the Israelites saying, "Let's go back to Egypt?" Could they possibly be serious? Did they not remember their lives as slaves? Conversely, did they not remember the many acts of providence God had shown them since they left Egypt? Surely they wouldn't give up on the promises of God for the "security" of slavery.

Or would they?

I've seen it happen today. I've seen people turn their backs on God for the slavery of addictions. I've seen people becomes slaves to debt after buying houses too big, cars too fast, and a host of gadgets they didn't need. I've seen people who are slaves to food, slaves to fashion, or slaves to fun.

Why did the children of Israel want to go back to Egypt? Perhaps slavery was comfortable. It was the same every day. Get up, do what the master says, and go to bed. No choices, no risks, no free will. But, on the other hand, no starvation, no wandering in the desert, and no looking for water. Perhaps the stability of slavery was preferable to the instability of freedom.

The apostle Paul compared sin to a slave master in his Letter to the Romans, and appealed to his readers to not be comfortable with their former lives as slaves. He writes, "In the past you were slaves to sin, and goodness did not control you. You did evil things, and now you are ashamed of them. Those things only bring death. But now you are free from sin and have become slaves of God. This brings you a life that is only for God, and this gives you life forever" (Romans 6:20–22).

The children of Israel could have chosen to serve God, but they preferred to return and serve the Egyptians. For this rebellion, their punishment was long— forty years in the wilderness, long enough for every adult to die in the desert. They would get neither the routine of slavery nor the thrill of freedom for the rest of their lives.

THOUGHTS TO PONDER

Does anything hold you captive? Do you know anyone who is a slave to sin? What can we do to escape the entanglements of sin? What can we do to help others trapped in the grip of sin?

PRAYER

God, help us cherish our freedom. Help us never to exchange our freedom for a life of slavery to sin. Amen.

A TIME OF RENEWAL

NUMBERS 15:27–36

[27]" 'If just one person sins without meaning to, a year-old female goat must be brought for a sin offering. [28]The priest will remove the sin of the person who sinned accidentally. He will remove it before the LORD, and the person will be forgiven. [29]The same teaching is for everyone who sins accidentally—for those born Israelites and for foreigners living among you.

[30]" 'But anyone who sins on purpose is against the LORD and must be cut off from the people, whether it is someone born among you or a foreigner. [31]That person has turned against the LORD's word and has not obeyed his commands. Such a person must surely be cut off from the others. He is guilty.' "

[32]When the Israelites were still in the desert, they found a man gathering wood on the Sabbath day. [33]Those who found him gathering wood brought him to Moses and Aaron and all the people. [34]They held the man under guard, because they did not know what to do with him. [35]Then the LORD said to Moses, "The man must surely die. All the people must kill him by throwing stones at him outside the camp." [36]So all the people took him outside the camp and stoned him to death, as the LORD commanded Moses.

DEVOTION

THE WHOLE OF ISRAEL was linked together in its fate, as you can see from the passage above. God could not abide sin in the camp—intentional or not—so he made provisions for the people to remedy unintentional sin.

But note the different way that God treats intentional sin. The person guilty of intentional sin was to be cut off from the people entirely. He or she was no longer a part of the community. By their own willful behavior, they cut themselves off from the people, and God commands the people to do the same to them.

Right after God issued these commands, the man in the story was caught breaking the commandments regarding the Sabbath. When Israel was camped at the base of the mountain in the Desert of Sinai, God gave Moses the Ten Commandments. The one regarding the Sabbath is found in Exodus 20:8–11 where we read, "Remember to keep the Sabbath holy. Work and get everything done during six days each week, but the seventh day is a day of rest to honor the LORD your God. On that day no one may do any work: not you, your son or daughter, your male or female slaves, your animals, or the foreigners living in your cities. The reason is that in six days the LORD made everything—the sky, the earth, the sea, and everything in them. On the seventh day he rested. So the LORD blessed the Sabbath day and made it holy."

While the penalty for ignoring the law of the Sabbath seems harsh, disobedience to the law is a direct insult to God, the one the Sabbath is designed to honor. It was the type of willful sin referred to in God's talk with Moses. However, this sin carried a specific penalty: the man was to be killed, and his executioners were to be all the people so that they would take a lesson away from his misdeeds.

So why did Jesus argue so often with the religious leaders in the New Testament days over the Sabbath? From performing healings on the Sabbath to gathering a few grains of wheat on the Sabbath as he and his followers walked through a field, Jesus seemed to be constantly on the defense about observing the Sabbath.

But Jesus never broke the law of the Sabbath as laid down in Exodus 20. He broke the religious leaders' interpretation of the law. By the time of the ministry of Jesus, the law of the Sabbath had become dozens of little rules regarding what constituted work. The rules were so complex that only the keepers of the law—known as scribes and Pharisees—knew all of them. This criticism of Jesus' activities was mainly because the religious leaders wanted to get him out of the way and they had nothing else to accuse him of.

Jesus used those opportunities to teach the real intent of the Sabbath. In a statement recorded by Mark in his Gospel, Jesus tells the Pharisees, "The Sabbath day was made to help people; they were not made to be ruled by the Sabbath day. So then, the Son of Man is Lord even of the Sabbath day" (Mark 2:27).

If the Sabbath was made to help people, do I still need it today? If you mean a time of rest and reflection, yes, I do—and so do you. Even the perversion of the Sabbath by the professional religious men in the days of Jesus can't take away its basic good as a time to restore and renew our spirits.

THOUGHTS TO PONDER

Why do you think the penalty for the Sabbath infraction was death? Why would all the people need to be involved? When do you find time for devotion to God? How do you protect that time?

PRAYER

Father, we pray that we will halt our busy lives frequently to worship you and reflect on your many good gifts to us, including the greatest gift of all—your Son. Amen.

A Life of Submission

NUMBERS 16:1–5, 12–14, 20–33

Read the entire story in Numbers 16:1–50.

16 Korah, Dathan, Abiram, and On turned against Moses. ²These men gathered two hundred fifty other Israelite men, well-known leaders chosen by the community, and challenged Moses. ³They came as a group to speak to Moses and Aaron and said, "You have gone too far. All the people are holy, every one of them, and the LORD is among them. So why do you put yourselves above all the people of the LORD?"

⁴When Moses heard this, he bowed facedown. ⁵Then he said to Korah and all his followers: "Tomorrow morning the LORD will show who belongs to him. He will bring the one who is holy near to him; he will bring to himself the person he chooses.

¹²Then Moses called Dathan and Abiram, the sons of Eliab, but they said, "We will not come! ¹³You have brought us out of a fertile land to this desert to kill us, and now you want to order us around. ¹⁴You haven't brought us into a fertile land; you haven't given us any land with fields and vineyards. Will you put out the eyes of these men? No! We will not come!"

²⁰The LORD said to Moses and Aaron, ²¹"Move away from these men so I can destroy them quickly."

²²But Moses and Aaron bowed facedown and cried out, "God, you are the God over the spirits of all people. Please don't be angry with this whole group. Only one man has really sinned."

²³Then the LORD said to Moses, ²⁴"Tell everyone to move away from the tents of Korah, Dathan, and Abiram."

²⁵Moses stood and went to Dathan and Abiram; the elders of Israel followed him. ²⁶Moses warned the people, "Move away from the tents of these evil men! Don't touch anything of theirs, or you will be destroyed because of their sins." ²⁷So they moved away from the tents of Korah, Dathan, and Abiram. Dathan and Abiram were standing outside their tents with their wives, children, and little babies.

²⁸Then Moses said, "Now you will know that the LORD has sent me to do all these things; it was not my idea. ²⁹If these men die a normal death—the way men usually die—then the LORD did not really send me. ³⁰But if the LORD does something new, you will know they have insulted the LORD. The ground will open and swallow them. They will be buried alive and will go to the place of the dead, and everything that belongs to them will go with them."

³¹When Moses finished saying these things, the ground under the men split open. ³²The earth opened and swallowed them and all their families. All Korah's

men and everything they owned went down. [33]They were buried alive, going to the place of the dead, and everything they owned went with them. Then the earth covered them. They died and were gone from the community.

DEVOTION

AT LEAST TWO complaints were being lodged against Moses and Aaron here. First, Korah, a Levite, wanted more authority in the temple duties. His tribe had been given that task, but now he chafed under the leadership of Aaron, the high priest. "Aren't we all holy?" he asks Moses. Next, Dathan and Abiram represent the Israelites who actually longed for a return to the fertile area of Goshen even though they had been the slaves of the king there. Better to be slaves in a land where crops would grow and cattle could graze than to be free in the desert, they surmised, and at least 250 of their fellow Israelites agreed.

God's wrath was quick. He wanted to destroy them all, and only the intervention of Moses limited the destruction to the three leaders and their families. Their death was a lesson to the entire community.

I see a parallel today. "Who's really in charge here?" I often want to ask God. Yet I am constantly called by Scripture to lead a life of submission—to God (James 4:7), to political powers (Romans 13:1), to my spouse (Ephesians 5:21), and to leaders in the church (Hebrews 13:17).

Why? Because Jesus set the example. In his Letter to the Philippians, Paul admonishes us to be like Jesus when he says in Philippians 2:8, "And when he was living as a man, he humbled himself and was fully obedient to God, even when that caused his death—death on a cross." The result? God exalted Jesus to his current throne (Philippians 2:9–11).

The difference is clear. We can either exalt ourselves on earth like Korah and face the consequences, or submit ourselves on earth and reap the reward. The choice is ours.

THOUGHTS TO PONDER

What does it mean to live a life of submission? Does submission automatically signal weakness? Why does God not exhibit his wrath against insubordination in a direct way today?

PRAYER

God, we pray that when it is our time to lead, we will lead, but when it is our time to submit, we will submit, and so glorify you. Amen.

Fruit-Bearing Followers

NUMBERS 16:41—17:11

⁴¹The next day all the Israelites complained against Moses and Aaron and said, "You have killed the LORD's people."

⁴²When the people gathered to complain against Moses and Aaron, they turned toward the Meeting Tent, and the cloud covered it. The glory of the LORD appeared. ⁴³Then Moses and Aaron went in front of the Meeting Tent.

⁴⁴The LORD said to Moses, ⁴⁵"Move away from these people so I can destroy them quickly." So Moses and Aaron bowed facedown.

⁴⁶Then Moses said to Aaron, "Get your pan, and put fire from the altar and incense in it. Hurry to the people and remove their sin. The LORD is angry with them; the sickness has already started." ⁴⁷So Aaron did as Moses said. He ran to the middle of the people, where the sickness had already started among them. So Aaron offered the incense to remove their sin. ⁴⁸He stood between the dead and the living, and the sickness stopped there. ⁴⁹But 14,700 people died from that sickness, in addition to those who died because of Korah. ⁵⁰Then Aaron went back to Moses at the entrance to the Meeting Tent. The terrible sickness had been stopped.

17 The LORD said to Moses, ²"Speak to the people of Israel and get twelve walking sticks from them—one from the leader of each tribe. Write the name of each man on his stick, and ³on the stick from Levi, write Aaron's name. There must be one stick for the head of each tribe. ⁴Put them in the Meeting Tent in front of the Ark of the Agreement, where I meet with you. ⁵I will choose one man whose walking stick will begin to grow leaves; in this way I will stop the Israelites from always complaining against you."

⁶So Moses spoke to the Israelites. Each of the twelve leaders gave him a walking stick—one from each tribe—and Aaron's walking stick was among them. ⁷Moses put them before the LORD in the Tent of the Agreement.

⁸The next day, when Moses entered the Tent, he saw that Aaron's stick (which stood for the family of Levi) had grown leaves. It had even budded, blossomed, and produced almonds. ⁹So Moses brought out to the Israelites all the walking sticks from the LORD's presence. They all looked, and each man took back his stick.

¹⁰Then the LORD said to Moses, "Put Aaron's walking stick back in front of the Ark of the Agreement. It will remind these people who are always turning against me to stop their complaining against me so they won't die." ¹¹So Moses obeyed what the LORD commanded him.

DEVOTION

WHAT'S THE PROOF that God is working in you? Look for the blooms. God blossoms in those who are chosen by him for his purposes. In the story above, to prove that Aaron was the chosen spiritual leader of the nation of Israel, God put life into an inanimate stick—a dead piece of wood that bloomed and came to life.

I think the same principle is at work today. When God wants to use us, he "inspires" us, a word that in the language of the Greek New Testament literally means "God-breathed." When we are inspired to do good works, we literally have the breath of God in us giving us life and energy. As surely as God put life into that lifeless stick of Aaron's to show that Aaron was his chosen high priest, God breathed eternal life into me so that I can be among the chosen for all eternity.

The result is that we can now all be priests. As Peter told his readers: "But you are a chosen people, royal priests, a holy nation, a people for God's own possession. You were chosen to tell about the wonderful acts of God, who called you out of darkness into his wonderful light" (1 Peter 2:9). God has chosen us for priesthood. Where he once had a physical nation in Israel, he now has a holy nation of those who have taken God's offer to step out of the darkness into the light.

Want further proof that God is working in you? Look for the fruit. In the story above, Aaron's walking stick produced almonds as proof that God was working through Aaron. When we bear fruit, we show the world that we belong to him as well. In his last discourse with his followers at the end of his life, Jesus told them that the fruit they bore would be the proof that they belong to him: "You should produce much fruit and show that you are my followers, which brings glory to my Father" (John 15:8).

Like Aaron's walking stick, when we bloom and bear fruit, it sends testimony to the world that we have been chosen by God to do his good works.

THOUGHTS TO PONDER

Why do you think God chose this method to show his favor with Aaron? What impact might it have had on the people? How can you tell when someone is bearing fruit for God?

PRAYER

Father, we pray that we will bloom and bear fruit for you in our lives today. Amen.

HONOR THE HOLINESS OF GOD

NUMBERS 20:1–13; 27:12–14

20 In the first month all the people of Israel arrived at the Desert of Zin, and they stayed at Kadesh. There Miriam died and was buried. ²There was no water for the people, so they came together against Moses and Aaron. ³They argued with Moses and said, "We should have died in front of the LORD as our brothers did. ⁴Why did you bring the LORD's people into this desert? Are we and our animals to die here? ⁵Why did you bring us from Egypt to this terrible place? It has no grain, figs, grapevines, or pomegranates, and there's no water to drink!"

⁶So Moses and Aaron left the people and went to the entrance of the Meeting Tent. There they bowed facedown, and the glory of the LORD appeared to them. ⁷The LORD said to Moses, ⁸"Take your walking stick, and you and your brother Aaron should gather the people. Speak to that rock in front of them so that its water will flow from it. When you bring the water out from that rock, give it to the people and their animals."

⁹So Moses took the stick from in front of the LORD, as he had said. ¹⁰Moses and Aaron gathered the people in front of the rock, and Moses said, "Now listen to me, you who turn against God! Do you want us to bring water out of this rock?" ¹¹Then Moses lifted his hand and hit the rock twice with his stick. Water began pouring out, and the people and their animals drank it.

¹²But the LORD said to Moses and Aaron, "Because you did not believe me, and because you did not honor me as holy before the people, you will not lead them into the land I will give them."

¹³These are the waters of Meribah, where the Israelites argued with the LORD and where he showed them he was holy.

¹²Then the LORD said to Moses, "Climb this mountain in the Abarim Mountains, and look at the land I have given to the Israelites. ¹³After you have seen it, you will die and join your ancestors as your brother Aaron did, ¹⁴because you both acted against my command in the Desert of Zin. You did not honor me as holy before the people at the waters of Meribah."

DEUTERONOMY 34:1–5

34 Then Moses climbed Mount Nebo from the plains of Moab to the top of Mount Pisgah, across from Jericho. From there the LORD showed him all the land from Gilead to Dan, ²all of Naphtali and the lands of Ephraim and Manasseh, all the land of Judah as far as the Mediterranean Sea, ³as well as the southern desert and the whole Valley of Jericho up to Zoar. (Jericho is called the city of palm trees.) ⁴Then the LORD said to Moses, "This is the land I promised to Abraham, Isaac, and Jacob when I said to them, 'I will give this land to your descendants.' I have let you look at it, Moses, but you will not cross over there."

⁵Then Moses, the servant of the LORD, died there in Moab, as the LORD had said.

DEVOTION

THE PEOPLE HAD GRUMBLED almost since the first day Moses led them out of captivity. They grumbled when they saw the Egyptian king's army approaching at the Red Sea. They complained in the wilderness about a lack of food and water. When God gave them manna to eat, they complained about a lack of meat.

In addition, they were a rebellious people. While Moses was on the mountain receiving the Law from God, they were in the plains below fashioning a golden calf to worship in the place of God. Korah the Levite and his followers challenged the priesthood of Aaron. Repeatedly, Moses found himself interceding with God on behalf of the nation to prevent them from being destroyed.

So it comes as no surprise that on this day in Kadesh, already emotional from the death of his sister, Miriam, Moses lashed out at the people. And in his anger, Moses struck the rock rather than speaking to it as God had commanded. It was an understandable mistake, but it was also an affront to God.

The holiness of God is to be feared and to be respected. His commands are to be followed. We do not have the right to pick and choose which ones we want to follow, nor do we have the right to alter them in any way. God's nature demands obedience and God's nature demands justice. Because Moses did not honor the holiness of God on that frustrating day in the desert, he only got a glimpse of the Promised Land.

THOUGHTS TO PONDER

Was God's punishment harsh? Does God's punishment overlook the many good things Moses did in his life? How do you reconcile the justice of God with the mercy of God in your own life?

PRAYER

God, we pray that we will always remember that you are a holy God, a God to be obeyed in all your commands. Amen.

SECOND FIDDLE

NUMBERS 20:22–29

²²All the Israelites moved from Kadesh to Mount Hor, ²³near the border of Edom. There the LORD said to Moses and Aaron, ²⁴"Aaron will die. He will not enter the land that I'm giving to the Israelites, because you both acted against my command at the waters of Meribah. ²⁵Take Aaron and his son Eleazar up on Mount Hor, ²⁶and take off Aaron's special clothes and put them on his son Eleazar. Aaron will die there; he will join his ancestors."

²⁷Moses obeyed the LORD's command. They climbed up Mount Hor, and all the people saw them go. ²⁸Moses took off Aaron's clothes and put them on Aaron's son Eleazar. Then Aaron died there on top of the mountain. Moses and Eleazar came back down the mountain, ²⁹and when all the people learned that Aaron was dead, everyone in Israel cried for him for thirty days.

DEVOTION

A FAMOUS CONDUCTOR was once asked which instrument was the most difficult to play. "Second fiddle," he replied. "Because no one wants to play it." Aaron will forever live in the shadow of Moses, but he lived an interesting and important life, and the national month of mourning at his death is just one indication of the deep respect the people had for this complex man.

We know that Aaron was the brother of Moses, but we have no record of how he escaped the decree of the Egyptian king that all baby boys born to the Israelites were to be thrown into the Nile, although it is probable that he was born before the decree. When Moses was picked by God to lead his people out of Egyptian slavery, it was Aaron who acted as his spokesman because of the stammer that Moses was afflicted with. He was right there with Moses when he drew the wrath of the king (Exodus 5:4) and he was beside Moses when the Hebrew people turned against them for making their work under the king harder (Exodus 5:20–21). It was Aaron's walking stick that turned into a serpent to show the king of Egypt the power of God (Exodus 7:8–13) and it was his stick that was stretched out to begin several of the plagues.

But Aaron was a complex individual with flaws and sorrows. When Moses tarried forty days on the mountain in the presence of God, Aaron gave in to the people and fashioned them an idol to worship (Exodus 32:1–6). Along with his sister Miriam, Aaron criticized the leadership of Moses, an act that resulted in a skin disease for Miriam and a rebuke for Aaron (Numbers 12:1–15). He had seen two of his sons, Nadab and Abihu, killed by God for not following God's orders exactly in their roles as priests (Leviticus 10:1–3). So devoted was Aaron to his duties that Scripture tells us he kept silent at the death of his sons for their dis-obedience to God's orders.

It is interesting to note in this story that the reason God gives for Aaron not entering the Promised Land—the fact that Moses disobeyed God at the waters of Meribah—was not even a sin of Aaron's. However, it demonstrates the close re-lationship between the two leaders that God held Aaron, the spiritual leader of the nation, equally accountable for the sin of Moses.

But despite his flaws, Aaron had been the unquestioned head of the priest-hood of the nation of Israel. In a time when God was only approached by special ceremonies and sins had to be forgiven by ritual sacrifices, no duty was more im-portant that Aaron's. He oversaw the building of the Holy Tent as a temporary dwelling place for God and the work of the priests and Levites who served in it.

But Aaron will always be remembered as being second—first to his brother Moses and later to the perfect priesthood of Jesus. We read in Hebrews 5:3–5, "Because he is weak, the high priest must offer sacrifices for his own sins and also for the sins of the people. To be a high priest is an honor, but no one chooses himself for this work. He must be called by God as Aaron was. So also Christ did not choose himself to have the honor of being a high priest, but God chose him."

There are worse legacies than to be the mouthpiece for Moses and forerun-ner for Christ's priesthood. In the story above, Aaron climbed the mountain aware that he would not climb back down. And, in a sense, the same is true of all of us. We go up the mountain once, and any role we play in God's kingdom along the way is an important one.

THOUGHTS TO PONDER

What qualities must Aaron have possessed to fulfill his role as spokesperson for Moses? What qualities must he have had to be named high priest? Why would God want the political and spiri-tual leaders of his chosen nation to be as close as brothers? What does this say about them?

PRAYER

God, we pray that we will serve in whatever role you give us. If we are called to lead, give us the courage to lead. If we are called to fol-low, give us the strength to follow. Amen.

VICTORY OVER DEATH

NUMBERS 21:1–9

21 The Canaanite king of Arad lived in the southern area. When he heard that the Israelites were coming on the road to Atharim, he attacked them and captured some of them. ²Then the Israelites made this promise to the LORD: "If you will help us defeat these people, we will completely destroy their cities." ³The LORD listened to the Israelites, and he let them defeat the Canaanites. The Israelites completely destroyed the Canaanites and their cities, so the place was named Hormah.

⁴The Israelites left Mount Hor and went on the road toward the Red Sea, in order to go around the country of Edom. But the people became impatient on the way ⁵and grumbled at God and Moses. They said, "Why did you bring us out of Egypt to die in this desert? There is no bread and no water, and we hate this terrible food!"

⁶So the LORD sent them poisonous snakes; they bit the people, and many of the Israelites died. ⁷The people came to Moses and said, "We sinned when we grumbled at you and the LORD. Pray that the LORD will take away these snakes." So Moses prayed for the people.

⁸The LORD said to Moses, "Make a bronze snake, and put it on a pole. When anyone who is bitten looks at it, that person will live." ⁹So Moses made a bronze snake and put it on a pole. Then when a snake bit anyone, that person looked at the bronze snake and lived.

DEVOTION

THE STORY ABOVE is yet another example of the constant grumbling of the Israelites and, therefore, nearly forgettable. (More on the "nearly" in a moment.) It's a familiar refrain: Why did you bring us out of Egypt to die here? The food's no good, the water is scarce and we haven't had bread for as long as we can remember.

The Israelites had grumbled before, but this time is different. This time God reacts. The desert floor swarms with snakes—deadly ones that kill the people who are bitten. You might remember that God told them that every adult over the age of twenty at the time of the exodus from Egypt would die in the desert because the people chose to believe the report of the unfaithful spies. Many of those adults would die on this day.

But the people repent, so God works with Moses to fashion a way of escape for the people to be saved. By looking up at the bronze snake on the pole, the people live.

If that was all, this would be just one more story of the children of Israel grumbling and facing the wrath of God. But this story gains added stature when Jesus uses it as an analogy in one of the most important passages in all of Scripture. In the Gospel of John (3:14–17) Jesus, speaking to Nicodemus, says, "Just as Moses lifted up the snake in the desert, the Son of Man must also be lifted up. So that everyone who believes can have eternal life in him. God loved the world so much that he gave his one and only Son so that whoever believes in him may not be lost, but have eternal life. God did not send his Son into the world to judge the world guilty, but to save the world through him."

Although Nicodemus doesn't understand it at the time, Jesus compares his coming role on the cross with that long-ago day in the desert. The serpent was lifted up on the pole; Jesus will be lifted up on the cross on Golgotha.

Just as the children of Israel suffered the consequences of their grumbling, you and I deserve to suffer the consequences of our sins. Those bit by the snakes suffered physical death, but sin causes a spiritual death. We battle the original serpent, the one who tricked Eve in the Garden of Eden. And once we feel the sting of sin, we face an eternity without hope.

But God loved us too much to let us suffer that fate, so he sent his only Son to pay the price (John 3:16). And just as the serpent lifted up on the pole was an antidote to the serpent's sting, Jesus lifted up on the cross is the antidote to the sting of death. Later, Paul would tell his readers in Corinth (1 Corinthians 15:55–57) that even the sting of death had been taken away by the victory in Jesus. That victory is still available to us today.

Feel caught in sin? Feel afraid to die? Then look up and see Jesus.

THOUGHTS TO PONDER

Why do you think God would choose snakes to punish the people?
What was the symbolism of the bronze snake that Moses created?
Why do you think Jesus used this story?

PRAYER

Father, we thank you for the way of escape you have given us from our sins. We pray that we will always keep our eyes on Jesus, the source of our salvation. Amen.

Selling Out

NUMBERS 22:1–19

22 Then the people of Israel went to the plains of Moab, and they camped near the Jordan River across from Jericho.

²Balak son of Zippor saw everything the Israelites had done to the Amorites. ³And Moab was scared of so many Israelites; truly, Moab was terrified by them.

⁴The Moabites said to the elders of Midian, "These people will take everything around us like an ox eating grass."

Balak son of Zippor was the king of Moab at this time. ⁵He sent messengers to Balaam son of Beor at Pethor, near the Euphrates River in his native land. Balak said, "A nation has come out of Egypt that covers the land. They have camped next to me, ⁶and they are too powerful for me. So come and put a curse on them. Maybe then I can defeat them and make them leave the area. I know that if you bless someone, the blessings happen, and if you put a curse on someone, it happens."

⁷The elders of Moab and Midian went with payment in their hands. When they found Balaam, they told him what Balak had said.

⁸Balaam said to them, "Stay here for the night, and I will tell you what the LORD tells me." So the Moabite leaders stayed with him.

⁹God came to Balaam and asked, "Who are these men with you?"

¹⁰Balaam said to God, "The king of Moab, Balak son of Zippor, sent them to me with this message: ¹¹'A nation has come out of Egypt that covers the land. So come and put a curse on them, and maybe I can fight them and force them out of my land.'"

¹²But God said to Balaam, "Do not go with them. Don't put a curse on those people, because I have blessed them."

¹³The next morning Balaam awoke and said to Balak's leaders, "Go back to your own country; the LORD has refused to let me go with you."

¹⁴So the Moabite leaders went back to Balak and said, "Balaam refused to come with us."

¹⁵So Balak sent other leaders—this time there were more of them, and they were more important. ¹⁶They went to Balaam and said, "Balak son of Zippor says this: Please don't let anything stop you from coming to me. ¹⁷I will pay you very well, and I will do what you say. Come and put a curse on these people for me."

¹⁸But Balaam answered Balak's servants, "King Balak could give me his palace full of silver and gold, but I cannot disobey the LORD my God in anything, great or small. ¹⁹You stay here tonight as the other men did, and I will find out what more the LORD tells me."

DEVOTION

THE KING OF MOAB had never seen a million people before, as ancient nations were not that large, but here they were, camped on his border. Besides the sheer number of the Israelites, King Balak was frightened by the stories. The miraculous escape from Egypt. The absolute defeat of the Amorites. The deaths of Sihon and Og.

For years, Bible story books called Balaam a prophet, but that's a bit misleading, and unsupported by the text. He would more accurately be called a psychic, someone who makes a living by purportedly telling the future. In fact, Peter would call Balaam a man "who loved being paid for doing wrong" (2 Peter 2:15).

Balak had heard of Balaam, and sent his messengers to ask Balaam to prophesy for hire. Because the journey was probably several days, Balaam extended them hospitality to stay in his home.

Given where he was located, it is possible that Balaam had never heard of the Israelites. But he did recognize God. The next morning when he declined the offer, he referred to God by the name Yahweh, which is always translated "LORD" in the text of the Old Testament. It is the most holy name for God, and Balaam uses it in refusing to go with the men.

Notice what God said to Balaam: leave the Israelites alone, because I have blessed them. These are the same people who, in fear, turned their back on God's offer to give them the land of Canaan. These are the people wandering in the desert for their rebellion, yet God still loved them and wanted to bless them . . . and he used this wayward soothsayer to do it.

Temptation rarely goes away and it often comes back even stronger. So when the messengers became more important and the offer more generous, Balaam petitioned God again for permission to go to Moab, not knowing the trouble he is asking for.

THOUGHTS TO PONDER

Why do you think God chose to reveal himself to Balaam in the night? Why would it matter what Balaam prophesied before Balak since God was ultimately in control? Have you known anyone tempted by money to turn his or her back on God?

PRAYER

God, we pray that we will always bless you and never curse you, no matter what circumstances we face, for we know all good gifts come from you. Amen.

Unexpected Messengers

NUMBERS 22:20–35

²⁰That night God came to Balaam and said, "These men have come to ask you to go with them. Go, but only do what I tell you."

²¹Balaam got up the next morning and put a saddle on his donkey. Then he went with the Moabite leaders. ²²But God became angry because Balaam went, so the angel of the LORD stood in the road to stop Balaam. Balaam was riding his donkey, and he had two servants with him. ²³When the donkey saw the angel of the LORD standing in the road with a sword in his hand, the donkey left the road and went into the field. Balaam hit the donkey to force her back on the road.

²⁴Later, the angel of the LORD stood on a narrow path between two vineyards, with walls on both sides. ²⁵Again the donkey saw the angel of the LORD, and she walked close to one wall, crushing Balaam's foot against it. So he hit her again.

²⁶The angel of the LORD went ahead again and stood at a narrow place, too narrow to turn left or right. ²⁷When the donkey saw the angel of the LORD, she lay down under Balaam. This made him so angry that he hit her with his stick. ²⁸Then the LORD made the donkey talk, and she said to Balaam, "What have I done to make you hit me three times?"

²⁹Balaam answered the donkey, "You have made me look foolish! I wish I had a sword in my hand! I would kill you right now!"

³⁰But the donkey said to Balaam, "I am your very own donkey, which you have ridden for years. Have I ever done this to you before?"

"No," Balaam said.

³¹Then the LORD let Balaam see the angel of the LORD, who was standing in the road with his sword drawn. Then Balaam bowed facedown on the ground.

³²The angel of the LORD asked Balaam, "Why have you hit your donkey three times? I have stood here to stop you, because what you are doing is wrong. ³³The donkey saw me and turned away from me three times. If she had not turned away, I would have killed you by now, but I would have let her live."

³⁴Then Balaam said to the angel of the LORD, "I have sinned; I did not know you were standing in the road to stop me. If I am wrong, I will go back."

³⁵The angel of the LORD said to Balaam, "Go with these men, but say only what I tell you." So Balaam went with Balak's leaders.

DEVOTION

THE WORD "REPENTANCE" is used frequently in the New Testament. In the Greek language of New Testament times, the word had a fairly simple definition: it meant to turn around. If you set out in the wrong direction, and then turned around, you repented. It was a secular word that gained a religious meaning when it came to mean turning from a life of sin to a life of righteousness.

I think this story is the clearest case of the literal meaning of repentance that you'll find. Balaam is going the wrong way—literally and spiritually—and when he finally discovers that fact, he says what each of us must say at some point: "If I am wrong, I will go back" (Numbers 22:34).

Why did God allow him to go? It seems that at the beginning of the story God is being fickle, but that's not in his nature. I think—and this is just an opinion here—that Balaam acted like an adolescent wanting to go to the party and God is the weary parent. Finally, God decides to relent, knowing that he can teach Balaam a lesson here. Balaam is allowed to go despite God's displeasure.

So Balaam, too proud to say no to the king a second time and too greedy to pass up the possibility of a good payday, mounts his donkey for the long journey to Moab only to be taught a lesson by his beast.

The wisdom of the donkey reminds me of a story of the owner of a chain of health clubs. Perplexed by the disappearance of the expensive shampoo from the showers, he asked his managers to solve the problem. But the signs they came up with actually caused more people to want the shampoo. Finally, a janitor offered this solution: leave the lids off the shampoo bottles. The thefts stopped immediately.

It's amazing where wisdom can come from if we only listen. To protect us from spectacular mistakes, perhaps God puts angels in our paths. Will we hear the messenger he chooses? Or will we be forced to repent later?

THOUGHTS TO PONDER

Have you ever been taught a profound lesson from an unlikely source? A child? A student? A pet? An employee? Why do we confuse wisdom with status? What could we learn if we were more open-minded?

PRAYER

God, we pray we will hear your wisdom and follow it no matter what the source. Help us be attuned to your message and your messengers today. Amen.

A Nonnegotiable Message

NUMBERS 22:36—23:12

³⁶When Balak heard that Balaam was coming, he went out to meet him at Ar in Moab, which was beside the Arnon, at the edge of his country. ³⁷Balak said to Balaam, "I had asked you before to come quickly. Why didn't you come to me? I am able to reward you well."

³⁸But Balaam answered, "I have come to you now, but I can't say just anything. I can only say what God tells me to say."

³⁹Then Balaam went with Balak to Kiriath Huzoth. ⁴⁰Balak offered cattle and sheep as a sacrifice and gave some meat to Balaam and the leaders with him.

⁴¹The next morning Balak took Balaam to Bamoth Baal; from there he could see the edge of the Israelite camp.

23 Balaam said to Balak, "Build me seven altars here, and prepare seven bulls and seven male sheep for me." ²Balak did what Balaam asked, and they offered a bull and a male sheep on each of the altars.

³Then Balaam said to Balak, "Stay here beside your burnt offering and I will go. If the LORD comes to me, I will tell you whatever he shows me." Then Balaam went to a higher place.

⁴God came to Balaam there, and Balaam said to him, "I have prepared seven altars, and I have offered a bull and a male sheep on each altar."

⁵The LORD told Balaam what he should say. Then the LORD said, "Go back to Balak and give him this message."

⁶So Balaam went back to Balak. Balak and all the leaders of Moab were still standing beside his burnt offering ⁷when Balaam gave them this message:

"Balak brought me here from Aram;
      the king of Moab brought me from the eastern mountains.
   Balak said, 'Come, put a curse on the people of Jacob for me.
      Come, call down evil on the people of Israel.'
⁸But God has not cursed them,
      so I cannot curse them.
   The LORD has not called down evil on them,
      so I cannot call down evil on them.
⁹I see them from the top of the mountains;
      I see them from the hills.
   I see a people who live alone,
      who think they are different from other nations.

[10]No one can number the many people of Jacob,
> and no one can count a fourth of Israel.
Let me die like good men,
> and let me end up like them!"

[11]Balak said to Balaam, "What have you done to me? I brought you here to curse my enemies, but you have only blessed them!"

[12]But Balaam answered, "I must say what the LORD tells me to say."

DEVOTION

GOD HAD BALAAM'S attention, so when Balaam appeared before Balak, he spoke only the words of God. Balaam's reply to the rebuke of Balak is similar to the one Peter and Paul would give centuries later when they were arrested for preaching that Jesus had been raised from the dead.

Peter replied to the Council of the Jews who had ordered the men to be silent, "You decide what God would want. Should we obey you or God? We cannot keep quiet. We must speak about what we have seen and heard" (Acts 4:19–20). Did those religious leaders realize they were acting like Balak did those many years ago in trying to stop the message of God? I doubt it. But Peter and Paul knew what Balaam discovered: when you are the messenger of God, the message is nonnegotiable.

Do we have "Balaams" in our midst today? Would Balaam today preach a social gospel of God's love without preaching about his commandments? Would he bend the ancient message to fit into a politically correct world? Would he preach what people wish to hear, gathering huge audiences along the way? Possibly.

When we hear false teaching today we must be like Peter. We cannot—and should not—keep quiet.

THOUGHTS TO PONDER

How do you check the accuracy of the messages you hear today? How do you know what you are hearing is the true message of God? Do you think God directly blesses his people today?

PRAYER

God, we pray that we will be your faithful messengers—unconcerned with popularity and unafraid of consequences. Give us the courage to speak. Amen.

Sin's Destructive Power

NUMBERS 25:1–18

25 While the people of Israel were still camped at Acacia, the men began sinning sexually with Moabite women. ²The women invited them to their sacrifices to their gods, and the Israelites ate food there and worshiped these gods. ³So the Israelites began to worship Baal of Peor, and the LORD was very angry with them.

⁴The LORD said to Moses, "Get all the leaders of the people and kill them in open daylight in the presence of the LORD. Then the LORD will not be angry with the people of Israel."

⁵So Moses said to Israel's judges, "Each of you must put to death your people who have become worshipers of Baal of Peor."

⁶Moses and the Israelites were gathered at the entrance to the Meeting Tent, crying there. Then an Israelite man brought a Midianite woman to his brothers in plain sight of Moses and all the people. ⁷Phinehas son of Eleazar, the son of Aaron, the priest, saw this, so he left the meeting and got his spear. ⁸He followed the Israelite into his tent and drove his spear through both the Israelite man and the Midianite woman. Then the terrible sickness among the Israelites stopped.

⁹This sickness had killed twenty-four thousand people.

¹⁰The LORD said to Moses, ¹¹"Phinehas son of Eleazar, the son of Aaron, the priest, has saved the Israelites from my anger. He hates sin as much as I do. Since he tried to save my honor among them, I will not kill them. ¹²So tell Phinehas that I am making my peace agreement with him. ¹³He and his descendants will always be priests, because he had great concern for the honor of his God. He removed the sins of the Israelites so they would belong to God."

¹⁴The Israelite man who was killed with the Midianite woman was named Zimri son of Salu. He was the leader of a family in the tribe of Simeon. ¹⁵And the name of the Midianite woman who was put to death was Cozbi daughter of Zur, who was the chief of a Midianite family.

¹⁶The LORD said to Moses, ¹⁷"The Midianites are your enemies, and you should kill them. ¹⁸They have already made you their enemies, because they tricked you at Peor and because of their sister Cozbi, the daughter of a Midianite leader. She was the woman who was killed when the sickness came because the people sinned at Peor."

DEVOTION

THIS IS NOT an uplifting story. In fact, it's quite depressing. But it's a lesson in how sin works, and a lesson we should hear today.

When the children of Israel approached the land of Moab, the Moabite leaders were justifiably terrified. Israel had just defeated Og, king of Bashan, and Si-hon, king of the Amorites, and traveled right through their lands. They were camped on the edge of Moab when we read these words: "Moab was scared of so many Israelites; truly, Moab was terrified by them. The Moabites said to the elders of Midian, 'These people will take everything around us like an ox eating grass'" (Numbers 22:3–4).

The king of Moab tried everything. He wanted an alliance with Midian. He wanted the prophet, Balaam, to prophesy against Israel. But what he never figured was that Israel would not be defeated by a mighty enemy; they would be brought low by their own sin.

Camped on the plains of Moab, the men of Israel began sinning with the women of Moab in rituals that probably mixed sexual immorality with the worship of idols. The sin became so acute that Zimri, a prominent man in the tribe of Simeon, brought a Moabite woman into the camp where he took her into his tent for sexual relations. Evidently, God's wrath could be contained no longer and he sent a terrible sickness throughout the camp that almost instantly killed twenty-four thousand people. The dying did not stop until Phinehas, the grandson of Aaron, killed Zimri and the woman with a single thrust of his spear.

Twenty-four thousand dead. More than Balak, king of Moab, could have ever hoped to kill on the field of battle. And he didn't even mount an army. That's the power of sin. It can do more damage than the most powerful army.

But the good news is this: sin and Satan have been defeated by Jesus on the cross. He fought the enemy for me and won. It is now my role to claim the victory in him. To paraphrase the statement of God to Moses above, he removed my sin so I would belong to God.

THOUGHTS TO PONDER

Why would Israel turn so soon to worshiping Baal after the incident of the golden calf? What would be the appeal of idols over the one true God? What have you seen sin do in your life or the lives of ones you love?

PRAYER

Father, we pray that we will stay far away from sin and its temptations and that we will always prefer you over the world's "idols" of fame or wealth or power. Amen.

LEADERSHIP QUALITIES

NUMBERS 27:12–23

¹²Then the LORD said to Moses, "Climb this mountain in the Abarim Mountains, and look at the land I have given to the Israelites. ¹³After you have seen it, you will die and join your ancestors as your brother Aaron did, ¹⁴because you both acted against my command in the Desert of Zin. You did not honor me as holy before the people at the waters of Meribah." (This was at Meribah in Kadesh in the Desert of Zin.)

¹⁵Moses said to the LORD, ¹⁶"The LORD is the God of the spirits of all people. May he choose a leader for these people, ¹⁷who will go in and out before them. He must lead them out like sheep and bring them in; the LORD's people must not be like sheep without a shepherd."

¹⁸So the LORD said to Moses, "Take Joshua son of Nun, because my Spirit is in him. Put your hand on him, ¹⁹and have him stand before Eleazar the priest and all the people. Then give him his orders as they watch. ²⁰Let him share your honor so that all the Israelites will obey him. ²¹He must stand before Eleazar the priest, and Eleazar will get advice from the LORD by using the Urim. At his command all the Israelites will go out, and at his command they will all come in."

²²Moses did what the LORD told him. He took Joshua and had him stand before Eleazar the priest and all the people, ²³and he put his hands on him and gave him orders, just as the LORD had told him.

DEUTERONOMY 34:1–9

34 Then Moses climbed Mount Nebo from the plains of Moab to the top of Mount Pisgah, across from Jericho. From there the LORD showed him all the land from Gilead to Dan, ²all of Naphtali and the lands of Ephraim and Manasseh, all the land of Judah as far as the Mediterranean Sea, ³as well as the southern desert and the whole Valley of Jericho up to Zoar. (Jericho is called the city of palm trees.) ⁴Then the LORD said to Moses, "This is the land I promised to Abraham, Isaac, and Jacob when I said to them, 'I will give this land to your descendants.' I have let you look at it, Moses, but you will not cross over there."

⁵Then Moses, the servant of the LORD, died there in Moab, as the LORD had said. ⁶He buried Moses in Moab in the valley opposite Beth Peor, but even today no one knows where his grave is. ⁷Moses was one hundred twenty years old when he died. His eyes were not weak, and he was still strong. ⁸The Israelites cried for Moses for thirty days, staying in the plains of Moab until the time of sadness was over.

⁹Joshua son of Nun was then filled with wisdom, because Moses had put his hands on him. So the Israelites listened to Joshua, and they did what the LORD had commanded Moses.

DEVOTION

MOSES HAD PERFORMED one of the most miraculous feats of leadership in human history. He had taken motley slaves out of Egypt and made them into not only a great nation but also a military force. He had interceded on their behalf numerous times in the presence of an angry God. He had spoken with God as one man speaks to another. But he was not allowed to enter the Promised Land as the penalty for striking the rock to receive the waters of Meribah instead of addressing the rock as he was told (Numbers 20:1–13).

But even faced with the disappointment of not being able to enter into the Land of Promise, Moses thought first of his people, not himself. He knew they would need another leader, and for that leader to succeed, the people needed to see that he was chosen by God. So Moses petitioned God to pick the next leader. And what God said next is a primer in how leaders are made. God told Moses, "Take Joshua son of Nun, because my Spirit is in him." Want to know who should be leading your local church? Look for the ones who have God's Spirit in them. Want good leaders in the home? Make sure parents have God's Spirit in them. Want better politicians? Elect people with God's Spirit in them.

In these two accounts above, we see the peaceful, orderly transition of power from one great leader to the next. Moses would forever be remembered as the one who led the nation out of slavery while Joshua would be known as the one who led them into the Promised Land. "Let him share your honor" God said to Moses. And in an act of true leadership, Moses shared the stage with Joshua before making his gracious, eternal exit to be buried by the very hand of God.

THOUGHTS TO PONDER

Why do you think the penalty for Moses striking the rock was so severe? What does this say about God? What does it mean to have the Spirit of God in us?

PRAYER

Father, we pray that we will have your Spirit in us and that we will be leaders in your kingdom here on earth. Amen.

Gifts from God

NUMBERS 31:1–12, 48–54

31 The LORD spoke to Moses and said, ²"Pay back the Midianites for what they did to the Israelites; after that you will die."

³So Moses said to the people, "Get some men ready for war. The LORD will use them to pay back the Midianites. ⁴Send to war a thousand men from each of the tribes of Israel." ⁵So twelve thousand men got ready for war, a thousand men from each tribe. ⁶Moses sent those men to war; Phinehas son of Eleazar the priest was with them. He took with him the holy things and the trumpets for giving the alarm. ⁷They fought the Midianites as the LORD had commanded Moses, and they killed every Midianite man. ⁸Among those they killed were Evi, Rekem, Zur, Hur, and Reba, who were the five kings of Midian. They also killed Balaam son of Beor with a sword.

⁹The Israelites captured the Midianite women and children, and they took all their flocks, herds, and goods. ¹⁰They burned all the Midianite towns where they had settled and all their camps, ¹¹but they took all the people and animals and goods. ¹²Then they brought the captives, the animals, and the goods back to Moses and Eleazar the priest and all the Israelites. Their camp was on the plains of Moab near the Jordan River, across from Jericho.

⁴⁸Then the officers of the army, the commanders of a thousand men and commanders of a hundred men, came to Moses. ⁴⁹They told Moses, "We, your servants, have counted our soldiers under our command, and not one of them is missing. ⁵⁰So we have brought the LORD a gift of the gold things that each of us found: arm bands, bracelets, signet rings, earrings, and necklaces. These are to remove our sins so we will belong to the LORD."

⁵¹So Moses and Eleazar the priest took the gold from them, which had been made into all kinds of objects. ⁵²The commanders of a thousand men and the commanders of a hundred men gave the LORD the gold, and all of it together weighed about 420 pounds; ⁵³each soldier had taken something for himself. ⁵⁴Moses and Eleazar the priest took the gold from the commanders of a thousand men and the commanders of a hundred men. Then they put it in the Meeting Tent as a memorial before the LORD for the people of Israel.

DEVOTION

TO THE VICTOR belong the spoils. It's a rule of war as ancient as the ritual of war. In the passage above, God punished the Midianites for the way they had treated the Israelites. They had attempted to cooperate with Moab in the destruction of Israel and it was time to pay. With the help of God, the battle went incredibly well for the Israelites. Not a single man from the army of Israel was killed, while the Midianite army was totally annihilated.

When the leaders of the army discovered that no man was missing, they asked every soldier to give them something from the spoils of war they had plundered. Soon, 420 pounds of gold lay at the feet of Moses by the Meeting Tent.

There was a time when God had to do battle for us, defeating our enemy Satan who held us captive for our sins. And the cost to him was dear, as Jesus had to die on the cross to claim this victory. So now, by rights, we are his captives.

But we serve an unusual king. We serve the ruler of the entire universe. When he takes captives, he does something absolutely unprecedented. Rather than asking for tribute from the captives, he give gifts to them, as Paul tells the Ephesians in the following passage: "There is one God and Father of everything. He rules everything and is everywhere and is in everything. Christ gave each one of us the special gift of grace, showing how generous he is. That is why it says in the Scriptures, 'When he went up to the heights, he led a parade of captives, and he gave gifts to people'" (Ephesians 4:6–8).

We belong to God because he won the battle over sin for us. But by his special gift of grace, we are not his captives, but his sons and daughters. And like any good Father, God gives his children gifts.

THOUGHTS TO PONDER

What are some of the gifts that God gives to us? What does it say about God that he showers gifts on us rather than demanding payment for our debt of sin?

PRAYER

Father, we see your kindness as you give us gifts out of your good mercy and grace even though we don't deserve it. Thank you for your kindness to us. Amen.

Faithful to the End

NUMBERS 32:1–24

32 The people of Reuben and Gad had large flocks and herds. When they saw that the lands of Jazer and Gilead were good for the animals, ²they came to Moses, Eleazar the priest, and the leaders of the people. ³⁻⁴They said, "We, your servants, have flocks and herds. The LORD has captured for the Israelites a land that is good for animals—the land around Ataroth, Dibon, Jazer, Nimrah, Heshbon, Elealeh, Sebam, Nebo, and Beon. ⁵If it pleases you, we would like this land to be given to us. Don't make us cross the Jordan River."

⁶Moses told the people of Gad and Reuben, "Shall your brothers go to war while you stay behind? ⁷You will discourage the Israelites from going over to the land the LORD has given them. ⁸Your ancestors did the same thing. I sent them from Kadesh Barnea to look at the land. ⁹They went as far as the Valley of Eshcol, and when they saw the land, they discouraged the Israelites from going into the land the LORD had given them. ¹⁰The LORD became very angry that day and made this promise: ¹¹'None of the people who came from Egypt and who are twenty years old or older will see the land that I promised to Abraham, Isaac, and Jacob. These people have not followed me completely. ¹²Only Caleb son of Jephunneh the Kenizzite and Joshua son of Nun followed the LORD completely.'

¹³"The LORD was angry with Israel, so he made them wander in the desert for forty years. Finally all the people who had sinned against the LORD died, ¹⁴and now you are acting just like your ancestors! You sinful people are making the LORD even more angry with Israel. ¹⁵If you quit following him, it will add to their stay in the desert, and you will destroy all these people."

¹⁶Then the Reubenites and Gadites came up to Moses and said, "We will build pens for our animals and cities for our children here. ¹⁷Then our children will be in strong, walled cities, safe from the people who live in this land. Then we will prepare for war. We will help the other Israelites get their land, ¹⁸and we will not return home until every Israelite has received his land. ¹⁹We won't take any of the land west of the Jordan River; our part of the land is east of the Jordan."

²⁰So Moses told them, "You must do these things. You must go before the LORD into battle ²¹and cross the Jordan River armed, until the LORD forces out the enemy. ²²After the LORD helps us take the land, you may return home. You will have done your duty to the LORD and Israel, and you may have this land as your own.

²³"But if you don't do these things, you will be sinning against the LORD; know for sure that you will be punished for your sin. ²⁴Build cities for your children and pens for your animals, but then you must do what you promised."

DEVOTION

WHAT DOES GOD ask of you before you receive your reward? Just as the tribes were to receive the land that had been promised to Abraham, Isaac, and Jacob so many years ago, we have been promised a home in heaven. But just as the people of Reuben and Gad had some obligations to fulfill before they could inherit their promised land, we have an obligation as well. It's found in Revelation 2:10 where John writes to the church in Smyrna: "But be faithful, even if you have to die, and I will give you the crown of life."

So simple—"be faithful"—yet so difficult—"even if you have to die"—all in one command. Part of me wants to say, "Is that all there is?" and part of me wants to so say, "Are you kidding me, that's too hard!"

Being faithful—doing what you promised you would do—has always been important to God. Remember the Sabbath. Keep the wedding vows sacred. Give to Caesar what belongs to Caesar, and to God what belongs to God.

But the interesting thing about being faithful is that, while it sounds simple, it can be so difficult. It's no surprise, then, that Jesus asked this question: "When the Son of Man comes again, will he find those on earth who believe in him?" (Luke 18:8). Jesus wants to know if the people who wear his name will be doing his will when he returns.

Here's the hard thing about faithfulness: it calls for the same behavior regardless of whether anyone is watching. But Moses wants the people of Reuben and Gad to know there is a heavenly audience for their behavior, the same one watching today. "But if you don't do these things, you will be sinning against the Lord; know for sure that you will be punished for your sin" (Numbers 32:23).

THOUGHTS TO PONDER

In what areas are you being asked to be faithful? What is the biggest challenge to living a faithful life?

PRAYER

God, we pray you will find us faithful and that we will inherit the home in heaven promised to the faithful. Amen.

NOTHING TO FEAR

JOSHUA 1:1–11, 16–18

1 After Moses, the servant of the LORD, died, the LORD spoke to Joshua son of Nun, Moses' assistant. ²The LORD said, "My servant Moses is dead. Now you and all these people go across the Jordan River into the land I am giving to the Israelites. ³I promised Moses I would give you this land, so I will give you every place you go in the land. ⁴All the land from the desert in the south to Lebanon in the north will be yours. All the land from the great river, the Euphrates, in the east, to the Mediterranean Sea in the west will be yours, too, including the land of the Hittites. ⁵No one will be able to defeat you all your life. Just as I was with Moses, so I will be with you. I will not leave you or forget you.

⁶"Joshua, be strong and brave! You must lead these people so they can take the land that I promised their fathers I would give them. ⁷Be strong and brave. Be sure to obey all the teachings my servant Moses gave you. If you follow them exactly, you will be successful in everything you do. ⁸Always remember what is written in the Book of the Teachings. Study it day and night to be sure to obey everything that is written there. If you do this, you will be wise and successful in everything. ⁹Remember that I commanded you to be strong and brave. Don't be afraid, because the LORD your God will be with you everywhere you go."

¹⁰Then Joshua gave orders to the officers of the people: ¹¹"Go through the camp and tell the people, 'Get your supplies ready. Three days from now you will cross the Jordan River and take the land the LORD your God is giving you.'"

¹⁶Then the people answered Joshua, "Anything you command us to do, we will do. Any place you send us, we will go. ¹⁷Just as we fully obeyed Moses, we will obey you. We ask only that the LORD your God be with you just as he was with Moses. ¹⁸Whoever refuses to obey your commands or turns against you will be put to death. Just be strong and brave!"

DEVOTION

THE MOST COMMON command in all Scripture is this: Don't be afraid. It occurs more than 360 times throughout the Bible, and it is the major theme of the passage above.

Be brave. Don't fear. From the shepherds who saw the angels announcing the birth of Jesus to the apostles seeing Jesus walking on the water toward their boat, the Bible is full of admonitions to not be afraid, including this admonition to Israel found in Isaiah 41:8–10:

[8]The LORD says, "People of Israel, you are my servants.
>People of Jacob, I chose you.
>You are from the family of my friend Abraham.
[9]I took you from places far away on the earth
>and called you from a faraway country.
>I said, 'You are my servants.'
>I have chosen you and have not turned against you.
[10]So don't worry, because I am with you.
>Don't be afraid, because I am your God."

I think the command to not fear is so common in Scripture because fear paralyzes us. Fear made the children of Israel reject the message of Joshua and Caleb and believe the ten spies who said the land couldn't be conquered. Now, only fear stood between Israel and their inheritance.

Even today, fear can rob Christians of their inheritance. "I was afraid and went and hid your money in the ground. Here is your bag of gold," said the servant to the master in one of the parables of Jesus (Matthew 25:25–26). Paralyzed into doing nothing other than hiding the money in the ground, the servant was called "wicked and lazy" by his master. Trying to do nothing wrong, the servant did nothing at all.

Where do we get our courage? Try this statement, recorded by Mark at the end of his Gospel: "Don't be afraid. You are looking for Jesus from Nazareth, who has been crucified. He has risen from the dead" (Mark 16:6). Once death is conquered, what else is there to fear?

THOUGHTS TO PONDER

What makes you afraid? Have you ever feared following the call of God? Have you ever been hesitant to ask his will because you feared the answer?

PRAYER

God, we pray that we will live with courage. Let us never be afraid to go wherever your will takes us. Amen.

THE RED CORD
OF SALVATION

JOSHUA 2:1–14

Read the entire story in Joshua 2:1–24.

2Joshua son of Nun secretly sent out two spies from Acacia and said to them, "Go and look at the land, particularly at the city of Jericho."

So the men went to Jericho and stayed at the house of a prostitute named Rahab.

²Someone told the king of Jericho, "Some men from Israel have come here tonight to spy out the land."

³So the king of Jericho sent this message to Rahab: "Bring out the men who came to you and entered your house. They have come to spy out our whole land."

⁴But the woman had hidden the two men. She said, "They did come here, but I didn't know where they came from. ⁵In the evening, when it was time to close the city gate, they left. I don't know where they went, but if you go quickly, maybe you can catch them." ⁶(The woman had taken the men up to the roof and had hidden them there under stalks of flax that she had spread out.) ⁷So the king's men went out looking for the spies on the road that leads to the crossings of the Jordan River. The city gate was closed just after the king's men left the city.

⁸Before the spies went to sleep for the night, Rahab went up to the roof. ⁹She said to them, "I know the LORD has given this land to your people. You frighten us very much. Everyone living in this land is terribly afraid of you ¹⁰because we have heard how the LORD dried up the Red Sea when you came out of Egypt. We have heard how you destroyed Sihon and Og, two Amorite kings who lived east of the Jordan. ¹¹When we heard this, we were very frightened. Now our men are afraid to fight you because the LORD your God rules the heavens above and the earth below! ¹²So now, promise me before the LORD that you will show kindness to my family just as I showed kindness to you. Give me some proof that you will do this. ¹³Allow my father, mother, brothers, sisters, and all of their families to live. Save us from death."

¹⁴The men agreed and said, "It will be our lives for your lives if you don't tell anyone what we are doing. When the LORD gives us the land, we will be kind and true to you."

DEVOTION

HAVE YOU EVER WONDERED how the two spies happened to be in the house of Rahab the harlot? Surely God's providence played a role, but it is likely she ran an inn where she not only housed her visitors but plied her trade as well, as was the custom of the time. As foreigners, the spies would fit in there, where almost everyone was a traveler.

But there must have been a couple of locals in the inn as well, because word quickly got to the king that Rahab was harboring spies. But Rahab's quick action to save the spies was an act of faith (Hebrews 11:31).

I see in Rahab three qualities that God saw in her when he selected her to aid the spies, and I think we need those qualities as well.

First, Rahab recognized God's messengers when they arrived. She knew they were special and hid them from the king's men, using her flax roof for cover. Who are God's messengers to you? A minister or pastor? A mentor? A friend or spouse? God's messengers come in many forms, and like Rahab, we need to recognize them when he sends them our way.

Second, Rahab realized God's power, and she knew that his power that delivered the Israelites across the Red Sea could deliver her from her life of sin. All around her in Jericho, hearts were melting and courage was in short supply, but Rahab was brave. Why? In her words: "The LORD your God rules the heavens above and the earth below!" (Joshua 2:11). That admission should be our source of courage as well. No matter what life throws at us, the God we serve is in control.

Third, Rahab saw her means of salvation, both from destruction and from her sin, and she grabbed it. Perhaps demonstrating the brassy nature of a harlot, she boldly asked to be saved for the favor she had done the spies.

God has promised to save all those who believe and follow his instructions. Christ is our "red cord" of salvation. Will you grab hold?

THOUGHTS TO PONDER

What qualities did God see in Rahab that she would be trusted with the spies? Who have you met who is making a significant impact on the world, in spite of seeming like the most unlikely candidate? How was he or she able to do it?

PRAYER

Father, we are thankful that you can use even flawed people for your tasks. Take our lives and use them for your purposes. Amen.

Tomorrow Holds Hope

JOSHUA 3:1–17

3 Early the next morning Joshua and all the Israelites left Acacia. They traveled to the Jordan River and camped there before crossing it. ²After three days the officers went through the camp ³and gave orders to the people: "When you see the priests and Levites carrying the Ark of the Agreement with the LORD your God, leave where you are and follow it. ⁴That way you will know which way to go since you have never been here before. But do not follow too closely. Stay about a thousand yards behind the Ark."

⁵Then Joshua told the people, "Make yourselves holy, because tomorrow the LORD will do amazing things among you."

⁶Joshua said to the priests, "Take the Ark of the Agreement and go ahead of the people." So the priests lifted the Ark and carried it ahead of the people.

⁷Then the LORD said to Joshua, "Today I will begin to make you great in the opinion of all the Israelites so the people will know I am with you just as I was with Moses. ⁸Tell the priests who carry the Ark of the Agreement to go to the edge of the Jordan River and stand in the water."

⁹Then Joshua said to the Israelites, "Come here and listen to the words of the LORD your God. ¹⁰Here is proof that the living God is with you and that he will force out the Canaanites, Hittites, Hivites, Perizzites, Girgashites, Amorites, and Jebusites. ¹¹The Ark of the Agreement with the Lord of the whole world will go ahead of you into the Jordan River. ¹²Now choose twelve men from among you, one from each of the twelve tribes of Israel. ¹³The priests will carry the Ark of the LORD, the Master of the whole world, into the Jordan ahead of you. When they step into the water, it will stop. The river will stop flowing and will stand up in a heap."

¹⁴So the people left the place where they had camped, and they followed the priests who carried the Ark of the Agreement across the Jordan River. ¹⁵During harvest the Jordan overflows its banks. When the priests carrying the Ark came to the edge of the river and stepped into the water, ¹⁶the water upstream stopped flowing. It stood up in a heap a great distance away at Adam, a town near Zarethan. The water flowing down to the Sea of Arabah (the Dead Sea) was completely cut off. So the people crossed the river near Jericho. ¹⁷The priests carried the Ark of the Agreement with the LORD to the middle of the river and stood there on dry ground. They waited there while all the people of Israel walked across the Jordan River on dry land.

DEVOTION

A GREAT THING ABOUT being a follower of God is that there is always the promise of a better tomorrow. Whether that promise is fulfilled here or in eternity, tomorrow holds hope for the believer.

For that reason, I love the words of Joshua to the people: "Make yourselves holy, because tomorrow the LORD will do amazing things among you." Do you realize each day for being the amazing gift of God that it is? Or does one day pretty much seem like another?

In the play *Our Town* by Thornton Wilder, Emily—the young mother who dies in childbirth—asks the Stage Manager, who is the "emcee" of the play, if she can return to earth for just a day. When he reluctantly gives in, the stage is set again for Emily to be with her mom and dad just one more time. She is fully aware she must return to the dead after just a day, but no one else is.

But within a few minutes Emily realizes that her mother and father are living the day exactly like they lived it the first time. They're oblivious to the fact that Emily will not live a long life and they fail to see each moment for the precious gift it is. She asks the Stage Manager to take her back to the cemetery long before her day is over.

Emily and the stage manager contemplate that only a small number of humans really appreciate life while they are living it.

As I write these words, it is dawn of the last day of the year. Almost universally, people will view tomorrow as something special—the turning of a page, the chance to start over. But by the time you read this passage, that New Year's Day will be long past. Did anything amazing happen?

God is willing to do amazing things, but it is up to us to recognize his works. Some days will be Jordan River crossings; some days will be waiting by the banks. But any day can be amazing if we live it God's way.

THOUGHTS TO PONDER

What is the most "amazing" thing God has done in your life or the life of a loved one lately? What are some of the amazing things in our lives that we take for granted?

PRAYER

Father, we pray that we will see the truly amazing things in the world around us and that we will see your hand in it all. Amen.

Monuments to God's Faithfulness

JOSHUA 4:1–24

4 After all the people had finished crossing the Jordan, the LORD said to Joshua, [2]"Choose twelve men from among the people, one from each tribe. [3]Tell them to get twelve rocks from the middle of the river, from where the priests stood. Carry the rocks and put them down where you stay tonight."

[4]So Joshua chose one man from each tribe. Then he called the twelve men together [5]and said to them, "Go out into the river where the Ark of the LORD your God is. Each of you bring back one rock, one for each tribe of Israel, and carry it on your shoulder. [6]They will be a sign among you. In the future your children will ask you, 'What do these rocks mean?' [7]Tell them the water stopped flowing in the Jordan when the Ark of the Agreement with the LORD crossed the river. These rocks will always remind the Israelites of this."

[8]So the Israelites obeyed Joshua and carried twelve rocks from the middle of the Jordan River, one rock for each of the twelve tribes of Israel, just as the LORD had commanded Joshua. They carried the rocks with them and put them down where they made their camp. [9]Joshua also put twelve rocks in the middle of the Jordan River where the priests had stood while carrying the Ark of the Agreement. These rocks are still there today.

[10]The priests carrying the Ark continued standing in the middle of the river until everything was done that the LORD had commanded Joshua to tell the people, just as Moses had told Joshua. The people hurried across the river. [11]After they finished crossing the river, the priests carried the Ark of the LORD to the other side as the people watched.

Editor's note: The soldiers prepared for war cross the river in verses 12–13.

[14]That day the LORD made Joshua great in the opinion of all the Israelites. They respected Joshua all his life, just as they had respected Moses.

[15]Then the LORD said to Joshua, [16]"Command the priests to bring the Ark of the Agreement out of the river."

[17]So Joshua commanded the priests, "Come up out of the Jordan."

[18]Then the priests carried the Ark of the Agreement with the LORD out of the river. As soon as their feet touched dry land, the water began flowing again. The river again overflowed its banks, just as it had before they crossed.

[19]The people crossed the Jordan on the tenth day of the first month and camped at Gilgal, east of Jericho. [20]They carried with them the twelve rocks taken from the Jordan, and Joshua set them up at Gilgal. [21]Then he spoke to the Israelites: "In the future your children will ask you, 'What do these rocks mean?' [22]Tell them, 'Israel

crossed the Jordan River on dry land. ²³The LORD your God caused the water to stop flowing until you finished crossing it, just as the LORD did to the Red Sea. He stopped the water until we crossed it. ²⁴The LORD did this so all people would know he has great power and so you would always respect the LORD your God.'"

DEVOTION

IF YOU SPEND enough time in the mountains, you realize that every pile of rocks means something. Air is too thin and energy too precious for wasting breath and energy creating meaningless piles of rocks.

There are the piles of rocks that mark the trail for those who will follow behind. Hiker tradition is that you add one rock to the pile, or if you find it toppled, you repair it. Circles of rocks denote past campfires. You can find rock piles that cover a hole, perhaps burrowed by an animal, so that future hikers will not sprain or break an ankle. Then there are stepping stones, large and flat on top, to help hikers cross a stream, too perfect to be an accident of nature.

Every pile of rocks in the wild sends a message. Here's the way to walk. Here's a spot to avoid. Here's a path across rushing waters.

So the command to Joshua makes sense. God is going to perform a wonderful act tomorrow and he wants a monument of the event left for future generations. These twelve large river stones stacked into an altar would stand out unmistakably from their surroundings and provoke the inevitable question: "What does this mean?"

Notice that the text says *when* your children ask, not *if* they ask. The writer assumes the curiosity of a child, what educators call "teachable moments." Christian parents must be ready for teachable moments, even to the point of creating them. Even today, our family monuments point the way to faith for our children.

THOUGHTS TO PONDER

What are the "monuments" in your family that cause a child to ask, "What is the meaning of this?" Have you made a point of documenting for your children the times that God has delivered you from illness? Financial problems? Other issues?

PRAYER

Father, thank you for parting the waters of the many problems we face in life. Help us to make monuments to your power in our lives so that others might ask about you. Amen.

God's Mark on Us

JOSHUA 5:1–15

5 All the kings of the Amorites west of the Jordan and the Canaanite kings living by the Mediterranean Sea heard that the LORD dried up the Jordan River until the Israelites had crossed it. After that they were scared and too afraid to face the Israelites.

²At that time the LORD said to Joshua, "Make knives from flint stones and circumcise the Israelites." ³So Joshua made knives from flint stones and circumcised the Israelites at Gibeath Haaraloth.

⁴This is why Joshua circumcised the men: After the Israelites left Egypt, all the men old enough to serve in the army died in the desert on the way out of Egypt. ⁵The men who had come out of Egypt had been circumcised, but none of those who were born in the desert on the trip from Egypt had been circumcised. ⁶The Israelites had moved about in the desert for forty years. During that time all the fighting men who had left Egypt had died because they had not obeyed the LORD. So the LORD swore they would not see the land he had promised their ancestors to give them, a fertile land. ⁷Their sons took their places. But none of the sons born on the trip from Egypt had been circumcised, so Joshua circumcised them. ⁸After all the Israelites had been circumcised, they stayed in camp until they were healed.

⁹Then the LORD said to Joshua, "As slaves in Egypt you were ashamed, but today I have removed that shame." So Joshua named that place Gilgal, which it is still named today.

¹⁰The people of Israel were camped at Gilgal on the plains of Jericho. It was there, on the evening of the fourteenth day of the month, they celebrated the Passover Feast. ¹¹The day after the Passover, the people ate food grown on that land: bread made without yeast and roasted grain. ¹²The day they ate this food, the manna stopped coming. The Israelites no longer got the manna from heaven. They ate the food grown in the land of Canaan that year.

¹³Joshua was near Jericho when he looked up and saw a man standing in front of him with a sword in his hand. Joshua went to him and asked, "Are you a friend or an enemy?"

¹⁴The man answered, "I am neither. I have come as the commander of the LORD's army."

Then Joshua bowed facedown on the ground and asked, "Does my master have a command for me, his servant?"

¹⁵The commander of the LORD's army answered, "Take off your sandals, because the place where you are standing is holy." So Joshua did.

DEVOTION

BY THE TIME this seemingly insignificant (but truly important) story starts, the enemies of Israel had lost their courage to fight. They had heard about how Jehovah dried up the Jordan to let the Israelites cross over on dry land; perhaps their spies had even seen it happen.

With the lull in fighting, it was time to return to God's laws given when he freed them from slavery in Egypt. Circumcision—which dated back to God's agreement with Abraham to give his descendents the very land in which they were now standing—had been abandoned for forty years. As part of putting years of bondage, wandering, and fighting behind them, it was necessary to return to God's Law . . . and that meant a return to circumcision.

If the act of circumcision had been ignored for forty years, it is probable that the teaching of its significance had been ignored as well. No one alive had heard God's promise to Abraham. Faced with the prospect of the flint knife, it's a completely logical response to ask, *Why? What in the world does something so personal have to do with my agreement with God?*

But God's ways are not my ways. His wisdom is not my wisdom. And he still makes requests of his people today that are counterintuitive to our wisdom. That's what Jesus did. Want to be first? Try being the last, he told the apostles. Want eternal life? Give all you have to the poor, he told the rich young ruler. Hard words for those who heard them; hard words for us today.

On the day he rewrote the tablets holding the Ten Commandments, God requested that his people give themselves completely to serving God (Deuteronomy 10:16), an act of commitment far greater than the ritual of circumcision. From the Israelites, the crowds who followed Jesus, and now me, God asks, "May I put my mark on you? Can I look into your heart and cut out envy? Lust? Pride?"

Allow him to change your heart, and the promise made to Israel will be yours: he will roll away the reproach of your past.

THOUGHTS TO PONDER

In what way are you different because you claim to be a follower of God? What is your "mark" that God has placed on you? What is your response when the commands of God seem to make no sense to you?

PRAYER

God, help us to be like the children of Israel who obeyed your command and fulfilled the agreement so long ago. Help us live in an agreement relationship with you all the days of our lives. Amen.

VICTORY COMES FROM GOD

JOSHUA 6:1–21

6The people of Jericho were afraid because the Israelites were near. They closed the city gates and guarded them. No one went into the city, and no one came out. ²Then the LORD said to Joshua, "Look, I have given you Jericho, its king, and all its fighting men. ³March around the city with your army once a day for six days. ⁴Have seven priests carry trumpets made from horns of male sheep and have them march in front of the Ark. On the seventh day march around the city seven times and have the priests blow the trumpets as they march. ⁵They will make one long blast on the trumpets. When you hear that sound, have all the people give a loud shout. Then the walls of the city will fall so the people can go straight into the city."

⁶So Joshua son of Nun called the priests together and said to them, "Carry the Ark of the Agreement. Tell seven priests to carry trumpets and march in front of it." ⁷Then Joshua ordered the people, "Now go! March around the city. The soldiers with weapons should march in front of the Ark of the Agreement with the LORD."

⁸When Joshua finished speaking to the people, the seven priests began marching before the LORD. They carried the seven trumpets and blew them as they marched. The priests carrying the Ark of the Agreement with the LORD followed them. ⁹Soldiers with weapons marched in front of the priests, and armed men walked behind the Ark. The priests were blowing their trumpets. ¹⁰But Joshua had told the people not to give a war cry. He said, "Don't shout. Don't say a word until the day I tell you. Then shout." ¹¹So Joshua had the Ark of the LORD carried around the city one time. Then they went back to camp for the night.

¹²Early the next morning Joshua got up, and the priests carried the Ark of the LORD again. ¹³The seven priests carried the seven trumpets and marched in front of the Ark of the LORD, blowing their trumpets. Soldiers with weapons marched in front of them, and other soldiers walked behind the Ark of the LORD. All this time the priests were blowing their trumpets. ¹⁴So on the second day they marched around the city one time and then went back to camp. They did this every day for six days.

¹⁵On the seventh day they got up at dawn and marched around the city, just as they had on the days before. But on that day they marched around the city seven times. ¹⁶The seventh time around the priests blew their trumpets. Then Joshua gave the command: "Now, shout! The LORD has given you this city! ¹⁷The city and everything in it are to be destroyed as an offering to the LORD. Only Rahab the prostitute and everyone in her house should remain alive. They must not be killed, because Rahab hid the two spies we sent out. ¹⁸Don't take any of the

things that are to be destroyed as an offering to the LORD. If you take them and bring them into our camp, you yourselves will be destroyed, and you will bring trouble to all of Israel. [19]All the silver and gold and things made from bronze and iron belong to the LORD and must be saved for him."

[20]When the priests blew the trumpets, the people shouted. At the sound of the trumpets and the people's shout, the walls fell, and everyone ran straight into the city. So the Israelites defeated that city. [21]They completely destroyed with the sword every living thing in the city—men and women, young and old, cattle, sheep, and donkeys.

DEVOTION

IT APPEARS THAT only Joshua knew the full instructions from God. The others took instructions and followed orders. If you think about it, the plan for defeating the great city of Jericho made little sense and required great faith. Marching around the wall of the city day after day put both the priests and the soldiers at risk of being killed by the soldiers of Jericho guarding the way.

Why? Perhaps God wanted to put the army in the most vulnerable position possible—right below the enemy—to show Israel that he planned to protect them. Not only in this battle, but in all the battles to come until the land God promised was at last in their possession. So God begins with a victory in the most dramatic fashion possible, proving that the victories would not come from military might but from trust in God. And God not only takes care of his people as a whole; he takes care of them individually, as demonstrated by the fact that Rahab is saved for her act of kindness to the spies.

THOUGHTS TO PONDER

In what ways has God shown his protection for you? In what ways has he asked you to step out in faith like the army of Israel marching below the walls of Jericho?

PRAYER

God, help us to remember that your ways are the right ways and that you call on us to obey, even when we might not understand. Give us the maturity to reach that point in our lives. Amen.

THROW AWAY SIN

JOSHUA 7:1-15

7But the Israelites did not obey the LORD. There was a man from the tribe of Judah named Achan. (He was the son of Carmi and grandson of Zabdi, who was the son of Zerah.) Because Achan kept some of the things that were to be given to the LORD, the LORD became very angry at the Israelites.

²Joshua sent some men from Jericho to Ai, which was near Beth Aven, east of Bethel. He told them, "Go to Ai and spy out the area." So the men went to spy on Ai.

³Later they came back to Joshua and said, "There are only a few people in Ai, so we will not need all our people to defeat them. Send only two or three thousand men to fight. There is no need to send all of our people." ⁴So about three thousand men went up to Ai, but the people of Ai beat them badly. ⁵The people of Ai killed about thirty-six Israelites and then chased the rest from the city gate all the way down to the canyon, killing them as they went down the hill. When the Israelites saw this, they lost their courage.

⁶Then Joshua tore his clothes in sorrow. He bowed facedown on the ground before the Ark of the LORD and stayed there until evening. The leaders of Israel did the same thing. They also threw dirt on their heads to show their sorrow. ⁷Then Joshua said, "Lord GOD, you brought our people across the Jordan River. Why did you bring us this far and then let the Amorites destroy us? We would have been happy to stay on the other side of the Jordan. ⁸Lord, there is nothing I can say now. Israel has been beaten by the enemy. ⁹The Canaanites and all the other people in this country will hear about this and will surround and kill us all! Then what will you do for your own great name?"

¹⁰The LORD said to Joshua, "Stand up! Why are you down on your face? ¹¹The Israelites have sinned; they have broken the agreement I commanded them to obey. They took some of the things I commanded them to destroy. They have stolen and lied and have taken those things for themselves. ¹²That is why the Israelites cannot face their enemies. They turn away from the fight and run, because I have commanded that they be destroyed. I will not help you anymore unless you destroy everything as I commanded you.

¹³"Now go! Make the people holy. Tell them, 'Set yourselves apart to the LORD for tomorrow. The LORD, the God of Israel, says some of you are keeping things he commanded you to destroy. You will never defeat your enemies until you throw away those things.

¹⁴" 'Tomorrow morning you must be present with your tribes. The LORD will choose one tribe to stand alone before him. Then the LORD will choose one family group from that tribe to stand before him. Then the LORD will choose one

family from that family group to stand before him, person by person. [15]The one who is keeping what should have been destroyed will himself be destroyed by fire. Everything he owns will be destroyed with him. He has broken the agreement with the LORD and has done a disgraceful thing among the people of Israel!' "

DEVOTION

IF THE POWER to defeat the enemy came from the Lord, then he could remove that power as well. Although the number of Israelite soldiers vastly outnumbered the small town of Ai, Israel was defeated badly, suffering its first casualties of the mission to gain the Promised Land. And it was all because a man named Achan took contraband from Jericho.

Put yourself in Joshua's place. The stakes couldn't have been higher. Show weakness, and the enemies of Israel will surround them and annihilate them. Try again, and without God's help, they would never defeat even the most minor of towns. So Joshua tears his clothes and throws himself to the ground in frustration.

God tells Joshua of the sin that has caused the problem, saying, "You will never defeat your enemies until you throw away these things."

The words are still true today. As I fight my old enemy, Satan, there are things I have to throw away in my life. If I am to defeat Satan, I have to throw away pride and greed and all the other things I've picked up from the world that don't belong in the life of a Christian. Only then can I set myself apart for God, as the people of Israel were commanded to do.

THOUGHTS TO PONDER

Why do you think God punished the entire nation for the sins of one individual? What does this say about the nature of God? What does it say about the nature of Israel as his chosen people?

PRAYER

God, help us remember that the things we think are hidden deep within our lives are visible to your eyes. We know that our sin can impact those that we love, so we pray that you would help us remove it. Amen.

The Same Inside and Out

JOSHUA 7:16—8:2

¹⁶Early the next morning Joshua led all of Israel to present themselves in their tribes, and the LORD chose the tribe of Judah. ¹⁷So the family groups of Judah presented themselves, and the LORD then chose the family group of Zerah. When all the families of Zerah presented themselves, the family of Zabdi was chosen. ¹⁸And Joshua told all the men in that family to present themselves. The LORD chose Achan son of Carmi. (Carmi was the son of Zabdi, who was the son of Zerah.)

¹⁹Then Joshua said to Achan, "My son, tell the truth. Confess to the LORD, the God of Israel. Tell me what you did, and don't try to hide anything from me."

²⁰Achan answered, "It is true! I have sinned against the LORD, the God of Israel. This is what I did: ²¹Among the things I saw was a beautiful coat from Babylonia and about five pounds of silver and more than one and one-fourth pounds of gold. I wanted these things very much for myself, so I took them. You will find them buried in the ground under my tent, with the silver underneath."

²²So Joshua sent men who ran to the tent and found the things hidden there, with the silver. ²³The men brought them out of the tent, took them to Joshua and all the Israelites, and spread them out on the ground before the LORD. ²⁴Then Joshua and all the people led Achan son of Zerah to the Valley of Trouble. They also took the silver, the coat, the gold, Achan's sons, daughters, cattle, donkeys, sheep, tent, and everything he owned. ²⁵Joshua said, "I don't know why you caused so much trouble for us, but now the LORD will bring trouble to you." Then all the people threw stones at Achan and his family until they died. Then the people burned them. ²⁶They piled rocks over Achan's body, and they are still there today. That is why it is called the Valley of Trouble. After this the LORD was no longer angry.

8 Then the LORD said to Joshua, "Don't be afraid or give up. Lead all your fighting men to Ai. I will help you defeat the king of Ai, his people, his city, and his land. ²You will do to Ai and its king what you did to Jericho and its king. Only this time you may take all the wealth and keep it for yourselves. Now tell some of your soldiers to set up an ambush behind the city."

DEVOTION

FOLLOWING THE ORDERS of God, Joshua goes through the elimination of all the people from tribes to families to individuals, until Achan is identified as the cause of Israel's problems. Even though God knew the culprit, this most public display was undoubtedly staged to get the attention of the entire nation about the seriousness of God's commands.

One of the most interesting parts of the story above is when the contraband Achan stole from Jericho—a coat, some gold, and some silver—was laid it out on the ground before God. I don't think there is a better metaphor for sin in the entire Bible than Achan's stolen goods being laid out before God. Even if I never have my sins laid bare in public like Achan, they are laid bare before God. He knows where I have hidden sin in my life, even if I have managed to keep it a secret from others.

Achan's sin affected his entire family and the nation as a whole. It was a costly sin. Many men were killed in battle. Widows and orphans were created because of Achan's sin. His family was stoned and burned because of Achan's greed.

Even today we see sins that destroy an entire family. One parent gets caught up in an adulterous affair and the children suffer the effects of the divorce. A greedy spouse embezzles at work and the entire family suffers the effects of the legal problems it causes.

I once saw a young man answer the invitation, or altar call, of a local church. He requested the prayers of the assembled group, and in his request for prayer, he said, "Pray for me that I'll be the same person on the inside that I appear to be on the outside."

I think that's an excellent aspiration for all of us. That lack of true character was definitely Achan's downfall in this story. Be the person on the inside that you appear to be on the outside—a good goal for today.

THOUGHTS TO PONDER

If Achan had known the consequences of his sin, do you think he would have continued with it? What are some of the foreseeable consequences of the activities in your life that you have managed to hide so far?

PRAYER

God, we've betrayed you for far less than a few coins and a coat. Forgive us when we betray you, and give us strength to be the same people in public that we are in private. Amen.

BY THEIR OWN MIGHT

JOSHUA 8:3–22

³So Joshua led his whole army toward Ai. Then he chose thirty thousand of his best fighting men and sent them out at night. ⁴Joshua gave them these orders: "Listen carefully. You must set up an ambush behind the city. Don't go far from it, but continue to watch and be ready. ⁵I and the men who are with me will march toward the city, and the men in the city will come out to fight us, just as they did before. Then we will turn and run away from them. ⁶They will chase us away from the city, thinking we are running away from them as we did before. When we run away, ⁷come out from your ambush and take the city. The LORD your God will give you the power to win. ⁸After you take the city, burn it. See to it! You have your orders."

⁹Then Joshua sent them to wait in ambush between Bethel and Ai, to the west of Ai. But Joshua stayed the night with his people.

¹⁰Early the next morning Joshua gathered his men together. He and the older leaders of Israel led them up to Ai. ¹¹All of the soldiers who were with Joshua marched up to Ai and stopped in front of the city and made camp north of it. There was a valley between them and the city. ¹²Then Joshua chose about five thousand men and set them in ambush in the area west of the city between Bethel and Ai. ¹³So the people took their positions; the main camp was north of the city, and the other men were hiding to the west. That night Joshua went down into the valley.

¹⁴Now when the king of Ai saw the army of Israel, he and his people got up early the next morning and hurried out to fight them. They went out to a place east of the city, but the king did not know soldiers were waiting in ambush behind the city. ¹⁵Joshua and all the men of Israel let the army of Ai push them back. Then they ran toward the desert. ¹⁶The men in Ai were called to chase Joshua and his men, so they left the city and went after them. ¹⁷All the men of Ai and Bethel chased the army of Israel. The city was left open; not a man stayed to protect it.

¹⁸Then the LORD said to Joshua, "Hold your spear toward Ai, because I will give you that city." So Joshua held his spear toward the city of Ai. ¹⁹When the Israelites who were in ambush saw this, they quickly came out of their hiding place and hurried toward the city. They entered the city, took control of it, and quickly set it on fire.

²⁰When the men of Ai looked back, they saw smoke rising from their city. At the same time the Israelites stopped running and turned against the men of Ai, who could not escape in any direction. ²¹When Joshua and all his men saw that the army had taken control of the city and saw the smoke rising from it, they stopped running and turned to fight the men of Ai. ²²The men who were in ambush also came out of the city to help with the fight. So the men of Ai were caught between the armies of Israel. None of the enemy escaped.

DEVOTION

ALTHOUGH GOD HAS given the city of Ai to the Israelites, it is up to Joshua to handle the military operation, and in this story we see some of the genius he possessed that made him God's choice to follow Moses as the leader of Israel.

The different outcomes of the two battles for Ai teach a stark lesson to us today. When we operate outside of God's will, he will not bless our plans. But when we get the stain of sin out of our lives, he blesses our plans. The difference in the two battles is not the difference in the size of the army, though Joshua takes ten times as many men for the second effort to take the city. The difference is in the power of the Lord to deliver the enemy into the hands of Israel.

It's a lesson Israel would need to learn repeatedly in the years to come. The lesson of Ai was not learned permanently so it would have to be learned repeatedly.

The question is whether we will learn the lesson of Ai. God blesses those who honor him with their lives and resists those who try to fight their battles by their own might.

THOUGHTS TO PONDER

Have you ever had to learn "the lesson of Ai" in your own life? That is, has God ever said "no" to you at first, and then said "yes" to you later? What was the difference? Are there currently any closed doors in your life that might be opened if you align yourself with God's will?

PRAYER

God, we pray that we will never make plans outside your will. Defeat us when we run counter to your will and bless us when we do your will. Amen.

DEPEND ON GOD

JOSHUA 9:3–23

³When the people of Gibeon heard how Joshua had defeated Jericho and Ai, ⁴they decided to trick the Israelites. They gathered old sacks and old leather wine bags that were cracked and mended, and they put them on the backs of their donkeys. ⁵They put old sandals on their feet and wore old clothes, and they took some dry, moldy bread. ⁶Then they went to Joshua in the camp near Gilgal.

The men said to Joshua and the Israelites, "We have traveled from a faraway country. Make a peace agreement with us."

⁷The Israelites said to these Hivites, "Maybe you live near us. How can we make a peace agreement with you?"

⁸The Hivites said to Joshua, "We are your servants."

But Joshua asked, "Who are you? Where do you come from?"

⁹The men answered, "We are your servants who have come from a far country, because we heard of the fame of the LORD your God. We heard about what he has done and everything he did in Egypt. ¹⁰We heard that he defeated the two kings of the Amorites from the east side of the Jordan River—Sihon king of Heshbon and Og king of Bashan who ruled in Ashtaroth. ¹¹So our elders and our people said to us, 'Take food for your journey and go and meet the Israelites. Tell them, "We are your servants. Make a peace agreement with us."'

¹²"Look at our bread. On the day we left home to come to you it was warm and fresh, but now it is dry and moldy. ¹³Look at our leather wine bags. They were new and filled with wine, but now they are cracked and old. Our clothes and sandals are worn out from the long journey."

¹⁴The men of Israel tasted the bread, but they did not ask the LORD what to do. ¹⁵So Joshua agreed to make peace with the Gibeonites and to let them live. And the leaders of the Israelites swore an oath to keep the agreement.

¹⁶Three days after they had made the agreement, the Israelites learned that the Gibeonites lived nearby. ¹⁷So the Israelites went to where they lived and on the third day came to their cities: Gibeon, Kephirah, Beeroth, and Kiriath Jearim. ¹⁸But the Israelites did not attack those cities, because they had made a promise to them before the LORD, the God of Israel.

All the Israelites grumbled against the leaders. ¹⁹But the leaders answered, "We have given our promise before the LORD, the God of Israel, so we cannot attack them now. ²⁰This is what we must do. We must let them live. Otherwise, God's anger will be against us for breaking the oath we swore to them. ²¹So let them live, but they will cut wood and carry water for our people." So the leaders kept their promise to them.

²²Joshua called for the Gibeonites and asked, "Why did you lie to us? Your

241

land was near our camp, but you told us you were from a far country. ²³Now, you will be placed under a curse to be our slaves. You will have to cut wood and carry water for the house of my God."

DEVOTION

THE PLAN WAS as ingenious as it was devious. The leaders of Gibeon set out to get a promise from the nation of Israel that they would not attack their cities by pretending that they were from far away when in reality they lived right in the path of the Israelites conquest.

The folly of the Israelites began when they relied on their own intuition and neglected to ask God what to do with these strangers. In a day when an oath was as binding as a contract, the shrewd Gibeonites extracted a promise from Joshua and the leaders of Israel that they would leave their cities intact. And even after the ruse was discovered, the Israelites had no remedy to go back on the promise. They could only make slaves of them, not destroy them.

Just as he did with Israel, God will let me make mistakes. It's called free will. But he will give success to those who call on him, the writer of Proverbs reminds us, "Trust the LORD with all your heart, and don't depend on your own understanding. Remember the LORD in all you do, and he will give you success" (Proverbs 3:5–6).

We don't have to repeat the mistake of the Israelites. God stands ready to help those who don't depend on their own understanding. Like a longsuffering parent, God will help his children when they ask.

THOUGHTS TO PONDER

Have you ever been fooled by anyone? How did you feel? When he realized he had been fooled, what does Joshua's response tell you about his character?

PRAYER

God, we so often make our plans and our alliances without first consulting you. Help us break that habit and come to rely on you more often in our lives and in our choices. Amen.

POWERFUL PRAYER

JOSHUA 10:1–15

10At this time Adoni-Zedek king of Jerusalem heard that Joshua had defeated Ai and completely destroyed it, as he had also done to Jericho and its king. The king also learned that the Gibeonites had made a peace agreement with Israel and that they lived nearby. ²Adoni-Zedek and his people were very afraid because of this. Gibeon was not a little town like Ai; it was a large city, as big as a city that had a king, and all its men were good fighters. ³So Adoni-Zedek king of Jerusalem sent a message to Hoham king of Hebron, Piram king of Jarmuth, Japhia king of Lachish, and Debir king of Eglon. He begged them, ⁴"Come with me and help me attack Gibeon, which has made a peace agreement with Joshua and the Israelites."

⁵Then these five Amorite kings—the kings of Jerusalem, Hebron, Jarmuth, Lachish, and Eglon—gathered their armies, went to Gibeon, surrounded it, and attacked it.

⁶The Gibeonites sent this message to Joshua in his camp at Gilgal: "Don't let us, your servants, be destroyed. Come quickly and help us! Save us! All the Amorite kings from the mountains have joined their armies and are fighting against us."

⁷So Joshua marched out of Gilgal with his whole army, including his best fighting men. ⁸The LORD said to Joshua, "Don't be afraid of those armies, because I will hand them over to you. None of them will be able to stand against you."

⁹Joshua and his army marched all night from Gilgal for a surprise attack. ¹⁰The LORD confused those armies when Israel attacked, so Israel defeated them in a great victory at Gibeon. They chased them along the road going up to Beth Horon and killed men all the way to Azekah and Makkedah. ¹¹As they chased the enemy down the Beth Horon Pass to Azekah, the LORD threw large hailstones on them from the sky and killed them. More people were killed by the hailstones than by the Israelites' swords.

¹²On the day that the LORD gave up the Amorites to the Israelites, Joshua stood before all the people of Israel and said to the LORD:

"Sun, stand still over Gibeon.

Moon, stand still over the Valley of Aijalon."

¹³So the sun stood still,

and the moon stopped

until the people defeated their enemies.

These words are written in the Book of Jashar.

The sun stopped in the middle of the sky and waited to go down for a full day. ¹⁴That has never happened at any time before that day or since. That was the day the LORD listened to a human being. Truly the LORD was fighting for Israel!

¹⁵After this, Joshua and his army went back to the camp at Gilgal.

DEVOTION

NO SOONER HAD the nation of Israel made a pact with the Gibeonites, allowing them to be servants of Israel rather than putting them to the sword, than they had to defend their new slaves. Five Amorite kings, afraid of the power of Gibeon, conspired to attack them. Joshua was now forced to protect his newly acquired servants.

But God was going to be fighting on this day, and his weapons would be the forces of nature at his disposal. The text tells us that the hailstones sent by God killed more than the swords of the Israelites. Then God, prompted by a request from Joshua, did something he had never done before and hasn't done since: he stopped the sun to allow for a longer day.

There's a wonderful sentence embedded in this story. We're told, "That was the day the Lord listened to a human being" (Joshua 10:14). Even though he hasn't made the sun stand still for us, or rained down hailstones on our enemies, God still listens to his people today. Through the avenue of prayer, God listens, and through the avenue of his word, God speaks.

So keen is God to listen to you that he even sent his Holy Spirit to pray with you and for you when you no longer have the words to talk with him. As Paul tells the believers in Rome, "the Spirit helps us with our weakness. We do not know how to pray as we should. But the Spirit himself speaks to God for us, even begs God for us with deep feelings that words cannot explain" (Romans 8:26).

Prayer is a great gift of God. James tells his readers, "When a believing person prays, great things happen" (James 5:16). I may not be able to pray and stop the sun in its tracks, but I can pray and stop sin in its tracks and that's a powerful thing.

THOUGHTS TO PONDER

When has God heard your prayers and helped you in your life? Did you recognize it at the time? Did you remember to thank him?

PRAYER

God, you have all power over the universe, including the sun, moon, and stars. Yet you are mindful of us. We worship your majesty today. Amen.

OUR GOD WILL FIGHT FOR US

JOSHUA 10:28–43

Read the entire story in Judges 10:16—12:24.

²⁸That day Joshua defeated Makkedah. He killed the king and completely destroyed all the people in that city as an offering to the LORD; no one was left alive. He did the same thing to the king of Makkedah that he had done to the king of Jericho.

²⁹Joshua and all the Israelites traveled from Makkedah to Libnah and attacked it. ³⁰The LORD handed over the city and its king. They killed every person in the city; no one was left alive. And they did the same thing to that king that they had done to the king of Jericho.

³¹Then Joshua and all the Israelites left Libnah and went to Lachish, which they surrounded and attacked. ³²The LORD handed over Lachish on the second day. The Israelites killed everyone in that city just as they had done to Libnah. ³³During this same time Horam king of Gezer came to help Lachish, but Joshua also defeated him and his army; no one was left alive.

³⁴Then Joshua and all the Israelites went from Lachish to Eglon. They surrounded Eglon, attacked it, and ³⁵captured it the same day. They killed all its people and completely destroyed everything in it as an offering to the LORD, just as they had done to Lachish.

³⁶Then Joshua and the Israelites went from Eglon to Hebron and attacked it, ³⁷capturing it and all the little towns near it. The Israelites killed everyone in Hebron; no one was left alive there. Just as they had done to Eglon, they completely destroyed the city and all its people as an offering to the LORD.

³⁸Then Joshua and the Israelites went back to Debir and attacked it. ³⁹They captured that city, its king, and all the little towns near it, completely destroying everyone in Debir as an offering to the LORD; no one was left alive there. Israel did to Debir and its king just as they had done to Libnah and its king, just as they had done to Hebron.

⁴⁰So Joshua defeated all the kings of the cities of these areas: the mountains, southern Canaan, the western hills, and the slopes. The LORD, the God of Israel, had told Joshua to completely destroy all the people as an offering to the LORD, so he left no one alive in those places. ⁴¹Joshua captured all the cities from Kadesh Barnea to Gaza, and from Goshen to Gibeon. ⁴²He captured all these cities and their kings on one trip, because the LORD, the God of Israel, was fighting for Israel.

⁴³Then Joshua and all the Israelites returned to their camp at Gilgal.

DEVOTION

WE HAVE NO extrabiblical record of these kings or kingdoms, though most of them were probably city-nations with just enough land to support their people. Joshua, moving from south to north completely annihilates the enemy and captures the land to be given to the tribes of Israel.

Although we do not know how long the conquest took, we do know that Joshua is now old and that he has led in the conquest of thirty-one kings (Judges 13:1). In virtually every one of the cities, all of the people were destroyed as an offering to God. At the end of the battles above, which included the hill country of southern Canaan, we get this reminder: "the God of Israel was fighting for Israel." It's a repeat of the promise that Moses made to the people as they quaked in fear at the sight of the chariots of the king pursuing them after they had fled Egypt. "You only need to remain calm; the LORD will fight for you," Moses told them (Exodus 14:14).

What a wonderful thought—in our warfare against Satan, God is right there in the trenches with us. That is why Paul could tell his readers in Corinth, "We do live in the world, but we do not fight in the same way the world fights. We fight with weapons that are different from those the world uses. Our weapons have power from God that can destroy the enemy's strong places" (2 Corinthians 10:3–4).

God not only fights for us; he gives us the equipment we need in the spiritual battles we fight each day. This is why Paul encourages his readers in Ephesus to "be strong in the Lord and in his great power. Put on the full armor of God so that you can fight against the devil's evil tricks" (Ephesians 6:10–11). Protected by our God-given armor, we can proclaim like Nehemiah did to the men rebuilding the wall of Jerusalem: "Our God will fight for us" (Nehemiah 4:20).

THOUGHTS TO PONDER

What does it mean for God to fight for us? When have you felt a divine hand in your battle against sin? How do we enlist God in our battle against Satan?

PRAYER

God, we know you will help us in our battles as you helped the children of Israel long ago. Help us to feel your protection today. Amen.

HILL COUNTRY

JOSHUA 14:6–15

⁶One day some men from the tribe of Judah went to Joshua at Gilgal. Among them was Caleb son of Jephunneh the Kenizzite. He said to Joshua, "You remember what the LORD said at Kadesh Barnea when he was speaking to the prophet Moses about you and me. ⁷Moses, the LORD's servant, sent me to look at the land where we were going. I was forty years old then. When I came back, I told Moses what I thought about the land. ⁸The other men who went with me frightened the people, but I fully believed the LORD would allow us to take the land. ⁹So that day Moses promised me, 'The land where you went will become your land, and your children will own it forever. I will give you that land because you fully believed in the LORD, my God.'

¹⁰"Now then, the LORD has kept his promise. He has kept me alive for forty-five years from the time he said this to Moses during the time we all wandered in the desert. Now here I am, eighty-five years old. ¹¹I am still as strong today as I was the day Moses sent me out, and I am just as ready to fight now as I was then. ¹²So give me the mountain country the LORD promised me that day long ago. Back then you heard that the Anakite people lived there and the cities were large and well protected. But now with the LORD helping me, I will force them out, just as the LORD said."

¹³Joshua blessed Caleb son of Jephunneh and gave him the city of Hebron as his own. ¹⁴Hebron still belongs to the family of Caleb son of Jephunneh the Kenizzite because he had faith and obeyed the LORD, the God of Israel. ¹⁵(In the past it was called Kiriath Arba, named for Arba, the greatest man among the Anakites.)

After this there was peace in the land.

DEVOTION

CAN YOU IMAGINE waiting forty-five years for the fulfillment of a promise? Could you be as single-minded as Caleb, wanting the same thing at age eighty-five as you did at age forty?

Caleb had been one of the twelve spies sent into the land of Canaan by Moses (see Numbers 13) to scout the land God was going to give to the Israelites. The twelve men spent forty days living off the bounty of the land and spying on its people. But even though God had promised them the land, ten of the twelve spies gave negative reports to Moses, and the people believed them. Only Joshua and Caleb believed that the Israelites could take the land.

So the children of Israel were forced to wander the desert for forty years—one year for every day the spies were in Canaan—until all the adults who had left Egyptian bondage had died. But Moses had promised Caleb the land he had seen. Because of their faithfulness, Caleb and Joshua would live long enough to enter the land.

I love this statement: "I am as strong today as I was the day Moses sent me out." Here was Caleb—the oldest man in the nation—wanting to keep fighting even while everyone else was thinking about settling into their new land. Imagine an eighty-five-year-old man ready to go to war.

I've been on the Washington, D.C., mall on Memorial Day making my way between the various war memorials—World War II, Korea, Vietnam. At every turn I saw veterans proudly wearing their uniforms, ready to talk about the war with total strangers. These were men in their sixties, seventies and eighties. Some of them stretched the buttons of their well-worn uniforms. Some of them propped themselves up with canes. A few were stooped.

But as I saw these men and listened, I could imagine the young man behind those years, and I could see old men who were ready even at that moment to defend their country if asked. The bodies had changed, but the fierce love of country and freedom hadn't dimmed a bit. They were modern day "Calebs."

Caleb had been promised the hill country and now was the time to claim that promise. It wouldn't be easy. The army of Israel had left it occupied by the heathen nations. Mountainous land is the hardest to capture. The fortified enemy had the high ground, and Caleb would be facing an "uphill battle" to claim his promised land.

Those of us who claim to be Christians are at war also, and we must never tire of carrying out the battle. Our fight is with Satan, and it sometimes seems that this battle is an uphill one for all of us.

I've been a Christian for about as long as Caleb had been waiting for his land. But the battle against sin is still going on in my life, just like it's going on in yours. But the longer I fight, the more the victories outnumber the defeats.

I have the same weapon against Satan that Caleb had against the fortified cities—the Lord's help. Caleb would use that help to force the inhabitants out who held claim to his promised land. We call on the help of the Lord to loose the claims of Satan on us, his children of the promise.

THOUGHTS TO PONDER

What is the one thing you have hoped for longer than anything else? What keeps your hope alive?

PRAYER

Almighty God, we pray you will be with us when we face the "hill country" in our own lives and that you will give us the victory. Amen.

Salvation Only through God

JOSHUA 24:14–29

[14]Then Joshua said to the people, "Now respect the LORD and serve him fully and sincerely. Throw away the gods that your ancestors worshiped on the other side of the Euphrates River and in Egypt. Serve the LORD. [15]But if you don't want to serve the LORD, you must choose for yourselves today whom you will serve. You may serve the gods that your ancestors worshiped when they lived on the other side of the Euphrates River, or you may serve the gods of the Amorites who lived in this land. As for me and my family, we will serve the LORD."

[16]Then the people answered, "We will never stop following the LORD to serve other gods! [17]It was the LORD our God who brought our ancestors out of Egypt. We were slaves in that land, but the LORD did great things for us there. He brought us out and protected us while we traveled through other lands. [18]Then he forced out all the people living in these lands, even the Amorites. So we will serve the LORD, because he is our God."

[19]Then Joshua said, "You are not able to serve the LORD, because he is a holy God and a jealous God. If you turn against him and sin, he will not forgive you. [20]If you leave the LORD and serve other gods, he will send you great trouble. The LORD may have been good to you, but if you turn against him, he will destroy you."

[21]But the people said to Joshua, "No! We will serve the LORD."

[22]Then Joshua said, "You are your own witnesses that you have chosen to serve the LORD."

The people said, "Yes, we are."

[23]Then Joshua said, "Now throw away the gods that you have. Love the LORD, the God of Israel, with all your heart."

[24]Then the people said to Joshua, "We will serve the LORD our God, and we will obey him."

[25]On that day at Shechem Joshua made an agreement for the people. He made rules and laws for them to follow. [26]Joshua wrote these things in the Book of the Teachings of God. Then he took a large stone and set it up under the oak tree near the LORD's Holy Tent.

[27]Joshua said to all the people, "See this stone! It will remind you of what we did today. It was here the LORD spoke to us today. It will remind you of what happened so you will not turn against your God."

[28]Then Joshua sent the people back to their land.

[29]After that, Joshua son of Nun died at the age of one hundred ten.

DEVOTION

I WAS IN THE PRESS BOX working on a story on the day Hall of Fame pitcher Nolan Ryan pitched his last game. Several events were planned. One of the most interesting was when they had all the Little Leaguers who had been named "Nolan" or "Ryan" in honor of the great pitcher file onto the field. They covered the base paths.

I read a study recently that said that children with names like "Christian" or "Charity" or biblical names like "Joshua" or "Mary" got into trouble less frequently than children with secular names. Perhaps the dads with all those "Nolans" and "Ryans" were trying to will themselves a future major-leaguer someday.

Names are important in the Bible. In the Old Testament, most names have significance. For instance, Moses means "drawn forth" because he was rescued out of the Nile as a baby. And even though the name of God (*Yahweh*, which we pronounce "Jehovah") was not spoken aloud, it was incorporated into several names such as Abijah ("God is his father"), Elijah ("my God is Yahweh"), and Jonathan ("gift of Yahweh").

But no name is more meaningful than the name Joshua, which means "Yahweh is salvation." The name was given to him by Moses right before the twelve spies went on their mission. And even though his faithful report didn't convince the Israelites that day, he would eventually be vindicated when Jehovah did indeed save the Israelites and give them their promised land, led by Joshua.

Now he stands before the assembled people once again with his final message to them. Yes, God can save, but God is a severe God and will not tolerate idolatry. Could they be faithful to only one God? Joshua, whose very name indicates that salvation is found only in God, warns the people against trying to find salvation in any other god.

Years later another would come, named Jesus. His name is a transliteration into Greek of the Hebrew Joshua. He would be the fulfillment of that great name, for salvation truly comes through God's work in Jesus.

THOUGHTS TO PONDER

> What is the significance of the final words of Joshua? What did he fear the most? What does it require to live up to these great words—"As for me and my family, we will serve the LORD"—in our lives today?

PRAYER

> Father, we pray that we will serve only you and not chase the false gods of wealth, popularity, or any other idol the world asks us to worship. Amen.

TEACH YOUR CHILDREN

JUDGES 2:6–22

⁶Then Joshua sent the people back to their land. ⁷The people served the LORD during the lifetime of Joshua and during the lifetimes of the elders who lived after Joshua and who had seen what great things the LORD had done for Israel. ⁸Joshua son of Nun, the servant of the LORD, died at the age of one hundred ten. ⁹They buried him in his own land at Timnath Serah in the mountains of Ephraim, north of Mount Gaash.

¹⁰After those people had died, their children grew up and did not know the LORD or what he had done for Israel. ¹¹So they did what the LORD said was wrong, and they worshiped the Baal idols. ¹²They quit following the LORD, the God of their ancestors who had brought them out of Egypt. They began to worship the gods of the people who lived around them, and that made the LORD angry. ¹³The Israelites quit following the LORD and worshiped Baal and Ashtoreth. ¹⁴The LORD was angry with the people of Israel, so he handed them over to robbers who took their possessions. He let their enemies who lived around them defeat them; they could not protect themselves. ¹⁵When the Israelites went out to fight, they always lost, because the LORD was not with them. The LORD had sworn to them this would happen. So the Israelites suffered very much.

¹⁶Then the LORD chose leaders called judges, who saved the Israelites from the robbers. ¹⁷But the Israelites did not listen to their judges. They were not faithful to God but worshiped other gods instead. Their ancestors had obeyed the LORD's commands, but they quickly turned away and did not obey. ¹⁸When their enemies hurt them, the Israelites cried for help. So the LORD felt sorry for them and sent judges to save them from their enemies. The LORD was with those judges all their lives. ¹⁹But when the judges died, the Israelites again sinned and worshiped other gods. They became worse than their ancestors. The Israelites were very stubborn and refused to change their evil ways.

²⁰So the LORD became angry with the Israelites. He said, "These people have broken the agreement I made with their ancestors. They have not listened to me. ²¹I will no longer defeat the nations who were left when Joshua died. ²²I will use them to test Israel, to see if Israel will keep the LORD's commands as their ancestors did."

DEVOTION

ONE OF THE AWESOME responsibilities of parents is to help their children grow into a personal and real faith. As a teacher of college students on a Christian university campus, I teach about one hundred first-time students each fall. Some of them are already on their way to a personal walk with God; others are still living off the faith of their parents. The semester goes on and the split between the two becomes quite obvious when you ask probing questions. They miss class; they miss worship services. Quite frankly, most of the students without a spiritual foundation leave before graduation. They don't feel comfortable inside a community of faith.

One of the saddest statements in Scripture is found above when the writer tells us that "their children grew up and did not know the LORD or what he had done for Israel." All of the eyewitnesses to God's providence for his people in the desert were gone. The ones who had observed the children of Israel walk across the Jordan on dry land were dead. The warriors who had taken the Promised Land in mighty battles—the ones who had seen the sun stand still—were all gone. And because that generation had not passed down those stories, the current generation was spiritually lost, looking to the local gods of wood and stone for spiritual comfort.

If we don't tell our children the great stories, who will? God said to the prophet Hosea, "My people will be destroyed because they have no knowledge" (Hosea 4:6).

The most frightening thing about leaving God is leaving his protection. Once Israel decided to live outside the agreement relationship with God, they were on their own. They fought their battles without his help. They planted their crops without his blessings. They treated their illnesses without his help. They never knew the many benefits of following God.

So God introduces the judges, and for the decades that span this great Book of Judges, the nation of Israel will go through the cycle of idol worship, punishment, repentance, and deliverance more than a dozen times. Yet the lessons never stick because the foundational stories of their faith had been forgotten.

THOUGHTS TO PONDER

Who told you the great stories of God found in the Bible? What have you done to pass along these stories to the next generation?

PRAYER

God, we know you from your Word and from the great witnesses who took the time to teach us. Help us to teach our children your wonders and your ways. Amen.

CONDEMNED TO REPEAT IT

JUDGES 3:12–30

¹²Again the people of Israel did what the LORD said was wrong. So the LORD gave Eglon king of Moab power to defeat Israel because of the evil Israel did. ¹³Eglon got the Ammonites and the Amalekites to join him. Then he attacked Israel and took Jericho, the city of palm trees. ¹⁴So the people of Israel were ruled by Eglon king of Moab for eighteen years.

¹⁵When the people cried to the LORD, he sent someone to save them. He was Ehud, son of Gera from the people of Benjamin, who was left-handed. Israel sent Ehud to give Eglon king of Moab the payment he demanded. ¹⁶Ehud made himself a sword with two edges, about eighteen inches long, and he tied it to his right hip under his clothes. ¹⁷Ehud gave Eglon king of Moab the payment he demanded. Now Eglon was a very fat man. ¹⁸After he had given Eglon the payment, Ehud sent away the people who had carried it. ¹⁹When he passed the statues near Gilgal, he turned around and said to Eglon, "I have a secret message for you, King Eglon."

The king said, "Be quiet!" Then he sent all of his servants out of the room. ²⁰Ehud went to King Eglon, as he was sitting alone in the room above his summer palace.

Ehud said, "I have a message from God for you." As the king stood up from his chair, ²¹Ehud reached with his left hand and took out the sword that was tied to his right hip. Then he stabbed the sword deep into the king's belly! ²²Even the handle sank in, and the blade came out his back. The king's fat covered the whole sword, so Ehud left the sword in Eglon. ²³Then he went out of the room and closed and locked the doors behind him.

²⁴When the servants returned just after Ehud left, they found the doors to the room locked. So they thought the king was relieving himself. ²⁵They waited for a long time. Finally they became worried because he still had not opened the doors. So they got the key and unlocked them and saw their king lying dead on the floor!

²⁶While the servants were waiting, Ehud had escaped. He passed by the statues and went to Seirah. ²⁷When he reached the mountains of Ephraim he blew the trumpet. The people of Israel heard it and went down from the hills with Ehud leading them.

²⁸He said to them, "Follow me! The LORD has helped you to defeat your enemies, the Moabites." So Israel followed Ehud and captured the crossings of the Jordan River. They did not allow the Moabites to cross the Jordan River. ²⁹Israel killed about ten thousand strong and able men from Moab; not one escaped. ³⁰So that day Moab was forced to be under the rule of Israel, and there was peace in the land for eighty years.

DEVOTION

THE FIRST FOUR of the judges are handled by the author in rapid succession and Ehud, the second, is fairly typical of the pattern we see emerging. First, the people sin. Then God empowers an enemy to punish his people. A period of captivity ensues, eighteen years in this case. The people cry out to God and he sends a deliverer. Israel is freed and peace comes once again, this time for eighty years. An entire century passes for one cycle to play out. But after the death of Ehud, the cycle will start all over again.

You may have heard the phrase: "Those who cannot remember the past are condemned to repeat it." Are we in danger today of failing to learn the lessons of history? Israel's troubles began when God was no longer a central fixture in the everyday lives of the people. Sacrifices were ignored. Tithes were forgotten. The institution of the priesthood was delegated to do all the worshiping for all the people. Eventually the nation turned from the unseen God to the gods of wood and stone that they could see.

Are we in danger? Ask yourself this: is God any longer at the center of life in America? Is any kind of sacrifice—money, time, energy—in vogue today? Do we have a religious future when less than half our children regularly attend worship? As a nation once founded on faith, are we simply repeating the folly of the nation of Israel?

I have lived a semester in Europe in a culture that has long been considered "post-religious." They have simply moved beyond religion. Most of the people have never been inside a church building. Entire cathedrals are being boarded up and sold; some denominations have offices to handle unneeded church property.

What has replaced God? Idols. Not idols of stone or wood, but the things we "worship" today. Celebrity. Fame. Wealth. Youth. Where are we in the cycle?

THOUGHTS TO PONDER

What evidence, if any, do you see that we are less religious than we once were? What can we do as individuals to call our nation back to God?

PRAYER

God, we know that you sustain us with your hand. We pray that we will return to you and reap your blessings again. Amen.

Not Our Own Strength

JUDGES 6:11–24

[11]The angel of the LORD came and sat down under the oak tree at Ophrah that belonged to Joash, one of the Abiezrite people. Gideon, Joash's son, was separating some wheat from the chaff in a winepress to keep the wheat from the Midianites. [12]The angel of the LORD appeared to Gideon and said, "The LORD is with you, mighty warrior!"

[13]Then Gideon said, "Sir, if the LORD is with us, why are we having so much trouble? Where are the miracles our ancestors told us he did when the LORD brought them out of Egypt? But now he has left us and has handed us over to the Midianites."

[14]The LORD turned to Gideon and said, "Go with your strength and save Israel from the Midianites. I am the one who is sending you."

[15]But Gideon answered, "Lord, how can I save Israel? My family group is the weakest in Manasseh, and I am the least important member of my family."

[16]The LORD answered him, "I will be with you. It will seem as if the Midianites you are fighting are only one man."

[17]Then Gideon said to the LORD, "If you are pleased with me, give me proof that it is really you talking with me. [18]Please wait here until I come back to you. Let me bring my offering and set it in front of you."

And the LORD said, "I will wait until you return."

[19]So Gideon went in and cooked a young goat, and with twenty quarts of flour, made bread without yeast. Then he put the meat into a basket and the broth into a pot. He brought them out and gave them to the angel under the oak tree.

[20]The angel of God said to Gideon, "Put the meat and the bread without yeast on that rock over there. Then pour the broth on them." And Gideon did as he was told. [21]The angel of the LORD touched the meat and the bread with the end of the stick that was in his hand. Then fire jumped up from the rock and completely burned up the meat and the bread! And the angel of the LORD disappeared! [22]Then Gideon understood he had been talking to the angel of the LORD. So Gideon cried out, "Lord GOD! I have seen the angel of the LORD face to face!"

[23]But the LORD said to Gideon, "Calm down! Don't be afraid! You will not die!"

[24]So Gideon built an altar there to worship the LORD and named it The LORD Is Peace. It still stands at Ophrah, where the Abiezrites live.

DEVOTION

NOT KNOWING he was talking with an angel, Gideon let his frustration show. "If the LORD is with us, why are we having so much trouble?" (Judges 6:13).

I know that feeling. I've seen people lose their homes to disasters, and I've known folks who have lost a loved one to cancer. I've watched people lose their jobs just before Christmas and I've watched them lose their sons in battle. All of them Christians. All the losses in the past year. It makes me want to ask the same question as Gideon: "If God is with us, why are we having so much trouble?"

Where is our miracle, God? That was the question of Gideon. *You've helped in the past; where are you now?* You can feel Gideon's frustration. I, too, have often longed to see a miracle during this past year.

When the angel found him, Gideon was below ground in a winepress, hoping to thresh a little grain without being detected by the Midianites. Food was in very short supply. The Midianites, in a particularly cruel strategy, planned to defeat the Israelites by slowly destroying the food supplies and then destroying their emaciated enemy.

So Gideon was hiding from the enemy when the angel called him a "mighty warrior." It must have sounded like a taunt, but God saw something in Gideon even before Gideon himself did. God saw a man who could be molded into the leader that the nation of Israel needed to get past the current crisis.

And where was Gideon to find the strength to defeat the Midianites? "Go with your strength," he is told. The strength is in you, and remember, God says, I am the one sending you. I will be on your side as well.

Where are we going to find the strength to fight the discouragement that comes our way? The same place that Gideon did all those years ago. The strength is in us to start the fight, and the strength is in God to finish it.

THOUGHTS TO PONDER

What miracle would you most want to see from God? When you feel like Gideon felt at the beginning of this story, how do you find hope?

PRAYER

God, we know you are the source of our deliverance from whatever Satan hurls at us. Help us find our strength in you. Amen.

Knowing What
God Wants

JUDGES 6:25–40

²⁵That same night the LORD said to Gideon, "Take the bull that belongs to your father and a second bull seven years old. Pull down your father's altar to Baal, and cut down the Asherah idol beside it. ²⁶Then build an altar to the LORD your God with its stones in the right order on this high ground. Kill and burn a second bull on this altar, using the wood from the Asherah idol."

²⁷So Gideon got ten of his servants and did what the LORD had told him to do. But Gideon was afraid that his family and the men of the city might see him, so he did it at night, not in the daytime.

²⁸When the men of the city got up the next morning, they saw that the altar for Baal had been destroyed and that the Asherah idol beside it had been cut down! They also saw the altar Gideon had built and the second bull that had been sacrificed on it. ²⁹The men of the city asked each other, "Who did this?"

After they asked many questions, someone told them, "Gideon son of Joash did this."

³⁰So they said to Joash, "Bring your son out. He has pulled down the altar of Baal and cut down the Asherah idol beside it. He must die!"

³¹But Joash said to the angry crowd around him, "Are you going to take Baal's side? Are you going to defend him? Anyone who takes Baal's side will be killed by morning! If Baal is a god, let him fight for himself. It's his altar that has been pulled down." ³²So on that day Gideon got the name Jerub-Baal, which means "let Baal fight against him," because Gideon pulled down Baal's altar.

³³All the Midianites, the Amalekites, and other peoples from the east joined together and came across the Jordan River and camped in the Valley of Jezreel. ³⁴But the Spirit of the LORD entered Gideon, and he blew a trumpet to call the Abiezrites to follow him. ³⁵He sent messengers to all of Manasseh, calling them to follow him. He also sent messengers to the people of Asher, Zebulun, and Naphtali. So they also went up to meet Gideon and his men.

³⁶Then Gideon said to God, "You said you would help me save Israel. ³⁷I will put some wool on the threshing floor. If there is dew only on the wool but all of the ground is dry, then I will know that you will use me to save Israel, as you said." ³⁸And that is just what happened. When Gideon got up early the next morning and squeezed the wool, he got a full bowl of water from it.

³⁹Then Gideon said to God, "Don't be angry with me if I ask just one more thing. Please let me make one more test. Let only the wool be dry while the ground around it gets wet with dew." ⁴⁰That night God did that very thing. Just the wool was dry, but the ground around it was wet with dew.

DEVOTION

HAVE YOU EVER put down the fleece for God? By that I mean, have you ever asked God for a sign for what you should be doing with your life?

Wouldn't a sign be nice? An unmistakable miracle to tell me what God has in mind for my life. Sadly, God doesn't work that way today.

But he has a plan to reveal his will to me. I find it in Paul's Letter to the Romans when he says, "Do not be shaped by this world; instead be changed within by a new way of thinking. Then you will be able to decide what God wants for you; you will know what is good and pleasing to him and what is perfect" (Romans 12:2).

Want to know God's will in your life? Change your life. Change your way of thinking. Then, and only then, will you be able to know what God wants for you.

This is how it worked with Gideon. Before the fleece, there was the idol. Everyone worshiped multiple gods in those days, including Gideon's own father. Dare to be different from everyone else, God tells Gideon. Tear down the idol by your father's house.

After Gideon had proved that he was willing to go against the popular opinion of his people, he was ready to lead them. Then God revealed his plan for Gideon: you will lead the army that will save Israel, and this fleece will be a sign.

If you haven't found God's will for your life, instead of throwing down the fleece, throw out the idols of the world—money, power, fame. Stop worshiping what the world worships and then listen for God's voice.

THOUGHTS TO PONDER

Why would God put Gideon's life at risk by asking him to tear down the idol? Why would Gideon be asked to pull down the idol of his own father? How did this prepare him for what was ahead?

PRAYER

God, we ask that you will reveal your will to us, and that we will be ready to accept our role in your plan. Amen.

The True Source of Victories

JUDGES 7:1–15

7 Early in the morning Jerub-Baal (also called Gideon) and all his men set up their camp at the spring of Harod. The Midianites were camped north of them in the valley at the bottom of the hill called Moreh. ²Then the LORD said to Gideon, "You have too many men to defeat the Midianites. I don't want the Israelites to brag that they saved themselves. ³So now, announce to the people, 'Anyone who is afraid may leave Mount Gilead and go back home.'" So twenty-two thousand men returned home, but ten thousand remained.

⁴Then the LORD said to Gideon, "There are still too many men. Take the men down to the water, and I will test them for you there. If I say, 'This man will go with you, he will go. But if I say, 'That one will not go with you,' he will not go."

⁵So Gideon led the men down to the water. There the LORD said to him, "Separate them into those who drink water by lapping it up like a dog and those who bend down to drink." ⁶There were three hundred men who used their hands to bring water to their mouths, lapping it as a dog does. All the rest got down on their knees to drink.

⁷Then the LORD said to Gideon, "Using the three hundred men who lapped the water, I will save you and hand Midian over to you. Let all the others go home." ⁸So Gideon sent the rest of Israel to their homes. But he kept three hundred men and took the jars and the trumpets of those who left.

Now the camp of Midian was in the valley below Gideon. ⁹That night the LORD said to Gideon, "Get up. Go down and attack the camp of the Midianites, because I will give them to you. ¹⁰But if you are afraid to go down, take your servant Purah with you. ¹¹When you come to the camp of Midian, you will hear what they are saying. Then you will not be afraid to attack the camp."

So Gideon and his servant Purah went down to the edge of the enemy camp. ¹²The Midianites, the Amalekites, and all the peoples from the east were camped in that valley. There were so many of them they seemed like locusts. Their camels could not be counted because they were as many as the grains of sand on the seashore!

¹³When Gideon came to the enemy camp, he heard a man telling his friend about a dream. He was saying, "I dreamed that a loaf of barley bread rolled into the camp of Midian. It hit the tent so hard that the tent turned over and fell flat!"

¹⁴The man's friend said, "Your dream is about the sword of Gideon son of Joash, a man of Israel. God will hand Midian and the whole army over to him!"

¹⁵When Gideon heard about the dream and what it meant, he worshiped God. Then Gideon went back to the camp of Israel and called out to them, "Get up! The LORD has handed the army of Midian over to you!"

DEVOTION

EXPERIENCED PILOTS will tell you that there are three things in aviation that you cannot use: altitude that's above you, runway that's behind you, and fuel that's left on the ground. The lesson to young pilots: you can never be too prepared.

Military commanders would probably have their own list, and at the top of that list would have to be this: never leave able-bodied soldiers at home. But that is exactly what God is asking Gideon to do in this story. From a total of thirty-two thousand men, God allows Gideon to keep only three hundred. Why? Because he wants both the Israelites and the enemy to know who won the battle on that day.

By now, Gideon has to be having his doubts. First God answers his request about the fleece, proving to him that victory is at hand, but now God is taking away the very soldiers Gideon needs to claim that victory. But God knows Gideon's fears, so he wakes Gideon and sends him to the edge of the camp to hear the vision of the soldier. Gideon recognizes that man's dream as God's message to him; he immediately worships God and rallies his men for war.

I think we have to take care, even today, against forgetting that it is God who gives us victories. We marvel at the skill of surgeons or the efficacy of medicines, yet it is God who gives healing. God works through doctors and medicines to give healing just like he works through diet and exercise to give health. We use our God-given talents to earn a living.

The lesson of Gideon is still true today. All victories come from God.

THOUGHTS TO PONDER

What significance do you see in the two "tests" that culled the army from thirty-two thousand to three hundred men? What parallels do you see between this story and the fact that Jesus chose only twelve men to carry out his mission? What could God do with a small, dedicated "army" today?

PRAYER

God, our strength is not in numbers; our strength is not in medicine or technology. Our strength is in you. Help us remember that fact all our days. Amen.

Ongoing Idolatry

JUDGES 7:16—8:3

16Gideon divided the three hundred men into three groups. He gave each man a trumpet and an empty jar with a burning torch inside.

17Gideon told the men, "Watch me and do what I do. When I get to the edge of the camp, do what I do. 18Surround the enemy camp. When I and everyone with me blow our trumpets, you blow your trumpets, too. Then shout, 'For the LORD and for Gideon!'"

19So Gideon and the one hundred men with him came to the edge of the enemy camp just after they had changed guards. It was during the middle watch of the night. Then Gideon and his men blew their trumpets and smashed their jars. 20All three groups of Gideon's men blew their trumpets and smashed their jars. They held the torches in their left hands and the trumpets in their right hands. Then they shouted, "A sword for the LORD and for Gideon!" 21Each of Gideon's men stayed in his place around the camp, but the Midianites began shouting and running to escape.

22When Gideon's three hundred men blew their trumpets, the LORD made all the Midianites fight each other with their swords! The enemy army ran away to the city of Beth Shittah toward Zererah. They ran as far as the border of Abel Meholah, near the city of Tabbath. 23Then men of Israel from Naphtali, Asher, and all of Manasseh were called out to chase the Midianites. 24Gideon sent messengers through all the mountains of Ephraim, saying, "Come down and attack the Midianites. Take control of the Jordan River as far as Beth Barah before the Midianites can get to it."

So they called out all the men of Ephraim, who took control of the Jordan River as far as Beth Barah. 25The men of Ephraim captured two princes of Midian named Oreb and Zeeb. They killed Oreb at the rock of Oreb and Zeeb at the winepress of Zeeb, and they continued chasing the Midianites. They brought the heads of Oreb and Zeeb to Gideon, who was east of the Jordan River.

8The men of Ephraim asked Gideon, "Why did you treat us this way? Why didn't you call us when you went to fight against Midian?" They argued angrily with Gideon.

2But he answered them, "I have not done as well as you! The small part you did was better than all that my people of Abiezer did. 3God let you capture Oreb and Zeeb, the princes of Midian. How can I compare what I did with what you did?" When the men of Ephraim heard Gideon's answer, they were not as angry anymore.

DEVOTION

IT WAS LATE at night, and very dark. Gideon's strategy—perhaps given to him by God, although we're not told—was to surprise and confuse the enemy. In the previous passage, we're told that the Midianite army was so numerous they looked like a swarm of locusts in the valley below. But Gideon had the high ground and the element of surprise working for him on this night, as well as the promise of victory from God.

The jars referred to in the story were undoubtedly opaque clay jars. The jars would have hidden the flames of the torches until Gideon's signal. So here is what the sleeping army of Midian would have experienced: a deafening blast of trumpets from all around the camp, then the shouts of hundreds of men, followed by a blaze of light from three hundred torches.

Since trumpeters and torchbearers were a small part of any army, the impression would be that a huge army lay behind these men, ready to attack the sleeping Midianites. That fear caused a pandemonium as the Midianites began fighting one another in the dark. No doubt the noise startled the thousands of camels, so they were probably running amok as well. Soon the enemy began to run away in full retreat. God had brought the victory.

Gideon finished the battle by letting the local armies of the tribes of Naphtali, Asher and Manasseh give chase into the hills of Ephraim where the enemy was killed. Incidentally, this was the second great defeat of this enemy of Israel. You might recall that the last battle of Moses, recorded in Numbers 31, was a devastating defeat of Midian for the wrongs they had committed against Israel.

This battle marks the conclusion of a period of seven years of oppression of the Israelite people. The Midianites were God's instrument of punishment for the apostasy of the nation (see Judges 6:1–10 for details). But this victory was just the beginning of a long cycle of sin and repentance that would keep Israel at war with its neighbors for many years to come as God used one nation after another to punish his people for their persistent idolatry.

THOUGHTS TO PONDER

Why would God use an evil nation like Midian to punish his people? Does God punish us today? How might he guide us toward obedience today?

PRAYER

God, we know that you defeat all the "enemies" we face—doubt, fear, despair—if we only call on you for the victory. Help us to do so. Amen.

Satan's Earrings

JUDGES 8:22–35

²²The people of Israel said to Gideon, "You saved us from the Midianites. Now, we want you and your son and your grandson to rule over us."

²³But Gideon told them, "The LORD will be your ruler. I will not rule over you, nor will my son rule over you." ²⁴He said, "I want you to do this one thing for me. I want each of you to give me a gold earring from the things you took in the fighting." (The Ishmaelites wore gold earrings.)

²⁵They said, "We will gladly give you what you want." So they spread out a coat, and everyone threw down an earring from what he had taken. ²⁶The gold earrings weighed about forty-three pounds. This did not count the decorations, necklaces, and purple robes worn by the kings of Midian, nor the chains from the camels' necks. ²⁷Gideon used the gold to make a holy vest, which he put in his hometown of Ophrah. But all the Israelites were unfaithful to God and worshiped it, so it became a trap for Gideon and his family.

²⁸So Midian was under the rule of Israel; they did not cause trouble anymore. And the land had peace for forty years, as long as Gideon was alive.

²⁹Gideon son of Joash went to his home to live. ³⁰He had seventy sons of his own, because he had many wives. ³¹He had a slave woman who lived in Shechem, and he had a son by her, whom he named Abimelech. ³²So Gideon son of Joash died at a good old age. He was buried in the tomb of Joash, his father, in Ophrah, where the Abiezrites live.

³³As soon as Gideon died, the people of Israel were again unfaithful to God and followed the Baals. They made Baal-Berith their god. ³⁴The Israelites did not remember the LORD their God, who had saved them from all their enemies living all around them. ³⁵And they were not kind to the family of Jerub-Baal, also called Gideon, for all the good he had done for Israel.

DEVOTION

WITH GOD'S HELP, Gideon did great things. And along the way, he avoided many traps that a lesser man would have fallen into. He took God at his word and approached the Midianites with a numerically inferior army, relying only on Jehovah for the victory. He refused to engage in the polytheistic trends of the time and refused to worship Baal. He tore down an altar, risking the wrath of an angry mob as he did it. He even turned down the offer of his people to be made a king after delivering them from the Midianites.

But then Gideon did a curious thing. After his victory, he asked each one of his admirers to give him an earring. It was undoubtedly the plunder of war, as the Midianites were known to wear gold earrings.

And his adoring public did just that. Forty-three pounds worth of earrings in fact, from the more than one hundred twenty thousand enemy soldiers killed. And this didn't even count the decorations, necklaces, purple robes, or animal ornamentations that were offered in abundance as well.

Then Gideon stumbled. He took the gold and made a "holy vest" and placed it in his hometown. The text goes on to say, "so it [the vest] became a trap for Gideon and his family" (Judges 8:27).

Satan had tried fear with Gideon. He had tried vanity. He had even tried false gods before. But in the end, he got Gideon, one of God's greatest warriors, to stumble over some golden earrings. A man who trusted God and conquered a vastly superior army with only three hundred men was finally brought down by earrings. The man who risked his life to tear down idols was now bowing down to an ephod he had made.

Are there any earrings lying around in your life, placed there by Satan? Because that's how he's going to get the faithful. He's not going to arrive with horns and a pitchfork—we're looking for that and we're too sophisticated to fall for it. He's not going to look like a serpent, either. He's been there and done that in the Garden of Eden.

So he'll change tactics and throw "earrings" in our path. Maybe it will be an earring of fame. Or wealth. Or power. Or lust. It will seem small by itself, but the accumulation of the earrings he throws in our path will be far greater than the forty-three pounds that Gideon harvested from the spoils of battle.

Will we recognize Satan's earrings for what they are, and will we act? Our answer could have eternal consequences.

THOUGHTS TO PONDER

Why do you think Gideon committed this blunder late in life? What are some of the "earrings" that Satan throws your way? What are you doing to avoid falling into the trap?

PRAYER

God, we pray that when Satan makes sin attractive and shiny like gold, we will see it in all its true ugliness and avoid falling into its trap. Amen.

No Deals Required

JUDGES 11:1–9, 29–39

11 Jephthah was a strong soldier from Gilead. His father was named Gilead, and his mother was a prostitute. ²Gilead's wife had several sons. When they grew up, they forced Jephthah to leave his home, saying to him, "You will not get any of our father's property, because you are the son of another woman." ³So Jephthah ran away from his brothers and lived in the land of Tob. There some worthless men began to follow him.

⁴After a time the Ammonites fought against Israel. ⁵When the Ammonites made war against Israel, the elders of Gilead went to Jephthah to bring him back from Tob. ⁶They said to him, "Come and lead our army so we can fight the Ammonites."

⁷But Jephthah said to them, "Didn't you hate me? You forced me to leave my father's house. Why are you coming to me now that you are in trouble?"

⁸The elders of Gilead said to Jephthah, "It is because of those troubles that we come to you now. Please come with us and fight against the Ammonites. You will be the ruler over everyone who lives in Gilead."

⁹Then Jephthah answered, "If you take me back to Gilead to fight the Ammonites and the LORD helps me win, I will be your ruler."

²⁹Then the Spirit of the LORD entered Jephthah. Jephthah passed through Gilead and Manasseh and the city of Mizpah in Gilead to the land of the Ammonites. ³⁰Jephthah made a promise to the LORD, saying, "If you will hand over the Ammonites to me, ³¹I will give you as a burnt offering the first thing that comes out of my house to meet me when I return from the victory. It will be the LORD's."

³²Then Jephthah went over to fight the Ammonites, and the LORD handed them over to him. ³³In a great defeat Jephthah struck them down from the city of Aroer to the area of Minnith, and twenty cities as far as the city of Abel Keramim. So the Ammonites were defeated by the Israelites.

³⁴When Jephthah returned to his home in Mizpah, his daughter was the first one to come out to meet him, playing a tambourine and dancing. She was his only child; he had no other sons or daughters. ³⁵When Jephthah saw his daughter, he tore his clothes to show his sorrow. He said, "My daughter! You have made me so sad because I made a promise to the LORD, and I cannot break it!"

³⁶Then his daughter said, "Father, you made a promise to the LORD. So do to me just what you promised, because the LORD helped you defeat your enemies, the Ammonites." ³⁷She also said, "But let me do one thing. Let me be alone for two months to go to the mountains. Since I will never marry, let me and my friends go and cry together."

[38]Jephthah said, "Go." So he sent her away for two months. She and her friends stayed in the mountains and cried for her because she would never marry. [39]After two months she returned to her father, and Jephthah did to her what he had promised.

DEVOTION

FOR EIGHTEEN YEARS the Israelites had suffered under the oppression of the Ammonites. It began east of the Jordan River in the area of Gilead, and soon the marauders had crossed the river and begun possessing the lands there. The Israelites know it is their worship of Baal and other gods that caused this turn of fortune, but when they repent and appeal to God, at first he mocks them. Let your false gods save you, he says.

But God relents when he sees their suffering, and once again he raises up a quite ordinary man to do his work. The son of a prostitute, Jephthah is a little rough around the edges. Forced from his home by jealousy, he runs with the wrong crowd, but along the way he gets a reputation as a strong soldier. It says something about Israel that Jephthah is the best leader they can find, but he agrees to take the job.

Soon after, the Spirit of God enters him, preparing him for the victory ahead. But Jephthah will always be remembered for the foolish promise he makes to God, and that vow will cost him his daughter.

God is not some cosmic dealmaker, deciding on a whim whom to bless and whom to curse. The Israelites were still operating under the "law of blessing and cursing" outlined in Deuteronomy 27 and 28. They were cursed because they sinned, not because of some fickle mood of God. They would be blessed when they repented, not because they struck a good deal with God.

We are blessed to serve an unchanging God who doesn't require our "deals" to rain his blessings on us.

THOUGHTS TO PONDER

When faced with a challenge or problem, do you ever try to bargain with God? Why do we think that God will be impressed by our offers? What does that say of our view of God?

PRAYER

Father, we know you are the Alpha and the Omega, the Changeless One who is the same yesterday, today, and tomorrow. Help us take comfort in that fact today. Amen.

Righteous Anger

JUDGES 15:1–15

15 At the time of the wheat harvest, Samson went to visit his wife, taking a young goat with him. He said, "I'm going to my wife's room," but her father would not let him go in.

²He said to Samson, "I thought you really hated your wife, so I gave her to your best man. Her younger sister is more beautiful. Take her instead."

³But Samson said to them, "This time no one will blame me for hurting you Philistines!" ⁴So Samson went out and caught three hundred foxes. He took two foxes at a time, tied their tails together, and then tied a torch to the tails of each pair of foxes. ⁵After he lit the torches, he let the foxes loose in the grainfields of the Philistines so that he burned up their standing grain, the piles of grain, their vineyards, and their olive trees.

⁶The Philistines asked, "Who did this?"

Someone told them, "Samson, the son-in-law of the man from Timnah, did because his father-in-law gave his wife to his best man."

So the Philistines burned Samson's wife and her father to death. ⁷Then Samson said to the Philistines, "Since you did this, I won't stop until I pay you back!" ⁸Samson attacked the Philistines and killed many of them. Then he went down and stayed in a cave in the rock of Etam.

⁹The Philistines went up and camped in the land of Judah, near a place named Lehi. ¹⁰The men of Judah asked them, "Why have you come here to fight us?"

They answered, "We have come to make Samson our prisoner, to pay him back for what he did to our people."

¹¹Then three thousand men of Judah went to the cave in the rock of Etam and said to Samson, "What have you done to us? Don't you know that the Philistines rule over us?"

Samson answered, "I only paid them back for what they did to me."

¹²Then they said to him, "We have come to tie you up and to hand you over to the Philistines."

Samson said to them, "Promise me you will not hurt me yourselves."

¹³The men from Judah said, "We agree. We will just tie you up and give you to the Philistines. We will not kill you." So they tied Samson with two new ropes and led him up from the cave in the rock. ¹⁴When Samson came to the place named Lehi, the Philistines came to meet him, shouting for joy. Then the Spirit of the LORD entered Samson and gave him great power. The ropes on him weakened like burned strings and fell off his hands! ¹⁵Samson found the jawbone of a dead donkey, took it, and killed a thousand men with it!

DEVOTION

SAMSON LIVED LIFE on the edge. Sometimes he appeared to be out of control. A Nazirite since birth, he was blessed with incredible strength, but his life seemed to be one turmoil after another, mostly aimed at the Philistines.

At his wedding, Samson told a riddle, offering thirty sets of clothes to anyone who solved it. When his Philistine guests tricked his wife and got the answer, Samson responded by killing thirty men to get the clothing to pay the bet. He left his wife and went to sulk.

When he returned, she was no longer his wife. Samson destroyed the fields of the Philistines because of the affront of losing his wife to a Philistine man. The retaliations continued until Samson's wife, his father-in-law, and a thousand men were dead. Trapped in a cave and bound by ropes, Samson grabbed the first available weapon—the jawbone of a donkey—and killed a thousand men.

Why did God choose someone like Samson? Why bless a man of his temperament with this kind of power? In Judges 14:4 we read, "The LORD wanted this to happen because he was looking for a way to challenge the Philistines, who were ruling over Israel at this time." Even though Israel had sinned, after forty years of oppression, it was now time to overthrow the tyranny of the Philistines and restore the Israelites to their freedom.

God can use imperfect people like Samson to accomplish his perfect will. He can even use our less attractive traits to do his good. I think it's perfectly alright to get angry at Satan with his modern "ropes"—debt, depression, addictions, illness. If God can use Samson with his flaws, he can use me. There are times when Satan will try to bind me with his ropes. And when he does, God will give me the "jawbone" to fight back if I just look.

THOUGHTS TO PONDER

Where do you get your power? Samson got his power from a Nazirite vow. What vow do we take as Christians that gives us spiritual power?

PRAYER

God, we pray that your strength will be sufficient for whatever threatens to bind us. Amen.

Reckless with God's Gifts

⁴After this, Samson fell in love with a woman named Delilah, who lived in the Valley of Sorek. ⁵The Philistine rulers went to Delilah and said, "Find out what makes Samson so strong. Trick him into telling you how we can overpower him and capture him and tie him up. If you do this, each one of us will give you twenty-eight pounds of silver."

⁶So Delilah said to Samson, "Tell me why you are so strong. How can someone tie you up and capture you?"

⁷Samson answered, "Someone would have to tie me up with seven new bowstrings that have not been dried. Then I would be as weak as any other man."

⁸The Philistine rulers brought Delilah seven new bowstrings that had not been dried, and she tied Samson with them. ⁹Some men were hiding in another room. Delilah said to him, "Samson, the Philistines are here!" But Samson broke the bowstrings like pieces of burned string. So the Philistines did not find out the secret of Samson's strength.

¹⁰Then Delilah said to Samson, "You made a fool of me. You lied to me. Now tell me how someone can tie you up."

¹¹Samson said, "They would have to tie me with new ropes that have not been used before. Then I would become as weak as any other man."

¹²So Delilah took new ropes and tied Samson. Some men were hiding in another room. She called out to him, "Samson, the Philistines are here!" But he broke the ropes as easily as if they were threads.

¹³Then Delilah said to Samson, "Again you have made a fool of me. You lied to me. Tell me how someone can tie you up."

He said, "Using the loom, weave the seven braids of my hair into the cloth, and tighten it with a pin. Then I will be as weak as any other man."

While Samson slept, Delilah wove the seven braids of his hair into the cloth. ¹⁴Then she fastened it with a pin.

Again she said to him, "Samson, the Philistines are here!" Samson woke up and pulled out the pin and the loom with the cloth.

¹⁵Then Delilah said to him, "How can you say, 'I love you,' when you don't even trust me? This is the third time you have made a fool of me. You haven't told me the secret of your great strength." ¹⁶She kept bothering Samson about his secret day after day until he felt he was going to die!

¹⁷So he told her everything. He said, "I have never had my hair cut, because I have been set apart to God as a Nazirite since I was born. If someone shaved my head, I would lose my strength and be as weak as any other man."

[18]When Delilah saw that he had told her everything sincerely, she sent a message to the Philistine rulers. She said, "Come back one more time, because he has told me everything." So the Philistine rulers came back to Delilah and brought the silver with them. [19]Delilah got Samson to sleep, lying in her lap. Then she called in a man to shave off the seven braids of Samson's hair. In this way she began to make him weak, and his strength left him.

[20]Then she said, "Samson, the Philistines are here!"

He woke up and thought, "I'll leave as I did before and shake myself free." But he did not know that the LORD had left him.

DEVOTION

THE LAST WORDS in this passage haunt me even more than Samson's eventual fate at the hands of the Philistines. Three times Delilah had asked Samson the source of his strength, and three times he had lied to her. But the fourth time he told the truth: he had been set apart to God as a Nazirite, and if he broke that vow, his strength would be gone.

But the passage contains this interesting phrase: "But he did not know that the LORD had left him" (Judges 16:20).

Can this happen today? Peter calls his Christian readers "a chosen people, royal priests, a holy nation, a people for God's own possession" (1 Peter 2:9). Is it possible for us to turn away from that today? Is it possible to live a life so outside of God's plan that we don't even feel ourselves slipping farther away into sin? Are we like Samson, convinced that we can, of our own will, shake ourselves free of whatever sin we have indulged in?

The lesson of Samson is sobering. A judge of his people for twenty years, but reckless with the very trait that made him special. May we never grow too accustomed to the true source of our power.

THOUGHTS TO PONDER

Why would Samson reveal the secret of his strength to Delilah? Do you think he thought he would be caught? Do you know someone like Samson, risking everything in reckless behavior?

PRAYER

God, we acknowledge you as the source of our strength and we pray that we will never know a day without that strength. Amen.

YOUR "ESTHER MOMENT"

JUDGES 16:21–31

²¹Then the Philistines captured Samson and tore out his eyes. They took him down to Gaza, where they put bronze chains on him and made him grind grain in the prison. ²²But his hair began to grow again.

²³The Philistine rulers gathered to celebrate and to offer a great sacrifice to their god Dagon. They said, "Our god has handed Samson our enemy over to us." ²⁴When the people saw him, they praised their god, saying,

"This man destroyed our country.
>   He killed many of us!
But our god handed over
>   our enemy to us."

²⁵While the people were enjoying the celebration, they said, "Bring Samson out to perform for us." So they brought Samson from the prison, and he performed for them. They made him stand between the pillars. ²⁶Samson said to the servant holding his hand, "Let me feel the pillars that hold up the temple so I can lean against them." ²⁷Now the temple was full of men and women. All the Philistine rulers were there, and about three thousand men and women were on the roof watching Samson perform. ²⁸Then Samson prayed to the LORD, "Lord GOD, remember me. God, please give me strength one more time so I can pay these Philistines back for putting out my two eyes!" ²⁹Then Samson turned to the two center pillars that supported the whole temple. He braced himself between the two pillars, with his right hand on one and his left hand on the other. ³⁰Samson said, "Let me die with these Philistines!" Then he pushed as hard as he could, causing the temple to fall on the rulers and all the people in it. So Samson killed more of the Philistines when he died than when he was alive.

³¹Samson's brothers and his whole family went down to get his body. They brought him back and buried him in the tomb of Manoah, his father, between the cities of Zorah and Eshtaol. Samson was a judge for the people of Israel for twenty years.

DEVOTION

IT'S BEEN SAID that in life, there are no second acts; but Samson certainly gets one in this story. Blind and weak, he languishes in jail, working among the animals at the grinding wheel. But God has one more use for Samson, so his strength begins to return. His last act—pulling down the temple and killing the thousands in it and on its roof—was the greatest in all his storied life as a man of strength.

If you are alive—and presumably all readers of this book qualify here—then God still has a plan for you. Otherwise, we would have been swept into heaven at the moment of our salvation. But it didn't happen that way. God wanted us to raise our children in his ways. He wanted us to witness for him in our communities and in our workplaces. He wanted us to glorify him in worship—not just on Sundays, but every day of our lives. We were preserved for a purpose.

Samson couldn't have foreseen his purpose when he was being treated like a beast on the grinding floor. Remember, he didn't have any extraordinary power at this point. Here's this blind man of ordinary strength, perhaps wasting away from a poor prison diet, dragging his chains as he slowly turned the millstone to crush the grain. I'm sure he prayed for death. But he was being preserved for a purpose.

In the Book of Esther, the new Queen Esther is in a unique position to save her Jewish people from impending slaughter during their period of captivity. But there's a problem: she hasn't been invited in to see the king, and to go in unannounced could mean death. Her uncle, Mordecai, urges her to go anyway. In one of the most insightful passages in all of Scripture we read, "If you keep quiet at this time, someone else will help and save the Jewish people, but you and your father's family will all die. And who knows, you may have been chosen queen for just such a time as this" (Esther 4:14).

What will be your "Esther moment"? Samson was preserved for the destruction of the Philistines. Perhaps you're being preserved for the salvation of your spouse, or your children or your grandchildren. All of us will have an "Esther moment" in our lives, and some of us may have many of them. What is it that you are uniquely called to do in the service of God? And more importantly, will you do it?

THOUGHTS TO PONDER

How will we recognize our God-given purpose when it arrives? Do you pray to God to open your eyes to his will?

PRAYER

God, please let us see that we have been spared to this moment for a reason. Help us find our purpose and pursue it. Amen.

Love That Knows
No Borders

RUTH 1:1–17

1 Long ago when the judges ruled Israel, there was a shortage of food in the land. ²So a man named Elimelech left the town of Bethlehem in Judah to live in the country of Moab with his wife and his two sons. His wife was named Naomi, and his two sons were named Mahlon and Kilion. They were Ephrathahites from Bethlehem in Judah. When they came to Moab, they settled there.

³Then Naomi's husband, Elimelech, died, and she was left with her two sons. ⁴These sons married women from Moab. One was named Orpah, and the other was named Ruth. Naomi and her sons had lived in Moab about ten years ⁵when Mahlon and Kilion also died. So Naomi was left alone without her husband or her two sons.

⁶While Naomi was in Moab, she heard that the LORD had come to help his people and had given them food again. So she and her daughters-in-law got ready to leave Moab and return home. ⁷Naomi and her daughters-in-law left the place where they had lived and started back to the land of Judah. ⁸But Naomi said to her two daughters-in-law, "Go back home, each of you to your own mother's house. May the LORD be as kind to you as you have been to me and my sons who are now dead. ⁹May the LORD give you another happy home and a new husband."

When Naomi kissed the women good-bye, they began to cry out loud. ¹⁰They said to her, "No, we want to go with you to your people."

¹¹But Naomi said, "My daughters, return to your own homes. Why do you want to go with me? I cannot give birth to more sons to give you new husbands; ¹²go back, my daughters, to your own homes. I am too old to have another husband. Even if I told myself, 'I still have hope' and had another husband tonight, and even if I had more sons, ¹³should you wait until they were grown into men? Should you live for so many years without husbands? Don't do that, my daughters. My life is much too sad for you to share, because the LORD has been against me!"

¹⁴The women cried together out loud again. Then Orpah kissed her mother-in-law Naomi good-bye, but Ruth held on to her tightly.

¹⁵Naomi said to Ruth, "Look, your sister-in-law is going back to her own people and her own gods. Go back with her."

¹⁶But Ruth said, "Don't beg me to leave you or to stop following you. Where you go, I will go. Where you live, I will live. Your people will be my people, and your God will be my God. ¹⁷And where you die, I will die, and there I will be buried. I ask the LORD to punish me terribly if I do not keep this promise: Not even death will separate us."

DEVOTION

ONE OF THE BIBLE'S greatest stories of devotion is found in the Book of Ruth. Its author is unknown—probably an anonymous scribe who was led by the Spirit to write it down after the story had been handed down orally for generations.

Naomi never expected her daughters-in-law to follow back to Israel. They had relatives in Moab. They could remarry. Customs were different in Judah. The language was different. Naomi wished them well, and after a few tears, expected them to journey home. And one, Orpah, did just that.

But Ruth was different. She simply would not leave Naomi, even if it meant living the rest of her life in a foreign land. "Your people will be my people," she said.

As I write this, one of my colleagues is preparing to be a missionary in Rwanda, a land that tore itself apart with mass genocide a few years ago. It's one of the poorest countries in the world, and its people are suffering greatly.

Why go? For the same reason Ruth went: love compels us to make sacrifices that go beyond explanation. Could I ever summon up enough love for another person to leave my comfort zone for their welfare?

"Love your neighbor as yourself," Jesus said. "Who then is my neighbor?" he was asked. Jesus responds with the parable of the Good Samaritan, one of the great stories of sacrificial love in the Bible (Luke 10:25–37). Anyone in need is my neighbor.

Astronauts who look at the world from space frequently comment that there are no borders from that perspective—only land and water. Ruth's love for Naomi knew no borders. Eventually, Ruth marries Boaz, and joins the lineage of the Savior, her name recorded forever in the first chapter of the New Testament (Matthew 1:5).

THOUGHTS TO PONDER

Why do you think Orpah and Ruth made different decisions in the story above? What qualities must Naomi have had that would cause Ruth to want to stay with her?

PRAYER

Father, you've given us people to love and it has enriched our lives. We thank you for blessing us with loved ones like Ruth was blessed with Naomi, and we know that when we love, we are most like you. Amen.

Paid in Full

RUTH 2:1–12

2 Now Naomi had a rich relative named Boaz, from Elimelech's family.
²One day Ruth, the Moabite, said to Naomi, "I am going to the fields. Maybe someone will be kind enough to let me gather the grain he leaves behind."

Naomi said, "Go, my daughter."

³So Ruth went to the fields and gathered the grain that the workers cutting the grain had left behind. It just so happened that the field belonged to Boaz, from Elimelech's family.

⁴Soon Boaz came from Bethlehem and greeted his workers, "The LORD be with you!"

And the workers answered, "May the LORD bless you!"

⁵Then Boaz asked his servant in charge of the workers, "Whose girl is that?"

⁶The servant answered, "She is the young Moabite woman who came back with Naomi from the country of Moab. ⁷She said, 'Please let me follow the workers cutting grain and gather what they leave behind.' She came and has remained here, from morning until just now. She has stopped only a few moments to rest in the shelter."

⁸Then Boaz said to Ruth, "Listen, my daughter. Don't go to gather grain for yourself in another field. Don't even leave this field at all, but continue following closely behind my women workers. ⁹Watch to see into which fields they go to cut grain and follow them. I have warned the young men not to bother you. When you are thirsty, you may go and drink from the water jugs that the young men have filled."

¹⁰Then Ruth bowed low with her face to the ground and said to him, "I am not an Israelite. Why have you been so kind to notice me?"

¹¹Boaz answered her, "I know about all the help you have given your mother-in-law after your husband died. You left your father and mother and your own country to come to a nation where you did not know anyone. ¹²May the LORD reward you for all you have done. May your wages be paid in full by the LORD, the God of Israel, under whose wings you have come for shelter."

Devotion

THE BOOK OF RUTH is actually an account of two different kinds of love stories. The first is the love story between Ruth, the young widowed girl from Moab and her Israelite mother-in-law, Naomi. The second is the love story introduced in this passage between Ruth and Boaz, a man of means and a distant relative of Naomi.

When Ruth and Naomi returned from Moab, their prospects were bleak. Both widowed, the women had no means of support other than the generosity of others. Naomi is so discouraged by her plight that she chooses a new name— Mara, meaning "bitter." Reading her comments at the end of chapter one, it is obvious that she is angry at God for her current circumstance. Only Ruth remains to comfort her.

Soon, Ruth takes to the fields to gather grain left behind by the gleaners. It was tradition for the owners of the fields to allow the poor to follow the harvest and pick up whatever kernels fell to the ground. Ruth chooses the field of Boaz to practice this ancient form of welfare.

But Boaz does far more than tolerate her; he welcomes her. He gives her protection and water to drink. Later, he feeds her lunch with his workers and instructs the men to leave full heads of grain lying out for Ruth to gather. By the end of the day, her harvest is a half bushel of the barley kernels—far more than Naomi anticipated.

Boaz explains the reason for his largess: he has heard about the help Ruth has given her mother-in-law. He admires her for moving to a nation, where she knows no one, to make a new life with Naomi. I especially like the blessing of Boaz. "May your wages be paid in full by the LORD, the God of Israel" (Ruth 2:12).

What a wonderful thought! Doesn't it feel good to do random acts of kindness, even if you'll never be noticed or thanked? Giving an anonymous gift. Passing up the close parking space. Standing rather than sitting on the subway. Cooking a holiday meal for shut-ins.

That good feeling, it seems to me, is God paying your wages in full. And that's better than any earthly reward.

Even as Boaz was admiring Ruth for her generosity to Naomi, he was displaying acts of kindness of his own. And when he eventually takes Ruth for his bride, their son will be the grandfather of King David, someone the Scriptures refer to as a man after God's heart.

Perhaps it was genetic.

THOUGHTS TO PONDER

What have you done for others that gave you the most joy? Why do you think the Bible tells us that it is more blessed to give than to receive? What does this story tell you about the character of Boaz?

PRAYER

God, we pray that we will be generous to those less fortunate than us, knowing that those we help are your children too. Amen.

RUTH'S REDEEMER

RUTH 3:1–18

3 Then Naomi, Ruth's mother-in-law, said to her, "My daughter, I must find a suitable home for you, one that will be good for you. ²Now Boaz, whose young women you worked with, is our close relative. Tonight he will be working at the threshing floor. ³Wash yourself, put on perfume, change your clothes, and go down to the threshing floor. But don't let him know you're there until he has finished his dinner. ⁴Watch him so you will know where he lies down to sleep. When he lies down, go and lift the cover off his feet and lie down. He will tell you what you should do."

⁵Then Ruth answered, "I will do everything you say."

⁶So Ruth went down to the threshing floor and did all her mother-in-law told her to do. ⁷After his evening meal, Boaz felt good and went to sleep lying beside the pile of grain. Ruth went to him quietly and lifted the cover from his feet and lay down.

⁸About midnight Boaz was startled and rolled over. There was a woman lying near his feet! ⁹Boaz asked, "Who are you?"

She said, "I am Ruth, your servant girl. Spread your cover over me, because you are a relative who is supposed to take care of me."

¹⁰Then Boaz said, "The LORD bless you, my daughter. This act of kindness is greater than the kindness you showed to Naomi in the beginning. You didn't look for a young man to marry, either rich or poor. ¹¹Now, my daughter, don't be afraid. I will do everything you ask, because all the people in our town know you are a good woman. ¹²It is true that I am a relative who is to take care of you, but you have a closer relative than I. ¹³Stay here tonight, and in the morning we will see if he will take care of you. If he decides to take care of you, that is fine. But if he refuses, I will take care of you myself, as surely as the LORD lives. So stay here until morning."

¹⁴So Ruth stayed near his feet until morning but got up while it was still too dark to recognize anyone. Boaz thought, "People in town must not know that the woman came here to the threshing floor." ¹⁵So Boaz said to Ruth, "Bring me your shawl and hold it open."

So Ruth held her shawl open, and Boaz poured six portions of barley into it. Boaz then put it on her head and went back to the city.

¹⁶When Ruth went back to her mother-in-law, Naomi asked, "How did you do, my daughter?"

Ruth told Naomi everything that Boaz did for her. ¹⁷She said, "Boaz gave me these six portions of barley, saying, 'You must not go home without a gift for your mother-in-law.'"

[18]Naomi answered, "Ruth, my daughter, wait here until you see what happens. Boaz will not rest until he has finished doing what he should do today."

DEVOTION

RUTH WAS EVIDENTLY a stunning woman. From the start, Naomi told her to go home to Moab, knowing young men there would want to marry her. In Israel she has drawn the attention of Boaz, who treats her kindly as she gleans in his field. But even when she sleeps at his feet—an ancient symbol that a woman wanted to marry a man—he can't believe his fortune. Such a beauty could have had a younger, possibly even richer man, yet she chose Boaz.

And in God's providence, Boaz was one of the nearest relatives of the family of Naomi. In Bible times the closest relative could marry a widow without children so she could have children. He would care for this family, but they and their property would not belong to him. They would belong to the dead husband so that his name would be carried on for generations to come.

In her act on the threshing room floor, Naomi is asking Boaz to claim his official role as her "redeemer" in the eyes of the law. But Boaz is a proper man. His first concern is for her reputation and welfare, so he sends her off in the dark, loaded with barley, before the daylight reveals where she has spent the night. His next concern is for following the law. He knows of a closer relative, and that man must deny his claim before Boaz is free to proceed.

What a wonderful man God prepared for Ruth! He was kind to her before he even knew her. Even though I'm sure there was a part of him that wanted to cover Ruth in a symbolic gesture of accepting her offer, he had to wait to see if this beautiful woman would be his wife.

THOUGHTS TO PONDER

Why do you think God would create the "close relative" or "redeemer" laws? What good would these laws have done the nation of Israel? What traits of Ruth do we see in this story?

PRAYER

God, we thank you for the beauty of love and the feelings you have given us for one another. Help us to be faithful in our love to you and to others all of our days. Amen.

From Bitterness to Joy

RUTH 4:1–17

4 Boaz went to the city gate and sat there until the close relative he had mentioned passed by. Boaz called to him, "Come here, friend, and sit down." So the man came over and sat down. ²Boaz gathered ten of the elders of the city and told them, "Sit down here!" So they sat down.

³Then Boaz said to the close relative, "Naomi, who has come back from the country of Moab, wants to sell the piece of land that belonged to our relative Elimelech. ⁴So I decided to tell you about it: If you want to buy back the land, then buy it in front of the people who are sitting here and in front of the elders of my people. But if you don't want to buy it, tell me, because you are the only one who can buy it, and I am next after you."

The close relative answered, "I will buy back the land."

⁵Then Boaz explained, "When you buy the land from Naomi, you must also marry Ruth, the Moabite, the dead man's wife. That way, the land will stay in the dead man's name."

⁶The close relative answered, "I can't buy back the land. If I did, I might harm what I can pass on to my own sons. I cannot buy the land back, so buy it yourself."

⁷Long ago in Israel when people traded or bought back something, one person took off his sandal and gave it to the other person. This was the proof of ownership in Israel.

⁸So the close relative said to Boaz, "Buy the land yourself," and he took off his sandal.

⁹Then Boaz said to the elders and to all the people, "You are witnesses today. I am buying from Naomi everything that belonged to Elimelech and Kilion and Mahlon. ¹⁰I am also taking Ruth, the Moabite who was the wife of Mahlon, as my wife. I am doing this so her dead husband's property will stay in his name and his name will not be separated from his family and his hometown. You are witnesses today."

¹¹So all the people and elders who were at the city gate said, "We are witnesses. May the LORD make this woman, who is coming into your home, like Rachel and Leah, who had many children and built up the people of Israel. May you become powerful in the district of Ephrathah and famous in Bethlehem. ¹²As Tamar gave birth to Judah's son Perez, may the LORD give you many children through Ruth. May your family be great like his."

¹³So Boaz took Ruth home as his wife and had sexual relations with her. The LORD let her become pregnant, and she gave birth to a son. ¹⁴The women told Naomi, "Praise the LORD who gave you this grandson. May he become famous

in Israel. [15]He will give you new life and will take care of you in your old age because of your daughter-in-law who loves you. She is better for you than seven sons, because she has given birth to your grandson."

[16]Naomi took the boy, held him in her arms, and cared for him. [17]The neighbors gave the boy his name, saying, "This boy was born for Naomi." They named him Obed. Obed was the father of Jesse, and Jesse was the father of David.

DEVOTION

BOAZ GATHERED about him an impromptu "synagogue" of ten elders and confronted the only man who stood between him and his would-be bride. When the negotiations were over, only Boaz wanted both the land and the responsibility of Ruth. He gladly made a vow in the presence of the elders that he would pay Naomi for the land and take Ruth as his wife.

One thing I like about this story is that there is no more mention of the name "Mara" for Naomi. She took the name Mara—which means "bitter"—immediately after she returned from years in Moab with no husband and no sons. God had dealt with her severely, she thought, and she wanted everyone to know just how bitter she was.

But now, she is once again Naomi. All references to Mara are gone. The bitterness of the past is over. God has blessed her with a loving kinsman who treats her fairly and now a baby boy who can carry on the lineage of her beloved Elimelech. The boy will give her new life. And as he works the land that once belonged to his grandfather, Obed will take care of Naomi.

The odyssey of Naomi began with a famine that forced her out of Israel. But famines—literal and spiritual—last only for a season, and then comes the rain of blessings that turns our bitterness into joy once more.

THOUGHTS TO PONDER

How many times do you see the providence of God at work in this story? Why do you think the story of Ruth—the grandmother of David—is preserved for us in Scripture?

PRAYER

God, we see your hand at work in preparing the right people at the right time to someday bless the world with your Son. Please prepare us to proclaim his next coming. Amen.

No Hesitation

1 SAMUEL 1:2–3, 9–20, 24–28

²Elkanah had two wives named Hannah and Peninnah. Peninnah had children, but Hannah had none.

³Every year Elkanah left his town of Ramah and went up to Shiloh to worship the LORD All-Powerful and to offer sacrifices to him.

⁹Once, after they had eaten their meal in Shiloh, Hannah got up. Now Eli the priest was sitting on a chair near the entrance to the LORD's house. ¹⁰Hannah was so sad that she cried and prayed to the LORD. ¹¹She made a promise, saying, "LORD All-Powerful, see how sad I am. Remember me and don't forget me. If you will give me a son, I will give him back to you all his life, and no one will ever cut his hair with a razor."

¹²While Hannah kept praying, Eli watched her mouth. ¹³She was praying in her heart so her lips moved, but her voice was not heard. Eli thought she was drunk ¹⁴and said to her, "Stop getting drunk! Throw away your wine!"

¹⁵Hannah answered, "No, sir, I have not drunk any wine or beer. I am a deeply troubled woman, and I was telling the LORD about all my problems. ¹⁶Don't think I am an evil woman. I have been praying because I have many troubles and am very sad."

¹⁷Eli answered, "Go! I wish you well. May the God of Israel give you what you asked of him."

¹⁸Hannah said, "May I always please you." When she left and ate something, she was not sad anymore.

¹⁹Early the next morning Elkanah's family got up and worshiped the LORD. Then they went back home to Ramah. Elkanah had sexual relations with his wife Hannah, and the LORD remembered her. ²⁰So Hannah became pregnant, and in time she gave birth to a son. She named him Samuel, saying, "His name is Samuel because I asked the LORD for him."

²⁴When Samuel was old enough to eat, Hannah took him to the house of the LORD at Shiloh, along with a three-year-old bull, one-half bushel of flour, and a leather bag filled with wine. ²⁵After they had killed the bull for the sacrifice, Hannah brought Samuel to Eli. ²⁶She said to Eli, "As surely as you live, sir, I am the same woman who stood near you praying to the LORD. ²⁷I prayed for this child, and the LORD answered my prayer and gave him to me. ²⁸Now I give him back to the LORD. He will belong to the LORD all his life."

DEVOTION

THE PAIN OF BEING childless was particularly acute during biblical times, when a woman was measured by her ability to give heirs to her husband. Sarah offered her handmaiden to Abraham so he could have an heir when she judged herself too old to fulfill the promise of God to make a great nation of Abraham's seed. Rachel grieved as her sister Leah was able to give Jacob six sons and a daughter before she was able to become pregnant with Joseph.

In this story, Hannah makes a promise to God: give me a son and I'll give him back to you. The promise she made indicated the boy would be a Nazirite, a person who would be dedicated to God in a special way. Nazirites were marked by their long hair, which would not be cut as long as the Nazirite vow was in place (see Numbers 6:1–5). Perhaps the most famous example of a Nazirite was Samson, whose legendary strength left him after Delilah cut his hair.

When God blesses her with a child, Hannah keeps her promise to God. She delivers him to the Temple for a lifetime of service. She considered Samuel to be a gift from God, and now she was repaying that gift by giving him back to God.

I think that every Christian parent needs the attitude of Hannah. Our children are a gift from God, and it is our duty to return them to God. As I heard one Christian woman remark to her child, "You came from heaven and it's my job to make sure you get back there."

I heard a man once speak at the funeral of his own child. Trying to make sense of the tragedy, he said, was impossible until he came across this passage and realized that his child had been a gift from God. As with any gift, he said, the only proper response was gratitude over the years he had enjoyed, not bitterness over what might have been.

When it was time, Hannah didn't hesitate. She thanked God for the years she enjoyed her special gift from heaven and gave him back to God.

THOUGHTS TO PONDER

How can we let our children know that we consider them a gift from God? How does it change our attitude when we see our children as belonging to God?

PRAYER

Father, we are all your children, and we pray that, when you allow us to be earthly parents, we will treasure our children as blessings from you. Amen.

A Message from God

1 SAMUEL 3:1–21

3 The boy Samuel served the LORD under Eli. In those days the LORD did not speak directly to people very often; there were very few visions.

²Eli's eyes were so weak he was almost blind. One night he was lying in bed. ³Samuel was also in bed in the LORD's house, where the Ark of the Agreement was. God's lamp was still burning.

⁴Then the LORD called Samuel, and Samuel answered, "I am here!" ⁵He ran to Eli and said, "I am here. You called me."

But Eli said, "I didn't call you. Go back to bed." So Samuel went back to bed. ⁶The LORD called again, "Samuel!"

Samuel again went to Eli and said, "I am here. You called me."

Again Eli said, "I didn't call you. Go back to bed."

⁷Samuel did not yet know the LORD, and the LORD had not spoken directly to him yet.

⁸The LORD called Samuel for the third time. Samuel got up and went to Eli and said, "I am here. You called me."

Then Eli realized the LORD was calling the boy. ⁹So he told Samuel, "Go to bed. If he calls you again, say, 'Speak, LORD. I am your servant and I am listening.'" So Samuel went and lay down in bed.

¹⁰The LORD came and stood there and called as he had before, "Samuel, Samuel!"

Samuel said, "Speak, LORD. I am your servant and I am listening."

¹¹The LORD said to Samuel, "Watch, I am going to do something in Israel that will shock those who hear about it. ¹²At that time I will do to Eli and his family everything I promised, from beginning to end. ¹³I told Eli I would punish his family always, because he knew his sons were evil. They acted without honor, but he did not stop them. ¹⁴So I swore to Eli's family, 'Your guilt will never be removed by sacrifice or offering.'"

¹⁵Samuel lay down until morning. Then he opened the doors of the house of the LORD. He was afraid to tell Eli about the vision, ¹⁶but Eli called to him, "Samuel, my son!"

Samuel answered, "I am here."

¹⁷Eli asked, "What did the LORD say to you? Don't hide it from me. May God punish you terribly if you hide from me anything he said to you." ¹⁸So Samuel told Eli everything and did not hide anything from him. Then Eli said, "He is the LORD. Let him do what he thinks is best."

¹⁹The LORD was with Samuel as he grew up; he did not let any of Samuel's messages fail to come true. ²⁰Then all Israel, from Dan to Beersheba, knew Samuel was a true prophet of the LORD. ²¹And the LORD continued to show himself at Shiloh, and he showed himself to Samuel through his word.

DEVOTION

I DISTINCTLY RECALL hearing as a child the story of young Samuel answering God's call. But the Bible story books rarely talked about what God said to Samuel. Only as an adult did I hear what God told the boy who would be his future priest.

Why would God burden a young boy with the fact that he was displeased with Eli due to the behavior of Eli's sons? The two sons, Hophni and Phinehas, were evil to the core. They took more than their share of the burnt offerings, and often took raw meat that had not yet even been offered to the LORD. They had also engaged in sexual relations with the women who served at the entrance to the Meeting Tent.

Finally, God could contain his anger no longer. He told Eli his family had no future as priests for his people. He also told Eli that both Hophni and Phinehas would die on the same day. That day would come when the Philistines killed thirty thousand Israelites in a single day, including Hophni and Phinehas, and captured the Ark of the Agreement. Eli would die upon hearing the news that his sons were gone.

So why burden young Samuel with the news of God's anger toward Eli and his sons? I think it was probably a lesson for Samuel. God wanted to impress on Samuel at a young age the sanctity of the priesthood so that history would not repeat itself. Honor needed to be restored to the priesthood and Samuel was God's choice for the task.

Samuel went on to have an illustrious career as a representative for God. He announced God's choice for the first two kings of Israel. He was the religious leader of the nation during a tumultuous time when God rejected one king and installed another. But I doubt that he ever forgot the lesson of that first message: God is to be respected and his laws are to be obeyed.

THOUGHTS TO PONDER

How does God speak to us today? How can we tune in to what God is saying to us?

PRAYER

God, we ask that you will speak to us today as we read your Word and as we meditate on it. We pray that, like Samuel, we will be ready to hear. Amen.

DECISIONS AND CONSEQUENCES

1 SAMUEL 4:1–18

At that time the Israelites went out to fight the Philistines. The Israelites camped at Ebenezer and the Philistines at Aphek. ²The Philistines went to meet the Israelites in battle. And as the battle spread, they defeated the Israelites, killing about four thousand soldiers on the battlefield. ³When some Israelite soldiers went back to their camp, the elders of Israel asked, "Why did the LORD let the Philistines defeat us? Let's bring the Ark of the Agreement with the LORD here from Shiloh and take it with us into battle. Then God will save us from our enemies."

⁴So the people sent men to Shiloh. They brought back the Ark of the Agreement with the LORD All-Powerful, who sits between the gold creatures with wings. Eli's two sons, Hophni and Phinehas, were there with the Ark.

⁵When the Ark of the Agreement with the LORD came into the camp, all the Israelites gave a great shout of joy that made the ground shake. ⁶When the Philistines heard Israel's shout, they asked, "What's all this shouting in the Hebrew camp?"

Then the Philistines found out that the Ark of the LORD had come into the Hebrew camp. ⁷They were afraid and said, "A god has come into the Hebrew camp! We're in trouble! This has never happened before! ⁸How terrible it will be for us! Who can save us from these powerful gods? They are the ones who struck the Egyptians with all kinds of disasters in the desert. ⁹Be brave, Philistines! Fight like men! In the past they were our slaves. So fight like men, or we will become their slaves."

¹⁰So the Philistines fought hard and defeated the Israelites, and every Israelite soldier ran away to his own home. It was a great defeat for Israel, because thirty thousand Israelite soldiers were killed. ¹¹The Ark of God was taken by the Philistines, and Eli's two sons, Hophni and Phinehas, died.

¹²That same day a man from the tribe of Benjamin ran from the battle. He tore his clothes and put dust on his head to show his great sadness. ¹³When he arrived in Shiloh, Eli was by the side of the road. He was sitting there in a chair, watching, because he was worried about the Ark of God. When the Benjaminite entered Shiloh, he told the bad news. Then all the people in town cried loudly. ¹⁴Eli heard the crying and asked, "What's all this noise?"

The Benjaminite ran to Eli and told him what had happened. ¹⁵Eli was now ninety-eight years old, and he was blind. ¹⁶The Benjaminite told him, "I have come from the battle. I ran all the way here today."

Eli asked, "What happened, my son?"

[17]The Benjaminite answered, "Israel ran away from the Philistines, and the Israelite army has lost many soldiers. Your two sons are both dead, and the Philistines have taken the Ark of God."

[18]When he mentioned the Ark of God, Eli fell backward off his chair. He fell beside the gate, broke his neck, and died, because he was old and fat. He had led Israel for forty years.

DEVOTION

AS THE MOST HOLY symbol of the people of Israel, the Ark resided within the Meeting Tent, in the Most Holy Place. Whether the Israelites were on the move or camping, the Ark was always at the center of the people (Numbers 2:17), a physical symbol of God's presence among them. When it was in front of the people, it was a symbol that God was going before them into battle (Deuteronomy 1:30–33). Perhaps the best-known military use of the Ark is described in the story of Jericho when the great walls of that city fell to the ground after the people of Israel, carrying the Ark of the Agreement, repeatedly marched around the city for seven days.

In this story we also see the fulfillment of the prophecy that Hophni and Phinehas would die for the way they flagrantly abused their positions as priests by taking portions of the animal sacrifices before they had been offered to God. They had also engaged in sexual immorality with women who were in the service of the Temple. The prediction that they would die on the same day because of their sins came true (1 Samuel 2:34).

Although the reason for the defeat is not given, it can be inferred that the Israelites did not have the blessing of God to take the Ark into this particular battle. They wanted to use the Ark as a sort of "charm," and the results were calamitous. God has never promised to protect us from our own bad choices. Israel paid the price for the rash decision to take the Ark into battle.

THOUGHTS TO PONDER

Why did God punish the Israelites for taking the Ark into this battle? How does this battle differ from circling Jericho with the Ark? Do we ever expect God's protection from our own bad decisions?

PRAYER

Father, we pray that you will bless the decisions we make and that we will never abuse the protection that you offer us as your children. Amen.

EBENEZER STONES

I SAMUEL 7:2–17

²The Ark stayed at Kiriath Jearim a long time—twenty years in all. And the people of Israel began to follow the LORD again. ³Samuel spoke to the whole group of Israel, saying, "If you're turning back to the LORD with all your hearts, you must remove your foreign gods and your idols of Ashtoreth. You must give yourselves fully to the LORD and serve only him. Then he will save you from the Philistines."

⁴So the Israelites put away their idols of Baal and Ashtoreth, and they served only the LORD.

⁵Samuel said, "All Israel must meet at Mizpah, and I will pray to the LORD for you." ⁶So the Israelites met together at Mizpah. They drew water from the ground and poured it out before the LORD and fasted that day. They confessed, "We have sinned against the LORD." And Samuel served as judge of Israel at Mizpah.

⁷The Philistines heard the Israelites were meeting at Mizpah, so the Philistine kings came up to attack them. When the Israelites heard they were coming, they were afraid. ⁸They said to Samuel, "Don't stop praying to the LORD our God for us! Ask him to save us from the Philistines!" ⁹Then Samuel took a baby lamb and offered it to the LORD as a whole burnt offering. He called to the LORD for Israel's sake, and the LORD answered him.

¹⁰While Samuel was burning the offering, the Philistines came near to attack Israel. But the LORD thundered against them with loud thunder. They were so frightened they became confused. So the Israelites defeated the Philistines in battle. ¹¹The men of Israel ran out of Mizpah and chased the Philistines almost to Beth Car, killing the Philistines along the way.

¹²After this happened Samuel took a stone and set it up between Mizpah and Shen. He named the stone Ebenezer, saying, "The LORD has helped us to this point." ¹³So the Philistines were defeated and did not enter the Israelites' land again.

The LORD was against the Philistines all Samuel's life. ¹⁴Earlier the Philistines had taken towns from the Israelites, but the Israelites won them back, from Ekron to Gath. They also took back from the Philistines the lands near these towns. There was peace also between Israel and the Amorites.

¹⁵Samuel continued as judge of Israel all his life. ¹⁶Every year he went from Bethel to Gilgal to Mizpah and judged the Israelites in all these towns. ¹⁷But Samuel always went back to Ramah, where his home was. There he judged Israel and built an altar to the LORD.

DEVOTION

THE LONGER I LIVE, the less I believe in luck or coincidence and the more I am assured of God's providence. From a worldly point of view, I can see the attraction of giving credit to "good luck" when things work out. If I give God the credit when things work out in my life, I might end up "owing" him praise and gratitude (and worse, obedience) for his role in my success. If on the other hand I credit "luck," I owe nothing to anyone.

The Ebenezer stone was Samuel's way of calling the nation's attention to the fact that God was operating in the lives of the Israelites, individually and corporately. "By God's help we've come this far" was the message of the stone. Not good luck, not military prowess. Only God's help had led the Israelites to victory, and for that help, he was worthy of praise. Later, Israel would sadly forget that lesson, and they would find out too late that military might is no substitute for following the instructions of God and having him on your side in times of battle.

I am firmly convinced that our faith would be strengthened if we had more Ebenezer stones in our lives. Hard work is a must. Good fortune may play a part. But for day in and day out results, I'll take the hand of God any day. We need to hear more "By God's help, I got this promotion" or "By God's help, our children are healthy and well-adjusted" and less "knock on wood."

Ebenezer stones—in whatever form they take—should mark our birthdays, our achievements, and every milestone of our lives.

Why was the stone so important to Israel? Why should these "stones" populate the walls of our offices, the bookshelves of our homes? Why should we talk about them? The reason is that the Ebenezer stone calls me back to two facts: I am not alone and I am not in charge. Where I am in life is the result of my efforts being blessed by God's grace.

Ebenezer stones do not mark final resting places; they mark temporary respites before pursuing God's purpose in the rest of my life. If life is a journey, Ebenezer stones are the mile markers.

THOUGHTS TO PONDER

What are some of the "Ebenezer" events in your life where you can see that God was helping you? What can we do to remind ourselves daily that God "has helped us to this point"?

PRAYER

God, we know that it is only by your divine help that we have come this far. Help us, like Samuel, to erect the reminders of your providence so we see them and remember you each day. Amen.

OUR ONLY KING

1 SAMUEL 8:1–22

8 When Samuel was old, he made his sons judges for Israel. ²His first son was named Joel, and his second son was named Abijah. Joel and Abijah were judges in Beersheba. ³But Samuel's sons did not live as he did. They tried to get money dishonestly, and they accepted money secretly to make wrong judgments.

⁴So all the elders came together and met Samuel at Ramah. ⁵They said to him, "You're old, and your sons don't live as you do. Give us a king to rule over us like all the other nations."

⁶When the elders said that, Samuel was not pleased. He prayed to the LORD, ⁷and the LORD told Samuel, "Listen to whatever the people say to you. They have not rejected you. They have rejected me from being their king. ⁸They are doing as they have always done. When I took them out of Egypt, they left me and served other gods. They are doing the same to you. ⁹Now listen to the people, but warn them what the king who rules over them will do."

¹⁰So Samuel told those who had asked him for a king what the LORD had said. ¹¹Samuel said, "If you have a king ruling over you, this is what he will do: He will take your sons and make them serve with his chariots and his horses, and they will run in front of the king's chariot. ¹²The king will make some of your sons commanders over thousands or over fifties. He will make some of your other sons plow his ground and reap his harvest. He will take others to make weapons of war and equipment for his chariots. ¹³He will take your daughters to make perfume and cook and bake for him. ¹⁴He will take your best fields, vineyards, and olive groves and give them to his servants. ¹⁵He will take one-tenth of your grain and grapes and give it to his officers and servants. ¹⁶He will take your male and female servants, your best cattle, and your donkeys and use them all for his own work. ¹⁷He will take one-tenth of your flocks, and you yourselves will become his slaves. ¹⁸When that time comes, you will cry out because of the king you chose. But the LORD will not answer you then."

¹⁹But the people would not listen to Samuel. They said, "No! We want a king to rule over us. ²⁰Then we will be the same as all the other nations. Our king will judge for us and go with us and fight our battles."

²¹After Samuel heard all that the people said, he repeated their words to the LORD. ²²The LORD answered, "You must listen to them. Give them a king."

Then Samuel told the people of Israel, "Go back to your towns."

DEVOTION

I WANT TO BE LIKE everybody else. Why do I have to be different? Every parent of a teenager has heard it. Now the nation of Israel is acting like an impatient adolescent asking Samuel to appoint a king to replace him as the leader of the nation when he dies.

There is a very telling sentence in the first conversation God has with Samuel. He says: "They have not rejected you. They have rejected me from being their king." God had offered to be their King, and the people had rejected the offer. They opted for frail humans instead. And over the next few hundred years they got a series of good and bad leaders, starting a gradual decline into total apostasy and eventual slavery. And it all began right here with a single bad decision: we want a king.

God makes the same offer to us today: *I will be your King. I will be the Ruler of your life, and in exchange, you will be called my sons and daughters.* The interesting thing about God as ruler is that he doesn't want slaves. He wants children. Paul wrote about this to the Galatian believers: "But when the right time came, God sent his Son who was born of a woman and lived under the law. God did this so he could buy freedom for those who were under the law and so we could become his children. Since you are God's children, God sent the Spirit of his Son into your hearts, and the Spirit cries out, "Father." So now you are not a slave; you are God's child, and God will give you the blessing he promised, because you are his child" (Galatians 4:4–7).

The kings of Israel did to the people everything Samuel predicted, and more. But our King keeps all of his promises to his children and even more. As Paul wrote, "God can do much, much more than anything we can ask or imagine" (Ephesians 3:20). That sounds like the type of King I want to follow.

THOUGHTS TO PONDER

What does God's reaction to the desire of Israel to have a king say about God? What does it say about Israel? Why is it so hard to make him the King of our lives?

PRAYER

Father, we pray that we will place you on the throne of our lives and commit ourselves to serving you always. Amen.

HUMBLE BEGINNINGS

I SAMUEL 9:17–21; 10:1–7

¹⁷When Samuel first saw Saul, the LORD said to Samuel, "This is the man I told you about. He will organize my people."

¹⁸Saul approached Samuel at the gate and said, "Please tell me where the seer's house is."

¹⁹Samuel answered, "I am the seer. Go with me to the place of worship. Today you and your servant are to eat with me. Tomorrow morning I will answer all your questions and send you home. ²⁰Don't worry about the donkeys you lost three days ago, because they have been found. Soon all the wealth of Israel will belong to you and your family."

²¹Saul answered, "But I am from the tribe of Benjamin, the smallest tribe in Israel. And my family group is the smallest in the tribe of Benjamin. Why are you saying such things?"

10Samuel took a jar of olive oil and poured it on Saul's head. He kissed Saul and said, "The LORD has appointed you to lead his people. ²After you leave me today, you will meet two men near Rachel's tomb on the border of Benjamin at Zelzah. They will say to you, 'The donkeys you were looking for have been found. But now your father has stopped thinking about his donkeys and is worrying about you. He is asking, "What will I do about my son?" '

³"Then you will go on until you reach the big tree at Tabor. Three men on their way to worship God at Bethel will meet you there. One man will be carrying three goats. Another will be carrying three loaves of bread. And the third will have a leather bag full of wine. ⁴They will greet you and offer you two loaves of bread, which you must accept. ⁵Then you will go to Gibeah of God, where a Philistine camp is. When you approach this town, a group of prophets will come down from the place of worship. They will be playing harps, tambourines, flutes, and lyres, and they will be prophesying. ⁶Then the Spirit of the LORD will rush upon you with power. You will prophesy with these prophets, and you will be changed into a different man. ⁷After these signs happen, do whatever you find to do, because God will help you."

DEVOTION

IT'S A LIST of mostly forgettable places: Tampico, Illinois; Kinderhook, New York; West Branch, Iowa; Niles, Ohio; LaRue County, Kentucky; Barton County, Missouri. Off the beaten path. Not known as centers of commerce or industry. But each town or county above is the birthplace of a president of the United States. Men like Lincoln, Truman, and others came from these places and rose to one of the most powerful offices in the world.

God has never been impressed by addresses. When he chose a king for Israel, he chose a man from the smallest family of the smallest tribe in a time when family size equaled land and wealth. When he chose an earthly family for Jesus, he chose Joseph and Mary of Nazareth, a place so insignificant that one of the men who would become a followers of Jesus, Nathanael, scoffed at the idea of the Messiah coming from Nazareth.

John recorded this conversation: "Philip found Nathanael and told him, 'We have found the man that Moses wrote about in the law, and the prophets also wrote about him. He is Jesus, the son of Joseph, from Nazareth.' But Nathanael said to Philip, 'Can anything good come from Nazareth?' Philip answered, 'Come and see'" (John 1:45–46).

Great people can come from the most unlikely of places. God saw something in Saul, this boy looking across the countryside for his father's lost donkeys, and directed him to Samuel to be anointed as the first king of Israel. Jesus found his followers—the ones who would walk with him every day for three years and be entrusted with his message after he was gone—in unlikely places, too. He found them in fishing boats. He found one in a tax collector's booth. And he found Paul, the most prolific evangelist of the early church, in a very unlikely place: on the road to Damascus to throw some Christians in jail.

So it really doesn't matter where God found you—in a church pew or in an alleyway. Your former location is not relevant to God when he calls you. What does matter is your willingness to leave your former life and follow him. Or as Samuel told Saul, "Do whatever you find to do, because God will help you."

THOUGHTS TO PONDER

Where did God find you? Where is he calling you to go? How are you able to hear his will for your life?

PRAYER

Father, we're so glad you found us and that you have elevated us out of a life of sin and into a life of being your sons and daughters. Help us follow your path all our lives. Amen.

Changed Hearts

1 SAMUEL 10:9–27

⁹When Saul turned to leave Samuel, God changed Saul's heart. All these signs came true that day. ¹⁰When Saul and his servant arrived at Gibeah, Saul met a group of prophets. The Spirit of God rushed upon him, and he prophesied with the prophets. ¹¹When people who had known Saul before saw him prophesying with the prophets, they asked each other, "What has happened to Kish's son? Is even Saul one of the prophets?"

¹²A man who lived there said, "Who is the father of these prophets?" So this became a famous saying: "Is even Saul one of the prophets?" ¹³When Saul finished prophesying, he entered the place of worship.

¹⁴Saul's uncle asked him and his servant, "Where have you been?"

Saul said, "We were looking for the donkeys. When we couldn't find them, we went to talk to Samuel."

¹⁵Saul's uncle asked, "Please tell me. What did Samuel say to you?"

¹⁶Saul answered, "He told us the donkeys had already been found." But Saul did not tell his uncle what Samuel had said about his becoming king.

¹⁷Samuel called all the people of Israel to meet with the LORD at Mizpah. ¹⁸He said, "This is what the LORD, the God of Israel, says: 'I led Israel out of Egypt. I saved you from Egypt's control and from other kingdoms that were troubling you.' ¹⁹But now you have rejected your God. He saves you from all your troubles and problems, but you said, 'No! We want a king to rule over us.' Now come, stand before the LORD in your tribes and family groups."

²⁰When Samuel gathered all the tribes of Israel, the tribe of Benjamin was picked. ²¹Samuel had them pass by in family groups, and Matri's family was picked. Then he had each man of Matri's family pass by, and Saul son of Kish was picked. But when they looked for Saul, they could not find him. ²²They asked the LORD, "Has Saul come here yet?"

The LORD said, "Yes. He's hiding behind the baggage."

²³So they ran and brought him out. When Saul stood among the people, he was a head taller than anyone else. ²⁴Then Samuel said to the people, "See the man the LORD has chosen. There is no one like him among all the people."

Then the people shouted, "Long live the king!"

²⁵Samuel explained the rights and duties of the king and then wrote them in a book and put it before the LORD. Then he told the people to go to their homes.

²⁶Saul also went to his home in Gibeah. God touched the hearts of certain brave men who went along with him. ²⁷But some troublemakers said, "How can this man save us?" They disapproved of Saul and refused to bring gifts to him. But Saul kept quiet.

Devotion

WHEN GOD SELECTS men or women for his purposes, he changes their hearts. As Saul turned to leave Samuel, no doubt still stunned by the turn of events that had made him the king, the text tells us that "God changed Saul's heart" (1 Samuel 10:9). That's where it all starts. If we're to follow God and do his will in our lives, it is going to require a "heart transplant." I'm going to have to allow him to exchange my heart for the one he intends me to have.

As we look at the story above, we see at least two qualities of Saul's heart that would serve him well as king. First, we see the heart of humility when Saul, knowing that he was the chosen one, refused to join the parade of males passing before the people. The people found Saul hiding in the baggage—the future king of Israel.

Second we see the quality of discretion. Even though he was surrounded by bodyguards who had been touched by God to be supporters of Saul, the new king did not punish those who spoke ill of him and refused to give him tribute. Instead, he kept quiet before his critics. About a month later, there was a crisis in Gilead during which Saul proved his ability to rally the people. But on this day, he held his tongue even in the face of criticism.

Would Saul have troubles? Yes, he certainly would. Eventually his defects would be so serious that God would reject him, and Samuel would anoint another king—David, son of Jesse—even before the death of Saul, causing chaos in the land for a while. But on this day, with his entire political career ahead of him, Saul stood head and shoulders taller than those around him in many ways.

Thoughts to ponder

How do we know when God changes our hearts? What will we be capable of if we allow God to truly change our hearts?

Prayer

God, please change our hearts so we will be able to do great things for you. Amen.

GOD PREFERS OBEDIENCE

I SAMUEL 15:1–3, 7–10, 13–22

15 Samuel said to Saul, "The LORD sent me to appoint you king over Israel. Now listen to his message. ²This is what the LORD All-Powerful says: 'When the Israelites came out of Egypt, the Amalekites tried to stop them from going to Canaan. So I will punish them. ³Now go, attack the Amalekites and destroy everything they own as an offering to the LORD. Don't let anything live. Put to death men and women, children and small babies, cattle and sheep, camels and donkeys.'"

⁷Then Saul defeated the Amalekites. He fought them all the way from Havilah to Shur, at the border of Egypt. ⁸He took King Agag of the Amalekites alive, but he killed all of Agag's army with the sword. ⁹Saul and the army let Agag live, along with the best sheep, fat cattle, and lambs. They let every good animal live, because they did not want to destroy them. But when they found an animal that was weak or useless, they killed it.

¹⁰Then the LORD spoke his word to Samuel: ¹¹"I am sorry I made Saul king, because he has stopped following me and has not obeyed my commands." Samuel was upset, and he cried out to the LORD all night long.

¹³When Samuel came to Saul, Saul said, "May the LORD bless you! I have obeyed the LORD's commands."

¹⁴But Samuel said, "Then why do I hear cattle mooing and sheep bleating?"

¹⁵Saul answered, "The soldiers took them from the Amalekites. They saved the best sheep and cattle to offer as sacrifices to the LORD your God, but we destroyed all the other animals."

¹⁶Samuel said to Saul, "Stop! Let me tell you what the LORD said to me last night." Saul answered, "Tell me."

¹⁷Samuel said, "Once you didn't think much of yourself, but now you have become the leader of the tribes of Israel. The LORD appointed you to be king over Israel. ¹⁸And he sent you on a mission. He said, 'Go and destroy those evil people, the Amalekites. Make war on them until all of them are dead.' ¹⁹Why didn't you obey the LORD? Why did you take the best things? Why did you do what the LORD said was wrong?"

²⁰Saul said, "But I did obey the LORD. I did what the LORD told me to do. I destroyed all the Amalekites, and I brought back Agag their king. ²¹The soldiers took the best sheep and cattle to sacrifice to the LORD your God at Gilgal."

²²But Samuel answered,

"What pleases the LORD more:
    burnt offerings and sacrifices
    or obedience to his voice?

It is better to obey than to sacrifice.

It is better to listen to God than to offer the fat of sheep."

Devotion

GANDHI PREACHED civil disobedience to his followers—the refusal to obey unjust rules in a non-violent way. Martin Luther King, Jr. would preach the same strategy years later in the segregated South. Non-violent protesters, such as Rosa Parks who refused to move to the back of the bus in Montgomery, are now a part of our history.

In this passage, Saul is performing an act of "religious disobedience." Told to utterly destroy the Amalekites, Saul changes the orders and saves the best of the sheep and oxen for the purpose of sacrificing them to God . . . in defiance of God's specific orders.

As noble as his motive might sound, Saul's act was wrong and the prophet Samuel's rebuke to him is one of the great lessons of the Bible. Forget your sacrifice; God prefers obedience.

How easy it is for us to slip into Saul's trap. God won't mind, I think, that I work a seventy-hour week, ignoring my family in the process, if I tithe out of the big salary I'll get. God won't mind what I do on a Saturday night as long as I make it to worship, properly penitent, on Sunday.

But worshiping God doesn't start at a fixed time on Sunday morning; it continues. It's a continuation of my work offering, my family obligation offering, my devotional offering that I've lifted up all week long. When Saul failed to carry out God's orders, God was not impressed with his offering. The same principle is true today.

Sacrifice can be done quickly, but obedience is a 24-hour-a-day job. That's why I think we prefer our one-time acts of sacrifice—write a check, drop off some old clothes at the rescue mission—over the fulltime job of obedience. God holds the opposite preference.

Thoughts to ponder

Why would an act of worship be considered an act of rebellion? What does this story tell us about God? What does it tell us about how we are supposed to live?

Prayer

God, we are your children, and we pray we will obey your will. Forgive us when we fall short, and forgive us when we think you're pleased by gifts rather than obedience. Amen.

IDOLS OF FLESH
AND BLOOD

1 SAMUEL 16:1–13

16 The LORD said to Samuel, "How long will you continue to feel sorry for Saul? I have rejected him as king of Israel. Fill your container with olive oil and go. I am sending you to Jesse who lives in Bethlehem, because I have chosen one of his sons to be king."

²But Samuel said, "If I go, Saul will hear the news and will try to kill me."

The LORD said, "Take a young calf with you. Say, 'I have come to offer a sacrifice to the LORD.' ³Invite Jesse to the sacrifice. Then I will tell you what to do. You must appoint the one I show you."

⁴Samuel did what the LORD told him to do. When he arrived at Bethlehem, the elders of Bethlehem shook with fear. They met him and asked, "Are you coming in peace?"

⁵Samuel answered, "Yes, I come in peace. I have come to make a sacrifice to the LORD. Set yourselves apart to the LORD and come to the sacrifice with me." Then he set Jesse and his sons apart to the LORD, and he invited them to come to the sacrifice.

⁶When they arrived, Samuel saw Eliab, and he thought, "Surely the LORD has appointed this person standing here before him."

⁷But the LORD said to Samuel, "Don't look at how handsome Eliab is or how tall he is, because I have not chosen him. God does not see the same way people see. People look at the outside of a person, but the LORD looks at the heart."

⁸Then Jesse called Abinadab and told him to pass by Samuel. But Samuel said, "The LORD has not chosen this man either." ⁹Then Jesse had Shammah pass by. But Samuel said, "No, the LORD has not chosen this one." ¹⁰Jesse had seven of his sons pass by Samuel. But Samuel said to him, "The LORD has not chosen any of these."

¹¹Then he asked Jesse, "Are these all the sons you have?"

Jesse answered, "I still have the youngest son. He is out taking care of the sheep."

Samuel said, "Send for him. We will not sit down to eat until he arrives."

¹²So Jesse sent and had his youngest son brought in. He was a fine boy, tanned, and handsome.

The LORD said to Samuel, "Go, appoint him, because he is the one."

¹³So Samuel took the container of olive oil and poured it on Jesse's youngest son to appoint him in front of his brothers. From that day on, the LORD's Spirit worked in David. Samuel then went back to Ramah.

DEVOTION

IN HIS BOOK, *Blink*, author Malcolm Gladwell writes about former president Warren Harding. Harding is not thought to be one of the most effective American presidents of the twentieth century. But it has been suggested that he was nominated for and won the presidency thanks primarily to his "presidential" looks (Little, Brown and Company, 2005).

Even today, in a photo gallery of all U.S. presidents, it is undeniable that Harding looks like the prototype for the job. But he was scarcely qualified, and his inadequacies came to light once he achieved the highest office in the land.

Samuel was falling into the same trap in the story above. Eliab was tall and looked the part. Surely this is the one, Samuel thought. But God had another choice in mind. David. The youngest of the group. Still a boy working the flocks. The least "kingly" of all Jesse's sons became the greatest king of Israel.

God had a lesson for Samuel on that day that we need to hear: "God does not see the same way people see. People look at the outside of a person, but the LORD looks at the heart" (1 Samuel 16:7).

Our culture is obsessed with the way a person looks. How tall they are. How much they weigh. What type of clothing they wear. How young they look. And as an entire generation of baby boomers reaches the late stages of middle age, plastic surgery is at an all-time high as men and women wage a battle against the toll of time.

George Bernard Shaw observed that men once made idols of wood and stone, but today our idols are flesh and blood. One need only look at our preoccupation with celebrity in this country and the control Hollywood has over our society to see who our modern idols are. If God spoke directly to us today, he would say of them, "Don't look at how handsome these movie stars are or how tall these supermodels are, for I have not chosen all of them. I have chosen people according to what I see in their hearts."

THOUGHTS TO PONDER

Do you think God reads our thoughts today like he did those of Samuel in this story? What would your thoughts about the way people look say about you if they were made public?

PRAYER

God, we pray that we will see all people as your children, and that we will see the living soul in everyone no matter how they look on the outside. Amen.

DEFEAT THROUGH DISCOURAGEMENT

1 SAMUEL 17:1–24

17 The Philistines gathered their armies for war. They met at Socoh in Judah and camped at Ephes Dammim between Socoh and Azekah. ²Saul and the Israelites gathered in the Valley of Elah and camped there and took their positions to fight the Philistines. ³The Philistines controlled one hill while the Israelites controlled another. The valley was between them.

⁴The Philistines had a champion fighter from Gath named Goliath. He was about nine feet, four inches tall. He came out of the Philistine camp ⁵with a bronze helmet on his head and a coat of bronze armor that weighed about one hundred twenty-five pounds. ⁶He wore bronze protectors on his legs, and he had a bronze spear on his back. ⁷The wooden part of his larger spear was like a weaver's rod, and its blade weighed about fifteen pounds. The officer who carried his shield walked in front of him.

⁸Goliath stood and shouted to the Israelite soldiers, "Why have you taken positions for battle? I am a Philistine, and you are Saul's servants! Choose a man and send him to fight me. ⁹If he can fight and kill me, we will be your servants. But if I can kill him, you will be our servants." ¹⁰Then he said, "Today I stand and dare the army of Israel! Send one of your men to fight me!" ¹¹When Saul and the Israelites heard the Philistine's words, they were very scared.

¹²Now David was the son of Jesse, an Ephrathite from Bethlehem in Judah. Jesse had eight sons. In Saul's time Jesse was an old man. ¹³His three oldest sons followed Saul to the war. The first son was Eliab, the second was Abinadab, and the third was Shammah. ¹⁴David was the youngest. Jesse's three oldest sons followed Saul, ¹⁵but David went back and forth from Saul to Bethlehem, where he took care of his father's sheep.

¹⁶For forty days the Philistine came out every morning and evening and stood before the Israelite army.

¹⁷Jesse said to his son David, "Take this half bushel of cooked grain and ten loaves of bread to your brothers in the camp. ¹⁸Also take ten pieces of cheese to the commander and to your brothers. See how your brothers are and bring back some proof to show me that they are all right. ¹⁹Your brothers are with Saul and the army in the Valley of Elah, fighting against the Philistines."

²⁰Early in the morning David left the sheep with another shepherd. He took the food and left as Jesse had told him. When David arrived at the camp, the army was going out to their battle positions, shouting their war cry. ²¹The Israelites and Philistines were lining up their men to face each other in battle.

[22]David left the food with the man who kept the supplies and ran to the battle line to talk to his brothers. [23]While he was talking with them, Goliath, the Philistine champion from Gath, came out. He shouted things against Israel as usual, and David heard him. [24]When the Israelites saw Goliath, they were very much afraid and ran away.

DEVOTION

HE WAS NINE FEET of warrior—stronger than any two men. With his incredible height and unparalleled arm span, no battlefield would be safe with Goliath as one of its combatants. He was an ancient precursor to one of those science fiction villains who cannot be killed. Only Goliath was not some creation of a Hollywood writer—he was a real, blasphemous menace to Israel. For forty days, the battle ceased while he taunted the Israelites with his challenges and undoubtedly his opinions about their God and their king.

Back home, Jesse sent David off with special food for his brothers. Homemade food on the battlefield has always tasted sweet, and Jesse sent plenty to share. As he commanded David to go, Jesse made an interesting comment: your brothers are fighting the Philistines.

How disheartened would the Israelites have been if they knew one man had stopped the entire army of Israel? Jesse proudly thought his boys were fighting the enemy when, in reality, they were cowering behind the lines.

You see, if Satan can discourage us, he doesn't have to defeat us. Keeping us timid about our faith is about as good as making us faithless. At least timid faith doesn't spread anywhere. So Satan finds a "goliath" to put in our way. Maybe it's illness. Or marital discord. Or the wrong friends. Or a worldly work environment. Whatever he can use to bully us back into our spiritual trenches, he will use.

Goliaths can be beaten. Anything Satan puts in your path can be overcome. That's the first lesson of this story.

THOUGHTS TO PONDER

What "goliaths" have you seen Satan use in your life or in the lives of others to discourage you or someone you know? How do you avoid them or defeat them?

PRAYER

God, we pray that we will never be timid and always overcome discouragement so that we can be courageous for you. Amen.

THE RIGHT "ARMOR"

1 SAMUEL 17:32–51

³²David said to Saul, "Don't let anyone be discouraged. I, your servant, will go and fight this Philistine!"

³³Saul answered, "You can't go out against this Philistine and fight him. You're only a boy. Goliath has been a warrior since he was a young man."

³⁴But David said to Saul, "I, your servant, have been keeping my father's sheep. When a lion or bear came and took a sheep from the flock, ³⁵I would chase it. I would attack it and save the sheep from its mouth. When it attacked me, I caught it by its fur and hit it and killed it. ³⁶I, your servant, have killed both a lion and a bear! This uncircumcised Philistine will be like them, because he has spoken against the armies of the living God. ³⁷The LORD who saved me from a lion and a bear will save me from this Philistine."

Saul said to David, "Go, and may the LORD be with you." ³⁸Saul put his own clothes on David. He put a bronze helmet on his head and dressed him in armor. ³⁹David put on Saul's sword and tried to walk around, but he was not used to all the armor Saul had put on him.

He said to Saul, "I can't go in this, because I'm not used to it." Then David took it all off. ⁴⁰He took his stick in his hand and chose five smooth stones from a stream. He put them in his shepherd's bag and grabbed his sling. Then he went to meet the Philistine.

⁴¹At the same time, the Philistine was coming closer to David. The man who held his shield walked in front of him. ⁴²When Goliath looked at David and saw that he was only a boy, tanned and handsome, he looked down on David with disgust. ⁴³He said, "Do you think I am a dog, that you come at me with a stick?" He used his gods' names to curse David. ⁴⁴He said to David, "Come here. I'll feed your body to the birds of the air and the wild animals!"

⁴⁵But David said to him, "You come to me using a sword and two spears. But I come to you in the name of the LORD All-Powerful, the God of the armies of Israel! You have spoken against him. ⁴⁶Today the LORD will hand you over to me, and I'll kill you and cut off your head. Today I'll feed the bodies of the Philistine soldiers to the birds of the air and the wild animals. Then all the world will know there is a God in Israel! ⁴⁷Everyone gathered here will know the LORD does not need swords or spears to save people. The battle belongs to him, and he will hand you over to us."

⁴⁸As Goliath came near to attack him, David ran quickly to meet him. ⁴⁹He took a stone from his bag, put it into his sling, and slung it. The stone hit the Philistine and went deep into his forehead, and Goliath fell facedown on the ground.

[50]So David defeated the Philistine with only a sling and a stone. He hit him and killed him. He did not even have a sword in his hand. [51]Then David ran and stood beside him. He took Goliath's sword out of its holder and killed him by cutting off his head.

When the Philistines saw that their champion was dead, they turned and ran.

DEVOTION

IMAGINE THE SIGHT of David, a smallish boy, being dressed in the armor of Saul, a king who stood head and shoulders above all the men of Israel. It must have looked like a child putting on his daddy's clothes. A breastplate that hung to his knees. A sword that dragged the ground and got between his legs when he tried to walk. A too-large helmet that covered his eyes, making it impossible to see.

David must have looked and felt ridiculous.

You see, to Saul, the power was in the armor. It was where he put his trust, and if David was to have a chance, he had to be fully armed.

But to David, the power was in God. The same God that had rescued him before from the wild animals that threatened his flock. The same God he had heard about who saved his people from the Egyptians and made armies melt in front of the nation of Israel as they were claiming the Land of Promise. Surely that God was bigger than this one oversized infidel.

David went into battle with what he had tested—his sling. His aim had been true before, and he knew it would be true on this day. He trusted the sling because he had tested the sling.

THOUGHTS TO PONDER

What is your "armor" against Satan? Have you tested it? Are you trusting in the wrong armor—the faith of your parents, regular church attendance, etc.—that might fail in the hour of trial?

PRAYER

Father, you have given us your Word as a defense against Satan. Help us test and prove it repeatedly so we can face the tests that will come. Amen.

CONSUMED WITH ENVY

1 SAMUEL 18:1–16, 28–30

18 When David finished talking with Saul, Jonathan felt very close to David. He loved David as much as he loved himself. ²Saul kept David with him from that day on and did not let him go home to his father's house. ³Jonathan made an agreement with David, because he loved David as much as himself. ⁴He took off his coat and gave it to David, along with his armor, including his sword, bow, and belt.

⁵Saul sent David to fight in different battles, and David was very successful. Then Saul put David over the soldiers, which pleased Saul's officers and all the other people.

⁶After David had killed the Philistine, he and the men returned home. Women came out from all the towns of Israel to meet King Saul. They sang songs of joy, danced, and played tambourines and stringed instruments. ⁷As they played, they sang,

"Saul has killed thousands of his enemies,
    but David has killed tens of thousands."

⁸The women's song upset Saul, and he became very angry. He thought, "The women say David has killed tens of thousands, but they say I have killed only thousands. The only thing left for him to have is the kingdom!" ⁹So Saul watched David closely from then on, because he was jealous.

¹⁰The next day an evil spirit from God rushed upon Saul, and he prophesied in his house. David was playing the harp as he usually did, but Saul had a spear in his hand. ¹¹He threw the spear, thinking, "I'll pin David to the wall." But David escaped from him twice.

¹²The LORD was with David but had left Saul. So Saul was afraid of David. ¹³He sent David away and made him commander of a thousand soldiers. So David led them in battle. ¹⁴He had great success in everything he did because the LORD was with him. ¹⁵When Saul saw that David was very successful, he feared David even more. ¹⁶But all the people of Israel and Judah loved David because he led them well in battle.

²⁸Saul saw that the LORD was with David and that his daughter Michal loved David. ²⁹So he grew even more afraid of David, and he was David's enemy all his life.

³⁰The Philistine commanders continued to go out to fight the Israelites, but every time, David was more skillful than Saul's officers. So he became famous.

DEVOTION

WHEN I WAS A BOY, the nation was gripped by Daniel Boone fever. Not that I was alive during the life of Daniel Boone, who died in 1820, but I was alive for his reincarnation as a genuine Sunday night hero manufactured by Disney in the 1960s.

This Daniel Boone wore a coonskin cap and a fringed leather jacket. He was the prototypical American pioneer. Suddenly, every kid in the nation had to have a coonskin cap and leather jacket with fringe. Then there was the song that began the show every Sunday night. It described Daniel Boone as larger than life, eagle-eyed and mountain tall. We all sang along and bought the record, the lunch pail, and anything else with Daniel Boone's image on it. More than a century after his death, he was a real American hero.

I thought of that because it appears that it was the song that got under Saul's skin the most in the story above. Ever since antiquity, we've loved to sing about our heroes, and the Israelites were no exception. "Saul has killed thousands of his enemies, but David has killed tens of thousands," they sang. "David is greater than the king" was the not-so-subtle message between the lines. If there had been lunch pails and trading cards back then, David's would have outsold Saul's ten to one. He was an instant folk hero, a literal giant-killer.

Maybe you've heard it said, "keep your friends close, keep your enemies closer." Saul was going to keep David very close, fearing that the people might someday turn away from him to this far more popular war hero. So he kept David in his house, offering him choice military assignments (hoping the Philistines would kill him) and even one of his daughters in marriage.

This would begin an intrigue between David and Saul that would last for years, cost many lives (including the lives of Saul and his sons), and lead to civil war. The account of the rivalry is recorded in the rest of the Book of 1 Samuel.

Envy is one of the most consuming of all sins, and Saul had an unhealthy dose of it. Fueled by envy, his rage toward David would shorten his reign and eventually lead to his own death.

THOUGHTS TO PONDER

Why was Saul incapable of giving David his due? Have you ever known anyone like Saul in this regard? What do you think it means that "the LORD was with David but had left Saul"?

PRAYER

Father, we pray that we will always have a humble spirit, quick to praise others and quick to recognize that you give gifts and talents to us all. Amen.

BE A "JONATHAN"

I SAMUEL 20:1–17

20 Then David ran away from Naioth in Ramah. He went to Jonathan and asked, "What have I done? What is my crime? How did I sin against your father? Why is he trying to kill me?"

²Jonathan answered, "No! You won't die! See, my father doesn't do anything great or small without first telling me. Why would he keep this from me? It's not true!"

³But David took an oath, saying, "Your father knows very well that you like me. He says to himself, 'Jonathan must not know about it, or he will tell David.' As surely as the LORD lives and as you live, I am only a step away from death!"

⁴Jonathan said to David, "I'll do anything you want me to do."

⁵So David said, "Look, tomorrow is the New Moon festival. I am supposed to eat with the king, but let me hide in the field until the third evening. ⁶If your father notices I am gone, tell him, 'David begged me to let him go to his hometown of Bethlehem. Every year at this time his family group offers a sacrifice.' ⁷If your father says, 'Fine,' I am safe. But if he becomes angry, you will know that he wants to hurt me. ⁸Jonathan, be loyal to me, your servant. You have made an agreement with me before the LORD. If I am guilty, you may kill me yourself! Why hand me over to your father?"

⁹Jonathan answered, "No, never! If I learn that my father plans to hurt you, I will warn you!"

¹⁰David asked, "Who will let me know if your father answers you unkindly?"

¹¹Then Jonathan said, "Come, let's go out into the field." So the two of them went out into the field.

¹²Jonathan said to David, "I promise this before the LORD, the God of Israel: At this same time the day after tomorrow, I will find out how my father feels. If he feels good toward you, I will send word to you and let you know. ¹³But if my father plans to hurt you, I will let you know and send you away safely. May the LORD punish me terribly if I don't do this. And may the LORD be with you as he has been with my father. ¹⁴But show me the kindness of the LORD as long as I live so that I may not die. ¹⁵You must never stop showing your kindness to my family, even when the LORD has destroyed all your enemies from the earth."

¹⁶So Jonathan made an agreement with David. He said, "May the LORD hold David's enemies responsible." ¹⁷And Jonathan asked David to repeat his promise of love for him, because he loved David as much as he loved himself.

DEVOTION

DO YOU HAVE what it takes to help someone else succeed? Although I've seen dozens of books on what it takes to be a success, I don't recall any books where the focus was how to help others succeed. Perhaps we could take a lesson from the story of Jonathan.

The interesting thing about the loyalty Jonathan demonstrated is that David's success is coming at Jonathan's expense. David will rise to be the next king, not Jonathan. As King Saul's eldest son, Jonathan could rightly expect to ascend to the throne after his father, but Jonathan knew that God had rejected his father and embraced David. In an act of uncommon selflessness, Jonathan protected David from the murderous wrath of Saul.

I was recently asked back to my Christian high school to be honored as an outstanding alumnus. I felt unworthy of the award and I informed the committee of my decision to decline the honor. But I eventually reversed my decision and decided to accept the award. Why the change of heart? Because one of my mentors gently reminded me that the award wasn't simply about me. "Come honor the ones who helped you get where you are," he said.

No one succeeds alone, and the lucky ones are those who, like David, have a "Jonathan," someone who is willing to look after the interests of others even before his or her own. My parents. My teachers. My wife. They've all been like Jonathan to me, supporting me and assisting my growth. And now it's my turn to do the same for the university students I teach. The lesson is this: when you're not called to be a David, be a Jonathan.

Can you help someone else accomplish something great and then step back and watch it happen? Jonathan could. And because of that, David was protected from the anger of Saul, and a great king was allowed to ascend to the throne.

THOUGHTS TO PONDER

What characteristics does it take to help others succeed? Who has helped you succeed in life? Have you helped anyone else succeed?

PRAYER

Father, we know that you expect us to serve one another. Help us to be willing to aid others whenever possible, and to accept the help of others when it is our time. Amen.

REWARDED FOR LOYALTY

1 SAMUEL 26:7–24

⁷So that night David and Abishai went into Saul's camp. Saul was asleep in the middle of the camp with his spear stuck in the ground near his head. Abner and the army were sleeping around Saul. ⁸Abishai said to David, "Today God has handed your enemy over to you. Let me pin Saul to the ground with my spear. I'll only have to do it once. I won't need to hit him twice."

⁹But David said to Abishai, "Don't kill Saul! No one can harm the LORD's appointed king and still be innocent! ¹⁰As surely as the LORD lives, the LORD himself will punish Saul. Maybe Saul will die naturally, or maybe he will go into battle and be killed. ¹¹But may the LORD keep me from harming his appointed king! Take the spear and water jug that are near Saul's head. Then let's go."

¹²So David took the spear and water jug that were near Saul's head, and they left. No one saw them or knew about it or woke up, because the LORD had put them sound asleep.

¹³David crossed over to the other side of the hill and stood on top of the mountain far from Saul's camp. They were a long way away from each other. ¹⁴David shouted to the army and to Abner son of Ner, "Won't you answer me, Abner?"

Abner answered, "Who is calling for the king? Who are you?"

¹⁵David said, "You're the greatest man in Israel. Isn't that true? Why didn't you guard your master the king? Someone came into your camp to kill your master the king! ¹⁶You have not done well. As surely as the LORD lives, you and your men should die. You haven't guarded your master, the LORD's appointed king. Look! Where are the king's spear and water jug that were near his head?"

¹⁷Saul knew David's voice. He said, "Is that your voice, David my son?"

David answered, "Yes, it is, my master and king." ¹⁸David also said, "Why are you chasing me, my master? What wrong have I done? What evil am I guilty of? ¹⁹My master and king, listen to me. If the LORD made you angry with me, let him accept an offering. But if people did it, may the LORD curse them! They have made me leave the land the LORD gave me. They have told me, 'Go and serve other gods.' ²⁰Now don't let me die far away from the LORD's presence. The king of Israel has come out looking for a flea! You're just hunting a bird in the mountains!"

²¹Then Saul said, "I have sinned. Come back, David my son. Today you respected my life, so I will not try to hurt you. I have been very stupid and foolish."

²²David answered, "Here is your spear. Let one of your young men come here and get it. ²³The LORD rewards us for the things we do right and for our loyalty

to him. The LORD handed you over to me today, but I wouldn't harm the LORD's appointed king. ²⁴As I respected your life today, may the LORD also respect my life and save me from all trouble."

DEVOTION

DAVID HAD SPARED the life of Saul earlier when Saul wandered into a cave not knowing David and his men were hiding there (1 Samuel 24). And even though Saul had promised peace to David, even acknowledging that David would someday be king, Saul was once again chasing David, hoping to kill him. His motive was obvious: once David was eliminated, the house of Saul would have a firm grip on the throne.

So once again, David demonstrated to Saul that he meant him no physical harm. He sneaked into Saul's camp at night, but instead of killing him as Abishai wanted to do, he simply stole his spear and his jug. Later, safely on the top of the mountain, he called down to Saul and his commander, Abner, to bring attention to what he could have done.

In battle, a man without a spear was defenseless. David had rendered Saul defenseless and ashamed in the presence of Saul's men. And even though Saul promised to not harm David, their rivalry was far from over—and David knew it. He ignored Saul's invitation into the camp and walked away.

But before he went, David made a profound statement that is still true today: "The LORD rewards us for the things we do right and for our loyalty to him." Jesus later told his followers that if we so much as offer a cup of water in his name, we will receive a reward (Matthew 10:42). He later said that if we do an act of kindness even to the least of society—the poor, the hungry, the imprisoned—we do it to him (Matthew 25:40).

Have you felt his reward today?

THOUGHTS TO PONDER

What traits does David exhibit in this story? Why would he twice spare the life of Saul when he knew he, David, was the anointed king? In what ways does God ask us to be loyal?

PRAYER

Father, we know that you reward us for the things we do right and we know that you ask us to be loyal to you. Help us to be faithful to you always. Amen.

CROWDING OUT
GOD'S PRESENCE

I SAMUEL 31:1–10

31 The Philistines fought against Israel, and the Israelites ran away from them. Many Israelites were killed on Mount Gilboa. ²The Philistines fought hard against Saul and his sons, killing his sons Jonathan, Abinadab, and Malki-Shua. ³The fighting was heavy around Saul. The archers shot him, and he was badly wounded. ⁴He said to the officer who carried his armor, "Pull out your sword and kill me. Then those uncircumcised men won't make fun of me and kill me." But Saul's officer refused, because he was afraid. So Saul took his own sword and threw himself on it. ⁵When the officer saw that Saul was dead, he threw himself on his own sword, and he died with Saul. ⁶So Saul, his three sons, and the officer who carried his armor died together that day.

⁷When the Israelites who lived across the Jezreel Valley and those who lived across the Jordan River saw how the Israelite army had run away, and that Saul and his sons were dead, they left their cities and ran away. Then the Philistines came and lived there.

⁸The next day when the Philistines came to take all the valuable things from the dead soldiers, they found Saul and his three sons dead on Mount Gilboa. ⁹They cut off Saul's head and took off his armor. Then they sent messengers through all the land of the Philistines to tell the news in the temple of their idols and to their people. ¹⁰They put Saul's armor in the temple of the Ashtoreths and hung his body on the wall of Beth Shan.

DEVOTION

THERE'S A CERTAIN AMOUNT of symbolism in what happens to Saul in this story—both what was done to him and what he did to himself. You see, Saul had always been his own worst enemy. He failed to listen to the instructions of God concerning the destruction of his enemies. He didn't know how to handle the popularity of David. He was at odds with his own son, Jonathan, and tried to kill him as well. He killed those who helped David.

As his life was spinning out of control, Saul consulted a woman who was a spiritual medium, evidently capable of speaking to the dead (see 1 Samuel 28 for this story). He asked her to call up the spirit of Samuel, the prophet who had rebuked Saul for failing to totally eradicate the Amalekites. Amazingly, Samuel appears in spirit form and has this to say to Saul: "The LORD has left you and has become your enemy. So why do you call on me? He has done what he said he would do—the things he said through me. He has torn the kingdom out of your hands and given it to one of your neighbors, David. You did not obey the LORD; you did not show the Amalekites how angry he was with them. That's why he has done this to you today" (1 Samuel 28:16–18).

"The LORD has left you." It's one of the saddest indictments in the entire Bible. You might recall that it was also said of Samson when his hair was cut while he slept, rendering him powerless when he awoke (see Judges 16 for this story). It's frightening when God leaves you, because there's nothing left but a void where he once was.

We can create a situation where God no longer aids our endeavors, not only through blatant sin but also by the choices we make that crowd him out. By our sins or by our omissions we can create an environment where God is no longer welcome. But we are not left to wonder if God has left us, because John tells us how we can have assurance that we are in God and he is in us. He writes, "But if someone obeys God's teaching, then in that person God's love has truly reached its goal. This is how we can be sure we are living in God: Whoever says that he lives in God must live as Jesus lived" (1 John 2:5–6).

Here is John's formula to avoid the folly of Saul and to always have God dwelling in you: live like Jesus—live in God.

THOUGHTS TO PONDER

What had Saul done that contributed to his demise at the hands of the Philistines? What does it feel like to "live in God"? What are some of the things people do to crowd God out of their lives?

PRAYER

Father, we pray we will always make room for you in our lives and welcome your presence in us. Amen.

Seeking Unity

2 SAMUEL 2:8–12, 17—3:1

⁸Abner son of Ner was the commander of Saul's army. Abner took Saul's son Ish-Bosheth to Mahanaim ⁹and made him king of Gilead, Ashuri, Jezreel, Ephraim, Benjamin, and all Israel. ¹⁰Saul's son Ish-Bosheth was forty years old when he became king over Israel, and he ruled two years. But the people of Judah followed David. ¹¹David was king in Hebron for seven years and six months.

¹²Abner son of Ner and the servants of Ish-Bosheth son of Saul left Mahanaim and went to Gibeon.

¹⁷That day there was a terrible battle, and David's men defeated Abner and the Israelites.

¹⁸Zeruiah's three sons, Joab, Abishai, and Asahel, were there. Now Asahel was a fast runner, as fast as a deer in the field. ¹⁹Asahel chased Abner, going straight toward him. ²⁰Abner looked back and asked, "Is that you, Asahel?"

Asahel said, "Yes, it is."

²¹Then Abner said to Asahel, "Turn to your right or left and catch one of the young men and take his armor." But Asahel refused to stop chasing him.

²²Abner again said to Asahel, "Stop chasing me! If you don't stop, I'll have to kill you! Then I won't be able to face your brother Joab again!"

²³But Asahel refused to stop chasing Abner. So using the back end of his spear, Abner stabbed Asahel in the stomach, and the spear came out of his back. Asahel died right there, and everyone stopped when they came to the place where Asahel's body lay.

²⁴But Joab and Abishai continued chasing Abner. As the sun was going down, they arrived at the hill of Ammah, near Giah on the way to the desert near Gibeon. ²⁵The men of Benjamin came to Abner, and all stood together at the top of the hill.

²⁶Abner shouted to Joab, "Must the sword kill forever? Surely you must know this will only end in sadness! Tell the people to stop chasing their own brothers!"

²⁷Then Joab said, "As surely as God lives, if you had not said anything, the people would have chased their brothers until morning." ²⁸Then Joab blew a trumpet, and his people stopped chasing the Israelites. They did not fight them anymore.

²⁹Abner and his men marched all night through the Jordan Valley. They crossed the Jordan River, and after marching all day, arrived at Mahanaim.

³⁰After he had stopped chasing Abner, Joab came back and gathered the people together. Asahel and nineteen of David's men were missing. ³¹But David's men had killed three hundred sixty Benjaminites who had followed Abner. ³²David's

men took Asahel and buried him in the tomb of his father at Bethlehem. Then Joab and his men marched all night. The sun came up as they reached Hebron.

3 There was a long war between the people who supported Saul's family and those who supported David's family. The supporters of David's family became stronger and stronger, but the supporters of Saul's family became weaker and weaker.

DEVOTION

THE DEATH OF SAUL solved nothing. An active army still supported Saul's sons and their claims to the throne of Israel. Abner, the head of Saul's army, installed Ish-Bosheth on the throne of Israel for two years, isolating David in Hebron among the people of Judah.

Losses mounted on both sides, including Asahel, the brother of Joab, the leader of David's army. As he runs away, Abner calls out to Joab, "Surely you must know this will only end in sadness! Tell the people to stop chasing their own brothers!" And since it was twilight and the forces of Abner occupied the high ground, it seemed a sensible thing to Joab to call off the troops.

What good does fighting our brothers and sisters do? Too often, the world of Christianity gets a bad name because we are busier "chasing our own brothers" than going about the true work of the church. We give those with whom we differ the verbal equivalent of the blunt end of the spear and leave them injured in our wake.

I think we face the same question the Hebrew nation did: who is going to be on the throne? You see, if God is on the throne, then we find a way to come together in unity rather than fight one another over our religious differences. But if we put ourselves on the throne, then every difference is a reason to call names, divide, and go our separate ways. As Abner said long ago, when we fail to get along, it only ends in sadness.

THOUGHTS TO PONDER

Why do we so often fight our own brothers and sisters? Why does it seem easier to divide rather than compromise?

PRAYER

Father, we pray that we will be people of peace, and that by living together in harmony we may show the world that we are your children. Amen.

Brain Freeze

2 SAMUEL 6:1–8

6David again gathered all the chosen men of Israel—thirty thousand of them. [2]Then he and all his people went to Baalah in Judah to bring back the Ark of God. The Ark is called by the Name, the name of the LORD All-Powerful, whose throne is between the gold creatures with wings. [3]They put the Ark of God on a new cart and brought it out of Abinadab's house on the hill. Uzzah and Ahio, sons of Abinadab, led the new cart [4]which had the Ark of God on it. Ahio was walking in front of it. [5]David and all the Israelites were celebrating in the presence of the LORD. They were playing wooden instruments: lyres, harps, tambourines, rattles, and cymbals.

[6]When David's men came to the threshing floor of Nacon, the oxen stumbled. So Uzzah reached out to steady the Ark of God. [7]The LORD was angry with Uzzah and killed him because of what he did. So Uzzah died there beside the Ark of God. [8]David was angry because the LORD had killed Uzzah. Now that place is called the Punishment of Uzzah.

DEVOTION

WHEN YOU THINK of Babe Ruth, what comes to mind? Home run hitter, right? So what was he thinking in Game Seven of the 1926 World Series against the St. Louis Cardinals when, with two outs in the bottom of the ninth inning, he decided to steal second base after being walked?

I've seen the grainy black and white film. After being walked by an over-cautious St. Louis pitcher, Ruth trots to first base on those toothpick legs that made his running look awkward. Then, for reasons known only to him, the Babe heads for second base on the next pitch. It wasn't even close. He never even reached the base.

The tag was applied and the celebration began for St. Louis—their first World Series championship. Ruth trotted off the field only a little slower than his dash to second base moments earlier. From the time he walked to first base to the time he left the field—a victim of his own mental lapse—less than a minute had elapsed.

What possesses a person to do something totally out of character?

Whatever else he was, the Babe was no base runner. He just wasn't a sprinter; his legs seemed too small for his thick torso. It was as if God blessed him only from the waist up with the body of an athlete.

Babe barely talked about that mental lapse that dashed the hopes of Yankee fans. My children would call it a "brain freeze," meaning something done spontaneously that is completely out of character. Brain freezes are rarely a good thing. A few are funny, but many of them are deadly serious.

When Uzzah reached out and steadied the Ark of the Agreement as it toppled from the cart, it was a brain freeze. You didn't touch the Ark. Everyone knew the rules. And even the fact that the Ark might have been damaged in the fall was not a mitigating factor. He was struck dead by God.

What is the dumbest thing you have ever done spontaneously?

I've personally known people who went through the brain freeze of adultery. Not a long-term affair, but a classic one-night, no-thought-for-tomorrow fling. The consequences were huge. Shattered lives everywhere. I've known people who quit a job in a fit of anger and found out later, in a calmer moment, that it couldn't be taken back. And we've all heard of people who had disastrous consequences from a first-time experiment with drugs.

Some brain freezes are of the smaller variety, but nonetheless harmful. "I hate you!" someone shouts. "I hate you too!" comes the reply, and two people break off a relationship because neither one can say "I'm sorry."

I don't know what in the world possessed Babe Ruth to try to steal second base when the entire World Series hung in the balance of that decision. I do know this: he didn't think he was going to get caught. He thought he was going to be standing on second base, listening to the adoring fans, ninety feet closer to home plate. He thought he was going to get away with it.

The same is true with any of us. When we contemplate doing the stupidest thing we've ever done, we don't think we're going to get caught. But the lesson of Uzzah is this: some decisions have permanent consequences that all the remorse later in life can't take back.

THOUGHTS TO PONDER

> Why would the penalty be so great for what Uzzah did? What does this incident say about God? What does this lesson say to us?

PRAYER

> God, we know that even though you are a loving God, you are also to be obeyed and feared. Help us as we seek to do your will in every circumstance of our lives. Amen.

BE CONTENT
WITH YOUR PART

2 SAMUEL 7:1–17

7 King David was living in his palace, and the LORD had given him peace from all his enemies around him. ²Then David said to Nathan the prophet, "Look, I am living in a palace made of cedar wood, but the Ark of God is in a tent!"

³Nathan said to the king, "Go and do what you really want to do, because the LORD is with you."

⁴But that night the LORD spoke his word to Nathan, ⁵"Go and tell my servant David, 'This is what the LORD says: Will you build a house for me to live in? ⁶From the time I brought the Israelites out of Egypt until now I have not lived in a house. I have been moving around all this time with a tent as my home. ⁷As I have moved with the Israelites, I have never said to the tribes, whom I commanded to take care of my people Israel, "Why haven't you built me a house of cedar?" '

⁸"You must tell my servant David, 'This is what the LORD All-Powerful says: I took you from the pasture and from tending the sheep and made you leader of my people Israel. ⁹I have been with you everywhere you have gone and have defeated your enemies for you. I will make you as famous as any of the great people on the earth. ¹⁰Also I will choose a place for my people Israel, and I will plant them so they can live in their own homes. They will not be bothered anymore. Wicked people will no longer bother them as they have in the past ¹¹when I chose judges for my people Israel. But I will give you peace from all your enemies. I also tell you that I will make your descendants kings of Israel after you.

¹²"'When you die and join your ancestors, I will make one of your sons the next king, and I will set up his kingdom. ¹³He will build a house for me, and I will let his kingdom rule always. ¹⁴I will be his father, and he will be my son. When he sins, I will use other people to punish him. They will be my whips. ¹⁵I took away my love from Saul, whom I removed before you, but I will never stop loving your son. ¹⁶But your family and your kingdom will continue always before me. Your throne will last forever.' "

¹⁷Nathan told David everything God had said in this vision.

DEVOTION

IN THE WORK of God's kingdom, each of us plays a role. It was true in the time of David and it's still true today. David's motives were noble: he wanted to build a proper house for God. He was living in a house of cedar while God's house was a tent. But building was not to be David's role. David was a warrior. His son, Solomon, would be the builder of the Temple.

In a message to Hiram, the king of Tyre who would supply some of the labor for the Temple, Solomon later said, "You remember my father David had to fight many wars with the countries around him, so he was never able to build a temple for worshiping the LORD his God . . . But now the LORD my God has given me peace on all sides of my country . . . Now, I plan to build that temple for worshiping the LORD my God" (1 Kings 5:3–5). Because of the peace that David had secured, Solomon could perform the role his father had desired.

Paul would write about the idea of our various roles in the church to the Christians in Corinth. Evidently the Corinthian church was in discord and the worship services bordered on chaos. Paul wanted them to understand that every role was important in work of the church. He wrote, "There are different kinds of gifts, but they are all from the same Spirit. There are different ways to serve but the same Lord to serve. And there are different ways that God works through people but the same God. God works in all of us in everything we do. Something from the Spirit can be seen in each person, for the common good" (1 Corinthians 12:4–7). Paul went on to compare the church to the human body. Every part—eyes, ears, hands, feet—plays an important role just like each member plays an important role in the local church.

Like David, we might not get to perform every role in the kingdom that we desire. In fact, it might be our role to help others perform the very works we would like to do, just as David did for Solomon. God, in his wisdom, has endowed each of us with unique gifts. Our job is to find the opportunities that match our God-given gifts.

THOUGHTS TO PONDER

What is the role you've been called to play in your church? In your family? In your community? How do we find the role God wants us to play to further his will in the world?

PRAYER

Father, please bless us with the talents we need in order to accomplish your work, and please bless us with contentment to be satisfied with the roles you give us. Amen.

Debts of Gratitude

2 SAMUEL 9:1–13

9 David asked, "Is anyone still left in Saul's family? I want to show kindness to that person for Jonathan's sake!"

²Now there was a servant named Ziba from Saul's family. So David's servants called Ziba to him. King David said to him, "Are you Ziba?"

He answered, "Yes, I am your servant."

³The king asked, "Is anyone left in Saul's family? I want to show God's kindness to that person."

Ziba answered the king, "Jonathan has a son still living who is crippled in both feet."

⁴The king asked Ziba, "Where is this son?"

Ziba answered, "He is at the house of Makir son of Ammiel in Lo Debar."

⁵Then King David had servants bring Jonathan's son from the house of Makir son of Ammiel in Lo Debar. ⁶Mephibosheth, Jonathan's son, came before David and bowed facedown on the floor.

David said, "Mephibosheth!"

Mephibosheth said, "I am your servant."

⁷David said to him, "Don't be afraid. I will be kind to you for your father Jonathan's sake. I will give you back all the land of your grandfather Saul, and you will always eat at my table."

⁸Mephibosheth bowed to David again and said, "You are being very kind to me, your servant! And I am no better than a dead dog!"

⁹Then King David called Saul's servant Ziba. David said to him, "I have given your master's grandson everything that belonged to Saul and his family. ¹⁰You, your sons, and your servants will farm the land and harvest the crops. Then your family will have food to eat. But Mephibosheth, your master's grandson, will always eat at my table."

(Now Ziba had fifteen sons and twenty servants.) ¹¹Ziba said to King David, "I, your servant, will do everything my master, the king, commands me."

So Mephibosheth ate at David's table as if he were one of the king's sons. ¹²Mephibosheth had a young son named Mica. Everyone in Ziba's family became Mephibosheth's servants. ¹³Mephibosheth lived in Jerusalem, because he always ate at the king's table. And he was crippled in both feet.

DEVOTION

JONATHAN HAD STOOD beside David as a friend even while Jonathan's own father, King Saul, had plotted to kill David. Now both Jonathan and Saul were dead, killed in battle against the Philistines at Mount Gilboa. David had bitterly mourned for them (2 Samuel 1:17–27) and now it was time for him to repay the favor that Jonathan had done for him during those dark days when Saul hunted David to kill him.

This story began when David realized that there was one heir left in the family of Jonathan. He was living across the Jordan River in Lo Debar. The text tells us he was crippled. Going back to 2 Samuel 4:4 we learn the reason why: "Saul's son Jonathan had a son named Mephibosheth, who was crippled in both feet. He was five years old when the news came from Jezreel that Saul and Jonathan were dead. Mephibosheth's nurse had picked him up and run away. But as she hurried to leave, she dropped him, and now he was lame."

David repaid his debt of gratitude to Jonathan by taking in Mephibosheth as one of his own sons. He provided him food and servants and gave him all the lands that had belonged to King Saul. Later, when David turned over the sons of Saul to the Gibeonites to be killed in retribution for the wrong that Saul had done to them, he spared Mephibosheth from death.

How do you repay your debts—not monetary ones, but debts of gratitude or debts of honor? More importantly, how do you repay God for what he has done for you? It's a question David contemplated in one of his Psalms: "What can I give the LORD for all the good things he has given to me? I will lift up the cup of salvation, and I will pray to the LORD. I will give the LORD what I promised in front of all his people" (Psalm 116:12–14).

David repaid his debt to Jonathan by taking in his son and feeding him at his table. Today, we repay our debt to God by trusting in his Son and drinking from the cup of salvation.

THOUGHTS TO PONDER

To whom do you owe a debt of gratitude? How can you express your thankfulness today? How do we show our thankfulness to God for the wonderful gift of his Son?

PRAYER

Father, we are grateful to you for our very lives and for the hope we have of eternal life through your Son. Help us to be ever thankful for this matchless gift. Amen.

"Nicked Up" Individuals

2 SAMUEL 11:1–17

11 In the spring, when the kings normally went out to war, David sent out Joab, his servants, and all the Israelites. They destroyed the Ammonites and attacked the city of Rabbah. But David stayed in Jerusalem. ²One evening David got up from his bed and walked around on the roof of his palace. While he was on the roof, he saw a woman bathing. She was very beautiful. ³So David sent his servants to find out who she was. A servant answered, "That woman is Bathsheba daughter of Eliam. She is the wife of Uriah the Hittite." ⁴So David sent messengers to bring Bathsheba to him. When she came to him, he had sexual relations with her. (Now Bathsheba had purified herself from her monthly period.) Then she went back to her house. ⁵But Bathsheba became pregnant and sent word to David, saying, "I am pregnant."

⁶So David sent a message to Joab: "Send Uriah the Hittite to me." And Joab sent Uriah to David. ⁷When Uriah came to him, David asked him how Joab was, how the soldiers were, and how the war was going. ⁸Then David said to Uriah, "Go home and rest."

So Uriah left the palace, and the king sent a gift to him. ⁹But Uriah did not go home. Instead, he slept outside the door of the palace as all the king's officers did.

¹⁰The officers told David, "Uriah did not go home."

Then David said to Uriah, "You came from a long trip. Why didn't you go home?"

¹¹Uriah said to him, "The Ark and the soldiers of Israel and Judah are staying in tents. My master Joab and his officers are camping out in the fields. It isn't right for me to go home to eat and drink and have sexual relations with my wife!"

¹²David said to Uriah, "Stay here today. Tomorrow I'll send you back to the battle." So Uriah stayed in Jerusalem that day and the next. ¹³Then David called Uriah to come to see him, so Uriah ate and drank with David. David made Uriah drunk, but he still did not go home. That evening Uriah again slept with the king's officers.

¹⁴The next morning David wrote a letter to Joab and sent it by Uriah. ¹⁵In the letter David wrote, "Put Uriah on the front lines where the fighting is worst and leave him there alone. Let him be killed in battle."

¹⁶Joab watched the city and saw where its strongest defenders were and put Uriah there. ¹⁷When the men of the city came out to fight against Joab, some of David's men were killed. And Uriah the Hittite was one of them.

DEVOTION

ADULTERY AND MURDER. These are the deeds David committed, yet Scripture calls Jesus the "Son of David" or the "seed of David" repeatedly. Despite his sin, David was still "the kind of man [the LORD] wants" (1 Sam. 13:14).

What does the sin and the subsequent repentance and restoration of David tell us about God? That he uses imperfect individuals because those are the only kind he has available for his purposes.

In 1845, Robert Patterson unpacked a statue for display at the birthplace of golf—St. Andrews in Scotland. But the packing around the statue interested him as well. It was called "gutta percha," a rubber-like substance. Patterson melted the sap into the first rubber-like golf ball, an innovation that flew far past the existing "featherie" balls. The gutta-percha ball would be the standard for golf balls for a half century.

These new golf balls were made smooth, but they easily nicked or scratched with play. But before long, golfers discovered that the scratched and nicked balls flew farther and straighter than the new ones, something we now figure into the dimpled design of golf balls.

I think there's a principle of life in those golf balls that worked better after a few nicks and cuts. All of us try our best to navigate our way through life, and all of us pick up a few dents and dings along the way. We pick up the scratches from bad decisions we have made. We pick up nicks from relationships that have wounded us. We get a cut or two from our jobs when careers don't go as we've planned. We even inflict a few wounds on ourselves like David did above.

But, when used properly, those blemishes can help us go through life straighter and smoother than we otherwise would have. We can learn from our mistakes and use that knowledge to go farther than before. If God uses "nicked up" individuals like David, then he can use you and me as well.

THOUGHTS TO PONDER

What are some of the scrapes you've accumulated in life that have taught you a lesson? What do you think God wants to teach David through the mistakes David made?

PRAYER

God, we pray not for a life free from occasional cuts and bruises, for that is not possible. But we pray that from every experience we will become better people than before. Amen.

An Eternal Solution

2 SAMUEL 12:1–18

12 The LORD sent Nathan to David. When he came to David, he said, "There were two men in a city. One was rich, but the other was poor. ²The rich man had many sheep and cattle. ³But the poor man had nothing except one little female lamb he had bought. The poor man fed the lamb, and it grew up with him and his children. It shared his food and drank from his cup and slept in his arms. The lamb was like a daughter to him.

⁴"Then a traveler stopped to visit the rich man. The rich man wanted to feed the traveler, but he didn't want to take one of his own sheep or cattle. Instead, he took the lamb from the poor man and cooked it for his visitor."

⁵David became very angry at the rich man. He said to Nathan, "As surely as the LORD lives, the man who did this should die! ⁶He must pay for the lamb four times for doing such a thing. He had no mercy!"

⁷Then Nathan said to David, "You are the man! This is what the LORD, the God of Israel, says: 'I appointed you king of Israel and saved you from Saul. ⁸I gave you his kingdom and his wives. And I made you king of Israel and Judah. And if that had not been enough, I would have given you even more. ⁹So why did you ignore the LORD's command? Why did you do what he says is wrong? You killed Uriah the Hittite with the sword of the Ammonites and took his wife to be your wife! ¹⁰Now there will always be people in your family who will die by a sword, because you did not respect me; you took the wife of Uriah the Hittite for yourself.'

¹¹"This is what the LORD says: 'I am bringing trouble to you from your own family. While you watch, I will take your wives from you and give them to someone who is very close to you. He will have sexual relations with your wives, and everyone will know it. ¹²You had sexual relations with Bathsheba in secret, but I will do this so all the people of Israel can see it.'"

¹³Then David said to Nathan, "I have sinned against the LORD."

Nathan answered, "The LORD has taken away your sin. You will not die. ¹⁴But what you did caused the LORD's enemies to lose all respect for him. For this reason the son who was born to you will die."

¹⁵Then Nathan went home. And the LORD caused the son of David and Bathsheba, Uriah's widow, to be very sick. ¹⁶David prayed to God for the baby. David fasted and went into his house and stayed there, lying on the ground all night. ¹⁷The elders of David's family came to him and tried to pull him up from the ground, but he refused to get up or to eat food with them.

¹⁸On the seventh day the baby died.

DEVOTION

I WAS SEVEN when I went to Dad's warehouse where he kept supplies for his gas stations. In those days, it was full of oil cans, belts, and hoses that every full-service gas station stocked. One day, I explored out back and found a junk yard. I thought cars went there to die. But these were alive with unbroken glass, so I picked up rocks to kill their windshields.

When the owner heard the third crash he ran to the noise. I admitted my name and he told me to go away. He would talk to my dad, who would talk to me when he got home.

Nothing hurts like disappointing your father. Do I remember getting a spanking? No. Do I remember making restitution? No. Perhaps I did repay in some way, but that's long forgotten. I do remember forty-five years later that Dad never brought it up again. As far as the east is from the west, Psalm 103:12 says—that's how far God removes our sin.

David has disappointed God and his remorse knows no depth. Later, his servants were afraid to inform him when the sick child died. He aches in his bones and in his soul. He prays and cries to the Lord that the child from his illegitimate relationship with Bathsheba will be spared, but in the end, his prayer goes unanswered.

Will God deliver us from our messes when we ask him in earnest? David laments in Psalm 6:3, "I am very upset. LORD, how long will it be?" Like David, I want deliverance from my problems right now—poor health, financial reversals, strained relationships. But it's only when we remember that God's silence might indicate an eternal solution (invisible to us) that we gain the confidence that he hears us—even when we might think he doesn't.

THOUGHTS TO PONDER

Have you ever not given a child everything he or she wanted? What was your reasoning? What have you persistently prayed about to God and still not received? What might God be teaching you by withholding what you want?

PRAYER

Father, we disappoint you daily. But Lord, we know that you have "unfailing love." Please extend it to us today, as we do our best to reflect you in our lives. Amen.

DEADLY TREES

2 SAMUEL 18:1–17

18David counted his men and placed over them commanders of thousands and commanders of hundreds. ²He sent the troops out in three groups. Joab commanded one-third of the men. Joab's brother Abishai son of Zeruiah commanded another third. And Ittai from Gath commanded the last third. King David said to them, "I will also go with you."

³But the men said, "You must not go with us! If we run away in the battle, Absalom's men won't care. Even if half of us are killed, Absalom's men won't care. But you're worth ten thousand of us! You can help us most by staying in the city."

⁴The king said to his people, "I will do what you think is best." So the king stood at the side of the gate as the army went out in groups of a hundred and a thousand.

⁵The king commanded Joab, Abishai, and Ittai, "Be gentle with young Absalom for my sake." Everyone heard the king's orders to the commanders about Absalom.

⁶David's army went out into the field against Absalom's Israelites, and they fought in the forest of Ephraim. ⁷There David's army defeated the Israelites. Many died that day—twenty thousand men. ⁸The battle spread through all the country, but that day more men died in the forest than in the fighting.

⁹Then Absalom happened to meet David's troops. As Absalom was riding his mule, it went under the thick branches of a large oak tree. Absalom's head got caught in the tree, and his mule ran out from under him. So Absalom was left hanging above the ground.

¹⁰When one of the men saw it happen, he told Joab, "I saw Absalom hanging in an oak tree!"

¹¹Joab said to him, "You saw him? Why didn't you kill him and let him fall to the ground? I would have given you a belt and four ounces of silver!"

¹²The man answered, "I wouldn't touch the king's son even if you gave me twenty-five pounds of silver. We heard the king command you, Abishai, and Ittai, 'Be careful not to hurt young Absalom.' ¹³If I had killed him, the king would have found out, and you would not have protected me!"

¹⁴Joab said, "I won't waste time here with you!" Absalom was still alive in the oak tree, so Joab took three spears and stabbed him in the heart. ¹⁵Ten young men who carried Joab's armor also gathered around Absalom and struck him and killed him.

¹⁶Then Joab blew the trumpet, so the troops stopped chasing the Israelites. ¹⁷Then Joab's men took Absalom's body and threw it into a large pit in the forest and filled the pit with many stones. All the Israelites ran away to their homes.

DEVOTION

WHEN YOU READ the story of the rebellion of Absalom, the most enduring visual is that of Absalom hanging by his hair and Joab driving the three darts into his heart. But I see in this passage an interesting verse that highlights the brutality of the battle between father and son for the throne of Israel, and teaches a lesson in the process.

The battle takes place in the forest of Ephraim. The text tells us that twenty thousand men were killed on that day, about the same amount each side lost in the Battle of Gettysburg.

But here's the strange part. Scripture tells us that the forest devoured more of the combatants than the sword (1 Samuel 18:8). Grasp that fact for a moment. More than ten thousand men killed running into trees, falling out of trees, being impaled by limbs. Perhaps even a fire erupted.

And of course one of those casualties of the trees was Absalom—caught by his long hair in the branch of a tree, ripe for the darts of Joab and the swords of his men. At that point, Joab called off the battle, as it was senseless to continue slaughtering the very people of Israel that David would once again rule.

I think I've seen an analogy to the "slaughter of the trees" played out over and over. I've seen parents who avoid the sword of the paddle but slay the spirit of their children with their words. "You're stupid." "Can't you do anything right?" Killed by the tree, not the sword. I've seen bosses that avoid the sword of firing, but kill the effectiveness of their employees with the tree of criticism.

Conflict is inevitable. Families quarrel. Differences erupt in the workplace. Just remember that the trees can be just as deadly as the sword.

THOUGHTS TO PONDER

When we try to live a Christian life, what are some of the "trees" that don't appear to be dangerous but can actually be deadly? How do we recognize the trees? How do we avoid them?

PRAYER

Father, we pray that you'll protect us from every kind of harm. Forgive us when we rebel against you, and bring us back into your fold. Amen.

NOT BY MIGHT

2 SAMUEL 24:1–16

24 The LORD was angry with Israel again, and he caused David to turn against the Israelites. He said, "Go, count the people of Israel and Judah."

²So King David said to Joab, the commander of the army, "Go through all the tribes of Israel, from Dan to Beersheba, and count the people. Then I will know how many there are."

³But Joab said to the king, "May the LORD your God give you a hundred times more people, and may my master the king live to see this happen. Why do you want to do this?"

⁴But the king commanded Joab and the commanders of the army, so they left the king to count the Israelites.

⁵After crossing the Jordan River, they camped near Aroer on the south side of the city in the ravine. They went through Gad and on to Jazer. ⁶Then they went to Gilead and the land of Tahtim Hodshi and to Dan Jaan and around to Sidon. ⁷They went to the strong, walled city of Tyre and to all the cities of the Hivites and Canaanites. Finally, they went to southern Judah, to Beersheba. ⁸After nine months and twenty days, they had gone through all the land. Then they came back to Jerusalem.

⁹Joab gave the list of the people to the king. There were eight hundred thousand men in Israel who could use the sword and five hundred thousand men in Judah.

¹⁰David felt ashamed after he had counted the people. He said to the LORD, "I have sinned greatly by what I have done. LORD, I beg you to forgive me, your servant, because I have been very foolish."

¹¹When David got up in the morning, the LORD spoke his word to Gad, who was a prophet and David's seer. ¹²The LORD told Gad, "Go and tell David, 'This is what the LORD says: I offer you three choices. Choose one of them and I will do it to you.'"

¹³So Gad went to David and said to him, "Should three years of hunger come to you and your land? Or should your enemies chase you for three months? Or should there be three days of disease in your land? Think about it. Then decide which of these things I should tell the LORD who sent me."

¹⁴David said to Gad, "I am in great trouble. Let the LORD punish us, because the LORD is very merciful. Don't let my punishment come from human beings!"

¹⁵So the LORD sent a terrible disease on Israel. It began in the morning and continued until the chosen time to stop. From Dan to Beersheba seventy thousand people died. ¹⁶When the angel raised his arm toward Jerusalem to destroy it, the LORD felt very sorry about the terrible things that had happened. He said to the angel who was destroying the people, "That is enough! Put down your arm!"

DEVOTION

THE ARMY OF ISRAEL had never won its battles because of superior military numbers; they had won because God favored them. And because God fought along with the army of Israel they had been able to defeat some vastly superior forces. You might recall the story of Gideon who was instructed by God to reduce his army from 82,000 men to only 300 before going up against the powerful Midianite army (Judges 7). On another occasion, God helped the Israelites defeat the Midianites without losing a single man in battle (Numbers 31).

Surely David had heard the stories. God had made the sun stand still so Israel could continue to defeat the five Amorite kings (Joshua 10). God had given Joshua and the Israelites a victory over the Amalekites as long as Moses held up his arms, aided by his brother, Aaron (Exodus 17:8–16). God had always supplied the victory for Israel as long as its leaders trusted in him.

For that reason, the census that David undertook of his fighting men was an affront to God. Even David's commander, Joab, knew it was a bad idea, but David persisted. The effort took more than nine months and the answer came back: 800,000 men in Israel and another 500,000 in Judah. Plenty of military might, but no protection against the wrath of God. Seventy thousand people died because of David's bad judgment.

God has never used overwhelming numbers to do his work. All of the creatures of the earth had been saved by Noah and his family of eight in a single boat. Jesus picked twelve common men to carry on his work after he returned to heaven. God can accomplish great things with modest numbers even today.

THOUGHTS TO PONDER

Why did God repeatedly intercede in the military affairs of Israel? How does God work in our lives today?

PRAYER

Father, we know you can do great things in the face of all odds. We pray that we will have faith to trust in you for our victories. Amen.

KEEPING GOD ON YOUR GUEST LIST

1 KINGS 1:5–25

⁵Adonijah was the son of King David and Haggith, and he was very proud. "I will be the king," he said. So he got chariots and horses for himself and fifty men for his personal bodyguard. ⁶Now David had never interfered with Adonijah by questioning what he did. Born next after Absalom, Adonijah was a very handsome man.

⁷Adonijah spoke with Joab son of Zeruiah and Abiathar the priest, and they agreed to help him. ⁸But Zadok the priest, Benaiah son of Jehoiada, Nathan the prophet, Shimei, Rei, and King David's special guard did not join Adonijah.

⁹Then Adonijah killed some sheep, cows, and fat calves for sacrifices at the Stone of Zoheleth near the spring of Rogel. He invited all his brothers, the other sons of King David, to come, as well as all the men of Judah. ¹⁰But Adonijah did not invite Nathan the prophet, Benaiah, his father's special guard, or his brother Solomon.

¹¹When Nathan heard about this, he went to Bathsheba, Solomon's mother. "Have you heard that Adonijah, Haggith's son, has made himself king?" Nathan asked. "Our real king, David, does not know it. ¹²I strongly advise you to save yourself and your sons. ¹³Go to King David and tell him, 'My master and king, you promised that my son Solomon would be king and would rule on your throne after you. Why then has Adonijah become king?' ¹⁴While you are still talking to the king, I will come in and tell him that what you have said about Adonijah is true."

¹⁵So Bathsheba went in to see the aged king in his bedroom, where Abishag, the girl from Shunam, was caring for him. ¹⁶Bathsheba bowed and knelt before the king. He asked, "What do you want?"

¹⁷She answered, "My master, you made a promise to me in the name of the LORD your God. You said, 'Your son Solomon will become king after me, and he will rule on my throne.' ¹⁸But now, unknown to you, Adonijah has become king. ¹⁹He has killed many cows, fat calves, and sheep for sacrifices. And he has invited all your sons, as well as Abiathar the priest and Joab the commander of the army, but he did not invite Solomon, who serves you. ²⁰My master and king, all the Israelites are watching you, waiting for you to decide who will be king after you. ²¹As soon as you die, Solomon and I will be treated as criminals."

²²While Bathsheba was still talking with the king, Nathan the prophet arrived. ²³The servants told the king, "Nathan the prophet is here." So Nathan went to the king and bowed facedown on the ground before him.

[24]Nathan said, "My master and king, have you said that Adonijah will be the king after you and that he will rule on your throne? [25]Today he has sacrificed many cows, fat calves, and sheep, and he has invited all your other sons, the commanders of the army, and Abiathar the priest. Right now they are eating and drinking with him. They are saying, 'Long live King Adonijah!'"

DEVOTION

WITH HIS FATHER, King David, old and frail and with his three older brothers out of the way, Adonijah decided to anoint himself king and the heir of his father. No doubt he felt it was his right—he was, after all, the next in line after Absalom. So he gathered his men and all his brothers except his younger brother Solomon—who was David's choice for king—and offered sacrifices to seal his position as the next king.

But missing from the guest list is the prophet Nathan. This is the man who had been the true oracle of God for years. He was the one who confronted David about his sin with Bathsheba, and he had been a trusted confidante of David ever since. If the will of God was to be determined, surely Nathan would be invited to do it. But he was not on the guest list of Adonijah on this day.

This tells us all we need to know about the gathering. Isn't it true that whenever we want to go against God's will, the last thing we want is a reminder of what his will is? Before we head down the road toward sin, we remove people and reminders that would prick our conscience and call us back to what's right. What parent hasn't told a child to remember that God is with them when they are away from home?

If you want to keep God's will, keep him on the guest list of your life. Keep him in your car. Keep him at your office. Keep him in your home. Nathan was kept away from the Stone of Zoheleth because Adonijah didn't want to hear what God had to say. Don't fall into the same trap.

THOUGHTS TO PONDER

Are you tuned in to God's voice in your life? Who are some of the people God uses to tell you how to live? A spouse? A trusted friend? A pastor? How do you treat their messages?

PRAYER

Father, we pray that we will listen to you and your will for us and that we will surround ourselves with people we can trust to direct us in the right way. Amen.

OUR FAITHFUL GOD

1 KINGS 1:28–35, 49–53; 2:1–4

²⁸Then the king said, "Tell Bathsheba to come in!" So she came in and stood before the king.

²⁹Then the king made this promise, "The LORD has saved me from all trouble. As surely as he lives, ³⁰I will do today what I have promised you in the name of the LORD, the God of Israel. I promised that your son Solomon would be king after me and rule on my throne in my place."

³¹Then Bathsheba bowed facedown on the ground and knelt before the king and said, "Long live my master King David!"

³²Then King David said, "Tell Zadok the priest, Nathan the prophet, and Benaiah son of Jehoiada to come in." When they came before the king, ³³he said to them, "Take my servants with you and put my son Solomon on my own mule. Take him down to the spring called Gihon. ³⁴There Zadok the priest and Nathan the prophet should pour olive oil on him and make him king over Israel. Blow the trumpet and shout, 'Long live King Solomon!' ³⁵Then come back up here with him. He will sit on my throne and rule in my place, because he is the one I have chosen to be the ruler over Israel and Judah."

⁴⁹Then all of Adonijah's guests were afraid, and they left quickly and scattered. ⁵⁰Adonijah was also afraid of Solomon, so he went and took hold of the corners of the altar. ⁵¹Then someone told Solomon, "Adonijah is afraid of you, so he is at the altar, holding on to its corners. He says, 'Tell King Solomon to promise me today that he will not kill me.'"

⁵²So Solomon answered, "Adonijah must show that he is a man of honor. If he does that, I promise he will not lose even a single hair from his head. But if he does anything wrong, he will die." ⁵³Then King Solomon sent some men to get Adonijah. When he was brought from the altar, he came before King Solomon and bowed down. Solomon told him, "Go home."

2 Since it was almost time for David to die, he gave his son Solomon his last commands. ²David said, "My time to die is near. Be a good and strong leader. ³Obey the LORD your God. Follow him by obeying his demands, his commands, his laws, and his rules that are written in the teachings of Moses. If you do these things, you will be successful in all you do and wherever you go. ⁴And if you obey the LORD, he will keep the promise he made to me. He said: 'If your descendants live as I tell them and have complete faith in me, a man from your family will always be king over the people of Israel.'"

329

DEVOTION

AFTER THE REBELLION of Absalom and after the insurrection of Adonijah, it was imperative for the aging King David to act in order to secure the succession to his throne. So he called for Solomon to be anointed king to the delight of Bathsheba and to the dismay of Adonijah.

What qualities, in David's opinion, would make Solomon a "good and strong leader"? The answer was simple: obey God. Obey his demands, his commands, his laws and his rules, all of which had been recorded in the teachings of Moses. And the reward for keeping God's commands? God would keep his promise to David's family.

Much is said about the need for the Christian to be faithful, and rightfully so. But it is interesting to note that writers of the New Testament also refer to the faithfulness of God. Paul, in writing to the Corinthians said, "God, who has called you into fellowship with his Son, Jesus Christ our Lord, is faithful" (1 Corinthians 1:9). God keeps his promises, just as David told his son Solomon.

And the promises of God are wonderful, indeed. In a letter to the Thessalonians, Paul wrote, "But the Lord is faithful and will give you strength and will protect you from the Evil One." (2 Thessalonians 3:3). John tells us that we can trust God: "But if we confess our sins, he will forgive our sins, because we can trust God to do what is right. He will cleanse us from all the wrongs we have done" (1 John 1:9). Protection from Satan. Cleansing from our sins. God will be faithful in these promises.

David knew the lessons of history. When the children of Israel had strayed away from God, they fell captive to the enemies around them. Conversely, when the nation had obeyed God, he blessed them with freedom and prosperity. The choice for Solomon then, and the choice for us today, is simple. Will we be faithful to a God who has promised to be faithful to us?

THOUGHTS TO PONDER

What promises does God expect us to keep? What promises does he offer to us?

PRAYER

God, we know you are faithful to us. Please help us to be faithful to you and to rely on your promises now and for all eternity. Amen.

LOSING SIGHT OF WHAT IS PRECIOUS

1 KINGS 3:4–9, 16–27

⁴King Solomon went to Gibeon to offer a sacrifice, because it was the most important place of worship. He offered a thousand burnt offerings on that altar. ⁵While he was at Gibeon, the LORD appeared to him in a dream during the night. God said, "Ask for whatever you want me to give you."

⁶Solomon answered, "You were very kind to your servant, my father David. He obeyed you, and he was honest and lived right. You showed great kindness to him when you allowed his son to be king after him. ⁷LORD my God, now you have made me, your servant, king in my father's place. But I am like a little child; I don't know how to do what must be done. ⁸I, your servant, am here among your chosen people, and there are too many of them to count. ⁹I ask that you give me a heart that understands, so I can rule the people in the right way and will know the difference between right and wrong. Otherwise, it is impossible to rule this great people of yours."

¹⁶One day two women who were prostitutes came to Solomon. As they stood before him, ¹⁷one of the women said, "My master, this woman and I live in the same house. I gave birth to a baby while she was there with me. ¹⁸Three days later this woman also gave birth to a baby. No one else was in the house with us; it was just the two of us. ¹⁹One night this woman rolled over on her baby, and he died. ²⁰So she took my son from my bed during the night while I was asleep, and she carried him to her bed. Then she put the dead baby in my bed. ²¹The next morning when I got up to feed my baby, I saw that he was dead! When I looked at him more closely, I realized he was not my son."

²²"No!" the other woman cried. "The living baby is my son, and the dead baby is yours!"

But the first woman said, "No! The dead baby is yours, and the living one is mine!" So the two women argued before the king.

²³Then King Solomon said, "One of you says, 'My son is alive and your son is dead.' Then the other one says, 'No! Your son is dead and my son is alive.'"

²⁴The king sent his servants to get a sword. When they brought it to him, ²⁵he said, "Cut the living baby into two pieces, and give each woman half."

²⁶The real mother of the living child was full of love for her son. So she said to the king, "Please, my master, don't kill him! Give the baby to her!"

But the other woman said, "Neither of us will have him. Cut him into two pieces!"

[27]Then King Solomon said, "Don't kill him. Give the baby to the first woman, because she is the real mother."

DEVOTION

WHY WOULD TWO PROSTITUTES each want a child so badly? After all, both babies were illegitimate. Either woman was going to face a harder life, adding the responsibility of raising a baby to the difficulty of living a lifestyle so cruel that the two women were forced to share a single existence.

Perhaps the baby boy represented a way out for the mother. Perhaps it would only be a matter of time before the boy became a man and took care of his mother, long after her prostitution days were behind her. Perhaps it was simply the bonding between mother and child that had occurred for each woman.

Either way, Solomon had to act, and in threatening to cut the baby in half, he finds the true mother. The baby was simply too valuable to her to be cut in half.

There's a lesson for us here. Satan is whispering in our ears to take valuable, even holy things and cut them in half. Devotion time with God? Why not just an hour a week on Sundays? Prayer life? Why not just a quick thank-you before each meal? Time for reflection? Why not just buy a good motivational CD and stick it in the car?

The true test of the mother is that she protested cutting the baby in half. Do I protest when life cuts into my time with God?

Satan wants us to take the precious things in life and cut them down until they are as superficial as possessing half a baby. And it doesn't take someone as wise as Solomon to figure out his motive: if he can make my faith a mere appendix to my being rather than its core, pretty soon it will wither away on its own.

THOUGHTS TO PONDER

How do you find the time for what's most important? How do you keep circumstances from cutting into what's important to you?

PRAYER

Father, help us never lose sight of what is precious in life. Help us keep the forces of the world from cutting into our time with you and our time with our families. Amen.

A TEMPLE FOR GOD

1 KINGS 6:1-6, 11-14

6Solomon began to build the Temple four hundred eighty years after the people of Israel had left Egypt. This was during the fourth year of King Solomon's rule over Israel.

²The Temple was ninety feet long, thirty feet wide, and forty-five feet high. ³The porch in front of the main room of the Temple was fifteen feet deep and thrity feet wide. This room ran along the front of the Temple itself. Its width was equal to that of the Temple. ⁴The Temple also had windows that opened and closed. ⁵Solomon also built some side rooms against the walls of the main room and the inner room of the Temple. He built rooms all around. ⁶The rooms on the bottom floor were seven and one-half feet wide. Those on the middle floor were nine feet wide, and the rooms above them were ten and one-half feet wide. The Temple wall that formed the side of each room was thinner than the wall in the room below. These rooms were pushed aganst the Temple wall, but they did not have their main beams built into the wall.

¹¹The LORD said to Solomon: ¹²"If you obey all my laws and commands, I will do for you what I promised your father David. ¹³I will live among the Israelites in this Temple, and I will never leave my people Israel."

¹⁴So Solomon finished building the Temple.

DEVOTION

ALTHOUGH CONCEIVED by his father, King David, the Temple was built during the reign of Solomon. David had been preoccupied with war, and the peace enjoyed by Solomon allowed him to turn the nation's attention at last to a permanent home for God to dwell among them.

The scope of the building was awe-inspiring, the materials exquisite, and the craftsmanship unparalleled. Not one nail was used in the construction. It took thousands of workers seven years to complete. Perched atop Mount Moriah, Solomon's Temple could be seen by all the people as a constant reminder of God's presence among them.

But not one remnant of that structure remains today. No archeological dig has ever found evidence of it. The Temple was completely destroyed by the Babylonian army in 587–586 B.C., and no evidence of it exists today.

A second temple was built only to be demolished later and rebuilt by King Herod (Ezra 1—6). Commonly called "Herod's temple," this was the structure

Jesus referred to when he told his followers that "not one stone will be left on another" (Matthew 24:2). And he was right: Herod's temple was destroyed by the Romans in A.D. 70.

Today, the temple of God is within us, and that is where he dwells. Paul tells his readers, "You should know that your body is a temple for the Holy Spirit who is in you. You have received the Holy Spirit from God" (1 Corinthians 6:19). But with this designation comes a warning: "Don't you know that you are God's temple and that God's Spirit lives in you? If anyone destroys God's temple, God will destroy that person, because God's temple is holy and you are that temple" (1 Corinthians 3:16–17).

Not one stone can be found from the great Temple built by Solomon. Why? Because when God was no longer worshiped there, it was no longer blessed and protected by God—a sober warning to those of us who would be his temple today.

THOUGHTS TO PONDER

What does it mean to be the "temple for the Holy Spirit" today? In what ways do people destroy the temple of God today?

PRAYER

Father, we pray that we will always be a fitting temple for your Holy Spirit to live in us. Help us to feel the power and the assurance that comes with that knowledge. Amen.

TRADING CONVICTIONS FOR COMPROMISES

1 KINGS 11:1–13

11 King Solomon loved many women who were not from Israel. He loved the daughter of the king of Egypt, as well as women of the Moabites, Ammonites, Edomites, Sidonians, and Hittites. ²The LORD had told the Israelites, "You must not marry people of other nations. If you do, they will cause you to follow their gods." But Solomon fell in love with these women. ³He had seven hundred wives who were from royal families and three hundred slave women who gave birth to his children. His wives caused him to turn away from God. ⁴As Solomon grew old, his wives caused him to follow other gods. He did not follow the LORD completely as his father David had done. ⁵Solomon worshiped Ashtoreth, the goddess of the people of Sidon, and Molech, the hated god of the Ammonites. ⁶So Solomon did what the LORD said was wrong and did not follow the LORD completely as his father David had done.

⁷On a hill east of Jerusalem, Solomon built two places for worship. One was a place to worship Chemosh, the hated god of the Moabites, and the other was a place to worship Molech, the hated god of the Ammonites. ⁸Solomon did the same thing for all his foreign wives so they could burn incense and offer sacrifices to their gods.

⁹The LORD had appeared to Solomon twice, but the king turned away from following the LORD, the God of Israel. The LORD was angry with Solomon, ¹⁰because he had commanded Solomon not to follow other gods. But Solomon did not obey the LORD's command. ¹¹So the LORD said to Solomon, "Because you have chosen to break your agreement with me and have not obeyed my commands, I will tear your kingdom away from you and give it to one of your officers. ¹²But I will not take it away while you are alive because of my love for your father David. I will tear it away from your son when he becomes king. ¹³I will not tear away all the kingdom from him, but I will leave him one tribe to rule. I will do this because of David, my servant, and because of Jerusalem, the city I have chosen."

DEVOTION

THE REIGN OF SOLOMON lasted for forty years. But even though he had asked for and been granted wisdom as a gift from God (1 Kings 3), he made grievous mistakes in his later years. Because of his many marriages to foreign women—especially those from royal families whom he married to ensure the peace—Solomon made allowances for his wives to worship their idols. It was a direct affront to God.

The penalty for introducing idol worship to God's people was severe. One of Solomon's officers inherited most of the kingdom, while Solomon's own son would lead only one tribe. This began the "Divided Kingdom" years which lasted until each of the two divided nations were carried off by enemy nations centuries later. The children of Israel would never again be united and free at the same time.

His political savvy had earned the country peace and made Solomon wealthier than any man had ever been. He had reached a trade agreement with the Queen of Sheba, who left great wealth with him. His vessels located at Ezion-Geber regularly returned with gold and other valuables. Vassal states paid tribute to him. He had an annual income of fifty thousand pounds of gold and income from other sources. He poured himself into the building of the Temple.

But compromise causes calamity. It was true for Solomon and it's still true today. The marriage of Solomon to the daughter of the king of Egypt (1 Kings 3:1) is but one example of Solomon using a political marriage rather than military might to accomplish peace. She came with the ransacked city of Gezer as her dowry and Solomon later rebuilt that town (1 Kings 9:16–17). And he followed that pattern seven hundred times.

Somewhere in that time, Solomon lost his way. His empire, soon to be split into two pieces, did not come apart because of a foreign invader; it fell apart from within. Every compromise he made—foreign wives, trade agreements, places of worship for foreign gods—brought the nation one step closer to doom without a single battle being fought.

Today, Satan only occasionally launches a frontal assault on God's people. Most likely, he's not going to come out hissing like a snake from the Garden of Eden. Instead, he takes his time, waiting for opportunities to offer us a concession to replace our convictions. An easy way to replace the difficult. A compromise rather than a cross. And eventually, our churches, our families, or whatever else Satan targets can fall apart from within.

THOUGHTS TO PONDER

Why do you think a wise man like Solomon made such a bad choice? What types of compromise does Satan offer us today?

PRAYER

God we pray that we will be vigilant to never take the compromises offered to us by Satan, but to live life in your path always. Amen.

THE RIGHT FRAME OF MIND

1 KINGS 11:27–40

²⁷This is the story of how Jeroboam turned against the king. Solomon was filling in the land and repairing the wall of Jerusalem, the city of David, his father. ²⁸Jeroboam was a capable man, and Solomon saw that this young man was a good worker. So Solomon put him over all the workers from the tribes of Ephraim and Manasseh.

²⁹One day as Jeroboam was leaving Jerusalem, Ahijah, the prophet from Shiloh, who was wearing a new coat, met him on the road. The two men were alone out in the country. ³⁰Ahijah took his new coat and tore it into twelve pieces. ³¹Then he said to Jeroboam, "Take ten pieces of this coat for yourself. The LORD, the God of Israel, says: 'I will tear the kingdom away from Solomon and give you ten tribes. ³²But I will allow him to control one tribe. I will do this for the sake of my servant David and for Jerusalem, the city I have chosen from all the tribes of Israel. ³³I will do this because Solomon has stopped following me and has worshiped the Sidonian god Ashtoreth, the Moabite god Chemosh, and the Ammonite god Molech. Solomon has not obeyed me by doing what I said is right and obeying my laws and commands, as his father David did.

³⁴" 'But I will not take all the kingdom away from Solomon. I will let him rule all his life because of my servant David, whom I chose, who obeyed all my commands and laws. ³⁵But I will take the kingdom away from his son, and I will allow you to rule over the ten tribes. ³⁶I will allow Solomon's son to continue to rule over one tribe so that there will always be a descendant of David, my servant, in Jerusalem, the city where I chose to be worshiped. ³⁷But I will make you rule over everything you want. You will rule over all of Israel, ³⁸and I will always be with you if you do what I say is right. You must obey all my commands. If you obey my laws and commands as David did, I will be with you. I will make your family a lasting family of kings, as I did for David, and give Israel to you. ³⁹I will punish David's children because of this, but I will not punish them forever.' "

⁴⁰Solomon tried to kill Jeroboam, but he ran away to Egypt, to Shishak king of Egypt, where he stayed until Solomon died.

DEVOTION

WHEN GOD REJECTED SOLOMON, God told him that ten of the tribes would be taken from the house of David. Only Judah would remain under the control of his descendants. But even though Jeroboam knew that he was being appointed king because of the idolatry of Solomon, he proved to be a weak king who actually set up idols to keep his people from traveling to Jerusalem to worship (1 Kings 12). God was so displeased with Jeroboam that he said the following through the prophet Ahijah:

> "I tore the kingdom away from David's family, and I gave it to you. But you are not like my servant David, who always obeyed my commands and followed me with all his heart. He did only what I said was right. ⁹But you have done more evil than anyone who ruled before you. You have quit following me and have made other gods and idols of metal. This has made me very angry, ¹⁰so I will soon bring disaster to your family. I will kill all the men in your family, both slaves and free men. I will destroy your family as completely as fire burns up manure." (1 Kings 14:8–10)

Did Jeroboam not listen when God told him that he would be blessed if he did what was right? Why did he have to make the same mistakes as Solomon?

I think pride played a huge role in his bad decisions. Once on the throne, Jeroboam ended his dependence on God. He was more concerned with creating his fortified capitals than in following God. But none of the great cities he built could protect him from the wrath of God. Because of his iniquity, only one of his sons would be buried in a grave; the others would die in battle and be eaten by the dogs and the birds.

It's no coincidence that the message of Jesus resonated with the downtrodden of the day. The rich, the politically powerful, and the religious establishment were all too proud to listen. Quoting from the Proverbs, James told his readers, "God is against the proud, but he gives grace to the humble" (James 4:6). Are you in the right frame of mind to receive God's grace?

THOUGHTS TO PONDER

What do you think was the attraction of the gods of the surrounding nations over the one true God? Why did Jeroboam make the same mistake as Solomon? Are we ever stubborn toward God?

PRAYER

Father, we pray that we will always obey you and learn from the mistakes of the past rather than repeat them. Amen.

WHO DO YOU RUN WITH?

1 KINGS 11:42—12:15

⁴²Solomon ruled in Jerusalem over all Israel for forty years. ⁴³Then he died and was buried in Jerusalem, the city of David, his father. And his son Rehoboam became king in his place.

12 Rehoboam went to Shechem, where all the Israelites had gone to make him king. ²Jeroboam son of Nebat was still in Egypt, where he had gone to escape from Solomon. When Jeroboam heard about Rehoboam being made king, he was living in Egypt. ³After the people sent for him, he and the people went to Rehoboam and said to him, ⁴"Your father forced us to work very hard. Now, make it easier for us, and don't make us work as hard as he did. Then we will serve you."

⁵Rehoboam answered, "Go away for three days, and then come back to me." So the people left.

⁶King Rehoboam asked the elders who had advised Solomon during his lifetime, "How do you think I should answer these people?"

⁷They said, "You should be like a servant to them today. If you serve them and give them a kind answer, they will serve you always."

⁸But Rehoboam rejected this advice. Instead, he asked the young men who had grown up with him and who served as his advisers. ⁹Rehoboam asked them, "What is your advice? How should we answer these people who said, 'Don't make us work as hard as your father did'?"

¹⁰The young men who had grown up with him answered, "Those people said to you, 'Your father forced us to work very hard. Now make our work easier.' You should tell them, 'My little finger is bigger than my father's legs. ¹¹He forced you to work hard, but I will make you work even harder. My father beat you with whips, but I will beat you with whips that have sharp points.'"

¹²Rehoboam had told the people, "Come back to me in three days." So after three days Jeroboam and all the people returned to Rehoboam. ¹³King Rehoboam spoke cruel words to them, because he had rejected the advice the elders had given him. ¹⁴He followed the advice of the young men and said to the people, "My father forced you to work hard, but I will make you work even harder. My father beat you with whips, but I will beat you with whips that have sharp points." ¹⁵So the king did not listen to the people. The LORD caused this to happen to keep the promise he had made to Jeroboam son of Nebat through Ahijah, a prophet from Shiloh.

Devotion

WHEN I RAN TRACK, the practice would end with the obligatory mile run to stretch our muscles and keep us in shape. It wasn't popular, but no one went home without running the four laps around the track.

I actually specialized in the longer races, at one point setting a middle school city record for the 600-yard run, when races were still measured in yards. But like everyone else, I griped about the workout-ending mile.

I discovered there were two distinct groups in those last laps. There were the true runners, who usually finished in about six or seven minutes and there were the "jumpers" and the "throwers" as we called them, who finished in about double that time, running disinterested laps along the way. I usually joined them.

My coach pulled me aside one day and told me to catch up with the runners and stay with them. He told me, "You're better than that. Who you run with tells me a lot about you." I think it's that way with all of us. You can tell a lot about a person by who they choose to run with.

When Rehoboam had an opportunity to seek advice, he decided to run with the younger crowd, who advised him to place a heavier yoke on the people than his father Solomon did. He rejected the wisdom of the elders who suggested he lead his people as a servant, lightening their load and winning their unending loyalty.

Taxes had been heavy under Solomon for the building of the Temple. With the Temple completed, he should have given the people relief, but Rehoboam chose to follow the younger crowd's harsh advice. His actions ultimately split the kingdom his father Solomon and grandfather David had led effectively. The split lasted until each weakened nation was taken into captivity.

A few years ago, the phrase "What Would Jesus Do?" was everywhere. Think about it for a minute: taking that phrase to heart means "running" with Jesus every day and making decisions in ways that honor him.

Thoughts to Ponder

Where do you go to get good advice? How do you test the advice you get? How do you know when the advice is within the will of God?

Prayer

Father, help us to weigh the counsel we are given and to always view it in the light of your Word. Amen.

Not My People

1 KINGS 12:20–33

²⁰When all the Israelites heard that Jeroboam had returned, they called him to a meeting and made him king over all Israel. Only the tribe of Judah continued to follow the family of David.

²¹When Rehoboam arrived in Jerusalem, he gathered one hundred eighty thousand of the best soldiers from the tribes of Judah and Benjamin. As son of Solomon, Rehoboam wanted to fight the people of Israel to take back his kingdom.

²²But God spoke his word to Shemaiah, a man of God, saying, ²³"Speak to Solomon's son Rehoboam, the king of Judah, and to all the people of Judah and Benjamin and the rest of the people. Say to them, ²⁴'The LORD says you must not go to war against your brothers, the Israelites. Every one of you should go home, because I made all these things happen.'" So they obeyed the LORD's command and went home as the LORD had commanded.

²⁵Then Jeroboam made Shechem in the mountains of Ephraim a very strong city, and he lived there. He also went to the city of Peniel and made it stronger.

²⁶Jeroboam said to himself, "The kingdom will probably go back to David's family. ²⁷If the people continue going to the Temple of the LORD in Jerusalem to offer sacrifices, they will want to be ruled again by Rehoboam. Then they will kill me and follow Rehoboam king of Judah."

²⁸King Jeroboam asked for advice. Then he made two golden calves. "It is too long a journey for you to go to Jerusalem to worship," he said to the people. "Israel, here are your gods who brought you out of Egypt." ²⁹Jeroboam put one golden calf in the city of Bethel and the other in the city of Dan. ³⁰This became a very great sin, because the people traveled as far as Dan to worship the calf there.

³¹Jeroboam built temples on the places of worship. He also chose priests from all the people, not just from the tribe of Levi. ³²And he started a new festival on the fifteenth day of the eighth month, just like the festival in Judah. During that time the king offered sacrifices on the altar, along with sacrifices to the calves in Bethel he had made. He also chose priests in Bethel to serve at the places of worship he had made. ³³So Jeroboam chose his own time for a festival for the Israelites—the fifteenth day of the eighth month. During that time he offered sacrifices on the altar he had built in Bethel. He set up a festival for the Israelites and offered sacrifices on the altar.

DEVOTION

EVEN IN THE BEST of times it had been difficult to hold the twelve tribes together. And with the calamitous decision of Rehoboam to increase the burden on the people, the kingdom was finally torn apart. The northern tribes found their leader and spokesman in Jeroboam. Their nation, made up of the rebel tribes that split from the house of David, was named Israel. The split would be permanent, although relations between the two nations would run hot and cold over the years. Probably because of its diversity and vast geographical range, Israel never enjoyed the stability of its sister kingdom, Judah, and it was the first to fall to foreign kings.

The only reason the twelve tribes had ever been stable was that they had shared a common religion. So when Solomon introduced false gods to the people and turned to idol worship in his old age, the stage was set for what happened to his son, Rehoboam. And the events of this story compounded the sin further.

To shore up his new kingdom, Jeroboam created two places of worship for his people. But the sanctuaries Jeroboam created were not for the worship of God, but for the worship of golden calves he created. He set them in Dan, at the far northern extreme of Israel, and Bethel in the south. The break with God was now complete.

Years later, God would send a prophet, Hosea, to Israel during its period of greatest decline. After the death of Jeroboam, the nation would have six kings in twenty years, four of them assassinated by their successors. They were only a few years away from captivity when Hosea came on the scene, prophesying for forty years. And in one of the most poignant application lessons in Scripture, God said this to Hosea: "The LORD said, 'Name him Lo-Ammi, because you are not my people, and I am not your God'" (Hosea 1:9). Give your son a name, God says, that reflects the nation's relationship to me: Lo-Ammi—not my people.

So we see how a nation goes from being favored by God to being disowned by him by turning away from him in worship.

THOUGHTS TO PONDER

What is the lesson of Jeroboam for us today? As a nation, are we truly God's people? What does God expect of us as a nation?

PRAYER

Father, we know that righteousness exalts a nation, but that sin tears it apart. Please help us as a people to turn to you, to do your will, and receive the blessings that come with faithful obedience. Amen.

GIVE WHAT YOU HAVE

1 KINGS 17:1–22

17Now Elijah the Tishbite was a prophet from the settlers in Gilead. "I serve the LORD, the God of Israel," Elijah said to Ahab. "As surely as the LORD lives, no rain or dew will fall during the next few years unless I command it."

²Then the LORD spoke his word to Elijah: ³"Leave this place and go east and hide near Kerith Ravine east of the Jordan River. ⁴You may drink from the stream, and I have commanded ravens to bring you food there." ⁵So Elijah did what the LORD said; he went to Kerith Ravine, east of the Jordan, and lived there. ⁶The birds brought Elijah bread and meat every morning and evening, and he drank water from the stream.

⁷After a while the stream dried up because there was no rain. ⁸Then the LORD spoke his word to Elijah, ⁹"Go to Zarephath in Sidon and live there. I have commanded a widow there to take care of you."

¹⁰So Elijah went to Zarephath. When he reached the town gate, he saw a widow gathering wood for a fire. Elijah asked her, "Would you bring me a little water in a cup so I may have a drink?" ¹¹As she was going to get his water, Elijah said, "Please bring me a piece of bread, too."

¹²The woman answered, "As surely as the LORD your God lives, I have no bread. I have only a handful of flour in a jar and only a little olive oil in a jug. I came here to gather some wood so I could go home and cook our last meal. My son and I will eat it and then die from hunger."

¹³"Don't worry," Elijah said to her. "Go home and cook your food as you have said. But first make a small loaf of bread from the flour you have, and bring it to me. Then cook something for yourself and your son. ¹⁴The LORD, the God of Israel, says, 'That jar of flour will never be empty, and the jug will always have oil in it, until the day the LORD sends rain to the land.'"

¹⁵So the woman went home and did what Elijah told her to do. And the woman and her son and Elijah had enough food every day. ¹⁶The jar of flour and the jug of oil were never empty, just as the LORD, through Elijah, had promised.

¹⁷Some time later the son of the woman who owned the house became sick. He grew worse and worse and finally stopped breathing. ¹⁸The woman said to Elijah, "Man of God, what have you done to me? Did you come here to remind me of my sin and to kill my son?"

¹⁹Elijah said to her, "Give me your son." Elijah took the boy from her, carried him upstairs, and laid him on the bed in the room where he was staying. ²⁰Then he prayed to the LORD: "LORD my God, this widow is letting me stay in her house. Why have you done this terrible thing to her and caused her son to

die?" ²¹Then Elijah lay on top of the boy three times. He prayed to the LORD, "LORD my God, let this boy live again!"

²²The LORD answered Elijah's prayer; the boy began breathing again and was alive.

DEVOTION

POSSIBLY THE GREATEST of the prophets, Elijah got a rather tough first assignment: tell King Ahab that God is stopping the rain. Elijah's next two stops—the stream in the ravine and the widow's house—were undoubtedly object lessons for Elijah in God's ability to provide. It was an important lesson for Elijah to learn, because God had another hazardous assignment in store for him.

But the interesting character in this story is the widow. No doubt the poor in society were the first to suffer the effects of the famine, and this woman, who probably lived off the charity of others, had already reached her end. She was ready to cook her final meal and die. Yet here was this stranger asking for that last morsel, promising God's blessings on her if she fed him. Amazingly, she believed him and was blessed.

Was the request too large? Should Elijah have asked the widow for her last meal? As you read the Bible, wealth is never a prerequisite for giving to God. We're not asked to give from our abundance; we're commanded to give—period. Jesus praised the widow who could only give two small coins to the Temple treasury and ignored the extravagant gifts of the wealthy (Mark 12:41–44). Jesus also took the lunch of a small boy and fed more than five thousand people with it (John 6:1–15).

The lesson is this: give God what you have and trust him to make the gift significant.

THOUGHTS TO PONDER

What small gift has someone given you that made a big difference in your life? What gift do you think God wants you to give?

PRAYER

Father, we know every blessing comes from you, and that when we give to others, we are sharing you. Amen.

DECIDING BETWEEN TWO CHOICES

1 KINGS 18:1–21

18 During the third year without rain, the LORD spoke his word to Elijah: "Go and meet King Ahab, and I will soon send rain." ²So Elijah went to meet Ahab.

By this time there was no food in Samaria. ³King Ahab sent for Obadiah, who was in charge of the king's palace. (Obadiah was a true follower of the LORD. ⁴When Jezebel was killing all the LORD's prophets, Obadiah hid a hundred of them in two caves, fifty in one cave and fifty in another. He also brought them food and water.) ⁵Ahab said to Obadiah, "Let's check every spring and valley in the land. Maybe we can find enough grass to keep our horses and mules alive and not have to kill our animals." ⁶So each one chose a part of the country to search; Ahab went in one direction and Obadiah in another.

⁷While Obadiah was on his way, Elijah met him. Obadiah recognized Elijah, so he bowed down to the ground and said, "Elijah? Is it really you, master?"

⁸"Yes," Elijah answered. "Go tell your master that I am here."

⁹Then Obadiah said, "What wrong have I done for you to hand me over to Ahab like this? He will put me to death. ¹⁰As surely as the LORD your God lives, the king has sent people to every country to search for you. If the ruler said you were not there, Ahab forced the ruler to swear you could not be found in his country. ¹¹Now you want me to go to my master and tell him, 'Elijah is here'? ¹²The Spirit of the LORD may carry you to some other place after I leave. If I go tell King Ahab you are here, and he comes and doesn't find you, he will kill me! I have followed the LORD since I was a boy. ¹³Haven't you been told what I did? When Jezebel was killing the LORD's prophets, I hid a hundred of them, fifty in one cave and fifty in another. I brought them food and water. ¹⁴Now you want me to go and tell my master you are here? He will kill me!"

¹⁵Elijah answered, "As surely as the LORD All-Powerful lives, whom I serve, I will be seen by Ahab today."

¹⁶So Obadiah went to Ahab and told him where Elijah was. Then Ahab went to meet Elijah.

¹⁷When he saw Elijah, he asked, "Is it you—the biggest troublemaker in Israel?"

¹⁸Elijah answered, "I have not made trouble in Israel. You and your father's family have made all this trouble by not obeying the LORD's commands. You have gone after the Baals. ¹⁹Now tell all Israel to meet me at Mount Carmel. Also bring the four hundred fifty prophets of Baal and the four hundred prophets of Asherah, who eat at Jezebel's table."

[20]So Ahab called all the Israelites and those prophets to Mount Carmel. [21]Elijah approached the people and said, "How long will you not decide between two choices? If the LORD is the true God, follow him, but if Baal is the true God, follow him!" But the people said nothing.

DEVOTION

THERE HAD BEEN THREE years without rain, and Elijah was perhaps the most hated man in Samaria. Droughts had always been an aspect of the cyclical weather patterns of that desert part of the world, but rarely had a drought lasted more than a year before being interrupted by the rainy season.

But this was no ordinary weather pattern. This drought was initiated by God and would not end until he was appeased by an idolatrous nation that had forgotten him. Queen Jezebel had responded to the crisis by killing all of the true prophets in the land, and only those hidden by Obadiah were saved. At the same time, she was supporting 850 false prophets by feeding them at the royal tables.

I like the challenge Elijah issued to the assembly: "How long will you not decide between two choices?" (1 Kings 18:21). I think we have two choices today. Jesus called it the narrow road and the wide road when he said, "Enter through the narrow gate. The gate is wide and the road is wide that leads to hell, and many people enter through that gate. But the gate is small and the road is narrow that leads to true life. Only a few people find that road" (Matthew 7:13–14).

The nation of Israel had a choice to make. So do you and I. While others are following the false gods of money or fame, we take the narrow path that leads to true life. The people did not answer Elijah, but we cannot be silent. Someday we will answer to "the LORD All-Powerful" about the path we have chosen in life. What will you say?

THOUGHTS TO PONDER

Why do you think the people stayed silent when Elijah called for them to choose to follow God? Are we ever guilty of being silent about our choice to follow God today?

PRAYER

Father, we pray that we will always choose your path and that you will give us the strength to walk in it. Amen.

CHASING FALSE GODS

1 KINGS 18:22–40

²²Elijah said, "I am the only prophet of the LORD here, but there are four hundred fifty prophets of Baal. ²³Bring two bulls. Let the prophets of Baal choose one bull and kill it and cut it into pieces. Then let them put the meat on the wood, but they are not to set fire to it. I will prepare the other bull, putting the meat on the wood but not setting fire to it. ²⁴You prophets of Baal, pray to your god, and I will pray to the LORD. The god who answers by setting fire to his wood is the true God."

All the people agreed that this was a good idea.

²⁵Then Elijah said to the prophets of Baal, "There are many of you, so you go first. Choose a bull and prepare it. Pray to your god, but don't start the fire."

²⁶So they took the bull that was given to them and prepared it. They prayed to Baal from morning until noon, shouting "Baal, answer us!" But there was no sound, and no one answered. They danced around the altar they had built.

²⁷At noon Elijah began to make fun of them. "Pray louder!" he said. "If Baal really is a god, maybe he is thinking, or busy, or traveling! Maybe he is sleeping so you will have to wake him!" ²⁸The prophets prayed louder, cutting themselves with swords and spears until their blood flowed, which was the way they worshiped. ²⁹The afternoon passed, and the prophets continued to act like this until it was time for the evening sacrifice. But no voice was heard; Baal did not answer, and no one paid attention.

³⁰Then Elijah said to all the people, "Now come to me." So they gathered around him, and Elijah rebuilt the altar of the LORD, which had been torn down. ³¹He took twelve stones, one stone for each of the twelve tribes, the number of Jacob's sons. (The LORD changed Jacob's name to Israel.) ³²Elijah used these stones to rebuild the altar in honor of the LORD. Then he dug a ditch around the altar that was big enough to hold about thirteen quarts of seed. ³³Elijah put the wood on the altar, cut the bull into pieces, and laid the pieces on the wood. ³⁴Then he said, "Fill four jars with water, and pour it on the meat and on the wood." Then Elijah said, "Do it again," and they did it again. Then he said, "Do it a third time," and they did it the third time. ³⁵So the water ran off the altar and filled the ditch.

³⁶At the time for the evening sacrifice, the prophet Elijah went near the altar. "LORD, you are the God of Abraham, Isaac, and Israel," he prayed. "Prove that you are the God of Israel and that I am your servant. Show these people that you commanded me to do all these things. ³⁷LORD, answer my prayer so these people will know that you, LORD, are God and that you will change their minds."

³⁸Then fire from the LORD came down and burned the sacrifice, the wood,

the stones, and the ground around the altar. It also dried up the water in the ditch. [39]When all the people saw this, they fell down to the ground, crying, "The LORD is God! The LORD is God!"

[40]Then Elijah said, "Capture the prophets of Baal! Don't let any of them run away!" The people captured all the prophets. Then Elijah led them down to the Kishon Valley, where he killed them.

DEVOTION

THEY BEAT THEMSELVES into a frenzy trying to get their gods to hear. Dancing, shouting, mutilations—all to get the attention of nonexistent gods.

As strange as this behavior seems, we've all seen folks whose "gods" have turned their backs, and the results weren't pretty. There are folks who have followed the god of popularity, only to be dumped. There are people who have worshiped the god of worldly success, only to fall apart when they stall out during their climb to the top. There are people who don't know where to turn because their god was another person who stopped loving them and doesn't want them around anymore.

There are other fickle gods. Alcohol, drugs, and all other forms of addiction. Gambling, pornography, and other vices. Millions call on them for recreation or for diversion. But before long the same hit no longer gives the same high. So they call louder and louder. But eventually, the god is so distant it can't even be reached.

Elijah's name means "Jehovah is my God," and on this day, he proves it. Is Jehovah your God? Our task is to rid our lives of all the rival gods that get in the way of our true service to him.

THOUGHTS TO PONDER

What thoughts do you think were running through Elijah's mind as he prepared the altar? What does his prayer to God tell you about his attitude? What are the "gods" you've had to defeat in your life?

PRAYER

God, we pray that our lives will show people that you are the one true God. Amen.

Don't Give Up

1 KINGS 19:1–14

19 King Ahab told Jezebel every thing Elijah had done and how Elijah had killed all the prophets with a sword. ²So Jezebel sent a messenger to Elijah, saying, "May the gods punish me terribly if by this time tomorrow I don't kill you just as you killed those prophets."

³When Elijah heard this, he was afraid and ran for his life, taking his servant with him. When they came to Beersheba in Judah, Elijah left his servant there. ⁴Then Elijah walked for a whole day into the desert. He sat down under a bush and asked to die. "I have had enough, LORD," he prayed. "Let me die. I am no better than my ancestors." ⁵Then he lay down under the tree and slept.

Suddenly an angel came to him and touched him. "Get up and eat," the angel said. ⁶Elijah saw near his head a loaf baked over coals and a jar of water, so he ate and drank. Then he went back to sleep.

⁷Later the LORD's angel came to him a second time. The angel touched him and said, "Get up and eat. If you don't, the journey will be too hard for you." ⁸So Elijah got up and ate and drank. The food made him strong enough to walk for forty days and nights to Mount Sinai, the mountain of God. ⁹There Elijah went into a cave and stayed all night.

Then the LORD spoke his word to him: "Elijah! Why are you here?"

¹⁰He answered, "LORD God All-Powerful, I have always served you as well as I could. But the people of Israel have broken their agreement with you, destroyed your altars, and killed your prophets with swords. I am the only prophet left, and now they are trying to kill me, too."

¹¹The LORD said to Elijah, "Go, stand in front of me on the mountain, and I will pass by you." Then a very strong wind blew until it caused the mountains to fall apart and large rocks to break in front of the LORD. But the LORD was not in the wind. After the wind, there was an earthquake, but the LORD was not in the earthquake. ¹²After the earthquake, there was a fire, but the LORD was not in the fire. After the fire, there was a quiet, gentle sound. ¹³When Elijah heard it, he covered his face with his coat and went out and stood at the entrance to the cave.

Then a voice said to him, "Elijah! Why are you here?"

¹⁴He answered, "LORD God All-Powerful, I have always served you as well as I could. But the people of Israel have broken their agreement with you, destroyed your altars, and killed your prophets with swords. I am the only prophet left, and now they are trying to kill me, too."

DEVOTION

HAVE YOU EVER WANTED to just give up like Elijah? If you have, the following story should encourage you.

Olin Browne had a solid golf career on the PGA Tour, but his recent lackluster play had forced him to qualify for the 2005 U.S. Open, the nation's golfing championship, rather than enjoy an exemption into the field like the well-known pros.

The odds were long. More than nine thousand golfers wanted the few slots available to qualifiers, and two-day tournaments around the country would decide who got to pursue their dream of playing in the U.S. Open. Browne had been in the Open before, but now was forced to qualify against college players about half his age.

He shot a 73 the first day—respectable but disappointing. Feeling like he had no chance in the short two-day tournament, Browne looked for a tournament official to ask how to withdraw. Not finding an official, he decided to go ahead and play the next day.

Haven't you had that feeling? You didn't do your best and you knew it. You looked for a way out, but didn't find it. You trudged on.

Good thing for Browne that he missed that official. The next day he shot a 59—a score that only a handful of golfers have ever attained. It put him into the U.S. Open.

And the story doesn't end there. He was in the top three the first three days of the Open. Even when he faded on the final day, he finished tied for fifteenth, on the nation's biggest golf stage—good enough for an automatic qualification the next year.

I've had more than my share of "73's" in life and so have you. But we can't quit. You have to believe you're capable of a "59" and that it just might happen tomorrow.

With God's help, Elijah would have better days, and so will you and I.

THOUGHTS TO PONDER

If you've ever felt like Elijah, what circumstances made you feel that way? How did you crawl out of your "cave"? How do you remain upbeat even when your current situation isn't what you want it to be?

PRAYER

God, help us to see that you never leave us. Help us to see you in the many ways you manifest yourself to us each day. Amen.

LIFE-DESTROYING LIES

Read the entire story at 1 Kings 21:1–28.

21 After these things had happened, this is what followed. A man named Naboth owned a vineyard in Jezreel, near the palace of Ahab king of Israel. ²One day Ahab said to Naboth, "Give me your vineyard. It is near my palace, and I want to make it into a vegetable garden. I will give you a better vineyard in its place, or, if you prefer, I will pay you what it is worth."

³Naboth answered, "May the LORD keep me from ever giving my land to you. It belongs to my family."

⁴Ahab went home angry and upset, because he did not like what Naboth from Jezreel had said. (Naboth had said, "I will not give you my family's land.") Ahab lay down on his bed, turned his face to the wall, and refused to eat.

⁵His wife, Jezebel, came in and asked him, "Why are you so upset that you refuse to eat?"

⁶Ahab answered, "I talked to Naboth, the man from Jezreel. I said, 'Sell me your vineyard, or, if you prefer, I will give you another vineyard for it.' But Naboth refused."

⁷Jezebel answered, "Is this how you rule as king over Israel? Get up, eat something, and cheer up. I will get Naboth's vineyard for you."

⁸So Jezebel wrote some letters, signed Ahab's name to them, and used his own seal to seal them. Then she sent them to the elders and important men who lived in Naboth's town. ⁹The letter she wrote said: "Declare a day during which the people are to fast. Call the people together, and give Naboth a place of honor among them. ¹⁰Seat two troublemakers across from him, and have them say they heard Naboth speak against God and the king. Then take Naboth out of the city and kill him with stones."

¹¹The elders and important men of Jezreel obeyed Jezebel's command, just as she wrote in the letters. ¹²They declared a special day on which the people were to fast. And they put Naboth in a place of honor before the people. ¹³Two troublemakers sat across from Naboth and said in front of everybody that they had heard him speak against God and the king. So the people carried Naboth out of the city and killed him with stones. ¹⁴Then the leaders sent a message to Jezebel, saying, "Naboth has been killed."

¹⁵When Jezebel heard that Naboth had been killed, she told Ahab, "Naboth of Jezreel is dead. Now you may go and take for yourself the vineyard he would not sell to you." ¹⁶When Ahab heard that Naboth of Jezreel was dead, he got up and went to the vineyard to take it for his own.

¹⁷At this time the LORD spoke his word to the prophet Elijah the Tishbite.

The LORD said, [18]"Go to Ahab king of Israel in Samaria. He is at Naboth's vineyard, where he has gone to take it as his own. [19]Tell Ahab that I, the LORD, say to him, 'You have murdered Naboth and taken his land. So I tell you this: In the same place the dogs licked up Naboth's blood, they will also lick up your blood!' "

DEVOTION

YOU MIGHT RECALL the story the prophet Nathan told King David when David sinned by sleeping with Bathsheba and later trying to cover his sin by having her husband killed in battle. It was a story of a poor man with one lamb, which he loved and treated as a pet, and a rich man who took that lamb and cooked it for his own feast. David—outraged by the story—said the rich man must die for his sin. "You are the man," Nathan said to David (2 Samuel 12:7). David had taken Uriah's wife for his own, even though he had a palace full of wives and concubines. But David would pay dearly for his sin.

Ahab reenacted the parable of Nathan in real life. He could have had any vineyard in the kingdom, but he wanted only Naboth's. Queen Jezebel—whose name is synonymous with evil today—plotted to get the vineyard for Ahab at the expense of Naboth's life.

You can see from this story why Israel was warned about perjury. "You must not tell lies about your neighbor" was one of the Ten Commandments to the people (Exodus 20:16). Lies destroy reputations. Lies destroy relationships. And as we see in the story above, lies can destroy lives.

Ahab and Jezebel paid dearly for their sin. Ahab died in battle. His blood, pooled in the floor of his chariot, was licked up by dogs (1 Kings 22:29–38). Jezebel was thrown down from the heights of the palace and dogs ate her, leaving only her skull, her feet, and the palms of her hands (2 Kings 9:30–37).

THOUGHTS TO PONDER

Why would Ahab envy the vineyard of Naboth when he could have had any property he wanted? What does this tell us about the sin of envy?

PRAYER

Father, we pray that we will be content with the bounty you have given us and we pray that we will quench the fire of envy that threatens to burn in each of us. Amen.

HEARING WHAT WE WANT TO HEAR

1 KINGS 22:1–9, 13–17

22 For three years there was peace between Israel and Aram. ²During the third year Jehoshaphat king of Judah went to visit Ahab king of Israel.

³At that time Ahab asked his officers, "Do you remember that the king of Aram took Ramoth in Gilead from us? Why have we done nothing to get it back?" ⁴So Ahab asked King Jehoshaphat, "Will you go with me to fight at Ramoth in Gilead?"

"I will go with you," Jehoshaphat answered. "My soldiers are yours, and my horses are yours." ⁵Jehoshaphat also said to Ahab, "But first we should ask if this is the LORD's will."

⁶Ahab called about four hundred prophets together and asked them, "Should I go to war against Ramoth in Gilead or not?"

They answered, "Go, because the Lord will hand them over to you."

⁷But Jehoshaphat asked, "Isn't there a prophet of the LORD here? Let's ask him what we should do."

⁸Then King Ahab said to Jehoshaphat, "There is one other prophet. We could ask the LORD through him, but I hate him. He never prophesies anything good about me, but something bad. He is Micaiah son of Imlah."

Jehoshaphat said, "King Ahab, you shouldn't say that!"

⁹So Ahab king of Israel told one of his officers to bring Micaiah to him at once.

¹³The messenger who had gone to get Micaiah said to him, "All the other prophets are saying King Ahab will succeed. You should agree with them and give the king a good answer."

¹⁴But Micaiah answered, "As surely as the LORD lives, I can tell him only what the LORD tells me."

¹⁵When Micaiah came to Ahab, the king asked him, "Micaiah, should we attack Ramoth in Gilead or not?"

Micaiah answered, "Attack and win! The LORD will hand them over to you."

¹⁶But Ahab said to Micaiah, "How many times do I have to tell you to speak only the truth to me in the name of the LORD?"

¹⁷So Micaiah answered, "I saw the army of Israel scattered over the hills like sheep without a shepherd. The LORD said, 'They have no leaders. They should go home and not fight.'"

DEVOTION

ABRAHAM LINCOLN WON the Republican nomination for president over three highly regarded rivals, and then he won over his opponents by creating a very unexpected cabinet. He invited his former opponents into his inner circle to help him through the troubled times. It was a measure of his genius and confidence that he could mold a unit and glean the wisdom from these former political enemies.

Ahab was no Abraham—Lincoln or biblical. He gathered four hundred prophets who "saw" only what the king wanted them to see. Their bias was so transparent that Jehoshaphat—the king of Judah who was thinking about allying with Ahab—asked if there was not a true prophet of God whom they could ask about the battle for Ramoth in Gilead.

Enter Micaiah, one of the heroes of the Bible, a man of great integrity. Ahab despised him because he knew Micaiah would only prophesy the truth. At first, Micaiah was sarcastic: "*Attack and win!*" he said, knowing that was what Ahab wanted to hear. But in truth, the battle would be a disaster and Israel would be left as an army without leaders.

Do we have false prophets today? Sure. If you listen closely, you may hear their voices; claiming to speak for God, they actually preach a message based on whatever they think people desire to hear. Easy religion is all the rage, despite the teachings of Jesus to the contrary. "Can I win the battle against Satan without any great sacrifice?" the world asks. "Sure," answer the modern-day false prophets. It sounds true because we want it to be.

But Paul told the young minister Timothy (2 Timothy 4:3) that "the time will come when people will not listen to the true teaching but will find many more teachers who please them by saying the things they want to hear." Ignoring the truth cost Ahab his life. What price will we pay if we listen to the false teachers?

THOUGHTS TO PONDER

What are some lies that people want to believe? How can you know the truth about what God wants you to do with your life?

PRAYER

God, we seek your direction in our lives, and we ask that we will hear what you want us to hear, not what we want to hear. Amen.

GAMBLING WITH
THE TRUTH

1 KINGS 22:18–38

¹⁸Then Ahab king of Israel said to Jehoshaphat, "I told you! He never prophesies anything good about me, but only bad."

¹⁹But Micaiah said, "Hear the message from the LORD: I saw the LORD sitting on his throne with his heavenly army standing near him on his right and on his left. ²⁰The LORD said, 'Who will trick Ahab into attacking Ramoth in Gilead where he will be killed?'

"Some said one thing; some said another. ²¹Then one spirit came and stood before the LORD and said, 'I will trick him.'

²²"The LORD asked, 'How will you do it?'

"The spirit answered, 'I will go to Ahab's prophets and make them tell lies.'

"So the LORD said, 'You will succeed in tricking him. Go and do it.'"

²³Micaiah said, "Ahab, the LORD has made your prophets lie to you, and the LORD has decided that disaster should come to you."

²⁴Then Zedekiah son of Kenaanah went up to Micaiah and slapped him in the face. Zedekiah said, "Has the LORD's spirit left me to speak through you?"

²⁵Micaiah answered, "You will find out on the day you go to hide in an inside room."

²⁶Then Ahab king of Israel ordered, "Take Micaiah and send him to Amon, the governor of the city, and to Joash, the king's son. ²⁷Tell them I said to put this man in prison and give him only bread and water until I return safely from the battle."

²⁸Micaiah said, "Ahab, if you come back safely from battle, the LORD has not spoken through me. Remember my words, all you people!"

²⁹So Ahab king of Israel and Jehoshaphat king of Judah went to Ramoth in Gilead. ³⁰King Ahab said to Jehoshaphat, "I will go into battle, but I will wear other clothes so no one will recognize me. But you wear your royal clothes." So Ahab wore other clothes and went into battle.

³¹The king of Aram had ordered his thirty-two chariot commanders, "Don't fight with anyone—important or unimportant—except the king of Israel." ³²When these commanders saw Jehoshaphat, they thought he was certainly the king of Israel, so they turned to attack him. But Jehoshaphat began shouting. ³³When they saw he was not King Ahab, they stopped chasing him.

³⁴By chance, a soldier shot an arrow, but he hit Ahab king of Israel between the pieces of his armor. King Ahab said to his chariot driver, "Turn around and get me out of the battle, because I am hurt!" ³⁵The battle continued all day. King Ahab was held up in his chariot and faced the Arameans. His blood flowed down

to the bottom of the chariot. That evening he died. [36]Near sunset a cry went out through the army of Israel: "Each man go back to his own city and land."

[37]In that way King Ahab died. His body was carried to Samaria and buried there. [38]The men cleaned Ahab's chariot at a pool in Samaria where prostitutes bathed, and the dogs licked his blood from the chariot. These things happened as the LORD had said they would.

DEVOTION

SOMETIMES JUSTICE TAKES an odd course. Bored by his king's command to attack only Ahab, a soldier aimlessly shoots an arrow into the air, only to have it come down right between the joints of Ahab's armor. Mortally wounded, Ahab is carted to Samaria where the dogs lick his blood just as they did Naboth's blood after Jezebel had him unjustly murdered in order to procure his vineyard.

The one and only time I was tempted to gamble came during my senior year in college. I bet the spread on my favorite team, wagering what was a good deal of money for me at the time. But as the week wore on and the game got closer, I got cold feet and placed another bet, this time with another gambler, and this time against my team. I would lose one bet and win the other—no harm done.

But the line had shifted, and there was one mathematical possibility to lose both bets if the score turned out exactly right. There was a one-point margin for the worst possible scenario. Surely it wouldn't happen. But it did. It took me two weeks of work over the holidays to pay the debt. I never bet again. That game was my arrow shot by chance that turned me away from a possibly addictive behavior. I've always been grateful for that.

But Ahab didn't have to meet his arrow on that day. He could have listened to the prophet Micaiah and refused to go to war. But he didn't.

Is God going to get your attention through his Word or through his "arrows"? The choice is yours.

THOUGHTS TO PONDER

Why would Ahab go to war even after he heard the prophecy of Micaiah? Have you ever ignored the warnings of others and regretted it? Have you ever ignored your conscience?

PRAYER

God, we pray that we will listen to you when you try to direct our paths. May we never willfully disobey you in our desire to do our own will. Amen.

Taking up the Cloak

2 KINGS 2:1–15

2 It was almost time for the LORD to take Elijah by a whirlwind up into heaven. While Elijah and Elisha were leaving Gilgal, ²Elijah said to Elisha, "Please stay here. The LORD has told me to go to Bethel."

But Elisha said, "As the LORD lives, and as you live, I won't leave you." So they went down to Bethel. ³The groups of prophets at Bethel came out to Elisha and said to him, "Do you know the LORD will take your master away from you today?"

Elisha said, "Yes, I know, but don't talk about it."

⁴Elijah said to him, "Stay here, Elisha, because the LORD has sent me to Jericho."

But Elisha said, "As the LORD lives, and as you live, I won't leave you."

So they went to Jericho. ⁵The groups of prophets at Jericho came to Elisha and said, "Do you know that the LORD will take your master away from you today?"

Elisha answered, "Yes, I know, but don't talk about it."

⁶Elijah said to Elisha, "Stay here. The LORD has sent me to the Jordan River." Elisha answered, "As the LORD lives, and as you live, I won't leave you."

So the two of them went on. ⁷Fifty men of the groups of prophets came and stood far from where Elijah and Elisha were by the Jordan. ⁸Elijah took off his coat, rolled it up, and hit the water. The water divided to the right and to the left, and Elijah and Elisha crossed over on dry ground.

⁹After they had crossed over, Elijah said to Elisha, "What can I do for you before I am taken from you?"

Elisha said, "Leave me a double share of your spirit."

¹⁰Elijah said, "You have asked a hard thing. But if you see me when I am taken from you, it will be yours. If you don't, it won't happen."

¹¹As they were walking and talking, a chariot and horses of fire appeared and separated Elijah from Elisha. Then Elijah went up to heaven in a whirlwind. ¹²Elisha saw it and shouted, "My father! My father! The chariots of Israel and their horsemen!" And Elisha did not see him anymore. Then Elisha grabbed his own clothes and tore them to show how sad he was.

¹³He picked up Elijah's coat that had fallen from him. Then he returned and stood on the bank of the Jordan. ¹⁴Elisha hit the water with Elijah's coat and said, "Where is the LORD, the God of Elijah?" When he hit the water, it divided to the right and to the left, and Elisha crossed over.

¹⁵The groups of prophets at Jericho were watching and said, "Elisha now has the spirit Elijah had."

DEVOTION

ELISHA HAD BEEN with Elijah for quite a while, and he had been the appointed heir to the spiritual powers of his master (1 Kings19:16) since God had commanded the elder prophet to lay his cloak on Elisha as a symbol that he had been chosen. Now it was time for the succession, and everyone in this story had received a revelation from God that today was the day. And even though Elijah urges Elisha to stay behind, three times Elisha refuses and accompanies his master on his final journey.

The request of Elisha is an interesting one: "Leave me a double share of your spirit." The request probably refers to the Jewish rules of inheritance. By law, the first son in a family would inherit a double share of his father's possessions. The other sons would divide the rest. So Elisha is asking to inherit an extra share of his master's power as his closest follower. He is not asking for twice as much power as Elijah had. After Elijah is gone—taken up to heaven in a whirlwind—Elisha picks up the cloak of Elijah. There is symmetry here as the cloak is probably the same one used when he was named successor to Elijah. Putting on the cloak, Elisha carries on.

I see an important concept for the work of the kingdom of God here. Most of us are like Elisha—carrying on for someone else. We are doing the work in churches we did not start. We are contributing to ministries we did not found. We are taking up the cloak of those who have gone on to their reward. At the same time, each of us who has been entrusted as a leader in God's work must find our "Elisha"—the person who will carry on after we are gone.

As each of us takes our place in this cycle—trainee, leader, mentor—we ensure that the work of the Lord continues until he comes to take each of us home.

THOUGHTS TO PONDER

Why do you think Elijah was carried into heaven without experiencing death? What impression would that event have on Elisha? Who are you training to do your work after you are gone?

PRAYER

Father, we pray that someday, like Elijah, you will take all of us into your kingdom. Amen.

THOSE WHO HAVE GONE BEFORE

2 KINGS 2:11–22

¹¹As they were walking and talking, a chariot and horses of fire appeared and separated Elijah from Elisha. Then Elijah went up to heaven in a whirlwind. ¹²Elisha saw it and shouted, "My father! My father! The chariots of Israel and their horsemen!" And Elisha did not see him anymore. Then Elisha grabbed his own clothes and tore them to show how sad he was.

¹³He picked up Elijah's coat that had fallen from him. Then he returned and stood on the bank of the Jordan. ¹⁴Elisha hit the water with Elijah's coat and said, "Where is the LORD, the God of Elijah?" When he hit the water, it divided to the right and to the left, and Elisha crossed over.

¹⁵The groups of prophets at Jericho were watching and said, "Elisha now has the spirit Elijah had." And they came to meet him, bowing down to the ground before him. ¹⁶They said to him, "There are fifty strong men with us. Please let them go and look for your master. Maybe the Spirit of the LORD has taken Elijah up and set him down on some mountain or in some valley."

But Elisha answered, "No, don't send them."

¹⁷When the groups of prophets had begged Elisha until he couldn't refuse them anymore, he said, "Send them." So they sent fifty men who looked for three days, but they could not find him. ¹⁸Then they came back to Elisha at Jericho where he was staying. He said to them, "I told you not to go, didn't I?"

¹⁹The people of the city said to Elisha, "Look, master, this city is a nice place to live as you can see. But the water is so bad the land cannot grow crops."

²⁰Elisha said, "Bring me a new bowl and put salt in it." So they brought it to him.

²¹Then he went out to the spring and threw the salt in it. He said, "This is what the LORD says: 'I have healed this water. From now on it won't cause death, and it won't keep the land from growing crops.'" ²²So the water has been healed to this day just as Elisha had said.

DEVOTION

ELIJAH WAS GONE, and no amount of searching would bring him back. The fifty "strong men" sent out by the prophets of Jericho found no trace of him. Elijah had moved on; it was time for Elisha to take his place.

How do you follow an Elijah? Who followed Coach Bear Bryant at the

University of Alabama? Who took the place of Justice Oliver Wendell Holmes on the Supreme Court? History is not often kind to those who follow a legend.

Following an Elijah is tough. President Andrew Johnson couldn't walk in the shoes of Abraham Lincoln. Did anyone comfortably slip into the role Martin Luther King filled in the civil rights movement? Isn't history full of organizations or movements that stalled when a charismatic leader stepped down?

Elisha was not intimidated by the fact that the prophets of Jericho wanted Elijah back. He didn't take it personally when they searched for three days. He simply waited for his inevitable vindication as God's selected successor to Elijah and then went about the business of improving the lot of the people who came to him for help.

We all follow others. We carry the name and often the reputation—good or bad—of our parents and grandparents who have gone before us. We follow predecessors in our jobs. I call it the "halo or horns" effect. For better or worse, we're either an "angel" or a "devil" compared to those we follow.

Elisha's first act was to bring life back to a community by making the waters drinkable. I love the phrase that the waters had been "healed." It reminds me of my native West Texas where farmers would occasionally leave a field fallow for a year to let it rest and heal in order to grow crops in future seasons. Because of the undrinkable water, the community was dying, and God, working through Elisha, brought it back to life. And in doing so, he validated Elisha as the anointed successor to Elijah.

Years later, Jesus would follow John. Both would teach and both would call the people to repentance. But Jesus would be special. He would be greater than the one he followed—something that even John himself understood. God himself made this proclamation: "This is my Son, whom I love, and I am very pleased with him" (Matthew 3:17).

Whether you're greater than those you follow or not, take a lesson from Elisha: take the initiative in helping and serving others and sooner or later you'll be a leader.

THOUGHTS TO PONDER

Who have you followed when it comes to your faith? What legacy are you leaving for those who will follow you?

PRAYER

God, we thank you for those who have gone before us and led the way. We pray that we will be a beacon for those who follow in our steps. Amen.

GOD WILL PROVIDE

2 KINGS 4:1–7

4 The wife of a man from the groups of prophets said to Elisha, "Your servant, my husband, is dead. You know he honored the LORD. But now the man he owes money to is coming to take my two boys as his slaves!"

²Elisha answered, "How can I help you? Tell me, what do you have in your house?"

The woman said, "I don't have anything there except a pot of oil."

³Then Elisha said, "Go and get empty jars from all your neighbors. Don't ask for just a few. ⁴Then go into your house and shut the door behind you and your sons. Pour oil into all the jars, and set the full ones aside."

⁵So she left Elisha and shut the door behind her and her sons. As they brought the jars to her, she poured out the oil. ⁶When the jars were all full, she said to her son, "Bring me another jar."

But he said, "There are no more jars." Then the oil stopped flowing.

⁷She went and told Elisha. And the prophet said to her, "Go, sell the oil and pay what you owe. You and your sons can live on what is left."

DEVOTION

HOW MUCH WILL GOD bless you when you ask? The answer might be found in how many "pots" we set out in faith.

Go get all the empty jars you can find, Elisha told the woman. Not just a few, but as many as you can. Then, miraculously, each and every one was filled with oil. Enough to sell. Enough to use. And most importantly, enough to keep her sons from becoming the slaves of the man to whom she was indebted.

When I was a child, my grandfather took me on a few occasions to a small country supermarket that had a candy aisle. This was well before the days of the convenience store on every corner, loaded with snacks and drinks. This was an old-fashioned country market stocked with a mile of candy by the estimation of my five-year-old eyes. My grandfather's instructions to me: get anything you want.

This created quite a dilemma for me. Did anything really mean *anything*? Could I go too far and stretch the limits of his generosity? Did I dare risk the humiliation of putting candy back? What would my mother allow when I walked back into my grandparents house? All these questions acted as a built-in limiter on my shopping, and I always went home with a handful of penny candy and perhaps one candy bar.

From the instructions given by Elisha, the widow knew to expect a bounty from God. All she had to do was provide the jars. I wonder if she had the same doubts about God's bounty that I did about my grandfather's generosity. I wonder if her windfall of oil was limited because she quit gathering jars, or whether she got every available jar.

As a child, I never reached the limit of my grandfather's generosity at Andy's Market in Kress, Texas. And so far, five decades into my life, I've never reached the limits of God's generosity either.

While I don't buy into the concept that God automatically rewards us right now in this life for gifts we give to him, I know he certainly takes care of his own. God stands ready to bless us spiritually when we ask, while being mindful of our physical needs as well. Jesus spoke strongly about this when he said: "Don't have so little faith! Don't worry and say, 'What will we eat?' or 'What will we drink?' or 'What will we wear?' The people who don't know God keep trying to get these things, and your Father in heaven knows you need them" (Matthew 6:30–32).

God wants to shower his blessings on us, as Jesus tells his followers in Matthew 7:7–11:

> "Ask, and God will give to you. Search, and you will find. Knock, and the door will open for you. Yes, everyone who asks will receive. Everyone who searches will find. And everyone who knocks will have the door opened. If your children ask for bread, which of you would give them a stone? Or if your children ask for a fish, would you give them a snake? Even though you are bad, you know how to give good gifts to your children. How much more your heavenly Father will give good things to those who ask him!"

Get out your jars, Jesus would tell us today, for we have a loving God ready to help.

THOUGHTS TO PONDER

Why do you think we turn to God last, after our own efforts have failed, when he urges us to ask for what we need? How hard is it to follow the command of Jesus to not worry about our need for sustenance?

PRAYER

God, we know you supply all our needs more abundantly than we deserve, and we thank you for the mercy and grace you have shown us. Amen.

GOD'S POWER OVER DEATH

2 KINGS 4:18–37

Read the entire story at 2 Kings 4:8–37.

Editor's note: Elisha promised a Shunammite woman a son in her old age. The next year, the son was born.

¹⁸The boy grew up and one day went out to his father, who was with the grain harvesters. ¹⁹The boy said to his father, "My head! My head!"

The father said to his servant, "Take him to his mother!" ²⁰The servant took him to his mother, and he lay on his mother's lap until noon. Then he died. ²¹So she took him up and laid him on Elisha's bed. Then she shut the door and left.

²²She called to her husband, "Send me one of the servants and one of the donkeys. Then I can go quickly to the man of God and return."

²³The husband said, "Why do you want to go to him today? It isn't the New Moon or the Sabbath day."

She said, "It will be all right."

²⁴Then she saddled the donkey and said to her servant, "Lead on. Don't slow down for me unless I tell you." ²⁵So she went to Elisha, the man of God, at Mount Carmel.

When he saw her coming from far away, he said to his servant Gehazi, "Look, there's the Shunammite woman! ²⁶Run to meet her and ask, 'Are you all right? Is your husband all right? Is the boy all right?'"

She answered, "Everything is all right."

²⁷Then she came to Elisha at the hill and grabbed his feet. Gehazi came near to pull her away, but Elisha said to him, "Leave her alone. She's very upset, and the LORD has not told me about it. He has hidden it from me."

²⁸She said, "Master, did I ask you for a son? Didn't I tell you not to lie to me?"

²⁹Then Elisha said to Gehazi, "Get ready. Take my walking stick in your hand and go quickly. If you meet anyone, don't say hello. If anyone greets you, don't respond. Lay my walking stick on the boy's face."

³⁰The boy's mother said, "As surely as the LORD lives and as you live, I won't leave you!" So Elisha got up and followed her.

³¹Gehazi went on ahead and laid the walking stick on the boy's face, but the boy did not talk or move. Then Gehazi went back to meet Elisha. "The boy has not awakened," he said.

³²When Elisha came into the house, the boy was lying dead on his bed. ³³Elisha entered the room and shut the door, so only he and the boy were in the room. Then he prayed to the LORD. ³⁴He went to the bed and lay on the boy, putting his mouth on the boy's mouth, his eyes on the boy's eyes, and his hands on the

boy's hands. He stretched himself out on top of the boy. Soon the boy's skin became warm. [35]Elisha turned away and walked around the room. Then he went back and put himself on the boy again. The boy sneezed seven times and opened his eyes.

[36]Elisha called Gehazi and said, "Call the Shunammite!" So he did. When she came, Elisha said, "Pick up your son." [37]She came in and fell at Elisha's feet, bowing facedown to the floor. Then she picked up her son and went out.

DEVOTION

WHEN JESUS ASKED his followers who people thought he was, one of the answers was that people had taken him for a prophet. The perception is understandable because most of the miracles that Jesus was able to do—from healings to mass feedings to resurrection from the dead—had been done by the prophets in the Old Testament. The followers of Jesus who knew the stories undoubtedly thought that God had sent another prophet in the mold of Elijah and Elisha to help his people.

The Shunammite woman had shown Elisha hospitality on his visits through her region, even preparing a room for him on her roof. In Bible times houses were built with flat roofs used for drying flax and fruit. It could be used as an extra room, a place for worship, or a cool place to sleep in the summer. God had rewarded her hospitality to Elisha by giving her a son to watch out for her in her old age . . . and now he was dead.

Note the faith of the woman in this story. Nowhere in the history of the prophets up to this point do we have an account of a resurrection from the dead, but from the moment her son dies, she knows she must find the prophet of God who promised her the son. She is rewarded for her faith with the first recorded resurrection by a prophet of God in the Bible.

THOUGHTS TO PONDER

How did the widow know Elisha had the power to raise her son? How do we know today that God has the power to raise us from the dead?

PRAYER

God, we thank you that you have promised us a resurrection someday, not in this physical body, but in a new spiritual form, to be with you forever. Amen.

PREACHING WITHOUT WORDS

2 KINGS 4:38–44; 6:1–6

³⁸When Elisha returned to Gilgal, there was a shortage of food in the land. While the groups of prophets were sitting in front of him, he said to his servant, "Put the large pot on the fire, and boil some stew for these men."

³⁹One of them went out into the field to gather plants. Finding a wild vine, he picked fruit from the vine and filled his robe with it. Then he came and cut up the fruit into the pot. But they didn't know what kind of fruit it was. ⁴⁰They poured out the stew for the others to eat. When they began to eat it, they shouted, "Man of God, there's death in the pot!" And they could not eat it.

⁴¹Elisha told them to bring some flour. He threw it into the pot and said, "Pour it out for the people to eat." Then there was nothing harmful in the pot.

⁴²A man from Baal Shalishah came to Elisha, bringing him twenty loaves of barley bread from the first harvest. He also brought fresh grain in his sack. Elisha said, "Give it to the people to eat."

⁴³Elisha's servant asked, "How can I feed a hundred people with so little?"

"Give the bread to the people to eat," Elisha said. "This is what the LORD says: 'They will eat and will have food left over.'" ⁴⁴After he gave it to them, the people ate and had food left over, as the LORD had said.

6 The groups of prophets said to Elisha, "The place where we meet with you is too small for us. ²Let's go to the Jordan River. There everyone can get a log, and let's build a place there to live."

Elisha said, "Go."

³One of them said, "Please go with us."

Elisha answered, "I will go," ⁴so he went with them. When they arrived at the Jordan, they cut down some trees. ⁵As one man was cutting down a tree, the head of his ax fell into the water. He yelled, "Oh, my master! I borrowed that ax!"

⁶Elisha asked, "Where did it fall?" The man showed him the place. Then Elisha cut down a stick and threw it into the water, and it made the iron head float. ⁷Elisha said, "Pick up the axhead." Then the man reached out and took it.

DEVOTION

THE THREE STORIES above clearly outline one of the duties of a prophet during biblical times. While we often think of them in their "prophecy mode," hearing the message of God and proclaiming it to the people, we sometimes overlook the fact that these were men of God who worked every day among the people.

Clearly the miracles above and others set a precedent for what Jesus would do in his ministry. They also give us a clear vision of what God's people should be in the world today.

In the Gospel of Luke, when Jesus raised the son of a widow from the dead, there was an interesting statement that followed: "All the people were amazed and began praising God, saying, 'A great prophet has come to us! God has come to help his people'" (Luke 7:16).

I once heard this advice: "Preach the gospel. If necessary, use words." A prophet was not merely a speaker of God's words. A prophet was a helper.

Why are we reminded that an axhead floated hundreds of years ago? Because it shows the prophet engaged in the day-to-day lives of the people. And if we are to touch people today with the message God has given us, we must touch their lives first.

Virtually every Sunday I'm at my home congregation, my wife and I sit in the worship assembly with a man who never attended church services until after his son died in the war in Afghanistan. His son had been a student at the Christian university where I teach before he was called to active duty. When he died, hundreds of members of our congregation sent cards, flowers, and food, or attended the funeral. Within weeks, the father was converted. His reason: this is the church that reached out to me in my time of need and this is where I want to be.

God came to help his people through Jesus, and it is our job to model his life's work and help others as well.

THOUGHTS TO PONDER

What acts of kindness have been shown to you in the name of the Lord? What acts have you done to others to show them that Jesus is working in you?

PRAYER

God, we pray that through the acts of kindness we do that others will see you in us and be drawn to a knowledge of you. Amen.

The Message That Sounds Foolish

2 KINGS 5:1-14

5 Naaman was commander of the army of the king of Aram. He was honored by his master, and he had much respect because the LORD used him to give victory to Aram. He was a mighty and brave man, but he had a skin disease.

²The Arameans had gone out to raid the Israelites and had taken a little girl as a captive. This little girl served Naaman's wife. ³She said to her mistress, "I wish my master would meet the prophet who lives in Samaria. He would cure him of his disease."

⁴Naaman went to the king and told him what the girl from Israel had said. ⁵The king of Aram said, "Go ahead, and I will send a letter to the king of Israel." So Naaman left and took with him about seven hundred fifty pounds of silver, as well as one hundred fifty pounds of gold and ten changes of clothes. ⁶He brought the letter to the king of Israel, which read, "I am sending my servant Naaman to you so you can heal him of his skin disease."

⁷When the king of Israel read the letter, he tore his clothes to show how upset he was. He said, "I'm not God! I can't kill and make alive again! Why does this man send someone with a skin disease for me to heal? You can see that the king of Aram is trying to start trouble with me."

⁸When Elisha, the man of God, heard that the king of Israel had torn his clothes, he sent the king this message: "Why have you torn your clothes? Let Naaman come to me. Then he will know there is a prophet in Israel." ⁹So Naaman went with his horses and chariots to Elisha's house and stood outside the door.

¹⁰Elisha sent Naaman a messenger who said, "Go and wash in the Jordan River seven times. Then your skin will be healed, and you will be clean."

¹¹Naaman became angry and left. He said, "I thought Elisha would surely come out and stand before me and call on the name of the LORD his God. I thought he would wave his hand over the place and heal the disease. ¹²The Abana and the Pharpar, the rivers of Damascus, are better than all the waters of Israel. Why can't I wash in them and become clean?" So Naaman went away very angry.

¹³Naaman's servants came near and said to him, "My father, if the prophet had told you to do some great thing, wouldn't you have done it? Doesn't it make more sense just to do it? After all, he only told you, 'Wash, and you will be clean.'" ¹⁴So Naaman went down and dipped in the Jordan seven times, just as Elisha had said. Then his skin became new again, like the skin of a child. And he was clean.

DEVOTION

THERE ARE AT LEAST two good lessons in this brief story. Notice first the events that led up to the healing. A foreign king sent generous gifts to the king of Israel, even though their nations lived uneasily side by side. Evidently, Naaman was quite valuable to his king as witnessed by the personal letter and the enormous wealth he sent with him.

The first lesson I see is this: God can do what governments and kings cannot do. With all his armies and power, the king of Israel was totally powerless to heal even a skin disease. In fact, he was convinced the king of Aram was looking for an excuse to go to war. In his distress, he tore his clothes, an ancient sign of mourning.

But the disease presented no problem to the prophet of God. In fact, Elisha invited the opportunity to show the foreign king that God had a representative in Israel. God's power could do what no army could do—cleanse Naaman of his disease.

The second lesson I see is that we cannot second-guess God's ways. God chose the muddy Jordan River as the means to wash away Naaman's disease. It was so simple—so humble—that Naaman scoffed at the idea. But until he obeyed, he wouldn't be made clean.

Paul told the Corinthians that God has his own ideas about how to save us, even if the world considers them foolish. He wrote: "So God chose to use the message that sounds foolish to save those who believe. The Jews ask for miracles, and the Greeks want wisdom. But we preach a crucified Christ. This causes the Jews to stumble and is foolishness to non-Jews" (1 Corinthians 1:21–23).

Want the healing of Jesus? The only way is through the Cross. It will seem foolish to some, but it's a beautiful sight to those who believe.

THOUGHTS TO PONDER

Why do you think Naaman wasn't allowed to dip in the cleaner and more convenient rivers in Damascus? What similarities do you see in Naaman's cleansing and our Christian baptism?

PRAYER

Father, we thank you for washing us clean with the blood of your Son that heals all our spiritual diseases. Amen.

RESTORED IN THE END

2 KINGS 5:15-27

¹⁵Naaman and all his group returned to Elisha. He stood before Elisha and said, "Look, I now know there is no God in all the earth except in Israel. Now please accept a gift from me."

¹⁶But Elisha said, "As surely as the LORD lives whom I serve, I won't accept anything." Naaman urged him to take the gift, but he refused.

¹⁷Then Naaman said, "If you won't take the gift, then please give me some soil—as much as two of my mules can carry. From now on I'll not offer any burnt offering or sacrifice to any other gods but the LORD. ¹⁸But let the LORD pardon me for this: When my master goes into the temple of Rimmon to worship, he leans on my arm. Then I must bow in that temple. May the LORD pardon me when I do that."

¹⁹Elisha said to him, "Go in peace."

Naaman left Elisha and went a short way. ²⁰Gehazi, the servant of Elisha the man of God, thought, "My master has not accepted what Naaman the Aramean brought. As surely as the LORD lives, I'll run after him and get something from him." ²¹So Gehazi went after Naaman.

When Naaman saw someone running after him, he got off the chariot to meet Gehazi. He asked, "Is everything all right?"

²²Gehazi said, "Everything is all right. My master has sent me. He said, 'Two young men from the groups of prophets in the mountains of Ephraim just came to me. Please give them seventy-five pounds of silver and two changes of clothes.'"

²³Naaman said, "Please take one hundred fifty pounds," and he urged Gehazi to take it. He tied one hundred fifty pounds of silver in two bags with two changes of clothes. Then he gave them to two of his servants to carry for Gehazi. ²⁴When they came to the hill, Gehazi took these things from Naaman's servants and put them in the house. Then he let Naaman's servants go, and they left.

²⁵When he came in and stood before his master, Elisha said to him, "Where have you been, Gehazi?"

"I didn't go anywhere," he answered.

²⁶But Elisha said to him, "My spirit was with you. I knew when the man turned from his chariot to meet you. This isn't a time to take money, clothes, olives, grapes, sheep, oxen, male servants, or female servants. ²⁷So Naaman's skin disease will come on you and your children forever." When Gehazi left Elisha, he had the disease and was as white as snow.

DEVOTION

IF NAAMAN COULDN'T leave his gift in Samaria, he at least wanted to take a part of Samaria with him. And while the request for the soil might seem a little strange, it wasn't without precedent. Immediately after giving the Israelites the laws that we know as the Ten Commandments, God made this request: "Make an altar of dirt for me, and sacrifice on it your whole burnt offerings and fellowship offerings, your sheep and your cattle. Worship me in every place that I choose, and I will come and bless you" (Exodus 20:24).

Perhaps that was the use Naaman had for the soil. Or perhaps he wanted some of the soil simply to create a hallowed ground on which to worship when he returned to Aram. Naaman had met the one true God, and even though his relationship with the king would force him to enter the pagan temples of Aram, he wanted the soil where Elisha stood so he could be close to the God of Elisha.

Elisha wanted no profit from the healing of Naaman, even though prophets were entitled to accept such gifts, as we see in 1 Samuel 9:7–8 when Saul looked for a gift so he could consult the seer about where his father's donkeys had gone.

Gehazi had been a faithful servant. When the Shunammite woman had been kind to Elisha and Gehazi, it had been Gehazi's idea to tell the prophet that a son for this childless woman would be a good reward for her hospitality. And when that child had died, it was Gehazi who ran ahead of Elisha with the prophet's staff to lay on the face of the child to be raised.

But now Gehazi made a terrible mistake. He coveted the gifts that Naaman offered. He paid the steep price of contracting a skin disease similar to Naaman's. Years later—undoubtedly cured from the disease since he was no longer considered unclean—Gehazi gave a good account of the prophet to Jehoram, king of Israel (2 Kings 8:4–5).

I think that makes Gehazi like most of us—capable of both good and bad, but in the end, always restored to a cleansed state, thanks to the grace of God.

THOUGHTS TO PONDER

How do you think Gehazi rationalized his actions to himself when he pursued Naaman for payment? Can greed make us do things we might not otherwise do?

PRAYER

God, we pray that you will cleanse our hearts from greed and help us to be content with the many blessings you give us continually. Amen.

Right There with Us

2 KINGS 6:8–23

⁸The king of Aram was at war with Israel. He had a council meeting with his officers and said, "I will set up my camp in this place."

⁹Elisha, the man of God, sent a message to the king of Israel, saying, "Be careful! Don't pass that place, because the Arameans are going down there!"

¹⁰The king of Israel checked the place about which Elisha had warned him. Elisha warned him several times, so the king protected himself there.

¹¹The king of Aram was angry about this. He called his officers together and demanded, "Tell me who of us is working for the king of Israel."

¹²One of the officers said, "None, my master and king. It's Elisha, the prophet from Israel. He can tell you what you speak in your bedroom."

¹³The king said, "Go and find him so I can send men and catch him."

The servants came back and reported, "He is in Dothan."

¹⁴Then the king sent horses, chariots, and many troops to Dothan. They arrived at night and surrounded the city.

¹⁵Elisha's servant got up early, and when he went out, he saw an army with horses and chariots all around the city. The servant said to Elisha, "Oh, my master, what can we do?"

¹⁶Elisha said, "Don't be afraid. The army that fights for us is larger than the one against us."

¹⁷Then Elisha prayed, "Lord, open my servant's eyes, and let him see."

The Lord opened the eyes of the young man, and he saw that the mountain was full of horses and chariots of fire all around Elisha.

¹⁸As the enemy came down toward Elisha, he prayed to the Lord, "Make these people blind." So he made the Aramean army blind, as Elisha had asked.

¹⁹Elisha said to them, "This is not the right road or the right city. Follow me and I'll take you to the man you are looking for." Then Elisha led them to Samaria.

²⁰After they entered Samaria, Elisha said, "Lord, open these men's eyes so they can see." So the Lord opened their eyes, and the Aramean army saw that they were inside the city of Samaria!

²¹When the king of Israel saw the Aramean army, he said to Elisha, "My father, should I kill them? Should I kill them?"

²²Elisha answered, "Don't kill them. You wouldn't kill people whom you captured with your sword and bow. Give them food and water, and let them eat and drink and then go home to their master." ²³So he prepared a great feast for the Aramean army. After they ate and drank, the king sent them away, and they went home to their master. The soldiers of Aram did not come anymore into the land of Israel.

DEVOTION

WHAT CAN WE DO? It's a question the unnamed servant of Elisha asked, and it's a question I've often asked, too. Perhaps you have as well.

Sometimes life's problems gang up on us, and it hardly seems fair. Aging parents to care for and time-consuming, maybe even rebellious teenagers at the same time. Debts compounded by a loss of job or a loss of health. Layoffs at work and nobody hiring experienced workers.

It makes you want to cry out to God: "Oh, my master, what can we do?"

At times like that, it's hard to see the invisible protection of God, but it's there. Even today, "the army that fights for us is larger than the one against us." But only those who open their eyes will ever see. Our prayer should be the prayer that Elisha prayed for his servant: Lord, open my eyes and let me see.

Lord, open my eyes because my spouse has cancer. Lord, open my eyes because I can't seem to reach my teenager. Open my eyes, Lord, because my company has announced they will be downsizing soon and I'm afraid.

"Don't be afraid," Elisha says. The most common command in all of Scripture. Don't be afraid. Have courage. Be brave. God wants us to live our lives free of fear.

Read again God's commands to Joshua on the day he became the leader of God's people in Joshua 1:1–9, and focus on the conclusion: "Remember that I commanded you to be strong and brave. Don't be afraid, because the LORD your God will be with you everywhere you go" (Joshua 1:9).

What does the future hold for you? I don't know. But I do know two things: the future will require all of us to be strong and brave, and God will be right there with us.

THOUGHTS TO PONDER

When have you felt the most overwhelmed by life? How did you get through it? When we are going through trials, how can we see the help that God offers us?

PRAYER

Father, may our eyes be open to your divine help in all the circumstances of our lives. Amen.

DON'T REMAIN SILENT!

2 KINGS 6:24–31; 7:1–9

²⁴Later, Ben-Hadad king of Aram gathered his whole army and surrounded and attacked Samaria. ²⁵There was a shortage of food in Samaria. It was so bad that a donkey's head sold for about two pounds of silver, and half of a pint of dove's dung sold for about two ounces of silver.

²⁶As the king of Israel was passing by on the wall, a woman yelled out to him, "Help me, my master and king!"

²⁷The king said, "If the LORD doesn't help you, how can I? Can I get help from the threshing floor or from the winepress?" ²⁸Then the king said to her, "What is your trouble?"

She answered, "This woman said to me, 'Give up your son so we can eat him today. Then we will eat my son tomorrow.' ²⁹So we boiled my son and ate him. Then the next day I said to her, 'Give up your son so we can eat him.' But she had hidden him."

³⁰When the king heard the woman's words, he tore his clothes in grief. As he walked along the wall, the people looked and saw he had on rough cloth under his clothes to show his sadness. ³¹He said, "May God punish me terribly if the head of Elisha son of Shaphat isn't cut off from his body today!"

7 Elisha said, "Listen to the LORD's word. This is what the LORD says: 'About this time tomorrow seven quarts of fine flour will be sold for two-fifths of an ounce of silver, and thirteen quarts of barley will be sold for two-fifths of an ounce of silver. This will happen at the gate of Samaria.'"

²Then the officer who was close to the king answered Elisha, "Even if the LORD opened windows in the sky, that couldn't happen."

Elisha said, "You will see it with your eyes, but you will not eat any of it."

³There were four men with a skin disease at the entrance to the city gate. They said to each other, "Why do we sit here until we die? ⁴There is no food in the city. So if we go into the city, we will die there. If we stay here, we will die. So let's go to the Aramean camp. If they let us live, we will live. If they kill us, we die."

⁵So they got up at twilight and went to the Aramean camp, but when they arrived, no one was there. ⁶The Lord had caused the Aramean army to hear the sound of chariots, horses, and a large army. They had said to each other, "The king of Israel has hired the Hittite and Egyptian kings to attack us!" ⁷So they got up and ran away in the twilight, leaving their tents, horses, and donkeys. They left the camp standing and ran for their lives.

⁸When the men with the skin disease came to the edge of the camp, they

went into one of the tents and ate and drank. They carried silver, gold, and clothes out of the camp and hid them. Then they came back and entered another tent. They carried things from this tent and hid them, also. ⁹Then they said to each other, "We're doing wrong. Today we have good news, but we are silent. If we wait until the sun comes up, we'll be discovered. Let's go right now and tell the people in the king's palace."

DEVOTION

THE FAMINE WAS SEVERE and the king was playing "blame the prophet." But Elisha had a message from God: tomorrow you will have more food than you can eat. The officer was skeptical, but Elisha kept his head.

The lucky men who found the bounty the Aramean army left behind were likely lepers—outcasts from the city. And like the people within the walls, they were starving too. So when they decided to cast their fate on the kindness of the Aramean army, they had little to lose.

But what happened next is one of the great lessons of the Bible. Overjoyed at their good fortune and reveling in the food and drink, they suddenly stopped and remembered the starving people inside the walls who knew nothing about the saving food that lay just outside. "We're doing wrong. Today we have good news, but we are silent," they said.

I think this is one of the great lessons of "evangelism" in the entire Bible. The lepers had good news, and they knew it was wrong to keep it to themselves. Isn't that our situation as Christians? Don't we have the Good News that our spiritually starving world needs? How can we possibly be silent?

In the end, Elisha survived. The people of Samaria survived. The only casualty was the doubter—the man told by Elisha that he would not see God's bounty. He was trampled at the gate by the crowds rushing to be fed.

THOUGHTS TO PONDER

What is the Good News we have for the world? What have you done to ensure that others hear it?

PRAYER

Father, we pray that we will be your messengers to the world, telling the world of your bountiful blessings that await them if they turn to you. Amen.

JUSTICE IN THE END

2 KINGS 9:1–10, 30–37

9 At the same time, Elisha the prophet called a man from the groups of prophets. Elisha said, "Get ready, and take this small bottle of olive oil in your hand. Go to Ramoth in Gilead. ²When you arrive, find Jehu son of Jehoshaphat, the son of Nimshi. Go in and make Jehu get up from among his brothers, and take him to an inner room. ³Then take the bottle and pour the oil on Jehu's head and say, 'This is what the LORD says: I have appointed you king over Israel.' Then open the door and run away. Don't wait!"

⁴So the young man, the prophet, went to Ramoth in Gilead. ⁵When he arrived, he saw the officers of the army sitting together. He said, "Commander, I have a message for you."

Jehu asked, "For which one of us?"

The young man said, "For you, commander."

⁶Jehu got up and went into the house. Then the young prophet poured the olive oil on Jehu's head and said to him, "This is what the LORD, the God of Israel says: 'I have appointed you king over the LORD's people Israel. ⁷You must destroy the family of Ahab your master. I will punish Jezebel for the deaths of my servants the prophets and for all the LORD's servants who were murdered. ⁸All of Ahab's family must die. I will not let any male child in Ahab's family live in Israel, whether slave or free. ⁹I will make Ahab's family like the family of Jeroboam son of Nebat and like the family of Baasha son of Ahijah. ¹⁰The dogs will eat Jezebel at Jezreel, and no one will bury her.'"

Then the young prophet opened the door and ran away.

Editor's note: Jehu kills Joram, the king of Israel and son of Jezebel, in battle.

³⁰When Jehu came to Jezreel, Jezebel heard about it. She put on her eye makeup and fixed her hair. Then she looked out the window. ³¹When Jehu entered the city gate, Jezebel said, "Have you come in peace, you Zimri, you who killed your master?"

³²Jehu looked up at the window and said, "Who is on my side? Who?" Two or three servants looked out the window at Jehu. ³³He said to them, "Throw her down." So they threw Jezebel down, and the horses ran over her. Some of her blood splashed on the wall and on the horses.

³⁴Jehu went into the house and ate and drank. Then he said, "Now see about this cursed woman. Bury her, because she is a king's daughter."

³⁵The men went to bury Jezebel, but they could not find her. They found only her skull, feet, and the palms of her hands. ³⁶When they came back and told Jehu, he said, "The LORD said this through his servant Elijah the Tishbite: 'The

dogs will eat Jezebel at Jezreel. [37]Her body will be like manure on the field in the land at Jezreel. No one will be able to say that this is Jezebel.'"

DEVOTION

THE SHADOW OF JEZEBEL had loomed large over Israel for years. The daughter of the king of Sidon, she was influential in getting her husband, King Ahab, to turn away from God and to worship Baal. She had gone on a murderous rampage, killing the prophets, prompting Obadiah to hide one hundred of them in caves and causing Elijah to flee for his life. She had conspired to kill Naboth so that Ahab could have his vineyard (see story in 1 Kings 21). It was at that point that Elijah had prophesied that Jezebel would die and the dogs would eat her flesh.

Even after the death of her husband, Jezebel continued to wield power through her son, Ahaziah. When he was killed in battle, she still remained influential as another son, Joram, ascended to the throne. But now they were both gone, and Jehu was fulfilling the prophecy of Elijah.

We read of God's judgment on evil leaders such as Ahab, Jezebel, and their sons in Psalm 94:20–23: "Crooked leaders cannot be your friends. They use the law to cause suffering. They join forces against people who do right and sentence to death the innocent. But the LORD is my defender; my God is the rock of my protection. God will pay them back for their sins and will destroy them for their evil. The LORD our God will destroy them."

Elijah didn't live to see justice done. Naboth never saw vindication for his murder. But God's justice was sure and Jezebel died unmourned and unburied in Israel. Centuries later, Paul would write: "Do not be fooled: You cannot cheat God. People harvest only what they plant." (Galatians 6:7). Evil people like Jezebel may appear to win an occasional skirmish, but the battle always belongs to God.

THOUGHTS TO PONDER

Have you ever thought that evil was triumphing over good? How do you keep faith when it appears that the wicked are prospering?

PRAYER

God, we know you are in control and that you have told us we will harvest what we plant. Help us to plant the seeds of righteousness in our lives in order to gain an eternal harvest. Amen.

Diminished by Sin

2 KINGS 10:17–33

¹⁷When Jehu came to Samaria, he killed all of Ahab's family in Samaria. He destroyed all those who were left, just as the LORD had told Elijah it would happen.

¹⁸Then Jehu gathered all the people together and said to them, "Ahab served Baal a little, but Jehu will serve Baal much. ¹⁹Now call for me all Baal's prophets and priests and all the people who worship Baal. Don't let anyone miss this meeting, because I have a great sacrifice for Baal. Anyone who is not there will not live." But Jehu was tricking them so he could destroy the worshipers of Baal. ²⁰He said, "Prepare a holy meeting for Baal." So they announced the meeting. ²¹Then Jehu sent word through all Israel, and all the worshipers of Baal came; not one stayed home. They came into the temple of Baal, and the temple was filled from one side to the other.

²²Jehu said to the man who kept the robes, "Bring out robes for all the worshipers of Baal." After he brought out robes for them, ²³Jehu and Jehonadab son of Recab went into the temple of Baal. Jehu said to the worshipers of Baal, "Look around, and make sure there are no servants of the LORD with you. Be sure there are only worshipers of Baal." ²⁴Then the worshipers of Baal went in to offer sacrifices and burnt offerings.

Jehu had eighty men waiting outside. He had told them, "Don't let anyone escape. If you do, you must pay with your own life."

²⁵As soon as Jehu finished offering the burnt offering, he ordered the guards and the captains, "Go in and kill the worshipers of Baal. Don't let anyone come out." So the guards and captains killed the worshipers of Baal with the sword and threw their bodies out. Then they went to the inner rooms of the temple ²⁶and brought out the pillars of the temple of Baal and burned them. ²⁷They tore down the stone pillar of Baal, as well as the temple of Baal. And they made it into a sewage pit, as it is today.

²⁸So Jehu destroyed Baal worship in Israel, ²⁹but he did not stop doing the sins Jeroboam son of Nebat had done. Jeroboam had led Israel to sin by worshiping the golden calves in Bethel and Dan.

³⁰The LORD said to Jehu, "You have done well in obeying what I said was right. You have done to the family of Ahab as I wanted. Because of this, your descendants as far as your great-great-grandchildren will be kings of Israel." ³¹But Jehu was not careful to follow the teachings of the LORD, the God of Israel, with all his heart. He did not stop doing the same sins Jeroboam had done, by which he had led Israel to sin.

³²At that time the LORD began to make Israel smaller. Hazael defeated the Israelites in all the land of Israel, ³³taking all the land of the Jordan known as the land of Gilead.

DEVOTION

JEHU HAD BEEN APPOINTED by God and anointed by the prophet to over-throw the evil King Ahab and take his place on the throne. He appears to have been brutally efficient in his task, killing Ahab's sons, Ahab's wife Jezebel, and eventually the entire royal family for their many sins.

Now Jehu, a former military commander, turned his sights on the wor-shipers of Baal. The story above began with a trick. The idol worshipers were led to believe they were coming to a religious ceremony; in reality, they were walk-ing into a trap. Once Jehu had them all in the temple of Baal, he ordered his eighty men to slaughter them and destroy the temple. In one of the most vivid images in the nation's history, Jehu turned the temple into a cesspool, a use that lasted for years.

But there was trouble. Jehu saw no problem with leaving the golden calves in Bethel and Dan—idols placed there by Jeroboam to solidify his northern king-dom after God separated the nations of Israel and Judah. Because the idols had been there for so many years, they were probably not considered "foreign" gods like Baal was. Like so many of his predecessors before him, Jehu ignored them. But this time, God reacted. Jehu had continued the sins of Jeroboam, and for that Israel would pay.

"At that time, the LORD began to make Israel smaller" we're told. I think there's an important principle here: sin diminishes the sinner. Sin can limit our ability to be a witness for God in our communities. Sin can bring reproach on our families or our churches. Sin makes us "smaller" people.

God had made a promise to Moses on top of Mount Sinai: "I will force out nations ahead of you and expand the borders of your land" (Exodus 34:24). Now, the opposite was happening. Sin was shrinking the geographic borders of Israel. Soon, sin would bring an end to the nation entirely.

THOUGHTS TO PONDER

Why do you think Jehu ignored the golden calves? What sins do we seem to ignore today? In what ways have you seen sin diminish people? In what ways does sin diminish our nation today?

PRAYER

God, we pray for our nation. Help us to honor and worship only you and not the idols of wealth and success so that we will always be strong. Amen.

JUST A MAN

2 CHRONICLES 26:3–10, 16–21

³Uzziah was sixteen years old when he became king, and he ruled fifty-two years in Jerusalem. His mother's name was Jecoliah, and she was from Jerusalem. ⁴He did what the LORD said was right, just as his father Amaziah had done. ⁵Uzziah obeyed God while Zechariah was alive, because he taught Uzziah how to respect and obey God. And as long as Uzziah obeyed the LORD, God gave him success.

⁶Uzziah fought a war against the Philistines. He tore down the walls around their towns of Gath, Jabneh, and Ashdod and built new towns near Ashdod and in other places among the Philistines. ⁷God helped Uzziah fight the Philistines, the Arabs living in Gur Baal, and the Meunites. ⁸Also, the Ammonites made the payments Uzziah demanded. He was very powerful, so his name became famous all the way to the border of Egypt.

⁹Uzziah built towers in Jerusalem at the Corner Gate, the Valley Gate, and where the wall turned, and he made them strong. ¹⁰He also built towers in the desert and dug many wells, because he had many cattle on the western hills and in the plains. He had people who worked his fields and vineyards in the hills and in the fertile lands, because he loved the land.

¹⁶But when Uzziah became powerful, his pride led to his ruin. He was unfaithful to the LORD his God; he went into the Temple of the LORD to burn incense on the altar for incense. ¹⁷Azariah and eighty other brave priests who served the LORD followed Uzziah into the Temple. ¹⁸They told him he was wrong and said to him, "You don't have the right to burn incense to the LORD. Only the priests, Aaron's descendants, should burn the incense, because they have been made holy. Leave this holy place. You have been unfaithful, and the LORD God will not honor you for this."

¹⁹Uzziah was standing beside the altar for incense in the Temple of the LORD, and in his hand was a pan for burning incense. He was very angry with the priests. As he was standing in front of the priests, a skin disease broke out on his forehead. ²⁰Azariah, the leading priest, and all the other priests looked at him and saw the skin disease on his forehead. So they hurried him out of the Temple. Uzziah also rushed out, because the LORD was punishing him. ²¹So King Uzziah had the skin disease until the day he died. He had to live in a separate house and could not enter the Temple of the LORD. His son Jotham was in charge of the palace, and he governed the people of the land.

Devotion

UZZIAH WAS A BOY WONDER. At age sixteen, he became the king of Judah following the death of his father, Amaziah, who had fought an ill-advised battle against Israel.

Scripture tells us he did what was right in the sight of God and he was blessed for it. He routed the Philistines, rebuilt the towers of Jerusalem and trained more than 300,000 men to go to war. But this great success story has a twist. At the point that Uzziah became powerful, he also became proud. Pride did what no army could: pride toppled Uzziah.

Note the order indicated in the verse: the pride followed the power. Like a parasite on a healthy plant or rust on exposed metal, pride often attaches itself to people with significant accomplishments and begins eating away.

Pride has toppled politicians, business leaders, and evangelists alike. Great accomplishments like the ones that came almost naturally to the boy wonder, King Uzziah, seem to become a form of "body armor" that can lead successful people to feel invincible. And when that feeling comes, danger is always right behind.

There's a story that when a returning Roman general was riding through the Coliseum of Rome being hailed by the population for a glorious victory, there was a slave riding in the chariot whispering in the conqueror's ear: "Remember, you are only a man."

I don't know if the story is true, but the point is well taken. When I think I'm something, I need to remember that I am only a man—capable of both incredible feats and deep disappointments.

In Acts 5:36 we hear the story of the ill-fated Theudas, a pseudo-Messiah. The text tells us that "He said he was a great man," but he proved to be quite mortal and his movement failed. No one is a great man who has to proclaim his greatness.

Uzziah failed to realize that the source of his power was God. He was just a man.

Thoughts to Ponder

Why is power so corrupting? What precautions should the powerful take to avoid falling into the trap of Uzziah?

Prayer

Father, we ask that when you give us power, you would also give us humility. Help us not to seek the first without asking for the latter. Amen.

BECOMING USELESS

2 KINGS 17:1-18

17 Hoshea son of Elah became king over Israel during Ahaz's twelfth year as king of Judah. Hoshea ruled in Samaria nine years. ²He did what the LORD said was wrong, but he was not as bad as the kings of Israel who had ruled before him.

³Shalmaneser king of Assyria came to attack Hoshea. Hoshea had been Shalmaneser's servant and had made the payments to Shalmaneser that he had demanded. ⁴But the king of Assyria found out that Hoshea had made plans against him by sending messengers to So, the king of Egypt. Hoshea had also stopped giving Shalmaneser the payments, which he had paid every year in the past. For that, the king put Hoshea in prison. ⁵Then the king of Assyria came and attacked all the land of Israel. He surrounded Samaria and attacked it for three years. ⁶He defeated Samaria in the ninth year Hoshea was king, and he took the Israelites away to Assyria. He settled them in Halah, in Gozan on the Habor River, and in the cities of the Medes.

⁷All these things happened because the Israelites had sinned against the LORD their God. He had brought them out of Egypt and had rescued them from the power of the king of Egypt, but the Israelites had honored other gods. ⁸They lived like the nations the LORD had forced out of the land ahead of them. They lived as their evil kings had shown them, ⁹secretly sinning against the LORD their God. They built places to worship gods in all their cities, from the watchtower to the strong, walled city. ¹⁰They put up stone pillars to gods and Asherah idols on every high hill and under every green tree. ¹¹The Israelites burned incense everywhere gods were worshiped, just as the nations who lived there before them had done, whom the LORD had forced out of the land. The Israelites did wicked things that made the LORD angry. ¹²They served idols when the LORD had said, "You must not do this." ¹³The LORD used every prophet and seer to warn Israel and Judah. He said, "Stop your evil ways and obey my commands and laws. Follow all the teachings that I commanded your ancestors, the teachings that I gave you through my servants the prophets."

¹⁴But the people would not listen. They were stubborn, just as their ancestors had been who did not believe in the LORD their God. ¹⁵They rejected the LORD's laws and the agreement he had made with their ancestors. And they refused to listen to his warnings. They worshiped useless idols and became useless themselves. They did what the nations around them did, which the LORD had warned them not to do.

¹⁶The people rejected all the commands of the LORD their God. They molded statues of two calves, and they made an Asherah idol. They worshiped all

the stars of the sky and served Baal. [17]They made their sons and daughters pass through fire and tried to find out the future by magic and witchcraft. They always chose to do what the LORD said was wrong, which made him angry. [18]Because he was very angry with the people of Israel, he removed them from his presence. Only the tribe of Judah was left.

DEVOTION

TUCKED INTO THE LONG LIST of indictments against the people of Israel is this interesting phrase: "They worshiped useless idols and became useless themselves." Is it possible that this will someday be the indictment of America? "They worshiped the gods of power, wealth, and success and became useless," God might say. "They worshiped fame and all those who claimed to be famous and their altar was the home entertainment center, so they became useless."

Observe the saturation coverage of celebrities by all the entertainment shows. Rock stars, athletes, actors and actresses, rappers, and a whole host of people "famous for being famous" have become the idols for us and our children. Meanwhile, we are losing our place in the world. Are we at risk of becoming useless?

Throughout history, nations disintegrated from within long before outside forces finished the job. The story above gives a long list of the many ways that Israel turned its back on God and turned to idols instead. So the army of Assyria in 722 B.C. simply finished what the nation of Israel herself had started generations ago—a long, slow slide into apostasy and captivity.

Scripture tells us, "Doing what is right makes a nation great, but sin will bring disgrace to any people" (Proverbs 14:34). Israel had fallen. Judah was not far behind. Once great; now disgraced. What will be the fate of our nation?

THOUGHTS TO PONDER

From the long list of the sins of Israel, which ones can be said to be true of our nation? How can a Christian hope to be "salt" and "light" as commanded in Matthew chapter 6?

PRAYER

Father, we pray for our nation. We pray that we will turn again to you as the one source of our strength. Amen.

THREE STEPS

2 CHRONICLES 31:20—32:8, 20—22

²⁰This is what King Hezekiah did in Judah. He did what was good and right and obedient before the LORD his God. ²¹Hezekiah tried to obey God in his service of the Temple of God, and he tried to obey God's teachings and commands. He gave himself fully to his work for God. So he had success.

32After Hezekiah did all these things to serve the LORD, Sennacherib king of Assyria came and attacked Judah. He and his army surrounded and attacked the strong, walled cities, hoping to take them for himself. ²Hezekiah knew that Sennacherib had come to Jerusalem to attack it. ³So Hezekiah and his officers and army commanders decided to cut off the water from the springs outside the city. So the officers and commanders helped Hezekiah. ⁴Many people came and cut off all the springs and the stream that flowed through the land. They said, "The king of Assyria will not find much water when he comes here." ⁵Then Hezekiah made Jerusalem stronger. He rebuilt all the broken parts of the wall and put towers on it. He also built another wall outside the first one and strengthened the area that was filled in on the east side of the old part of Jerusalem. He also made many weapons and shields.

⁶Hezekiah put army commanders over the people and met with them at the open place near the city gate. Hezekiah encouraged them, saying, ⁷"Be strong and brave. Don't be afraid or worried because of the king of Assyria or his large army. There is a greater power with us than with him. ⁸He only has men, but we have the LORD our God to help us and to fight our battles." The people were encouraged by the words of Hezekiah king of Judah.

²⁰King Hezekiah and the prophet Isaiah son of Amoz prayed to heaven about this. ²¹Then the LORD sent an angel who killed all the soldiers, leaders, and officers in the camp of the king of Assyria. So the king went back to his own country in disgrace. When he went into the temple of his god, some of his own sons killed him with a sword.

²²So the LORD saved Hezekiah and the people in Jerusalem from Sennacherib king of Assyria and from all other people. He took care of them on every side.

DEVOTION

THINGS LOOKED BLEAK for the nation of Judah. Sennacherib and his Assyrian army had already plundered much of the nation—forty-six cities by Sennacherib's own count (recorded on a stone called the "Taylor Prism" now housed in the British Museum). Now the city of Jerusalem was in his sights. According to Sennacherib's ancient account, Hezekiah and the Israelites were trapped like a caged bird. Yet God intervened with his angel of death, killing the enemy—as many as 185,000 men according to the account in 2 Kings 19:35—and sending Sennacherib back to his own country in disgrace where, according to Assyrian history, he was murdered by his sons.

I think the actions and words of Hezekiah in the story above show us a good three-step formula for God's followers when they face perplexing problems. Step one is this: get in shape spiritually. Hezekiah went into the problem with Assyria spiritually fit. He had purified the Temple. He had reinstated the priesthood and the religious observances. He had eliminated all altars other than the one in Jerusalem. He was fully devoted to God.

Step two: fix the problems that you can. Hezekiah immediately went into action. He fortified the walls. He stopped the flow of water outside the city to frustrate the enemy. He built an entire second wall around the city and put men to work manufacturing weapons. Rather than sit back and suffer a long siege by a determined enemy, Hezekiah did what he could to protect his people.

And finally, step three: trust God to take care of the things you can't control. Hezekiah assured his people that God was on their side and that their God was greater than even the great army of the Assyrians. Judah's deliverance would not come from the strength of its army, it would come from God, and Hezekiah knew this well. The enemy would be fighting with men; Judah would have God on their side.

You don't have to be going up against a great army to put Hezekiah's method to work. No matter what adversity Satan throws at you, you can win provided you keep yourself in good spiritual condition, work to change the things you can control, and turn over to God the things you can't.

The words of Hezekiah were true then and they're true now: "We have the LORD our God to help us and to fight our battles."

THOUGHTS TO PONDER

If God was going to fight the battle for Judah, was all the work on the wall in vain? Even though God has promised us a victory over Satan, what does he expect us to do?

PRAYER

God, we know that all victories, big and small, come from you. Help us to be like Hezekiah and do the things we know to do and trust you for the rest. Amen.

OUR TRUE HOME

2 KINGS 20:1–11

20At that time Hezekiah became so sick he almost died. The prophet Isaiah son of Amoz went to see him and told him, "This is what the LORD says: Make arrangements because you are not going to live, but die."

²Hezekiah turned toward the wall and prayed to the LORD, ³"LORD, please remember that I have always obeyed you. I have given myself completely to you and have done what you said was right." Then Hezekiah cried loudly.

⁴Before Isaiah had left the middle courtyard, the LORD spoke his word to Isaiah: ⁵"Go back and tell Hezekiah, the leader of my people: 'This is what the LORD, the God of your ancestor David, says: I have heard your prayer and seen your tears, so I will heal you. Three days from now you will go up to the Temple of the LORD. ⁶I will add fifteen years to your life. I will save you and this city from the king of Assyria; I will protect the city for my sake and for the sake of my servant David.'"

⁷Then Isaiah said, "Make a paste from figs." So they made it and put it on Hezekiah's boil, and he got well.

⁸Hezekiah had asked Isaiah, "What will be the sign that the LORD will heal me and that I will go up to the Temple of the LORD on the third day?"

⁹Isaiah said, "The LORD will do what he says. This is the sign from the LORD to show you: Do you want the shadow to go forward ten steps or back ten steps?"

¹⁰Hezekiah answered, "It's easy for the shadow to go forward ten steps. Instead, let it go back ten steps."

¹¹Then Isaiah the prophet called to the LORD, and the LORD brought the shadow ten steps back up the stairway of Ahaz that it had gone down.

DEVOTION

DO YOU WANT to live to see next year? For most of us, I think the answer would be "yes." If I asked whether you wanted to live fifteen more years, I think most of would still answer "yes." But if I asked the question every year: "Do you want to live fifteen more years?" at some point you would begin to wonder if that's what you really wanted. Does anyone really want to live in our fragile bodies forever?

Hezekiah knew from the time he was healed that his days were numbered. Is there an advantage to that? Would we look on death, or life for that matter, any differently if we knew how long we would live?

What should be the Christian's response to death? I think any parent wants to live long enough to see his or her children become self-sufficient adults. But then, I've observed that most grandparents want to be there for their grandchildren as well. What is the balance between a healthy attachment to the things we love here and a desire to be with God? I haven't worked that one out yet.

The psalmist said this about death: "The death of one that belongs to the LORD is precious in his sight" (Psalm 116:15). But even for those of us who look at death as a "homecoming," it's hard to get excited about beginning the celebration. However, the apostle Paul was ready to die and go to his true home. He had endured his share of hardships because of his role as an ambassador for the Good News to the early church, and in a very candid passage of his letter to the church in Philippi, he wrote: "To me the only important thing about living is Christ, and dying would be profit for me. If I continue living in my body, I will be able to work for the Lord. I do not know what to choose—living or dying. It is hard to choose between the two. I want to leave this life and be with Christ, which is much better, but you need me here in my body. Since I am sure of this, I know I will stay with you to help you grow and have joy in your faith" (Philippians 1:21–25).

Like Paul, I still have things on earth I want to do—family to care for, work I enjoy, etc. Where I differ from Paul is that I don't know if I can honestly say, "I want to leave this life and be with Christ." I think I get a little closer to being able to say it every year, and perhaps that's part of maturing spiritually. It's tempting to ask God for a "revolving" fifteen-year reprieve from death where the counter starts all over every year. But eventually, this body wears out. Friends and relatives die. Jobs end. Eventually we realize that this world is not our home, and strangely enough, it never was. It's a fact that Abraham, Isaac, and Jacob knew all along (Hebrews 11:13–16), and it's a lesson we all need to learn.

THOUGHTS TO PONDER

What do you think the psalmist means by the death of the saints being "precious" to God? What things do you want to remain on earth for? What makes you yearn for heaven?

PRAYER

Father, thank you for the hope we have in an eternal home with you. Help us to be ready for your call to that heavenly place no matter when it comes. Amen.

A Temple Not Built
by Human Hands

2 KINGS 22:1–11; 23:1–3

22 Josiah was eight years old when he became king, and he ruled thirty-one years in Jerusalem. His mother's name was Jedidah daughter of Adaiah, who was from Bozkath. ²Josiah did what the LORD said was right. He lived as his ancestor David had lived, and he did not stop doing what was right.

³In Josiah's eighteenth year as king, he sent Shaphan to the Temple of the LORD. Shaphan son of Azaliah, the son of Meshullam, was the royal secretary. Josiah said, ⁴"Go up to Hilkiah the high priest, and have him empty out the money the gatekeepers have gathered from the people. This is the money they have brought into the Temple of the LORD. ⁵Have him give the money to the supervisors of the work on the Temple of the LORD. They must pay the workers who repair the Temple of the LORD— ⁶the carpenters, builders, and bricklayers. Also use the money to buy timber and cut stone to repair the Temple. ⁷They do not need to report how they use the money given to them, because they are working honestly."

⁸Hilkiah the high priest said to Shaphan the royal secretary, "I've found the Book of the Teachings in the Temple of the LORD." He gave it to Shaphan, who read it.

⁹Then Shaphan the royal secretary went to the king and reported to Josiah, "Your officers have paid out the money that was in the Temple of the LORD. They have given it to the workers and supervisors at the Temple." ¹⁰Then Shaphan the royal secretary told the king, "Hilkiah the priest has given me a book." And Shaphan read from the book to the king.

¹¹When the king heard the words of the Book of the Teachings, he tore his clothes to show how upset he was.

23 Then the king gathered all the elders of Judah and Jerusalem together. ²He went up to the Temple of the LORD, and all the people from Judah and Jerusalem went with him. The priests, prophets, and all the people—from the least important to the most important—went with him. He read to them all the words of the Book of the Agreement that was found in the Temple of the LORD. ³The king stood by the pillar and made an agreement in the presence of the LORD to follow the LORD and obey his commands, rules, and laws with his whole being, and to obey the words of the agreement written in this book. Then all the people promised to obey the agreement.

DEVOTION

EVERYBODY KNEW BOB: college professor, avid fisherman, encourager everyone wanted to be around.

He and a fellow professor celebrated the end of each spring semester by loading up the fishing gear and heading for Colorado. But the trip in the spring of 1995 ended in tragedy. One moment his friend was driving late into the night and the next, the car flipped and Bob was paralyzed, with no feeling below his chest.

Bob was flown to Albuquerque, where he stayed for months before returning to a home remodeled by members of our congregation to fit his wheelchair. Our large church building was literally over Bob's back fence and for months, members came with help, food, and encouragement. Eventually, Bob returned to teaching and worshiping; he was even able to escort his daughter down the aisle at her wedding.

This would be a great story of perseverance and Christian hospitality even if it ended here. But there's more. Bob's neighbors observed the daily evidence of Christians acting as Christians do when one is in distress. And those neighbors began to visit our congregation, eventually becoming members.

In all the years our large building sat across the back fence from Bob's neighbors, we hadn't made a single impression on them with our building expansions and our billboards about upcoming events. But when this couple saw Christianity in action, the pull was almost magnetic.

At the time of Josiah, the Temple had been the center of the Jewish community for generations, but it was in such disrepair that it was a remarkable find when a single copy of the Law was found. You can imagine for yourself how little effect that structure had on the hearts of the people.

Scripture tells us that God doesn't dwell in temples (or church buildings) built by hand. He lives inside us. And if the world is ever going to find God, it will be through his people, not the temples we build.

THOUGHTS TO PONDER

Are we ever guilty of wrapping up the message of God in our buildings, hiding it from the world? How do we get the message out of the building and into the world?

PRAYER

God, you've given us your Word to guide our lives. Help us to live it boldly and share it freely so that others may see you. Amen.

PRESERVE THAT WHICH IS PRECIOUS

2 KINGS 22:1–13

Read the entire story in 2 Kings 22:1–20.

22 Josiah was eight years old when he became king, and he ruled thirty-one years in Jerusalem. His mother's name was Jedidah daughter of Adaiah, who was from Bozkath. ²Josiah did what the LORD said was right. He lived as his ancestor David had lived, and he did not stop doing what was right.

³In Josiah's eighteenth year as king, he sent Shaphan to the Temple of the LORD. Shaphan son of Azaliah, the son of Meshullam, was the royal secretary. Josiah said, ⁴"Go up to Hilkiah the high priest, and have him empty out the money the gatekeepers have gathered from the people. This is the money they have brought into the Temple of the LORD. ⁵Have him give the money to the supervisors of the work on the Temple of the LORD. They must pay the workers who repair the Temple of the LORD— ⁶the carpenters, builders, and bricklayers. Also use the money to buy timber and cut stone to repair the Temple. ⁷They do not need to report how they use the money given to them, because they are working honestly."

⁸Hilkiah the high priest said to Shaphan the royal secretary, "I've found the Book of the Teachings in the Temple of the LORD." He gave it to Shaphan, who read it.

⁹Then Shaphan the royal secretary went to the king and reported to Josiah, "Your officers have paid out the money that was in the Temple of the LORD. They have given it to the workers and supervisors at the Temple." ¹⁰Then Shaphan the royal secretary told the king, "Hilkiah the priest has given me a book." And Shaphan read from the book to the king.

¹¹When the king heard the words of the Book of the Teachings, he tore his clothes to show how upset he was. ¹²He gave orders to Hilkiah the priest, Ahikam son of Shaphan, Acbor son of Micaiah, Shaphan the royal secretary, and Asaiah the king's servant. These were the orders: ¹³"Go and ask the LORD about the words in the book that was found. Ask for me, for all the people, and for all Judah. The LORD's anger is burning against us, because our ancestors did not obey the words of this book; they did not do all the things written for us to do."

DEVOTION

I STOOD IN THE GLOW of the glass that preserved the two-hundred-year-old document, the only person in the rotunda of the National Archives fifteen minutes before closing time on a raw, rainy February afternoon. The threat of frozen roads during rush hour had scattered all the tour buses and only a few hearty pedestrians were on the streets of Washington, D.C. That is how I came to have fifteen minutes alone with the Constitution and the Declaration of Independence, our nation's two most precious documents.

"Can I stand here for a minute?" I asked the guard. I had been in the rotunda before, but always under strict instructions to keep moving to accommodate the huge crowds wanting to see the documents.

"As long as you don't lean on the glass," he replied. "If you do, the documents will go straight down into the vault below ground." So I stood there, hands clasped behind my back, leaning forward to read the ornate writing through the faint green glow of the gas that preserved the documents.

The words were all there. The preamble we memorized in grade school. The bold signature of John Hancock. The Bill of Rights. As a teacher of First Amendment law, I was mesmerized by reading those words from the very paper on which they had first been written.

As I considered all the safeguards surrounding the documents—guards, glass, alarms, a deep unseen vault below—it dawned on me that these precious documents had never been lost or unattended since the day they were penned. Even though their words appear in countless civics books, Americans still derive great comfort from knowing that the original documents are available for us to see.

Imagine then how little the nation of Israel must have regarded the Law in order for it to be lost. In a day when every manuscript was carefully hand copied by scribes, books were precious commodities, yet this most important one had been, sadly, lost for many years. When he heard the words he knew to be from God, Josiah grieved at the loss and ordered his men to see what God would do about this affront.

At the end of the chapter, the word of Huldah, the prophetess whom Shaphan sought out, was not good: Israel would pay a steep price for forgetting its responsibilities under the Law. But because he was a righteous man, Josiah would not see the ruin of his country in his days as king.

THOUGHTS TO PONDER

What is the most precious thing you have ever lost? Why was it precious? What did you do to try to find it? Why would the priesthood of Israel have allowed the holy Book of the Law to be lost?

PRAYER

God, we pray that your words will be written on our hearts so that we will never be far away from them. Amen.

The Price of Sin

2 KINGS 23:4–7, 21–30

⁴The king commanded Hilkiah the high priest and the priests of the next rank and the gatekeepers to bring out of the Temple of the LORD everything made for Baal, Asherah, and all the stars of the sky. Then Josiah burned them outside Jerusalem in the open country of the Kidron Valley and carried their ashes to Bethel. ⁵The kings of Judah had chosen priests for these gods. These priests burned incense in the places where gods were worshiped in the cities of Judah and the towns around Jerusalem. They burned incense to Baal, the sun, the moon, the planets, and all the stars of the sky. But Josiah took those priests away. ⁶He removed the Asherah idol from the Temple of the LORD and took it outside Jerusalem to the Kidron Valley, where he burned it and beat it into dust. Then he threw the dust on the graves of the common people. ⁷He also tore down the houses of the male prostitutes who were in the Temple of the LORD, where the women did weaving for Asherah.

²¹The king commanded all the people, "Celebrate the Passover to the LORD your God as it is written in this Book of the Agreement." ²²The Passover had not been celebrated like this since the judges led Israel. Nor had one like it happened while there were kings of Israel and kings of Judah. ²³This Passover was celebrated to the LORD in Jerusalem in the eighteenth year of King Josiah's rule.

²⁴Josiah destroyed the mediums, fortune-tellers, house gods, and idols. He also destroyed all the hated gods seen in the land of Judah and Jerusalem. This was to obey the words of the teachings written in the book Hilkiah the priest had found in the Temple of the LORD.

²⁵There was no king like Josiah before or after him. He obeyed the LORD with all his heart, soul, and strength, following all the Teachings of Moses.

²⁶Even so, the LORD did not stop his strong and terrible anger. His anger burned against Judah because of all Manasseh had done to make him angry. ²⁷The LORD said, "I will send Judah out of my sight, as I have sent Israel away. I will reject Jerusalem, which I chose. And I will take away the Temple about which I said, 'I will be worshiped there.'"

²⁸Everything else Josiah did is written in the book of the history of the kings of Judah.

²⁹While Josiah was king, Neco king of Egypt went to help the king of Assyria at the Euphrates River. King Josiah marched out to fight against Neco, but at Megiddo, Neco faced him and killed him. ³⁰Josiah's servants carried his body in a chariot from Megiddo to Jerusalem and buried him in his own grave. Then the people of Judah chose Josiah's son Jehoahaz and poured olive oil on him to make him king in his father's place.

Devotion

SIN WAS EVERYWHERE in the kingdom, and Josiah was determined to eliminate it. Once he had heard the recently rediscovered Book of the Agreement read aloud, he went to work to restore his kingdom to a right relationship with God. There were idols to remove, altars to destroy, even idolatrous priests to kill. And then it was time to reinstate the Passover, perhaps the most important ceremony required by the Book of the Agreement—a ceremony which reminded the people of their miraculous delivery from Egyptian bondage by God.

Even though Josiah did what was pleasing to God, there was still a terrible price to pay for the sins of the nation. The people were eventually overrun by foreign nations and scattered to the winds. The Temple where God desired to be worshiped was eventually destroyed.

Sin still has consequences. Even though forgiveness is possible, the effects of sin often last long after the sin has occurred. Lives are forever shattered because of a reckless decision like drunken driving or an extramarital fling. A moment of cheating at work can lead to a multitude of consequences.

This leads us to one of the great paradoxes about God: he is forgiving, but he is also just. And in the case of Israel, their continued sin demanded that God's justice be satisfied. Because of the righteousness of Josiah, it did not happen during his reign. But the day was coming when the children of Israel would pay a steep price for their sins. Today, because of the blood of Jesus, God can protect us from the eternal penalty of sin, but the earthly consequences often remain.

Thoughts to Ponder

When God forgives our sins, why does he allow the earthly consequences to remain? What does that fact tell you about his nature?

Prayer

Father, we pray that we will have the strength to resist sin in all its forms and that your Word will never be far from our hearts. Amen.

WHEN DID THE LOVE
GO OUT?

2 KINGS 24:18—25:12

¹⁸Zedekiah was twenty-one years old when he became king, and he was king in Jerusalem for eleven years. His mother's name was Hamutal daughter of Jeremiah from Libnah. ¹⁹Zedekiah did what the LORD said was wrong, just as Jehoiakim had done. ²⁰All this happened in Jerusalem and Judah because the LORD was angry with them. Finally, he threw them out of his presence.

Zedekiah turned against the king of Babylon.

25Nebuchadnezzar king of Babylon marched against Jerusalem with his whole army during Zedekiah's ninth year as king, on the tenth day of the tenth month. He made a camp around the city and piled dirt against the city walls to attack it. ²The city was under attack until Zedekiah's eleventh year as king. ³By the ninth day of the fourth month, the hunger was terrible in the city. There was no food for the people to eat. ⁴Then the city was broken into, and the whole army ran away at night through the gate between the two walls by the king's garden. While the Babylonians were still surrounding the city, Zedekiah and his men ran away toward the Jordan Valley. ⁵But the Babylonian army chased King Zedekiah and caught up with him in the plains of Jericho. All of his army was scattered from him, ⁶so they captured Zedekiah and took him to the king of Babylon at Riblah. There he passed sentence on Zedekiah. ⁷They killed Zedekiah's sons as he watched. Then they put out his eyes and put bronze chains on him and took him to Babylon.

⁸Nebuzaradan was the commander of the king's special guards. This officer of the king of Babylon came to Jerusalem on the seventh day of the fifth month, in Nebuchadnezzar's nineteenth year as king of Babylon. ⁹Nebuzaradan set fire to the Temple of the LORD and the palace and all the houses of Jerusalem. Every important building was burned.

¹⁰The whole Babylonian army, led by the commander of the king's special guards, broke down the walls around Jerusalem. ¹¹Nebuzaradan, the commander of the guards, captured the people left in Jerusalem, those who had surrendered to the king of Babylon, and the rest of the people. ¹²But the commander left behind some of the poorest people of the land to take care of the vineyards and fields.

DEVOTION

AT WHAT POINT does God decide to throw Judah "out of his presence"? I don't think it happened suddenly when this story occurred. In fact, Nebuchadnezzar had raided Judah on two previous occasions, imposing his will. So the people of Judah hadn't been truly free for some time.

But the end still brings grief—a certain finality that things will never be the same. A lawyer once told me of his divorce clients who go to pieces after their final divorce decree even though they had been fighting with their spouse for perhaps a year or more. Why? Because there's something about even a bad marriage ending that seems totally final and that brings sadness to many of the participants.

God's marriage with the children of Abraham had reached a low point. And even though God would never quit loving them, this part of their relationship was at an end. Already the northern kingdom had fallen to the Assyrians. Now the kingdom of Judah was in the hands of the Babylonians.

When does the love go out of a marriage headed for divorce? When did the exclusive love for God go out of the people?

When did the slide into infidelity begin? When the people asked Aaron for a god of gold? When they refused to believe the spies in the desert and were punished with forty years of wilderness wandering? When they demanded a king for their nation? When the prophets were persecuted? When the people began to intermarry with the nations around them and incorporate their customs? When idols were erected so that people could worship close to home without going to Jerusalem?

A slide as steep and deep as Israel's has many reasons and many milestones. And even if you can't point to where it started, you can point to where it ended—with a scattered army on the very plains of Jericho where God once proudly went before his people into battle.

THOUGHTS TO PONDER

Is your love for God stronger today than when you first met him? What steps do you take to stay close to God?

PRAYER

Father, we pray that we will never slide into apathy in our relationship with you, but that we will renew our vows to you each day that you let us live. Amen.

FINDING THE "NEW NORMAL"

EZRA 2:64—3:6, 10–13

⁶⁴The total number of those who returned was 42,360. ⁶⁵This is not counting their 7,337 male and female servants and the 200 male and female singers they had with them. ⁶⁶They had 736 horses, 245 mules, ⁶⁷435 camels, and 6,720 donkeys.

⁶⁸When they arrived at the Temple of the LORD in Jerusalem, some of the leaders of families gave offerings to rebuild the Temple of God on the same site as before. ⁶⁹They gave as much as they could to the treasury to rebuild the Temple—about 1,100 pounds of gold, about 6,000 pounds of silver, and 100 pieces of clothing for the priests.

⁷⁰All the Israelites settled in their hometowns. The priests, Levites, singers, gatekeepers, and Temple servants, along with some of the other people, settled in their own towns as well.

3 In the seventh month, after the Israelites were settled in their hometowns, they met together in Jerusalem. ²Then Jeshua son of Jozadak and his fellow priests joined Zerubbabel son of Shealtiel and began to build the altar of the God of Israel where they could offer burnt offerings, just as it is written in the Teachings of Moses, the man of God. ³Even though they were afraid of the people living around them, they built the altar where it had been before. And they offered burnt offerings on it to the LORD morning and evening. ⁴Then, to obey what was written, they celebrated the Feast of Shelters. They offered the right number of sacrifices for each day of the festival. ⁵After the Feast of Shelters, they had regular sacrifices every day, as well as sacrifices for the New Moon and all the festivals commanded by the LORD. Also there were special offerings brought as gifts to the LORD. ⁶On the first day of the seventh month they began to bring burnt offerings to the LORD, but the foundation of the LORD's Temple had not yet been laid.

¹⁰The builders finished laying the foundation of the Temple of the LORD. Then the priests, dressed in their robes, stood with their trumpets, and the Levites, the sons of Asaph, stood with their cymbals. They all took their places and praised the LORD just as David king of Israel had said to do. ¹¹With praise and thanksgiving, they sang to the LORD:

"He is good;
        his love for Israel continues forever."

And then all the people shouted loudly, "Praise the LORD! The foundation of his Temple has been laid." ¹²But many of the older priests, Levites, and family leaders who had seen the first Temple cried when they saw the foundation of this Temple. Most of the other people were shouting with joy. [13]The people made so much noise it could be heard far away, and no one could tell the difference between the joyful shouting and the sad crying.

DEVOTION

"THERE WILL NEVER BE CLOSURE," the woman said to me, and I immediately regretted having asked the question. I was a journalist, working the story of the bombing of the Oklahoma City federal building on the one-year anniversary of the event. I was interviewing Patti, who had been in a coma for several days after the event and I had just asked what I quickly realized was a dumb question. I had asked her when closure would occur for her and the other victims, as if the bombing were a door that could be easily shut.

"Closure? There will never be closure. What we have is a 'new normal' and we make the best of it," she said.

Following their return to their home from Babylonian captivity, the children of Israel faced a "new normal," and nowhere is that more evident than the reaction of the young and the old at the laying of the foundation of the Temple. Most of the people rejoiced, but the older priests wept. Depending on your perspective, the rebuilt Temple was either a return to normal for the nation after years of worshiping in a foreign land or it was a reminder that things would never be the same as they were when Solomon built the first magnificent Temple.

We go through life accumulating "losses." For many of us, we lose loved ones. Sadly, too many lose trust in those around them. Others lose their fortunes or their health. And with every loss, we mourn the fact that things will never be the same. But at the same time, we have to find the "new normal" and honor God by persevering through our losses, because "he is good" and his love for us lasts forever.

THOUGHTS TO PONDER

What do the size of the contributions and the immediate restoration of the sacrifices say about this group of people? What events in your life have led you to a "new normal"?

PRAYER

Father, we pray that no matter what our circumstances, we will worship you and praise you for being good to us. Amen.

Walls for Spiritual Protection

NEHEMIAH 2:1–7, 11–17

2 It was the month of Nisan in the twentieth year Artaxerxes was king. He wanted some wine, so I took some and gave it to the king. I had not been sad in his presence before. ²So the king said, "Why does your face look sad even though you are not sick? Your heart must be sad."

Then I was very afraid. ³I said to the king, "May the king live forever! My face is sad because the city where my ancestors are buried lies in ruins, and its gates have been destroyed by fire."

⁴Then the king said to me, "What do you want?"

First I prayed to the God of heaven. ⁵Then I answered the king, "If you are willing and if I have pleased you, send me to the city in Judah where my ancestors are buried so I can rebuild it."

⁶The queen was sitting next to the king. He asked me, "How long will your trip take, and when will you get back?" It pleased the king to send me, so I set a time.

⁷I also said to him, "If you are willing, give me letters for the governors of Trans-Euphrates. Tell them to let me pass safely through their lands on my way to Judah.

¹¹I went to Jerusalem and stayed there three days. ¹²Then at night I started out with a few men. I had not told anyone what God had caused me to do for Jerusalem. There were no animals with me except the one I was riding.

¹³I went out at night through the Valley Gate. I rode toward the Dragon Well and the Trash Gate, inspecting the walls of Jerusalem that had been broken down and the gates that had been destroyed by fire. ¹⁴Then I rode on toward the Fountain Gate and the King's Pool, but there was not enough room for the animal I was riding to pass through. ¹⁵So I went up the valley at night, inspecting the wall. Finally, I turned and went back in through the Valley Gate. ¹⁶The guards did not know where I had gone or what I was doing. I had not yet said anything to the Jewish people, the priests, the important men, the officers, or any of the others who would do the work.

¹⁷Then I said to them, "You can see the trouble we have here. Jerusalem is a pile of ruins, and its gates have been burned. Come, let's rebuild the wall of Jerusalem so we won't be full of shame any longer."

Devotion

IN THE DAYS OF NEHEMIAH, walls defined a city. Walls kept the people in and the enemy out. Walls provided a vantage point for watchmen and "high ground" in time of battle.

Some walls were elaborate, able to accommodate two chariots across. Some walls allowed a water source inside or enclosed the livestock, making the city less vulnerable to siege. But if a fortified city with walls was a wonderful thing to behold, a city without walls was a disgrace to its people, a mere step up from a tent city.

This was the fate of the city of Jerusalem. Once the crown jewel of Israel, it had been leveled in 587 B.C. by Nebuchadnezzar, king of Babylon, and the people were carried off into captivity. Now, approximately 140 years later, a remnant of the Jews was allowed to repatriate the area under a new policy of the Persians who had defeated the Babylonians. But the Jews lacked the resources to rebuild the wall, and without a wall, the settlers were vulnerable to the kings and nations around them, far from the protection of Artaxerxes.

That situation grieved Nehemiah, a Jew, who had risen to the position of cupbearer for the king. He was so grieved by the shame of the city that he was willing to leave the comforts of life in the palace to return to the desolation that was Jerusalem. So Nehemiah went, with the permission of the king.

Like an ancient city, our families today have "walls" too. These invisible walls are our traditions, values, and even rules that separate us from the world, keeping our identity in and the world's identity out. But the walls can be breached by media or by peers. The walls can fall into disrepair by our own negligence. Our job as Christians is to live *in the world* but not be *of the world*. When our spiritual walls fall down, what is the difference between us and the outside world? We become like that ancient city that Nehemiah encountered—"full of shame."

Jesus calls us "a city that is built on a hill" that cannot easily be hidden (Matthew 5:14). How visible is your city? How fortified is it?

Thoughts to ponder

Why would the king allow the Jews to rebuild their city wall? Why didn't the early settlers share Nehemiah's vision for the wall? What are some of the traditions that make up the "wall" of your family?

Prayer

God, we pray that we will find a way to live in this world and even influence this world without it influencing us. Give us walls where we need walls and gates where we need gates. Amen.

FIGHTING FOR WHAT'S RIGHT

NEHEMIAH 4:1–20

4 When Sanballat heard we were rebuilding the wall, he was very angry, even furious. He made fun of the Jewish people. ²He said to his friends and those with power in Samaria, "What are these weak Jews doing? Will they rebuild the wall? Will they offer sacrifices? Can they finish it in one day? Can they bring stones back to life from piles of trash and ashes?"

³Tobiah the Ammonite, who was next to Sanballat, said, "If a fox climbed up on the stone wall they are building, it would break it down."

⁴I prayed, "Hear us, our God. We are hated. Turn the insults of Sanballat and Tobiah back on their own heads. Let them be captured and stolen like valuables. ⁵Do not hide their guilt or take away their sins so that you can't see them, because they have insulted the builders."

⁶So we rebuilt the wall to half its height, because the people were willing to work.

⁷But Sanballat, Tobiah, the Arabs, the Ammonites, and the people from Ashdod were very angry when they heard that the repairs to Jerusalem's walls were continuing and that the holes in the wall were being closed. ⁸So they all made plans to come to Jerusalem and fight and stir up trouble. ⁹But we prayed to our God and appointed guards to watch for them day and night.

¹⁰The people of Judah said, "The workers are getting tired. There is so much trash we cannot rebuild the wall."

¹¹And our enemies said, "The Jews won't know or see anything until we come among them and kill them and stop the work."

¹²Then the Jewish people who lived near our enemies came and told us ten times, "Everywhere you turn, the enemy will attack us." ¹³So I put people behind the lowest places along the wall—the open places—and I put families together with their swords, spears, and bows. ¹⁴Then I looked around and stood up and said to the important men, the leaders, and the rest of the people: "Don't be afraid of them. Remember the Lord, who is great and powerful. Fight for your brothers, your sons and daughters, your wives, and your homes."

¹⁵Then our enemies heard that we knew about their plans and that God had ruined their plans. So we all went back to the wall, each to his own work.

¹⁶From that day on, half my people worked on the wall. The other half was ready with spears, shields, bows, and armor. The officers stood in back of the people of Judah ¹⁷who were building the wall. Those who carried materials did their work with one hand and carried a weapon with the other. ¹⁸Each builder wore his

sword at his side as he worked. The man who blew the trumpet to warn the people stayed next to me.

[19]Then I said to the important people, the leaders, and everyone else, "This is a very big job. We are spreading out along the wall so that we are far apart. [20]Wherever you hear the sound of the trumpet, assemble there. Our God will fight for us."

DEVOTION

MANY GOOD WORKS have failed because the leadership failed to anticipate opposition. Even when we think we are in the right, and even when we think we are doing what God wants us to do, opposition will come from somewhere. Satan doesn't give us a pass, especially when we're trying to do what is right.

Nehemiah ignored the ridicule of the foreign kings who hurled their insults at the workers. But when the wall reached half its height and completion was in sight, their insults turned to threats. Nehemiah was forced to take action to protect his workers while still keeping up with the work he'd set out to accomplish.

There's an important lesson here. There are times to ignore our critics and there are times to take action. Part of our spiritual growth is learning to anticipate criticism and react appropriately. Sometimes we ignore our critics; sometimes we take action.

Jesus told his followers that there would be a price to pay for following him. Speaking to a large crowd on the mountainside, he said: "People will insult you and hurt you. They will lie and say all kinds of evil things about you because you follow me. But when they do, you will be blessed. Rejoice and be glad, because you have a great reward waiting for you in heaven. People did the same evil things to the prophets who lived before you" (Matthew 5:11–12).

Have you ever had to fight for what you knew was right? Take comfort in the words of Nehemiah: "Our God will fight for us."

THOUGHTS TO PONDER

Have you been ridiculed or criticized for doing what was right? How did it feel? How do you think the workers felt building the wall in full sight of their enemy?

PRAYER

God, we pray that we will have the courage to do what is right in spite of the opposition that Satan tries to throw our way. Amen.

SPIRITUAL EROSION

NEHEMIAH 6:15–16; 7:1–3; 8:1–3, 9–14

Read the entire story in Nehemiah 6:15—8:14

¹⁵The wall of Jerusalem was completed on the twenty-fifth day of the month of Elul. It took fifty-two days to rebuild. ¹⁶When all our enemies heard about it and all the nations around us saw it, they were shamed. They then understood that the work had been done with the help of our God.

7After the wall had been rebuilt and I had set the doors in place, the gatekeepers, singers, and Levites were chosen. ²I put my brother Hanani, along with Hananiah, the commander of the palace, in charge of Jerusalem. Hananiah was honest and feared God more than most people. ³I said to them, "The gates of Jerusalem should not be opened until the sun is hot. While the gatekeepers are still on duty, have them shut and bolt the doors. Appoint people who live in Jerusalem as guards, and put some at guard posts and some near their own houses."

8All the people of Israel gathered together in the square by the Water Gate. They asked Ezra the teacher to bring out the Book of the Teachings of Moses, which the LORD had given to Israel.

²So on the first day of the seventh month, Ezra the priest brought out the Teachings for the crowd. Men, women, and all who could listen and understand had gathered. ³At the square by the Water Gate Ezra read the Teachings out loud from early morning until noon to the men, women, and everyone who could listen and understand. All the people listened carefully to the Book of the Teachings.

⁹Then Nehemiah the governor, Ezra the priest and teacher, and the Levites who were teaching said to all the people, "This is a holy day to the LORD your God. Don't be sad or cry." All the people had been crying as they listened to the words of the Teachings.

¹⁰Nehemiah said, "Go and enjoy good food and sweet drinks. Send some to people who have none, because today is a holy day to the Lord. Don't be sad, because the joy of the LORD will make you strong."

¹¹The Levites helped calm the people, saying, "Be quiet, because this is a holy day. Don't be sad."

¹²Then all the people went away to eat and drink, to send some of their food to others, and to celebrate with great joy. They finally understood what they had been taught.

¹³On the second day of the month, the leaders of all the families, the priests, and the Levites met with Ezra the teacher. They gathered to study the words of

the Teachings. ¹⁴This is what they found written in the Teachings: The LORD commanded through Moses that the people of Israel were to live in shelters during the feast of the seventh month.

DEVOTION

MANY OF THE PEOPLE gathered on this day of celebration had never heard God's laws read aloud. Their people had been in exile for more than a century. Many had to rely on the Levites to translate the Hebrew, a tongue that some had probably never heard during their exile.

But whether they understood the reading or relied on the translation, the entire nation realized that they had fallen short of the standards written in the Teachings. It was a scene reminiscent of 2 Kings 22 when King Josiah discovered the missing Book of the Teachings in the Temple and had it read aloud before the entire nation.

How does a nation lose its most holy book? How does a nation forget one of its most holy days like the Feast of the Tabernacles mentioned at the end of this story?

It doesn't happen all at once. It happens a step at a time. When copies of the Ten Commandments are banned from public buildings. When prayer is banned from public schools. When "Merry Christmas" becomes "Happy Holidays." It happens when we as Christians fail to stand up against the gradual erosion of our spiritual foundation from our everyday lives.

As incredible as it seems that the most holy book of the nation of Israel could be lost, it is equally incredible that we stand by as the Scriptures become marginalized in our increasingly secular society. The writer of the Proverbs gives a sobering reminder when he says, "Doing what is right makes a nation great, but sin will bring disgrace to any people" (Proverbs 14:34).

When Israel ceased doing what was right, they fell. It was too late for repentance. And when Nehemiah, Ezra, and the remnant returned years later, they were forced to rebuild the city—physically and spiritually—one stone and one tradition at a time.

THOUGHTS TO PONDER

Why were the people crying at the reading of the Law? Why would Nehemiah tell them to be happy? What do you think God would say about our notion of a separation between church and state?

PRAYER

God, we acknowledge you as the giver of law and the sustainer of life. We pray we will live our days inside your will. Amen.

A Life That Demands
an Explanation

ESTHER 1:1–15

1 This is what happened during the time of King Xerxes, the king who ruled the one hundred twenty-seven states from India to Cush. ²In those days King Xerxes ruled from his capital city of Susa. ³In the third year of his rule, he gave a banquet for all his important men and royal officers. The army leaders from the countries of Persia and Media and the important men from all Xerxes' empire were there.

⁴The banquet lasted one hundred eighty days. All during that time King Xerxes was showing off the great wealth of his kingdom and his own great riches and glory. ⁵When the one hundred eighty days were over, the king gave another banquet. It was held in the courtyard of the palace garden for seven days, and it was for everybody in the palace at Susa, from the greatest to the least. ⁶The courtyard had fine white curtains and purple drapes that were tied to silver rings on marble pillars by white and purple cords. And there were gold and silver couches on a floor set with tiles of white marble, shells, and gems. ⁷Wine was served in gold cups of various kinds. And there was plenty of the king's wine, because he was very generous. ⁸The king commanded that the guests be permitted to drink as much as they wished. He told the wine servers to serve each man what he wanted.

⁹Queen Vashti also gave a banquet for the women in the royal palace of King Xerxes.

¹⁰On the seventh day of the banquet, King Xerxes was very happy, because he had been drinking much wine. He gave a command to the seven eunuchs who served him—Mehuman, Biztha, Harbona, Bigtha, Abagtha, Zethar, and Carcas. ¹¹He commanded them to bring him Queen Vashti, wearing her royal crown. She was to come to show her beauty to the people and important men, because she was very beautiful. ¹²The eunuchs told Queen Vashti about the king's command, but she refused to come. Then the king became very angry; his anger was like a burning fire.

¹³It was a custom for the king to ask advice from experts about law and order. So King Xerxes spoke with the wise men who would know the right thing to do. ¹⁴The wise men the king usually talked to were Carshena, Shethar, Admatha, Tarshish, Meres, Marsena, and Memucan, seven of the important men of Persia and Media. These seven had special privileges to see the king and had the highest rank in the kingdom. ¹⁵The king asked them, "What does the law say must be done to Queen Vashti? She has not obeyed the command of King Xerxes, which the eunuchs took to her."

DEVOTION

THE ROYAL BANQUET had gone on for seven days. This was after a full half-year of celebration in the capital city of Susa for all the royal officers of King Xerxes.

Xerxes must have been a vain man, intent on showing his officers the bounty of his wealth. From the finest furnishings to marble floors, the palace was a testament to the great wealth and influence of Xerxes. But perhaps his greatest possession—and in that day she was considered a possession—was Vashti, no doubt picked to be queen from all the beautiful women in the land.

So after showing off his palace, his food, and his wine, Xerxes decides to show off his wife. There is good reason to believe that his command to Vashti to parade in front of the drunken officers wearing her crown meant wearing *only* her crown. Xerxes, vain and probably inebriated, wanted to show the officers the physical charms of his wife.

But Vashti was modest. And the king heard something from her that the king would never hear from any advisor, general, or expert in the law. He heard her say, "No."

I love the question above: What are we going to do with Vashti?

The world has never known exactly what to do with people of higher moral standards. People who don't laugh at the dirty jokes. People who don't cheat on their taxes or their spouses. People who do what's right even when it comes at great personal cost.

What do we do with Shadrach, Meshach, and Abednego, who refused to bow down to the idol of the king? What do we do with Daniel, who refused to pray to the king? What do we do with the followers of Jesus, who continued to preach about their risen Savior even after being warned and beaten? It demands an explanation.

Vashti was banished from the palace for her modesty. But her example stands for us today.

THOUGHTS TO PONDER

Have you lived a life that demands an explanation? And are you ready to pay the price for your choices?

PRAYER

Father, we pray that we always will make the right choice in every situation, no matter what the cost. Amen.

COME HUMBLY OR NOT AT ALL

ESTHER 3:1–14

3 After these things happened, King Xerxes honored Haman son of Hamme-datha the Agagite. He gave him a new rank that was higher than all the important men. ²All the royal officers at the king's gate would bow down and kneel before Haman, as the king had ordered. But Mordecai would not bow down or show him honor.

³Then the royal officers at the king's gate asked Mordecai, "Why don't you obey the king's command?" ⁴And they said this to him every day. When he did not listen to them, they told Haman about it. They wanted to see if Haman would accept Mordecai's behavior because Mordecai had told them he was Jewish.

⁵When Haman saw that Mordecai would not bow down to him or honor him, he became very angry. ⁶He thought of himself as too important to try to kill only Mordecai. He had been told who the people of Mordecai were, so he looked for a way to destroy all of Mordecai's people, the Jews, in all of Xerxes' kingdom.

⁷It was in the first month of the twelfth year of King Xerxes' rule—the month of Nisan. Pur (that is, the lot) was thrown before Haman to choose a day and a month. So the twelfth month, the month of Adar, was chosen.

⁸Then Haman said to King Xerxes, "There is a certain group of people scattered among the other people in all the states of your kingdom. Their customs are different from those of all the other people, and they do not obey the king's laws. It is not right for you to allow them to continue living in your kingdom. ⁹If it pleases the king, let an order be given to destroy those people. Then I will pay seven hundred fifty thousand pounds of silver to those who do the king's business, and they will put it into the royal treasury."

¹⁰So the king took his signet ring off and gave it to Haman son of Hamme-datha, the Agagite, the enemy of the Jewish people. ¹¹Then the king said to Haman, "The money and the people are yours. Do with them as you please."

¹²On the thirteenth day of the first month, the royal secretaries were called, and they wrote out all of Haman's orders. They wrote to the king's governors and to the captains of the soldiers in each state and to the important men of each group of people. The orders were written in the writing of each state and in the language of each people. They were written in the name of King Xerxes and sealed with his signet ring. ¹³Letters were sent by messengers to all the king's empire ordering them to destroy, kill, and completely wipe out all the Jewish people. That meant young and old, women and little children, too. It was to happen on a single day—the thirteenth day of the twelfth month, which was Adar. And

they could take everything the Jewish people owned. [14]A copy of the order was given out as a law in every state so all the people would be ready for that day.

DEVOTION

IF EVER A PERSON was tripped up by his own hubris, it was Haman. Honored by the king, bowed down to by all the officers at the palace gate—Haman seemingly had everything. But he didn't have the obedience of Mordecai, who refused to grovel when Haman passed by. Haman's rage at this slight proved to be his undoing.

It wasn't enough for Haman to just kill Mordecai. He wanted to kill all of Mordecai's people as well. By convincing the king that the Jews were a threat to his throne, Haman obtained what amounted to a license to kill all Jews on the thirteenth day of the twelfth month of the year. From young to old, the entire captive nation of Israel was to be annihilated, all because of Haman's wounded pride.

What have you seen pride destroy? I've seen it destroy marriages when two people are unable or unwilling to say "I'm sorry" and put the other's needs above their own. I've seen it bring down leaders, even in ministry, who begin to think their success is of their own doing and not from God.

Jesus told a parable about a proud man. Blessed with great crops, the man congratulated himself by building bigger barns to store his bounty rather than giving thanks to God and sharing his good fortune (Luke 12:13–21). Jesus called him a fool. Pride is a foolish activity, and Haman set himself up for a great fall in this story.

Want to get close to God? Come humbly or not at all, James tells his readers (James 4:6). God refuses to enter a heart located in a puffed-out chest.

THOUGHTS TO PONDER

What is the source of most pride that you see today? Why do you think it is such a potent weapon for Satan? How do you resist the temptation of pride?

PRAYER

God, we humble ourselves before you, and we pray that you will help us remain humble in every aspect of our lives. Amen.

For Just Such a Time

ESTHER 4:1–14

4 When Mordecai heard about all that had been done, he tore his clothes, put on rough cloth and ashes, and went out into the city crying loudly and painfully. ²But Mordecai went only as far as the king's gate, because no one was allowed to enter that gate dressed in rough cloth. ³As the king's order reached every area, there was great sadness and loud crying among the Jewish people. They fasted and cried out loud, and many of them lay down on rough cloth and ashes to show how sad they were.

⁴When Esther's servant girls and eunuchs came to her and told her about Mordecai, she was very upset and afraid. She sent clothes for Mordecai to put on instead of the rough cloth, but he would not wear them. ⁵Then Esther called for Hathach, one of the king's eunuchs chosen by the king to serve her. Esther ordered him to find out what was bothering Mordecai and why.

⁶So Hathach went to Mordecai, who was in the city square in front of the king's gate. ⁷Mordecai told Hathach everything that had happened to him, and he told Hathach about the amount of money Haman had promised to pay into the king's treasury for the killing of the Jewish people. ⁸Mordecai also gave him a copy of the order to kill the Jewish people, which had been given in Susa. He wanted Hathach to show it to Esther and to tell her about it. And Mordecai told him to order Esther to go into the king's presence to beg for mercy and to plead with him for her people.

⁹Hathach went back and reported to Esther everything Mordecai had said. ¹⁰Then Esther told Hathach to tell Mordecai, ¹¹"All the royal officers and people of the royal states know that no man or woman may go to the king in the inner courtyard without being called. There is only one law about this: Anyone who enters must be put to death unless the king holds out his gold scepter. Then that person may live. And I have not been called to go to the king for thirty days."

¹²Esther's message was given to Mordecai. ¹³Then Mordecai sent back word to Esther: "Just because you live in the king's palace, don't think that out of all the Jewish people you alone will escape. ¹⁴If you keep quiet at this time, someone else will help and save the Jewish people, but you and your father's family will all die. And who knows, you may have been chosen queen for just such a time as this."

DEVOTION

THE BOOK OF ESTHER never mentions the name of God directly. Because of this unusual omission, some have argued that it does not belong in the "canon," the group of books commonly acknowledged to make up our Christian Bible. According to its critics, the book exists only as a way of explaining how the Jews came to celebrate the Feast of Purim, their day of delivery.

But when I read Esther, I see several themes worthy of inclusion in the Bible: the modesty of Vashti, the bravery of Esther, and perhaps the greatest reason of all, the clear view of the providence of God expressed by Mordecai, the uncle of Esther who had raised her as his own child.

Mordecai powerfully communicates two points to Esther as she ponders whether to risk the wrath of the king by going in unannounced. First, he says, deliverance from the evil plan of Haman will come from somewhere. Second, he points out that perhaps she has been placed in the king's palace for just such a time as this.

And while there is no doubt that her beauty has landed her the role as the successor to the banished Vashti, perhaps God has been working behind the scenes all along to ensure Esther would be at the right place at exactly the right time.

What is God calling you to do? Finding the answer to that question is one of life's biggest challenges for Christians. But accepting that role once we've found it is often an even bigger challenge.

But know this: God's work will be done. His purposes go far beyond my willingness and my ability. Those whom God calls, he empowers. Think Moses, Daniel, Joseph, Paul. But make no mistake about it, his will is always done.

So our question is this: Am I a parent for just such a time as this? Am I an employee for just such a time as this? Am I a neighbor for just such a time as this?

How can we turn our circumstances into God's will today?

THOUGHTS TO PONDER

How can we recognize the providence of God in all the situations that happen to us? How can we see God's hand where others simply see luck or circumstance? What is God's will for your life?

PRAYER

God, we know we are in a particular time and place because of your will. Please help us find that good and perfect will and follow it in our lives. Amen.

THE PATH OF BRAVERY

ESTHER 4:15—5:8; 7:1–6

¹⁵Then Esther sent this answer to Mordecai: ¹⁶"Go and get all the Jewish people in Susa together. For my sake, fast; do not eat or drink for three days, night and day. I and my servant girls will also fast. Then I will go to the king, even though it is against the law, and if I die, I die."

¹⁷So Mordecai went away and did everything Esther had told him to do.

5 On the third day Esther put on her royal robes and stood in the inner court-yard of the king's palace, facing the king's hall. The king was sitting on his royal throne in the hall, facing the doorway. ²When the king saw Queen Esther standing in the courtyard, he was pleased. He held out to her the gold scepter that was in his hand, so Esther went forward and touched the end of it.

³The king asked, "What is it, Queen Esther? What do you want to ask me? I will give you as much as half of my kingdom."

⁴Esther answered, "My king, if it pleases you, come today with Haman to a banquet that I have prepared for you."

⁵Then the king said, "Bring Haman quickly so we may do what Esther asks."

So the king and Haman went to the banquet Esther had prepared for them. ⁶As they were drinking wine, the king said to Esther, "Now, what are you asking for? I will give it to you. What is it you want? I will give you as much as half of my kingdom."

⁷Esther answered, "This is what I want and what I ask for. ⁸My king, if you are pleased with me and if it pleases you, give me what I ask for and do what I want. Come with Haman tomorrow to the banquet I will prepare for you. Then I will answer your question about what I want."

7 So the king and Haman went in to eat with Queen Esther. ²As they were drinking wine on the second day, the king asked Esther again, "What are you asking for? I will give it to you. What is it you want? I will give you as much as half of my kingdom."

³Then Queen Esther answered, "My king, if you are pleased with me, and if it pleases you, let me live. This is what I ask. And let my people live, too. This is what I want. ⁴My people and I have been sold to be destroyed, to be killed and completely wiped out. If we had been sold as male and female slaves, I would have kept quiet, because that would not be enough of a problem to bother the king."

⁵Then King Xerxes asked Queen Esther, "Who is he, and where is he? Who has done such a thing?"

⁶Esther said, "Our enemy and foe is this wicked Haman!"

Devotion

ESTHER FACED A LIFE-THREATENING SITUATION no matter what she chose. She could choose to do nothing, and the massacre of the Jews planned by Haman would eventually reach her family and perhaps her as well. Or she could act, and risk losing her life by angering the king, who might not extend his scepter to her.

But the risks are not equal. By choosing to go to the king, Esther put herself in personal and immediate danger as opposed to the possibility of being found out as a Jew on the day of the proposed slaughter of the Jews. She chose the harder path.

In this story, Esther showed herself to be both cunning and brave as she gained the king's favor and revealed to him the evil plot of Haman. Because of her bravery, Haman was hanged from a gallows he prepared for Mordecai. Unable to reverse his first decree, the king issued a second one allowing the Jews to arm themselves against their enemies (the right to fight could only be granted by law) and defend themselves on the appointed day. The result was the salvation of all her people, an event still celebrated by the Feast of Purim on the thirteenth day of the twelfth month.

How did Esther ready herself for the task? She fasted for three days and undoubtedly prayed as well. She also recruited all her people in the city of Susa and her personal handmaidens to do the same.

How do you approach a big decision? Perhaps it's a change of job, or a move, or even both. How much time do you spend in prayer? In fasting? The next time you're faced with a challenge, remember the example of Esther and bring God into all the major decisions of your life.

Thoughts to ponder

Have you ever fasted? Do you look on fasting as a spiritual discipline required of a Christian or an outmoded activity we read about only in the Bible? What are the spiritual benefits of fasting?

Prayer

God, we pray that we will draw close to you in our lives at all times, but especially when we face the major decisions in life. Thank you for the example of Esther. Amen.

MORE THAN FAIR

JOB 1:1–12

1 A man named Job lived in the land of Uz. He was an honest and innocent man; he honored God and stayed away from evil. ²Job had seven sons and three daughters. ³He owned seven thousand sheep, three thousand camels, five hundred teams of oxen, and five hundred female donkeys. He also had a large number of servants. He was the greatest man among all the people of the East.

⁴Job's sons took turns holding feasts in their homes and invited their sisters to eat and drink with them. ⁵After a feast was over, Job would send and have them made clean. Early in the morning Job would offer a burnt offering for each of them, because he thought, "My children may have sinned and cursed God in their hearts." Job did this every time.

⁶One day the angels came to show themselves before the LORD, and Satan was with them. ⁷The LORD said to Satan, "Where have you come from?"

Satan answered the LORD, "I have been wandering around the earth, going back and forth in it."

⁸Then the LORD said to Satan, "Have you noticed my servant Job? No one else on earth is like him. He is an honest and innocent man, honoring God and staying away from evil."

⁹But Satan answered the LORD, "Job honors God for a good reason. ¹⁰You have put a wall around him, his family, and everything he owns. You have blessed the things he has done. His flocks and herds are so large they almost cover the land. ¹¹But reach out your hand and destroy everything he has, and he will curse you to your face."

¹²The LORD said to Satan, "All right, then. Everything Job has is in your power, but you must not touch Job himself." Then Satan left the LORD's presence.

DEVOTION

SATAN CLAIMED that the only reason Job was faithful was that God had placed a protective wall around him and his family. I sometimes wonder: Do I have a providential wall around me? With my relatively good health and my measure of wealth, my stable job, and my freedoms, do I have an untested faith? Is that my reason for honoring God?

Some of you have tasted illness. Some of you have tasted the loss of a job, the loss of a spouse, or the loss of a loved one. For many good people, the wall has been breached, not once but often. And it's in those moments that we see what we are made of.

The text chronicles Job's losses: his livestock, his servants—even his sons and daughters. And Job's reaction to all this calamity? "When Job heard this, he got up and tore his robe and shaved his head to show how sad he was. Then he bowed down to the ground to worship God" (Job 1:20). He worshiped! He praised God! If it's me, I'm shaking my fist at heaven and daring lightning to strike. "I've served you, God. I've been faithful. So where are you?" I'd shout.

We want life to be fair, and the things that happened to Job, and sometimes happen to us, don't seem fair at all. But if you think it through, I don't think we *want* fair.

You see, fair would mean that I pay the penalty for my sins. No hope of heaven. No hope of being in the presence of a perfect God who cannot abide with sin. That's what "fair" gets you.

I want much more than "fair." I want grace and mercy to cover my sins. I want to claim the blood of Jesus Christ. I want an eternal reward I could never earn. And thanks to the atonement of Jesus, I can get that reward.

But along the way, sin takes its toll. It takes its toll in disease, broken relationships, financial reversals, and the final price: death. But that's all sin can do. Sin can't take away the victory in Jesus. Strip me of my possessions and even my loved ones, and I still stand as a titleholder to a mansion in heaven (John 14:1–4).

Did Job know all this? I don't know the extent of his grasp of the afterlife, but I do know what he thought about his current situation: "I was naked when I was born, and I will be naked when I die. The LORD gave these things to me, and he has taken them away. Praise the name of the LORD" (Job 1:21).

Can I hope to find that attitude in me when the time of testing comes?

THOUGHTS TO PONDER

What is the toughest situation you have ever had to face? What did it do to your faith? How do you think Job found the inner strength to face the adversity the way he did?

PRAYER

God we pray that when adversity comes we will find our comfort in you and that we will be found faithful in the time of testing. Amen.

BLESS GOD TO THE END

JOB 2:1–10

2 On another day the angels came to show themselves before the LORD, and Satan was with them again. [2]The LORD said to Satan, "Where have you come from?"

Satan answered the LORD, "I have been wandering around the earth, going back and forth in it."

[3]Then the LORD said to Satan, "Have you noticed my servant Job? No one else on earth is like him. He is an honest and innocent man, honoring God and staying away from evil. You caused me to ruin him for no good reason, but he continues to be without blame."

[4]"One skin for another!" Satan answered. "A man will give all he has to save his own life. [5]But reach out your hand and destroy his flesh and bones, and he will curse you to your face."

[6]The LORD said to Satan, "All right, then. Job is in your power, but you may not take his life."

[7]So Satan left the LORD's presence. He put painful sores on Job's body, from the top of his head to the soles of his feet. [8]Job took a piece of broken pottery to scrape himself, and he sat in ashes in misery.

[9]Job's wife said to him, "Why are you trying to stay innocent? Curse God and die!"

[10]Job answered, "You are talking like a foolish woman. Should we take only good things from God and not trouble?" In spite of all this Job did not sin in what he said.

DEVOTION

I ATTENDED THE FUNERAL of a friend and colleague today. She died of cancer at age 46. This woman was incredible—a mother, a wife, a university professor, an active member of her local church. But more than that, during her four-year struggle with cancer, she was living proof to those around us that Satan was wrong in the passage above.

Kim lost her health to a most aggressive form of cancer. She lost her hair. She lost her energy. Some days she even lost the ability to get out of bed. But one thing she never lost: she never lost her faith.

When she got her initial diagnosis, Kim could have done nothing and died within six months. It would have been less painful. But she fought, and fought hard. And because she did, her family, her friends, and her colleagues at the university benefited from four more years of her smile, her courage, her silent testimony, and that wonderful singing voice.

During a thirteen-year teaching career, Kim taught hundreds of students; scores of them went on to medical school. But the greatest lesson she ever taught them was this: Christians need not fear death. A philosopher who survived the holocaust once noted that our children will not fear life if their elders do not fear death. The courage with which we face illness speaks volumes to our children.

In this story, Job was covered in sores from head to foot. He probably wanted to die. His wife even recommended a way out: "Curse God and die!" Let him strike you dead for your blasphemy, Job.

But Job had it right. Do we try to accept the good things from God and not the occasional troubles that are inevitable in a fallen world? Do I accept the bounty of the good health I have been given and not accept the possibility of disease? Do I accept the benefits of family without the inevitability of separation?

Did Job get angry? Sure. Check out this passage from the next chapter: "Let the day I was born be destroyed, and the night it was said, 'A boy is born!'" (Job 3:3). Or this: "Why didn't I die as soon as I was born? Why didn't I die when I came out of the womb?" (Job 3:11).

This glimpse of Job as an angry, confused man—remember that in his culture it was thought bad things happened only to bad people—tells me that it's alright when I don't understand why bad things happen to me. But even though you hear Job's frustration, what you don't hear is a man blaming God.

You see, we are only temporary custodians of health, wealth, or any other blessing from God. We might get to keep these gifts until the end of life or they might be taken from us before we die. Kim lost the gift of health long before she lost the gift of life, but she never complained.

I'll miss Kim, like I miss so many others who have lost the battle to disease, but I won't ever forget the testimony of her life. Satan was wrong. A person can see flesh and bones destroyed, and literally waste away, and still bless God until the end.

THOUGHTS TO PONDER

Who do you know who has faced illness courageously and kept faith with God? What is it about them that is different from the rest of the world? How should a Christian face the end of life?

PRAYER

God, we pray that you will give us health for all our days. But we also pray that when health fails us, that we will never fail to trust you. Amen.

REMEMBER WHO GOD IS

JOB 38:1–7, 12–18

Read the full text of this speech in Job 38:1—41:34.

38 Then the LORD answered Job from the storm. He said:
²"Who is this that makes my purpose unclear
  by saying things that are not true?
³Be strong like a man!
  I will ask you questions,
  and you must answer me.
⁴Where were you when I made the earth's foundation?
  Tell me, if you understand.
⁵Who marked off how big it should be? Surely you know!
  Who stretched a ruler across it?
⁶What were the earth's foundations set on,
  or who put its cornerstone in place
⁷while the morning stars sang together
  and all the angels shouted with joy?

¹²"Have you ever ordered the morning to begin,
  or shown the dawn where its place was
¹³in order to take hold of the earth by its edges
  and shake evil people out of it?
¹⁴At dawn the earth changes like clay being pressed by a seal;
  the hills and valleys stand out like folds in a coat.
¹⁵Light is not given to evil people;
  their arm is raised to do harm, but it is broken.

¹⁶"Have you ever gone to where the sea begins
  or walked in the valleys under the sea?
¹⁷Have the gates of death been opened to you?
  Have you seen the gates of the deep darkness?
¹⁸Do you understand how wide the earth is?
  Tell me, if you know all these things.

DEVOTION

AFTER THE THREE FRIENDS of Job had their say, and after Job—a good person to whom bad things had happened—vented at God with some angry remarks, God made an appearance. And if the text above can be summed up in a few words it would be these: "Job, you don't know everything."

Neither do I. Neither do you. While I might ponder the seeming inequities of why my wife has MS or why my son has diabetes, I rarely consider the inherent inequity of things that have gone my way. Like being born in the wealthiest nation in the world. Like being blessed with political and religious freedom. Or being given the intellect to earn a living the way I want. I seldom ponder those benefits; I only consider the things that don't go my way.

God says to Job—and to you and me today—you can't master my ways any more than you can master all the mysteries of nature. If God and I are to have a relationship at all, it must be based on me respecting God for who he is while remembering who I am.

Paul addresses the problem of God's perceived injustice in his Letter to the Romans: "Is God unfair? In no way. God said to Moses, 'I will show kindness to anyone to whom I want to show kindness, and I will show mercy to anyone to whom I want to show mercy.' So God will choose the one to whom he decides to show mercy; his choice does not depend on what people want or try to do" (Romans 9:14–16). He goes on to compare God to a potter and us to clay. He is the Creator; we are the creation.

Evidence of God's kindness is all around us—the beauty of nature, the bounty of the harvest. But so are the results of living in a fallen world—the ugliness of disease, famine, wars. Our job is to see both sides through the lens of faith in a loving God who cares for us.

THOUGHTS TO PONDER

Why is it easier to count our problems than to count our blessings? Have you ever noticed that occasional problems help us enjoy more fully the blessings that do come our way? What should that tell us about our attitudes toward suffering?

PRAYER

God, we know that you are the source of more blessings than we can count. Help us to remember that each day. Amen.

WAITING ON GOD

JOB 42:1–6, 10–16

42¹Then Job answered the LORD:
²"I know that you can do all things
and that no plan of yours can be ruined.
³You asked, 'Who is this that made my purpose unclear by saying things
that are not true?'
Surely I spoke of things I did not understand;
I talked of things too wonderful for me to know.
⁴You said, 'Listen now, and I will speak.
I will ask you questions,
and you must answer me.'
⁵My ears had heard of you before,
but now my eyes have seen you.
⁶So now I hate myself;
I will change my heart and life.
I will sit in the dust and ashes."

Editor's note: God chastises the friends of Job here and demands a sacrifice for what they had spoken.

¹⁰After Job had prayed for his friends, the LORD gave him success again. The LORD gave Job twice as much as he had owned before. ¹¹Job's brothers and sisters came to his house, along with everyone who had known him before, and they all ate with him there. They comforted him and made him feel better about the trouble the LORD had brought on him, and each one gave Job a piece of silver and a gold ring.

¹²The LORD blessed the last part of Job's life even more than the first part. Job had fourteen thousand sheep, six thousand camels, a thousand teams of oxen, and a thousand female donkeys. ¹³Job also had seven sons and three daughters. ¹⁴He named the first daughter Jemimah, the second daughter Keziah, and the third daughter Keren-Happuch. ¹⁵There were no other women in all the land as beautiful as Job's daughters. And their father Job gave them land to own along with their brothers.

¹⁶After this, Job lived one hundred forty years. He lived to see his children, grandchildren, great-grandchildren, and great-great-grandchildren. ¹⁷Then Job died; he was old and had lived many years.

DEVOTION

IN HIS LETTER to the church, James, the brother of Jesus, wrote this about Job: "You have heard about Job's patience, and you know the Lord's purpose for him in the end. You know the Lord is full of mercy and is kind" (James 5:11).

What was God's purpose for Job? I think the answer is found in the latter part of the verse. God's purpose for Job was to use him to show that God is merciful and kind to us. Even when it looked like all of Job's fortunes had reversed, God had a plan for him. And the same is true for us today.

The context of the above passage from James is a reminder to his readers to be patient in waiting for the coming of the Lord. He knew some of them might even face persecution during their wait, and Job was a lesson to these Christians. James wrote: "Brothers and sisters, be patient until the Lord comes again. A farmer patiently waits for his valuable crop to grow from the earth and for it to receive the autumn and spring rains. You, too, must be patient. Do not give up hope, because the Lord is coming soon" (James 5:7–8).

There were two rainy seasons in the regions where James's letter was sent. They were called the early and the late rains, and each was needed for a crop to succeed. Be patient like a farmer, James wrote. And be patient like Job.

I think I'm often caught in life between the early and late rains. I remember that God has blessed me in the past. I pray that God will bless me in the future. But it doesn't seem like rainy weather right now. I just came through a tough season, God, so answer me this: where is my rain?

Job had been blessed early in life. But during his trial, he had no way of knowing that a "late rain" would make the last part of his life more blessed than the first. Waiting on God is the hardest thing in the world to do. But sometimes, it is the only thing in the world to do.

THOUGHTS TO PONDER

How hard is it for you to be patient? What are the kinds of things in life that teach us patience? Are we really willing to go through what is necessary in order for us to become more patient?

PRAYER

Father, we know you love us and are watching over us even when we are going through the inevitable tests of life. Please help us feel your presence always. Amen.

"HERE I AM . . . SEND ME!"

ISAIAH 6:1–11

6In the year that King Uzziah died, I saw the Lord sitting on a very high throne. His long robe filled the Temple. ²Heavenly creatures of fire stood above him. Each creature had six wings: It used two wings to cover its face, two wings to cover its feet, and two wings for flying. ³Each creature was calling to the others:

"Holy, holy, holy is the LORD All-Powerful.
     His glory fills the whole earth."

⁴Their calling caused the frame around the door to shake, as the Temple filled with smoke.

⁵I said, "Oh, no! I will be destroyed. I am not pure, and I live among people who are not pure, but I have seen the King, the LORD All-Powerful."

⁶One of the heavenly creatures used a pair of tongs to take a hot coal from the altar. Then he flew to me with the hot coal in his hand. ⁷The creature touched my mouth with the hot coal and said, "Look, your guilt is taken away, because this hot coal has touched your lips. Your sin is taken away."

⁸Then I heard the Lord's voice, saying, "Whom can I send? Who will go for us?"

So I said, "Here I am. Send me!"

⁹Then the Lord said, "Go and tell this to the people:

'You will listen and listen, but you will not understand.
     You will look and look, but you will not learn.'
¹⁰Make the minds of these people dumb.
     Shut their ears. Cover their eyes.
Otherwise, they might really understand
     what they see with their eyes
     and hear with their ears.
They might really understand in their minds
     and come back to me and be healed."

¹¹Then I asked, "Lord, how long should I do this?"
He answered,
"Until the cities are destroyed
     and the people are gone,
until there are no people left in the houses,
     until the land is destroyed and left empty."

DEVOTION

THE REACTIONS OF ISAIAH in the story above are, I think, fairly typical of a religious experience. Whether we encounter God on the top of a mountain peak or cradle our newborn infant in our arms, whether we see God in the powerful hurricane or the still April shower, there are two almost universal reactions. First: I am not worthy to be in the presence of God. And second: what can I possibly do for God in response to everything he's done for me? Isaiah goes through both reactions in the story above.

Ironically, Isaiah was in the Temple when he had his religious experience, yet it still surprised him. I've been there and done that. One worship service blurs into another. Christmas pageants quickly give way to Easter morning and our prayers seem to go no higher than the roof. Then—all of a sudden—God wants into my life.

So this dialogue with God follows: "I'm not pure!" we shout. "I'll make you pure," God replies. "What do you want me to do?" we ask. "I need a messenger to the world," God replies. And like Isaiah we reply: "Here I am. Send me!"

As I look at God's messengers, from Moses to the prophets to the apostles, it seems that God does not require talent in those who are his messengers; he only requires a willing heart. He can work out all the other details.

"God, I'm not eloquent, I'm a stutterer," Moses argued. *I will help you with the words.* "God, I have a bad past—I even killed Christians," the apostle Paul said. *My grace is enough.*

I communicate to my college students that a great place to start is to simply show up. Show up. Try. I can help you with all the rest.

God is saying the same to us today. He's not promising that being his messenger will be easy—in fact, people might be as stubborn as they were in the days of Isaiah. But God only asks us to spread the seed of his word and trust him for the harvest.

THOUGHTS TO PONDER

Where have you been when you had some of the most moving religious experiences of your life? How did it make you feel? How did you respond?

PRAYER

God, we know you show yourself to us in so many ways. We pray that we will see you and respond willingly to you when you call. Amen.

BITTER OR BETTER?

JEREMIAH 38:1–13

38 Shephatiah son of Mattan, Gedaliah son of Pashhur, Jehucal son of Shelemiah, and Pashhur son of Malkijah heard what Jeremiah was telling all the people. He said: ²"This is what the LORD says: 'Everyone who stays in Jerusalem will die from war, or hunger, or terrible diseases. But everyone who surrenders to the Babylonian army will live; they will escape with their lives and live.' ³And this is what the LORD says: 'This city of Jerusalem will surely be handed over to the army of the king of Babylon. He will capture this city!'"

⁴Then the officers said to the king, "Jeremiah must be put to death! He is discouraging the soldiers who are still in the city, and all the people, by what he is saying to them. He does not want good to happen to us; he wants to ruin us."

⁵King Zedekiah said to them, "Jeremiah is in your control. I cannot do anything to stop you."

⁶So the officers took Jeremiah and put him into the well of Malkijah, the king's son, which was in the courtyard of the guards. The officers used ropes to lower Jeremiah into the well, which did not have any water in it, only mud. And Jeremiah sank down into the mud.

⁷But Ebed-Melech, a Cushite and a servant in the palace, heard that the officers had put Jeremiah into the well. As King Zedekiah was sitting at the Benjamin Gate, ⁸Ebed-Melech left the palace and went to the king. Ebed-Melech said to him, ⁹"My master and king, these rulers have acted in an evil way. They have treated Jeremiah the prophet badly. They have thrown him into a well and left him there to die! When there is no more bread in the city, he will starve to death."

¹⁰Then King Zedekiah commanded Ebed-Melech the Cushite, "Take thirty men from the palace and lift Jeremiah the prophet out of the well before he dies."

¹¹So Ebed-Melech took the men with him and went to a room under the storeroom in the palace. He took some old rags and worn-out clothes from that room. Then he let those rags down with some ropes to Jeremiah in the well. ¹²Ebed-Melech the Cushite said to Jeremiah, "Put these old rags and worn-out clothes under your arms to be pads for the ropes." So Jeremiah did as Ebed-Melech said. ¹³The men pulled Jeremiah up with the ropes and lifted him out of the well. And Jeremiah stayed under guard in the courtyard of the guard.

DEVOTION

HAVE YOU EVER felt like Jeremiah—stuck in the mud by your enemies? Have you ever been unpopular for telling the truth?

Judah was about to be overrun by the Babylonians as God's punishment for their disobedience, an account that can be found in 2 Kings 25. Jeremiah, a prophet, was warning people to escape to the enemy. Since they were all eventually going to be Babylonian captives, better to go before the battle than risk being killed in it. It was not a popular message with the king's officials.

Earlier, Jeremiah had been imprisoned and now he was only allowed to stay in the courtyard under the watchful gaze of the king's guard. From this position, it was a brave thing for Jeremiah to encourage his people to leave the city and throw themselves on the mercy of their captors. For his candor, he was lowered into the muddy well.

Think about the low points in your life, particularly those where you felt the distress was especially unjustified. Did you waver or did it make you stronger? As the old saying about difficulties goes: they can either make you bitter or better.

What I like about Jeremiah is when he was rescued from the mud he preached the same prophecy as before. He had been beaten, jailed, and lowered into the well, but there he was, later in this chapter, telling King Zedekiah that unless he surrendered to the Babylonians, the city would be burned.

This is the lesson of Jeremiah: when life mistreats you, stick with your convictions and God will deliver you. David put it this way in a song: "I waited patiently for the LORD. He turned to me and heard my cry. He lifted me out of the pit of destruction, out of the sticky mud. He stood me on a rock and made my feet steady. He put a new song in my mouth, a song of praise to our God" (Psalm 40:1–3).

You may feel stuck in the mud today, but look for God's rock and listen for his song. They're on the way.

THOUGHTS TO PONDER

When have you told the truth and suffered consequences for doing it? How did it feel? Looking back on it, did it make you "bitter" or "better"?

PRAYER

God, we pray for courage to stick up for the truth and continue to do the right thing in every circumstance, knowing our reward will be in heaven. Amen.

New Life

EZEKIEL 37:1–14

37 I felt the power of the LORD on me, and he brought me out by the Spirit of the LORD and put me down in the middle of a valley. It was full of bones. ²He led me around among the bones, and I saw that there were many bones in the valley and that they were very dry. ³Then he asked me, "Human, can these bones live?"

I answered, "Lord GOD, only you know."

⁴He said to me, "Prophesy to these bones and say to them, 'Dry bones, hear the word of the LORD. ⁵This is what the Lord GOD says to the bones: I will cause breath to enter you so you will come to life. ⁶I will put muscles on you and flesh on you and cover you with skin. Then I will put breath in you so you will come to life. Then you will know that I am the LORD.'"

⁷So I prophesied as I was commanded. While I prophesied, there was a noise and a rattling. The bones came together, bone to bone. ⁸I looked and saw muscles come on the bones, and flesh grew, and skin covered the bones. But there was no breath in them.

⁹Then he said to me, "Prophesy to the wind. Prophesy, human, and say to the wind, 'This is what the Lord GOD says: Wind, come from the four winds, and breathe on these people who were killed so they can come back to life.'" ¹⁰So I prophesied as the LORD commanded me. And the breath came into them, and they came to life and stood on their feet, a very large army.

¹¹Then he said to me, "Human, these bones are like all the people of Israel. They say, 'Our bones are dried up, and our hope has gone. We are destroyed.' ¹²So, prophesy and say to them, 'This is what the Lord GOD says: My people, I will open your graves and cause you to come up out of your graves. Then I will bring you into the land of Israel. ¹³My people, you will know that I am the LORD when I open your graves and cause you to come up from them. ¹⁴And I will put my Spirit inside you, and you will come to life. Then I will put you in your own land. And you will know that I, the LORD, have spoken and done it, says the LORD.'"

DEVOTION

EZEKIEL HAD BEEN CARRIED into captivity by King Nebuchadnezzar of Babylonia in 597 B.C. Based on events in the book that bears his name, Ezekiel was apparently a prophet for more than two decades.

The story above occurs in the third section of the book. The purpose of the latter part of the book was to give hope and consolation to the exiled nation of Israel. In the vision above, Israel in exile is compared to bones without life. Even though they had been carried far away from their home by Nebuchadnezzar, the children of Israel could be made alive again by God. He would breathe life into them, and once again the people would know that God is the LORD.

The message from Ezekiel was clear: God would return Israel to their home. Even though their hope was currently gone, it would be back. The exile would not be permanent. God would not forsake his people forever.

The reason I like this story is that God has made the same provision for us today. He has breathed life back into us even when we were dead in our sins. As Paul wrote to the church in Ephesus: "In the past you were spiritually dead because of your sins and the things you did against God . . . But God's mercy is great, and he loved us very much. Though we were spiritually dead because of the things we did against God, he gave us new life with Christ. You have been saved by God's grace" (Ephesians 2:1, 4–5).

I had exiled myself from God. I was held captive by sin just as surely as the Israelites were held by Nebuchadnezzar. But God rescued me and put new life into this old spirit. And because of that, I will never be dead in my sins again. "I will put my Spirit inside you, and you will come to life," God told Ezekiel, and he says the same thing to us today.

THOUGHTS TO PONDER

Why would God still be interested in the nation of Israel after they had abandoned him for the idols of the nations around them? What does this story tell us about the nature of God?

PRAYER

God, we pray that you will breathe new life into us and that your Spirit will give us a new walk and a new talk so that others will see you living in us. Amen.

Your Body Is a Temple

DANIEL 1:1–16

1 During the third year that Jehoiakim was king of Judah, Nebuchadnezzar king of Babylon came to Jerusalem and surrounded it with his army. ²The Lord allowed Nebuchadnezzar to capture Jehoiakim king of Judah. Nebuchadnezzar also took some of the things from the Temple of God, which he carried to Babylonia and put in the temple of his gods.

³Then King Nebuchadnezzar ordered Ashpenaz, his chief officer, to bring some of the men of Judah into his palace. He wanted them to be from important families, including the family of the king of Judah. ⁴King Nebuchadnezzar wanted only young Israelite men who had nothing wrong with them. They were to be handsome and well educated, capable of learning and understanding, and able to serve in his palace. Ashpenaz was to teach them the language and writings of the Babylonians. ⁵The king gave the young men a certain amount of food and wine every day, just like the food he ate. The young men were to be trained for three years, and then they would become servants of the king of Babylon. ⁶Among those young men were Daniel, Hananiah, Mishael, and Azariah from the people of Judah.

⁷Ashpenaz, the chief officer, gave them Babylonian names. Daniel's new name was Belteshazzar, Hananiah's was Shadrach, Mishael's was Meshach, and Azariah's was Abednego.

⁸Daniel decided not to eat the king's food or drink his wine because that would make him unclean. So he asked Ashpenaz for permission not to make himself unclean in this way.

⁹God made Ashpenaz, the chief officer, want to be kind and merciful to Daniel, ¹⁰but Ashpenaz said to Daniel, "I am afraid of my master, the king. He ordered me to give you this food and drink. If you begin to look worse than other young men your age, the king will see this. Then he will cut off my head because of you."

¹¹Ashpenaz had ordered a guard to watch Daniel, Hananiah, Mishael, and Azariah. ¹²Daniel said to the guard, "Please give us this test for ten days: Don't give us anything but vegetables to eat and water to drink. ¹³After ten days compare how we look with how the other young men look who eat the king's food. See for yourself and then decide how you want to treat us, your servants."

¹⁴So the guard agreed to test them for ten days. ¹⁵After ten days they looked healthier and better fed than all the young men who ate the king's food. ¹⁶So the guard took away the king's special food and wine, feeding them vegetables instead.

Devotion

LET'S BE HONEST: America is overweight. As a nation, we eat too much and exercise too little. And although there are valid medical reasons for many who suffer from obesity, for many of us the battle of the bulge is a matter of willpower.

In the story above, Daniel and his friends thrived when they rejected the rich foods from the king's table and ate vegetables instead. They knew then what we understand now: what goes in our bodies matters. And by that I mean *anything* that goes in: food, drink, tobacco, drugs, media. Yes, even media—the content we "ingest" with our minds.

What is your consumption problem? Too much food? Too much alcohol or tobacco? Too much media every day? Too many painkillers? Too much caffeine? I'm not preaching here; I struggle in some of these categories as well. Perhaps you do, too.

Paul challenged his readers in Corinth to pay attention to their bodies because they are the temples of God. He wrote, "You should know that your body is a temple for the Holy Spirit who is in you. You have received the Holy Spirit from God. So you do not belong to yourselves, because you were bought by God for a price. So honor God with your bodies" (1 Corinthians 6:19–20). What goes into our mouths and into our minds matters, because our bodies house the Holy Spirit, the very embodiment of God inside us.

I don't know if this is possible in every case, but perhaps we could take a cue from Daniel and his friends. Could you go on a diet just for ten days? Could you exercise for ten days? Could you go on a "media fast" for ten days? Or eliminate caffeine or alcohol for ten days? Could you take the challenge of Daniel and see how you feel in ten days?

But here's a warning: don't try any major change in your life without immersing the process in prayer. From the later stories in the book, we know they were men of prayer. Shadrach, Meshach, and Abednego were able to face a fiery furnace (Daniel 3) and Daniel braved a den of lions (Daniel 6) because they had full trust in God and his ability to deliver them. And God can deliver us from our self-imposed prisons as well.

Thoughts to ponder

What was Daniel's motivation for not wanting the king's food? Where did the Hebrew laws of diet originate? What can you do to better feed the spirit within you over the next ten days?

Prayer

God, we pray that we will treat our bodies as the temples you made them to be. Amen.

GOD IS NEAR

DANIEL 2:1–12, 24

2During Nebuchadnezzar's second year as king, he had dreams that bothered him and kept him awake at night. ²So the king called for his fortune-tellers, magicians, wizards, and wise men, because he wanted them to tell him what he had dreamed. They came in and stood in front of the king.

³Then the king said to them, "I had a dream that bothers me, and I want to know what it means."

⁴The wise men answered the king in the Aramaic language, "O king, live forever! Please tell us, your servants, your dream. Then we will tell you what it means."

⁵King Nebuchadnezzar said to them, "I meant what I said. You must tell me the dream and what it means. If you don't, I will have you torn apart, and I will turn your houses into piles of stones. ⁶But if you tell me my dream and its meaning, I will reward you with gifts and great honor. So tell me the dream and what it means."

⁷Again the wise men said to the king, "Tell us, your servants, the dream, and we will tell you what it means."

⁸King Nebuchadnezzar answered, "I know you are trying to get more time, because you know that I meant what I said. ⁹If you don't tell me my dream, you will be punished. You have all agreed to tell me lies and wicked things, hoping things will change. Now, tell me the dream so that I will know you can tell me what it really means!"

¹⁰The wise men answered the king, saying, "No one on earth can do what the king asks! No great and powerful king has ever asked the fortune-tellers, magicians, or wise men to do this; ¹¹the king is asking something that is too hard. Only the gods could tell the king this, but the gods do not live among people."

¹²When the king heard their answer, he became very angry. He ordered that all the wise men of Babylon be killed.

²⁴Then Daniel went to Arioch, the man King Nebuchadnezzar had chosen to kill the wise men of Babylon. Daniel said to him, "Don't put the wise men of Babylon to death. Take me to the king, and I will tell him what his dream means."

DEVOTION

DOES GOD LIVE among us today? Is he at work in lives today? Or has God wound this world up like an enormous clock only to sit passively and watch it wind down? For centuries, there have been honest arguments over whether God is involved in the everyday lives of his people.

I thought of that when I read the statement of the panicking fortune-tellers and magicians above, scrambling to save their lives. Nebuchadnezzar wanted his dream interpreted and he wasn't even going to divulge the content of the dream to those who were supposed to interpret it. Failure was not an option. They cried out that his request was too hard. "Only the gods could tell the king this, but the gods do not live among people," they said.

What a sad view of a god. Distant. Detached. Unable to help. But I understand their comment. Sometimes it's hard to comprehend the whole day-to-day activity of God. I've known folks who added "God willing" after every sentence that involved the future, even if the future was only lunch in fifteen minutes. On the other hand, I've known folks who scarcely believed that God would intervene in the life of a terminally ill person and heal them, claiming that such prayers were futile because everything was predetermined.

In the Gospel of Luke, Jesus stopped a funeral procession (Luke 7:11–17). A widow's son had died. The dead son was likely his mother's only means of support, and now he was gone. But Jesus had compassion on the woman and raised the son back to life. Immediately the people reacted with joy, shouting the news across the countryside: "God has come to help his people!" (Luke 7:16). To the mourners, the concept of a God close enough to help was good news indeed.

It's still Good News today. Paul told the crowd at Athens that God "is not far from any of us: 'By his power we live and move and exist'" (Acts 17:27–28). Close enough to hear; close enough to care.

The dream of Nebuchadnezzar foretold the future of the kingdoms that would follow Babylonia. The interpretation pleased the king so sufficiently that he made Daniel and his Jewish friends, Shadrach, Meshach, and Abednego, leaders over the area of Babylon. And whether it was facing a fiery furnace (Daniel 3) or a lion's den (Daniel 6), these young men always felt the presence of a God who was nearby—a God who was ready to help.

THOUGHTS TO PONDER

What does it say about their "gods" that the magicians didn't think that even they could interpret the dream? Do you think God intervenes directly in our lives today? If so, in what ways?

PRAYER

Father, we pray that we will always feel your presence near us when we pray and that we will feel your power in us as we live. Amen.

But Even If . . .

DANIEL 3:1–18

3 King Nebuchadnezzar made a gold statue ninety feet high and nine feet wide and set it up on the plain of Dura in the area of Babylon. ²Then he called for the leaders: the governors, assistant governors, captains of the soldiers, people who advised the king, keepers of the treasury, judges, rulers, and all other officers in his kingdom. He wanted them to come to the special service for the statue he had set up. ³So they all came for the special service and stood in front of the statue that King Nebuchadnezzar had set up. ⁴Then the man who made announcements for the king said in a loud voice, "People, nations, and those of every language, this is what you are commanded to do: ⁵When you hear the sound of the horns, flutes, lyres, zithers, harps, pipes, and all the other musical instruments, you must bow down and worship the gold statue that King Nebuchadnezzar has set up. ⁶Anyone who doesn't bow down and worship will immediately be thrown into a blazing furnace."

⁷Now people, nations, and those who spoke every language were there. When they heard the sound of the horns, flutes, lyres, zithers, pipes, and all the other musical instruments, they bowed down and worshiped the gold statue King Nebuchadnezzar had set up.

⁸Then some Babylonians came up to the king and began speaking against the men of Judah. ⁹They said to King Nebuchadnezzar, "O king, live forever! ¹⁰O king, you gave a command that everyone who heard the horns, lyres, zithers, harps, pipes, and all the other musical instruments would have to bow down and worship the gold statue. ¹¹Anyone who wouldn't do this was to be thrown into a blazing furnace. ¹²O king, there are some men of Judah whom you made officers in the area of Babylon that did not pay attention to your order. Their names are Shadrach, Meshach, and Abednego. They do not serve your gods and do not worship the gold statue you have set up."

¹³Nebuchadnezzar became very angry and called for Shadrach, Meshach, and Abednego. When they were brought to the king, ¹⁴Nebuchadnezzar said, "Shadrach, Meshach, and Abednego, is it true that you do not serve my gods nor worship the gold statue I have set up? ¹⁵In a moment you will again hear the sound of the horns, flutes, lyres, zithers, harps, pipes, and all the other musical instruments. If you bow down and worship the statue I made, that will be good. But if you do not worship it, you will immediately be thrown into the blazing furnace. What god will be able to save you from my power then?"

¹⁶Shadrach, Meshach, and Abednego answered the king, saying, "Nebuchadnezzar, we do not need to defend ourselves to you. ¹⁷If you throw us into the blazing furnace, the God we serve is able to save us from the furnace. He will save us

from your power, O king. [18]But even if God does not save us, we want you, O king, to know this: We will not serve your gods or worship the gold statue you have set up."

DEVOTION

WHAT A POWERFUL STATEMENT of faith the three men make at the end of this story. On the one hand, they proclaimed that God was great enough to provide deliverance from the fiery fate of those who opposed the king. "But even if" the next sentence begins—three of the most significant words in the entire Bible—"But even if God does not save us . . . we will not serve your gods." They were faithful to God. So they didn't bow.

How many of us have the kind of faith demonstrated by Shadrach, Meshach, and Abednego? Do you have a deep enough faith to look at two drastically different outcomes—one attractive and one disastrous—and allow that either outcome is God's will in the matter?

I think that all of us have faith enough to pray to God before any big event in life. Trying out for a new job. Making a cross-country move. Having a baby. Looking for a lifelong companion. But do we have the faith to accept a negative outcome in any of the events above? Do we have the faith of Shadrach, Meshach, and Abednego? Can we honestly add to our prayer, "But even if God does not . . ." and mean it?

"Lord, take this illness away from me. But if not, help me to live with the measure of health you give me." "Lord, help me to close the loan on this dream house. But if not, help us to be content where we are." I know people who could pray these prayers in all honesty. I also know that, try as I might, the second half of these prayers sticks in my throat. But Shadrach, Meshach, and Abednego knew their God, and the more I get to know him, the easier it will become to accept any outcome in my life and not lose faith.

THOUGHTS TO PONDER

Do you think God works directly today when we pray for him to protect us from harm? Does it shake your faith when harm comes anyway, even after your prayers?

PRAYER

God, we pray that when we ask for your blessings we will be open to your answer, no matter what form it takes. Amen.

THERE BESIDE YOU

DANIEL 3:19–30

[19]Then Nebuchadnezzar was furious with Shadrach, Meshach, and Abednego, and he changed his mind. He ordered the furnace to be heated seven times hotter than usual. [20]Then he commanded some of the strongest soldiers in his army to tie up Shadrach, Meshach, and Abednego and throw them into the blazing furnace.

[21]So Shadrach, Meshach, and Abednego were tied up and thrown into the blazing furnace while still wearing their robes, trousers, turbans, and other clothes. [22]The king's command was very strict, and the furnace was made so hot that the flames killed the strong soldiers who threw Shadrach, Meshach, and Abednego into the furnace. [23]Firmly tied, Shadrach, Meshach, and Abednego fell into the blazing furnace.

[24]Then King Nebuchadnezzar was so surprised that he jumped to his feet. He asked the men who advised him, "Didn't we tie up only three men and throw them into the fire?"

They answered, "Yes, O king."

[25]The king said, "Look! I see four men walking around in the fire. They are not tied up, and they are not burned. The fourth man looks like a son of the gods."

[26]Then Nebuchadnezzar went to the opening of the blazing furnace and shouted, "Shadrach, Meshach, and Abednego, come out! Servants of the Most High God, come here!"

So Shadrach, Meshach, and Abednego came out of the fire. [27]When they came out, the governors, assistant governors, captains of the soldiers, and royal advisers crowded around them and saw that the fire had not harmed their bodies. Their hair was not burned, their robes were not burned, and they didn't even smell like smoke!

[28]Then Nebuchadnezzar said, "Praise the God of Shadrach, Meshach, and Abednego. Their God has sent his angel and saved his servants from the fire! These three men trusted their God and refused to obey my command. They were willing to die rather than serve or worship any god other than their own. [29]So I now give this command: Anyone from any nation or language who says anything against the God of Shadrach, Meshach, and Abednego will be torn apart and have his house turned into a pile of stones. No other god can save his people like this." [30]Then the king promoted Shadrach, Meshach, and Abednego in the area of Babylon.

DEVOTION

WHEN I LOOK BACK on my worst and most difficult trials, I can clearly see that I was not alone. The story of Shadrach, Meshach, and Abednego tells us that God will be right there in the furnace with us if we only have faith in him to deliver us.

A few months ago, I made the decision to quit taking all pain medication for my back. I had suffered for years with degenerated discs and I'd had a few of them fused, but the pain always returned. Then, one spring morning, I decided to quit the round-the-clock morphine that had made my life bearable but had clouded my memory.

I didn't tell anyone of my decision—not my wife, not my doctor. For the first couple of days, I was coasting by. A little more pain, but nothing I couldn't handle.

On the third day, however, my entire body was on fire. The fact that the drug was legal and arguably necessary didn't change the fact that I was in full-fledged withdrawal. All night long I threw up until I was dehydrated. I looked at the clock every few minutes, counting the time until I would be the first patient at the doctor's office in the morning.

I had two choices that night. I could go find that bottle of medication in the bathroom and start the cycle of chemical dependency all over again, or I could rely on God to get me through. I chose the latter, and through my pain I kept a constant dialogue with God all night. At a couple of points, I actually prayed for God to take me right then, but morning came and I made it to my doctor, a good friend and coauthor of one of my earlier books.

It was five more days before I was able to come home from the hospital, but I eventually became free of pain medication. Through the whole ordeal—and there were many more bad hours—I completely felt the presence of God. And even now when I suffer the pains of a bad back, I remember what God told Paul (2 Corinthians 12:9) about Paul's physical illness: "My grace is enough for you. When you are weak, my power is made perfect in you."

I don't wish you a trial like Shadrach, Meshach, and Abednego went through in order to fully feel the presence of God. But I do hope that when the trials come, you will feel him right there beside you in the flames.

THOUGHTS TO PONDER

What is the greatest period of testing you have ever endured? How did you get through it? Why do trials make us turn to God?

PRAYER

Father, you are with us in every circumstance of our lives. Help us to feel your presence even in the firestorm of our trials. Amen.

MEASURED AND WEIGHED

DANIEL 5:1–7, 13–17, 23–31

5 King Belshazzar gave a big banquet for a thousand royal guests and drank wine with them. ²As Belshazzar was drinking his wine, he gave orders to bring the gold and silver cups that his ancestor Nebuchadnezzar had taken from the Temple in Jerusalem. This was so the king, his royal guests, his wives, and his slave women could drink from those cups. ³So they brought the gold cups that had been taken from the Temple of God in Jerusalem. And the king and his royal guests, his wives, and his slave women drank from them. ⁴As they were drinking, they praised their gods, which were made from gold, silver, bronze, iron, wood, and stone.

⁵Suddenly the fingers of a person's hand appeared and began writing on the plaster of the wall, near the lampstand in the royal palace. The king watched the hand as it wrote.

⁶King Belshazzar was very frightened. His face turned white, his knees knocked together, and he could not stand up because his legs were too weak. ⁷The king called for the magicians, wise men, and wizards of Babylon and said to them, "Anyone who can read this writing and explain it will receive purple clothes fit for a king and a gold chain around his neck. And I will make that person the third highest ruler in the kingdom."

¹³So they brought Daniel to the king, and the king asked, "Is your name Daniel? Are you one of the captives my father the king brought from Judah? ¹⁴I have heard that the spirit of the gods is in you, and that you are very wise and have knowledge and extraordinary understanding. ¹⁵The wise men and magicians were brought to me to read this writing and to explain what it means, but they could not explain it. ¹⁶I have heard that you are able to explain what things mean and can find the answers to hard problems. Read this writing on the wall and explain it to me. If you can, I will give you purple clothes fit for a king and a gold chain to wear around your neck. And you will become the third highest ruler in the kingdom."

¹⁷Then Daniel answered the king, "You may keep your gifts for yourself, or you may give those rewards to someone else. But I will read the writing on the wall for you and will explain to you what it means.

²³You ordered the drinking cups from the Temple of the Lord to be brought to you. Then you and your royal guests, your wives, and your slave women drank wine from them. You praised the gods of silver, gold, bronze, iron, wood, and stone that are not really gods; they cannot see or hear or understand anything. You did not honor God, who has power over your life and everything you do. ²⁴So God sent the hand that wrote on the wall.

²⁵"These are the words that were written on the wall: 'Mene, mene, tekel, and parsin.'

²⁶"This is what the words mean: Mene: God has counted the days until your kingdom will end. ²⁷Tekel: You have been weighed on the scales and found not good enough. ²⁸Parsin: Your kingdom is being divided and will be given to the Medes and the Persians."

²⁹Then Belshazzar gave an order for Daniel to be dressed in purple clothes and to have a gold chain put around his neck. And it was announced that Daniel was the third highest ruler in the kingdom. ³⁰That very same night Belshazzar, king of the Babylonian people, was killed. ³¹So Darius the Mede became the new king when he was sixty-two years old.

DEVOTION

"YOU HAVE BEEN WEIGHED on the scales and found not good enough," God told Belshazzar. He had seen what happened to his father, Nebuchadnezzar, when for his arrogance he was forced to live like a wild beast for seven years. But he had not learned a lesson. His action of drinking from the golden cups of the Temple, captured by his father, was considered blasphemous by God, and the price would be very high: Belshazzar would die that very night.

God is measuring you and he is measuring me. Do we meet his standards? Jesus was measuring the rich young man in Luke 18 when he asked the man questions about keeping the commandments. When the young man replied that he had kept all the commandments, Jesus said, "There is still one more thing you need to do. Sell everything you have and give it to the poor, and you will have treasure in heaven. Then come and follow me" (Luke 18:22). In that one request, Jesus weighed the young man and found him lacking. The story concludes with the young man going away without following Jesus.

When you're weighed, what will the scales say?

THOUGHTS TO PONDER

How does God measure his followers today? Can you ever measure up to God's standards on your own?

PRAYER

Father, we pray that when you weigh us on the scales of life that we will be found "good enough," not because of what we do, but because of who we are—Christians saved by your grace. Amen.

OBEYING GOD'S LAWS

DANIEL 6:1–12

6Darius thought it would be a good idea to choose one hundred twenty governors who would rule his kingdom. ²He chose three men as supervisors over those governors, and Daniel was one of the supervisors. The supervisors were to ensure that the governors did not try to cheat the king. ³Daniel showed that he could do the work better than the other supervisors and governors, so the king planned to put Daniel in charge of the whole kingdom. ⁴Because of this, the other supervisors and governors tried to find reasons to accuse Daniel about his work in the government. But they could not find anything wrong with him or any reason to accuse him, because he was trustworthy and not lazy or dishonest. ⁵Finally these men said, "We will never find any reason to accuse Daniel unless it is about the law of his God."

⁶So the supervisors and governors went as a group to the king and said: "King Darius, live forever! ⁷The supervisors, assistant governors, governors, the people who advise you, and the captains of the soldiers have all agreed that you should make a new law for everyone to obey: For the next thirty days no one should pray to any god or human except to you, O king. Anyone who doesn't obey will be thrown into the lions' den. ⁸Now, O king, make the law and sign your name to it so that it cannot be changed, because then it will be a law of the Medes and Persians and cannot be canceled." ⁹So King Darius signed the law.

¹⁰Even though Daniel knew that the new law had been written, he went to pray in an upstairs room in his house, which had windows that opened toward Jerusalem. Three times each day Daniel would kneel down to pray and thank God, just as he always had done.

¹¹Then those men went as a group and found Daniel praying and asking God for help. ¹²So they went to the king and talked to him about the law he had made. They said, "Didn't you sign a law that says no one may pray to any god or human except you, O king? Doesn't it say that anyone who disobeys during the next thirty days will be thrown into the lions' den?"

The king answered, "Yes, that is the law, and the laws of the Medes and Persians cannot be canceled."

DEVOTION

KING DARIUS KNEW that power could corrupt. So when he created a system of governors to oversee his vast kingdom, he put in an extra layer of protection— three supervisors over the governors. When it became obvious Daniel was far superior to all of the other appointees, he was placed in charge of the entire kingdom. You might recall a similar situation in Genesis 41 where Joseph rose from slavery and prison to become the Egyptian king's right-hand man. Using the principles of integrity expected of God's children, these men rose to the top in these kingdoms, despite being foreigners.

I find it interesting that Daniel's enemies admitted that they would never find a valid reason to accuse him before King Darius. Wouldn't that be a wonderful thing to have said about us? Wouldn't it be great if the only accusation that could be made about us would be that we obeyed our consciences rather than an unjust human law?

So his enemies constructed a law Daniel was bound to disobey.

Are Christians ever called to civil disobedience? What should our reaction be if acts of government violate our conscience and our interpretation of Scripture? It's a thorny issue.

Just a few weeks before this writing, civil rights pioneer Rosa Parks died, decades after catalyzing the civil rights movement by refusing to yield her seat at the front of a Montgomery, Alabama bus to a white man, as the law of the day required. Her simple act of defiance—"I was tired at the end of the day and just didn't want to give up my seat," she would explain—is still a landmark in race relations in America. Decades later, in a photo seen around the world, a young man stood in front of a long line of tanks in China's Tiananmen Square to try to stop the bloodshed in his country.

But, as I said, this is thorny. Others assert they're following their consciences when they bomb abortion clinics and may even murder the doctors in the name of following God. Others create Web sites claiming, "God hates" certain groups of people. All *claim* to be following the Word of God.

How do we know the difference between acts that honor God and acts that dishonor him and disgrace his church? We can sharpen our discernment by knowing his Word and growing closer to him. Perhaps we should follow the example of Daniel and get on our knees frequently to pray.

THOUGHTS TO PONDER

What does it say about Daniel that the other government leaders knew he would defy the order? What laws today test you as a Christian? Have you ever disobeyed them?

PRAYER

God, we pray that, like Daniel, we will always be found faithful to you. But we also pray that, like Daniel, we will always be found in prayer to you and listening for your answer. Amen.

Only Pure Worship

DANIEL 6:13–26

¹³Then they said to the king, "Daniel, one of the captives from Judah, is not paying attention to you, O king, or to the law you signed. Daniel still prays to his God three times every day." ¹⁴The king became very upset when he heard this. He wanted to save Daniel, and he worked hard until sunset trying to think of a way to save him.

¹⁵Then those men went as a group to the king. They said, "Remember, O king, the law of the Medes and Persians says that no law or command given by the king can be changed."

¹⁶So King Darius gave the order, and Daniel was brought in and thrown into the lions' den. The king said to Daniel, "May the God you serve all the time save you!" ¹⁷A big stone was brought and placed over the opening of the lions' den. Then the king used his signet ring and the rings of his royal officers to put special seals on the rock. This ensured that no one would move the rock and bring Daniel out. ¹⁸Then King Darius went back to his palace. He did not eat that night, he did not have any entertainment brought to him, and he could not sleep.

¹⁹The next morning King Darius got up at dawn and hurried to the lions' den. ²⁰As he came near the den, he was worried. He called out to Daniel, "Daniel, servant of the living God! Has your God that you always worship been able to save you from the lions?"

²¹Daniel answered, "O king, live forever! ²²My God sent his angel to close the lions' mouths. They have not hurt me, because my God knows I am innocent. I never did anything wrong to you, O king."

²³King Darius was very happy and told his servants to lift Daniel out of the lions' den. So they lifted him out and did not find any injury on him, because Daniel had trusted in his God.

²⁴Then the king commanded that the men who had accused Daniel be brought to the lions' den. They, their wives, and their children were thrown into the den. The lions grabbed them before they hit the floor of the den and crushed their bones.

²⁵Then King Darius wrote a letter to all people and all nations, to those who spoke every language in the world:

I wish you great peace and wealth.

²⁶I am making a new law for people in every part of my kingdom. All of you must fear and respect the God of Daniel.

DEVOTION

"MAY THE GOD YOU SERVE all the time save you!" Darius said as he sent Daniel into the lions' den. Even though he had been hemmed in by one of his own laws, Darius desperately wanted Daniel to survive, and based on what he knew about Daniel, this "God" was his best chance.

Daniel knew that he had nothing to fear. He had kept faith with God even in defiance of a law that had been tailored to trap him. God would judge him, Daniel knew as he entered the lions' den, and God would find him guilt-free.

Have you ever been thrown into the lions' den? Have you ever been persecuted for doing what you believed to be right? Perhaps you refused to cut corners on a project in order to maximize profits. Perhaps you refused to cheat at school. Or maybe you've personally been in the lions' den of having to blow the whistle on illegal or unethical behaviors in your workplace.

Sir Thomas Gresham, a financier in the days of Tudor England, claimed, "Bad money drives good money out of circulation." Many applications have been made of "Gresham's law" since that time, but here is my favorite. In the marketplaces of England, unscrupulous merchants would put a scant amount of metal shavings into the flour in order to make it heavier. Subsequently, they could sell this heavy, adulterated flour more cheaply to unsuspecting customers. And true to Gresham's law, soon it was hard to find pure flour in the marketplace as every dealer was forced to cheat to compete.

If Daniel had adulterated his religious life and sprinkled in a little worship of Darius with a little worship of Jehovah, he would likely have never faced the lions' den. But because he stood up, and offered only pure worship to God, he was able to make an incredible statement of faith to Darius and to the rest of the country. Standing up for what is right has never been easy, but it's never been more necessary than today.

THOUGHTS TO PONDER

What are some of the adjectives you would use to describe Darius based on his actions in Daniel 6? What are some adjectives to describe Daniel? What words would describe your actions when you face the lions' den?

PRAYER

God, we pray we will be faithful to you no matter what the cost, and that we, like Daniel, will stand up for you. Amen.

Harvest the Storm

HOSEA 1:1–9; 3:1–5

1 The Lord spoke his word to Hosea son of Beeri during the time that Uzziah, Jotham, Ahaz, and Hezekiah were kings of Judah and Jeroboam son of Jehoash was king of Israel.

²When the Lord began speaking through Hosea, the Lord said to him, "Go, and marry an unfaithful woman and have unfaithful children, because the people in this country have been completely unfaithful to the Lord." ³So Hosea married Gomer daughter of Diblaim, and she became pregnant and gave birth to Hosea's son.

⁴The Lord said to Hosea, "Name him Jezreel, because soon I will punish the family of Jehu for the people they killed at Jezreel. In the future I will put an end to the kingdom of Israel ⁵and break the power of Israel's army in the Valley of Jezreel."

⁶Gomer became pregnant again and gave birth to a daughter. The Lord said to Hosea, "Name her Lo-Ruhamah, because I will not pity Israel anymore, nor will I forgive them. ⁷But I will show pity to the people of Judah. I will save them, but not by using bows or swords, horses or horsemen, or weapons of war. I, the Lord their God, will save them."

⁸After Gomer had stopped nursing Lo-Ruhamah, she became pregnant again and gave birth to another son. ⁹The Lord said, "Name him Lo-Ammi, because you are not my people, and I am not your God."

3 The Lord said to me again, "Go, show your love to a woman loved by someone else, who has been unfaithful to you. In the same way the Lord loves the people of Israel, even though they worship other gods and love to eat the raisin cakes."

²So I bought her for six ounces of silver and ten bushels of barley. ³Then I told her, "You must wait for me for many days. You must not be a prostitute, and you must not have sexual relations with any other man. I will act the same way toward you."

⁴In the same way Israel will live many days without a king or leader, without sacrifices or holy stone pillars, and without the holy vest or an idol. ⁵After this, the people of Israel will return to the Lord their God and follow him and the king from David's family. In the last days they will turn in fear to the Lord, and he will bless them.

Devotion

GOD'S COMMAND TO HOSEA is among the strangest in Scripture. The God who told Abraham to sacrifice his own son, the God who told Sarah she would bear a child when she was in her nineties now tells Hosea to take a prostitute for a wife. Instead of looking for the best qualities in a spouse, the prophet Hosea is under direct instructions from God to look for the worst, and he finds those qualities in Gomer.

Not only is she is of dubious character when they are married, she leaves Hosea after the birth of their three children. Hosea is put in the humiliating position of having to buy her back from another man. When his six ounces of silver is not enough to pay the debt, he also offers about ten bushels of barley, undoubtedly leaving Hosea broke and facing hunger, but he obeys the voice of God.

All of this is to demonstrate the unfaithfulness of Israel to God. Like a harlot, they have strayed from their one true Lover, who led them out of Egypt and into the Promised Land, and asked only fidelity to him alone in return. Here is how Israel is described by Hosea: "Plead with your mother. Accuse her, because she is no longer my wife, and I am no longer her husband. Tell her to stop acting like a prostitute, to stop behaving like an unfaithful wife" (Hosea 2:2).

Israel had pursued other Gods just like Gomer pursued other men before and after her marriage to Hosea. So in one of the warnings in the prophets, "The foolish plans are like planting the wind, but they will harvest a storm" (Hosea 8:7).

I see in Hosea's willingness to bankrupt himself to reclaim Gomer a forerunner of God's willingness to reclaim me at great cost.

Although I've believed in and worshiped one God for as long as I can remember, I've been tempted by the idols of success, wealth, envy, and all the rest of Satan's pantheon of gods. More than once I've given in. I've planted the wind of overcrowded schedules and greed and reaped the whirlwind of stress and ulcers.

But the last verse of Hosea's prophecy is my guide out of Satan's temptations: "The LORD's ways are right. Good people live by following them, but those who turn against God die because of them" (Hosea 14:9). Which describes you?

THOUGHTS TO PONDER

Why did God ask Hosea to go through the heartache of an unfaithful marriage? Do you think the children of Israel noticed? What does this tell us about the way God views our sin?

PRAYER

God, we know we disappoint you. We know we're sometimes unfaithful to you. But we pray that we will see the error of our ways and come back into a right relationship with you. Amen.

Blessings or Locusts?

JOEL 1:1–4, 10–11; 2:12–14

Read the entire passage in Joel 1:1—2:32.

1 The LORD spoke his word to Joel son of Pethuel:
 ²Elders, listen to this message.
  Listen to me, all you who live in the land.
 Nothing like this has ever happened during your lifetime
  or during your ancestors' lifetimes.
³Tell your children about these things,
  let your children tell their children,
  and let your grandchildren tell their children.
⁴What the cutting locusts have left,
  the swarming locusts have eaten;
 what the swarming locusts have left,
  the hopping locusts have eaten,
 and what the hopping locusts have left,
  the destroying locusts have eaten.

¹⁰The fields are ruined;
  the ground is dried up.
 The grain is destroyed,
  the new wine is dried up,
  and the olive oil runs out.
¹¹Be sad, farmers.
  Cry loudly, you who grow grapes.
 Cry for the wheat and the barley.
  Cry because the harvest of the field is lost.

¹²The LORD says, "Even now, come back to me with all your heart.
  Fast, cry, and be sad."

¹³Tearing your clothes is not enough to show you are sad;
  let your heart be broken.
 Come back to the LORD your God,
  because he is kind and shows mercy.
 He doesn't become angry quickly,
  and he has great love.
  He can change his mind about doing harm.
¹⁴Who knows? Maybe he will turn back to you
  and leave behind a blessing for you.

DEVOTION

THEIR ANCESTORS had seen something like it in Egypt when God brought a plague of locusts on the Egyptians when they refused to let his people go into the desert to worship him. But even if this generation of Israelites had heard that story, this swarm of locusts was unprecedented as God prepared to release the fury of nature on his disobedient children who once again chose to worship the idols of the nations around them.

God had already used the armies of the surrounding nations to punish the Israelites. But this was an army of a different sort—a cruelly efficient army that left nothing behind. An army so vast that even the sun was blotted out. Cattle died in the fields from lack of food. Wild animals died from lack of water. Nothing was spared.

But there was hope. God could change his mind. He is slow to become angry. There was still time for true, heartfelt repentance.

The same is true for us today. God's wrath is very real, but so are his kindness and mercy. The word for repentance in the New Testament literally means "to turn around." If we repent, God repents. If we turn away from sin, he turns away from wrath. The ending is left for us to write.

But this is important—we must turn first. God will only work with a penitent heart. Blessings or locusts? The choice was obvious then and it's obvious today. But the choice is up to us.

THOUGHTS TO PONDER

Do you think God directly punishes people today, or is his wrath against sin confined to eternal damnation? Does God directly bless people today? What supports your answers?

PRAYER

God, we pray that we will serve you all of our days and that we will experience your love and kindness. Please be slow to anger with us, today and always. Amen.

RUNNING FROM GOD'S WILL

JONAH 1:1–17

1 The LORD spoke his word to Jonah son of Amittai: ²"Get up, go to the great city of Nineveh, and preach against it, because I see the evil things they do."

³But Jonah got up to run away from the LORD by going to Tarshish. He went to the city of Joppa, where he found a ship that was going to the city of Tarshish. Jonah paid for the trip and went aboard, planning to go to Tarshish to run away from the LORD.

⁴But the LORD sent a great wind on the sea, which made the sea so stormy that the ship was in danger of breaking apart. ⁵The sailors were afraid, and each man cried to his own god. They began throwing the cargo from the ship into the sea to make the ship lighter.

But Jonah had gone down far inside the ship to lie down, and he fell fast asleep. ⁶The captain of the ship came and said, "Why are you sleeping? Get up and pray to your god! Maybe your god will pay attention to us, and we won't die!"

⁷Then the men said to each other, "Let's throw lots to see who caused these troubles to happen to us."

When they threw lots, the lot showed that the trouble had happened because of Jonah. ⁸Then they said to him, "Tell us, who caused our trouble? What is your job? Where do you come from? What is your country? Who are your people?"

⁹Then Jonah said to them, "I am a Hebrew. I fear the LORD, the God of heaven, who made the sea and the land."

¹⁰The men were very afraid, and they asked Jonah, "What terrible thing did you do?" (They knew he was running away from the LORD because he had told them.)

¹¹Since the wind and the waves of the sea were becoming much stronger, they said to him, "What should we do to you to make the sea calm down for us?"

¹²Jonah said to them, "Pick me up, and throw me into the sea, and then it will calm down. I know it is my fault that this great storm has come on you."

¹³Instead, the men tried to row the ship back to the land, but they could not, because the sea was becoming more stormy.

¹⁴So the men cried to the LORD, "LORD, please don't let us die because of this man's life; please don't think we are guilty of killing an innocent person. LORD, you have caused all this to happen; you wanted it this way." ¹⁵So they picked up Jonah and threw him into the sea, and the sea became calm. ¹⁶Then they began to fear the LORD very much; they offered a sacrifice to the LORD and made promises to him.

¹⁷The LORD caused a big fish to swallow Jonah, and Jonah was inside the fish three days and three nights.

DEVOTION

CARL WAS A BIG GUY with a big voice. He wrestled and played football—the types of activities that big boys do—but his friends urged him to join the chorus. And even though he became a soloist in high school and later studied at the Shenandoah Conservatory of Music, Carl never pursued a musical career.

Instead, Carl drove a truck by day and worked as a bounty hunter at night. But he never stopped singing in his truck, especially the opera arias that he loved.

On a single day, three people told him to get smart and follow his destiny as a singer. The first was a lady who heard his singing in the truck. The second was his partner in the bounty hunting business who told him to move to New York. The third was his father, who said, "You know what you're supposed to do and you're not doing it."

Carl moved to New York, but once he arrived, he again settled into driving a truck. It took him four years to work up the nerve to sing one night at a Greenwich Village restaurant with singing waiters. In the audience was a man who offered Carl a chance at the opera's apprentice program.

Fourteen years later, Carl has been around the world, singing with major operas in Europe and with the New York Metropolitan Opera. He sang "O Holy Night" at the White House Christmas tree lighting. He made a triumphant return to the Santa Fe Opera, where he related his unique story to the local paper.

"You know what you're supposed to do and you're not doing it." Those could have been God's words to Jonah. Jonah knew his mission was in Nineveh, but he fled in the opposite direction on a boat. It took a detour in the belly of a fish to get his attention.

How many of us need to hear that same message?

THOUGHTS TO PONDER

What is your mission? What is your talent? And most importantly, are you running toward God or away from him?

PRAYER

God, reveal to us your paths and bless us as we walk in them. Help us to always run toward your will for our lives, never away from it. Amen.

Priorities on a Lifeboat

JONAH 3:3–10; 4:5–11

³So Jonah obeyed the LORD and got up and went to Nineveh. It was a very large city; just to walk across it took a person three days. ⁴After Jonah had entered the city and walked for one day, he preached to the people, saying, "After forty days, Nineveh will be destroyed!"

⁵The people of Nineveh believed God. They announced that they would fast for a while, and they put on rough cloth to show their sadness. All the people in the city did this, from the most important to the least important.

⁶When the king of Nineveh heard this news, he got up from his throne, took off his robe, and covered himself with rough cloth and sat in ashes to show how upset he was.

⁷He sent this announcement through Nineveh:

By command of the king and his important men: No person or animal, herd or flock, will be allowed to taste anything. Do not let them eat food or drink water. ⁸But every person and animal should be covered with rough cloth, and people should cry loudly to God. Everyone must turn away from evil living and stop doing harm all the time. ⁹Who knows? Maybe God will change his mind. Maybe he will stop being angry, and then we will not die.

¹⁰When God saw what the people did, that they stopped doing evil, he changed his mind and did not do what he had warned. He did not punish them.

⁵Jonah went out and sat down east of the city. There he made a shelter for himself and sat in the shade, waiting to see what would happen to the city. ⁶The LORD made a plant grow quickly up over Jonah, which gave him shade and helped him to be more comfortable. Jonah was very pleased to have the plant. ⁷But the next day when the sun rose, God sent a worm to attack the plant so that it died.

⁸As the sun rose higher in the sky, God sent a very hot east wind to blow, and the sun became so hot on Jonah's head that he became very weak and wished he were dead. He said, "It is better for me to die than to live."

⁹But God said to Jonah, "Do you think it is right for you to be angry about the plant?"

Jonah answered, "It is right for me to be angry! I am so angry I could die!"

¹⁰And the LORD said, "You are so concerned for that plant even though you did nothing to make it grow. It appeared one day, and the next day it died. ¹¹Then shouldn't I show concern for the great city Nineveh, which has more than one hundred twenty thousand people who do not know right from wrong, and many animals, too?"

DEVOTION

THERE'S A TREND, especially in big-city churches, that is both exciting and frightening. Auditoriums now boast concert stages, huge video screens, and state-of-the art sound systems. Outlying buildings house youth activity centers, counseling centers, and the occasional retirement home. I recently visited a congregation whose facility featured a coffee shop franchise.

While it's exciting to see innovations that reach the non-member, it's frightening to think that all this activity might lead us to fall victim to the same malady as Jonah in this chapter. Check our church budgets. If we're spending more on air-conditioning the gym or blacktopping the parking lot than we are in reaching out to lost souls, we might be imitating Jonah, lounging under the vine.

Jonah was more concerned about his shade than the souls of the people in Nineveh. And when it was taken away, I think God let the sun blaze on Jonah's head to give him a little taste of hell on earth. Still, Jonah didn't get it. One hundred twenty thousand souls in Nineveh, and Jonah mourned the loss of his vine.

Do we get it? Six billion souls on earth, and the main way churches grow is to take members from one another. It's as if churches are in an "arms race" with one another for larger auditoriums and new gyms; meanwhile, this lost world is desperately waiting for the Good News.

Jesus stated his mission simply: to seek and save the lost. The same Savior who said, "Foxes have holes to live in, and the birds have nests, but the Son of Man has no place to rest his head" (Matthew 8:20) didn't worry about the seating during the Sermon on the Mount.

I love large churches and attend one each week. This is not to criticize comfortable places to worship or safe places for our children to gather. I only want us to remember that the church is not a club, it's a lifeboat, and none of us should worry about the comfort of the cushions while there are so many left to rescue.

THOUGHTS TO PONDER

Why do you think God provided the vine to Jonah and then took it away? What are the "vines" we have constructed that take up time and resources from our true mission?

PRAYER

Father, we pray that we will be more concerned with souls than with buildings. Help us to be more concerned with the lost than with our programs. Amen.

Our Offering to God

MICAH 6:6–8

6You say, "What can I bring with me
    when I come before the LORD,
    when I bow before God on high?
Should I come before him with burnt offerings,
    with year-old calves?
7Will the LORD be pleased with a thousand male sheep?
    Will he be pleased with ten thousand rivers of oil?
Should I give my first child for the evil I have done?
    Should I give my very own child for my sin?"
8The LORD has told you, human, what is good;
    he has told you what he wants from you:
to do what is right to other people,
    love being kind to others,
    and live humbly, obeying your God.

DEVOTION

THE OLDER I GET, the harder it is for me to shop for my dad at Christmas. I love him, and I enjoy the task, but I don't exactly relish the challenge.

You see, he's gotten older too, and as he's aged, his world has become smaller. When we were both younger, I could give him tools. He always needed tools to work at his car lot. He also traveled a lot, taking his cars to auction, so he needed coats and luggage, and he always seemed to enjoy the accessories I bought for his truck.

Later, as my dad slowed down, I made sure he had blankets or sweaters to keep him warm. He'd get the first copies of my manuscripts or books, bound nicely and wrapped for the season. I also picked most of his ties, as he always wears a suit to worship or to the all-too-frequent funerals of his friends.

Today, my dad has all he needs. In fact, he'd be happy if all I gave him was more of my time—more than I seem able to give these days. I pray that my work makes him proud, but I know it keeps me from having enough time to go home regularly.

But I still need to give him gifts. It seems to be the least awkward way I know of telling him how much he means to me. So even though the search for the right gift gets more difficult each year, I keep trying because it does me good.

Micah, representing all of Israel, has a big shopping problem. What do you give the one who has everything? How do you repay someone who is the source of all you own?

At the beginning of this chapter, God reminds Micah that he led the people out of slavery and that he saved them from the kings who possessed the land they had been promised. Now it's time for the offerings of thanks.

So here's the list of possibilities Micah comes up with: year-old calves, a thousand rams, ten thousand rivers of oil, and the most costly of all—our first born children.

However, God shows no interest in our extravagant gifts. But the gifts he does want are even more challenging. He wants our lives to be a gift to him. He wants us to live in a way that honors him in a way no mere sacrifice could.

Do what is right to other people. Love being kind to others. Live humbly, obeying your God. Let those be your gifts, God says.

God would say the same to us today. Don't think you can shop for me and somehow satisfy the tremendous debt you have accrued. But walk in my ways, and you'll never worry about that debt again, because the blood of my Son—yes, I gave my firstborn—will continually cleanse you from sin (1 John 1:7).

THOUGHTS TO PONDER

What is the best gift you have ever received? How did it make you feel? How do you compare that feeling to giving a gift?

PRAYER

Father, you've given us such good gifts that we can never repay you. However, help us to live our lives as you would have us live in response to your generosity. Amen.

Too Difficult for God?

LUKE 1:5–25

⁵During the time Herod ruled Judea, there was a priest named Zechariah who belonged to Abijah's group. Zechariah's wife, Elizabeth, came from the family of Aaron. ⁶Zechariah and Elizabeth truly did what God said was good. They did everything the Lord commanded and were without fault in keeping his law. ⁷But they had no children, because Elizabeth could not have a baby, and both of them were very old.

⁸One day Zechariah was serving as a priest before God, because his group was on duty. ⁹According to the custom of the priests, he was chosen by lot to go into the Temple of the Lord and burn incense. ¹⁰There were a great many people outside praying at the time the incense was offered. ¹¹Then an angel of the Lord appeared to Zechariah, standing on the right side of the incense table. ¹²When he saw the angel, Zechariah was startled and frightened. ¹³But the angel said to him, "Zechariah, don't be afraid. God has heard your prayer. Your wife, Elizabeth, will give birth to a son, and you will name him John. ¹⁴He will bring you joy and gladness, and many people will be happy because of his birth. ¹⁵John will be a great man for the Lord. He will never drink wine or beer, and even from birth, he will be filled with the Holy Spirit. ¹⁶He will help many people of Israel return to the Lord their God. ¹⁷He will go before the Lord in spirit and power like Elijah. He will make peace between parents and their children and will bring those who are not obeying God back to the right way of thinking, to make a people ready for the coming of the Lord."

¹⁸Zechariah said to the angel, "How can I know that what you say is true? I am an old man, and my wife is old, too."

¹⁹The angel answered him, "I am Gabriel. I stand before God, who sent me to talk to you and to tell you this good news. ²⁰Now, listen! You will not be able to speak until the day these things happen, because you did not believe what I told you. But they will really happen."

²¹Outside, the people were still waiting for Zechariah and were surprised that he was staying so long in the Temple. ²²When Zechariah came outside, he could not speak to them, and they knew he had seen a vision in the Temple. He could only make signs to them and remained unable to speak. ²³When his time of service at the Temple was finished, he went home.

²⁴Later, Zechariah's wife, Elizabeth, became pregnant and did not go out of her house for five months. Elizabeth said, ²⁵"Look what the Lord has done for me! My people were ashamed of me, but now the Lord has taken away that shame."

DEVOTION

WHAT'S THE MOST unbelievably good news you've ever had? Getting into the college or the job that you wanted? Getting engaged? Landing that promotion you had worked so hard to attain?

For many, the announcement that a baby was on the way was the best news they ever received. I remember exactly where I was and exactly how I reacted when I heard from my wife that I would be a father the following March, now more than twenty-five years ago. Zechariah probably never forgot the announcement of his imminent fatherhood, either. But the happiness of the memory was likely marred by the fact that he doubted the news, even though it was delivered directly by an angel.

What's interesting here is that, as a priest, Zechariah would have known the similar story of Abraham and Sarah found in Genesis 18. Abraham's messengers looked like three men, and after offering them hospitality, Abraham got the word that he and Sarah would have a child within a year, even though they were advanced in age. Sarah laughed to herself at the prospect, but her laughter was heard by the Lord. God's response to her doubt should have been known by Zechariah: "Is anything too hard for the LORD?" (Genesis 18:14).

You of all people know all the great stories, Zechariah. You know that God delivers on his promises, Zechariah, Gabriel said. The writer of Hebrews calls the heroes of the Old Testament a cloud of witnesses (Hebrews 12:1) and Zechariah fell short of their standard in a circumstance far less trying.

Is anything too difficult for the Lord? That's still a valid question today. You see, as long as I think there's something too difficult for him, it's easier to leave that problem out of my prayer life. If I think God can't help my rebellious teens, my irrational boss, my troubled relationship with my spouse, then I won't have the faith to take the problem to him.

"For God all things are possible," Jesus told his followers (Mark 10:27). Do I have the faith of Moses, or the faith of Zechariah when it comes to believing that statement?

THOUGHTS TO PONDER

Have you ever been reluctant to take an issue, an illness for instance, to God because you thought it was impossible? What does that say about our faith? Or our view of God?

PRAYER

Father, we know that your Son has said that all things are possible with you. Help us to take you at your word and ask in faith so that we might receive. Amen.

TAKE GOD AT HIS WORD

LUKE 1:26–45

[26]During Elizabeth's sixth month of pregnancy, God sent the angel Gabriel to Nazareth, a town in Galilee, [27]to a virgin. She was engaged to marry a man named Joseph from the family of David. Her name was Mary. [28]The angel came to her and said, "Greetings! The Lord has blessed you and is with you."

[29]But Mary was very startled by what the angel said and wondered what this greeting might mean.

[30]The angel said to her, "Don't be afraid, Mary; God has shown you his grace. [31]Listen! You will become pregnant and give birth to a son, and you will name him Jesus. [32]He will be great and will be called the Son of the Most High. The Lord God will give him the throne of King David, his ancestor. [33]He will rule over the people of Jacob forever, and his kingdom will never end."

[34]Mary said to the angel, "How will this happen since I am a virgin?"

[35]The angel said to Mary, "The Holy Spirit will come upon you, and the power of the Most High will cover you. For this reason the baby will be holy and will be called the Son of God. [36]Now Elizabeth, your relative, is also pregnant with a son though she is very old. Everyone thought she could not have a baby, but she has been pregnant for six months. [37]God can do anything!"

[38]Mary said, "I am the servant of the Lord. Let this happen to me as you say!" Then the angel went away.

[39]Mary got up and went quickly to a town in the hills of Judea. [40]She came to Zechariah's house and greeted Elizabeth. [41]When Elizabeth heard Mary's greeting, the unborn baby inside her jumped, and Elizabeth was filled with the Holy Spirit. [42]She cried out in a loud voice, "God has blessed you more than any other woman, and he has blessed the baby to which you will give birth. [43]Why has this good thing happened to me, that the mother of my Lord comes to me? [44]When I heard your voice, the baby inside me jumped with joy. [45]You are blessed because you believed that what the Lord said to you would really happen."

DEVOTION

"HOW IS THIS POSSIBLE?" Mary asked. "God can do anything!" Gabriel replied. And Mary responded in faith: "Let this happen to me as you say!"

When you think of the circumstances, this is a remarkable exchange. Mary, who had never had sexual relations, is told she is to give birth to a son. And not just any son, but the Son of God, the occupier of the throne of David, the one the descendants of David had anticipated through generations of captivity and occupation.

Notice that Elizabeth immediately realized that Mary was carrying the baby who was to be her Lord. She went on to say that Mary would be blessed "because you believed that what the Lord said to you would really happen."

What would life be like if all of us who claim to be believers in God carried this attitude around with us all the time? How blessed would our lives be if we believed God's words as readily as Mary did and acted accordingly? Look at these words from the first recorded sermon of Jesus:

> [25]"So I tell you, don't worry about the food or drink you need to live, or about the clothes you need for your body. Life is more than food, and the body is more than clothes. [26]Look at the birds in the air. They don't plant or harvest or store food in barns, but your heavenly Father feeds them. And you know that you are worth much more than the birds. [27]You cannot add any time to your life by worrying about it.
>
> [28]"And why do you worry about clothes? Look at how the lilies in the field grow. They don't work or make clothes for themselves. [29]But I tell you that even Solomon with his riches was not dressed as beautifully as one of these flowers. [30]God clothes the grass in the field, which is alive today but tomorrow is thrown into the fire. So you can be even more sure that God will clothe you. Don't have so little faith!" (Matthew 6:25–30)

He could have said, "Be more like my mother. Take God at his word, and trust him to work out the details."

THOUGHTS TO PONDER

Have you, like Mary, ever asked God, "How will this happen?" Do you think the things that happen in life are merely coincidental, or accomplished by the hand of God? How can we know?

PRAYER

Father, thank you for the wonderful faith of Mary who took you at your word and blessed the entire world through the Son she brought into this world. Amen.

Big Promises

LUKE 1:39–66

³⁹Mary got up and went quickly to a town in the hills of Judea. ⁴⁰She came to Zechariah's house and greeted Elizabeth. ⁴¹When Elizabeth heard Mary's greeting, the unborn baby inside her jumped, and Elizabeth was filled with the Holy Spirit. ⁴²She cried out in a loud voice, "God has blessed you more than any other woman, and he has blessed the baby to which you will give birth. ⁴³Why has this good thing happened to me, that the mother of my Lord comes to me? ⁴⁴When I heard your voice, the baby inside me jumped with joy. ⁴⁵You are blessed because you believed that what the Lord said to you would really happen."

⁴⁶Then Mary said,

"My soul praises the Lord;
⁴⁷   my heart rejoices in God my Savior,
⁴⁸because he has shown his concern for his humble servant girl.
From now on, all people will say that I am blessed,
⁴⁹   because the Powerful One has done great things for me.
      His name is holy.
⁵⁰God will show his mercy forever and ever
      to those who worship and serve him.
⁵¹He has done mighty deeds by his power.
      He has scattered the people who are proud
      and think great things about themselves.
⁵²He has brought down rulers from their thrones
      and raised up the humble.
⁵³He has filled the hungry with good things
      and sent the rich away with nothing.
⁵⁴He has helped his servant, the people of Israel,
      remembering to show them mercy
⁵⁵as he promised to our ancestors,
      to Abraham and to his children forever."

⁵⁶Mary stayed with Elizabeth for about three months and then returned home.

⁵⁷When it was time for Elizabeth to give birth, she had a boy. ⁵⁸Her neighbors and relatives heard how good the Lord was to her, and they rejoiced with her.

⁵⁹When the baby was eight days old, they came to circumcise him. They wanted to name him Zechariah because this was his father's name, ⁶⁰but his mother said, "No! He will be named John."

⁶¹The people said to Elizabeth, "But no one in your family has this name." ⁶²Then they made signs to his father to find out what he would like to name him.

⁶³Zechariah asked for a writing tablet and wrote, "His name is John," and everyone was surprised. ⁶⁴Immediately Zechariah could talk again, and he began praising God. ⁶⁵All their neighbors became alarmed, and in all the mountains of Judea people continued talking about all these things. ⁶⁶The people who heard about them wondered, saying, "What will this child be?" because the Lord was with him.

DEVOTION

YOU HAVE TO LIKE the statement of Elizabeth to Mary in the story above. "You are blessed because you believed that what the Lord said to you would really happen."

Each was to have a baby under extraordinary circumstances. Mary was a virgin; Elizabeth was old and believed to be barren. And each was to have an extraordinary child. Mary's would be the Savior of the world and Elizabeth's would get the people ready for the Savior's coming.

Big promises to both. Yet each believed through faith and each accepted her role gladly in bringing the Savior into the world and into his ministry.

What has God told you would really happen? Have you believed Him?

God has promised that if we're faithful to death, a crown is waiting for us in heaven (Revelation 2:10). God has promised if we give to others, we'll receive full measure, and more, in return, (Luke 6:38). God has promised that if we cease our worrying, he will take care of us just like he does the birds of the air (Matthew 6:26–27).

Do we believe him? Do we act like we believe him? Mary believed and was blessed. When we truly believe, we will be blessed as well.

THOUGHTS TO PONDER

How does God create a believing heart? How do we cultivate a spirit of belief in the promises of God so that the blessings of belief rain down on us?

PRAYER

God, you've promised us so many blessings that it strains our belief that you would shower so much mercy on us. Help us to believe, and in our belief to be blessed. Amen.

UNQUESTIONING FAITH

MATTHEW 1:16–25

¹⁶Jacob was the father of Joseph.
Joseph was the husband of Mary,
and Mary was the mother of Jesus.
Jesus is called the Christ.

¹⁷So there were fourteen generations from Abraham to David. And there were fourteen generations from David until the people were taken to Babylon. And there were fourteen generations from the time when the people were taken to Babylon until Christ was born.

¹⁸This is how the birth of Jesus Christ came about. His mother Mary was engaged to marry Joseph, but before they married, she learned she was pregnant by the power of the Holy Spirit. ¹⁹Because Mary's husband, Joseph, was a good man, he did not want to disgrace her in public, so he planned to divorce her secretly.

²⁰While Joseph thought about these things, an angel of the Lord came to him in a dream. The angel said, "Joseph, descendant of David, don't be afraid to take Mary as your wife, because the baby in her is from the Holy Spirit. ²¹She will give birth to a son, and you will name him Jesus, because he will save his people from their sins."

²²All this happened to bring about what the Lord had said through the prophet: ²³"The virgin will be pregnant. She will have a son, and they will name him Immanuel," which means "God is with us."

²⁴When Joseph woke up, he did what the Lord's angel had told him to do. Joseph took Mary as his wife, ²⁵but he did not have sexual relations with her until she gave birth to the son. And Joseph named him Jesus.

DEVOTION

THEY STOOD IN A LONG LINE without realizing they were even in it. Each one, from Abraham to Joseph, a total of forty-two men, carried the promise of a Messiah forward. But none had the role that Joseph did.

Engagements at the time of Joseph and Mary were binding agreements. Breaking it required a divorce, not unlike a marriage. Any breach of fidelity during an engagement was considered adultery and the guilty party could be put to death.

Mary's pregnancy created a predicament for Joseph. Being an upright man, he knew he wasn't the father of the child. But to divorce Mary would disgrace her at best and put her life in jeopardy at worst. But while he was pondering his situation, Joseph was visited by an angel in a dream.

And even though the origin of the baby Mary was carrying was explained to him, Joseph still had a difficult circumstance. He would have to bear the insinuating remarks about Mary's pregnancy knowing both he and she were innocent of wrongdoing. He was a simple carpenter, engaged to the woman he loved. Who could ask him to bear this burden?

God could, and God did. God looked at Joseph and said, in essence, "Help me to fulfill prophecy and bring my Son into the world."

His name would be Jesus, meaning "salvation," God said. The angel gave him an additional name, Immanuel, meaning "God is with us."

Help me bring salvation to the world, God asked Joseph. Help me bring a part of me to people who need it badly. Don't think of your own circumstances, Joseph, think of a world without a Savior.

He asks the same of us today. And like Joseph, his request can upset our comfortable worlds. Take his name to the nations. Be light and salt in a world which needs it. Get out of my comfort zone and love my enemies, do good to those who persecute me.

It's never comfortable taking the name of God where it hasn't been proclaimed, but it's always rewarding. The story tells us that Joseph woke up and did what he was requested to do. Perhaps that's a good example for all of us today.

THOUGHTS TO PONDER

What does Joseph's willingness to continue with the engagement tell you about his personal characteristics? Knowing that each of us plays a part in bringing Jesus and the Good News into unreached parts of the world, what is your role?

PRAYER

Father, help us model the unquestioning faith of Joseph when we hear your voice in our lives. Amen.

OPPORTUNITIES OR OBSTACLES?

LUKE 2:1-21

2At that time, Augustus Caesar sent an order that all people in the countries under Roman rule must list their names in a register. ²This was the first registration; it was taken while Quirinius was governor of Syria. ³And all went to their own towns to be registered.

⁴So Joseph left Nazareth, a town in Galilee, and went to the town of Bethlehem in Judea, known as the town of David. Joseph went there because he was from the family of David. ⁵Joseph registered with Mary, to whom he was engaged and who was now pregnant. ⁶While they were in Bethlehem, the time came for Mary to have the baby, ⁷and she gave birth to her first son. Because there were no rooms left in the inn, she wrapped the baby with pieces of cloth and laid him in a feeding trough.

⁸That night, some shepherds were in the fields nearby watching their sheep. ⁹Then an angel of the Lord stood before them. The glory of the Lord was shining around them, and they became very frightened. ¹⁰The angel said to them, "Do not be afraid. I am bringing you good news that will be a great joy to all the people. ¹¹Today your Savior was born in the town of David. He is Christ, the Lord. ¹²This is how you will know him: You will find a baby wrapped in pieces of cloth and lying in a feeding box."

¹³Then a very large group of angels from heaven joined the first angel, praising God and saying:

¹⁴"Give glory to God in heaven,
    and on earth let there be peace among the people who please God."

¹⁵When the angels left them and went back to heaven, the shepherds said to each other, "Let's go to Bethlehem. Let's see this thing that has happened which the Lord has told us about."

¹⁶So the shepherds went quickly and found Mary and Joseph and the baby, who was lying in a feeding trough. ¹⁷When they had seen him, they told what the angels had said about this child. ¹⁸Everyone was amazed at what the shepherds said to them. ¹⁹But Mary treasured these things and continued to think about them. ²⁰Then the shepherds went back to their sheep, praising God and thanking him for everything they had seen and heard. It had been just as the angel had told them.

²¹When the baby was eight days old, he was circumcised and was named Jesus, the name given by the angel before the baby began to grow inside Mary.

DEVOTION

THE CHURCH ORGAN was out of commission and the midnight Christmas Eve service was just a few hours away. Without music, the program would be a disaster, so Father Joseph Mohr set out to write a simple song that could be sung by the congregation without accompaniment.

The idled organist, Franz Gruber, wrote the tune in time for the service in the small Austrian village of Oberndorf in 1818. The result was "Silent Night," perhaps the most beloved Christmas hymn of all time, incorporating several facts from the story above.

What's especially interesting is that if it weren't for the broken organ, we wouldn't have this great Christmas song.

But it's fitting that this beloved Christmas carol was a last-minute replacement. So was the feeding trough. So was the barn. Everything about the situation surrounding Christ's birth was improvised by Joseph and Mary.

Forced to travel in the late stages of Mary's pregnancy by the registration; forced to stay in the stable when there were no rooms at the inn; forced to use the feed box for a cradle. The King, announced to lowly shepherds first, rather than nobles. But it was all a part of God's plan.

There's a lesson here for us as well. We must take the broken organs of our lives and turn them into beautiful songs to Jesus. We need to see inns with no vacancy as opportunities, not obstacles. From lowly circumstances come great results.

THOUGHTS TO PONDER

Why would the first announcement of the birth of Jesus be to shepherds, among the lowliest members of Galilean society? What does this say about the eventual ministry of Jesus?

PRAYER

Father, we know you chose a lowly station in life when you sent your Son. Help us to use his example to take ourselves off the throne of our lives and elevate Jesus instead. Amen.

WAITING FOR THE MESSIAH

LUKE 2:22–40

²²When the time came for Mary and Joseph to do what the law of Moses taught about being made pure, they took Jesus to Jerusalem to present him to the Lord. ²³(It is written in the law of the Lord: "Every firstborn male shall be given to the Lord.") ²⁴Mary and Joseph also went to offer a sacrifice, as the law of the Lord says: "You must sacrifice two doves or two young pigeons."

²⁵In Jerusalem lived a man named Simeon who was a good man and godly. He was waiting for the time when God would take away Israel's sorrow, and the Holy Spirit was in him. ²⁶Simeon had been told by the Holy Spirit that he would not die before he saw the Christ promised by the Lord. ²⁷The Spirit led Simeon to the Temple. When Mary and Joseph brought the baby Jesus to the Temple to do what the law said they must do, ²⁸Simeon took the baby in his arms and thanked God:

²⁹"Now, Lord, you can let me, your servant,
    die in peace as you said.
³⁰With my own eyes I have seen your salvation,
³¹   which you prepared before all people.
³²It is a light for the non-Jewish people to see
    and an honor for your people, the Israelites."

³³Jesus' father and mother were amazed at what Simeon had said about him. ³⁴Then Simeon blessed them and said to Mary, "God has chosen this child to cause the fall and rise of many in Israel. He will be a sign from God that many people will not accept ³⁵so that the thoughts of many will be made known. And the things that will happen will make your heart sad, too."

³⁶There was a prophetess, Anna, from the family of Phanuel in the tribe of Asher. Anna was very old. She had once been married for seven years. ³⁷Then her husband died, and she was a widow for eighty-four years. Anna never left the Temple but worshiped God, going without food and praying day and night. ³⁸Standing there at that time, she thanked God and spoke about Jesus to all who were waiting for God to free Jerusalem.

³⁹When Joseph and Mary had done everything the law of the Lord commanded, they went home to Nazareth, their own town in Galilee. ⁴⁰The little child grew and became strong. He was filled with wisdom, and God's goodness was upon him.

DEVOTION

THE RITUAL REFERRED TO in Luke 2 is the rite of circumcision, required under the Law of Moses for every Jewish boy on the eighth day after birth, as prescribed in Leviticus 12:3. The practice had been initiated by God himself when he made his agreement with Abraham and had been reinstated by the Jews after it was abandoned during their forty years of wandering in the wilderness.

So Mary and Joseph arrived at the Temple to dedicate their newborn to God and to participate in the purification rites for Mary following her childbirth, also as prescribed in the Law. We get a glimpse of their financial circumstances when they chose the two birds as a sacrifice, an allowance made in the Law for those who could not afford a lamb (Leviticus 12:8).

Present in the Temple were two elderly individuals—Simeon and Anna— each of whom was given a message to deliver to the parents. Each of them had a poignant story. Simeon had been allowed to live until he saw the Christ, and that time had finally arrived. Rather than face his inevitable death with gloom, he was overjoyed at the baby he took in his arms, having seen with his ancient eyes the salvation of both Jews and non-Jews alike. The words after his prayer (verse 34) were particularly prescient: Jesus was destined to shake up things in Israel.

Anna was married only seven years before being widowed and had now lived to the age of eighty-four. She was a resident of the Temple, quite likely depending on the sacrifices for her sustenance. She served in a capacity of "prophetess," evidently having the powers to prophesy. With her gifts, she recognized the baby as the one who would "free Jerusalem," that is, establish a spiritual kingdom which could not be toppled by earthly governments.

The theme of the entire passage is fulfillment—fulfillment of the requirements of the Law and fulfillment of promises and scriptural prophecies about the Messiah. Jesus was brought up in a home where the traditions of his people were respected.

THOUGHTS TO PONDER

Anna had lived more than a hundred years anticipating the birth of the Savior. What do you hope to see in your lifetime? What do you hope to accomplish before you die?

PRAYER

Father, we know your Son fulfilled the many prophecies about the Savior. Help us to accept him as the Savior of our lives. Amen.

GIVE GOD YOUR BEST

MATTHEW 2:1–15

1 Jesus was born in the town of Bethlehem in Judea during the time when Herod was king. When Jesus was born, some wise men from the east came to Jerusalem. ²They asked, "Where is the baby who was born to be the king of the Jews? We saw his star in the east and have come to worship him."

³When King Herod heard this, he was troubled, as were all the people in Jerusalem. ⁴Herod called a meeting of all the leading priests and teachers of the law and asked them where the Christ would be born. ⁵They answered, "In the town of Bethlehem in Judea. The prophet wrote about this in the Scriptures:

⁶'But you, Bethlehem, in the land of Judah,
>   are not just an insignificant village in Judah.
> A ruler will come from you
>   who will be like a shepherd for my people Israel.'"   *Micah 5:2*

⁷Then Herod had a secret meeting with the wise men and learned from them the exact time they first saw the star. ⁸He sent the wise men to Bethlehem, saying, "Look carefully for the child. When you find him, come tell me so I can worship him too."

⁹After the wise men heard the king, they left. The star that they had seen in the east went before them until it stopped above the place where the child was. ¹⁰When the wise men saw the star, they were filled with joy. ¹¹They came to the house where the child was and saw him with his mother, Mary, and they bowed down and worshiped him. They opened their gifts and gave him treasures of gold, frankincense, and myrrh. ¹²But God warned the wise men in a dream not to go back to Herod, so they returned to their own country by a different way.

¹³After they left, an angel of the Lord came to Joseph in a dream and said, "Get up! Take the child and his mother and escape to Egypt, because Herod is starting to look for the child so he can kill him. Stay in Egypt until I tell you to return."

¹⁴So Joseph got up and left for Egypt during the night with the child and his mother. ¹⁵And Joseph stayed in Egypt until Herod died. This happened to bring about what the Lord had said through the prophet: "I called my son out of Egypt."

DEVOTION

WHEN YOU LOOK at the list of gifts above, one of the first impressions you get is that guys shouldn't be allowed to buy gifts for baby showers. None of the gifts seemed appropriate for a baby. But they were suited for a king. Why? Because of their value. Each of the choices represented an expensive gift fit for royalty.

God has always wanted and deserved our best gifts. From the days of Abraham, God asked his people for unblemished animals for the altar of sacrifice. When Jesus visited with a rich young man, he asked him to sell everything he owned in order to follow him. He made no apologies in asking for the best.

Yet sacrifice seems like a dated concept today. The pattern seems to be that the more we earn, the less we give.

Following Hurricane Katrina, some of the evacuees were sent to an abandoned military camp near my home. A local church helped them move in. The pastor helped one family who had lost absolutely everything in the floods that engulfed New Orleans. They owed a mortgage on a house that was totally gone and insurance would not pay.

Like other families, this one received an emergency check for $2,000 from the federal government. The next Sunday, the pastor who had worked with the evacuees welcomed this family as they came to visit his congregation. He noticed later in the service that when the offering was passed, the father took two crisp, new hundred-dollar bills out of his pocket and put them in the plate. He had tithed out of his government stipend.

After the service, the pastor tried to tell the man that the church could not accept his money. But the man protested saying, "Don't take away my dignity by not allowing me to give."

Paul told the Corinthians that the Macedonians were giving, even though they had come through a recent severe trial (2 Corinthians 8:2). In fact, they pleaded for the privilege of giving.

Giving like that is hard to fathom, yet totally in line with God's will. Being wealthy has never been a prerequisite for being asked to give to God, who gave us the greatest gift of all.

THOUGHTS TO PONDER

What gifts have you brought to Jesus? What does God expect from each of us?

PRAYER

Father, we pray that we will always be grateful recipients of your gifts and that, like the wise men above, we will give you only the best. Amen.

SAVED BY HIS BLOOD

MATTHEW 2:1–16

2 Jesus was born in the town of Bethlehem in Judea during the time when Herod was king. When Jesus was born, some wise men from the east came to Jerusalem. ²They asked, "Where is the baby who was born to be the king of the Jews? We saw his star in the east and have come to worship him."

³When King Herod heard this, he was troubled, as were all the people in Jerusalem. ⁴Herod called a meeting of all the leading priests and teachers of the law and asked them where the Christ would be born. ⁵They answered, "In the town of Bethlehem in Judea. The prophet wrote about this in the Scriptures:

⁶'But you, Bethlehem, in the land of Judah,

are not just an insignificant village in Judah.

A ruler will come from you

who will be like a shepherd for my people Israel.'"   *Micah 5:2*

⁷Then Herod had a secret meeting with the wise men and learned from them the exact time they first saw the star. ⁸He sent the wise men to Bethlehem, saying, "Look carefully for the child. When you find him, come tell me so I can worship him too."

⁹After the wise men heard the king, they left. The star that they had seen in the east went before them until it stopped above the place where the child was. ¹⁰When the wise men saw the star, they were filled with joy. ¹¹They came to the house where the child was and saw him with his mother, Mary, and they bowed down and worshiped him. They opened their gifts and gave him treasures of gold, frankincense, and myrrh. ¹²But God warned the wise men in a dream not to go back to Herod, so they returned to their own country by a different way.

¹³After they left, an angel of the Lord came to Joseph in a dream and said, "Get up! Take the child and his mother and escape to Egypt, because Herod is starting to look for the child so he can kill him. Stay in Egypt until I tell you to return."

¹⁴So Joseph got up and left for Egypt during the night with the child and his mother. ¹⁵And Joseph stayed in Egypt until Herod died. This happened to bring about what the Lord had said through the prophet: "I called my son out of Egypt."

¹⁶When Herod saw that the wise men had tricked him, he was furious. So he gave an order to kill all the baby boys in Bethlehem and in the surrounding area who were two years old or younger.

DEVOTION

IN THE MIDDLE of the seventeenth century, "tulipomania" struck Europe—the discovery of the tulip flower, seemingly overnight, by an entire continent of garden-loving people. Suddenly, everyone had to have them. With bulbs imported from the Netherlands by investors, endless fields of tulips suddenly burgeoned on various countrysides of the European continent to be sold in the cities.

But the speculators soon discovered their investment had decreased by up to 95 percent due to overplanting. To recover, the importers sent mercenary soldiers into the fields to stomp down the emerging tulips, sending up the prices of those that remained unharmed, an act captured in a famous painting by Romereo entitled "The Tulip Stompers."

Put yourself in the position of these soldiers. How would it feel to be a trained soldier out in the fields stomping down tulips? Killing delicate flowers for no good reason at all?

Now put yourself in the position of the soldiers who were under orders from Herod to kill every male baby under the age of two. No exceptions. No mercy. All done in brutal haste so that none got away. Except one—the Son of God—taken to safety by his mother and father.

Now put yourself in yet another situation: how would you feel upon the discovery that your sins killed that perfect Lamb of God who earlier escaped the wrath of Herod? That your sins had actually condemned him to a worse fate? But how does it feel to know that the very blood you helped to shed is your means of redemption?

Millions have been killed from various causes—wars, famines, etc.—but only one death, and one Resurrection matters eternally to you and to me.

THOUGHTS TO PONDER

How successful do you think Herod's program of infanticide was? Do you think Jesus grew up as the only boy of his age in the Bethlehem area? Might some babies have been hidden, like Moses so many years before?

PRAYER

God, we can't understand the unspeakable cruelty that Herod inflicted in his attempt to thwart your plan, but we know that Satan does the same today. Help us to always find the way of escape in every situation. Amen.

In My Father's House

LUKE 2:41–52

⁴¹Every year Jesus' parents went to Jerusalem for the Passover Feast. ⁴²When he was twelve years old, they went to the feast as they always did. ⁴³After the feast days were over, they started home. The boy Jesus stayed behind in Jerusalem, but his parents did not know it. ⁴⁴Thinking that Jesus was with them in the group, they traveled for a whole day. Then they began to look for him among their family and friends. ⁴⁵When they did not find him, they went back to Jerusalem to look for him there. ⁴⁶After three days they found Jesus sitting in the Temple with the teachers, listening to them and asking them questions. ⁴⁷All who heard him were amazed at his understanding and answers. ⁴⁸When Jesus' parents saw him, they were astonished. His mother said to him, "Son, why did you do this to us? Your father and I were very worried about you and have been looking for you."

⁴⁹Jesus said to them, "Why were you looking for me? Didn't you know that I must be in my Father's house?" ⁵⁰But they did not understand the meaning of what he said.

⁵¹Jesus went with them to Nazareth and was obedient to them. But his mother kept in her mind all that had happened. ⁵²Jesus became wiser and grew physically. People liked him, and he pleased God.

Devotion

THE ONLY GLIMPSE we have into the childhood of Jesus comes from this passage describing an incident that occurred when he was a twelve-year-old boy. From other scriptures we know Jesus had brothers and sisters. From Joseph's absence in stories where Mary is present, such as the wedding in Cana (John 2:1–11) or the moment at the foot of the cross when Jesus asked the apostle John to care for Mary (John 19:26–27), we infer that he may have died before the adult ministry of Jesus.

So what do we know from this brief story?

First, Jesus was raised in a home that kept the traditions of God's chosen people, the Jews. The Passover was the major event in the Jewish calendar. At the time of the New Testament, it is estimated that as many as two million of the faithful made their way to Jerusalem as commanded in the Law (Deuteronomy 16:16) for the celebration. Entire families traveled together, allowing for Jesus' absence to go undetected when his mother and father left Jerusalem. They assumed Jesus was somewhere in the group of travelers.

The Passover was the Jews' commemoration of their deliverance from slavery in Egypt. After sending numerous plagues on the Egyptian king and his people, God sent the angel of death to kill every firstborn boy in the land. Only in those families who had killed the sacrificial lamb, and sprinkled its blood on the doorposts, did the death angel "pass over" the house and not kill the firstborn male. By Jesus' day, the Passover observance was combined with the Festival of Unleavened Bread, which commemorated the haste with which the Israelites had left Egypt—so fast the bread had no time to rise.

Second, we see that Jesus was knowledgeable in the Law, and curious about it as well. The text indicates that he was listening and asking questions as well as answering them. This is in keeping with the teaching style of the day—a series of unending questions between student and teacher designed to lead the student to deduce the answer on his own. Jesus was probably both asking and answering questions in this way, amazing the teachers of the law. His age is also significant here. He was not even required to go to Jerusalem for Passover until he reached the age of thirteen, yet there he was, a boy in the traditional sense, showing deep knowledge of the Law.

Third, we see Jesus as the obedient son—both to his earthly mother and father and to his heavenly Father. He obeyed the call of God to stay in the Temple and learn from the scholars, and the last verse tells us that he was obedient to his parents as well. As he grew, he became the type of boy people liked, while at the same time pleasing God.

The fact that he grew up in Nazareth, a small town of no repute, was a source of amazement for Nathanael, one of the twelve men Jesus called to follow him (John 1:46). But it was the ideal place for Jesus to grow physically strong and spiritually wise at the same time. His small-town roots helped him relate to the types of people who were drawn to his message in the years that followed.

THOUGHTS TO PONDER

How do you think Jesus acquired his understanding of the Law? Was it the result of hours of study or was it a miracle? Where do you think Jesus acquired his abilities to teach like no one else before him?

PRAYER

Father, may we be always hungry, like Jesus, to learn more about your Word, and may it be said of us that we are pleasing to you. Amen.

Preparing for Another's Success

MARK 1:1–15

1 This is the beginning of the Good News about Jesus Christ, the Son of God, ²as the prophet Isaiah wrote:

"I will send my messenger ahead of you,
who will prepare your way." *Malachi 3:1*

³"This is a voice of one
who calls out in the desert:
'Prepare the way for the Lord.
Make the road straight for him.'" *Isaiah 40:3*

⁴John was baptizing people in the desert and preaching a baptism of changed hearts and lives for the forgiveness of sins. ⁵All the people from Judea and Jerusalem were going out to him. They confessed their sins and were baptized by him in the Jordan River. ⁶John wore clothes made from camel's hair, had a leather belt around his waist, and ate locusts and wild honey. ⁷This is what John preached to the people: "There is one coming after me who is greater than I; I am not good enough even to kneel down and untie his sandals. ⁸I baptize you with water, but he will baptize you with the Holy Spirit."

⁹At that time Jesus came from the town of Nazareth in Galilee and was baptized by John in the Jordan River. ¹⁰Immediately, as Jesus was coming up out of the water, he saw heaven open. The Holy Spirit came down on him like a dove, ¹¹and a voice came from heaven: "You are my Son, whom I love, and I am very pleased with you."

¹²Then the Spirit sent Jesus into the desert. ¹³He was in the desert forty days and was tempted by Satan. He was with the wild animals, and the angels came and took care of him.

¹⁴After John was put in prison, Jesus went into Galilee, preaching the Good News from God. ¹⁵He said, "The right time has come. The kingdom of God is near. Change your hearts and lives and believe the Good News!"

Devotion

WHEN ROGER BANNISTER prepared to become the first human to break the four-minute barrier for the mile run, he enlisted the help of two of his Oxford classmates, each of them world-class runners as well. His plan was for them to act as "forerunners" for him, setting a pace that would help him stay on pace for his goal, then stepping off the track at the appropriate time and allowing Roger to do what many experts claimed couldn't be done.

The first forerunner set the pace for two laps, or a half-mile, and stepped off the track with Roger two seconds ahead of pace. The second set the pace for the third lap and stepped off the track leaving Roger one second ahead of pace. Roger finished the race in just over 3:59, breaking the world record and the four-minute mark at the same time. When he took his victory lap, Roger included his two forerunners, running with lifted hands around the track.

The Gospel of Mark begins with the story of John, the forerunner of Jesus. Luke tells us about his birth and Matthew records a brief but fiery sermon from him. Like the other writers, Mark points out that John's role was prophesied and that he was indeed the one who pointed the way to Jesus.

The baptism of Jesus marks the point where John steps off the track, as it were. In fact, before this section is finished, Mark tells us that John was imprisoned after falling out of favor with King Herod. He didn't get out alive.

Do you have the attitude of John? Can you prepare the way for someone else's success? It's been said that a good leader picks people better than him- or herself and then helps them do their jobs. Some of us are called to be leaders; others of us are called to be followers. Most of us do both in our various roles.

John fulfilled his role of preparing the people for Christ and then putting the spotlight on Jesus. What better legacy could any of us have?

Thoughts to Ponder

What personality traits must John have had to fulfill his role as the predecessor of Jesus? How challenging is it to take a lesser role in the church to prepare the way for others who are better equipped take the lead roles?

Prayer

God, you've given us various talents to further your work in the world. Help us to accept whatever role we're given and to do it to the best of our ability. Amen.

Don't Play the Enemy's Game

MATTHEW 4:1–11

4 Then the Spirit led Jesus into the desert to be tempted by the devil. [2]Jesus fasted for forty days and nights. After this, he was very hungry. [3]The devil came to Jesus to tempt him, saying, "If you are the Son of God, tell these rocks to become bread."

[4]Jesus answered, "It is written in the Scriptures, 'A person lives not on bread alone, but by everything God says.'"

[5]Then the devil led Jesus to the holy city of Jerusalem and put him on a high place of the Temple. [6]The devil said, "If you are the Son of God, jump down, because it is written in the Scriptures:

'He has put his angels in charge of you.
    They will catch you in their hands
so that you will not hit your foot on a rock.'"   *Psalm 91:11–12*

[7]Jesus answered him, "It also says in the Scriptures, 'Do not test the Lord your God.'"

[8]Then the devil led Jesus to the top of a very high mountain and showed him all the kingdoms of the world and all their splendor. [9]The devil said, "If you will bow down and worship me, I will give you all these things."

[10]Jesus said to the devil, "Go away from me, Satan! It is written in the Scriptures, 'You must worship the Lord your God and serve only him.'"

[11]So the devil left Jesus, and angels came and took care of him.

Devotion

WHEN I WAS A JUNIOR in high school, I played on a basketball team that went 32-4. Three of the losses were to the same team—by one, two and three points—a team that went on to win a Texas public school state championship. This story is about that fourth loss.

We dispatched teams nightly with ease. We won a private school state championship. We won five of the six tournaments we entered.

But this is the game I remember. We were playing a game against a team about twenty miles from my hometown. We scheduled this team every year, and no one could remember the last time we had lost to them—home, away, or neutral court. We owned this team.

But on that night, we were flat. We went through the motions of playing a game, but we played flat. And as the clock wound down, they made the shots we missed and beat us by three points. The gym floor erupted with fans; having to run through them to leave the court was an added insult to the outcome of the evening. We hung our heads and ran for the safety of the locker room.

Our van ride home was in total silence, unlike the many nights we joked and laughed and replayed the night's game. Coach didn't say a word until the van stopped and then he only announced the time of the next day's practice. Since we all knew the time, we could read between the lines that he wanted us to expect the practice to be a serious one.

Why had we lost? We had played their game on their court. We were used to running; they walked the ball up the court. We took quick shots; they were patient. We walked right into their trap and paid the price when we failed to adjust to the schemes of our opponents.

Satan had a game plan to trip up Jesus. He planned to prey on his physical hunger. If that failed, he would get him to sin by testing God to catch him in a plunge from the top of the Temple. And in possibly the greatest temptation of all, Satan offered Jesus the opportunity to rule over the world without the painful death on the cross that would eventually accomplish the same purpose.

All of the things that Satan offered—freedom from hunger, protection by the Father, and lordship over the world—eventually came to Jesus without giving in to Satan's temptations. He met Satan and won. And in every test, Jesus replied with Scripture. He was ready for the game plan of Satan.

Years later, I coached basketball teams at the Christian school where my children attended. I emphasized to them the importance of being prepared for whatever the opponent threw at them—on the court and off.

THOUGHTS TO PONDER

When Satan tempts you, what does he dangle in front of you? Power? Money? Fleshly desires? How do we prepare for his assaults so we're not taken by surprise? How do we stick to our game plan?

PRAYER

Father, we see that even Jesus was tempted by Satan. Help us to be neither surprised nor disappointed at his tactics, but help us to be ever vigilant. Amen.

THE SACRIFICE
SEEMS LIGHTER

MATTHEW 5:1–16

5 When Jesus saw the crowds, he went up on a hill and sat down. His followers came to him, ²and he began to teach them, saying:

³"They are blessed who realize their spiritual poverty,
for the kingdom of heaven belongs to them.
⁴They are blessed who grieve,
for God will comfort them.
⁵They are blessed who are humble,
for the whole earth will be theirs.
⁶They are blessed who hunger and thirst after justice,
for they will be satisfied.
⁷They are blessed who show mercy to others,
for God will show mercy to them.
⁸They are blessed whose thoughts are pure,
for they will see God.
⁹They are blessed who work for peace,
for they will be called God's children.
¹⁰They are blessed who are persecuted for doing good,
for the kingdom of heaven belongs to them.

¹¹"People will insult you and hurt you. They will lie and say all kinds of evil things about you because you follow me. But when they do, you will be blessed. ¹²Rejoice and be glad, because you have a great reward waiting for you in heaven. People did the same evil things to the prophets who lived before you.

¹³"You are the salt of the earth. But if the salt loses its salty taste, it cannot be made salty again. It is good for nothing, except to be thrown out and walked on.

¹⁴"You are the light that gives light to the world. A city that is built on a hill cannot be hidden. ¹⁵And people don't hide a light under a bowl. They put it on a lampstand so the light shines for all the people in the house. ¹⁶In the same way, you should be a light for other people. Live so that they will see the good things you do and will praise your Father in heaven.

DEVOTION

KNOW YOUR AUDIENCE, speakers are taught. No one was a better master of this than Jesus. "A farmer went out to plant his seed . . ." He would begin a parable. "A woman lost a coin . . ." Everyone related.

When Jesus saw the crowds and climbed the mountain for his longest recorded sermon, He knew his audience. Look at the way they were dressed, sitting in the dirt. Hardly any had provisions for lunch. Not exactly the religious elite.

So he started with a list that they could relate to: the poor in spirit, the mourners, the meek, the religiously hungry, the merciful, the pure, the peacemakers. In short, the backbones of society that no one applauds for the trials they face and the lives they lead. The ones far more likely to be victims than perpetrators of the many evils in Jewish society under Roman rule.

In this passage, Jesus recognizes the quiet heroism of a faithful life and lists its rewards: a place in heaven, comfort, spiritual satisfaction, reciprocal mercy, a chance to see God and to be called his children.

But there's a caveat. If you lead a faithful life, you may be persecuted. If so, consider yourselves blessed. You're in company with the prophets and you're headed for an eternal reward.

Having connected with the crowd, Jesus had them ready to listen to the lifestyle changes they needed to make. Be salt. Be light. No more lust. Turn the other cheek. Go the second mile.

Because once you identify with the reward and the Giver of it, the sacrifice seems lighter.

THOUGHTS TO PONDER

Which of the beatitudes most describes you and why? Which one or ones do you need the most work on and what one step can you take today to begin?

PRAYER

Father, we see in these words a picture of what you want your children to be. Lord, please mold us until the light of the world shines through us. Amen.

Welcome at His Table

LUKE 5:1–11, 27–32

5 One day while Jesus was standing beside Lake Galilee, many people were pressing all around him to hear the word of God. ²Jesus saw two boats at the shore of the lake. The fishermen had left them and were washing their nets. ³Jesus got into one of the boats, the one that belonged to Simon, and asked him to push off a little from the land. Then Jesus sat down and continued to teach the people from the boat.

⁴When Jesus had finished speaking, he said to Simon, "Take the boat into deep water, and put your nets in the water to catch some fish."

⁵Simon answered, "Master, we worked hard all night trying to catch fish, and we caught nothing. But you say to put the nets in the water, so I will." ⁶When the fishermen did as Jesus told them, they caught so many fish that the nets began to break. ⁷They called to their partners in the other boat to come and help them. They came and filled both boats so full that they were almost sinking.

⁸When Simon Peter saw what had happened, he bowed down before Jesus and said, "Go away from me, Lord. I am a sinful man!" ⁹He and the other fishermen were amazed at the many fish they caught, as were ¹⁰James and John, the sons of Zebedee, Simon's partners.

Jesus said to Simon, "Don't be afraid. From now on you will fish for people." ¹¹When the men brought their boats to the shore, they left everything and followed Jesus.

²⁷After this, Jesus went out and saw a tax collector named Levi sitting in the tax collector's booth. Jesus said to him, "Follow me!" ²⁸So Levi got up, left everything, and followed him.

²⁹Then Levi gave a big dinner for Jesus at his house. Many tax collectors and other people were eating there, too. ³⁰But the Pharisees and the men who taught the law for the Pharisees began to complain to Jesus' followers, "Why do you eat and drink with tax collectors and sinners?"

³¹Jesus answered them, "It is not the healthy people who need a doctor, but the sick. ³²I have not come to invite good people but sinners to change their hearts and lives."

Devotion

WHAT DOES IT SAY about Jesus that rough fishermen would recognize him as Lord and leave their nets to follow him? What does it say when a tax collector would walk away from the lucrative tax franchise he had purchased from the Romans and follow Jesus?

Simon, who was later called Peter by Christ, recognized him as "Master," a term of respect for a Jewish teacher, before the miraculous catch of fish had even occurred. He recognized him as "Lord" after the haul, which was so great they had to ask for help from a nearby boat.

There was something about Jesus that commanded respect. Scripture tells us it wasn't his physical presence. But Scripture also records that even the Temple guards sent to arrest Jesus by the leading priest and Pharisees replied with reluctance: "The words he says are greater than the words of any other person who has ever spoken" (John 7:46). Matthew tells us that crowds were amazed at his teachings because he spoke as one "who had authority," unlike the teachers of the law (Matthew 7:28–29).

Perhaps it was his bearing, his voice, his way of turning a phrase. But for whatever reason, twelve men left their livelihoods to follow him. And according to his critics he was none too choosy about those he called.

Two bold brothers, he called the "sons of thunder." There were fishermen, the tax collector, the original skeptic, Nathanael, and his excited brother Philip. None was a scholar of the law. None was a member of the clergy. In fact, one, Judas, was rotten to the core, always with his eye on the group's purse and later the one to betray Jesus.

What does it say about Jesus? That he can use me. That I am welcome at his table. If he dined with the likes of Levi, who had been the curse of his own people for years levying the Romans' taxes, surely I'm welcome at his table as well.

He tells us that he still stands at the door and knocks today (Revelation 3:20). Listen and open the door of your heart to him.

THOUGHTS TO PONDER

If Jesus was gathering his apostles today, what professions would they come from? Why do you think that? What qualities do you think Jesus saw in these men apart from their occupations?

PRAYER

God, you've shown that you can use good people from all backgrounds. Take our talents and use them for your purposes. Amen.

THE HUMBLE MESSIAH

JOHN 1:35-51

[35]The next day John was there again with two of his followers. [36]When he saw Jesus walking by, he said, "Look, the Lamb of God!"

[37]The two followers heard John say this, so they followed Jesus. [38]When Jesus turned and saw them following him, he asked, "What are you looking for?"

They said, "Rabbi, where are you staying?" ("Rabbi" means "Teacher.")

[39]He answered, "Come and see." So the two men went with Jesus and saw where he was staying and stayed there with him that day. It was about four o-clock in the afternoon.

[40]One of the two men who followed Jesus after they heard John speak about him was Andrew, Simon Peter's brother. [41]The first thing Andrew did was to find his brother Simon and say to him, "We have found the Messiah." ("Messiah" means "Christ.")

[42]Then Andrew took Simon to Jesus. Jesus looked at him and said, "You are Simon son of John. You will be called Cephas." ("Cephas" means "Peter.")

[43]The next day Jesus decided to go to Galilee. He found Philip and said to him, "Follow me."

[44]Philip was from the town of Bethsaida, where Andrew and Peter lived. [45]Philip found Nathanael and told him, "We have found the man that Moses wrote about in the law, and the prophets also wrote about him. He is Jesus, the son of Joseph, from Nazareth."

[46]But Nathanael said to Philip, "Can anything good come from Nazareth?"

Philip answered, "Come and see."

[47]As Jesus saw Nathanael coming toward him, he said, "Here is truly an Israelite. There is nothing false in him."

[48]Nathanael asked, "How do you know me?"

Jesus answered, "I saw you when you were under the fig tree, before Philip told you about me."

[49]Then Nathanael said to Jesus, "Teacher, you are the Son of God; you are the King of Israel."

[50]Jesus said to Nathanael, "Do you believe simply because I told you I saw you under the fig tree? You will see greater things than that." [51]And Jesus said to them, "I tell you the truth, you will all see heaven open and 'angels of God going up and coming down on the Son of Man."

Devotion

ONE PHENOMENON COMMON to small towns is the billboard or painted water tower that announces the "favorite son" or "favorite daughter" who managed to emerge from the clutches of the small community and gain fame.

There may be signs proclaiming that a Miss America grew up here. One or two might brag about country-western singers who long ago left for Nashville. Then there are the "Friday night heroes," the listing of teams who won the hearts of the community by being the best in the state in some sport.

If the entire significant output of a town can be reduced to a billboard or a water tower, it doesn't surprise me that Nathanael wasn't impressed by Philip's claim that the Messiah had come out of a one-stoplight town like Nazareth. Are you kidding me? Surely the Messiah would have a better zip code than Nazareth.

But Philip had seen and heard Jesus, and Nathanael hadn't. Something about the man drew fishermen out of their boats and tax collectors out of their toll booths.

We call Thomas the doubter because he wanted to see the nail prints in Jesus' hands, but Nathanael was the first doubter. It took the miracle of Jesus telling him he had been under a fig tree to get Nathanael's attention, and even then Jesus said, in modern terms, "You haven't seen anything yet."

Paul tells us that the lowly circumstances were Christ's own choice as he left heaven to become flesh (Philippians 2:5). He could have come as a king—there were certainly those who expected that—and he would have drawn larger, adoring crowds. But by coming as a carpenter's son in Nazareth, he found his true followers, and the same principle is true today.

Thoughts to ponder

What do you think it was about Jesus that caused John to immediately recognize his deity? Why would Philip care if Nathanael met Jesus? Have you been a "Philip" to anyone, introducing them to Jesus? What would you tell someone who didn't know Jesus about why they should follow him?

Prayer

Lord, help us to have the spirit we see in this story and to be willing to leave our comfort zones and our routines to go wherever you take us. Amen.

In His Name

JOHN 2:1–11

2 Two days later there was a wedding in the town of Cana in Galilee. Jesus' mother was there, ²and Jesus and his followers were also invited to the wedding. ³When all the wine was gone, Jesus' mother said to him, "They have no more wine."

⁴Jesus answered, "Dear woman, why come to me? My time has not yet come."

⁵His mother said to the servants, "Do whatever he tells you to do."

⁶In that place there were six stone water jars that the Jews used in their washing ceremony. Each jar held about twenty or thirty gallons.

⁷Jesus said to the servants, "Fill the jars with water." So they filled the jars to the top.

⁸Then he said to them, "Now take some out and give it to the master of the feast."

So they took the water to the master. ⁹When he tasted it, the water had become wine. He did not know where the wine came from, but the servants who had brought the water knew. The master of the wedding called the bridegroom ¹⁰and said to him, "People always serve the best wine first. Later, after the guests have been drinking awhile, they serve the cheaper wine. But you have saved the best wine till now."

¹¹So in Cana of Galilee Jesus did his first miracle. There he showed his glory, and his followers believed in him.

Devotion

THE FIRST MIRACLE of Jesus was remarkably understated. First, there was the setting—a small wedding with only the invited guests. Second, there was the reluctance of Jesus—"my time has not yet come." Third, it was done in secret. Even the master of the banquet didn't know the source of the wine.

To have run out of wine was a potentially embarrassing situation for the groom, the host of the wedding. The celebration would often last for days with many guests, and a good host would never run out of food or drink. It would be an insult to his guests. Mary was hoping that Jesus would step in and prevent this source of embarrassment from spoiling the day for the groom.

Why didn't Jesus want the credit for this miracle? He gave us a hint: "My time has not yet come." Interestingly, a man who would demonstrate his mastery of the Law with the teachers in the Temple at age twelve was not yet ready to demonstrate his power over natural law with his friends at a wedding at age thirty. But he does it out of respect for his mother and to keep the groom from embarrassment.

How did Mary know he had the power to turn water into wine? The angel's visitation. The Virgin Birth. The Temple incident when Jesus was twelve were all "kept in her mind" (Luke 2:51). She knew who he was and she knew his powers.

Jesus never performed a miracle to draw a crowd. He performed miracles because he saw the sick hurting. He saw relatives grieving over their dead. He saw the lame, the blind, and the lepers being treated as outcasts.

Did these acts draw a crowd? Scripture tells us so many brought their lame and ill to him for healing that he had to board a boat or go to the mountains to get away.

But Jesus didn't come to end physical disease; he came to end spiritual disease. "It is not the healthy people who need a doctor, but the sick" he said, and he wasn't referring to the physically sick (Matthew 9:12). Miracles were a means to the end of bringing God's message to the lost.

I think there's an analogy today. As Christians, we can run soup kitchens, free clinics, and homeless shelters. But unless it's a means to the end of bringing the less fortunate to Jesus—the very type of people he preferred while he was on earth—then the "miracles" we do are in vain. On the other hand, Jesus said that if we offer even a cup of water in his name, it will be rewarded. We must always ensure that God gets the credit for the good we do in his name.

THOUGHTS TO PONDER

Tradition tells us that Jesus was about thirty years old at the time his ministry started. Why do you think Jesus prepared thirty years for what would be a three year ministry? How do you think Mary knew that the time was right for Jesus to reveal his supernatural power?

PRAYER

God, you sent your Son at just the right moment in history so that word of his ministry could spread throughout the world. Help us to continue that work even today using all the tools you've blessed us with. Amen.

INSTRUCTIVE DISCIPLINE

MATTHEW 21:12-17

¹²Jesus went into the Temple and threw out all the people who were buying and selling there. He turned over the tables of those who were exchanging different kinds of money, and he upset the benches of those who were selling doves. ¹³Jesus said to all the people there, "It is written in the Scriptures, 'My Temple will be called a house for prayer.' But you are changing it into a 'hideout for robbers.'"

¹⁴The blind and crippled people came to Jesus in the Temple, and he healed them. ¹⁵The leading priests and the teachers of the law saw that Jesus was doing wonderful things and that the children were praising him in the Temple, saying, "Praise to the Son of David." All these things made the priests and the teachers of the law very angry.

¹⁶They asked Jesus, "Do you hear the things these children are saying?"

Jesus answered, "Yes. Haven't you read in the Scriptures, 'You have taught children and babies to sing praises'?"

¹⁷Then Jesus left and went out of the city to Bethany, where he spent the night.

JOHN 2:12-17

¹²After this, Jesus went to the town of Capernaum with his mother, brothers, and followers. They stayed there for just a few days. ¹³When it was almost time for the Jewish Passover Feast, Jesus went to Jerusalem. ¹⁴In the Temple he found people selling cattle, sheep, and doves. He saw others sitting at tables, exchanging different kinds of money. ¹⁵Jesus made a whip out of cords and forced all of them, both the sheep and cattle, to leave the Temple. He turned over the tables and scattered the money of those who were exchanging it. ¹⁶Then he said to those who were selling pigeons, "Take these things out of here! Don't make my Father's house a place for buying and selling!"

¹⁷When this happened, the followers remembered what was written in the Scriptures: "My strong love for your Temple completely controls me."

DEVOTION

BY THE DAYS OF JESUS, Temple sacrifices in Jerusalem had become a profitable business for many powerful and influential people.

If you came from far away, chances were you had to buy an animal at inflated Temple prices. If you brought your own, Temple workers might likely find a blemish on it and you'd be sent to buy another. If you brought money for the purchase, it had to be exchanged into Temple currency at unfavorable rates.

All of this activity happened with the knowledge of the priests and the teachers of the law who taught in the Temple. The system worked—God was "pleased" through the sacrifices and the many dependents of the Temple were fed. The penitent went away both forgiven and fleeced.

So Jesus was taking on a powerful economic and "religious" structure when he entered the Temple to drive out the sellers and the traders.

John's Gospel includes a significant fact: before he flew into his righteous fury, Jesus sat down and wove a whip from strips of leather. How long did that take? We don't know, but it's significant. It means that Christ thought out his righteous indignation rather than flying into a rage.

When his time of reflection and whip-making was over, he did the part we all remember: overturning tables, scattering money, driving out animals and sellers alike. But then he did one more thing. He taught the stunned crowd a lesson.

"My Temple will be called a house for prayer," he quoted Isaiah. But instead, you have made it a "hideout for robbers." Penitents, at their most vulnerable point and often at the end of a long journey, had been robbed at the very place that was supposed to represent mercy and forgiveness.

In this story, Jesus sets two good precedents for biblical discipline. First, control your wrath, and second, make sure your discipline includes instruction. It's a good formula for parents, teachers, bosses, and anyone in authority.

THOUGHTS TO PONDER

Why would Jesus take the time to weave the whip? Did he need the whip or did he need the time to think about his acts? You see no opposition to Jesus in this passage. Why do you think that is?

PRAYER

Father, we pray that our own places of worship will never be a disgrace to you. Help us to focus on maintaining houses of prayer. Amen.

Simple Wisdom

JOHN 3:1–21

3 There was a man named Nicodemus who was one of the Pharisees and an important Jewish leader. ²One night Nicodemus came to Jesus and said, "Teacher, we know you are a teacher sent from God, because no one can do the miracles you do unless God is with him."

³Jesus answered, "I tell you the truth, unless you are born again, you cannot be in God's kingdom."

⁴Nicodemus said, "But if a person is already old, how can he be born again? He cannot enter his mother's womb again. So how can a person be born a second time?"

⁵But Jesus answered, "I tell you the truth, unless you are born from water and the Spirit, you cannot enter God's kingdom. ⁶Human life comes from human parents, but spiritual life comes from the Spirit. ⁷Don't be surprised when I tell you, 'You must all be born again.' ⁸The wind blows where it wants to and you hear the sound of it, but you don't know where the wind comes from or where it is going. It is the same with every person who is born from the Spirit."

⁹Nicodemus asked, "How can this happen?"

¹⁰Jesus said, "You are an important teacher in Israel, and you don't understand these things? ¹¹I tell you the truth, we talk about what we know, and we tell about what we have seen, but you don't accept what we tell you. ¹²I have told you about things here on earth, and you do not believe me. So you will not believe me if I tell you about things of heaven. ¹³The only one who has ever gone up to heaven is the One who came down from heaven—the Son of Man.

¹⁴"Just as Moses lifted up the snake in the desert, the Son of Man must also be lifted up. ¹⁵So that everyone who believes can have eternal life in him.

¹⁶"God loved the world so much that he gave his one and only Son so that whoever believes in him may not be lost, but have eternal life. ¹⁷God did not send his Son into the world to judge the world guilty, but to save the world through him. ¹⁸People who believe in God's Son are not judged guilty. Those who do not believe have already been judged guilty, because they have not believed in God's one and only Son. ¹⁹They are judged by this fact: The Light has come into the world, but they did not want light. They wanted darkness, because they were doing evil things. ²⁰All who do evil hate the light and will not come to the light, because it will show all the evil things they do. ²¹But those who follow the true way come to the light, and it shows that the things they do were done through God."

DEVOTION

THIS PASSAGE is perhaps the most famous in the New Testament, and many people are familiar with it; but few realize that only one listener heard it initially.

"God loved the world so much that he gave his one and only Son so that whoever believes in him may not be lost, but have eternal life." It's the central thought of the Good News and it's told to one confused Pharisee, a member of the sect that claimed to be experts in the keeping of the law. He had seen the miracles and knew that Jesus must be a special teacher, but he didn't understand the message.

However, Nicodemus fell victim to what Paul calls "the foolishness of the cross" in a letter to the Corinthians. He wrote, "The teaching about the cross is foolishness to those who are being lost, but to us who are being saved it is the power of God. It is written in the Scriptures: 'I will cause the wise to lose their wisdom; I will make the wise unable to understand.' Where is the wise person? Where is the educated person? Where is the skilled talker of this world? God has made the wisdom of the world foolish" (1 Corinthians 1:18–20).

God has made his plan of salvation so simple, and in its simplicity, it trips up the wise, like the Pharisee Nicodemus. But Jesus tried to help Nicodemus understand what had to happen by referring to an Old Testament story he should have known well. In it, the complaining children of Israel were being killed by venomous snakes until God interceded through Moses and had him lift up a bronze serpent so that those who looked on it would survive the sting of the serpents (Numbers 21:4–9).

Jesus was referring to the fact that he, too, would be lifted up on the cross of Calvary, and everyone who looked to the cross, believed in him, and was born again would be saved.

It's that simple.

THOUGHTS TO PONDER

Why did Nicodemus fail to understand the metaphor in the remarks of Jesus? How do you interpret the command that we must be "born again"? What does this mean to you?

PRAYER

Father, we pray that, as we are reborn in you, we will spread that news to others as well. Amen.

IN SPIRIT AND IN TRUTH

JOHN 4:5—26

⁵In Samaria Jesus came to the town called Sychar, which is near the field Jacob gave to his son Joseph. ⁶Jacob's well was there. Jesus was tired from his long trip, so he sat down beside the well. It was about twelve o'clock noon. ⁷When a Samaritan woman came to the well to get some water, Jesus said to her, "Please give me a drink." ⁸(This happened while Jesus' followers were in town buying some food.)

⁹The woman said, "I am surprised that you ask me for a drink, since you are a Jewish man and I am a Samaritan woman." (Jewish people are not friends with Samaritans.)

¹⁰Jesus said, "If you only knew the free gift of God and who it is that is asking you for water, you would have asked him, and he would have given you living water."

¹¹The woman said, "Sir, where will you get this living water? The well is very deep, and you have nothing to get water with. ¹²Are you greater than Jacob, our father, who gave us this well and drank from it himself along with his sons and flocks?"

¹³Jesus answered, "Everyone who drinks this water will be thirsty again, ¹⁴but whoever drinks the water I give will never be thirsty. The water I give will become a spring of water gushing up inside that person, giving eternal life."

¹⁵The woman said to him, "Sir, give me this water so I will never be thirsty again and will not have to come back here to get more water."

¹⁶Jesus told her, "Go get your husband and come back here."

¹⁷The woman answered, "I have no husband."

Jesus said to her, "You are right to say you have no husband. ¹⁸Really you have had five husbands, and the man you live with now is not your husband. You told the truth."

¹⁹The woman said, "Sir, I can see that you are a prophet. ²⁰Our ancestors worshiped on this mountain, but you say that Jerusalem is the place where people must worship."

²¹Jesus said, "Believe me, woman. The time is coming when neither in Jerusalem nor on this mountain will you actually worship the Father. ²²You Samaritans worship something you don't understand. We understand what we worship, because salvation comes from the Jews. ²³The time is coming when the true worshipers will worship the Father in spirit and truth, and that time is here already. You see, the Father too is actively seeking such people to worship him. ²⁴God is spirit, and those who worship him must worship in spirit and truth."

²⁵The woman said, "I know that the Messiah is coming." (Messiah is the One called Christ.) "When the Messiah comes, he will explain everything to us."

²⁶Then Jesus said, "I am he—I, the one talking to you."

DEVOTION

THE MORE YOU GET to know Jesus, the more remarkable he appears. In the story above, this Samaritan woman, hardened from what life has thrown her way, softens the longer she talks to Jesus. She goes from calling him "Sir" (verse 11) to recognizing him as a "prophet" (verse 19) to contemplating whether he just might be the "Messiah" (verse 25).

That a Samaritan woman was waiting for the Messiah is interesting. The Jews called the Samaritans "dogs" and wouldn't allow them to worship in the Temple in Jerusalem. Subsequently, the Samaritans had built their own temple on Mount Gerazim, which loomed in the background of the scene in this story.

Yet in spite of her past, the woman recognized Jesus as something more than a man—and just perhaps he was the one they had been looking for. As she deftly shifted the subject off her marital past and current living arrangement and brought up the subject of worship, it is possible she was scanning the horizon for anything to change the topic and saw the mountain as a handy diversion.

Where is the right place to worship? Worship is not about the location of the temple but the inclination of the heart.

In the Old Testament, the prophet Micah pondered what sacrifice to offer God for his sins. He asked: "Will the LORD be pleased with a thousand male sheep? Will he be pleased with ten thousand rivers of oil? Should I give my first child for the evil I have done?" (Micah 6:7). God replied: "The LORD has told you, human, what is good; he has told you what he wants from you: to do what is right to other people, love being kind to others, and live humbly, obeying your God" (Micah 6:8).

You can be in the "right place" and not be worshiping. You can give a fancy gift to the offering and not be worshiping. Only when we meet the two conditions of Jesus—worship in spirit and in truth—can we please God.

THOUGHTS TO PONDER

Where are some of the places you go to meditate? What steps do you take to guard this time? What do you think worshiping in "spirit and truth" looks like?

PRAYER

Father, may our worship to you be constant, and may it always be in spirit and in truth. Amen.

Seeing the Harvest

JOHN 4:27–42

27Just then his followers came back from town and were surprised to see him talking with a woman. But none of them asked, "What do you want?" or "Why are you talking with her?"

28Then the woman left her water jar and went back to town. She said to the people, 29"Come and see a man who told me everything I ever did. Do you think he might be the Christ?" 30So the people left the town and went to see Jesus.

31Meanwhile, his followers were begging him, "Teacher, eat something."

32But Jesus answered, "I have food to eat that you know nothing about."

33So the followers asked themselves, "Did somebody already bring him food?"

34Jesus said, "My food is to do what the One who sent me wants me to do and to finish his work. 35You have a saying, 'Four more months till harvest.' But I tell you, open your eyes and look at the fields ready for harvest now. 36Already, the one who harvests is being paid and is gathering crops for eternal life. So the one who plants and the one who harvests celebrate at the same time. 37Here the saying is true, 'One person plants, and another harvests.' 38I sent you to harvest a crop that you did not work on. Others did the work, and you get to finish up their work."

39Many of the Samaritans in that town believed in Jesus because of what the woman said: "He told me everything I ever did." 40When the Samaritans came to Jesus, they begged him to stay with them, so he stayed there two more days. 41And many more believed because of the things he said.

42They said to the woman, "First we believed in Jesus because of what you said, but now we believe because we heard him ourselves. We know that this man really is the Savior of the world."

Devotion

THREE TIMES in two chapters of John's Gospel Jesus spoke in metaphor, and three times the hearer didn't understand. With Nicodemus he talked about the need to be born a second time. With the woman at the well, he talked about water that quenches thirst permanently. With his followers he talked about heavenly food and an eternal harvest. The receivers didn't understand. But the words are preserved for us, the readers.

We now understand being born again. We now understand the ability of God's Word to be as permanently satisfying as a well that never runs out of water. We now understand our role as harvesters of souls who have already been purchased by the blood of Jesus and who now need to hear the Good News—the literal interpretation of the word "gospel."

Jesus often talked on two levels—using the literal objects around him to teach a heavenly lesson. Although his followers didn't always understand him, Luke tells us that Jesus "opened their minds so they could understand the Scriptures" before he ascended to heaven (Luke 24:45).

If they looked around with literal eyes, it was still four months until harvest. The plants were mere seedlings. Who would take a sickle to ankle high plants?

But here they were, sitting in the middle of the spiritual harvest and they didn't even know it. Here were Samaritans so willing to hear the Teacher at the well that they begged Jesus to stay a couple of days. The ones that the Jews called "dogs" were the first to recognize that Jesus was the Promised One—the "Savior of the world." It was an object lesson the followers wouldn't forget.

Do we prejudge the crop before we go about our job of harvesting? Do we see the homeless and the downtrodden as candidates for our congregations, or do we simply look for more candidates like ourselves? In the story, the followers were startled that Jesus had talked to a woman as an equal. Do we prejudge who should get the message of salvation?

THOUGHTS TO PONDER

Do you have eyes for the harvest? Do you see the many people around you who need to be introduced to Jesus? Find the two ways in the passage above that people in the town were led to believe. How can we lead people to believe?

PRAYER

Father, open our eyes to the harvest. Help us to see the many in the world that need you and help us to be the Good News for them, that they may see you in our lives. Amen.

PEACE OR A SWORD

LUKE 4:14–30

[14]Jesus returned to Galilee in the power of the Holy Spirit, and stories about him spread all through the area. [15]He began to teach in their synagogues, and everyone praised him.

[16]Jesus traveled to Nazareth, where he had grown up. On the Sabbath day he went to the synagogue, as he always did, and stood up to read. [17]The Book of Isaiah the prophet was given to him. He opened the book and found the place where this is written:

[18]"The Lord has put his Spirit in me,

because he appointed me to tell the Good News to the poor.

He has sent me to tell the captives they are free

and to tell the blind that they can see again.   *Isaiah 61:1*

God sent me to free those who have been treated unfairly   *Isaiah 58:6*

[19]   and to announce the time when the Lord will show his kindness."

Isaiah 61:2

[20]Jesus closed the book, gave it back to the assistant, and sat down. Everyone in the synagogue was watching Jesus closely. [21]He began to say to them, "While you heard these words just now, they were coming true!"

[22]All the people spoke well of Jesus and were amazed at the words of grace he spoke. They asked, "Isn't this Joseph's son?"

[23]Jesus said to them, "I know that you will tell me the old saying: 'Doctor, heal yourself.' You want to say, 'We heard about the things you did in Capernaum. Do those things here in your own town!'" [24]Then Jesus said, "I tell you the truth, a prophet is not accepted in his hometown. [25]But I tell you the truth, there were many widows in Israel during the time of Elijah. It did not rain in Israel for three and one-half years, and there was no food anywhere in the whole country. [26]But Elijah was sent to none of those widows, only to a widow in Zarephath, a town in Sidon. [27]And there were many with skin diseases living in Israel during the time of the prophet Elisha. But none of them were healed, only Naaman, who was from the country of Syria."

[28]When all the people in the synagogue heard these things, they became very angry. [29]They got up, forced Jesus out of town, and took him to the edge of the cliff on which the town was built. They planned to throw him off the edge, [30]but Jesus walked through the crowd and went on his way.

DEVOTION

THERE'S SOMETHING DIFFERENT about speaking in your hometown. In the audience are people who knew you before the degrees, the promotions, the accomplishments. I agree with the comedians who say to stay away from where you began your craft.

Jesus, fresh off his battle with Satan, returns to his hometown of Nazareth where he was the carpenter's son for thirty years. So here he is, beginning his preaching ministry where people saw him play in the streets, go to synagogue, and work with his father.

But Jesus was there on that day to reintroduce himself not as the son of Joseph but the Son of Man—his favorite term for his own deity. And from the text, he was well-received. Teaching from the scroll handed to him, he claims to be the fulfillment of the prophecy of Isaiah.

He would be the bearer of Good News. He would be the healer of the blind, the deliverer of those captive to sin. And the crowd was amazed.

But it wasn't his task to please the hometown crowd on this day. He came to tell them a hard truth: the "words of grace" he spoke were not only for the Jews, but for the non-Jews as well. And to prove his point, he told the stories of Elijah and Elisha, two prophets who took their miracles to non-Jews.

The crowd went from being amazed to furious. That the Good News would also be for non-Jews as well as the Jews turned out to be a sticking point for the entire ministry of Jesus and one of the causes of his betrayal.

Jesus didn't seek to be popular. Later, he would say: "Don't think that I came to bring peace to the earth. I did not come to bring peace, but a sword" (Matthew 10:34).

Peace or a sword—the choice is up to you.

THOUGHTS TO PONDER

Why do you think Jesus chose to stir up the crowd in his first sermon in his hometown? Why did the people act as they did? Why did they go from amazement to dismay based on the last part of Jesus' message?

PRAYER

God, help us to take your words and accept them gladly, even when they are not what we want to hear. Convict us daily with your Word. Amen.

BELIEVING JESUS' WORDS

JOHN 4:43–54

⁴³Two days later, Jesus left and went to Galilee. ⁴⁴(Jesus had said before that a prophet is not respected in his own country.) ⁴⁵When Jesus arrived in Galilee, the people there welcomed him. They had seen all the things he did at the Passover Feast in Jerusalem, because they had been there, too.

⁴⁶Jesus went again to visit Cana in Galilee where he had changed the water into wine. One of the king's important officers lived in the city of Capernaum, and his son was sick. ⁴⁷When he heard that Jesus had come from Judea to Galilee, he went to Jesus and begged him to come to Capernaum and heal his son, because his son was almost dead. ⁴⁸Jesus said to him, "You people must see signs and miracles before you will believe in me."

⁴⁹The officer said, "Sir, come before my child dies."

⁵⁰Jesus answered, "Go. Your son will live."

The man believed what Jesus told him and went home. ⁵¹On the way the man's servants came and met him and told him, "Your son is alive."

⁵²The man asked, "What time did my son begin to get well?"

They answered, "Yesterday at one o'clock the fever left him."

⁵³The father knew that one o'clock was the exact time that Jesus had said, "Your son will live." So the man and all the people who lived in his house believed in Jesus.

⁵⁴That was the second miracle Jesus did after coming from Judea to Galilee.

DEVOTION

THIS IS THE SECOND recorded miracle and the first healing of Jesus in John's Gospel. Jesus had been recruited earlier by his mother to perform a miracle in Cana (John 2:1–11) even though he protested that his time had not yet come. His miracle on that day—turning water to wine at a wedding when the supply of wine had run out—showed two things about Jesus. First, his respect for his mother who asked him to help, and second, his compassion for the groom who would suffer a great loss of reputation if he failed to be a proper host at the multi-day affair that was a Jewish wedding.

Now Jesus was heading back to Galilee, his native area, after a successful visit to Samaria where, after two days of teaching, many believed in him. And even though Galilee was his home country, he knew he would not be respected there. Events proved him correct when his message in the synagogue at Nazareth, his hometown, angered the crowd so much that they tried to throw him off a cliff (Luke 4:14–30).

With the success in Samaria behind him and the perils of Galilee ahead, Jesus encountered this officer of the king on the road. His son was sick in Capernaum, a distance of several miles away, and he wanted Jesus to visit his home to heal him.

How did he know about the powers of Jesus? According to John, only one miracle had occurred so far, and that was at a private wedding in Cana. So the request of the royal official demonstrated a leap of faith. So far, this Jesus had turned water to wine and had purged the Temple of the money changers, and now the official was ready to believe Jesus could heal his son. Three times in Jesus' ministry he healed from a distance—this time, the centurion's son (Matthew 8:4–13), and the daughter of the Syrophoenician woman (Mark 7:24–30).

And even though Jesus didn't follow the official to Capernaum, there is a powerful statement in verse 50 in which we're told "the man believed what Jesus told him" and went on his way.

What if we did the same? Jesus tells us not to worry (Matthew 6:25). Do we believe what Jesus tells us? Jesus tells us that God will clothe and feed us (Matthew 6:31). Do we believe him? We're told that "you have been saved by God's grace" (Ephesians 2:5) and that "you did not save yourselves; it was a gift from God" (Ephesians 2:8).

Do we, like the official with the sick boy, believe what we've been told? The stakes are high. John ends his Gospel with these words: "Jesus did many other miracles in the presence of his followers that are not written in this book. But these are written so that you may believe that Jesus is the Christ, the Son of God. Then, by believing, you may have life through his name" (John 20:30–31).

The story of the official's son and dozens of others like it, complete with eyewitnesses to the events, are written so I can believe and have eternal life out of the reach of earthly diseases.

THOUGHTS TO PONDER

Where did the Roman official get word of Jesus? What did he risk by coming to Jesus for help with his son? What faith was he demonstrating? Do we have that level of faith today?

PRAYER

Father, you are the great Healer of all our problems and diseases, whether here on earth or in heaven. Help us come to you in faith and ask boldly for your help. Amen.

BUILT TO WITHSTAND THE STORMS

MATTHEW 7:18–29

18A good tree cannot produce bad fruit, and a bad tree cannot produce good fruit. 19Every tree that does not produce good fruit is cut down and thrown into the fire. 20In the same way, you will know these false prophets by what they do.

21"Not all those who say 'You are our Lord' will enter the kingdom of heaven. The only people who will enter the kingdom of heaven are those who do what my Father in heaven wants. 22On the last day many people will say to me, 'Lord, Lord, we spoke for you, and through you we forced out demons and did many miracles.' 23Then I will tell them clearly, 'Get away from me, you who do evil. I never knew you.'

24"Everyone who hears my words and obeys them is like a wise man who built his house on rock. 25It rained hard, the floods came, and the winds blew and hit that house. But it did not fall, because it was built on rock. 26Everyone who hears my words and does not obey them is like a foolish man who built his house on sand. 27It rained hard, the floods came, and the winds blew and hit that house, and it fell with a big crash."

28When Jesus finished saying these things, the people were amazed at his teaching, 29because he did not teach like their teachers of the law. He taught like a person who had authority.

DEVOTION

THE TELLTALE SIGNS showed up a few years ago. A hairline crack that shot out of a door frame and snaked its way up to the ceiling. A chunk of concrete that jumped off the doorstep one day. A stuck window. A shower door that didn't want to close.

Our house was cracking up, the victim of settling in the shifting soil underneath. It would have to be raised by driving beams from the foundation to bedrock many feet below. It would be painfully expensive.

Experts told us that the building site, like many in our neighborhood, was never suitably prepared for the structure we built on it. For a few years it looked solid. But several seasons of rain, followed by seasons of drought, had expanded and contracted the soil, and because the house was not anchored, it began its slow slide down the hill of our neighborhood. So we hired a crew and did what had to be done: we anchored the home to the solid bedrock many feet below the structure.

In this parable, Jesus is telling his listeners that he alone is the anchor to get our spiritual house through the storms of life.

When the 2004 hurricane season hit Florida four times in a matter of a few weeks, some communities were hit by more than one of the storms. I was fascinated to hear the mayor of one community speaking after the fourth storm, Jeanne, had destroyed much of his community with its Category III winds. Just weeks earlier, Hurricane Frances had hit with its Category I winds and the damage had been relatively mild. The difference in the categories was only about twenty miles per hour.

Why the massive difference in devastation? he was asked.

The answer: The buildings were built to withstand a Category I storm, but not a Category III. The extra twenty-mile-per-hour winds had torn through buildings that were built before codes had been toughened to require all buildings to withstand a Category III storm. The buildings had done what they were designed to do when Frances hit. But when Jeanne hit, the storm exceeded the built-in capability of the structures to withstand the storm.

Satan doesn't whisper in my ear to urge me to build a spiritual house on sand. He knows I'd recognize that trick and reject that shoddy foundation for my life. Instead, Satan does an effective job of convincing Christians that we will never get a Category III blow in life—so why prepare for it? Surely a loving God would never allow one of his own to lose his or her health and job at the same time. Surely no child of God will ever suffer the storm of rebellious teens and aging parents at the same time. But when that "perfect storm" comes, we blame God instead of Satan, and Satan wins—game, set, and match—because we fail to predict the severity of the storms of life.

Watch out for that extra twenty miles per hour that Satan has in his arsenal. Job survived it, and you can too by preparing before the storm arrives.

THOUGHTS TO PONDER

> What are you doing today about the storms of life that lie ahead? What can we do to avoid being surprised and spiritually devastated when illness, divorce, bankruptcy, or any other of life's problems strikes our "spiritual house"?

PRAYER

> God, we pray that our lives are built on the solid rock of your word and that we successfully weather the storms of life as we await an eternal home with you. Amen.

RETYING LOOSE ENDS

MATTHEW 8:1-4

8 When Jesus came down from the hill, great crowds followed him. [2]Then a man with a skin disease came to Jesus. The man bowed down before him and said, "Lord, you can heal me if you will."

[3]Jesus reached out his hand and touched the man and said, "I will. Be healed!" And immediately the man was healed from his disease. [4]Then Jesus said to him, "Don't tell anyone about this. But go and show yourself to the priest and offer the gift Moses commanded for people who are made well. This will show the people what I have done."

DEVOTION

DESPITE ITS BREVITY, this story of a man with a skin disease is nonetheless packed with significance.

First, I like its position in the Gospel of Matthew. This man is the first person to walk up to Jesus immediately after his longest recorded sermon (Matthew 5—7) often called the Sermon on the Mount. Jesus had spoken to the crowd on the side of the mountain about justice, purity, love, generosity, and godly living. He had taught them how to pray. He had admonished them to store treasures in heaven. He had warned them about the folly of worry and the problems with judging others.

Now it was time to leave the mountaintop. And as Jesus walked away from his greatest oration, he was confronted with this diseased man.

I think the same thing happens to us. We leave the mountaintop of a wonderful worship service and drive past the homeless on our way to apply the great lessons we've heard. We thank God for our daily bread and sometimes forget that some people do not know where their next meal will come from.

Jesus was just as comfortable with this man and his diseased skin as he was with teaching on the mountainside. And that's a lesson to us today. Religion is not an insular activity; it's an outreach.

Second, I like the fact that Jesus touched the man. We don't know his exact disease. Older translations of the Bible called the disease leprosy, but we don't know for sure. Under Old Testament law, this would make Jesus ceremonially unclean. And, as a practical matter, he risked contracting the infection himself. Jesus could have healed the man any way he wanted, but he chose to touch the diseased skin of the man.

There are so many people who need to be touched. The runaway teenager.

493

The senior citizen who can no longer leave the house. The junior-high student eating alone in the cafeteria, unable or too afraid to make friends in a new school. The elderly couple who lose their pension when a company goes bankrupt.

If we don't touch them, who will?

Third, the story demonstrates that when Jesus heals, there will still be things to work out. The diseased man had been ceremonially unclean, unable to worship in the Temple, and perhaps even banned from living inside the city. He still had much to do: "Go show yourself to the priest," Jesus said.

According to Leviticus 14, there were several steps to follow. He would need to wash his clothes. He would have to shave off all his hair. He would possibly be required to live outside his home for the next seven days. After that, he would be required to offer two perfect lambs. If he was poor—and with no way to earn an income during his disease he might have been very poor—then his sacrifice might be as little as a grain offering.

After all of that, the man would be able to rejoin Jewish society.

Jesus can heal our sins. All of them. He can heal adultery, ambition, or greed. But it may take several steps before we can fully regain the trust of others. We may go through the modern equivalent of living outside the city before we can get back.

But make no mistake: Jesus came off the mountainside to heal sinners like me. He came to touch sinners like me. And he came to reinstate sinners like me into a saved relationship with God.

The word "religion" comes from Latin, and literally means "to re-tie." Jesus comes in and reties the loose ends, whether it's a leper outside the city gates or a sinner outside the kingdom.

THOUGHTS TO PONDER

Why would Jesus instruct the man with the skin disease to tell no one about the source of his healing? What do you think the reaction was in the Temple when the formerly diseased man walked in?

PRAYER

God, we come to you with unclean hearts, more concealed but no less diseased than the man with the skin disease. Please make us clean. Amen.

PHYSICAL AND SPIRITUAL HEALING

LUKE 7:1–10

7 When Jesus finished saying all these things to the people, he went to Capernaum. ²There was an army officer who had a servant who was very important to him. The servant was so sick he was nearly dead. ³When the officer heard about Jesus, he sent some Jewish elders to him to ask Jesus to come and heal his servant. ⁴The men went to Jesus and begged him, saying, "This officer is worthy of your help. ⁵He loves our people, and he built us a synagogue."

⁶So Jesus went with the men. He was getting near the officer's house when the officer sent friends to say, "Lord, don't trouble yourself, because I am not worthy to have you come into my house. ⁷That is why I did not come to you myself. But you only need to command it, and my servant will be healed. ⁸I, too, am a man under the authority of others, and I have soldiers under my command. I tell one soldier, 'Go,' and he goes. I tell another soldier, 'Come,' and he comes. I say to my servant, 'Do this,' and my servant does it."

⁹When Jesus heard this, he was amazed. Turning to the crowd that was following him, he said, "I tell you, this is the greatest faith I have found anywhere, even in Israel."

¹⁰Those who had been sent to Jesus went back to the house where they found the servant in good health.

DEVOTION

THERE WAS A TIME when I was simultaneously a chairman of my academic department at the university where I teach and the president of an association of Christian schools which accredited schools across the nation. My children joked that I was the "boss" everywhere I worked, even though I answered, of course, to two boards.

This army officer was an important man. He was a "centurion," a word that comes from the same root as "century," meaning that one hundred Roman soldiers were under his command. His authority over them was absolute. He was also a good man, as demonstrated by his use of government resources to build a synagogue for the Jews of Capernaum. But regardless of all he had accomplished, he could not heal his own servant.

Here is where I begin to really relate to this story. Even with my two titles, my three college degrees, and my published books, I was helpless when MS struck my wife. I was unable to change anything when my son was diagnosed with diabetes or my daughter with rheumatoid arthritis, even though I would have taken their places without hesitation.

The Matthew account of this story contains this line from the centurion: "Lord, I am not worthy for you to come into my house. You only need to command it, and my servant will be healed" (Matthew 8:8). He realized that the power of Jesus was not confined to his touch, but resided in his divinity. Jesus did not need to enter his house for the servant to be healed.

Jesus was obviously touched by his faith, calling it the greatest faith he had seen anywhere, including the nation of Israel, whose people should have been recognizing the miracles as signs of the Messiah for which they had waited. Matthew recorded these words of Jesus: "I tell you the truth, this is the greatest faith I have found, even in Israel. Many people will come from the east and from the west and will sit and eat with Abraham, Isaac, and Jacob in the kingdom of heaven. But those people who should be in the kingdom will be thrown outside into the darkness, where people will cry and grind their teeth with pain" (Matthew 8:10–12).

The healing and the teaching that followed were undeniable signals that Jesus was taking his ministry, including his healing touch, to non-Jews. In the future, people from every direction experienced not only the physical healing but the spiritual healing of Jesus.

Jesus does not physically come to my house today, but his healing power reaches me still. And those diseases not healed here on earth? They'll be gone when I sit to eat with Abraham, Isaac, and Jacob in the kingdom of heaven.

THOUGHTS TO PONDER

What do we know about the army officer based on the story above? What type of man must he have been—a Roman soldier loved by the Jewish population? Why would Jesus call his faith, "the greatest faith" he had seen?

PRAYER

God, let us break down our pride or any other barrier that keeps us from bringing our problems to you. Amen.

MUSTARD SEED FAITH

MARK 4:30–41

³⁰Then Jesus said, "How can I show you what the kingdom of God is like? What story can I use to explain it? ³¹The kingdom of God is like a mustard seed, the smallest seed you plant in the ground. ³²But when planted, this seed grows and becomes the largest of all garden plants. It produces large branches, and the wild birds can make nests in its shade."

³³Jesus used many stories like these to teach the crowd God's message—as much as they could understand. ³⁴He always used stories to teach them. But when he and his followers were alone, Jesus explained everything to them.

³⁵That evening, Jesus said to his followers, "Let's go across the lake." ³⁶Leaving the crowd behind, they took him in the boat just as he was. There were also other boats with them. ³⁷A very strong wind came up on the lake. The waves came over the sides and into the boat so that it was already full of water. ³⁸Jesus was at the back of the boat, sleeping with his head on a cushion. His followers woke him and said, "Teacher, don't you care that we are drowning!"

³⁹Jesus stood up and commanded the wind and said to the waves, "Quiet! Be still!" Then the wind stopped, and it became completely calm.

⁴⁰Jesus said to his followers, "Why are you afraid? Do you still have no faith?"

⁴¹The followers were very afraid and asked each other, "Who is this? Even the wind and the waves obey him!"

DEVOTION

THIS PASSAGE BEGINS with a parable about the mustard seed. It's a seed so small it seems to be insignificant, but it produces a plant so hearty that birds can make nests in its shade. Jesus used it to illustrate the way the kingdom of God would grow large, around the world within one generation in fact, from the small seeds he was planting in the countrysides of Judea and Israel. Other accounts (Matthew 13:32; Luke 13:19) add a second short parable about a woman who puts a small amount of yeast in her bread and from that small ingredient, the whole bread rises.

Jesus returned to the tiny mustard seed on another occasion when his disciples failed in an attempt to heal a small boy. On that occasion, he said to his disciples, "I tell you the truth, if your faith is as big as a mustard seed, you can say to this mountain, 'Move from here to there,' and it will move. All things will be possible for you" (Matthew 17:20).

That type of faith is in short supply in the second part of this passage. Jesus and the followers got in a boat at dusk to go to the other side of the water, to a region called the Gerasenes, where Jesus performed several miracles. On this evening, Jesus was exhausted and quickly fell into a deep sleep despite the strong winds. When the storm began to rage, the followers panicked.

"Teacher, don't you care that we are drowning!" they cried.

I think I've asked that question several times in my life. Jesus, do you care that I'm drowning here? I've got more work than I can do, small children who need my attention, debts greater than my income. Can't you help a drowning man?

And his reply comes back to me, the same as above: "Why are you afraid? Do you still have no faith?"

I actually think the single word "faith" covers two acts in the Christian life. The first faith is the faith that Jesus is the Son of God and is the only way to eternal life. This type of faith trips up most people in the world who choose not to acknowledge Jesus as Lord of their lives. The second type of faith is trust in God to sustain his people, to give us what we need when we ask in prayer. This type of faith has to grow in those of us who are believers. At this point in the story, the followers were still lacking.

So when I pray to God for good health, prosperity, etc., I am committing an act of faith, trusting that the answer I get is the right answer, even if it's not the one I was looking for. That's "mustard seed faith," and it is all too rare, even among believers.

THOUGHTS TO PONDER

After having seen Jesus heal diseases of all kinds, why would the stilling of the storm frighten his closest followers? What do you think they meant by the question: "Who is this?"

PRAYER

God, we know you have the power over all of nature, yet you still care about each of us. Thank you for your awesome power and your tender love. Amen.

HIS POWER IS GREATER

MARK 5:1–20

5 Jesus and his followers went to the other side of the lake to the area of the Gerasene people. ²When Jesus got out of the boat, instantly a man with an evil spirit came to him from the burial caves. ³This man lived in the caves, and no one could tie him up, not even with a chain. ⁴Many times people had used chains to tie the man's hands and feet, but he always broke them off. No one was strong enough to control him. ⁵Day and night he would wander around the burial caves and on the hills, screaming and cutting himself with stones. ⁶While Jesus was still far away, the man saw him, ran to him, and fell down before him.

⁷The man shouted in a loud voice, "What do you want with me, Jesus, Son of the Most High God? I command you in God's name not to torture me!" ⁸He said this because Jesus was saying to him, "You evil spirit, come out of the man."

⁹Then Jesus asked him, "What is your name?"

He answered, "My name is Legion, because we are many spirits." ¹⁰He begged Jesus again and again not to send them out of that area.

¹¹A large herd of pigs was feeding on a hill near there. ¹²The demons begged Jesus, "Send us into the pigs; let us go into them." ¹³So Jesus allowed them to do this. The evil spirits left the man and went into the pigs. Then the herd of pigs—about two thousand of them—rushed down the hill into the lake and were drowned.

¹⁴The herdsmen ran away and went to the town and to the countryside, telling everyone about this. So people went out to see what had happened. ¹⁵They came to Jesus and saw the man who used to have the many evil spirits, sitting, clothed, and in his right mind. And they were frightened. ¹⁶The people who saw this told the others what had happened to the man who had the demons living in him, and they told about the pigs. ¹⁷Then the people began to beg Jesus to leave their area.

¹⁸As Jesus was getting back into the boat, the man who was freed from the demons begged to go with him. ¹⁹But Jesus would not let him. He said, "Go home to your family and tell them how much the Lord has done for you and how he has had mercy on you." ²⁰So the man left and began to tell the people in the Ten Towns about what Jesus had done for him. And everyone was amazed.

DEVOTION

THE STORY OF LEGION is one of the most vivid in all of Scripture. First you have the image of the man, probably wild-eyed and hairy, covered with self-inflicted wounds. You have his home of choice—the burial caves. And you have the two thousand pigs hurling themselves down the hill to be drowned, leaving hundreds of carcasses floating in the lake.

It had already been an eventful day for the apostles. Just hours earlier, they had feared death in a sudden storm as they crossed the lake in their boat. When Jesus aroused from his unconcerned sleep and commanded the storm to be still, the apostles were simultaneously relieved and terrified by the fact that Jesus had authority even over the weather.

Demons are relatively rare in the Old Testament and are not depicted as the free agents they seem to be in the New Testament. Jesus deals with demon possession frequently in the New Testament and the demons seem to have wills and emotions of their own.

From the first chapter of the Gospel of Mark, Jesus drove demons out of the possessed and commanded them to obey him (Mark 1:34). The Gospels record at least eight cases of Jesus casting them out of the possessed, and numerous other general references to demons. His followers eventually gained the power to cast out demons as well (Luke 9:1).

How did demon possessions happen? We're not told. Were the possessed culpable in allowing demons to occupy their body? It doesn't seem to be the case. While Jesus tells at least two of his healing recipients to stop sinning or face worse problems, he doesn't accuse the demon possessed of causing their own woes, nor does he give them warnings afterward.

Treatment of demons in the New Testament is rather matter-of-fact. They simply happened with little text given to explanation. This story is the longest of the eight accounts and the earliest, yet none of the three Gospels that record this story answers any of the questions we might ask about demon possession today.

THOUGHTS TO PONDER

What do you believe about demon possession during the time of Jesus? Was it a medical phenomenon like epilepsy or bipolar disorder? Was it a paranormal phenomenon in which a spirit inhabited the body? What do you believe about demon possession today?

PRAYER

God, even if we don't understand everything about how and why Satan works, we do understand that you have given us the Holy Spirit to dwell in us and that your power is greater than any other force in the world. Amen.

POTENTIAL BEAUTY

MATTHEW 8:28–34

28When Jesus arrived at the other side of the lake in the area of the Gadarene people, two men who had demons in them met him. These men lived in the burial caves and were so dangerous that people could not use the road by those caves. 29They shouted, "What do you want with us, Son of God? Did you come here to torture us before the right time?"

30Near that place there was a large herd of pigs feeding. 31The demons begged Jesus, "If you make us leave these men, please send us into that herd of pigs."

32Jesus said to them, "Go!" So the demons left the men and went into the pigs. Then the whole herd rushed down the hill into the lake and were drowned. 33The herdsmen ran away and went into town, where they told about all of this and what had happened to the men who had demons. 34Then the whole town went out to see Jesus. When they saw him, they begged him to leave their area.

DEVOTION

AT THE BEGINNING of the week of camp, the heavy object looked like an ordinary chunk of concrete. Its most distinguishing feature was the fact that it was cylindrical, sort of like a roll of cookie dough.

Each of the campers, kids from inner-city Los Angeles who had been taken to a serene mountain setting for the week by a local church, examined the hard tube of concrete. Dull, gray concrete. Rock hard.

Then, with the help of a diamond saw, we began to saw slices off the cylinder, making wafers of concrete out of the long roll—one for each child. Now, interesting differences began to show up in these disks of concrete, each about the size of a paperweight. Deep black chunks of rocks were exposed on the smooth surface of the concrete, set in contrast to the occasional white rocks and specks of pink rock. Although they had come out of the same cylinder of concrete, no two disks were the same. Each was like an abstract piece of art.

Next we put the concrete disks into a rock washing and polishing machine where they tumbled for two days and nights. What emerged was nothing short of a miracle. The surface of the concrete was now gleaming, polished by the contact with the other rocks and the diamond brushes. The blacks, whites, and pinks shown against the gray of the concrete that bound them together. Each child now had a shiny paperweight to take home, out of a lump of concrete no different from the cracking sidewalks of their neighborhood.

The lesson was this: inside the ordinary gray concrete was a beautiful piece of art with brilliant colors shining through. And inside each of those campers were beautiful traits waiting to shine though.

Why did Jesus bother with men so despised by civilized society that they were forced to live on the edge of town among the tombs for the dead? Perhaps because he saw through their hard veneer and saw the beautiful traits inside. Perhaps he was thinking about how those traits could be utilized when their lives were devoted to God.

You might notice that this story is like the previous story from Mark, particularly the part where the demons were cast into the herd of pigs. The difference in this account is that there are two men in Matthew's story and one in Mark's. The accounts are probably reconciled by the fact that Mark (and Luke in his Gospel) focuses on the one who does the talking for both of them.

Jesus always saw right through people. He saw the potential in the demon possessed. He rejected the notion that sick people were being punished for their sins. And he certainly saw past the religious leaders of the day with their flowing robes and long tassels and scriptures bound on their foreheads and arms (Matthew 23:5). He could see the heart of a woman of ill repute washing his feet with her tears and he could see the hypocrisy in the religious leaders who would have never allowed her to touch them. He could see through teachers of the law who, though they scrupulously tithed even out of their spice jars, had no idea how to dispense from God's deep wells of justice and mercy (Matthew 23:23).

He could also see through an entire town that thought more of their pigs than they did these men. Go away, Jesus, before we lose any more livestock.

What does God see when he looks deep inside me? Does he see my "demons" of lust, envy, gossip, or pride? Or does he see only the blood of Jesus?

The choice is mine, and the choice is yours.

THOUGHTS TO PONDER

> What do you see inside the hearts of the townsfolk when they asked Jesus to go away? What do you see in your own heart when you examine it carefully? Do you fear or welcome Jesus?

PRAYER

> Father, you know our hearts and there are no secrets from you. We pray that we will have an inner heart that is beautiful for the entire world to see. Amen.

THE OPPORTUNITY GATE

MARK 2:1–17

2 A few days later, when Jesus came back to Capernaum, the news spread that he was at home. ²Many people gathered together so that there was no room in the house, not even outside the door. And Jesus was teaching them God's message. ³Four people came, carrying a paralyzed man. ⁴Since they could not get to Jesus because of the crowd, they dug a hole in the roof right above where he was speaking. When they got through, they lowered the mat with the paralyzed man on it. ⁵When Jesus saw the faith of these people, he said to the paralyzed man, "Young man, your sins are forgiven."

⁶Some of the teachers of the law were sitting there, thinking to themselves, ⁷"Why does this man say things like that? He is speaking as if he were God. Only God can forgive sins."

⁸Jesus knew immediately what these teachers of the law were thinking. So he said to them, "Why are you thinking these things? ⁹Which is easier: to tell this paralyzed man, 'Your sins are forgiven,' or to tell him, 'Stand up. Take your mat and walk'? ¹⁰But I will prove to you that the Son of Man has authority on earth to forgive sins." So Jesus said to the paralyzed man, ¹¹"I tell you, stand up, take your mat, and go home." ¹²Immediately the paralyzed man stood up, took his mat, and walked out while everyone was watching him.

The people were amazed and praised God. They said, "We have never seen anything like this!"

¹³Jesus went to the lake again. The whole crowd followed him there, and he taught them. ¹⁴While he was walking along, he saw a man named Levi son of Alphaeus, sitting in the tax collector's booth. Jesus said to him, "Follow me," and he stood up and followed Jesus.

¹⁵Later, as Jesus was having dinner at Levi's house, many tax collectors and "sinners" were eating there with Jesus and his followers. Many people like this followed Jesus. ¹⁶When the teachers of the law who were Pharisees saw Jesus eating with the tax collectors and "sinners," they asked his followers, "Why does he eat with tax collectors and sinners?"

¹⁷Jesus heard this and said to them, "It is not the healthy people who need a doctor, but the sick. I did not come to invite good people but to invite sinners."

DEVOTION

NEARLY A CENTURY AGO, a boarding school was begun for farm boys in an attempt by one woman to bring literacy to rural Georgia. Since young boys were needed so badly on the family farm, they often missed out on a public education. In fact, many small communities in the Deep South had no school for their children to attend at that time.

Those families, who could scarcely spare their sons from farm chores for public school, surely couldn't be expected to pay tuition for this new private school being run by "Miss Berry." So the "opportunity gate" was born.

The opportunity gate stood at the end of a long lane that led to the main building of the school. Young boys were brought to the opportunity gate with a pig or a dairy cow that would serve as tuition. The donation would feed the boys throughout the semester; the school also had a working farm on the premises. A boy had only to arrive at the opportunity gate, animal in tow, ready to learn, and he would be given an opportunity for an education and a chance for a better existence than the hardscrabble farm life of rural Georgia.

The friends of the paralyzed man in this passage created his "opportunity gate" by peeling back the roof and lowering their friend down through the opening. Their faith was rewarded when Jesus healed their friend.

But notice what Jesus did. He healed the soul first, gathering the criticism of the religious leaders who were there. Then he did the visible act—caused the man to walk—silencing his critics. Jesus confounded his critics once again in this passage when he called Levi (also called Matthew) to be one of his followers. Levi walked through his "opportunity gate" and entered the Master's circle.

Ironically, the only ones who didn't see the opportunity that Jesus offered were the religious leaders who stood aside and criticized. And they were left to their ignorance.

THOUGHTS TO PONDER

How can you create an opportunity for someone you know to find Jesus? What barriers can you eliminate to help others make their way to him?

PRAYER

Father, help us to be deeply involved in seeing that those who need you will find you. Help us to crawl out on the "roofs" of our lives to bring others to you. Amen.

Your Sins Are Forgiven

LUKE 5:17–26

¹⁷One day as Jesus was teaching the people, the Pharisees and teachers of the law from every town in Galilee and Judea and from Jerusalem were there. The Lord was giving Jesus the power to heal people. ¹⁸Just then, some men were carrying on a mat a man who was paralyzed. They tried to bring him in and put him down before Jesus. ¹⁹But because there were so many people there, they could not find a way in. So they went up on the roof and lowered the man on his mat through the ceiling into the middle of the crowd right before Jesus. ²⁰Seeing their faith, Jesus said, "Friend, your sins are forgiven."

²¹The Jewish teachers of the law and the Pharisees thought to themselves, "Who is this man who is speaking as if he were God? Only God can forgive sins."

²²But Jesus knew what they were thinking and said, "Why are you thinking these things? ²³Which is easier: to say, 'Your sins are forgiven,' or to say, 'Stand up and walk'? ²⁴But I will prove to you that the Son of Man has authority on earth to forgive sins." So Jesus said to the paralyzed man, "I tell you, stand up, take your mat, and go home."

²⁵At once the man stood up before them, picked up his mat, and went home, praising God. ²⁶All the people were fully amazed and began to praise God. They were filled with much respect and said, "Today we have seen amazing things!"

Devotion

IN THE DAYS WHEN JESUS walked the earth, a rather simple notion of sin was quite prevalent. If you had a physical infirmity, such as blindness or lameness, you were probably a sinner. Or at the very least, your parents had sinned and that sin had been manifested in your handicap. In this simple system, good things happened to good people and bad things happened only to bad people.

Even the apostles bought into this concept. Seeing a blind man beside the road, they asked, "Teacher, whose sin caused this man to be born blind—his own sin or his parents' sin?" (John 9:1). Neither, said Jesus. But he could use the man's blindness to confirm the power of God working through him.

This issue arose in Matthew 9 as well. Jesus was locked in a battle with the entrenched religious authorities, the Pharisees, over this very same belief system, and the paralytic man was the battlefield.

Seeing the man, Jesus told him, "Be encouraged, young man. Your sins are forgiven" (Matthew 9:2). This comment threw the teachers of the law into a frenzy, and Jesus asked, "Which is easier: to say, 'Your sins are forgiven,' or to tell him, 'Stand up and walk'?" (Matthew 9:5). Obviously, if he could do what the

Pharisees perceived as the "harder" act—causing the man to walk—then, by inference, he must have the powers of God and only God could forgive sin. So Jesus commanded the man to walk, further proving his divinity and confounding his critics.

Lost in this story, however, is the cost to Jesus. At the very point that Jesus forgave the sins of the man, quite early in his ministry, he assured his own place on a cross. There was no going back. If the man's sins were to be forgiven, a price had to be paid, and Jesus had just signed a promissory note that he would be good for the debt.

And even though many more months were left in his time on earth, Jesus was now headed toward the Cross. The Cross was not the result of Judas' treachery or Pilate's political weakness, although those circumstances might have played a part in the timing. The Cross was a part of the providential plan of God, predicted by Jesus early in his ministry.

And that date with his destiny was coming thanks to his promise to forgive sins. Forgiveness would require a sacrifice, and that sacrifice could only occur on the cross of Calvary. But it was a price he was willing to pay. Paul told the Philippians that "Christ himself was like God in everything. But he did not think that being equal with God was something to be used for his own benefit. But he gave up his place with God and made himself nothing. He was born as a man and became like a servant. And when he was living as a man, he humbled himself and was fully obedient to God, even when that caused his death—death on a cross" (Philippians 2:6–8).

He went to that cross for the paralytic man brought to him on the mat and he went to that cross for you and me, so that we can be complete and whole with him in heaven. No matter what your infirmity—spiritual or physical—healing is on the way, thanks to Jesus' work on the Cross.

THOUGHTS TO PONDER

Why would Jesus forgive the man's sins first and then his physical illness second? What message was he sending?

PRAYER

God, we know the Cross was in your plan. We thank you for providing a way through your suffering to bridge the separation caused by our sin. Amen.

A HEALTHY FAITH

JOHN 5:1–18

5 Later Jesus went to Jerusalem for a special feast. ²In Jerusalem there is a pool with five covered porches, which is called Bethesda in the Hebrew language. This pool is near the Sheep Gate. ³Many sick people were lying on the porches beside the pool. Some were blind, some were crippled, and some were paralyzed [, and they waited for the water to move. ⁴Sometimes an angel of the Lord came down to the pool and stirred up the water. After the angel did this, the first person to go into the pool was healed from any sickness he had]. ⁵A man was lying there who had been sick for thirty-eight years. ⁶When Jesus saw the man and knew that he had been sick for such a long time, Jesus asked him, "Do you want to be well?"

⁷The sick man answered, "Sir, there is no one to help me get into the pool when the water starts moving. While I am coming to the water, someone else always gets in before me."

⁸Then Jesus said, "Stand up. Pick up your mat and walk." ⁹And immediately the man was well; he picked up his mat and began to walk.

The day this happened was a Sabbath day. ¹⁰So the Jews said to the man who had been healed, "Today is the Sabbath. It is against our law for you to carry your mat on the Sabbath day."

¹¹But he answered, "The man who made me well told me, 'Pick up your mat and walk.' "

¹²Then they asked him, "Who is the man who told you to pick up your mat and walk?"

¹³But the man who had been healed did not know who it was, because there were many people in that place, and Jesus had left.

¹⁴Later, Jesus found the man at the Temple and said to him, "See, you are well now. Stop sinning so that something worse does not happen to you."

¹⁵Then the man left and told his people that Jesus was the one who had made him well.

¹⁶Because Jesus was doing this on the Sabbath day, some evil people began to persecute him. ¹⁷But Jesus said to them, "My Father never stops working, and so I keep working, too."

¹⁸This made them try still harder to kill him. They said, "First Jesus was breaking the law about the Sabbath day. Now he says that God is his own Father, making himself equal with God!"

DEVOTION

THIS STORY, which is told only by John, raises an interesting and perplexing question about sin and disease that has puzzled people of faith for ages.

Did sin cause the man to be ill? It was a common theory. Job's friends in the Old Testament story found in the Book of Job believed it. Check the apostles' reaction to the blind man in John 9:2 when they asked Jesus whose sin—the man's or his parent's—caused the blindness. To the people of the day it was simple cosmic symmetry—good health was a reflection of a good life while disease was a sign of sin. God was the source of good health while Satan was the source of disease.

Jesus didn't condemn the man for sinning. Instead, he healed the man and only later warned him to stop sinning lest something worse should happen. Was he referring to another disease? To eternal punishment?

What is the relationship between health and faith? Do I see good health as an opportunity to praise God, or am I a person who requires disease or physical weakness to find my way to my knees in prayer? Is that what Jesus meant in his warning to the lame man—that he would use anything, including disease, to keep him focused on God?

The apostle Paul told the Corinthians that he had "a painful physical problem" (2 Corinthians 12:7). We don't know what it was, but we do know that he asked God three times to take it away. But God declined. He told Paul, "My grace is enough for you. When you are weak, my power is made perfect in you" (2 Corinthians 12:8). Paul accepted the answer and even bragged about his physical weakness, saying that it made Christ's power all the more evident in his life.

Jesus knew the temptations that would face the healed man by the pool. He could now walk. He could become self-reliant. He could become proud. He could find sin.

Jesus' warning is an appropriate one for anyone who enjoys good health. Don't put your trust in good health, he's saying, because when it leaves, so will your faith.

THOUGHTS TO PONDER

How do you think the pool worked? Do you think its powers were real or simply folklore? When Jesus commanded the man to "stop sinning" or something worse would happen, was he speaking of a spiritual calamity or a physical one?

PRAYER

God, our health is in your hands. Help us to not tie our spiritual stability to our physical health, and give us a good measure of both. Amen.

THE GOD OF THE SABBATH

MARK 2:23—3:6

²³One Sabbath day, as Jesus was walking through some fields of grain, his followers began to pick some grain to eat. ²⁴The Pharisees said to Jesus, "Why are your followers doing what is not lawful on the Sabbath day?"

²⁵Jesus answered, "Have you never read what David did when he and those with him were hungry and needed food? ²⁶During the time of Abiathar the high priest, David went into God's house and ate the holy bread, which is lawful only for priests to eat. And David also gave some of the bread to those who were with him."

²⁷Then Jesus said to the Pharisees, "The Sabbath day was made to help people; they were not made to be ruled by the Sabbath day. ²⁸So then, the Son of Man is Lord even of the Sabbath day."

3 Another time when Jesus went into a synagogue, a man with a crippled hand was there. ²Some people watched Jesus closely to see if he would heal the man on the Sabbath day so they could accuse him.

³Jesus said to the man with the crippled hand, "Stand up here in the middle of everyone."

⁴Then Jesus asked the people, "Which is lawful on the Sabbath day: to do good or to do evil, to save a life or to kill?" But they said nothing to answer him.

⁵Jesus was angry as he looked at the people, and he felt very sad because they were stubborn. Then he said to the man, "Hold out your hand." The man held out his hand and it was healed. ⁶Then the Pharisees left and began making plans with the Herodians about a way to kill Jesus.

DEVOTION

THE COMMON DENOMINATOR in these two stories is Jesus' attitude about the Sabbath—the day that God declared to be holy and observed as a day of rest by the Jews ever since the Ten Commandments were given to them. To Jesus, the spirit of the Sabbath was about revival, not rigid enforced rest, and both of the activities above—eating and healing—are acts of revival.

Jesus was not breaking the law of the Sabbath. The law simply said to remember the Sabbath and keep it holy. Jesus was breaking the interpretation of the law of the Sabbath imposed by the Pharisees, the religious leaders of the day. It was the Pharisees who determined how far you could travel on the Sabbath or how much you could lift. None of these interpretations were in the Torah—that is the Law of Moses found in the Old Testament—but in writings such as the Haggadah.

But the Haggadah had to constantly change with the times. Any innovation required a new ruling. Look at any modern appliance we enjoy and imagine a ruling being made as to whether pushing an elevator button constitutes "work" on the Sabbath (it does, according to modern orthodox groups).

It's no wonder that the average person couldn't relate to the Pharisees and their many interpretations of the Law of Moses. Confounding the issue, there were at least two schools of thought in the Pharisees and they didn't always agree. But the average person could relate to Jesus with his easy-to-understand parables and his compassion for the sick and the lame.

So the seeds of bad blood between the Pharisees and Jesus began early. By Mark's account here, the plot to kill Jesus began at the same time he was gathering his twelve apostles to train them. It was three years before the plot culminated at the cross, but it began here.

As you look through the healings in the New Testament, it seems that an unusual number of them occur on the Sabbath. The Pharisees were never able to see past their rules to the true goodness of Jesus' actions.

THOUGHTS TO PONDER

Why would Jesus feel justified in breaking any of the plethora of man-made rules governing the Sabbath? What do we do today to protect the sanctity of our day of worship?

PRAYER

Father, we know you are the God of the Sabbath and of every other day. We pray that we give you the time you deserve in our routines. Amen.

A GOD WHO HELPS

[11]Soon afterwards Jesus went to a town called Nain, and his followers and a large crowd traveled with him. [12]When he came near the town gate, he saw a funeral. A mother, who was a widow, had lost her only son. A large crowd from the town was with the mother while her son was being carried out. [13]When the Lord saw her, he felt very sorry for her and said, "Don't cry." [14]He went up and touched the coffin, and the people who were carrying it stopped. Jesus said, "Young man, I tell you, get up!" [15]And the son sat up and began to talk. Then Jesus gave him back to his mother.

[16]All the people were amazed and began praising God, saying, "A great prophet has come to us! God has come to help his people."

[17]This news about Jesus spread through all Judea and into all the places around there.

DEVOTION

SCRIPTURE RECORDS SEVERAL TIMES when Jesus chose to raise people from the dead. He raised a young girl who had died (Mark 5:21–43), telling her parents that she was only sleeping. He raised Lazarus, his friend, even though Lazarus had been dead several days by the time Jesus arrived, and his body had already been laid to rest.

A whole body of laws had developed about the surviving relatives' responsibilities to a woman when her husband had died. This was a particularly sad funeral procession. The widow had depended on her son, an only child, for support, and he had always provided it.

Now she was alone, a widow without family or any means of support. But she wasn't thinking about that as the procession went through the gate. She couldn't worry about the future when her heart was breaking over the present.

Jesus and his apostles were approaching Nain from Capernaum, where he had healed the servant of a Roman centurion. When the followers saw the procession exit the town gate, they no doubt stopped, some out of respect, and some out of distaste for going near a dead body. But Jesus headed straight for the coffin. Following Jewish tradition of the day, the coffin was probably being carried with the lid off for all to see the body. Taking the young man's hand, in a loud voice Jesus told him to rise.

The widow must have looked at Jesus in amazement. Who is this madman to interrupt this burial? But before she could utter a protest, her son sat up in his coffin and began to speak. The crowds began to shout. Some said, "A great prophet has come to us!" Others, recognizing that this was not the work of an ordinary prophet, shouted. "God has come to help his people!"

Around the countryside the cry went, "God has come to help his people!"

That's one of my favorite verses in Scripture: "God has come to help his people."

The very idea of a helper-God was radically different from what the people were being taught by their religious leaders. They had heard of a God who would come to *judge* his people. They were wary of a God who would come to *punish* his people. They had prayed for a God who would come to *rule* his people.

But here was God—in the form of a man—who had come to *help* his people. Not to organize, not to conquer, but to help—a far different God than they had heard about in the Temple and the synagogues.

Jesus still stands ready to help you today. He's only a prayer away.

THOUGHTS TO PONDER

What does the choice of the people who Jesus chose to raise from the dead tell you about him and his ministry? Why only certain people and not all the dead? What did raising individuals from the dead say about his power that healings did not?

PRAYER

Father, we thank you that death is not the final stage of life, but merely the way we enter an eternity with you. Thank you for that hope. Amen.

FORGIVEN OF MUCH

LUKE 7:36-50

³⁶One of the Pharisees asked Jesus to eat with him, so Jesus went into the Pharisee's house and sat at the table. ³⁷A sinful woman in the town learned that Jesus was eating at the Pharisee's house. So she brought an alabaster jar of perfume ³⁸and stood behind Jesus at his feet, crying. She began to wash his feet with her tears, and she dried them with her hair, kissing them many times and rubbing them with the perfume. ³⁹When the Pharisee who asked Jesus to come to his house saw this, he thought to himself, "If Jesus were a prophet, he would know that the woman touching him is a sinner!"

⁴⁰Jesus said to the Pharisee, "Simon, I have something to say to you."

Simon said, "Teacher, tell me."

⁴¹Jesus said, "Two people owed money to the same banker. One owed five hundred coins and the other owed fifty. ⁴²They had no money to pay what they owed, but the banker told both of them they did not have to pay him. Which person will love the banker more?"

⁴³Simon, the Pharisee, answered, "I think it would be the one who owed him the most money."

Jesus said to Simon, "You are right." ⁴⁴Then Jesus turned toward the woman and said to Simon, "Do you see this woman? When I came into your house, you gave me no water for my feet, but she washed my feet with her tears and dried them with her hair. ⁴⁵You gave me no kiss of greeting, but she has been kissing my feet since I came in. ⁴⁶You did not put oil on my head, but she poured perfume on my feet. ⁴⁷I tell you that her many sins are forgiven, so she showed great love. But the person who is forgiven only a little will love only a little."

⁴⁸Then Jesus said to her, "Your sins are forgiven."

⁴⁹The people sitting at the table began to say among themselves, "Who is this who even forgives sins?"

⁵⁰Jesus said to the woman, "Because you believed, you are saved from your sins. Go in peace."

DEVOTION

TO UNDERSTAND THIS STORY, you have to understand the characters. Jesus had agreed to eat at the house of a Pharisee. They were the ultra-strict keepers of the law—so strict, in fact, that their name means "those who separate themselves." And you can bet that this woman, likely a prostitute, was one of those from whom they separated.

There are at least two mysteries surrounding this woman. First, how did she get into the dinner? Second, how did she come into possession of such expensive perfume? Scripture doesn't tell us, but we are told what she did once she made her way in.

Jesus had undoubtedly observed the practice of removing his shoes when he entered Simon's house so that the dust of the roads didn't defile his house. But Simon had not responded with the traditional washing of his guest's feet. They would be reclining at a table to eat. Foot washing was a part of the necessary hygiene of a formal meal, and the conversation that followed that might last for hours.

Simon was a professional at parsing the law. The Pharisees, about six thousand in number at the time of Jesus, had taken the 613 laws of the Torah and interpreted them into thousands of applications. For instance, the simple command of "Remember the Sabbath and keep it holy" had led to hundreds of rules about what could and could not be done on the Sabbath—interpretations that Jesus flaunted on more than one occasion.

For all his correctness in keeping the law, Simon lacked the insight of this common sinful woman. She saw the enormity of her shortcomings. He only saw the shortcomings of others. She saw a need for forgiveness; Simon saw no such need. And only one of them went away that evening saved from their sins.

I think being "good" can be the enemy of being forgiven. If I look at my life and see only that I'm not as bad as others, I risk missing out on the chance to be fully forgiven and a chance to deepen my love for God.

THOUGHTS TO PONDER

Do those who have been forgiven of much have an advantage over those who have been forgiven of little? Is grace sweeter to the woman in the story than to the Pharisees who don't keenly feel its need? How do we find those in our society who need the message of grace?

PRAYER

Father, you've forgiven our sins. And we know that our sin is a blot on our lives, regardless of how the world categorizes it. Help us to not judge the sins of others, but to clean up the sins in our lives. Amen.

Rocky Ground

MATTHEW 13:1–13; 18–23

13 That same day Jesus went out of the house and sat by the lake. ²Large crowds gathered around him, so he got into a boat and sat down, while the people stood on the shore. ³Then Jesus used stories to teach them many things. He said: "A farmer went out to plant his seed. ⁴While he was planting, some seed fell by the road, and the birds came and ate it all up. ⁵Some seed fell on rocky ground, where there wasn't much dirt. That seed grew very fast, because the ground was not deep. ⁶But when the sun rose, the plants dried up, because they did not have deep roots. ⁷Some other seed fell among thorny weeds, which grew and choked the good plants. ⁸Some other seed fell on good ground where it grew and produced a crop. Some plants made a hundred times more, some made sixty times more, and some made thirty times more. ⁹Let those with ears use them and listen."

¹⁰The followers came to Jesus and asked, "Why do you use stories to teach the people?"

¹¹Jesus answered, "You have been chosen to know the secrets about the kingdom of heaven, but others cannot know these secrets. ¹²Those who have understanding will be given more, and they will have all they need. But those who do not have understanding, even what they have will be taken away from them. ¹³This is why I use stories to teach the people: They see, but they don't really see. They hear, but they don't really hear or understand."

¹⁸"So listen to the meaning of that story about the farmer. ¹⁹What is the seed that fell by the road? That seed is like the person who hears the message about the kingdom but does not understand it. The Evil One comes and takes away what was planted in that person's heart. ²⁰And what is the seed that fell on rocky ground? That seed is like the person who hears the teaching and quickly accepts it with joy. ²¹But he does not let the teaching go deep into his life, so he keeps it only a short time. When trouble or persecution comes because of the teaching he accepted, he quickly gives up. ²²And what is the seed that fell among the thorny weeds? That seed is like the person who hears the teaching but lets worries about this life and the temptation of wealth stop that teaching from growing. So the teaching does not produce fruit in that person's life. ²³But what is the seed that fell on the good ground? That seed is like the person who hears the teaching and understands it. That person grows and produces fruit, sometimes a hundred times more, sometimes sixty times more, and sometimes thirty times more."

DEVOTION

UNTIL I TRIED to plant fescue grass at our cabin in northern New Mexico, I hadn't fully understood one of the types of ground in this parable. It's that second ground—the rocky ground.

The other types of ground, I understand. I see far too many people who are like the seed which fell beside the road. The seed of the Word never makes it into their hardened lives. They don't see any need for God, and Satan stands ready to make sure the seed never takes hold.

I understand the thorny weeds. It's the folks who may have embraced the Word of God if they hadn't been surrounded with bad relationships. Perhaps a spouse or a peer group. Surrounded by folks who have already consigned themselves to a life without God, these "friends" choke out the Spirit in anyone near them.

I see people every day like the fourth type of ground. They are strongly rooted in the Word of God, growing the fruits of the Spirit such as "love, joy, peace, patience, kindness, goodness, faithfulness, gentleness and self-control" (Galatians 5:22–23). Their roots are deep, and their lives are strong against the storms of life.

Now back to the second type of ground. When I planted my grass, I picked out hundreds of rocks from the soil. Convinced I had them all, I added a layer of topsoil and put the seed in the dark soil. It sprouted in five days. But soon, the roots hit the rocks still in the ground (they're called the Rocky Mountains for good reason) and my chance for a mountain lawn was over.

Any of us who think we're in the fertile ground category need to take care. We've gladly accepted the Word, but rocks lurk just under the surface—bad health, financial reversal, etc. They're Satan's way of choking the life out of fruit-bearing Christians.

So what is our response? Follow the advice of Jesus to his listeners above: hear and understand.

THOUGHTS TO PONDER

What is your ground type? How can we know that we are firmly rooted in the Word and not merely like those among the rocky ground—temporarily rooted until disaster strikes and proves us wrong? What steps can we take to keep that from happening?

PRAYER

God, you know our hearts and you know the type of ground we represent. We know we can't fool you; help us to not fool ourselves. Keep us firmly rooted in you. Amen.

A Good Harvest

MATTHEW 13:24–30, 36–43

²⁴Then Jesus told them another story: "The kingdom of heaven is like a man who planted good seed in his field. ²⁵That night, when everyone was asleep, his enemy came and planted weeds among the wheat and then left. ²⁶Later, the wheat sprouted and the heads of grain grew, but the weeds also grew. ²⁷Then the man's servants came to him and said, 'You planted good seed in your field. Where did the weeds come from?' ²⁸The man answered, 'An enemy planted weeds.' The servants asked, 'Do you want us to pull up the weeds?' ²⁹The man answered, 'No, because when you pull up the weeds, you might also pull up the wheat. ³⁰Let the weeds and the wheat grow together until the harvest time. At harvest time I will tell the workers, "First gather the weeds and tie them together to be burned. Then gather the wheat and bring it to my barn."'"

³⁶Then Jesus left the crowd and went into the house. His followers came to him and said, "Explain to us the meaning of the story about the weeds in the field."

³⁷Jesus answered, "The man who planted the good seed in the field is the Son of Man. ³⁸The field is the world, and the good seed are all of God's children who belong to the kingdom. The weeds are those people who belong to the Evil One. ³⁹And the enemy who planted the bad seed is the devil. The harvest time is the end of the age, and the workers who gather are God's angels.

⁴⁰"Just as the weeds are pulled up and burned in the fire, so it will be at the end of the age. ⁴¹The Son of Man will send out his angels, and they will gather out of his kingdom all who cause sin and all who do evil. ⁴²The angels will throw them into the blazing furnace, where the people will cry and grind their teeth with pain. ⁴³Then the good people will shine like the sun in the kingdom of their Father. Let those with ears use them and listen.

Devotion

THE REACTION OF THE OWNER of the field in this parable amazes me. He counsels patience where I would have had none.

"Get the weeds out!" "Find out who did this!" I'd be screaming. But the owner of the field has a different thought. Let the weeds and the crop grow together until the harvest reveals them for what they are. Separate them then, he says, sending each to its proper end.

All of us have weeds in our lives. We even know who helped to plant them—

Satan, who has been spoiling gardens since Eden. But those of us who have been redeemed have the fruits of the Spirit growing too (Galatians 5:22–23). Peace. Patience. Goodness. Self-control. In fact, Paul tells the Corinthians that we are growing more like God, which "brings ever greater glory" (2 Corinthians 3:18).

My role is to make sure my crop of the fruits of the Spirit grows to be completely and undeniably distinguishable from the weeds in my life. I'm instructed to be slow to wrath while I'm growing my patience as tall as it will grow. When the harvest comes, I want my qualities that are most like Jesus to rise high above Satan's weeds, by the grace of God.

Peter reminds his readers that everything we see—everything we accumulate—will someday be consumed by the fire of the coming of the Lord. He writes: "But the day of the Lord will come like a thief. The skies will disappear with a loud noise. Everything in them will be destroyed by fire, and the earth and everything in it will be exposed. In that way everything will be destroyed. So what kind of people should you be? You should live holy lives and serve God, as you wait for and look forward to the coming of the day of God" (2 Peter 3:10–12).

Notice that when he asked his readers, "What kind of people should you be?" that he answers his own question: "You should live holy lives and serve God." Why? Because only those lives will survive the flames, just like the crop intended by the master escapes the flames in this story. If I am to escape the flames, the stalks of my fruits of the Spirit must grow higher than the weeds Satan attempts to plant.

THOUGHTS TO PONDER

What are some of the tallest "stalks" of the fruits of the spirit in your life right now? What are the thorniest of the weeds? What is your strategy for removing them?

PRAYER

God, we know you have told us of a time when the harvest will come. Help us to be ready and anticipating its arrival. Amen.

NOTHING TO LOSE

MARK 5:21–42

²¹When Jesus went in the boat back to the other side of the lake, a large crowd gathered around him there. ²²A leader of the synagogue, named Jairus, came there, saw Jesus, and fell at his feet. ²³He begged Jesus, saying again and again, "My daughter is dying. Please come and put your hands on her so she will be healed and will live." ²⁴So Jesus went with him.

A large crowd followed Jesus and pushed very close around him. ²⁵Among them was a woman who had been bleeding for twelve years. ²⁶She had suffered very much from many doctors and had spent all the money she had, but instead of improving, she was getting worse. ²⁷When the woman heard about Jesus, she came up behind him in the crowd and touched his coat. ²⁸She thought, "If I can just touch his clothes, I will be healed." ²⁹Instantly her bleeding stopped, and she felt in her body that she was healed from her disease.

³⁰At once Jesus felt power go out from him. So he turned around in the crowd and asked, "Who touched my clothes?"

³¹His followers said, "Look at how many people are pushing against you! And you ask, 'Who touched me?' "

³²But Jesus continued looking around to see who had touched him. ³³The woman, knowing that she was healed, came and fell at Jesus' feet. Shaking with fear, she told him the whole truth. ³⁴Jesus said to her, "Dear woman, you are made well because you believed. Go in peace; be healed of your disease."

³⁵While Jesus was still speaking, some people came from the house of the synagogue leader. They said, "Your daughter is dead. There is no need to bother the teacher anymore."

³⁶But Jesus paid no attention to what they said. He told the synagogue leader, "Don't be afraid; just believe."

³⁷Jesus let only Peter, James, and John the brother of James go with him. ³⁸When they came to the house of the synagogue leader, Jesus found many people there making lots of noise and crying loudly. ³⁹Jesus entered the house and said to them, "Why are you crying and making so much noise? The child is not dead, only asleep." ⁴⁰But they laughed at him. So, after throwing them out of the house, Jesus took the child's father and mother and his three followers into the room where the child was. ⁴¹Taking hold of the girl's hand, he said to her, "Talitha, koum!" (This means, "Young girl, I tell you to stand up!") ⁴²At once the girl stood right up and began walking. (She was twelve years old.) Everyone was completely amazed.

DEVOTION

OF ALL THE ATTEMPTS to go over the Niagara Falls, this was perhaps the most novel. First, the would-be adventurer planned to go upstream and use a jet-powered ski to clear the cascading waters. Next, a parachute would supposedly come out of his backpack and he would glide to safety below. It could have worked; but it didn't.

In full sight of a number of startled onlookers, the hopeful hero sped downstream in his jet-powered ski and was momentarily suspended in the air. The parachute popped out hard, tearing itself from the backpack in the process, and the young man plunged to his death as his parachute blew away in the breeze.

Have you ever put your faith in an escape—from pain, from debt, from unemployment—only to be let down? The woman in this passage had tried doctors and medicines until she was bankrupt, but she had only grown worse from the barbaric treatments. But she had heard about Jesus, and in him, she saw a means of escape. She had nothing left to lose.

Jairus had much to lose. As a synagogue ruler, he shouldn't have been seen asking a favor of Jesus, a radical who had defied the laws of the Sabbath with his apostles. Already the Pharisees had begun the plot to kill the very Jesus he was now beseeching on behalf of his daughter.

Much to lose; nothing to lose. They find themselves seeking help at the feet of Jesus. Even now, there's no better place to be when trials come.

What will you try before you try Jesus? Will you believe in your "parachutes" of savings, insurance, medicine, or hard work to see you through hard times? Or will you, like these two, ask Jesus for his help?

Why do people resist Jesus? Because their current parachutes are still holding them up. Jesus told his hearers that it was not the healthy people who needed a doctor but the sick (Mark 2:17). It's not a question of whether we will need him to hold us up, but when.

THOUGHTS TO PONDER

Are we ever tempted to try other things before we turn to God for help with our daily problems? How could the woman have known that just touching the clothes of Jesus would cure her illness? What does this say about her faith?

PRAYER

God, we pray that we would have the faith of these two people who made their way to Jesus. Help us to make our way to you daily with our needs. Amen.

WORKERS TO GATHER
HIS HARVEST

MATTHEW 9:27–38

²⁷When Jesus was leaving there, two blind men followed him. They cried out, "Have mercy on us, Son of David!"

²⁸After Jesus went inside, the blind men went with him. He asked the men, "Do you believe that I can make you see again?"

They answered, "Yes, Lord."

²⁹Then Jesus touched their eyes and said, "Because you believe I can make you see again, it will happen." ³⁰Then the men were able to see. But Jesus warned them strongly, saying, "Don't tell anyone about this." ³¹But the blind men left and spread the news about Jesus all around that area.

³²When the two men were leaving, some people brought another man to Jesus. This man could not talk because he had a demon in him. ³³After Jesus forced the demon to leave the man, he was able to speak. The crowd was amazed and said, "We have never seen anything like this in Israel."

³⁴But the Pharisees said, "The prince of demons is the one that gives him power to force demons out."

³⁵Jesus traveled through all the towns and villages, teaching in their synagogues, preaching the Good News about the kingdom, and healing all kinds of diseases and sicknesses. ³⁶When he saw the crowds, he felt sorry for them because they were hurting and helpless, like sheep without a shepherd. ³⁷Jesus said to his followers, "There are many people to harvest but only a few workers to help harvest them. ³⁸Pray to the Lord, who owns the harvest, that he will send more workers to gather his harvest."

DEVOTION

IF YOU REMEMBER the televised images of Hurricane Katrina in the late summer of 2005, you'll recall the flooding of New Orleans. For four hot, muggy days, tens of thousands of New Orleans residents were stranded in the Superdome or the convention center or on the rooftops of their houses. They were out of food. They were out of drinking water. No electricity. No toilets. No medical supplies.

Never has there been a more poignant illustration of a time in America when the need was so great and the workers were so few. A few hospital workers trying to keep patients alive. A few law enforcement personnel trying to guard property and direct people to safety. The small numbers seemed almost ludicrous compared to the overwhelming need. It wasn't until the fifth day after the disaster that an army of buses, helicopters, and trucks came to the rescue of the thousands of displaced people.

That must have been the situation Jesus saw as he walked through the towns of villages. There was no cure for blindness, no cure for leprosy. A person born lame remained lame. Even simple infections could kill in an era before antibiotics, and demon possession was a real problem as well.

But more importantly, Jesus knew as he walked through the countryside that there was no permanent cure for sin, either. There were sacrifices to atone for sin, but the blood of animals provided only a temporary remedy. The rituals had to be repeated at regular intervals.

Between sacrifices, the people carried with them the burden of keeping the Law. And looking over their shoulders were the Pharisees. It was the Pharisees who interpreted the basic laws of the Old Testament into the daily lives of the people. "Remember the Sabbath and keep it holy" in the hands of the Pharisees became dozens of rules about travel, work, and other requirements and prohibitions.

Just like those victims of Katrina had to be plucked from their roofs one person at a time, Jesus looked at the swelling crowds around him, with their many physical and spiritual needs, and healed them one at a time. The blind. The demon-possessed. The unnamed ones in the towns and villages who had "all kinds of diseases and sicknesses" according to Matthew.

Yes, the harvest is plentiful; the need is great. Yes, it sometimes looks like the workers are too few. But the solution is the same as it was in the days of Jesus: meet their needs––physically and spiritually—one person at a time.

Can we make any headway in a world that is drowning in sin when the workers are so few? Yes, because God is the owner of the harvest, according to Matthew, and we are in his employ. We know the solution to sin because we have experienced it, and now we work in his vineyard.

THOUGHTS TO PONDER

The text says Jesus hurt for those who were hurting. How do we spread that spirit into our churches? Why are we more ready to respond to a tragedy or disaster than the everyday poverty we see around us?

PRAYER

God, open our eyes to the needs around us and help us to have the heart of Jesus. We pray that we would be deeply sorrowed by the hurting and illness around us, and that we would be moved to action. Amen.

SEARCH FOR THE LOST

MATTHEW 10:1–22

10 Jesus called his twelve followers together and gave them authority to drive out evil spirits and to heal every kind of disease and sickness. ²These are the names of the twelve apostles: Simon (also called Peter) and his brother Andrew; James son of Zebedee, and his brother John; ³Philip and Bartholomew; Thomas and Matthew, the tax collector; James son of Alphaeus, and Thaddaeus; ⁴Simon the Zealot and Judas Iscariot, who turned against Jesus.

⁵Jesus sent out these twelve men with the following order: "Don't go to the non-Jewish people or to any town where the Samaritans live. ⁶But go to the people of Israel, who are like lost sheep. ⁷When you go, preach this: 'The kingdom of heaven is near.' ⁸Heal the sick, raise the dead to life again, heal those who have skin diseases, and force demons out of people. I give you these powers freely, so help other people freely. ⁹Don't carry any money with you—gold or silver or copper. ¹⁰Don't carry a bag or extra clothes or sandals or a walking stick. Workers should be given what they need.

¹¹"When you enter a city or town, find some worthy person there and stay in that home until you leave. ¹²When you enter that home, say, 'Peace be with you.' ¹³If the people there welcome you, let your peace stay there. But if they don't welcome you, take back the peace you wished for them. ¹⁴And if a home or town refuses to welcome you or listen to you, leave that place and shake its dust off your feet. ¹⁵I tell you the truth, on the Judgment Day it will be better for the towns of Sodom and Gomorrah than for the people of that town.

¹⁶"Listen, I am sending you out like sheep among wolves. So be as clever as snakes and as innocent as doves. ¹⁷Be careful of people, because they will arrest you and take you to court and whip you in their synagogues. ¹⁸Because of me you will be taken to stand before governors and kings, and you will tell them and the non-Jewish people about me. ¹⁹When you are arrested, don't worry about what to say or how to say it. At that time you will be given the things to say. ²⁰It will not really be you speaking but the Spirit of your Father speaking through you.

²¹"Brothers will give their own brothers to be killed, and fathers will give their own children to be killed. Children will fight against their own parents and have them put to death. ²²All people will hate you because you follow me, but those people who keep their faith until the end will be saved.

DEVOTION

IT WAS ANTON CHEKHOV who said, "Any idiot can face a crisis, it's the day-to-day living that's hard." When Jesus sent out the Twelve, they were going to face both crises and day-to-day living while carrying out his instructions.

The key to this story, and a similar story in Luke 10 where Jesus sent out seventy-two followers in pairs, is in the statement of Jesus just before this story: "There are many people to harvest but only a few workers to help harvest them" (Matthew 9:37). If his work is to be done, his power must be multiplied through his believers. Even the meaning of the name "apostle," which is first used in this passage, indicates Christ's intentions for them. They are literally "the sent out."

According to Jesus, his immediate priority was to look for his lost sheep in Israel. Why? Because they had been waiting for him for hundreds of years.

The message to Israel was that the kingdom they were looking for was near. The Messiah they had been waiting for had arrived. Even though the Good News of his life, death, and resurrection would eventually be for all peoples, he wanted to work first with the nation of Israel. And he did this knowing that they would reject him, lie about him, and deliver him to the Romans to be crucified.

The message to the apostles is this: travel light, do good wherever you go, stay among the believers, avoid those who would oppose you, and be shrewd, yet maintain an innocence that looks for the lost sheep everywhere.

I think it's a perfect model for evangelism still. Find the lost sheep among the wolves and bring them back to the Shepherd. But they might be sleeping under a bridge. They may be in prison. They might not smell nice in our assemblies or know any of our church music. But when we look through the eyes of Jesus, they just might be the "lost sheep of Israel" in our time.

THOUGHTS TO PONDER

Where do we go today to find those most receptive to the Good News? How do we best glorify God in our missions programs?

PRAYER

God, help us to find the lost sheep that belong in your fold wherever they are, and help us to welcome them into our churches and fellowship with them when we find them. Amen.

TRUTH AND CONSEQUENCES

MATTHEW 14:1–12

14 At that time Herod, the ruler of Galilee, heard the reports about Jesus. ²So he said to his servants, "Jesus is John the Baptist, who has risen from the dead. That is why he can work these miracles."

³Sometime before this, Herod had arrested John, tied him up, and put him into prison. Herod did this because of Herodias, who had been the wife of Philip, Herod's brother. ⁴John had been telling Herod, "It is not lawful for you to be married to Herodias." ⁵Herod wanted to kill John, but he was afraid of the people, because they believed John was a prophet.

⁶On Herod's birthday, the daughter of Herodias danced for Herod and his guests, and she pleased him. ⁷So he promised with an oath to give her anything she wanted. ⁸Herodias told her daughter what to ask for, so she said to Herod, "Give me the head of John the Baptist here on a platter." ⁹Although King Herod was very sad, he had made a promise, and his dinner guests had heard him. So Herod ordered that what she asked for be done. ¹⁰He sent soldiers to the prison to cut off John's head. ¹¹And they brought it on a platter and gave it to the girl, and she took it to her mother. ¹²John's followers came and got his body and buried it. Then they went and told Jesus.

DEVOTION

HAVE YOU EVER TOLD the truth and paid a price for it? Or, even worse, have you ever decided to not tell the truth because you feared the consequences?

As you'll recall from the Gospel of Mark, John, often called "John the Baptist," was divinely designated to prepare the people for the coming of the Promised One (Mark 1:1–12). It was John that Jesus turned to when he wished to be baptized in order to please his Father.

Matthew recorded one of John's fiery sermons against the Pharisees and Sadducees. Beginning in 3:7, we read, "When John saw them, he said, 'You are snakes! Who warned you to run away from God's coming punishment? Do the things that show you really have changed your hearts and lives. And don't think you can say to yourselves, "Abraham is our father." I tell you that God could make children for Abraham from these rocks.'"

John boldly called the religious leaders of his day "snakes" and said that their heritage from Abraham meant nothing. Clearly, this man—dressed in camel's hair and eating locusts and honey—cut a large figure in the desert of Judea and was afraid of no one.

But Herod, the Roman-appointed head of the region, was tired of John's preaching. Herod was particularly perturbed by the fact that John condemned him for living with Herodias, the wife of his brother, Philip. Herod had taken his sister-in-law for his wife, and this pesky prophet was stirring up the people.

It is important to note that only political expedience prevented Herod from killing John immediately. The text tells us that Herod was afraid of the people, so John languished in jail. And even when the text says he was "sad" at his step-daughter's request for John's head on a platter, Herod was undoubtedly glad to have John silenced. He only feared a revolt, for John was popular.

Herod's job was a tenuous one. As tetrarch, his main responsibility was to keep the peace of Rome and make sure his small part of the world contributed financially to the wealth of the Roman Empire. Any revolt that required military help from Rome would be a problem for Herod, so he kept a close eye on the Jews who thought that John was a prophet.

But Herod reluctantly granted the request of Salome (the daughter of Herodias) and had John's head brought in on a platter. John's role as the forerunner of Christ was completed. After John's death, some of his followers buried him. Even in death, John continued to haunt Herod as some said that Jesus was actually John, returned from the dead. Note that the story above is told in "flashback." It begins with Herod obsessing about whether John was back, and then tells the story of John's death.

The weakness of Herod and the boldness of John stand in stark contrast in this story. Truth is not always popular. Truth does not always change hearts or minds. But truth, John would tell us today, is truth regardless of the consequences.

THOUGHTS TO PONDER

How do you explain it when bad things like this happen to a very good person like John? Have you ever suffered for telling the truth? How did it feel?

PRAYER

God, we appreciate the boldness of people like John who give us an example of being fearless in speaking the truth. Help us to do the same. Amen.

SMALL BUT SIGNIFICANT

JOHN 6:1–15

6After this, Jesus went across Lake Galilee (or, Lake Tiberias). ²Many people followed him because they saw the miracles he did to heal the sick. ³Jesus went up on a hill and sat down there with his followers. ⁴It was almost the time for the Jewish Passover Feast.

⁵When Jesus looked up and saw a large crowd coming toward him, he said to Philip, "Where can we buy enough bread for all these people to eat?" ⁶(Jesus asked Philip this question to test him, because Jesus already knew what he planned to do.)

⁷Philip answered, "Someone would have to work almost a year to buy enough bread for each person to have only a little piece."

⁸Another one of his followers, Andrew, Simon Peter's brother, said, ⁹"Here is a boy with five loaves of barley bread and two little fish, but that is not enough for so many people."

¹⁰Jesus said, "Tell the people to sit down." There was plenty of grass there, and about five thousand men sat down there. ¹¹Then Jesus took the loaves of bread, thanked God for them, and gave them to the people who were sitting there. He did the same with the fish, giving as much as the people wanted.

¹²When they had all had enough to eat, Jesus said to his followers, "Gather the leftover pieces of fish and bread so that nothing is wasted." ¹³So they gathered up the pieces and filled twelve baskets with the pieces left from the five barley loaves.

¹⁴When the people saw this miracle that Jesus did, they said, "He must truly be the Prophet who is coming into the world."

¹⁵Jesus knew that the people planned to come and take him by force and make him their king, so he left and went into the hills alone.

DEVOTION

IT HAD BEEN A YEAR since I had last used the chain saw, so I took a little extra time to clean it, oil it, and check the chain. It was far too loose. If left that way, the chain saw would have operated for about five minutes before the chain jumped off the bar.

I turned the screw to tighten it. Nothing happened. I loosened bolts and pulled on the bar by hand. No luck. I went to the manual for instructions on disassembling the chain saw. I'm not known in my family for being handy, so I fully expected to be taking the saw into the shop after I had torn it up, but I was willing to try.

Reversing the assembly instructions, I got into the saw and discovered that the tiniest part of the saw, called the "adjusting pin" had fallen out of place. That part, no bigger than my fingernail was the sole connection between the tightening screw and the chain bar. Without it, the entire saw was useless. Once installed, the chain tightened and the saw worked.

Jesus can work with small but important components. He told his followers that if their faith equaled the size of a mustard seed they could move mountains (Matthew 17:20). He praised the two small coins the widow put into the Temple offering more than all the larger gifts (Luke 21:1–2). And in this story, Jesus uses the small offering of five loaves and two fishes from a small boy to feed the masses who were following him.

Sometimes we look at the enormity of God's gift to us and get paralyzed in our response to that gift. But like that small chain saw part made the entire machine work, the gift of the loaves and fishes from the boy was the small part that put the miracle in motion. Even today, a seemingly insignificant gift from us can become part of God's wonderful plan for feeding the spiritually hungry of this world.

Jesus said that even a cup of water offered in his name would be worthy of a reward (Matthew 10:42). Where's your cup?

THOUGHTS TO PONDER

What can you offer God today that could become significant in his hands? What small deed has someone done for you that had big consequences? How did you attempt to repay it?

PRAYER

God, help me to find that mustard seed of faith divinely planted in each of us by you and to nurture it into something beautiful. Help me be your instrument today in doing some small act of kindness for someone in your name. Amen.

Keep Looking Forward

MATTHEW 14:22–36

²²Immediately Jesus told his followers to get into the boat and go ahead of him across the lake. He stayed there to send the people home. ²³After he had sent them away, he went by himself up into the hills to pray. It was late, and Jesus was there alone. ²⁴By this time, the boat was already far away from land. It was being hit by waves, because the wind was blowing against it.

²⁵Between three and six o'clock in the morning, Jesus came to them, walking on the water. ²⁶When his followers saw him walking on the water, they were afraid. They said, "It's a ghost!" and cried out in fear.

²⁷But Jesus quickly spoke to them, "Have courage! It is I. Do not be afraid."

²⁸Peter said, "Lord, if it is really you, then command me to come to you on the water."

²⁹Jesus said, "Come."

And Peter left the boat and walked on the water to Jesus. ³⁰But when Peter saw the wind and the waves, he became afraid and began to sink. He shouted, "Lord, save me!"

³¹Immediately Jesus reached out his hand and caught Peter. Jesus said, "Your faith is small. Why did you doubt?"

³²After they got into the boat, the wind became calm. ³³Then those who were in the boat worshiped Jesus and said, "Truly you are the Son of God!"

³⁴When they had crossed the lake, they came to shore at Gennesaret. ³⁵When the people there recognized Jesus, they told people all around there that Jesus had come, and they brought all their sick to him. ³⁶They begged Jesus to let them touch just the edge of his coat, and all who touched it were healed.

Devotion

TO REACH OUR MOUNTAIN CABIN, the final hurdle is a one-hundred-yard unpaved driveway. When it rains, it gets ruts. When it snows, it drifts as much as four feet high. We've had winter guests who chose to haul luggage the length of a football field rather than risk our driveway.

But the real challenge is not getting in, it's getting out. Turning around is a tight, tedious process, but it's the one my wife always chooses. I'm too impatient so I choose to back out. I'm embarrassed to admit it took me four summers to figure out how to do it right.

When I turned and looked out the back window, I would inevitably tug on the wheel and veer from side to side. When I looked in the rearview mirror I lost sight of the driveway since it slopes down several degrees off the mountain. Then one day it dawned on me. The driveway was straight enough that if I pointed the front of the car straight at the cabin, the backing up would take care of itself.

Here's the principle: Even when you're going backwards, keep looking forward for your direction.

I'm not perfect. Some days I feel as if I'm backing up in my Christian walk. But even in those days of doubts and misdeeds, I need to keep looking forward for my direction.

Peter was walking on the water, going in the right direction, headed for Jesus. Then the text says that he began to see the wind and the waves and he began to sink. Taking his eyes off Jesus and looking instead at the waves was Peter's downfall.

As you walk through life, are you seeing the wind and the waves, or are you seeing Jesus? Those who obsess about the challenges will inevitably be overwhelmed by them. Like Peter, they will sink in the very problems they are seeking to avoid. But those who fix their eyes on Jesus will make their way through the same waves toward safety.

Jesus called himself "the way" and claimed that "the only way to the Father is through me" (John 14:6). But followers of Jesus are not left to their own resources to find his path. John calls it living "in the light" (1 John 1:7). Always look ahead, straight at Jesus, not behind; because, as John reminds us, when we're in the light, our sins remain in the past, continually forgiven.

THOUGHTS TO PONDER

What are some of the "waves" that take our minds off the main objective of following Jesus? How do we take note of the waves without obsessing over them?

PRAYER

God, we thank you for guiding us through the uncertain waters of life. Help us to always focus on Jesus when the waves rise around us. Amen.

OVERCOMING PREJUDICE

MATTHEW 15:21–31

²¹Jesus left that place and went to the area of Tyre and Sidon. ²²A Canaanite woman from that area came to Jesus and cried out, "Lord, Son of David, have mercy on me! My daughter has a demon, and she is suffering very much."

²³But Jesus did not answer the woman. So his followers came to Jesus and begged him, "Tell the woman to go away. She is following us and shouting."

²⁴Jesus answered, "God sent me only to the lost sheep, the people of Israel."

²⁵Then the woman came to Jesus again and bowed before him and said, "Lord, help me!"

²⁶Jesus answered, "It is not right to take the children's bread and give it to the dogs."

²⁷The woman said, "Yes, Lord, but even the dogs eat the crumbs that fall from their masters' table."

²⁸Then Jesus answered, "Woman, you have great faith! I will do what you asked." And at that moment the woman's daughter was healed.

²⁹After leaving there, Jesus went along the shore of Lake Galilee. He went up on a hill and sat there.

³⁰Great crowds came to Jesus, bringing with them the lame, the blind, the crippled, those who could not speak, and many others. They put them at Jesus' feet, and he healed them. ³¹The crowd was amazed when they saw that people who could not speak before were now able to speak. The crippled were made strong. The lame could walk, and the blind could see. And they praised the God of Israel for this.

DEVOTION

HIS CLOSEST FOLLOWERS had never heard Jesus refuse to help someone before. Once a man had prefaced a request for a healing by asking Jesus, "If you can help," and Jesus had rebuked him. But even that man had been helped (Mark 9:21–25).

Nor had they heard him speak of anyone in the Jewish slang. I'm sure the apostles, with their rough pedigrees, still had some of their prejudices and would often use words like "dog" to describe the non-Jews who wandered into the crowds, but only when they thought he wouldn't hear, because they knew he wouldn't approve. He even gave equal status to the children who got under their feet. So it was surprising to hear the rejection of the Greek woman in this story and doubly surprising to hear the slur they perceived in his reply.

It is interesting to note the Greek word used here, *kunaria*, a term meaning a "house pet." When they intended it for a slur, the Jews called her people *kuon*, the street dogs that ran in packs and ate the town's refuse. Jesus seemed to call the woman begging for his help a "puppy" and she responded in kind. "Yes, Lord, but even the puppies eat the crumbs that fall from their master's table" is a fairly accurate English translation of her reply. Perhaps he had been testing her faith.

She had passed his test. He was probably smiling. "Woman, you have great faith. Your request is granted." She probably knelt at his feet once more and rose to run to her house where she found her daughter healed.

I think the audience for this healing was the apostles. They had just left the area of Gennesarat where Jesus had healed a number of people who simply touched the edge of his coat. But once again, he had been hassled by the teachers of the law over whether his followers would obey the unwritten laws of handwashing before eating. If the leaders of the Jews would rather talk about someone's dirty hands than examine their own hearts, then Jesus would take his ministry to places where the people would be more receptive.

His first comment to the woman about being sent to the lost sheep of Israel was a test. Would she go away or would she persist? When she persisted, even when he used the diminutive word for dog, he knew he had found faith—greater faith than in the Pharisees who were concerned only about their rules. The difference is quite stark and no doubt taught the followers much about both faith and prejudice.

There were other times when Jesus took his message and his miracles to non-Jews. He never ignored his ministry to the lineage of David, from which he came, but he also took the Good News of his salvation to others as well. But it was up to his apostles, his closest followers, to complete the mission after his death. This lesson was surely fresh on their minds.

THOUGHTS TO PONDER

Why do you think Jesus replied to the woman as he did? What lesson did he want to teach the apostles when he paid attention to the woman's request?

PRAYER

God, we know you are the God of all nations and now call all peoples to come to you. Help us to spread this Good News to every nation and every race. Amen.

INTENTIONAL OBSCURITY

MARK 7:24–37

[24]Jesus left that place and went to the area around Tyre. When he went into a house, he did not want anyone to know he was there, but he could not stay hidden. [25]A woman whose daughter had an evil spirit in her heard that he was there. So she quickly came to Jesus and fell at his feet. [26]She was Greek, born in Phoenicia, in Syria. She begged Jesus to force the demon out of her daughter.

[27]Jesus told the woman, "It is not right to take the children's bread and give it to the dogs. First let the children eat all they want."

[28]But she answered, "Yes, Lord, but even the dogs under the table can eat the children's crumbs."

[29]Then Jesus said, "Because of your answer, you may go. The demon has left your daughter."

[30]The woman went home and found her daughter lying in bed; the demon was gone.

[31]Then Jesus left the area around Tyre and went through Sidon to Lake Galilee, to the area of the Ten Towns. [32]While he was there, some people brought a man to him who was deaf and could not talk plainly. The people begged Jesus to put his hand on the man to heal him.

[33]Jesus led the man away from the crowd, by himself. He put his fingers in the man's ears and then spit and touched the man's tongue. [34]Looking up to heaven, he sighed and said to the man, "Ephphatha!" (This means, "Be opened.") [35]Instantly the man was able to hear and to use his tongue so that he spoke clearly.

[36]Jesus commanded the people not to tell anyone about what happened. But the more he commanded them, the more they told about it. [37]They were completely amazed and said, "Jesus does everything well. He makes the deaf hear! And those who can't talk he makes able to speak."

DEVOTION

THE PERFORMER had been in show business for more than five decades on stage, film, and television. But the years had taken a toll, and on this night, this performer (no gender cues here because I don't want to hurt any feelings) wasn't on top of his or her game anymore. Yet the performer was still trudging on.

What the program lacked in quality it made up for in length. As the time went on, songs were sung in a key just out of the performer's range. As about a third of the audience walked quietly out of the auditorium between numbers, it dawned on me: the performer needed the audience more than we needed the performer.

Most of the time, when I go to a concert, I "need" the performance, or at least strongly want it. I pay money to fill my need for aesthetic beauty in my life. But occasionally the tables are turned. Perhaps it's a young up-and-comer trying to make his or her way into show business. Or someone on the comeback trail after being out of the public eye for a while. Or, sadly, you have performers who keep going because it's the only thing they know how to do.

Jesus did not need the praise of people to get his work done. In fact, he went out of his way to avoid the adoration of the crowds. The Gospels record numerous commands from Jesus to individuals and crowds to tell no one about the miracle they had just witnessed. Yet the more he commanded them to stop, the more the word spread about his acts.

With his miraculous abilities, Jesus could have had any earthly throne he desired. He could have extracted money for his services. He could have had all the fame he wanted.

Yet he chose the small villages. In the story above, he was in a region where the towns were so nondescript that they were simply known as the Decapolis—the area of Ten Towns. There he taught and healed Jews and Greeks alike. He went alone to the mountainsides to pray. He retreated into the sanctuary of boats and private homes, like the one in Tyre above.

All these wonderful works, accompanied by constant reminders to tell no one. What a wonderful example of how we should conduct our own ministry of good works.

THOUGHTS TO PONDER

Why did Jesus not want the credit for his actions? What example does that set for us today? What did the people mean when they said "Jesus does everything well"?

PRAYER

Father, your mercy is shown in the fact that Jesus was never too tired to heal. He healed the Greeks and Jews alike. He healed the servants and children of the wealthy and he raised the dead children of widows. We thank you that any of us can ask for your power knowing you will hear us. Amen.

No Reason to Worry

MARK 8:1–21

8 Another time there was a great crowd with Jesus that had nothing to eat. So Jesus called his followers and said, [2]"I feel sorry for these people, because they have already been with me for three days, and they have nothing to eat. [3]If I send them home hungry, they will faint on the way. Some of them live a long way from here."

[4]Jesus' followers answered, "How can we get enough bread to feed all these people? We are far away from any town."

[5]Jesus asked, "How many loaves of bread do you have?"

They answered, "Seven."

[6]Jesus told the people to sit on the ground. Then he took the seven loaves, gave thanks to God, and divided the bread. He gave the pieces to his followers to give to the people, and they did so. [7]The followers also had a few small fish. After Jesus gave thanks for the fish, he told his followers to give them to the people also. [8]All the people ate and were satisfied. Then his followers filled seven baskets with the leftover pieces of food. [9]There were about four thousand people who ate. After they had eaten, Jesus sent them home. [10]Then right away he got into a boat with his followers and went to the area of Dalmanutha.

[11]The Pharisees came to Jesus and began to ask him questions. Hoping to trap him, they asked Jesus for a miracle from God. [12]Jesus sighed deeply and said, "Why do you people ask for a miracle as a sign? I tell you the truth, no sign will be given to you." [13]Then Jesus left the Pharisees and went in the boat to the other side of the lake.

[14]His followers had only one loaf of bread with them in the boat; they had forgotten to bring more. [15]Jesus warned them, "Be careful! Beware of the yeast of the Pharisees and the yeast of Herod."

[16]His followers discussed the meaning of this, saying, "He said this because we have no bread."

[17]Knowing what they were talking about, Jesus asked them, "Why are you talking about not having bread? Do you still not see or understand? Are your minds closed? [18]You have eyes, but you don't really see. You have ears, but you don't really listen. Remember when [19]I divided five loaves of bread for the five thousand? How many baskets did you fill with leftover pieces of food?"

They answered, "Twelve."

[20]"And when I divided seven loaves of bread for the four thousand, how many baskets did you fill with leftover pieces of food?"

They answered, "Seven."

[21]Then Jesus said to them, "Don't you understand yet?"

DEVOTION

THE PRIMARY AUDIENCE for this miracle was not the thousands who benefited from the food. In fact, many in the back might not have had a clue of its miraculous origin. And it certainly wasn't the Pharisees who wanted to see one more sign.

The audience for this miracle and the application that followed were the followers closest to Jesus. The very followers who had served food to the crowd of five thousand (John 6:1–15) and then again to the four thousand followers of Jesus in this story. The same followers who gathered more leftovers than the original amount of food.

Can't you hear them bickering in the boat? Who had forgotten the food? Was it Judas who carried the group's purse? Was it Peter who often took the lead? Who would get to eat the single loaf? Twelve hungry and tired guys in a boat with a single loaf of bread. Twelve guys wondering why each hadn't stuffed away a little food from the plenty they'd had access to a few hours earlier.

But Jesus wanted them to see beyond that day's meal and see him as the ultimate provider of every need. He had already taught them to pray to God for the food they needed daily (Matthew 6:11). He had also called himself the bread that gives life (John 6:35) in one of his sermons that the followers had undoubtedly heard but not understood.

If they began worrying about something as insignificant as bread, they would fall into the trap of the rest of the world, trusting in the law or the authorities—the two "yeasts" he refers to—rather than trusting God.

God will provide, Jesus had told the crowds on the mountainside (Matthew 6:25–34) and now he was reinforcing that lesson to his closest followers. Work still has a role in God's plan, but worry has no place. It won't even get you an extra loaf of bread.

THOUGHTS TO PONDER

What is your image of the followers based on this story? How confident should Jesus be that these men will take his message to the world? Why do you think these human glimpses of the followers are given to us?

PRAYER

God, you see through our childish behavior and you patiently wait on our maturity. Please help us to trust you for our daily bread. Amen.

May God Open Our Eyes

MARK 8:22–33

²²Jesus and his followers came to Bethsaida. There some people brought a blind man to Jesus and begged him to touch the man. ²³So Jesus took the blind man's hand and led him out of the village. Then he spit on the man's eyes and put his hands on the man and asked, "Can you see now?"

²⁴The man looked up and said, "Yes, I see people, but they look like trees walking around."

²⁵Again Jesus put his hands on the man's eyes. Then the man opened his eyes wide and they were healed, and he was able to see everything clearly. ²⁶Jesus told him to go home, saying, "Don't go into the town."

²⁷Jesus and his followers went to the towns around Caesarea Philippi. While they were traveling, Jesus asked them, "Who do people say I am?"

²⁸They answered, "Some say you are John the Baptist. Others say you are Elijah, and others say you are one of the prophets."

²⁹Then Jesus asked, "But who do you say I am?"

Peter answered, "You are the Christ."

³⁰Jesus warned his followers not to tell anyone who he was.

³¹Then Jesus began to teach them that the Son of Man must suffer many things and that he would be rejected by the Jewish elders, the leading priests, and the teachers of the law. He told them that the Son of Man must be killed and then rise from the dead after three days. ³²Jesus told them plainly what would happen. Then Peter took Jesus aside and began to tell him not to talk like that. ³³But Jesus turned and looked at his followers. Then he told Peter not to talk that way. He said, "Go away from me, Satan! You don't care about the things of God, but only about things people think are important."

Devotion

THIS IS NOT THE FIRST ACCOUNT of Jesus healing a blind man, nor is it the most remarkable account. The first is likely recorded by Matthew in chapter 9 of his Gospel when Jesus healed two blind men because of their faith. Since it was early in his ministry, he warned them to tell no one, but they went out and spread the word of their miraculous healing anyway.

Perhaps the most remarkable account is the entire ninth chapter of John when Jesus healed a blind man who then found himself in deep trouble with the Temple officials for acknowledging the obvious: a miracle had occurred.

This was a "quieter" miracle, but it has an interesting unfolding as Jesus healed the man in two stages. At first, his vision was blurry—the people looked like trees walking around, he said. From this I think we can infer that the man was not born blind, but had become blind later in life, since he had a reference point of trees for his impaired vision. Then Jesus completed the healing by touching him, and he was able to see everything clearly.

I think most of us have been in every state that this blind man went through. I think we see clearly what God wants of us, but at some point, we become blind to it. Then we begin making our way back, unclearly at first, but more clearly as we align our will to God's. It's no wonder that New Testament writers refer to sin as darkness. It's hard to see what God wants me to do when I'm in a state of rebellion to him.

But Jesus is described as light. He chases away the darkness. He improves my impaired spiritual vision. He helps me to see clearly.

I think the next event in this passage illustrates the state of clear vision pretty well. Jesus asked his closest followers, "Who do people say I am?" followed by, "Who do you say I am?" He wanted to see if the chosen ones—those who would be left to carry on his ministry after he was gone—realized that he was more than a prophet. Peter answered correctly: "You are the Christ" (Matthew 16:16).

This is no small admission. Because when I see clearly who Jesus is, I have to do something about it. I must respond. When I realize that Jesus is the Son of Man who came to suffer and die for my sins, it demands a response.

I'm often like Peter at the end of this story: I see clearly, but I still don't want to hear the hard truth that my sins were the reason for his coming. Like Peter, I can see clearly one moment and then blurry the next.

May God open our eyes.

THOUGHTS TO PONDER

Have you noticed any blind spots in your life? What is something you see clearly now that you formerly did not see? What caused you to see more clearly?

PRAYER

God, help us to have clear vision of what you want us to be and what you want us to do with our lives. Amen.

"Who Do You Say I Am?"

MATTHEW 16:13–23

¹³When Jesus came to the area of Caesarea Philippi, he asked his followers, "Who do people say the Son of Man is?"

¹⁴They answered, "Some say you are John the Baptist. Others say you are Elijah, and still others say you are Jeremiah or one of the prophets."

¹⁵Then Jesus asked them, "And who do you say I am?"

¹⁶Simon Peter answered, "You are the Christ, the Son of the living God."

¹⁷Jesus answered, "You are blessed, Simon son of Jonah, because no person taught you that. My Father in heaven showed you who I am. ¹⁸So I tell you, you are Peter. On this rock I will build my church, and the power of death will not be able to defeat it. ¹⁹I will give you the keys of the kingdom of heaven; the things you don't allow on earth will be the things that God does not allow, and the things you allow on earth will be the things that God allows." ²⁰Then Jesus warned his followers not to tell anyone he was the Christ.

²¹From that time on Jesus began telling his followers that he must go to Jerusalem, where the Jewish elders, the leading priests, and the teachers of the law would make him suffer many things. He told them he must be killed and then be raised from the dead on the third day.

²²Peter took Jesus aside and told him not to talk like that. He said, "God save you from those things, Lord! Those things will never happen to you!"

²³Then Jesus said to Peter, "Go away from me, Satan! You are not helping me! You don't care about the things of God, but only about the things people think are important."

Devotion

AS A TEACHER of discussion classes on the university level, I find that the students who offer the most right answers are sometimes the ones who give the most wrong answers as well. Why? It's a simple matter of percentages. They're participating at higher levels, so they'll be the sources of the most comments—right or wrong. They're high risk/high reward students that make class fun.

Peter was that type of person. The first one out of the boat to walk on the water to Jesus. The one who drew his sword in Gethsemane to prevent Jesus from being taken. The one who claimed he would never deny Jesus, only to break that promise three times before the Crucifixion.

So here was Peter in two episodes, getting it right and getting it wrong. "Who am I, Peter?" Jesus asked. "The Son of the living God," he correctly replied. "Peter, I must go to Jerusalem where I will be killed," Jesus taught. "Never!" Peter replied, only to be strongly rebuked by Jesus.

How could Peter be so right and so wrong in back-to-back contexts? I think it's because Jesus as the Son of God fit the template of the Messiah that Peter had in mind, while Jesus as the sacrificial lamb did not.

Peter could identify with the Jesus of the miracles and the teachings. Surely, this was the Son of God. No one could speak this way or perform these signs without divine affiliation. But Peter couldn't identify with the Jesus of the Passion, submitting himself to authorities who had no power over him and dying a cruel death when he was innocent. This image didn't compute for Peter, so he said, "Those things will never happen to you!" Even after the rebuke, Peter didn't truly understand until he spent time with the resurrected Jesus.

Even today, we run the same risk. We risk taking the parts of Jesus and his ministry that fit our template, but we leave the harder commands out. We want the Jesus of unconditional love, but not the Jesus who asks that we take up our crosses and follow him.

The lesson of Peter in this passage is to embrace Jesus in all his roles—Son of God, head of the church, and a willing sacrifice for our sins.

THOUGHTS TO PONDER

With what traits of Peter do you identify? Why do you think it was especially hard for Peter to accept the earthly fate of Jesus?

PRAYER

God, we see in Peter the earnestness and enthusiasm that you want in all of us. Help us rein in our skepticism and disbelief, and keep the childlike zeal for you that you long to see. Amen.

TAKING JESUS SERIOUSLY

LUKE 9:23–36

[23]Jesus said to all of them, "If people want to follow me, they must give up the things they want. They must be willing to give up their lives daily to follow me. [24]Those who want to save their lives will give up true life. But those who give up their lives for me will have true life. [25]It is worthless to have the whole world if they themselves are destroyed or lost. [26]If people are ashamed of me and my teaching, then the Son of Man will be ashamed of them when he comes in his glory and with the glory of the Father and the holy angels. [27]I tell you the truth, some people standing here will see the kingdom of God before they die."

[28]About eight days after Jesus said these things, he took Peter, John, and James and went up on a mountain to pray. [29]While Jesus was praying, the appearance of his face changed, and his clothes became shining white. [30]Then two men, Moses and Elijah, were talking with Jesus. [31]They appeared in heavenly glory, talking about his departure which he would soon bring about in Jerusalem. [32]Peter and the others were very sleepy, but when they awoke fully, they saw the glory of Jesus and the two men standing with him. [33]When Moses and Elijah were about to leave, Peter said to Jesus, "Master, it is good that we are here. Let us make three tents—one for you, one for Moses, and one for Elijah." (Peter did not know what he was talking about.)

[34]While he was saying these things, a cloud came and covered them, and they became afraid as the cloud covered them. [35]A voice came from the cloud, saying, "This is my Son, whom I have chosen. Listen to him!"

[36]When the voice finished speaking, only Jesus was there. Peter, John, and James said nothing and told no one at that time what they had seen.

DEVOTION

BEHIND MY OFFICE DOOR is a velvet painting of Elvis, bought by the side of the road near Branson, Missouri. It's my inside joke. The painting only shows when I shut my office door. But when I do, Velvet Elvis hangs proudly with the diplomas and the awards.

The few students who have seen it don't know how to act. They want to think it's a joke, but they dare not laugh just in case I'm weird enough to be serious. So they stare at the painting, and then look back at me for a cue on how to act.

Is he serious?

Not really.

Then there's the one boy whose face lit up. "I have one of those too," he cried. "Only mine has Jesus, John Wayne, and Elvis going into heaven." Now it was my turn to feel uncomfortable. He seemed genuinely enthused about his Velvet Elvis and happy to meet a fellow enthusiast.

Here's a big leap, but stay with me.

Peter didn't know what to do in the story above, so he jumped up from his sleep and decided to start building tents for dead people. His mind couldn't comprehend what his eyes were seeing. He decided to get busy with his hands so he wouldn't have to deal with the enormity of the situation.

For centuries, this event has been called the "transfiguration," a big word referring to the change in the appearance of Jesus. There's no simple everyday word for it because it had never happened before and hasn't happened since. This rarest event in history was witnessed by three frightened and confused men.

On top of that, God spoke out loud for only the second time in the lifetime of Jesus. The first had been at his baptism when God had expressed his approval of his Son. This time God had a command: *Listen to my Son*. Now they *really* didn't know what to make of the situation.

Jesus hits me with statements that make me as confused as those followers on the mountain or (excuse the analogy) as confused as those students staring at Velvet Elvis.

"If people want to follow me, they must give up the things they want."

"Those who want to save their lives will give up true life."

"It is worthless to have the whole world if they themselves are destroyed or lost."

Is he serious?

Yes, really.

THOUGHTS TO PONDER

How would you have handled seeing what Peter, James, and John saw? How do you handle Jesus' comments about what we must give up in order to follow him? Have you taken him seriously?

PRAYER

God, we pray that we will listen to your Son and follow his call to live sacrificial lives. Amen.

ONLY BY PRAYER

MARK 9:14–29

[14]When Jesus, Peter, James, and John came back to the other followers, they saw a great crowd around them and the teachers of the law arguing with them. [15]But as soon as the crowd saw Jesus, the people were surprised and ran to welcome him.

[16]Jesus asked, "What are you arguing about?"

[17]A man answered, "Teacher, I brought my son to you. He has an evil spirit in him that stops him from talking. [18]When the spirit attacks him, it throws him on the ground. Then my son foams at the mouth, grinds his teeth, and becomes very stiff. I asked your followers to force the evil spirit out, but they couldn't."

[19]Jesus answered, "You people have no faith. How long must I stay with you? How long must I put up with you? Bring the boy to me."

[20]So the followers brought him to Jesus. As soon as the evil spirit saw Jesus, it made the boy lose control of himself, and he fell down and rolled on the ground, foaming at the mouth.

[21]Jesus asked the boy's father, "How long has this been happening?"

The father answered, "Since he was very young. [22]The spirit often throws him into a fire or into water to kill him. If you can do anything for him, please have pity on us and help us."

[23]Jesus said to the father, "You said, 'If you can!' All things are possible for the one who believes."

[24]Immediately the father cried out, "I do believe! Help me to believe more!"

[25]When Jesus saw that a crowd was quickly gathering, he ordered the evil spirit, saying, "You spirit that makes people unable to hear or speak, I command you to come out of this boy and never enter him again!"

[26]The evil spirit screamed and caused the boy to fall on the ground again. Then the spirit came out. The boy looked as if he were dead, and many people said, "He is dead!" [27]But Jesus took hold of the boy's hand and helped him to stand up.

[28]When Jesus went into the house, his followers began asking him privately, "Why couldn't we force that evil spirit out?"

[29]Jesus answered, "That kind of spirit can only be forced out by prayer."

DEVOTION

IT MUST HAVE BEEN an unusual day for Jesus. He experienced walking and talking with Elijah and Moses in the presence of three of his most trusted followers—Peter, James, and John. God himself had spoken from the cloud: "This is my Son, whom I love. Listen to him!" (Mark 9:7). It was an object lesson to the three witnesses: the lawgiver, the prophet, and now, above both, the Messiah.

But for every mountaintop experience there is a valley, and Jesus walked right into one here. The other followers had caused a commotion. They had tried to heal a demon-possessed boy and failed. In the process they gathered a crowd, some wanting to believe, others hostile to anyone connected with Jesus.

Seeing the crowd, Jesus rebuked the spirit and got immediate results.

"Why couldn't we drive it out?" the followers asked later.

"This kind can come out only by prayer," he replied.

My question is this: what exactly had they tried? Had they honestly thought they had it within themselves to call out the spirit? Had their powers to heal and cast out spirits caused the followers to forget the very Source of their power?

But aren't we all capable of doing the same thing?

Let me just work my way out of this financial problem; no need to pray. Let the doctors handle this disease; medicine is what's needed, not prayer. Let's get counseling for this problem instead of spending hours in prayer together.

That's not to say there's anything wrong with hard work, medicine, or counseling, to name a few of the ways we try to get out of the situations we find ourselves in. We just need to be reminded that prayer isn't a last resource . . . it's a first defense. With faith, prayer can both prevent and heal life's problems. In Matthew's account of this healing, Jesus told his followers that if they had faith the size of a mustard seed, they could move mountains (Matthew 17:20).

What's in your life that will come out only with faithful prayer?

THOUGHTS TO PONDER

Have you ever deeply desired and prayed for something, but found yourself hesitant in your prayers? Are we sometimes like the man who approaches Jesus timidly? Are there times when we, like the apostles here, try hard work before we try prayer?

PRAYER

God, help us to turn to you first and turn to you boldly with all our needs. Amen.

A Room Prepared for Me

MATTHEW 17:24–27

²⁴When Jesus and his followers came to Capernaum, the men who collected the Temple tax came to Peter. They asked, "Does your teacher pay the Temple tax?"

²⁵Peter answered, "Yes, Jesus pays the tax."

Peter went into the house, but before he could speak, Jesus said to him, "What do you think? The kings of the earth collect different kinds of taxes. But who pays the taxes—the king's children or others?"

²⁶Peter answered, "Other people pay the taxes."

Jesus said to Peter, "Then the children of the king don't have to pay taxes. ²⁷But we don't want to upset these tax collectors. So go to the lake and fish. After you catch the first fish, open its mouth and you will find a coin. Take that coin and give it to the tax collectors for you and me."

DEVOTION

MOST MAJOR CITIES have a hotel tax levied on each night's stay in a guest room. As a frequent traveler, I have seen this tax vary from 8 percent all the way up to a whopping 20 percent in some major tourist destinations.

The tax is used to fund convention and visitors bureaus, which, in turn spend their time trying to get more people into town to visit and, of course, pay the tax. It's also used to fund public projects such as convention centers and tourist destinations, all designed to attract even more business and more tax revenue.

Other cities have toll roads or toll bridges. Each driver pays a share and the sum is used to pay the bonds on that project and often pays for other projects long after the original road or bridge is paid for.

Here's the attraction of the "bed tax" or the toll road to local politicians: non-residents pay the overwhelming majority of the tax. Millions of dollars are left behind in major convention cities by one-time visitors tacked on to their room bills. Millions are paid by truckers and cross-country drivers to build the roads in a community where they do not live. Politicians love it because none of their constituents who will ultimately be voting for them have to pay the tax.

When Jesus entered Capernaum, one of the collectors of the Temple tax immediately descended on Peter and asked for a two-drachma coin. The origin of this tax is probably found in Exodus 30 where every Israelite over the age of twenty paid half a shekel annually. Called "atonement money," these funds were used for the service of the Temple. The system was more random by Jesus' day.

Instead of collecting the tax in an annual census, the maintenance of the Temple was paid for by those who entered towns to conduct business.

Jesus' question to Simon had a point. Just as the residents of a community don't pay the hotel tax when they go to bed in their home, the Temple was Jesus' home, dedicated to the worship of his Father.

But there was a practical side to Jesus. The single-minded and possibly simple-minded Temple tax collector was not going to understand the analogy, so Jesus arranged to pay the tax.

Here's the point for us today. From his childhood he set an example of being in favor with God and man simultaneously (Luke 2:52). Even though he was ultimately the very object of the worship that the tax was designed to support, the Jews could not see it yet, and it was not the time to press the issue. He was consistent on this point. Later in Matthew Jesus advocated Jews paying taxes to Rome even though the more radical elements thought tribute ought only to be paid to God (Matthew 22:21).

No one is won over by followers of Christ ignoring the laws of the land. That's why Jesus paid the tax. That's why Paul advocated the paying of taxes by the Romans as well (Romans 13:7). So Peter went fishing, the unbelievers were satisfied for yet another day, and Jesus could once again return to ministry.

When I lay my head on a pillow in a distant city, I pay the tax. But when I reach heaven, I will dwell in a room prepared for me by Christ himself (John 14:1–4), where I will enjoy all the privileges of being a child of my heavenly Father.

THOUGHTS TO PONDER

Why do you think Jesus used a miracle to produce the coin? What lesson did it teach Peter? Should we as Christians obey laws even though we don't see the purpose of them or even if we don't support them? Why? Is there ever a time for "civil disobedience"?

PRAYER

Father, help us to see that obeying the laws of the leaders over us is obeying you. Grant us discernment concerning our civic responsibilities, knowing that our true citizenship is in heaven with you. Amen.

A Higher Calling

LUKE 17:11–19

¹¹While Jesus was on his way to Jerusalem, he was going through the area between Samaria and Galilee. ¹²As he came into a small town, ten men who had a skin disease met him there. They did not come close to Jesus ¹³but called to him, "Jesus! Master! Have mercy on us!"

¹⁴When Jesus saw the men, he said, "Go and show yourselves to the priests."

As the ten men were going, they were healed. ¹⁵When one of them saw that he was healed, he went back to Jesus, praising God in a loud voice. ¹⁶Then he bowed down at Jesus' feet and thanked him. (And this man was a Samaritan.) ¹⁷Jesus said, "Weren't ten men healed? Where are the other nine? ¹⁸Is this Samaritan the only one who came back to thank God?" ¹⁹Then Jesus said to him, "Stand up and go on your way. You were healed because you believed."

DEVOTION

THE LIFE OF ANYONE with a skin disease—and leprosy seems to be the most common one in the time of Jesus—was a hard life. The lepers (as I'll call them here) lived outside of town since it was believed that contact with non-infected persons would spread the disease. They probably lived in caves or other natural formations. It was rare for the towns to care enough about them to erect any shelter.

Their life was hard. The disease was always fatal, and progressed throughout the body, usually beginning at the extremities and working inward. Flesh would literally fall off the bone—fingers, toes, ears, noses. Eventually the organs would scar or harden and shut down, causing death. To prevent any casual contact, they would shout out, "Unclean, unclean!" whenever they saw strangers approaching. This is the sound that probably reached Jesus first, even before they recognized him.

Can you imagine having to call out your worst fault or your deepest secret? "Bankrupt!" "Divorced!" "Addicted!" How different would life be? How miserable would it be? But that was the plight of these ten men.

Now to the lesson of the story—the lack of gratitude among the lepers. I live in a football-rabid community in Oklahoma. We're a state with no professional football franchises, so our high school and college teams get all the adoration of a sports-hungry public. I watched along with everyone else in the state as one of our home-grown players, Jason White, won the 2003 Heisman Trophy, college football's most prestigious award, symbolic of the nation's best college football player.

Unfortunately, Jason had two games left to play after the award was announced—the conference and national championship games. And although he didn't tell anyone, Jason was hurt. Because of the injury he had lost his mobility. The team he quarterbacked, the OU Sooners, lost both games, twice looking bad on national television. It wasn't until he had surgery in the off-season that the world knew what was wrong with Jason.

After the two losses, the local boo-birds came out in force. The young man who had carried the team to an 11-0 start and won the highest award college football could give was now returning for a final season and angry callers to the sports radio talk shows wanted him replaced.

What have you done for us lately, Jason? What have you done for us lately, Jesus?

It's easy to forget what others have done for us. In fact, in my experience, the odds of one leper in ten coming back to thank Jesus is about right. And the one who came back was the least likely of all—a Samaritan, considered an inferior race by the very priests who would approve his reentry into society.

But we keep doing good works because, as Jesus taught and showed, we're not doing good works to be seen by men. In the parable of the sheep and goats in Matthew 25, he praised those he called the sheep because of their many good works—feeding the hungry, visiting the imprisoned, and clothing the naked. And the amazing thing about the praise is that these individuals don't even recall the incidents he is praising them for.

Praise is a nice motivator, but doing good because it's the right thing to do is a higher calling for all of us who wear the name of Christ.

THOUGHTS TO PONDER

What message is Jesus sending to the officials of the Temple, where the healed men would soon go, by healing the outcasts of society? What message is Jesus sending by reaching out and touching the diseased men? Who are the "lepers" of our society? What are we doing to touch them for Jesus?

PRAYER

God, we pray that you will help us leave our comfort zones and reach out to those we might consider unclean. Give us strength to do it and blessings when we do. Amen.

THROWING STONES

JOHN 8:1–11

8 Jesus went to the Mount of Olives. ²But early in the morning he went back to the Temple, and all the people came to him, and he sat and taught them. ³The teachers of the law and the Pharisees brought a woman who had been caught in adultery. They forced her to stand before the people. ⁴They said to Jesus, "Teacher, this woman was caught having sexual relations with a man who is not her husband. ⁵The law of Moses commands that we stone to death every woman who does this. What do you say we should do?" ⁶They were asking this to trick Jesus so that they could have some charge against him.

But Jesus bent over and started writing on the ground with his finger. ⁷When they continued to ask Jesus their question, he raised up and said, "Anyone here who has never sinned can throw the first stone at her." ⁸Then Jesus bent over again and wrote on the ground.

⁹Those who heard Jesus began to leave one by one, first the older men and then the others. Jesus was left there alone with the woman standing before him. ¹⁰Jesus raised up again and asked her, "Woman, where are they? Has no one judged you guilty?"

¹¹She answered, "No one, sir."

Then Jesus said, "I also don't judge you guilty. You may go now, but don't sin anymore."

DEVOTION

THIS STORY IS ONE of three attempts recorded in the Gospels where critics of Jesus try to put him in an untenable position. On another occasion he was asked whether to pay taxes to Caesar (Matthew 22:15–22). Later, he was asked a contorted question about marriage in heaven to disprove the idea of a resurrection (Matthew 22:23–32). And John 8 gives the account of when Jesus was asked whether a woman caught in the act of adultery should die.

Of the three "entrapment stories" as they are called, this one was the most personal. It wasn't about the existence of an afterlife and it wasn't about politics. It was about the fate of one woman. For her, the answer was life or death.

The accusers had a problem. Jewish law required the testimony of both parties, yet she wasn't allowed to speak. The law also required the punishment of both parties, yet she was alone. No man was brought before Jesus.

If Jesus answered that she should be stoned, it would negate his teachings of mercy and turn the crowds against him. If he answered that she should be spared, he would fly in the face of the law which prescribed death for her sin. The leaders of the Temple felt they had Jesus trapped. But again, Jesus managed to confound his own accusers with a reply they had not anticipated.

I think this story may sometimes seem too "easy" for us because the woman was caught in the act of adultery, a sin that some people may think they'll never have to deal with. But what if she was being accused of breaking a promise? Lying? Double-dealing in business? Or working on the Sabbath—the first-century equivalent of burning the candle at both ends?

Now what is our response? Can we see ourselves in any of these sins?

I don't understand the story of this woman until I understand that she is me. I'm one of the soldiers, mocking Jesus at the foot of the cross. I'm Peter denying Christ in words and actions. I'm John Mark, quitting a missionary journey before it is over. I know, because I have done the equivalent of all of these things in my life. I'm in no position to cast a stone, and I need the grace of God to keep the stones from coming at me.

My only response is to follow the instruction that Jesus gave the woman, caught there in the public square: "Go and leave your life of sin."

THOUGHTS TO PONDER

How understanding are you of the faults of others? Do you tend to "cast stones" or offer forgiveness for wrongs you see in others? Would you like to be forgiven in the same manner you forgive?

PRAYER

God, help us to be people who drop our stones of accusation and create peace and forgiveness as you have forgiven us. Amen.

WHO SINNED?

JOHN 9:1–15

9 As Jesus was walking along, he saw a man who had been born blind. [2]His followers asked him, "Teacher, whose sin caused this man to be born blind—his own sin or his parents' sin?"

[3]Jesus answered, "It is not this man's sin or his parents' sin that made him blind. This man was born blind so that God's power could be shown in him. [4]While it is daytime, we must continue doing the work of the One who sent me. Night is coming, when no one can work. [5]While I am in the world, I am the light of the world."

[6]After Jesus said this, he spit on the ground and made some mud with it and put the mud on the man's eyes. [7]Then he told the man, "Go and wash in the Pool of Siloam." (Siloam means Sent.) So the man went, washed, and came back seeing.

[8]The neighbors and some people who had earlier seen this man begging said, "Isn't this the same man who used to sit and beg?"

[9]Some said, "He is the one," but others said, "No, he only looks like him." The man himself said, "I am the man."

[10]They asked, "How did you get your sight?"

[11]He answered, "The man named Jesus made some mud and put it on my eyes. Then he told me to go to Siloam and wash. So I went and washed, and then I could see."

[12]They asked him, "Where is this man?"

"I don't know," he answered.

[13]Then the people took to the Pharisees the man who had been blind. [14]The day Jesus had made mud and healed his eyes was a Sabbath day. [15]So now the Pharisees asked the man, "How did you get your sight?"

He answered, "He put mud on my eyes, I washed, and now I see."

DEVOTION

WHEN THE FOLLOWERS saw the blind man beside the road, their natural response was the common belief of the time. For his misfortune, someone must have sinned. Was it him or was it his parents? There's even a hint of a belief in a reincarnation myth here: could he have sinned in a previous life and been born blind in this one as punishment?

It was a widely held worldview: good things happen to good people and bad things happen to bad people. It's a lazy philosophy meant to duck the hard questions of life. Why do bad things happen to good people? Why do the un-righteous seem to prosper?

The questions date back to the time of Job, who pondered his situation and God's motives, and the prophets, who often asked God why he would use the more unrighteous nations to punish Israel for its idolatry. Which leads us back to the blind man beside the road. Who did something wrong, Jesus?

Does Jesus' reply indicate that the man had suffered a lifetime of blindness for this one object lesson? I think not. I read his reply to mean that God can take any bad situation and use it to turn people's minds to him. Hardships such as famine, floods, war, and the like have for years turned people and nations to God.

As I write this, I am watching the damage from Hurricane Katrina that de-stroyed the Gulf Coast of Louisiana and Mississippi in the late summer of 2005. Good people and bad alike were affected. Had their sin brought the hurricane? No, but the hurricane, like any other hardship is a dividing line: will you curse God for your loss or bless God for your survival? The decision is up to each per-son affected.

The blind man was saved because he followed the instructions of Jesus with-out question. Note that the instructions, on the surface, make no sense at all. There is no medical reason why mud made from spit combined with the water from the Pool of Siloam would equal a cure from blindness. It was his faith that saved him.

I think it's easy to take the attitude of the followers even today. We look at people in financial trouble, relationship trouble, substance abuse trouble, and usually our initial response is to point the fingers at them.

"Who sinned?" we ask, rather than responding with immediate, unquestion-ing help. Jesus would tell us, "God can make something good of any situation. Trust him unconditionally, even when life doesn't seem to make sense."

THOUGHTS TO PONDER

Are we ever quick to judge when we see someone not as fortunate as we are? Can we see past the sin to help the addict? Can we see past our prejudice to help the homeless?

PRAYER

Father, help us to not be the ones who are blind. Open our eyes that we may see people as you see them. Amen.

Now I See

JOHN 9:18–41

¹⁸These leaders did not believe that he had been blind and could now see again. So they sent for the man's parents ¹⁹and asked them, "Is this your son who you say was born blind? Then how does he now see?"

²⁰His parents answered, "We know that this is our son and that he was born blind. ²¹But we don't know how he can now see. We don't know who opened his eyes. Ask him. He is old enough to speak for himself." ²²His parents said this because they were afraid of the elders, who had already decided that anyone who said Jesus was the Christ would be avoided. ²³That is why his parents said, "He is old enough. Ask him."

²⁴So for the second time, they called the man who had been blind. They said, "You should give God the glory by telling the truth. We know that this man is a sinner."

²⁵He answered, "I don't know if he is a sinner. One thing I do know: I was blind, and now I see."

²⁶They asked, "What did he do to you? How did he make you see again?"

²⁷He answered, "I already told you, and you didn't listen. Why do you want to hear it again? Do you want to become his followers, too?"

²⁸Then they insulted him and said, "You are his follower, but we are followers of Moses. ²⁹We know that God spoke to Moses, but we don't even know where this man comes from."

³⁰The man answered, "This is a very strange thing. You don't know where he comes from, and yet he opened my eyes. ³¹We all know that God does not listen to sinners, but he listens to anyone who worships and obeys him. ³²Nobody has ever heard of anyone giving sight to a man born blind. ³³If this man were not from God, he could do nothing."

³⁴They answered, "You were born full of sin! Are you trying to teach us?" And they threw him out.

³⁵When Jesus heard that they had thrown him out, Jesus found him and said, "Do you believe in the Son of Man?"

³⁶He asked, "Who is the Son of Man, sir, so that I can believe in him?"

³⁷Jesus said to him, "You have seen him. The Son of Man is the one talking with you."

³⁸He said, "Lord, I believe!" Then the man worshiped Jesus.

³⁹Jesus said, "I came into this world so that the world could be judged. I came so that the blind would see and so that those who see will become blind."

⁴⁰Some of the Pharisees who were nearby heard Jesus say this and asked, "Are you saying we are blind, too?"

[41]Jesus said, "If you were blind, you would not be guilty of sin. But since you keep saying you see, your guilt remains."

DEVOTION

IF THE BLIND MAN thought he had problems when he was handicapped, nothing could have prepared him for the firestorm that happened after he had been healed. He was now the battleground in the war of disbelief between the Pharisees and Jesus.

The evidence was indisputable: a blind man could now see. And it was the undeniable nature of that fact that made the leaders of the synagogue furious. They threatened to banish anyone from the synagogue who acknowledged the lordship of Jesus. And, according to Jewish interpretation of the law, banishment meant damnation. You can understand the hesitation of his parents who knew the consequences if they gave credit to the power of Jesus for the change in their son.

So for the second time, they bring the formerly blind man before them. It's at this point that the blind man makes a profound statement that I think many of us could make: "One thing I do know: I was blind and now I see." I love the simplicity and truth of that statement.

I think there are things I was formerly blind to, that I now see clearly. I was blind to overwork, and now I see its consequences. I was blind to rushing through my prayer and devotional life, but now I see the fallacy of that decision.

Here's the point of this story: no one sees Jesus if his people are living blind. But when we open our eyes to the lives he wants us to live, the world can't ignore the change in us. When I open my eyes to the life I'm called to live, the difference will be as obvious as the man healed of blindness in this story.

THOUGHTS TO PONDER

What does Jesus mean when he says that he came so that those who see would become blind? What is Jesus saying in his last remark to the Pharisees?

PRAYER

God, help us always to be among those who see. Help to not be blinded by ambition, by self-righteousness, or any of the other blinders Satan puts in our way. Amen.

COME AS A CHILD

MARK 9:33–42

³³Jesus and his followers went to Capernaum. When they went into a house there, he asked them, "What were you arguing about on the road?" ³⁴But the followers did not answer, because their argument on the road was about which one of them was the greatest.

³⁵Jesus sat down and called the twelve apostles to him. He said, "Whoever wants to be the most important must be last of all and servant of all."

³⁶Then Jesus took a small child and had him stand among them. Taking the child in his arms, he said, ³⁷"Whoever accepts a child like this in my name accepts me. And whoever accepts me accepts the One who sent me."

³⁸Then John said, "Teacher, we saw someone using your name to force demons out of a person. We told him to stop, because he does not belong to our group."

³⁹But Jesus said, "Don't stop him, because anyone who uses my name to do powerful things will not easily say evil things about me. ⁴⁰Whoever is not against us is with us. ⁴¹I tell you the truth, whoever gives you a drink of water because you belong to the Christ will truly get his reward.

⁴²"If one of these little children believes in me, and someone causes that child to sin, it would be better for that person to have a large stone tied around his neck and be drowned in the sea."

DEVOTION

WHEN YOU GET THE INVITATION to a party, you are generally given cues on how to dress. "Come as you are." "Black tie required." "Business casual," whatever that means.

So in this passage, Jesus, possibly tired of the squabbling among his followers about who was the greatest, tells us how to come to the kingdom of heaven. "Come as a child," he tells us. Come eager. Come without guile. Come without petty bickering or comparisons.

God's invitation to his kingdom says nothing about dress. No need for gifts, other than ourselves. No head of the table or foot of the table or assigned seating. God's invitation is simply, "Come as a child."

Children were expected to be invisible in the time of Jesus. In fact, in the Matthew account of this story, the followers were actively trying to keep the children in their place, away from the Teacher. But Jesus senses what is going on and says, "Let the little children come to me. Don't stop them, because the kingdom of heaven belongs to people who are like these children" (Matthew 19:14).

Rather than push them to the background, Jesus puts them at the center of this lesson. Children don't bicker about greatness. Children don't come jealous to the Master when they find others doing good works like John did. Children accept others for who they are—they can spot the genuine and see through the phonies.

I can never read the passage above about giving a drink of water without remembering a story from early in my marriage, more than twenty-five years ago. When a truck ran off a nearby road and plowed through the house across the street, it destroyed half the house, narrowly missing its occupants. I did the typical "man thing"—running across the street with tools and tarps, I worked until dark helping the neighbors keep the elements out of their now open-air house.

My wife took a more thoughtful approach. "I better make lemonade," she said. And soon she delivered iced lemonade, as well as a supply of disposable cups. As it turned out, our neighbors had no water or electricity for days. And even though they slept in a motel at night, they worked in the hot sun to salvage items from their home, and my wife's daily supply of lemonade was a welcome sight. Months later, when they had time to give thanks to us, they particularly mentioned Linda's lemonade as a help in troubled times. We saw the same thing in the aftermath of Hurricane Katrina in New Orleans. Nothing was more important than a drink of cold water in the sweltering heat that followed the storm.

Give a drink of water, Jesus said. Look for the greatest need you can fill, and fill it in my name; you will receive your reward.

THOUGHTS TO PONDER

Can you name some of the qualities of a child that Jesus would wish for his followers to have? In order to offer a person a drink of water in the days of Jesus, what steps would a person have to take? Why didn't Jesus stop the person referred to from casting out demons? What does that tell us?

PRAYER

God, help us come to you as the children we are, and help us to protect the children in our care. Amen.

A HOLE IN YOUR SWING

MATTHEW 19:16-30

¹⁶A man came to Jesus and asked, "Teacher, what good thing must I do to have life forever?"

¹⁷Jesus answered, "Why do you ask me about what is good? Only God is good. But if you want to have life forever, obey the commands."

¹⁸The man asked, "Which commands?"

Jesus answered, " 'You must not murder anyone; you must not be guilty of adultery; you must not steal; you must not tell lies about your neighbor; ¹⁹honor your father and mother; and love your neighbor as you love yourself.' "

²⁰The young man said, "I have obeyed all these things. What else do I need to do?"

²¹Jesus answered, "If you want to be perfect, then go and sell your possessions and give the money to the poor. If you do this, you will have treasure in heaven. Then come and follow me."

²²But when the young man heard this, he left sorrowfully, because he was rich.

²³Then Jesus said to his followers, "I tell you the truth, it will be hard for a rich person to enter the kingdom of heaven. ²⁴Yes, I tell you that it is easier for a camel to go through the eye of a needle than for a rich person to enter the kingdom of God."

²⁵When Jesus' followers heard this, they were very surprised and asked, "Then who can be saved?"

²⁶Jesus looked at them and said, "For people this is impossible, but for God all things are possible."

²⁷Peter said to Jesus, "Look, we have left everything and followed you. So what will we have?"

²⁸Jesus said to them, "I tell you the truth, when the age to come has arrived, the Son of Man will sit on his great throne. All of you who followed me will also sit on twelve thrones, judging the twelve tribes of Israel. ²⁹And all those who have left houses, brothers, sisters, father, mother, children, or farms to follow me will get much more than they left, and they will have life forever. ³⁰Many who are first now will be last in the future. And many who are last now will be first in the future.

DEVOTION

HITTING A CURVEBALL in baseball might be the hardest skill to acquire in all of sports. If the temperature, the humidity, and the pitcher's delivery all come together, the ball starts at twelve o'clock when it leaves the pitcher's hand and ends up at six o'clock in the catcher's glove, breaking almost straight down in the strike zone over the plate. Any player would prefer a ninety-mile-an-hour fastball to a nasty curve.

Many baseball players have washed out of the major leagues because they couldn't hit the curve. It's called "having a hole in your swing" and it's a career-breaker. When a player with the weakness is revealed, curves are all he'll see until he strikes out repeatedly.

The rich young man had a "hole" in his life, and Jesus found it. The young man had the commandments down cold, like a baseball player who could field, throw, and hit the fastball. But there was that gaping hole, and Jesus knew it.

One thing you lack. How the man's heart must have leaped! I'm nearly there! What is it Jesus? I'm ready!

Then *zing!* comes the curveball, right into the heart of the young man: sell all you have and distribute it to the poor. Trade your treasure on earth for treasure in heaven. Get rid of that earthly baggage that will hinder your journey to eternity. Like a particularly nasty curveball, the young ruler never saw it coming.

They say no one makes eye contact with a player sent down to the minor leagues as he cleans out his locker. They just go away much like this young man did—big dreams shattered by the reality of one's own weaknesses.

The standard sounded so high, the followers wondered, "Then who can be saved?" The answer to them is the answer to all of us: "For God all things are possible."

What's the "hole" in your life? Are you holding anything back from Jesus? And more importantly, what will you do about it?

THOUGHTS TO PONDER

What do you think this man's image of eternal life was? Since we are among the rich of the world, what lesson does this story have for us? What does Jesus mean by being "perfect" in this passage?

PRAYER

God, help us to enjoy the blessings you give us, but help them to not be a stumbling block as we try to enter heaven. Amen.

Culture Shock

LUKE 10:1–20

10After this, the Lord chose seventy-two others and sent them out in pairs ahead of him into every town and place where he planned to go. ²He said to them, "There are a great many people to harvest, but there are only a few workers. So pray to God, who owns the harvest, that he will send more workers to help gather his harvest. ³Go now, but listen! I am sending you out like sheep among wolves. ⁴Don't carry a purse, a bag, or sandals, and don't waste time talking with people on the road. ⁵Before you go into a house, say, 'Peace be with this house.' ⁶If peace-loving people live there, your blessing of peace will stay with them, but if not, then your blessing will come back to you. ⁷Stay in the same house, eating and drinking what the people there give you. A worker should be given his pay. Don't move from house to house. ⁸If you go into a town and the people welcome you, eat what they give you. ⁹Heal the sick who live there, and tell them, 'The kingdom of God is near you.' ¹⁰But if you go into a town, and the people don't welcome you, then go into the streets and say, ¹¹'Even the dirt from your town that sticks to our feet we wipe off against you. But remember that the kingdom of God is near.' ¹²I tell you, on the Judgment Day it will be better for the people of Sodom than for the people of that town.

¹³"How terrible for you, Korazin! How terrible for you, Bethsaida! If the miracles I did in you had happened in Tyre and Sidon, those people would have changed their lives long ago. They would have worn rough cloth and put ashes on themselves to show they had changed. ¹⁴But on the Judgment Day it will be better for Tyre and Sidon than for you. ¹⁵And you, Capernaum, will you be lifted up to heaven? No! You will be thrown down to the depths!

¹⁶"Whoever listens to you listens to me, and whoever refuses to accept you refuses to accept me. And whoever refuses to accept me refuses to accept the One who sent me."

¹⁷When the seventy-two came back, they were very happy and said, "Lord, even the demons obeyed us when we used your name!"

¹⁸Jesus said, "I saw Satan fall like lightning from heaven. ¹⁹Listen, I have given you power to walk on snakes and scorpions, power that is greater than the enemy has. So nothing will hurt you. ²⁰But you should not be happy because the spirits obey you but because your names are written in heaven."

Devotion

THIS STORY is similar to Jesus sending out his twelve followers a chapter earlier. We're not sure where he got the seventy-two followers, but by now the crowds around him had grown. It was time to ready his followers for when he would not be with them. By growing from twelve to seventy-two ambassadors in just a short time, Jesus expanded his base, reaching more people and towns.

Each summer, my Christian university and my congregation send scores of students to foreign countries to do mission work. The Sunday night in April when the groups assemble with the flags of their respective countries, they cover the entire stage.

These students know the message. They've had many preparation classes to ensure that. And even though these classes discuss cultural differences and what to expect from experienced missionaries-in-residence on our campus, there is always culture shock.

The locals worship differently. Signs are unreadable. Even if you know the fundamentals of the language, the locals speak too fast. The food is strange if not unrecognizable. Staying in the homes of the locals is a real eye-opener, especially for those lucky enough to get outhouses with their lodging.

All of this explains Jesus' instructions. Without a purse, they could not buy lodging, so they would stay with receptive people, who would likely be at the bottom rungs of society because they were the ones who welcomed Jesus' message. Be happy with your accommodations and don't move around to better ones, he says.

Most importantly, stick to the message: the kingdom of God is near. If that message resonates in a community, stay and teach; if not, move on.

It's no wonder the seventy-two came back excited with their results. Some of the most committed students on our campus have known the joy and anxiety of an international experience and seen how blessed we are. By sending out the seventy-two Jesus was not only looking for what they would do for the world, but for what the experience would do for them.

THOUGHTS TO PONDER

> Have you ever taken a trip without an itinerary? Or gone on a trip with no predetermined destination? Or had to leave on very short notice? How did it feel? How do you think the seventy-two felt at the end of their experience? What do you think Jesus wanted them to learn?

PRAYER

> God, we know you protect us in our homes and on our travels. Thank you for watching over us wherever we are. Amen.

LIMITATION OF LIABILITY

LUKE 10:25–37

²⁵Then an expert on the law stood up to test Jesus, saying, "Teacher, what must I do to get life forever?"

²⁶Jesus said, "What is written in the law? What do you read there?"

²⁷The man answered, "Love the Lord your God with all your heart, all your soul, all your strength, and all your mind." Also, "Love your neighbor as you love yourself."

²⁸Jesus said to him, "Your answer is right. Do this and you will live."

²⁹But the man, wanting to show the importance of his question, said to Jesus, "And who is my neighbor?"

³⁰Jesus answered, "As a man was going down from Jerusalem to Jericho, some robbers attacked him. They tore off his clothes, beat him, and left him lying there, almost dead. ³¹It happened that a priest was going down that road. When he saw the man, he walked by on the other side. ³²Next, a Levite came there, and after he went over and looked at the man, he walked by on the other side of the road. ³³Then a Samaritan traveling down the road came to where the hurt man was. When he saw the man, he felt very sorry for him. ³⁴The Samaritan went to him, poured olive oil and wine on his wounds, and bandaged them. Then he put the hurt man on his own donkey and took him to an inn where he cared for him. ³⁵The next day, the Samaritan brought out two coins, gave them to the innkeeper, and said, 'Take care of this man. If you spend more money on him, I will pay it back to you when I come again.' "

³⁶Then Jesus said, "Which one of these three men do you think was a neighbor to the man who was attacked by the robbers?"

³⁷The expert on the law answered, "The one who showed him mercy."

Jesus said to him, "Then go and do what he did."

DEVOTION

PERHAPS IT'S NO COINCIDENCE that it was a lawyer who asked the question: If I must love my neighbor as myself, then who is my neighbor? It's called "limitation of liability." Tell me just how many people I have to love, Jesus.

I recall Peter's question about forgiveness found in Matthew chapter 18. Although we don't know the circumstances, Peter came to Jesus, having obviously been provoked, and asked, "Lord, when my fellow believer sins against me, how many times must I forgive him? Should I forgive him as many as seven times?" (Matthew 18:21). Jesus' reply: not seven times, but up to seventy times seven.

With its status in Jewish tradition as a symbol of completeness, the number seven is important here. You will never complete your debt of forgiveness, Peter, Jesus was saying. No limitation of liability here.

The same principle was at work in this story. By answering with a parable, Jesus refused to place a limit on "who is my neighbor." Instead, he told a story so memorable that even today, the term "Good Samaritan" is a metaphor for anyone who does a favor for a stranger with no expectations of payment in return.

Notice that the "usual suspects" don't help. The priest might have been too concerned that touching the blood of the wounded man would make him "unclean" for his priestly duties, so he skirted by on the other side. The Levite came from a tribe designated to act in the service of God (Numbers 3:40–51). Supported by the tithes of the people, they were to do good works . . . but not on this day.

Jesus chose the Samaritan, a race considered to be "dogs" by the Jewish orthodoxy, to be the neighbor to the man. There is no limitation of liability here. Anyone and everyone is my neighbor.

Now comes the hard part: "Go and do what he did," Jesus said. To the sick, to the imprisoned, to the homeless. People who will never live in my neighborhood are my neighbors. But like the priest and the Levite, I must not be so blinded by my rush to do good works that I fail to see them as my neighbors.

THOUGHTS TO PONDER

Why do you think Jesus chose a Levite—a Temple worker—and a priest as the first two people to pass by the man in this parable? Why do you think he chose a Samaritan—someone from a race despised by the Jews—to be the one who helped? What does Jesus' parable tell us about who is our neighbor?

PRAYER

God, open our eyes to the many neighbors we have in the world. Help us to not pass them by on our way to complete our agendas. Amen.

APPROACHING GOD BOLDLY

LUKE 11:1–13

11 One time Jesus was praying in a certain place. When he finished, one of his followers said to him, "Lord, teach us to pray as John taught his followers."

²Jesus said to them, "When you pray, say:

'Father, may your name always be kept holy.

May your kingdom come.

³Give us the food we need for each day.

⁴Forgive us for our sins,

because we forgive everyone who has done wrong to us.

And do not cause us to be tempted.' "

⁵Then Jesus said to them, "Suppose one of you went to your friend's house at midnight and said to him, 'Friend, loan me three loaves of bread. ⁶A friend of mine has come into town to visit me, but I have nothing for him to eat.' ⁷Your friend inside the house answers, 'Don't bother me! The door is already locked, and my children and I are in bed. I cannot get up and give you anything.' ⁸I tell you, if friendship is not enough to make him get up to give you the bread, your boldness will make him get up and give you whatever you need. ⁹So I tell you, ask, and God will give to you. Search, and you will find. Knock, and the door will open for you. ¹⁰Yes, everyone who asks will receive. The one who searches will find. And everyone who knocks will have the door opened. ¹¹If your children ask for a fish, which of you would give them a snake instead? ¹²Or, if your children ask for an egg, would you give them a scorpion? ¹³Even though you are bad, you know how to give good things to your children. How much more your heavenly Father will give the Holy Spirit to those who ask him!"

DEVOTION

THE INSTRUCTIONS to the soldiers about to be first-time paratroopers were simple: jump out of the aircraft boldly or risk being slammed against the side of the plane. You could get hurt trying to go timidly into the vast expanse beyond the airplane door. Some things in life just can't be approached apprehensively.

Jesus wanted his followers to approach prayer boldly. Go with confidence before the throne of God expecting to be heard. Take him your needs, your hurts, your disappointment. Our promise from God is the same one he made to the children of Israel long ago: he will never leave us or forget us. If he seems distant, perhaps it's because we're the ones who moved away.

As a college professor, I'm in one of the most "beseeched" professions on earth dealing with some of the most persistent "beseechers" God ever made. How can I make up my absence? Can I have extra time on my paper? Is there any way I can change my grade? Do you have a policy for extra credit? Like the friend in the house at midnight in the parable above, I've been caught at church services, at the movies, at restaurants, and every other place imaginable by anxious students.

And though I try to be impartial to every request, I admit to having a preference for the bold ones. Rather than whining, they simply say: "I've messed up and I want to make it better. Is there any way?" And then we usually work things out.

In Matthew's account of this story we're told "your Father knows the things you need before you ask him" (Matthew 6:8). He knows I need forgiveness. He knows I need direction. He knows I need sustenance. There are no secrets between God and me, and there are no secrets between him and you, either. And because there are no secrets, each of us can go boldly to God in prayer. Even though I may not get everything I want, God has promised to give me what I need.

So if it helps, before you get on your knees in prayer, imagine those instructions to the first-time jumpers huddled in that plane: go boldly into the vast expanse of God's grace, more reliable than even the most carefully packed parachute.

THOUGHTS TO PONDER

When is the last time you approached God boldly in prayer? What are some of the opportunities that God offers those who ask? What are some of the things God requires of his children?

PRAYER

Father, we thank you that we are invited to approach you boldly in prayer. Help us to walk in a manner worthy of the grace you have given us as your children. Amen.

DRINKING THE CUP
GOD OFFERS

MARK 10:35–45

[35]Then James and John, sons of Zebedee, came to Jesus and said, "Teacher, we want to ask you to do something for us."

[36]Jesus asked, "What do you want me to do for you?"

[37]They answered, "Let one of us sit at your right side and one of us sit at your left side in your glory in your kingdom."

[38]Jesus said, "You don't understand what you are asking. Can you drink the cup that I must drink? And can you be baptized with the same kind of baptism that I must go through?"

[39]They answered, "Yes, we can."

Jesus said to them, "You will drink the same cup that I will drink, and you will be baptized with the same baptism that I must go through. [40]But I cannot choose who will sit at my right or my left; those places belong to those for whom they have been prepared."

[41]When the other ten followers heard this, they began to be angry with James and John.

[42]Jesus called them together and said, "The other nations have rulers. You know that those rulers love to show their power over the people, and their important leaders love to use all their authority. [43]But it should not be that way among you. Whoever wants to become great among you must serve the rest of you like a servant. [44]Whoever wants to become the first among you must serve all of you like a slave. [45]In the same way, the Son of Man did not come to be served. He came to serve others and to give his life as a ransom for many people."

DEVOTION

ONE OF THE GREAT IRONIES of effective leadership is that good leaders are first good servants. And while leadership gurus and authors have discovered this fact in recent years, Jesus was teaching it two thousand years ago.

The more I'm around leaders, the more I'm convinced that "leader" doesn't mean "boss." Leaders may have employees under them, but that's more an outcome than a goal. When I see effective leaders, I inevitably see effective servants. When I have been appointed to leadership roles, it became quickly obvious that my role was that of a facilitator, helping talented people have the resources they needed to do their jobs right.

Servanthood is the quickest route to leadership that I know. How rare is servanthood? It doesn't even show up in the spell checker of my computer.

There are two versions of this story in the Gospel accounts of Matthew and Mark. They are quite similar in the basics. The two petitioners are James and John, the sons of Zebedee, who had been called out of a boat where they were fishing with their father to follow Jesus (Mark 1:19). They had immediately joined him. The accounts agree that the request got back to the other ten and they became angry with the brothers.

Where the accounts of Matthew and Mark differ is in who makes the request. In the account above, from Mark, it is the brothers who do the asking. In the account in Matthew (20:20–28), it is their mother. The best way to reconcile the two accounts is to surmise that the idea came from a very proud mother who urged her boys and perhaps even accompanied them to Jesus to make the request.

The request also points out what was a very common belief among the followers of Jesus—that he would soon set up an earthly kingdom. Indeed, in the chapter that follows, his entry into Jerusalem had all the markings of the entry of a king with people lining the streets singing praises and putting palm branches in the road.

Because of this misconception, James and John didn't really even know what they were asking of Jesus. And even though I've never sought a special seat by Jesus in my prayers, I think I've prayed for something without realizing what I was requesting.

I've prayed for patience without knowing what I was asking for. Then came plenty of problems to teach me patience. I've prayed for a meaningful role in his kingdom. God sent me plenty of people to serve. At some points, I almost wanted to take back my requests.

When James and John said they could drink the same cup as Jesus, they didn't know what they had agreed to, but they found out. For them, it meant death for their beliefs. Each of us must drink of the cup we're offered from God, for in doing so, we become more like Jesus.

THOUGHTS TO PONDER

What did Jesus mean when he told James and John that they would drink of his cup and be baptized with his baptism? Why was it not up to Jesus who would sit in the seats on his left and right hand?

PRAYER

God, help us to not be blinded by ambition and help us to only ask for what you know we can bear. Amen.

"I Can't See My Sins"

MARK 10:46–52

⁴⁶Then they came to the town of Jericho. As Jesus was leaving there with his followers and a great many people, a blind beggar named Bartimaeus son of Timaeus was sitting by the road. ⁴⁷When he heard that Jesus from Nazareth was walking by, he began to shout, "Jesus, Son of David, have mercy on me!"

⁴⁸Many people warned the blind man to be quiet, but he shouted even more, "Son of David, have mercy on me!"

⁴⁹Jesus stopped and said, "Tell the man to come here."

So they called the blind man, saying, "Cheer up! Get to your feet. Jesus is calling you." ⁵⁰The blind man jumped up, left his coat there, and went to Jesus.

⁵¹Jesus asked him, "What do you want me to do for you?"

The blind man answered, "Teacher, I want to see."

⁵²Jesus said, "Go, you are healed because you believed." At once the man could see, and he followed Jesus on the road.

DEVOTION

TRY TO IMAGINE hearing these words after a lifetime of darkness: "Jesus is calling you." But something this dramatic has happened in each one of our lives: when we call, "Have mercy on me, a sinner," God responds with his wonderful saving grace.

The blind man's request was simple: "Teacher, I want to see." I wonder why we can't all make that same request of Jesus today. Even though we may have perfect eyesight, there is so much we need to see. We need to see God's will in our lives. We need to see the many physical and spiritual needs of everyone around us. We need to see our own sins.

The story is told of a young girl who immigrated to the United States from her native Cuba. A devout Catholic, the young girl was faithful in going to confession. She wasn't fluent in English, but there was one priest who spoke Spanish and she always sought him out to confess her sins in her native language.

However, one confessional day, the bilingual priest said he was going to be gone the next week. He told her that she would need to say her confession to an English-speaking priest.

So the Cuban girl asked an American friend to help her translate her sins into English and write them on a slip of paper for her to read phonetically. She would read them using her limited English skills. She memorized her opening line ("Forgive me, Father, for I have sinned") and then rehearsed the reading of her transgressions.

On the appointed day, she went into the booth and started by repeating in English the phrase she had memorized. "Forgive me, Father, for I have sinned." She then looked down at the list she was to read and discovered that it was too dark in the booth to read.

A little hesitantly now, she started again, "Forgive me, Father, for I have sinned."

She looked down, faltered, and then, frustrated, gave up.

"Forgive me, Father," she said for the third and final time and she slipped out of the booth. On her way out, through her tears, another bilingual confessant heard her say in her native tongue: "I can't see my sins."

"I can't see my sins." What a profound statement. How many of us truly "see our sins"?

How many of us can stand outside our lives and take an objective look at what we've become? The first step toward forgiveness is to recognize our sins. Until we can "see" them, we can't repent. Could the Pharisees who constantly criticized Jesus on the finer points of the law, ignoring the great good he was doing among the people, not to mention the fact that he was the long-awaited Messiah, see their sin of self-righteousness?

I like the end of the story of Bartimaeus. Now able to see, he was sent on his way by Jesus. "Go, you are healed because you believed," Jesus said. But of all the sights he could have gone to see, and of all the people he could go look in the eyes for the first time, Bartimaeus simply took up his place in the throngs who were following Jesus.

Why? He had seen Jesus. And once you've seen Jesus, everything is different. Try praying the prayer of Bartimaeus today: "Teacher, I want to see."

THOUGHTS TO PONDER

What are some of the things in this world that we can become "blind" to? What things would the world have us spend our time looking at? Can you truly see your own sins?

PRAYER

God, we pray that you will open our eyes so we may see you and see all your children in the world who have needs that we can serve today. Amen.

A Prayer Away

LUKE 10:38—11:13

³⁸While Jesus and his followers were traveling, Jesus went into a town. A woman named Martha let Jesus stay at her house. ³⁹Martha had a sister named Mary, who was sitting at Jesus' feet and listening to him teach. ⁴⁰But Martha was busy with all the work to be done. She went in and said, "Lord, don't you care that my sister has left me alone to do all the work? Tell her to help me."

⁴¹But the Lord answered her, "Martha, Martha, you are worried and upset about many things. ⁴²Only one thing is important. Mary has chosen the better thing, and it will never be taken away from her."

11 One time Jesus was praying in a certain place. When he finished, one of his followers said to him, "Lord, teach us to pray as John taught his followers."

²Jesus said to them, "When you pray, say:
'Father, may your name always be kept holy.
May your kingdom come.
³Give us the food we need for each day.
⁴Forgive us for our sins,
    because we forgive everyone who has done wrong to us.
And do not cause us to be tempted.' "

⁵Then Jesus said to them, "Suppose one of you went to your friend's house at midnight and said to him, 'Friend, loan me three loaves of bread. ⁶A friend of mine has come into town to visit me, but I have nothing for him to eat.' ⁷Your friend inside the house answers, 'Don't bother me! The door is already locked, and my children and I are in bed. I cannot get up and give you anything.' ⁸I tell you, if friendship is not enough to make him get up to give you the bread, your boldness will make him get up and give you whatever you need. ⁹So I tell you, ask, and God will give to you. Search, and you will find. Knock, and the door will open for you. ¹⁰Yes, everyone who asks will receive. The one who searches will find. And everyone who knocks will have the door opened. ¹¹If your children ask for a fish, which of you would give them a snake instead? ¹²Or, if your children ask for an egg, would you give them a scorpion? ¹³Even though you are bad, you know how to give good things to your children. How much more your heavenly Father will give the Holy Spirit to those who ask him!"

DEVOTION

JESUS HAD COME TO SEE his friends for a social occasion. Custom of the time dictated that a guest of Jesus' stature should be offered a meal of at least three courses, and Martha set about that task. Think of it: no electricity, no microwave, no refrigeration and a three course meal to prepare. No wonder she was miffed when her sister Mary went to sit at the feet of Jesus. She implored Jesus to send Mary into the kitchen. A proper guest required a proper meal.

Jesus' reply—"only one thing is needed"—has been alternatively interpreted as asking for a simple one-course meal to complimenting the one thing Mary chose to do—listen to the voice of the Master. I think he meant both. If you're going to hear my voice, he says to them and to us today, do the following: simplify your life by putting first things first.

Don't get me wrong; you can find peace in a traffic jam and you can say a silent prayer when you're wrestling with a paper jam in the copier. But for the clearest signal in our communication with God, one thing is needed, and Mary got it right: get your worries behind you and get at the feet of Jesus through his Word and through prayer. All too often I do only the latter—tell God what's on my mind and ask a few favors along the way—without looking into his mind as revealed by his Word. But both are required to hear the voice of God.

It would have been wonderful to sit at the feet of Jesus like Mary, but the opportunity is still there today if we only take it.

In the next passage, Jesus not only taught his followers how to pray; he encouraged them to be bold in doing so. The instructions to "ask," "search," and "find" are some of the most comforting assurances in all of Scripture. Our God is never further away than a prayer.

THOUGHTS TO PONDER

If you were at the feet of Jesus, what would be the first thing you would ask? Jesus says, "Only one thing is important." Can you emphasize that one thing in your life today? Are you bold when you approach God in prayer?

PRAYER

God, we thank you that you have invited us to pray to you. Let us clear away the worries of today and find a way to connect with you. Amen.

"Where Are You, God?"

JOHN 11:1–7, 20–28, 33–44

11 A man named Lazarus was sick. He lived in the town of Bethany, where Mary and her sister Martha lived. ²Mary was the woman who later put perfume on the Lord and wiped his feet with her hair. Mary's brother was Lazarus, the man who was now sick. ³So Mary and Martha sent someone to tell Jesus, "Lord, the one you love is sick."

⁴When Jesus heard this, he said, "This sickness will not end in death. It is for the glory of God, to bring glory to the Son of God." ⁵Jesus loved Martha and her sister and Lazarus. ⁶But when he heard that Lazarus was sick, he stayed where he was for two more days. ⁷Then Jesus said to his followers, "Let's go back to Judea."

²⁰When Martha heard that Jesus was coming, she went out to meet him, but Mary stayed home. ²¹Martha said to Jesus, "Lord, if you had been here, my brother would not have died. ²²But I know that even now God will give you anything you ask."

²³Jesus said, "Your brother will rise and live again."

²⁴Martha answered, "I know that he will rise and live again in the resurrection on the last day."

²⁵Jesus said to her, "I am the resurrection and the life. Those who believe in me will have life even if they die. ²⁶And everyone who lives and believes in me will never die. Martha, do you believe this?"

²⁷Martha answered, "Yes, Lord. I believe that you are the Christ, the Son of God, the One coming to the world."

²⁸After Martha said this, she went back and talked to her sister Mary alone. Martha said, "The Teacher is here and he is asking for you."

³³When Jesus saw Mary crying and the Jews who came with her also crying, he was upset and was deeply troubled. ³⁴He asked, "Where did you bury him?"

"Come and see, Lord," they said.

³⁵Jesus cried.

³⁶So the Jews said, "See how much he loved him."

³⁷But some of them said, "If Jesus opened the eyes of the blind man, why couldn't he keep Lazarus from dying?"

³⁸Again feeling very upset, Jesus came to the tomb. It was a cave with a large stone covering the entrance. ³⁹Jesus said, "Move the stone away."

Martha, the sister of the dead man, said, "But, Lord, it has been four days since he died. There will be a bad smell."

⁴⁰Then Jesus said to her, "Didn't I tell you that if you believed you would see the glory of God?"

[41]So they moved the stone away from the entrance. Then Jesus looked up and said, "Father, I thank you that you heard me. [42]I know that you always hear me, but I said these things because of the people here around me. I want them to believe that you sent me." [43]After Jesus said this, he cried out in a loud voice, "Lazarus, come out!" [44]The dead man came out, his hands and feet wrapped with pieces of cloth, and a cloth around his face.

Jesus said to them, "Take the cloth off of him and let him go."

DEVOTION

THE REACTION OF MARTHA comforts me because it sounds like me. She got a little testy with Jesus: "If you had been here, my brother would not have died," she told him. Martha believed in his power to heal, but Jesus hadn't come quickly enough when he had been summoned. Now her brother was dead.

Where were you Lord? It's a common question. Where were you when the terrorists struck? Where were you when the hurricane hit? Martha's reaction, which mirrored that of her sister, Mary, tells me that it's alright to question God at times like these. He's big enough to take it.

There will inevitably be times when I am disappointed with God. When I want relief but none is in sight, I can ask, "Where are you, God?" without fear of being struck down.

I serve a God who wept at the tomb of Lazarus, and he still feels my pain today. And even if he doesn't take away all the pain today, he has promised a time when there will be no more tears (Revelation 21:4).

Where is God when I need him? The same place he is when I ignore him. Just a prayer away.

THOUGHTS TO PONDER

Have you ever felt that something bad wouldn't have happened if God had been nearer? Have you ever wondered, "God, where were you?" How did Jesus handle that question?

PRAYER

God, we know that everything happens in your time, and that your timetable is not always ours. Help us to continue to beseech you, but help us to find comfort in the answers you give. Amen.

Lasting Treasures

LUKE 12:13–34

¹³Someone in the crowd said to Jesus, "Teacher, tell my brother to divide with me the property our father left us."

¹⁴But Jesus said to him, "Who said I should judge or decide between you?" ¹⁵Then Jesus said to them, "Be careful and guard against all kinds of greed. Life is not measured by how much one owns."

¹⁶Then Jesus told this story: "There was a rich man who had some land, which grew a good crop. ¹⁷He thought to himself, 'What will I do? I have no place to keep all my crops.' ¹⁸Then he said, 'This is what I will do: I will tear down my barns and build bigger ones, and there I will store all my grain and other goods. ¹⁹Then I can say to myself, "I have enough good things stored to last for many years. Rest, eat, drink, and enjoy life!" '

²⁰"But God said to him, 'Foolish man! Tonight your life will be taken from you. So who will get those things you have prepared for yourself?'

²¹"This is how it will be for those who store up things for themselves and are not rich toward God."

²²Jesus said to his followers, "So I tell you, don't worry about the food you need to live, or about the clothes you need for your body. ²³Life is more than food, and the body is more than clothes. ²⁴Look at the birds. They don't plant or harvest, they don't have storerooms or barns, but God feeds them. And you are worth much more than birds. ²⁵You cannot add any time to your life by worrying about it. ²⁶If you cannot do even the little things, then why worry about the big things? ²⁷Consider how the lilies grow; they don't work or make clothes for themselves. But I tell you that even Solomon with his riches was not dressed as beautifully as one of these flowers. ²⁸God clothes the grass in the field, which is alive today but tomorrow is thrown into the fire. So how much more will God clothe you? Don't have so little faith! ²⁹Don't always think about what you will eat or what you will drink, and don't keep worrying. ³⁰All the people in the world are trying to get these things, and your Father knows you need them. ³¹But seek God's kingdom, and all your other needs will be met as well.

³²"Don't fear, little flock, because your Father wants to give you the kingdom. ³³Sell your possessions and give to the poor. Get for yourselves purses that will not wear out, the treasure in heaven that never runs out, where thieves can't steal and moths can't destroy. ³⁴Your heart will be where your treasure is."

Devotion

TO BORROW A TERM from the gorilla kingdom, we have an "alpha male" hummingbird at our cabin this summer. He's slightly larger than the other hummingbirds and noticeably brighter in the red coloring around the neck and head.

He perches on the top of our hummingbird feeder, a long plastic tube with bright red sugar water and four feeding spigots at the bottom. In other years, it was not unusual to see two or three hummingbirds at a time around the feeder, but not this year. Our alpha male perches on the feeder, guarding it from any intruders.

During "rush hour" just after sunup, it's not unusual to see him chasing away as many as six hungry hummingbirds. The most timid are the all-green young females, but even the males go away after being closely buzzed by the bully.

Now, there's more sugary water in that tube than he would eat in a season. Plus, it gets replenished frequently. But he doesn't care. He wants it all for himself.

Our rich man in the story above had enjoyed a good crop. Having grown up in dry land cotton country, I know the "boom or bust" cycle of farming; this man had just enjoyed a bumper crop. Notice that Jesus says that it was the land that grew the crop. The man was just the beneficiary of a combination of good earth and good weather.

What he does next seals his fate. It is not the fact that he is rich that angers God. It's what he does with these riches, hoarding them for himself, that angers God. Like our alpha hummingbird, the rich man decides to keep the bounty for himself rather than sharing his good fortune with those less fortunate. I get the image of an Ebenezer Scrooge with grain in the place of coins.

God calls him foolish, condemns him to death, and reminds him that none of his good fortune will follow him in death. In the teaching that follows the parable, Jesus reminds us of two things. First, God takes care of his own, and second, the only lasting treasures are those stored in heaven.

Thoughts to ponder

What exactly was the rich man's sin? What does God's reaction to the rich man tell us about being wealthy today?

Prayer

God, we know that all wealth comes from you and we acknowledge you as its source. Please help us to be generous with your riches. Amen.

HUMAN RULES
VS. TRUE GOODNESS

LUKE 13:6–21

⁶Jesus told this story: "A man had a fig tree planted in his vineyard. He came looking for some fruit on the tree, but he found none. ⁷So the man said to his gardener, 'I have been looking for fruit on this tree for three years, but I never find any. Cut it down. Why should it waste the ground?' ⁸But the servant answered, 'Master, let the tree have one more year to produce fruit. Let me dig up the dirt around it and put on some fertilizer. ⁹If the tree produces fruit next year, good. But if not, you can cut it down.' "

¹⁰Jesus was teaching in one of the synagogues on the Sabbath day. ¹¹A woman was there who, for eighteen years, had an evil spirit in her that made her crippled. Her back was always bent; she could not stand up straight. ¹²When Jesus saw her, he called her over and said, "Woman, you are free from your sickness." ¹³Jesus put his hands on her, and immediately she was able to stand up straight and began praising God.

¹⁴The synagogue leader was angry because Jesus healed on the Sabbath day. He said to the people, "There are six days when one has to work. So come to be healed on one of those days, and not on the Sabbath day."

¹⁵The Lord answered, "You hypocrites! Doesn't each of you untie your work animals and lead them to drink water every day—even on the Sabbath day? ¹⁶This woman that I healed, a daughter of Abraham, has been held by Satan for eighteen years. Surely it is not wrong for her to be freed from her sickness on a Sabbath day!" ¹⁷When Jesus said this, all of those who were criticizing him were ashamed, but the entire crowd rejoiced at all the wonderful things Jesus was doing.

¹⁸Then Jesus said, "What is God's kingdom like? What can I compare it with? ¹⁹It is like a mustard seed that a man plants in his garden. The seed grows and becomes a tree, and the wild birds build nests in its branches."

²⁰Jesus said again, "What can I compare God's kingdom with? ²¹It is like yeast that a woman took and hid in a large tub of flour until it made all the dough rise."

DEVOTION

THIS IS THE LAST ACCOUNT we have of Jesus teaching in a synagogue. In fact, it is the last account of Jesus being in synagogue, and there is little doubt that his every move was now being watched by those who wanted to entrap him. So when Jesus healed the woman who had been stooped for eighteen years—apparently the work of an evil spirit—the leader of the synagogue was quick to point out that Jesus had just performed the act of healing on the Sabbath, the traditional day of rest for the Jews.

Notice in the story above that the leader of the synagogue did not even have the courage to address his comments to Jesus. Instead, he took his problem with the actions of Jesus directly to the people. Don't bring your illnesses in here on a Sabbath, he seemed to be saying, because our rules are more important than our compassion.

But Jesus pointed out that even animals could be given relief from their thirst on the Sabbath. Surely, this woman, with eighteen years of suffering deserved relief from her illness even though it was a Sabbath. The text tells us that his answer shamed his critics.

Have you ever been around someone like the leader of this synagogue? Someone who was so obsessed with legalistic versions of what was "right" that they couldn't see what was truly good? Have you ever known anyone who worshiped the rules more than the one who made the rules? It's an easy problem to slip into and a hard one to escape.

The ministry of Jesus was focused on people just like this woman in the story above. If Jesus brought his friends and acquaintances into our churches, how welcome would they be? Common fishermen. Tax collectors. The lame. Those who had been unclean from skin diseases. Prostitutes. How welcome would we make them feel? Don't they need to be freed from their sins on Sunday as surely as this woman needed to be freed from her handicap on the Sabbath?

THOUGHTS TO PONDER

What is an instance in which human rules about what's "right" don't match up with the truth of what's good and right in God's eyes? What message was Jesus sending by healing so often on the Sabbath?

PRAYER

Father, we pray that we will treat others with the compassion that Jesus showed for them and that we will seek to love and care for other people above our own rules and regulations. Amen.

A Seat at the Table

LUKE 14:7–24

⁷When Jesus noticed that some of the guests were choosing the best places to sit, he told this story: ⁸"When someone invites you to a wedding feast, don't take the most important seat, because someone more important than you may have been invited. ⁹The host, who invited both of you, will come to you and say, 'Give this person your seat.' Then you will be embarrassed and will have to move to the last place. ¹⁰So when you are invited, go sit in a seat that is not important. When the host comes to you, he may say, 'Friend, move up here to a more important place.' Then all the other guests will respect you. ¹¹All who make themselves great will be made humble, but those who make themselves humble will be made great."

¹²Then Jesus said to the man who had invited him, "When you give a lunch or a dinner, don't invite only your friends, your family, your other relatives, and your rich neighbors. At another time they will invite you to eat with them, and you will be repaid. ¹³Instead, when you give a feast, invite the poor, the crippled, the lame, and the blind. ¹⁴Then you will be blessed, because they have nothing and cannot pay you back. But you will be repaid when the good people rise from the dead."

¹⁵One of those at the table with Jesus heard these things and said to him, "Blessed are the people who will share in the meal in God's kingdom."

¹⁶Jesus said to him, "A man gave a big banquet and invited many people. ¹⁷When it was time to eat, the man sent his servant to tell the guests, 'Come. Everything is ready.'

¹⁸"But all the guests made excuses. The first one said, 'I have just bought a field, and I must go look at it. Please excuse me.' ¹⁹Another said, 'I have just bought five pairs of oxen; I must go and try them. Please excuse me.' ²⁰A third person said, 'I just got married; I can't come.' ²¹So the servant returned and told his master what had happened. Then the master became angry and said, 'Go at once into the streets and alleys of the town, and bring in the poor, the crippled, the blind, and the lame.' ²²Later the servant said to him, 'Master, I did what you commanded, but we still have room.' ²³The master said to the servant, 'Go out to the roads and country lanes, and urge the people there to come so my house will be full. ²⁴I tell you, none of those whom I invited first will eat with me.' "

Devotion

AT THE ANCIENT FEASTS, the guests literally reclined at the table, usually on their left arm and ate with their right from the common dishes placed in front of them on the low tables. Because of the arrangement, there was obviously a preferred side. Unlike today's tables where a host can be expected to entertain conversation from both sides, the ancient method of seating left some people unable to talk to the host. This important seat, probably to the right of the host, would have his full attention while the spot to the left would have only his back.

In reading these stories, I'm reminded of a time when my oldest daughter was about four years old. If anyone offended her, she would promptly let them know, "You're not invited to my birthday party." Now the date might be months away, but the threat was good for any season. The list of people not invited to her next birthday party grew quite long indeed and at one time included both her mother and me. It left us to wonder who was going to throw this party.

The host on this evening was not much more morally developed than my four-year-old daughter. It would have never occurred to him to invite those out of his class into his home. Public meals were a display of wealth—fine foods, servants, music. So many people came and went serving the guests that at one party it was even possible for a less-than-reputable woman to slip in and begin anointing the feet of Jesus with expensive perfume and her tears.

But if this man's feast was about favorites and tacky displays of wealth, God's feast will be different, Jesus says. Everyone is invited to this birthday party. But unfortunately, many will be too preoccupied to come. And the very ones left out of the earthly party—the poor, the crippled, and the blind—will be the ones who eat at God's table.

This is good news for me. I wasn't born into a special group or class that merits the favor of God. But because of Christ, I am family. I can claim a spot at the table where every seat is a good seat and everyone is welcome.

Thoughts to ponder

Do we leave people out of God's feast today? Have we made our churches accommodating to the homeless? The addict? The unwed mother? Would Jesus be eating with them today?

Prayer

God, we pray that we will give everyone a chance to sit at the table as we strive to worship you and try to be your kingdom here on this earth. Amen.

RARE AND VALUABLE

LUKE 15:1–10

15 The tax collectors and sinners all came to listen to Jesus. [2]But the Pharisees and the teachers of the law began to complain: "Look, this man welcomes sinners and even eats with them."

[3]Then Jesus told them this story: [4]"Suppose one of you has a hundred sheep but loses one of them. Then he will leave the other ninety-nine sheep in the open field and go out and look for the lost sheep until he finds it. [5]And when he finds it, he happily puts it on his shoulders [6]and goes home. He calls to his friends and neighbors and says, 'Be happy with me because I found my lost sheep.' [7]In the same way, I tell you there is more joy in heaven over one sinner who changes his heart and life, than over ninety-nine good people who don't need to change.

[8]"Suppose a woman has ten silver coins, but loses one. She will light a lamp, sweep the house, and look carefully for the coin until she finds it. [9]And when she finds it, she will call her friends and neighbors and say, 'Be happy with me because I have found the coin that I lost.' [10]In the same way, there is joy in the presence of the angels of God when one sinner changes his heart and life."

DEVOTION

AT A RECENT AUCTION, a rare nickel with a colorful history sold for $3 million. Here's the story of the nickel.

As the nation's mints prepared to move from the old Liberty Head nickel to the new Indian Head nickel at the end of 1912, five coins with the old Liberty Head were struck with the new 1913 date in Philadelphia, either by accident or, more likely, as a part of a plot by a mint employee to create a rare coin. Because of their unauthorized minting, the nickels were at one time illegal to own.

Thanks to their colorful heritage and extreme rarity, the five nickels have been notorious in coin collecting circles for nearly a hundred years. One of the five went out of circulation for more than four decades when the owners were mistakenly told by a dealer that it was a fake—a bit of irony for a coin that was a manufactured rare coin from its inception.

Whether created intentionally or accidentally, the coins are valuable because they are rare. In our story, the woman's coin is valuable because, to her, it is rare. It is one-tenth of what she owns. To the shepherd, each and every sheep is unique and valuable. To the woman, each coin is the same. So each went looking for what they valued.

Jesus was also looking for something. He told one repentant sinner that he came to "find lost people and save them" (Luke 19:10), and he's still looking today.

To God, you are rare and valuable. And he proves that to each of us over and over again. How do I know? He made us in his image. He sustains us with his hand. And he redeemed us with his Son.

Going by the last purchase price, a 1913 Liberty Head nickel is worth $3 million. Going by your purchase price, you are worth the blood of the Son of God. Even if you had been the only sinner in the world, he still would have sent his Son to redeem you. You're worth that much to him.

The context of these wonderful stories is a criticism by the Pharisees and the teachers of the law. Jesus had the audacity to call sinners such as tax collectors to listen to him, and he had even eaten with at least one of them as we see in the story of Zacchaeus. Jesus responds to their criticism with three stories—these two and the one to follow, commonly called the Prodigal Son.

The religion of the Pharisees and the leading priests was not a religion of outreach as we commonly view religion today. They showed no interest in enlarging their community of faith—at least, not in the recorded passages in the Gospels. In fact, on at least one occasion, with the blind man and his parents (John 9), we see them threatening to expel them from the Temple if they gave credit to Jesus for the miracle.

Jesus was attacking this view of religion. He was opening the doors that the religious hierarchy was trying to close, because he knew the value of a single person to God.

THOUGHTS TO PONDER

What are some of the most valuable items you own? Why are they valuable? What would you do if they were suddenly lost?

PRAYER

God, we're grateful that you value each and every one of us. Help us to take heart from that and live as worthily as we can of your love. Amen.

A Second Chance

LUKE 15:11–25, 28–32

[11]"A man had two sons. [12]The younger son said to his father, 'Give me my share of the property.' So the father divided the property between his two sons. [13]Then the younger son gathered up all that was his and traveled far away to another country. There he wasted his money in foolish living. [14]After he had spent everything, a time came when there was no food anywhere in the country, and the son was poor and hungry. [15]So he got a job with one of the citizens there who sent the son into the fields to feed pigs. [16]The son was so hungry that he wanted to eat the pods the pigs were eating, but no one gave him anything. [17]When he realized what he was doing, he thought, 'All of my father's servants have plenty of food. But I am here, almost dying with hunger. [18]I will leave and return to my father and say to him, "Father, I have sinned against God and against you. [19]I am no longer worthy to be called your son, but let me be like one of your servants."' [20]So the son left and went to his father.

"While the son was still a long way off, his father saw him and felt sorry for his son. So the father ran to him and hugged and kissed him. [21]The son said, 'Father, I have sinned against God and against you. I am no longer worthy to be called your son.' [22]But the father said to his servants, 'Hurry! Bring the best clothes and put them on him. Also, put a ring on his finger and sandals on his feet. [23]And get our fat calf and kill it so we can have a feast and celebrate. [24]My son was dead, but now he is alive again! He was lost, but now he is found!' So they began to celebrate.

[25]"The older son was in the field, and as he came closer to the house, he heard the sound of music and dancing."

[28]"The older son was angry and would not go in to the feast. So his father went out and begged him to come in. [29]But the older son said to his father, 'I have served you like a slave for many years and have always obeyed your commands. But you never gave me even a young goat to have at a feast with my friends. [30]But your other son, who wasted all your money on prostitutes, comes home, and you kill the fat calf for him!' [31]The father said to him, 'Son, you are always with me, and all that I have is yours. [32]We had to celebrate and be happy because your brother was dead, but now he is alive. He was lost, but now he is found.'"

DEVOTION

BEFORE HE WAS SIXTEEN, Jesse was in jail for his participation in a race riot at a New Mexico high school that left one boy dead. Approaching the age where juvenile detention could not keep him anymore, Jesse seemingly had no prospects. Going home probably meant more trouble.

But he had caught the eye of a Christian man, a veterinarian in a community about an hour north of the boys' detention facility in New Mexico. This man was respected in the horse country of northern New Mexico, and he had a plan for Jesse.

He arranged to have Jesse attend a Christian university in Texas. "Doc," as he was affectionately known, arranged transportation, tuition, and all the other details. He was possibly the first person to believe in Jesse.

Jesse thrived in his new environment of a Christian college campus, a complete turnaround from the lockup he had endured the preceding few years. He studied hard, and eventually got a job working with campus security at night. The boy who had once been locked up now held the keys to valuable offices, buildings, and labs.

Jesse found the Lord during this time. Several students and teachers had a role in the process, but no one was more important to Jesse's conversion than "Doc."

One day, Jesse was jogging on the road adjacent to the campus. He loved to stay in good physical condition. However, a large pickup with huge side mirrors came too close to Jesse and the right mirror hit him square on the back of the head. He died immediately.

But Jesse's future is assured because he got a second chance. Not from Doc, not from the university, but from the same one who gives you a second chance, our heavenly Father, the God of second chances. The God who sent his Son to ensure our second chance. The God who will run down the road to meet us when we return.

What will you do with your second chance?

THOUGHTS TO PONDER

What are some of the traits of God we see in this story as evidenced by the behavior of the father? Do we welcome sinners when they return? How can we avoid being the "older brother" in this story?

PRAYER

Father, it is truly an honor to call you our Father and to know that you long for us to be your obedient children. Forgive us when we sin and please run to us when we return to you. Amen.

HEAVEN'S CURRENCY

LUKE 16:19—17:4

¹⁹Jesus said, "There was a rich man who always dressed in the finest clothes and lived in luxury every day. ²⁰And a very poor man named Lazarus, whose body was covered with sores, was laid at the rich man's gate. ²¹He wanted to eat only the small pieces of food that fell from the rich man's table. And the dogs would come and lick his sores. ²²Later, Lazarus died, and the angels carried him to the arms of Abraham. The rich man died, too, and was buried. ²³In the place of the dead, he was in much pain. The rich man saw Abraham far away with Lazarus at his side. ²⁴He called, 'Father Abraham, have mercy on me! Send Lazarus to dip his finger in water and cool my tongue, because I am suffering in this fire!' ²⁵But Abraham said, 'Child, remember when you were alive you had the good things in life, but bad things happened to Lazarus. Now he is comforted here, and you are suffering. ²⁶Besides, there is a big pit between you and us, so no one can cross over to you, and no one can leave there and come here.' ²⁷The rich man said, 'Father, then please send Lazarus to my father's house. ²⁸I have five brothers, and Lazarus could warn them so that they will not come to this place of pain.' ²⁹But Abraham said, 'They have the law of Moses and the writings of the prophets; let them learn from them.' ³⁰The rich man said, 'No, father Abraham! If someone goes to them from the dead, they would believe and change their hearts and lives.' ³¹But Abraham said to him, 'If they will not listen to Moses and the prophets, they will not listen to someone who comes back from the dead.' "

17 Jesus said to his followers, "Things that cause people to sin will happen, but how terrible for the person who causes them to happen! ²It would be better for you to be thrown into the sea with a large stone around your neck than to cause one of these little ones to sin. ³So be careful!

"If another follower sins, warn him, and if he is sorry and stops sinning, forgive him. ⁴If he sins against you seven times in one day and says that he is sorry each time, forgive him."

DEVOTION

IF YOU'VE EVER TRAVELED ABROAD, perhaps you've watched or participated in the frenzy to spend up currency before leaving a country. Traveling through Europe during a semester abroad in the days before the Euro currency, we faced the dilemma many times—spend it or lose it. It's a strange sensation to be spending money before it becomes worthless, or at the very least, greatly devalued at the money changers.

And even though the Euro coins and bills introduced earlier this century have made travel between countries in Europe a little easier, sooner or later you have to come home, and when you do, chances are there will be a little (or a lot) of the local currency in your pocket.

The closer you get to the airport or train station, the worse the exchange rates and the higher the fee, which makes even the sane traveler a temporary "spendaholic." Another rule of traveling seems to be that the closer you are to embarking, the tackier the gifts in the gift stores. If you've ever received a really tacky gift from a globe-trotting friend, perhaps he or she thought of you during a frantic attempt to dump soon-to-be useless currency before getting on the plane.

The rich man in the parable above didn't know it, but in the journey called life, his money was eventually going to become worthless. This lesson is preserved for us today because it is hard, Jesus said, for a rich man to enter the kingdom of heaven (Matthew 19:24). In fact, Jesus taught more on money than any other topic, precisely because he didn't want any of us to fall into the trap of the rich man.

And don't think you're not among the rich. If you're not hungry tonight, if you have a permanent roof over your head tonight, you are rich by the world's standards, so the warnings apply to us. Jesus said "store your treasures in heaven" (Matthew 6:20) rather than on earth. Lazarus did; the rich man didn't. And only one had "currency" in heaven.

THOUGHTS TO PONDER

How do you think this parable was received by the ordinary people following Jesus? How do you think it was received by those in power? How do you counter the accusation of some that Jesus was anti-wealth?

PRAYER

God, we know that you will raise the lowly and resist the proud in your kingdom. We pray that you will find us always among the meek of the earth who will inherit eternal life. Amen.

PATIENT AND FORGIVING

MATTHEW 18:21–35

²¹Then Peter came to Jesus and asked, "Lord, when my fellow believer sins against me, how many times must I forgive him? Should I forgive him as many as seven times?"

²²Jesus answered, "I tell you, you must forgive him more than seven times. You must forgive him even if he wrongs you seventy times seven.

²³"The kingdom of heaven is like a king who decided to collect the money his servants owed him. ²⁴When the king began to collect his money, a servant who owed him several million dollars was brought to him. ²⁵But the servant did not have enough money to pay his master, the king. So the master ordered that everything the servant owned should be sold, even the servant's wife and children. Then the money would be used to pay the king what the servant owed.

²⁶"But the servant fell on his knees and begged, 'Be patient with me, and I will pay you everything I owe.' ²⁷The master felt sorry for his servant and told him he did not have to pay it back. Then he let the servant go free.

²⁸"Later, that same servant found another servant who owed him a few dollars. The servant grabbed him around the neck and said, 'Pay me the money you owe me!'

²⁹"The other servant fell on his knees and begged him, 'Be patient with me, and I will pay you everything I owe.'

³⁰"But the first servant refused to be patient. He threw the other servant into prison until he could pay everything he owed. ³¹When the other servants saw what had happened, they were very sorry. So they went and told their master all that had happened.

³²"Then the master called his servant in and said, 'You evil servant! Because you begged me to forget what you owed, I told you that you did not have to pay anything. ³³You should have showed mercy to that other servant, just as I showed mercy to you.' ³⁴The master was very angry and put the servant in prison to be punished until he could pay everything he owed.

³⁵"This king did what my heavenly Father will do to you if you do not forgive your brother or sister from your heart."

DEVOTION

CONSIDER A FEW of the unanswered questions of this parable. How could the first servant in this passage have gotten so deeply in debt? How does a servant go through millions of dollars of his master's money?

Conversely, where did that deeply indebted servant get the money to loan his fellow servant? Isn't it likely that it was truly the king's money?

This parable, told mainly for the benefit of Peter, is not only about forgiveness; it's about being patient with those around us. One is as important as the other. God is patient with me, allowing me to find my own way, not even forcing me to acknowledge him. But the patient nature of God is a two-edged sword. It keeps him from destroying me for my shortcomings, but it allows my "sin debt" to reach a point where it's as enormous as the millions the servant owed in this story.

But God's forgiveness is greater than my debt. God stands ready to forgive me based on the blood that Jesus shed on the cross. No debt of sin is greater than the price that was paid for me.

You and I could never pay that debt, but here's where it gets interesting. We get a little more like God each time we choose to forgive someone who has sinned against us. Forgiveness is perhaps the most godly trait we will ever take on.

Peter asked his question to limit his liability. *Jesus, when do I get to quit forgiving someone and simply write them off?* The answer from Jesus is "never." Because our God has never given up on us. He hasn't limited his forgiveness to a certain number of times or even a category of sins.

Perhaps the prophet Isaiah put it best in a vision about the nation of Judah: "Though your sins are like scarlet, they can be as white as snow. Though your sins are deep red, they can be white like wool" (Isaiah 1:18).

When I'm looking at my brother or my sister and seeing red from anger, I should look at them again through God's eyes and perhaps the color will change.

THOUGHTS TO PONDER

In your life, are you more often asking for forgiveness or being called on to forgive? Which is harder? Why is it important that Christians be forgiving people?

PRAYER

God, you have forgiven us of so much. Help us to be forgiving to others in the same manner. Amen.

PERSISTENCE AND GOD'S TIMETABLE

LUKE 18:1–14

18 Then Jesus used this story to teach his followers that they should always pray and never lose hope. ²"In a certain town there was a judge who did not respect God or care about people. ³In that same town there was a widow who kept coming to this judge, saying, 'Give me my rights against my enemy.' ⁴For a while the judge refused to help her. But afterwards, he thought to himself, 'Even though I don't respect God or care about people, ⁵I will see that she gets her rights. Otherwise she will continue to bother me until I am worn out.' "

⁶The Lord said, "Listen to what the unfair judge said. ⁷God will always give what is right to his people who cry to him night and day, and he will not be slow to answer them. ⁸I tell you, God will help his people quickly. But when the Son of Man comes again, will he find those on earth who believe in him?"

⁹Jesus told this story to some people who thought they were very good and looked down on everyone else: ¹⁰"A Pharisee and a tax collector both went to the Temple to pray. ¹¹The Pharisee stood alone and prayed, 'God, I thank you that I am not like other people who steal, cheat, or take part in adultery, or even like this tax collector. ¹²I fast twice a week, and I give one-tenth of everything I get!'

¹³"The tax collector, standing at a distance, would not even look up to heaven. But he beat on his chest because he was so sad. He said, 'God, have mercy on me, a sinner.' ¹⁴I tell you, when this man went home, he was right with God, but the Pharisee was not. All who make themselves great will be made humble, but all who make themselves humble will be made great."

DEVOTION

WHAT DO YOU ASK for in prayer? According to a survey by Silent Unity, an international prayer ministry, here is the order, by category, of the two million prayer requests it receives annually: healing, divine order, peace of mind, guidance, harmony, prosperity, success, employment, protection, and justice. In May of 1979, my wife and I had been in our new house in Lubbock, Texas for three months. It was a new subdivision of starter homes full of young couples we were getting to know. On May 30, a truck ran off the nearby loop that encircled Lubbock, over a ditch, across the two-lane service road, over another ditch, and then straight through the east bedroom of the house across the street. Its overturned tires were spinning a few feet from my mailbox.

Across the street, a third of the house was demolished and the wife was buried in her daughter's closet where she had been working. She had a broken back. The daughter, who was out, would surely have been killed if she had been home in her room.

I had thought of the event periodically over the years, and even written about it. Some time later, I saw an interview with the husband in the Lubbock paper. His wife had been both paralyzed and in pain for twenty-five years. But a fourth surgery a couple of months earlier had caused her to regain feeling in her legs and had relieved some pain.

"No matter what people might say," he wrote to the paper, "God answers prayers." He reported that she had actually felt tingling in her legs for the first time in twenty-five years the night *before* the surgery as family members gathered in prayer for her. "That could only have been the hand of God touching her that night," he said.

Pray hard and wait for an answer. That's the message of the first story above. And the second story tells us to pray humbly, for even God's "foolishness" is greater than our wisdom (1 Corinthians 1:25).

Our timetable is rarely God's, but God's deliverance from our present pain, even if it happens in eternity, is sure.

THOUGHTS TO PONDER

Looking again at the list above of the things that people ask for in prayer, what do you think explains the order? If you were to order the things you ask for in prayer, what would your list look like?

PRAYER

Father, thank you for the avenue of prayer. Help us to come to you often, not only with our needs, but also with our praise, for you alone are worthy. Amen.

Being Genuine with God

LUKE 18:9–17

⁹Jesus told this story to some people who thought they were very good and looked down on everyone else: ¹⁰"A Pharisee and a tax collector both went to the Temple to pray. ¹¹The Pharisee stood alone and prayed, 'God, I thank you that I am not like other people who steal, cheat, or take part in adultery, or even like this tax collector. ¹²I fast twice a week, and I give one-tenth of everything I get!'

¹³"The tax collector, standing at a distance, would not even look up to heaven. But he beat on his chest because he was so sad. He said, 'God, have mercy on me, a sinner.' ¹⁴I tell you, when this man went home, he was right with God, but the Pharisee was not. All who make themselves great will be made humble, but all who make themselves humble will be made great."

¹⁵Some people brought even their babies to Jesus so he could touch them. When the followers saw this, they told them to stop. ¹⁶But Jesus called for the children, saying, "Let the little children come to me. Don't stop them, because the kingdom of God belongs to people who are like these children. ¹⁷I tell you the truth, you must accept the kingdom of God as if you were a child, or you will never enter it."

Devotion

THIS IS ONE of the very few stories of Jesus that has a specific target audience. Fed up with the self-righteous leaders all around him, Jesus tells the story above.

In the late 1960s, long before the rise of the modern "megachurch," a great minister I knew ministered over a congregation that had grown to nearly two thousand members, the largest of its type in the nation. In a tradition where weekly communion and congregational singing were a part of each worship service, the minister quickly became an authority on "facilitating the assembly" as he called it. He felt that churches could only grow if members were comfortable that the assembly would end at a predictable time each week.

The worship leaders would meet in his office a few minutes before the services began. He would ask the prayer leaders, "Do you pray to God regularly?" Taken by surprise, most would mutter, "Sure," or, "Of course."

"Good!" the minister would reply. "Then you don't have to tell him everything that's on your mind today," he would say as a gentle reminder to the prayer leaders to be concise in their roles.

It seems that the Pharisee in this parable needed to remind God of his personal status. Maybe he didn't check in all that often, and he wanted God to remember him. In case you've forgotten, God, I'm a pretty good guy. Look what I don't do. Look at what I do. And the list is impressive.

But it's the prayer of the tax collector that's effective. Remember that tax collectors were the "bottom-feeders" of Jewish society. In most cases, they were Jews who had sold out to the Romans in the eyes of their friends by buying a tax franchise from the Roman Empire and then collecting taxes at the highest rate possible and keeping the excess for income.

His prayer is not really a formal prayer—it's a plea. Not even glancing heavenward, he mutters, "God, have mercy on me a sinner." I think he said it more than once, over and over like a chant, getting more plaintive with every repetition. I think that because I know I've used this phrase in exactly that way when I've messed up so badly I can't even pray a "formal" prayer.

In my life, I've heard prayers I didn't even think lifted through the roof, some of my own included. And I've heard other prayers that literally opened the doors to the throne of God for me. The difference, I think now, is how genuine was the heart of the one who prayed.

My preacher acquaintance wanted genuine prayers, not long-winded ones. Jesus wants the same. And his forgiveness hangs in the balance for those who are sincere.

And just to give us a lesson in being genuine, he touches the children brought to him. If you've ever heard the prayer of a young child, you've heard a genuine prayer.

THOUGHTS TO PONDER

What qualities does God look for in one who prays? What can we do to make our prayer life more acceptable to him?

PRAYER

God, we know you hear the prayer of the humble and that you resist the proud. Help us always to live our lives in a way that helps our prayers be heard. Amen.

JESUS' INVITATION

LUKE 18:35—19:10

³⁵As Jesus came near the city of Jericho, a blind man was sitting beside the road, begging. ³⁶When he heard the people coming down the road, he asked, "What is happening?"

³⁷They told him, "Jesus, from Nazareth, is going by."

³⁸The blind man cried out, "Jesus, Son of David, have mercy on me!"

³⁹The people leading the group warned the blind man to be quiet. But the blind man shouted even more, "Son of David, have mercy on me!"

⁴⁰Jesus stopped and ordered the blind man to be brought to him. When he came near, Jesus asked him, ⁴¹"What do you want me to do for you?"

He said, "Lord, I want to see."

⁴²Jesus said to him, "Then see. You are healed because you believed."

⁴³At once the man was able to see, and he followed Jesus, thanking God. All the people who saw this praised God.

19 Jesus was going through the city of Jericho. ²A man was there named Zacchaeus, who was a very important tax collector, and he was wealthy. ³He wanted to see who Jesus was, but he was not able because he was too short to see above the crowd. ⁴He ran ahead to a place where Jesus would come, and he climbed a sycamore tree so he could see him. ⁵When Jesus came to that place, he looked up and said to him, "Zacchaeus, hurry and come down! I must stay at your house today."

⁶Zacchaeus came down quickly and welcomed him gladly. ⁷All the people saw this and began to complain, "Jesus is staying with a sinner!"

⁸But Zacchaeus stood and said to the Lord, "I will give half of my possessions to the poor. And if I have cheated anyone, I will pay back four times more."

⁹Jesus said to him, "Salvation has come to this house today, because this man also belongs to the family of Abraham. ¹⁰The Son of Man came to find lost people and save them."

DEVOTION

ACCORDING TO THE GREEK MYTH, the sculptor Pygmalion fell madly in love with a female statue he had created. Because of his fervor for her, Venus, the goddess of love, brought her to life and the two married. Because he saw her as real, she became real.

Since that time, the term "Pygmalion effect" has been used to denote the tendency of a person to become what others believe them to be. You might recall

591

the modern telling of the Pygmalion story found in the musical "My Fair Lady," where Eliza Doolittle, a common flower girl, becomes a lady under the tutelage of Dr. Henry Higgins.

Jesus saw something in people even when society didn't. He paid attention to the blind man, even when those around the blind man wanted him to be quiet and not bother the Master. He saw something in a tax collector even though most Jews would have nothing to do with that hated class of Roman puppets. Jesus knew how his love could transform lives.

Is the Pygmalion effect simply a Greek myth or a musical comedy? Research shows that teachers who have been told they are teaching a class of bright children (actually selected at random) raised the achievement scores of the class to above average simply by believing that they were smart. Factory workers, told they were handpicked because they were the best (again at random) also began to produce more than their peers.

Jesus saw something in Zacchaeus that no one else did. Look at the response of the people when Jesus singled him out for a special visit. No way! Not in the house of a sinner! Surely, Jesus, you don't know who this guy is!

But Jesus not only knew exactly who Zacchaeus was; he knew what he could become. And because Jesus saw deep inside this hated tax collector and reached out to him, his vision of Zacchaeus actually came true.

He's seen something in you, too. And he wants to come to your house. John, in his revelation for the church at Laodicea, says this of God: "Here I am! I stand at the door and knock. If you hear my voice and open the door, I will come in and eat with you, and you will eat with me" (Revelation 3:20).

It's the same invitation Jesus gave Zacchaeus, and he's waiting for an answer from you.

THOUGHTS TO PONDER

What are some of the traits that you have overlooked in others, only to discover them later when you became better acquainted? What do others overlook in you that you know to be true? How can we see past the exterior of people to find the true person underneath?

PRAYER

God, we thank you that you see in us not only what we are but what we can become with your help. Amen.

Teachable Moments

MARK 11:1–11, 15–19

11 As Jesus and his followers were coming closer to Jerusalem, they came to the towns of Bethphage and Bethany near the Mount of Olives. From there Jesus sent two of his followers ²and said to them, "Go to the town you can see there. When you enter it, you will quickly find a colt tied, which no one has ever ridden. Untie it and bring it here to me. ³If anyone asks you why you are doing this, tell him its Master needs the colt, and he will send it at once."

⁴The followers went into the town, found a colt tied in the street near the door of a house, and untied it. ⁵Some people were standing there and asked, "What are you doing? Why are you untying that colt?" ⁶The followers answered the way Jesus told them to answer, and the people let them take the colt.

⁷They brought the colt to Jesus and put their coats on it, and Jesus sat on it. ⁸Many people spread their coats on the road. Others cut branches in the fields and spread them on the road. ⁹The people were walking ahead of Jesus and behind him, shouting,

"Praise God!
God bless the One who comes in the name of the Lord!   *Psalm 118:26*
¹⁰God bless the kingdom of our father David!
      That kingdom is coming!
Praise to God in heaven!"

¹¹Jesus entered Jerusalem and went into the Temple. After he had looked at everything, since it was already late, he went out to Bethany with the twelve apostles.

¹⁵When Jesus returned to Jerusalem, he went into the Temple and began to throw out those who were buying and selling there. He turned over the tables of those who were exchanging different kinds of money, and he upset the benches of those who were selling doves. ¹⁶Jesus refused to allow anyone to carry goods through the Temple courts. ¹⁷Then he taught the people, saying, "It is written in the Scriptures, 'My Temple will be called a house for prayer for people from all nations.' But you are changing God's house into a 'hideout for robbers.'"

¹⁸The leading priests and the teachers of the law heard all this and began trying to find a way to kill Jesus. They were afraid of him, because all the people were amazed at his teaching. ¹⁹That evening, Jesus and his followers left the city.

DEVOTION

THIS STORY TEACHES an important lesson about Jesus, and it's a valuable lesson for us to learn. In the story, Jesus is making what has traditionally been called the "triumphal entry" into Jerusalem for what will be his final week on earth. The outpouring of love from his followers is obvious from the paving of the way with coats and branches and the praises they call out as he rides into the city.

On his arrival in Jerusalem, Jesus looks into the Temple. Deciding it was late, he moves on. The next day, Jesus goes into the Temple where he turns over the tables of the money exchangers and the sellers of sacrifices.

What is the lesson? Not every wrong gets righted in a day. Sometimes it's best to sleep on our anger.

Mark tells us that Jesus looked at everything when he arrived the day before. Undoubtedly he saw the scandalous proceedings. If a person came without a sacrifice, he would be sold one at an inflated price. If he brought his own, the Temple priests would find a blemish on it and, again, sell one at an inflated price. And the would-be worshiper would lose money again on the currency exchange since only special Temple money could be used in the Temple.

But all that could be righted tomorrow.

I think Jesus looked into the Temple and noted the unscrupulous selling of sacrifices and the usurious lending of money the night before, but he saved the confrontation for the next day. Far from flying off the handle on the spur of the moment, Jesus spent the night, went back into the Temple, and began to cleanse it of the moneymakers. Then, the story tells us, he taught the people.

It's a lesson I've had to learn as a parent: sometimes things can be righted tomorrow. In my role as a college professor I've also come to learn that "teachable moments" do exist and they're rarely the first moment after some bad behavior occurs. The goal of correction is teaching, not punishment, and that takes time.

THOUGHTS TO PONDER

How do you correct your children, or anyone else you lead? Do you display the patience, but firmness that Jesus did in this story? Do you teach in your correction?

PRAYER

Father, we know that you have shown patience with us repeatedly. Help us to show patience with those who might do us wrong. Amen.

The Early Workers

MATTHEW 20:1–16

20"The kingdom of heaven is like a person who owned some land. One morning, he went out very early to hire some people to work in his vineyard. ²The man agreed to pay the workers one coin for working that day. Then he sent them into the vineyard to work. ³About nine o'clock the man went to the marketplace and saw some other people standing there, doing nothing. ⁴So he said to them, 'If you go and work in my vineyard, I will pay you what your work is worth.' ⁵So they went to work in the vineyard. The man went out again about twelve o'clock and three o'clock and did the same thing. ⁶About five o'clock the man went to the marketplace again and saw others standing there. He asked them, 'Why did you stand here all day doing nothing?' ⁷They answered, 'No one gave us a job.' The man said to them, 'Then you can go and work in my vineyard.'

⁸"At the end of the day, the owner of the vineyard said to the boss of all the workers, 'Call the workers and pay them. Start with the last people I hired and end with those I hired first.'

⁹"When the workers who were hired at five o'clock came to get their pay, each received one coin. ¹⁰When the workers who were hired first came to get their pay, they thought they would be paid more than the others. But each one of them also received one coin. ¹¹When they got their coin, they complained to the man who owned the land. ¹²They said, 'Those people were hired last and worked only one hour. But you paid them the same as you paid us who worked hard all day in the hot sun.' ¹³But the man who owned the vineyard said to one of those workers, 'Friend, I am being fair to you. You agreed to work for one coin. ¹⁴So take your pay and go. I want to give the man who was hired last the same pay that I gave you. ¹⁵I can do what I want with my own money. Are you jealous because I am good to those people?'

¹⁶"So those who are last now will someday be first, and those who are first now will someday be last."

Devotion

FOR THE LONGEST TIME, I read this parable with the assumption that I was one of the early workers in this story. I had been baptized at an early age and I couldn't remember a time when worship and God's work hadn't been a major part of my life.

I checked a lot of boxes. Worked at a Christian university. Wrote several Christian books. Spoke in hundreds of churches. I found myself nudging closer to the half-century mark of working in God's vineyard. Surely, I was an early hire.

Then I spent a semester in Europe with thirty-five university students. We were based in Vienna at the time of the horrible ethnic cleansing in Bosnia, only a few hours away. Vienna had become a crossroads—a way station in the fashion of Casablanca during World War II—full of people who had fled there with no hope of returning to their homes, and once their visas expired, no hope of getting out of Austria either. Some of them were Christians.

I met a young lady one Sunday at a small congregation of no more than fifty members. She had come from a Muslim family to study in Vienna. While she was there, she became a Christian. Her whole world changed.

She was no longer welcome to go home. If she dared to return, one of her more zealous relatives would kill her for her new faith. All of a sudden, I didn't look like one of the earlier workers anymore. She had already sacrificed more for her month-old faith than I had been asked to sacrifice in more than four decades of following Christ.

Because of the relative comforts of my Christian walk, I now realize that I am one of the late workers, blessed by God with one of the easiest paths to the reward. I can only thank God for his loving mercy in accepting my meager offering.

Even today, when I hear the message of the Resurrection, I realize I don't always live as if I believe it. It's a far greater challenge to acknowledge the Resurrection with your actions than with your head.

THOUGHTS TO PONDER

Of the workers in the vineyard above, which one explains best your work in God's kingdom and why? Who might Jesus be referring to in the passage above about the first and the last individuals?

PRAYER

God, we pray that we will labor in your kingdom all of our days. We know we don't deserve your eternal reward but you offer it freely to all who accept the salvation offered through Jesus. Amen.

PLOTTING AGAINST GOD

MATTHEW 21:33–46

³³"Listen to this story: There was a man who owned a vineyard. He put a wall around it and dug a hole for a winepress and built a tower. Then he leased the land to some farmers and left for a trip. ³⁴When it was time for the grapes to be picked, he sent his servants to the farmers to get his share of the grapes. ³⁵But the farmers grabbed the servants, beat one, killed another, and then killed a third servant with stones. ³⁶So the man sent some other servants to the farmers, even more than he sent the first time. But the farmers did the same thing to the servants that they had done before. ³⁷So the man decided to send his son to the farmers. He said, 'They will respect my son.' ³⁸But when the farmers saw the son, they said to each other, 'This son will inherit the vineyard. If we kill him, it will be ours!' ³⁹Then the farmers grabbed the son, threw him out of the vineyard, and killed him. ⁴⁰So what will the owner of the vineyard do to these farmers when he comes?"

⁴¹The priests and leaders said, "He will surely kill those evil men. Then he will lease the vineyard to some other farmers who will give him his share of the crop at harvest time."

⁴²Jesus said to them, "Surely you have read this in the Scriptures:

'The stone that the builders rejected
    became the cornerstone.
The Lord did this,
    and it is wonderful to us.'   *Psalm 118:22–23*

⁴³"So I tell you that the kingdom of God will be taken away from you and given to people who do the things God wants in his kingdom. ⁴⁴The person who falls on this stone will be broken, and on whomever that stone falls, that person will be crushed."

⁴⁵When the leading priests and the Pharisees heard these stories, they knew Jesus was talking about them. ⁴⁶They wanted to arrest him, but they were afraid of the people, because the people believed that Jesus was a prophet.

DEVOTION

JESUS KNEW THAT he was in his last days, and the tone and content of his stories began to reflect a sharper tone. In this one, Jesus condemned the nation of Israel at large and these priests and leaders in particular for what they first did to the prophets and what they were about to do him.

Did they get it? The end of the story indicates that the leading priests and Pharisees had indeed seen themselves in the story and they were mad enough to have him arrested right then. They knew he was speaking not only of the centuries of bloody hands their predecessors had possessed, but also the blood that was on their minds as they plotted his death.

Ironically, they were plotting to make the last part of this parable come true. They had already rejected Jesus, and now they were plotting to kill him. This put Jesus in the company of some of the heroes of the faith whose stories are told in the eleventh chapter of Hebrews. Read this section from Hebrews 11:36–38: "Some were laughed at and beaten. Others were put in chains and thrown into prison. They were stoned to death, they were cut in half, and they were killed with swords. Some wore the skins of sheep and goats. They were poor, abused, and treated badly. The world was not good enough for them! They wandered in deserts and mountains, living in caves and holes in the earth."

Telling the truth around these people had never been a good career move. Their forefathers had killed the prophets in horrible ways. The current leaders had threatened to throw out of the synagogue a man healed of blindness if he even acknowledged that his healing had come from Jesus. These were ruthless folks who would criticize a formerly lame man, who was walking for the first time ever, because he was carrying his mat on the Sabbath.

"So what will the owner of the vineyard do to these farmers when he comes?" Jesus asks his listeners. It's not just a question for them. You see, the Word has been planted in me and God will come and expect a return on that seed. To not grow is to reject the Master of the vineyard, and that puts us in the same company, and the same fate, as the Pharisees. What return will the Master get from you when he returns?

THOUGHTS TO PONDER

The text tells us that the leading priests and Pharisees in the audience knew that the story was about them. How might they have known that? Why would the followers of Jesus have thought that he was a prophet? Why had they not yet recognized him as the Son of God?

PRAYER

Father, we know that Jesus was your Son, the one you appointed to take away the sins of the world. Help us by our actions and our words to accept him as the master of our lives. Amen.

WEDDING CLOTHES

MATTHEW 22:1-14

22 Jesus again used stories to teach them. He said, ²"The kingdom of heaven is like a king who prepared a wedding feast for his son. ³The king invited some people to the feast. When the feast was ready, the king sent his servants to tell the people, but they refused to come.

⁴"Then the king sent other servants, saying, 'Tell those who have been invited that my feast is ready. I have killed my best bulls and calves for the dinner, and everything is ready. Come to the wedding feast.'

⁵"But the people refused to listen to the servants and left to do other things. One went to work in his field, and another went to his business. ⁶Some of the other people grabbed the servants, beat them, and killed them. ⁷The king was furious and sent his army to kill the murderers and burn their city.

⁸"After that, the king said to his servants, 'The wedding feast is ready. I invited those people, but they were not worthy to come. ⁹So go to the street corners and invite everyone you find to come to my feast.' ¹⁰So the servants went into the streets and gathered all the people they could find, both good and bad. And the wedding hall was filled with guests.

¹¹"When the king came in to see the guests, he saw a man who was not dressed for a wedding. ¹²The king said, 'Friend, how were you allowed to come in here? You are not dressed for a wedding.' But the man said nothing. ¹³So the king told some servants, 'Tie this man's hands and feet. Throw him out into the darkness, where people will cry and grind their teeth with pain.'

¹⁴"Yes, many are invited, but only a few are chosen."

DEVOTION

THE BEGINNING of this story parallels the way Israel treated the offers of God and the entreaties of the prophets that he sent to Israel. Beginning with the agreement with Abraham, God had a special place for the nation of Israel. He promised that they would be a great nation numerically. He promised them the land of Canaan. Through the nation of Israel, he would bless the entire world through his Son.

But time and again, the Israelite nation rejected God. They chose to intermarry with the women of the surrounding countries. They chose to worship foreign gods. They let the Temple fall into disrepair and even lost their copy of the Law given to Moses. And when God sent the prophets to call the nation back to repentance, they were ignored at best and persecuted at worst. Even the few times that the nation repented, they quickly relapsed back into the idol worship and unholy living that drew the wrath of God each time.

Finally, there were no more second chances. First the northern kingdom, followed by the southern kingdom of the divided Israel, was taken away into captivity. They were there for a long time. The prophets were instructed to tell the people to marry, buy fields, and get accustomed to their new lands, because they would not be returning to Israel soon. When they did return, shortly before the time of Jesus, it was under a Roman program that repatriated lands with their indigenous people in an attempt to keep the peace.

God wanted a relationship with the nation of Israel even though they had left him. And now he had sent his Son into the world, and the religious leaders rejected Jesus just like their forefathers rejected God for the idols of their neighbors many years before.

Rejection hurts. Rejection of unconditional love hurts even more. Jesus went first to the nation of Israel because they were God's chosen people. But like the ungrateful guests invited to the wedding, the people refused to listen. God then opened his invitation to all nations, a fact that was difficult for the Jewish nation to grasp, even though they had the first opportunity for a place at God's table.

It's amazing that the God of the universe wants a relationship with us. In fact, he sent his Son to make it possible for us to sit at his table for all eternity. Yet all too often, by our actions, we reject his offer. There is to be a certain reverence to our response, according to the last part of the story. No one enters into a relationship with God casually. My "clothes" for the occasion include a covering of reverence and humility and gratitude for the great cost of the wedding banquet he is preparing.

THOUGHTS TO PONDER

In what ways is this "rejection parable" like the one before? What new wrinkle does this story have? How do we receive the invitation of God? In what ways might we reject Jesus today?

PRAYER

God we thank you for inviting us into your banquet even though we are not worthy. Help us to accept your invitation with gladness and extend the news of your invitation to others. Amen.

An Agreement Stronger than Death

MATTHEW 22:15–33

[15]Then the Pharisees left that place and made plans to trap Jesus in saying something wrong. [16]They sent some of their own followers and some people from the group called Herodians. They said, "Teacher, we know that you are an honest man and that you teach the truth about God's way. You are not afraid of what other people think about you, because you pay no attention to who they are. [17]So tell us what you think. Is it right to pay taxes to Caesar or not?"

[18]But knowing that these leaders were trying to trick him, Jesus said, "You hypocrites! Why are you trying to trap me? [19]Show me a coin used for paying the tax." So the men showed him a coin. [20]Then Jesus asked, "Whose image and name are on the coin?"

[21]The men answered, "Caesar's."

Then Jesus said to them, "Give to Caesar the things that are Caesar's, and give to God the things that are God's."

[22]When the men heard what Jesus said, they were amazed and left him and went away.

[23]That same day some Sadducees came to Jesus and asked him a question. (Sadducees believed that people would not rise from the dead.) [24]They said, "Teacher, Moses said if a married man dies without having children, his brother must marry the widow and have children for him. [25]Once there were seven brothers among us. The first one married and died. Since he had no children, his brother married the widow. [26]Then the second brother also died. The same thing happened to the third brother and all the other brothers. [27]Finally, the woman died. [28]Since all seven men had married her, when people rise from the dead, whose wife will she be?"

[29]Jesus answered, "You don't understand, because you don't know what the Scriptures say, and you don't know about the power of God. [30]When people rise from the dead, they will not marry, nor will they be given to someone to marry. They will be like the angels in heaven. [31]Surely you have read what God said to you about rising from the dead. [32]God said, 'I am the God of Abraham, the God of Isaac, and the God of Jacob.' God is the God of the living, not the dead."

[33]When the people heard this, they were amazed at Jesus' teaching.

DEVOTION

TWO TRAPS WERE LAID for Jesus in this passage. Together, they show the tenacity of his critics and the ability of Jesus to discern their real intentions.

In the first trap, the Pharisees tried flattery before springing the trap: "So do we pay taxes to Caesar or not?" The Pharisees had engaged their followers and the Herodians, known supporters of King Herod, to ask the question. Surely Jesus' answer would reach higher levels no matter what he said. If he supported the tax, the Pharisees would whip up public sentiment against him as a supporter of the occupying Romans. If he opposed the tax, he could be charged with treason against Rome.

Jesus answered and amazed his listeners. There is a place for obeying local authorities and a place for obeying God. The challenge is to know the difference.

In the second trap, the Sadducees tried to create a scenario for Jesus to show the impossibility of the resurrection of the dead. They cited Jewish law mandating that a childless widow was to be married by her husband's surviving brother (Deuteronomy 25:5–10) so she could continue her husband's name. Using that law, the Sadducees created an improbable scenario in which such a woman accumulated seven husbands before dying. Whose wife would she be after the resurrection of the dead?

The Sadducees didn't understand the nature of the resurrection. Jesus said that not only would heaven operate under a different set of conditions (no marriage, for instance)—we would be different as well. We would be like angels. Surely they could understand that angels do not engage in earthly acts like marriage.

Then Jesus quoted from the agreement God made with Moses (Exodus 3:6). Surely God's oath to Abraham and his descendants and his spiritual agreement with Israel (Jeremiah 31:33) would not be broken by the physical limitations of death.

The passage closes with the amazement of the people, and the parties who tried to trap Jesus were embarrassed by his insights.

THOUGHTS TO PONDER

What is it about these teachings that in both cases they were called "amazing"? Why does Jesus avoid a debate on taxes? What do his answers tell you about the focus of Jesus?

PRAYER

God, we can get caught up in so many meaningless debates. Help us to focus on the saving message of the Good News and stand ready to give an answer for that each and every day. Amen.

OBEDIENCE FIRST, THEN SACRIFICE

MARK 12:28–40

²⁸One of the teachers of the law came and heard Jesus arguing with the Sadducees. Seeing that Jesus gave good answers to their questions, he asked Jesus, "Which of the commands is most important?"

²⁹Jesus answered, "The most important command is this: 'Listen, people of Israel! The Lord our God is the only Lord. ³⁰Love the Lord your God with all your heart, all your soul, all your mind, and all your strength.' ³¹The second command is this: 'Love your neighbor as you love yourself.' There are no commands more important than these."

³²The man answered, "That was a good answer, Teacher. You were right when you said God is the only Lord and there is no other God besides him. ³³One must love God with all his heart, all his mind, and all his strength. And one must love his neighbor as he loves himself. These commands are more important than all the animals and sacrifices we offer to God."

³⁴When Jesus saw that the man answered him wisely, Jesus said to him, "You are close to the kingdom of God." And after that, no one was brave enough to ask Jesus any more questions.

³⁵As Jesus was teaching in the Temple, he asked, "Why do the teachers of the law say that the Christ is the son of David? ³⁶David himself, speaking by the Holy Spirit, said:

'The Lord said to my Lord,
"Sit by me at my right side,
    until I put your enemies under your control." '   *Psalm 110:1*

³⁷David himself calls the Christ 'Lord,' so how can the Christ be his son?" The large crowd listened to Jesus with pleasure.

³⁸Jesus continued teaching and said, "Beware of the teachers of the law. They like to walk around wearing fancy clothes, and they love for people to greet them with respect in the marketplaces. ³⁹They love to have the most important seats in the synagogues and at feasts. ⁴⁰But they cheat widows and steal their houses and then try to make themselves look good by saying long prayers. They will receive a greater punishment."

DEVOTION

BY THE TIME this story started, Jesus had already met two verbal challenges from his critics. Now came the lawyer. Hearing the previous answers, he wanted to question Jesus for himself. Of the 613 commandments in the Torah, the first five books of the Old Testament handed down through the centuries, which one is the most important? Jesus quoted first from Deuteronomy 6:5—"Love the LORD your God with all your heart, all your soul, and all your strength"—and then went on to Leviticus 19:18—"Love your neighbor as you love yourself."

Note the response of the lawyer: living by the two statements of Jesus is more important than all the sacrifices required by the Law. This is a remarkable admission coming from a man whose job it was to point out people's shortcomings in keeping all 613 rules and their many thousands of interpretations. Jesus saw his wisdom and complimented his insight.

Does God want sacrifices or obedience? When King Saul got an order from God to totally destroy the Amalekite nation, he disobeyed. He spared some of the animals to sacrifice to God and took them back to Gilgal to lay them on the altar to God. But the prophet Samuel rebuked Saul saying, "It is better to obey than to sacrifice" (1 Samuel 15:22). God wants my heart more than he wants my tithe, because when he has my heart, my sacrifice will follow.

After that, since no one was brave enough to ask him any questions, Jesus poses one of his own. Why do the teachers of the law insist that he is a Son of David and not the Son of God? He has harsh words for the teachers of the law. God despises hypocrites, he says, and the teachers of the law are just that.

From the pleasure of the crowds, you can infer that they related to what Jesus was saying. They had seen the teachers of the law taking the best seats in the Temple, wearing the flowing robes, and praying the long prayers. They knew that these same men would foreclose on a widow one day—throwing her out on the streets, and quite likely into a life of prostitution—and worship the next.

Does God want perfection or mercy? When Micah was looking for a sacrifice for the sins of Israel, he runs through a list of gifts (Micah 6:6–8). Does God want calves? Rivers of oil? My firstborn child? No, Hosea is told. Here are the gifts the Lord requires: act justly, love mercy, and walk humbly.

It's a lesson the people knew, but the lawyer had yet to learn.

THOUGHTS TO PONDER

How do we put the most important command into practice? On a practical level, what does it mean to love the Lord with all your heart?

PRAYER

God, we pray that we never hold anything back in our love for you, and that we would also love our neighbors as ourselves. Amen.

CLOSED DOORS

MATTHEW 25:1–13

25 "At that time the kingdom of heaven will be like ten bridesmaids who took their lamps and went to wait for the bridegroom. ²Five of them were foolish and five were wise. ³The five foolish bridesmaids took their lamps, but they did not take more oil for the lamps to burn. ⁴The wise bridesmaids took their lamps and more oil in jars. ⁵Because the bridegroom was late, they became sleepy and went to sleep.

⁶"At midnight someone cried out, 'The bridegroom is coming! Come and meet him!' ⁷Then all the bridesmaids woke up and got their lamps ready. ⁸But the foolish ones said to the wise, 'Give us some of your oil, because our lamps are going out.' ⁹The wise bridesmaids answered, 'No, the oil we have might not be enough for all of us. Go to the people who sell oil and buy some for yourselves.'

¹⁰"So while the five foolish bridesmaids went to buy oil, the bridegroom came. The bridesmaids who were ready went in with the bridegroom to the wedding feast. Then the door was closed and locked.

¹¹"Later the others came back and said, 'Sir, sir, open the door to let us in.' ¹²But the bridegroom answered, 'I tell you the truth, I don't want to know you.'

¹³"So always be ready, because you don't know the day or the hour the Son of Man will come."

DEVOTION

AS A FREQUENT TRAVELER, I have missed my share of flights because of bad weather, mechanical delays, and the like. But one flight I missed was entirely my fault. It was at the end of a trip, the last leg to get home, a 9:40 p.m. flight. I had a three-hour layover and would get in just after midnight. After checking for earlier flights, I got my seat assignment for the late flight and found a cozy spot to begin a novel.

So I read. And read. I really got into the plot and before I knew it, it was 9:45. I ran to my gate and saw the plane, but the door to the jet way was locked. Even though the plane was just down the ramp, the door could not be unlocked for security reasons. They had called my name and I hadn't heard them. I wouldn't be able to travel until the next morning, I was told.

Perhaps you've experienced a closed door. Maybe it was a promotion that didn't come through. Or maybe someone you loved closed the door on the relationship. Closed doors—literal or figurative—have one thing in common: they sting.

In this parable and the ones that follow, Jesus warned his followers to be ready for his return. It must have seemed a strange message for his hearers since he hadn't yet left them.

In the tradition of weddings in the days of Jesus, the bridegroom would be the last to come. He would visit several friends and relatives along the way, making the time of his arrival an uncertain event. So the bridesmaids were to watch on behalf of the bride and announce the arrival of the groom whenever he arrived. Waiting and watching was the main duty of a bridesmaid.

The "lamps" above were likely torches with rags on the end that were soaked in olive oil to light the way for the procession of the groom to the house of the bride. When they awoke, five of the bridesmaids had reserve oil for the tips of their torches and five didn't.

This story and the two that follow are Jesus' longest discourses on the events surrounding his return. Although they are simple stories, it's doubtful that any of the hearers fully understood them, since they hadn't fully grasped the fact that Jesus would die and be resurrected and someday come again to reclaim his own.

So that makes these stories for those of us who know the full story and faithfully await his coming. This story is actually one of hope. It tells us that no one who prepares will have to watch the doors of heaven close from outside.

Thoughts to Ponder

Have you ever felt the sting of being left out? How do we follow the advice of Jesus to always be ready for his return? What does that state of readiness look like?

Prayer

Father, we know you are returning again to find the faithful. Please help us to always be among that number and to be ready when you return. Amen.

Two-Bag People

MATTHEW 25:14–30

14"The kingdom of heaven is like a man who was going to another place for a visit. Before he left, he called for his servants and told them to take care of his things while he was gone. 15He gave one servant five bags of gold, another servant two bags of gold, and a third servant one bag of gold, to each one as much as he could handle. Then he left. 16The servant who got five bags went quickly to invest the money and earned five more bags. 17In the same way, the servant who had two bags invested them and earned two more. 18But the servant who got one bag went out and dug a hole in the ground and hid the master's money.

19"After a long time the master came home and asked the servants what they did with his money. 20The servant who was given five bags of gold brought five more bags to the master and said, 'Master, you trusted me to care for five bags of gold, so I used your five bags to earn five more.' 21The master answered, 'You did well. You are a good and loyal servant. Because you were loyal with small things, I will let you care for much greater things. Come and share my joy with me.'

22"Then the servant who had been given two bags of gold came to the master and said, 'Master, you gave me two bags of gold to care for, so I used your two bags to earn two more.' 23The master answered, 'You did well. You are a good and loyal servant. Because you were loyal with small things, I will let you care for much greater things. Come and share my joy with me.'

24"Then the servant who had been given one bag of gold came to the master and said, 'Master, I knew that you were a hard man. You harvest things you did not plant. You gather crops where you did not sow any seed. 25So I was afraid and went and hid your money in the ground. Here is your bag of gold.' 26The master answered, 'You are a wicked and lazy servant! You say you knew that I harvest things I did not plant and that I gather crops where I did not sow any seed. 27So you should have put my gold in the bank. Then, when I came home, I would have received my gold back with interest.'

28"So the master told his other servants, 'Take the bag of gold from that servant and give it to the servant who has ten bags of gold. 29Those who have much will get more, and they will have much more than they need. But those who do not have much will have everything taken away from them.' 30Then the master said, 'Throw that useless servant outside, into the darkness where people will cry and grind their teeth with pain.' "

DEVOTION

THERE'S A FORGOTTEN CHARACTER here, an important one because he's like most of us. I'll call him Two-Bag Man or TBM for short. Most of the lessons taught from this parable are about the One-Bag Man who did nothing with his Master's trust and the Five-Bag Man who was obviously the most capable of the three and was even entrusted with more at the end of the story.

TBM is caught in the middle and gets little attention. He's not the worst of the three and he's not the best. In fact, if the amount of gold they were entrusted with is an indication of their talents, and it probably is, TBM is a little closer to the bottom than the top.

But TBM does what is expected of him—he gives the Master a good return for the trust that has been placed in him. He doesn't whine about not getting more gold and he doesn't hide his gold in the earth. He does the most with the abilities he has.

I think most of us are like TBM. We're not the natural leader, the top of the class, the quarterback who dates the head cheerleader. But we're not the class cutup either. We're the great middle—people given diverse abilities by God and expected to glorify him by using them. Are you a good listener—that's a "bag of gold" you're expected to use. Do you have the financial ability to aid those in greater need than you? That's another bag of gold.

We've all been entrusted with abilities from God and we're all expected to invest them in his work. It's not my job to worry about the depth or breadth of my abilities, and it's certainly not my role to be jealous of yours. I simply need to be the best TBM I am called to be.

THOUGHTS TO PONDER

What are the talents you can bring to the Master? How are you developing them?

PRAYER

God, we thank you for our talents as we know that you are the source of all our abilities. Help us to use these talents to further your work. Amen.

FAITHFUL REPETITION

MATTHEW 25:31–46

[31]"The Son of Man will come again in his great glory, with all his angels. He will be King and sit on his great throne. [32]All the nations of the world will be gathered before him, and he will separate them into two groups as a shepherd separates the sheep from the goats. [33]The Son of Man will put the sheep on his right and the goats on his left.

[34]"Then the King will say to the people on his right, 'Come, my Father has given you his blessing. Receive the kingdom God has prepared for you since the world was made. [35]I was hungry, and you gave me food. I was thirsty, and you gave me something to drink. I was alone and away from home, and you invited me into your house. [36]I was without clothes, and you gave me something to wear. I was sick, and you cared for me. I was in prison, and you visited me.'

[37]"Then the good people will answer, 'Lord, when did we see you hungry and give you food, or thirsty and give you something to drink? [38]When did we see you alone and away from home and invite you into our house? When did we see you without clothes and give you something to wear? [39]When did we see you sick or in prison and care for you?'

[40]"Then the King will answer, 'I tell you the truth, anything you did for even the least of my people here, you also did for me.'

[41]"Then the King will say to those on his left, 'Go away from me. You will be punished. Go into the fire that burns forever that was prepared for the devil and his angels. [42]I was hungry, and you gave me nothing to eat. I was thirsty, and you gave me nothing to drink. [43]I was alone and away from home, and you did not invite me into your house. I was without clothes, and you gave me nothing to wear. I was sick and in prison, and you did not care for me.'

[44]"Then those people will answer, 'Lord, when did we see you hungry or thirsty or alone and away from home or without clothes or sick or in prison? When did we see these things and not help you?'

[45]"Then the King will answer, 'I tell you the truth, anything you refused to do for even the least of my people here, you refused to do for me.'

[46]"These people will go off to be punished forever, but the good people will go to live forever."

DEVOTION

WE WERE HEADING to one of those "big box" stores where my son was going to use his birthday money to buy the biggest and newest video game system available. It was a Saturday, and the entire trip was via freeways flowing at posted speed limits, which was good because Joshua was anxious.

We were near our exit when we spotted a middle-aged, very well dressed woman, standing beside her car. Something told me to stop. My son was in an understandable hurry, but this situation looked different.

"I'm out of gas in my daughter's car," she said, nearly crying. "I'm headed to her wedding. It's still a couple of hours away, but I'll be late for the pictures if I don't get some help. She has my car to take on her honeymoon."

Birthdays happen every year, but this woman was having a once-in-a-lifetime problem and I welcomed her in our car.

The electronics store was next to a hardware store. Joshua and I dove into one to get our toy, now a little less important to me than it was just five minutes ago, and she ran into the other to buy a gallon gas can. We came out at the same time.

We were back at her car with a gallon of gas in less than fifteen minutes. I did the work to keep her from smelling of gas. Along the way, she kept talking about how good the Lord was and how kind I was, and all the time I felt small knowing how rare my actions that day really were.

In Matthew 25, those about to enter heaven don't even remember the kind acts they did. But Jesus does. Perhaps that's the mark of a true servant—forgetfulness brought on by faithful repetition.

THOUGHTS TO PONDER

When Jesus lists the criteria for entering the kingdom, why do you think he makes no references to religious acts such as prayer or fasting? What does it tell you about what our priorities are to be?

PRAYER

God, we know that when we help the least of your people, we serve you. We pray that we will honor you in the acts of kindness we do each day. Amen.

Press Releases

MARK 12:35–44

³⁵As Jesus was teaching in the Temple, he asked, "Why do the teachers of the law say that the Christ is the son of David? ³⁶David himself, speaking by the Holy Spirit, said:

> 'The Lord said to my Lord,
> "Sit by me at my right side,
>   until I put your enemies under your control." '   *Psalm 110:1*

³⁷David himself calls the Christ 'Lord,' so how can the Christ be his son?" The large crowd listened to Jesus with pleasure.

³⁸Jesus continued teaching and said, "Beware of the teachers of the law. They like to walk around wearing fancy clothes, and they love for people to greet them with respect in the marketplaces. ³⁹They love to have the most important seats in the synagogues and at feasts. ⁴⁰But they cheat widows and steal their houses and then try to make themselves look good by saying long prayers. They will receive a greater punishment."

⁴¹Jesus sat near the Temple money box and watched the people put in their money. Many rich people gave large sums of money. ⁴²Then a poor widow came and put in two small copper coins, which were only worth a few cents.

⁴³Calling his followers to him, Jesus said, "I tell you the truth, this poor widow gave more than all those rich people. ⁴⁴They gave only what they did not need. This woman is very poor, but she gave all she had; she gave all she had to live on."

Devotion

IN HIS ROLE as spokesperson for a publicly-traded company, my friend handled media requests for the large distribution company where he worked. With centers across the nation and a strong presence on Wall Street, it was a major corporation and he was a major cog in the wheel managing the public image of the corporation.

Under his first boss, the results were legendary. Quarter after quarter of profits, growth in every sector. And the company was generous with its good fortune, giving to a variety of charities and good works out of corporate profits and products. My friend's instructions from the top were plain: don't announce our gifts through press releases. We don't need to make a big deal out of sharing our blessings with the less fortunate, he was told.

But that boss retired. And following him was a leader with an entirely different personality. Every gift was to be trumpeted. Like the teachers of the law, the company issued a press release so that no good deed went unnoticed. The company thrived under the first leader; it fell into bankruptcy under the second. It doesn't exist today.

When Jesus entered the Temple with his followers to watch the giving of the gifts, he came upon a spectacle that was equal parts ego-stroking and peer pressure. The givers were lined up in the Temple by the workers according to the size of their gifts. When they got to the front of the line, the gift was announced aloud by a Temple worker. The givers would then take their place close to the front of the synagogue and watch the others as they gave in decreasing sums as the ceremony continued.

So the widow was at the end of the line with her small coins. Think a couple of pennies in America. Or even more vivid, two pesos or lire in those inflated currencies of Mexico or Italy. The coin only existed to make change. It was barely worth anything as currency.

But still she gave. Many wouldn't have bothered to give something so little. Others would have hoarded the last pennies for themselves. But this was no ordinary widow. She was special, and Jesus noticed.

You can be assured that she didn't want her gift announced. But Jesus noticed it. And Jesus saw through the "press releases" he had heard about all the other gifts, and he spotted the one that meant the most.

THOUGHTS TO PONDER

What did Jesus mean that the rich gave only what they didn't need? How do we compare to the generosity and the sacrifice of the widow?

PRAYER

God, we pray that our gifts will be pleasing and acceptable to you and that we will be motivated by love when we prepare our gifts for you. Amen.

WHAT'S YOUR PRICE?

LUKE 22:1–6

22 It was almost time for the Feast of Unleavened Bread, called the Passover Feast. ²The leading priests and teachers of the law were trying to find a way to kill Jesus, because they were afraid of the people.

³Satan entered Judas Iscariot, one of Jesus' twelve apostles. ⁴Judas went to the leading priests and some of the soldiers who guarded the Temple and talked to them about a way to hand Jesus over to them. ⁵They were pleased and agreed to give Judas money. ⁶He agreed and watched for the best time to hand Jesus over to them when he was away from the crowd.

DEVOTION

AT LEAST THE LEADING PRIESTS had a motive. Here was this Jesus, stirring up the people, upsetting the religious status quo. Making threats about tearing down the Temple and rebuilding it in three days. Making a scene by throwing out the money changers and sellers of sacrifices from the Temple, claiming that it was his Father's house. Healing on the Sabbath. Oh yeah, there was plenty of motive to want Jesus gone.

But Judas had none of these objections to Jesus. In fact, they were close. He had traveled with Jesus for three years. He had seen all the miracles, witnessed all the healings, and heard all the sermons. So he had no political or religious problems with Jesus.

For Judas, maybe the motive was money. If Jesus wasn't going to set up an earthly kingdom and make his inner circle rich and powerful, then perhaps Judas was going to get rich off Jesus any way he could. And that would make his motive for betraying Jesus even more evil than the motive of his employers who wished to kill Jesus.

Would money make you happier? I'm not talking about just a little bit to pay off some bills or make ends meet. I'm talking hitting the lottery. Would that make you happy?

It happened to a man and his estranged second wife, who shared a $34 million jackpot in 2000. When he won the money, he was driving a forklift and she was making corrugated boxes.

Each had lived a hard life. Never able to hold a steady job and always battling alcoholism, the husband had lived in an abandoned bus at one point. His wife had seen her life change drastically when her father and two brothers were sent to prison for dealing drugs and using the family's chain of transmission shops as fronts.

Within a year of winning the lottery, they were divorced, moving into separate mansions. He moved into a forty-three-acre estate in a house modeled after Mount Vernon. She opted for a modern geodesic-dome mansion on the Ohio River and a Mercedes.

Within five years of their windfall, they were both dead. The cause of his death was confirmed as complications related to alcoholism. The cause of her death baffled authorities, but a drug overdose was suspected; her body was discovered several days after her death. Neighbors suspected her house had become a place for drug use or even trafficking.

Their survivors weren't surprised. Her brother: "Any problems people have, money magnifies it." His first wife: "When you put that kind of money in the hands of somebody with problems, it just helps them kill themselves."

He was 45; she was 51. Only a fraction of their $34 million fortune remained.

Judas would be no happier with his thirty pieces of silver he received for betraying Jesus. In fact, he tried to give it back in a futile attempt to undo what he had started. The very same money was later used to buy his burial plot. It couldn't go back into the Temple treasury because it was "blood money."

Have you betrayed Jesus for your own base motives? Have you quietly put your Christianity on the shelf at work so you wouldn't offend anyone or so that you would fit in better? Have you betrayed Jesus for a chance to get ahead even though it meant cheating a little at work, or on your taxes? Have we betrayed Jesus by the way we act at our sporting events or our vacations when we don't think anyone else is looking?

There are many ways to betray Jesus even today. No money changes hands, and Satan even works to ensure no one finds out so that he keeps us hooked into our traitorous roles.

Judas had a price. It was thirty pieces of silver. What is Satan offering you to betray Jesus?

THOUGHTS TO PONDER

What do you think it means when the text tells us that Satan entered into Judas? What role did Judas play in being a welcome "host" for Satan? How does Satan try to get us to betray Jesus today?

PRAYER

God, we pray that in our actions and in our thoughts we will never betray you. Amen.

THE PASSOVER LAMB

LUKE 22:7–13

⁷The Day of Unleavened Bread came when the Passover lambs had to be sacrificed. ⁸Jesus said to Peter and John, "Go and prepare the Passover meal for us to eat."

⁹They asked, "Where do you want us to prepare it?" ¹⁰Jesus said to them, "After you go into the city, a man carrying a jar of water will meet you. Follow him into the house that he enters, ¹¹and tell the owner of the house, 'The Teacher says: "Where is the guest room in which I may eat the Passover meal with my followers?"' ¹²Then he will show you a large, furnished room upstairs. Prepare the Passover meal there."

¹³So Peter and John left and found everything as Jesus had said. And they prepared the Passover meal.

DEVOTION

BY THE TIME OF JESUS, the ancient ritual of the Feast of Passover had certain rules. All the lambs had to be slaughtered in the Temple, though they could be eaten in the home. Because the meat would be perishable and could not be transported far, this was a "pilgrimage festival" as many people came to Jerusalem for a proper Passover meal. Jesus was looking for a room in a city that would be crowded, so he gave specific instructions on how to find the man who would lead them to the room.

The pattern of the evening would include an opening prayer and the blessing of the cup. Then came the blessing and the breaking of the unleavened bread. The bread celebrated the time when the children of Israel took their dough before it was leavened and baked it into a hard, unleavened bread in anticipation of an imminent departure from Egypt. Ever since that time, as the day approached, the Jews were expected to eliminate all yeast from the house so that there was no chance of eating leavened bread during the time of the feast.

After the breaking and partaking of the bread, the head of the house would tell his children the story of the first Passover. The father would tell of how the angel of the Lord came to Egypt to kill all of the firstborn as Moses had warned the king. But the Israelites had been given a way to escape the calamity. They were to kill a lamb and brush blood on the doorposts of each house. Seeing the blood of the lamb, the angel of death would "pass over" the house and the firstborn would be saved. The feast would recall how God had used this greatest and last of the plagues to free his children from bondage in Egypt.

Following the recounting of the story came the eating of the Passover lamb. Typically, bitter herbs dipped in sauce would be served, reminiscent of what the Israelites ate at that first Passover meal. In later days, the tradition of some was to eat the meal standing, perhaps wearing traveling clothes, in memory of the journey the Israelites took immediately afterwards. Blessings and psalms were a part of the ceremony.

Even as he was about to be killed for alleged violations of the Jewish law and the "blasphemy" of calling himself the Son of God, Jesus was keeping the sacred feast. He was using his last hours on earth to wed traditions of the old physical kingdom of Israel—the Passover—with a tradition that would carry forward into the new spiritual kingdom of his church—the Lord's Supper, or communion, which we still observe today.

Jesus told his followers that he did not come to destroy the Law, but to fulfill it. In the first public sermon of his ministry, he said, "Don't think that I have come to destroy the law of Moses or the teaching of the prophets. I have not come to destroy them but to bring about what they said. I tell you the truth, nothing will disappear from the law until heaven and earth are gone. Not even the smallest letter or the smallest part of a letter will be lost until everything has happened" (Matthew 5:17–18).

Within a few hours of keeping this Passover Feast, Jesus would become the perfect sacrifice, the Passover Lamb for all people and the fulfillment of everything the Israelites had been looking for (1 Corinthians 5:7). But the religious leaders did not recognize him as the Messiah, the one who came to take away the sin of the world. They recognized him only as a dangerous teacher whose followers were capable of revolt.

THOUGHTS TO PONDER

Why would Jesus spend his last hours on earth obeying the Jewish observance of Passover? What does this tell you about him? What does it mean that "nothing will disappear from the law until heaven and earth are gone"?

PRAYER

Father, we pray that we will observe the occasion of the perfect sacrifice of Jesus in the way that you have instituted and that we will remember his sacrifice until he comes again. Amen.

LEADING WITH A SERVANT'S HEART

JOHN 13:1–20

13It was almost time for the Passover Feast. Jesus knew that it was time for him to leave this world and go back to the Father. He had always loved those who were his own in the world, and he loved them all the way to the end.

²Jesus and his followers were at the evening meal. The devil had already persuaded Judas Iscariot, the son of Simon, to turn against Jesus. ³Jesus knew that the Father had given him power over everything and that he had come from God and was going back to God. ⁴So during the meal Jesus stood up and took off his outer clothing. Taking a towel, he wrapped it around his waist. ⁵Then he poured water into a bowl and began to wash the followers' feet, drying them with the towel that was wrapped around him.

⁶Jesus came to Simon Peter, who said to him, "Lord, are you going to wash my feet?"

⁷Jesus answered, "You don't understand now what I am doing, but you will understand later."

⁸Peter said, "No, you will never wash my feet."

Jesus answered, "If I don't wash your feet, you are not one of my people."

⁹Simon Peter answered, "Lord, then wash not only my feet, but wash my hands and my head, too!"

¹⁰Jesus said, "After a person has had a bath, his whole body is clean. He needs only to wash his feet. And you men are clean, but not all of you." ¹¹Jesus knew who would turn against him, and that is why he said, "Not all of you are clean."

¹²When he had finished washing their feet, he put on his clothes and sat down again. He asked, "Do you understand what I have just done for you? ¹³You call me 'Teacher' and 'Lord,' and you are right, because that is what I am. ¹⁴If I, your Lord and Teacher, have washed your feet, you also should wash each other's feet. ¹⁵I did this as an example so that you should do as I have done for you. ¹⁶I tell you the truth, a servant is not greater than his master. A messenger is not greater than the one who sent him. ¹⁷If you know these things, you will be blessed if you do them.

¹⁸"I am not talking about all of you. I know those I have chosen. But this is to bring about what the Scripture said: 'The man who ate at my table has turned against me.' ¹⁹I am telling you this now before it happens so that when it happens, you will believe that I am he. ²⁰I tell you the truth, whoever accepts anyone I send also accepts me. And whoever accepts me also accepts the One who sent me."

DEVOTION

DIRTY FEET were the enemies of group dining in the days of Jesus. The tables were low to the ground and the guests sat on the floor, actually reclining onto one another as they ate. Perched on one elbow, each guest would stretch his legs out and eat with his free hand. This placed your feet in close proximity to the table and to someone else's head. Additionally, there was the fact that the guests had traveled over dusty roads wearing sandals; the problem of what to do with dirty feet before dining was a problem for any host.

So the servants would typically wash the feet of the guests. While it was the role of a good host to provide the service, it would be considered beneath him to stop his hosting duties to perform the chore personally. Washing feet was the lowliest form of service.

Alone in an upper room prepared to eat a Passover Feast, none of the followers had volunteered to be the one to wash feet. So Jesus took the task himself. The followers had argued before about who would be the greatest in the coming kingdom of Jesus—even though they didn't know what form it would take. So none of them were going to take on the lowly role of washing feet, even if it meant spending the evening next to someone's stinking feet.

So this act of Jesus was both a practical necessity and an object lesson. "Want to be a leader?" Jesus was asking. "Be ready to wash feet."

I have been a leader in various roles on different occasions and true leadership always comes down to service. True leadership is never about being the "boss." It's about being the servant.

THOUGHTS TO PONDER

Who are some of the greatest leaders you have been able to work with? What was their style of leadership? What do you know about the leadership of Jesus from what you've seen in the Gospels?

PRAYER

Father, we pray that you will raise up leaders among us who will have the hearts of servants so that your work will be done in the world. Amen.

A RITUAL OF REMEMBRANCE

MATTHEW 26:26–30

²⁶While they were eating, Jesus took some bread and thanked God for it and broke it. Then he gave it to his followers and said, "Take this bread and eat it; this is my body."

²⁷Then Jesus took a cup and thanked God for it and gave it to the followers. He said, "Every one of you drink this. ²⁸This is my blood which is the new agreement that God makes with his people. This blood is poured out for many to forgive their sins. ²⁹I tell you this: I will not drink of this fruit of the vine again until that day when I drink it new with you in my Father's kingdom."

³⁰After singing a hymn, they went out to the Mount of Olives.

ACTS 20:7

⁷On the first day of the week, we all met together to break bread, and Paul spoke to the group.

1 CORINTHIANS 11:23–26

²³The teaching I gave you is the same teaching I received from the Lord: On the night when the Lord Jesus was handed over to be killed, he took bread ²⁴and gave thanks for it. Then he broke the bread and said, "This is my body; it is for you. Do this to remember me." ²⁵In the same way, after they ate, Jesus took the cup. He said, "This cup is the new agreement that is sealed with the blood of my death. When you drink this, do it to remember me." ²⁶Every time you eat this bread and drink this cup you are telling others about the Lord's death until he comes.

DEVOTION

AT THE END of the meal with his followers, Jesus used the bread and the wine to teach them an object lesson. His body would soon be broken. His blood would soon be shed. And even though they didn't realize it at the time, the followers were witnessing a ceremony that would become the heart of Christian worship in the centuries to come.

Within a short time after the death of Christ, the eating of a symbolic meal became a part of the worship of the early church. And through the centuries, the formula has remained essentially the same—the bread to symbolize the body of Christ and the wine to symbolize his blood.

Three of the Gospel accounts tell us that the context of this event was the final celebration of the Passover by Jesus and his followers, just hours before Jesus was to be handed over to the authorities for his trial and crucifixion. Because of this, Christian tradition holds that Jesus used the unleavened bread eaten by Jews since the night of the original Passover in the ceremony. By the end of the first century, this was the predominant way the "Lord's Supper" or "Eucharist" was celebrated.

Paul told the Corinthian believers how to participate in this celebration, and then added a reason for the ceremony of the Lord's Supper: we are proclaiming the sacrifice of Jesus to the world, and ensuring that we never forget the price he paid for our sin. Unfortunately, the church in Corinth had perverted the Lord's Supper into a meal where the rich were gorging themselves while the poor went hungry. Paul took on this problem in the following passage: "So a person who eats the bread or drinks the cup of the Lord in a way that is not worthy of it will be guilty of sinning against the body and the blood of the Lord. Look into your own hearts before you eat the bread and drink the cup, because all who eat the bread and drink the cup without recognizing the body eat and drink judgment against themselves" (1 Corinthians 11:27–29).

Based on this teaching, religious communities have focused both on the manner in which the Lord's Supper is taken. It is to be both a time of remembrance of the death of Jesus on the cross and a time of introspection of our own lives. Paul issues a strict warning against any casual attitude toward this part of the worship.

Why would Jesus take the time—hours away from his capture and eventual death—to institute this ritual? Paul gives the answer in his instructions to the Corinthians. The communion ritual is to remember the sacrifice of the Lord. It's actually a look *backwards* at Jesus on the cross, a look *inward* at my own heart and a look *forward* to the day we drink it with Jesus in his kingdom. That's a lesson I need over and over as I make my way through this world.

Thoughts to Ponder

Why would Jesus institute this ritual to the followers before they could even understand it? What thoughts might have been going through their minds? What do you understand the communion ceremony to mean to a Christian today?

Prayer

Father, we pray that we will always remember the sacrifice of your Son, particularly at that moment when you call us to commune with you. Amen.

DENYING OUR LORD

JOHN 13:21–38

²¹After Jesus said this, he was very troubled. He said openly, "I tell you the truth, one of you will turn against me."

²²The followers all looked at each other, because they did not know whom Jesus was talking about. ²³One of the followers sitting next to Jesus was the follower Jesus loved. ²⁴Simon Peter motioned to him to ask Jesus whom he was talking about.

²⁵That follower leaned closer to Jesus and asked, "Lord, who is it?"

²⁶Jesus answered, "I will dip this bread into the dish. The man I give it to is the man who will turn against me." So Jesus took a piece of bread, dipped it, and gave it to Judas Iscariot, the son of Simon. ²⁷As soon as Judas took the bread, Satan entered him. Jesus said to him, "The thing that you will do—do it quickly." ²⁸No one at the table understood why Jesus said this to Judas. ²⁹Since he was the one who kept the money box, some of the followers thought Jesus was telling him to buy what was needed for the feast or to give something to the poor.

³⁰Judas took the bread Jesus gave him and immediately went out. It was night.

³¹When Judas was gone, Jesus said, "Now the Son of Man receives his glory, and God receives glory through him. ³²If God receives glory through him, then God will give glory to the Son through himself. And God will give him glory quickly."

³³Jesus said, "My children, I will be with you only a little longer. You will look for me, and what I told the Jews, I tell you now: Where I am going you cannot come.

³⁴"I give you a new command: Love each other. You must love each other as I have loved you. ³⁵All people will know that you are my followers if you love each other."

³⁶Simon Peter asked Jesus, "Lord, where are you going?"

Jesus answered, "Where I am going you cannot follow now, but you will follow later."

³⁷Peter asked, "Lord, why can't I follow you now? I am ready to die for you!"

³⁸Jesus answered, "Are you ready to die for me? I tell you the truth, before the rooster crows, you will say three times that you don't know me."

DEVOTION

WHEN I WAS IN COLLEGE, I did my best to disguise that I was majoring in religion. Although my graduate degrees and my current college teaching field are in journalism, that option wasn't available at the small Christian college in my hometown, so I studied religion and worked on the student newspaper.

But I sure didn't want to be considered one of the "preacher boys." So I perfected the back-of-the-class slouch to show I wasn't really into this stuff. When a teacher required that we write a commentary on a book of the Bible, I did it in pencil on a lined writing tablet instead of taking the time to type it out neatly.

I acted out in other ways, too. When others seemed incredulous that I was a Bible major, I took it as a source of pride. I would make the best grades in the class, but I wouldn't act "holy." In fact, I wouldn't even act religious. I was no preacher boy, I was just a guy smart enough to get a scholarship to study the Bible and convert it into a free education. So I thought.

What I didn't realize then, but fully realize now, is that I was behaving like Peter behaved on the night described in the story above: I was denying Jesus. I wasn't denying that he lived or even denying that he was the Son of God. I was simply denying by my actions that he was the Lord of my life.

But the writer of the Letter to the Hebrews tells us, "God's word is alive and working and is sharper than a double-edged sword. It cuts all the way into us, where the soul and the spirit are joined, to the center of our joints and bones. And it judges the thoughts and feelings in our hearts" (Hebrews 4:12). Soon, some of the words started to cut into my thick skin and enter my heart. Long after I recognized Christ was my Savior, my life began to reflect that he was also my Lord.

But it's still easy, and even a little tempting, to deny Jesus in our everyday lives. We want to worship him, but we don't want to be looked at differently because of him. So we ask him to wait outside the office while we get a day's work done. We put him aside when we get stuck in traffic or face any of life's other annoyances. Although we rarely deny him outright—for that would be blasphemous—we claim him when we need him, and we ignore him when he's "inconvenient."

Judas and Peter represent two opposites on the continuum of disassociating ourselves from Jesus. On the "Judas end," we betray him. On the "Peter end," we simply deny him. Which do you think is the greatest threat to Christians today?

THOUGHTS TO PONDER

What do you think it means in the text above when we are told, "As soon as Judas took the bread, Satan entered him"? In what ways do Christians today deny Jesus and his role in their lives?

PRAYER

God, we pray that we will neither betray you nor deny you in the way we act this day. Amen.

FINAL INSTRUCTIONS

JOHN 14:1–24

14Jesus said, "Don't let your hearts be troubled. Trust in God, and trust in me. ²There are many rooms in my Father's house; I would not tell you this if it were not true. I am going there to prepare a place for you. ³After I go and prepare a place for you, I will come back and take you to be with me so that you may be where I am. ⁴You know the way to the place where I am going."

⁵Thomas said to Jesus, "Lord, we don't know where you are going. So how can we know the way?"

⁶Jesus answered, "I am the way, and the truth, and the life. The only way to the Father is through me. ⁷If you really knew me, you would know my Father, too. But now you do know him, and you have seen him."

⁸Philip said to him, "Lord, show us the Father. That is all we need."

⁹Jesus answered, "I have been with you a long time now. Do you still not know me, Philip? Whoever has seen me has seen the Father. So why do you say, 'Show us the Father'? ¹⁰Don't you believe that I am in the Father and the Father is in me? The words I say to you don't come from me, but the Father lives in me and does his own work. ¹¹Believe me when I say that I am in the Father and the Father is in me. Or believe because of the miracles I have done. ¹²I tell you the truth, whoever believes in me will do the same things that I do. Those who believe will do even greater things than these, because I am going to the Father. ¹³And if you ask for anything in my name, I will do it for you so that the Father's glory will be shown through the Son. ¹⁴If you ask me for anything in my name, I will do it.

¹⁵"If you love me, you will obey my commands. ¹⁶I will ask the Father, and he will give you another Helper to be with you forever— ¹⁷the Spirit of truth. The world cannot accept him, because it does not see him or know him. But you know him, because he lives with you and he will be in you.

¹⁸"I will not leave you all alone like orphans; I will come back to you. ¹⁹In a little while the world will not see me anymore, but you will see me. Because I live, you will live, too. ²⁰On that day you will know that I am in my Father, and that you are in me and I am in you. ²¹Those who know my commands and obey them are the ones who love me, and my Father will love those who love me. I will love them and will show myself to them."

²²Then Judas (not Judas Iscariot) said, "But, Lord, why do you plan to show yourself to us and not to the rest of the world?"

²³Jesus answered, "If people love me, they will obey my teaching. My Father will love them, and we will come to them and make our home with them. ²⁴Those who do not love me do not obey my teaching. This teaching that you hear is not really mine; it is from my Father, who sent me.

DEVOTION

IN THE PASSAGE ABOVE, Jesus gave his followers a final address. Although they didn't grasp it yet, he was going to leave them soon. He wanted to impress on them these final thoughts: I will return for you, and in the meantime, I will not abandon you.

But as he speaks, he's interrupted three times by questions and comments from the followers. And I think the things they say reflect some of the same concerns we have today. You see, like Thomas, I would like a nice road map to heaven. Like Philip, I sometimes long for a little glimpse of God, just to know that my faith is justified. And like Judas—the son of James, not the one who will betray Jesus—I sometimes wonder why Jesus just didn't do some sign so overwhelmingly spectacular that it would have forced every knee in the world to bow to him.

But those wishes—both mine and the followers—are shortsighted. If I got my way on all those requests, my faith would not be necessary. But Jesus came to reveal God to us, and Jesus has shown us the way to the home he is preparing for us. On that night, Jesus answered each question and comment without judgment, just as he answers my doubts today with a measure of grace while he gently points me in the direction of an answer.

THOUGHTS TO PONDER

Which of the followers above do you most closely identify with? Why? What question would you ask Jesus if you had the opportunity?

PRAYER

God, we're thankful that you allow our questions and that you supply us with the answers we need in order find our way back to you. Amen.

A Spirit/Body Problem

MARK 14:32-42

³²Jesus and his followers went to a place called Gethsemane. He said to them, "Sit here while I pray." ³³Jesus took Peter, James, and John with him, and he began to be very sad and troubled. ³⁴He said to them, "My heart is full of sorrow, to the point of death. Stay here and watch."

³⁵After walking a little farther away from them, Jesus fell to the ground and prayed that, if possible, he would not have this time of suffering. ³⁶He prayed, "Abba, Father! You can do all things. Take away this cup of suffering. But do what you want, not what I want."

³⁷Then Jesus went back to his followers and found them asleep. He said to Peter, "Simon, are you sleeping? Couldn't you stay awake with me for one hour? ³⁸Stay awake and pray for strength against temptation. The spirit wants to do what is right, but the body is weak."

³⁹Again Jesus went away and prayed the same thing. ⁴⁰Then he went back to his followers, and again he found them asleep, because their eyes were very heavy. And they did not know what to say to him.

⁴¹After Jesus prayed a third time, he went back to his followers and said to them, "Are you still sleeping and resting? That's enough. The time has come for the Son of Man to be handed over to sinful people. ⁴²Get up, we must go. Look, here comes the man who has turned against me."

Devotion

THE SUPPER was over and darkness washed over the city of Jerusalem. Jesus decided to do what he had done so many times in his ministry: he went out alone to pray.

The group was getting smaller. Judas fled the supper in the upper room to find the leaders of the Temple who had paid him to deliver Jesus to them. Eight of the apostles had scattered. They were not to be together again until after the burial of Jesus as they awaited their fate in a sealed room.

But three remained with Jesus. Peter, James, and John—the followers closest to Jesus and the ones he wanted near him at the end of his time on earth. But even they failed him. It was late. They had enjoyed a large banquet meal, probably with wine. In his Gospel account, Luke says they were exhausted from their sorrow. For whatever reason, their eyes were too heavy and they fell asleep two times.

Luke's account also says that angels came to minister to Jesus as he sweated so profusely, it was like drops of blood. But while angels attended him, Jesus'

625

earthly friends had failed him. It would be a night of failures. Judas would betray him. The three followers would fall asleep on him. Peter would deny him three times. And none of his followers would stand up for him before the court of Pilate.

The words Jesus spoke to Peter still hold true today: "The spirit wants to do what is right, but the body is weak."

I can think of times in my life when I've had a spirit/body problem. I wanted to say something to a lost friend, but the words didn't come. I wanted to change my bad habits, but the temptation was too great. I wanted to be home with my family, but the work was piled up at the office. The spirit wants to do what is right, but the body is weak.

I could go on with my spirit/body problems and you could add yours. We all have good intentions at war with our human frailties. Paul writes of this problem: "I do not understand the things I do. I do not do what I want to do, and I do the things I hate" (Romans 7:15). He continues: "But I am not really the one who is doing these hated things; it is sin living in me that does them (7:17). But Paul's conclusion can encourage all of us: "Who will save me from this body that brings me death? I thank God for saving me through Jesus Christ our Lord!" (7:24–25).

Jesus doesn't condemn the three sleepers and he doesn't condemn you and me. Like Paul, I am sometimes amazed at the things I'm capable of doing even when I don't want to. But to all of us who struggle with a body weaker than our spirit, Jesus wakes us gently and encourages us with the same words he used to encourage Peter: pray for strength against temptation.

THOUGHTS TO PONDER

What are some things you do that you don't want to do? What are some things you wish you could do but can't seem to do? How can we overcome our weaknesses to do what we ought to do?

PRAYER

Father, we know we are called to watch for you, just as the followers in Gethsemane were called. Help us to be diligent as we wait. Amen.

THE BETRAYAL

LUKE 22:1–6, 14–23, 47–51

22 It was almost time for the Feast of Unleavened Bread, called the Passover Feast. ²The leading priests and teachers of the law were trying to find a way to kill Jesus, because they were afraid of the people.

³Satan entered Judas Iscariot, one of Jesus' twelve apostles. ⁴Judas went to the leading priests and some of the soldiers who guarded the Temple and talked to them about a way to hand Jesus over to them. ⁵They were pleased and agreed to give Judas money. ⁶He agreed and watched for the best time to hand Jesus over to them when he was away from the crowd.

¹⁴When the time came, Jesus and the apostles were sitting at the table. ¹⁵He said to them, "I wanted very much to eat this Passover meal with you before I suffer. ¹⁶I will not eat another Passover meal until it is given its true meaning in the kingdom of God."

¹⁷Then Jesus took a cup, gave thanks, and said, "Take this cup and share it among yourselves. ¹⁸I will not drink again from the fruit of the vine until God's kingdom comes."

¹⁹Then Jesus took some bread, gave thanks, broke it, and gave it to the apostles, saying, "This is my body, which I am giving for you. Do this to remember me." ²⁰In the same way, after supper, Jesus took the cup and said, "This cup is the new agreement that God makes with his people. This new agreement begins with my blood which is poured out for you.

²¹"But one of you will turn against me, and his hand is with mine on the table. ²²What God has planned for the Son of Man will happen, but how terrible it will be for that one who turns against the Son of Man."

²³Then the apostles asked each other which one of them would do that.

⁴⁷While Jesus was speaking, a crowd came up, and Judas, one of the twelve apostles, was leading them. He came close to Jesus so he could kiss him.

⁴⁸But Jesus said to him, "Judas, are you using the kiss to give the Son of Man to his enemies?"

⁴⁹When those who were standing around him saw what was happening, they said, "Lord, should we strike them with our swords?" ⁵⁰And one of them struck the servant of the high priest and cut off his right ear.

⁵¹Jesus said, "Stop! No more of this." Then he touched the servant's ear and healed him.

DEVOTION

HAVE YOU EVER WONDERED how Judas could betray Jesus? Hadn't he seen the miracles? Passed the baskets at the feedings? Watched the leper's skin become clean? Didn't he realize Jesus was the Son of God?

Perhaps Jesus disappointed Judas. Maybe Jesus' refusal to set up an earthly kingdom frustrated him. After all, with Jesus' power and the pent-up frustration of the Jewish nation, perhaps the Roman oppression could have been toppled.

But even if that wasn't the goal of Jesus, couldn't he be a little more concerned about money? Why did the followers have to live day to day when Jesus could have provided for their every need at a whim? Hadn't it been Judas who pointed out the extravagance of the woman who poured expensive perfume on the feet of Jesus (John 12:4–6)? As Judas's disappointment with Jesus burned, we're told that Satan entered Judas, and he made the deal with the leading priests to betray Jesus.

Ironically, it was when he was disappointed with his leaders and the general direction of the American Revolution that Benedict Arnold agreed to betray his country and hand over his garrison at West Point to the British. Disappointment is a powerful motivator to turn your back on that which was formerly important to you.

I think we have to be on guard against Judas-type behavior today. We get disappointed with God when we don't get the medical report we've prayed for. We question his guidance when our financial needs are not met. We wonder where he is when we lose a loved one.

And Satan is there, ready to turn that disappointment into betrayal. "Curse God and die," Job's wife told him (Job 2:9). Perhaps subtly or maybe brazenly, many Christians do just that when life hands them a major disappointment.

I won't always get my way with God. He's not a cosmic vending machine dispensing everything I ask for. But I have to resist the efforts of Satan to turn God's silence into my open rebellion.

THOUGHTS TO PONDER

Why do you think Judas betrayed Jesus? Why would Jesus have chosen a follower who would betray him? Why not let one of his many enemies turn him over to the Romans?

PRAYER

Jesus, we pray that we will never betray you, either by our words or our actions. Help us to be on guard against Satan's attempts to get us to turn our backs on you when times are tough. Amen.

IGNORING THE MIRACULOUS

JOHN 18:1–11

18 When Jesus finished praying, he went with his followers across the Kidron Valley. On the other side there was a garden, and Jesus and his followers went into it.

²Judas knew where this place was, because Jesus met there often with his followers. Judas was the one who turned against Jesus. ³So Judas came there with a group of soldiers and some guards from the leading priests and the Pharisees. They were carrying torches, lanterns, and weapons.

⁴Knowing everything that would happen to him, Jesus went out and asked, "Who is it you are looking for?"

⁵They answered, "Jesus from Nazareth."

"I am he," Jesus said. (Judas, the one who turned against Jesus, was standing there with them.) ⁶When Jesus said, "I am he," they moved back and fell to the ground.

⁷Jesus asked them again, "Who is it you are looking for?"

They said, "Jesus of Nazareth."

⁸"I told you that I am he," Jesus said. "So if you are looking for me, let the others go." ⁹This happened so that the words Jesus said before would come true: "I have not lost any of the ones you gave me."

¹⁰Simon Peter, who had a sword, pulled it out and struck the servant of the high priest, cutting off his right ear. (The servant's name was Malchus.) ¹¹Jesus said to Peter, "Put your sword back. Shouldn't I drink the cup the Father gave me?"

MATTHEW 26:52–56

⁵²Jesus said to the man, "Put your sword back in its place. All who use swords will be killed with swords. ⁵³Surely you know I could ask my Father, and he would give me more than twelve armies of angels. ⁵⁴But it must happen this way to bring about what the Scriptures say."

⁵⁵Then Jesus said to the crowd, "You came to get me with swords and clubs as if I were a criminal. Every day I sat in the Temple teaching, and you did not arrest me there. ⁵⁶But all these things have happened so that it will come about as the prophets wrote." Then all of Jesus' followers left him and ran away.

DEVOTION

WHEN I WAS IN COLLEGE, I was a counselor at a Bible camp, and one night we had to take a young camper to the emergency room of the hospital for a minor medical issue. On the other side of the curtain was a loud, profane, drunk man who had gotten into a knife fight and lost an ear. After being belligerent with all the nurses and then the doctor, the man announced he was leaving. He put his ear back into the plastic bag he had used to bring it in, and walked out as we looked at one another in amazement. Since this was the only hospital in town—indeed for miles around—he would undoubtedly lose the ear for his foolish behavior.

Which leads us to Malchus. As the servant of the high priest, he was an important part of the arresting party. In his role, he was probably in charge of administration, running the day-to-day affairs of the Temple and reporting directly to the high priest. He was also able to represent the high priest in his absence, and that was apparently what he was doing in the garden on the night of Jesus' betrayal.

So Peter was not picking some out-of-the-way servant on the edge of the crowd to attack. He was in the center of things—once again—striking at the man who would be reporting the arrest of Jesus back to the high priest. But Jesus quickly defused the situation by picking up the severed ear and healing Malchus, according to Luke's account of this story.

Didn't they see the miracle? Didn't this cause anyone in the arresting party to think, "Hey, this man just might be who he says he is"? But the answer, sadly, is that their hearts were so hardened by their hatred that they weren't going to be moved by a simple healing.

Just like that drunk man who ignored the doctors and went on to his fate of living a life with a missing ear, the members of the arresting party ignored the miracle and went on to their fate—living a life without seeing the very Son of God who was right in front of them.

THOUGHTS TO PONDER

Why would Peter be carrying a sword? What did he hope to accomplish? Why would Jesus heal Malchus when he knew his own fate was already sealed? What did Jesus mean by saying, "All who use swords will be killed with swords"?

PRAYER

Father, we pray that we will hear your words and that, because we have heard, we will believe. Amen.

STAGES OF DENIAL

MATTHEW 26:31–35, 57–58, 69–75

[31]Jesus told his followers, "Tonight you will all stumble in your faith on account of me, because it is written in the Scriptures:
'I will kill the shepherd,
and the sheep will scatter.'   *Zechariah 13:7*
[32]But after I rise from the dead, I will go ahead of you into Galilee."

[33]Peter said, "Everyone else may stumble in their faith because of you, but I will not."

[34]Jesus said, "I tell you the truth, tonight before the rooster crows you will say three times that you don't know me."

[35]But Peter said, "I will never say that I don't know you! I will even die with you!" And all the other followers said the same thing.

[57]Those people who arrested Jesus led him to the house of Caiaphas, the high priest, where the teachers of the law and the elders were gathered. [58]Peter followed far behind to the courtyard of the high priest's house, and he sat down with the guards to see what would happen to Jesus.

[69]At that time, as Peter was sitting in the courtyard, a servant girl came to him and said, "You also were with Jesus of Galilee."

[70]But Peter said to all the people there that he was never with Jesus. He said, "I don't know what you are talking about."

[71]When he left the courtyard and was at the gate, another girl saw him. She said to the people there, "This man was with Jesus of Nazareth."

[72]Again, Peter said he was never with him, saying, "I swear I don't know this man Jesus!"

[73]A short time later, some people standing there went to Peter and said, "Surely you are one of those who followed Jesus. The way you talk shows it."

[74]Then Peter began to place a curse on himself and swear, "I don't know the man." At once, a rooster crowed. [75]And Peter remembered what Jesus had told him: "Before the rooster crows, you will say three times that you don't know me." Then Peter went outside and cried painfully.

DEVOTION

THE PROGRESSION of Peter's three denials of Jesus fascinates me because it gives us a glimpse into how one begins to drift away from Jesus. In the beginning,

Peter could almost laugh off his association with Jesus. "I don't know what you are talking about," he said to the servant girl—a girl identified in other Gospel accounts as a servant of the high priest who was accusing Jesus of crimes against Rome.

But that wasn't the end. Another accuser came forward: "This man was with Jesus of Nazareth," she said. Since being a follower of Jesus didn't look like a good career prospect at the moment, Peter did some quick calculations. *Perhaps they'll believe an oath.* So he swore that he didn't know Jesus.

But that still didn't put the matter to rest. By the third time, Peter had multiple accusers and the heat was turned up. He sounded like someone from Jesus' part of the country. He didn't speak like someone from the city. Why would he be out here in the middle of the night watching this proceeding—warming himself by the fire, according to the Gospel of Mark—if he wasn't one of them?

So Peter decided to do something to convince the skeptics that he was not a follower of Jesus: he decided to act like the rest of the world. So he offered to put a curse on himself if his words weren't true. "I don't know the man," he swore with an oath.

There's a simple formula in this story, I think, and it's this: if you want the world to know you're a Christian, sound like one. On the other hand, if you don't want the world to know you're a Christian, just act like everybody else.

As long as Peter's talk gave him away, the crowd took him for a follower of Jesus. But as soon as he proved by his coarse words and reckless oath-taking that he was, indeed, worldly, then he was no longer mistaken for a follower of Jesus. If you were judged this week by your words and your actions, would anyone consider you to be a follower of Jesus? Do we, like Peter, try to warm ourselves by the fires of the world, thinking we will never get burned?

Thoughts to ponder

Why do you think Peter spoke up and made the boast that he would never deny Jesus? The text tells us that all the followers of Jesus ran away (Matthew 26:56). Why do you think Peter stayed close?

Prayer

Father, we pray that by our words and by our deeds we will never deny you or your presence in our lives. Amen.

A Legacy of a Traitor

MATTHEW 26:47–50; 27:1–10

⁴⁷While Jesus was still speaking, Judas, one of the twelve apostles, came up. With him were many people carrying swords and clubs who had been sent from the leading priests and the Jewish elders of the people. ⁴⁸Judas had planned to give them a signal, saying, "The man I kiss is Jesus. Arrest him." ⁴⁹At once Judas went to Jesus and said, "Greetings, Teacher!" and kissed him.

⁵⁰Jesus answered, "Friend, do what you came to do."

Then the people came and grabbed Jesus and arrested him.

27 Early the next morning, all the leading priests and elders of the people decided that Jesus should die. ²They tied him, led him away, and turned him over to Pilate, the governor.

³Judas, the one who had given Jesus to his enemies, saw that they had decided to kill Jesus. Then he was very sorry for what he had done. So he took the thirty silver coins back to the priests and the leaders, ⁴saying, "I sinned; I handed over to you an innocent man."

The leaders answered, "What is that to us? That's your problem, not ours."

⁵So Judas threw the money into the Temple. Then he went off and hanged himself.

⁶The leading priests picked up the silver coins in the Temple and said, "Our law does not allow us to keep this money with the Temple money, because it has paid for a man's death." ⁷So they decided to use the coins to buy Potter's Field as a place to bury strangers who died in Jerusalem. ⁸That is why that field is still called the Field of Blood. ⁹So what Jeremiah the prophet had said came true: "They took thirty silver coins. That is how little the Israelites thought he was worth. ¹⁰They used those thirty silver coins to buy the potter's field, as the Lord commanded me."

DEVOTION

APPARENTLY THE SOLDIERS that were hired by the Jewish religious leaders to arrest Jesus were not readily familiar with his appearance. For that reason, it was necessary for Judas to give a sign to show them who to seize. The sign was a betrayal kiss. So the scene was set for the final interaction between Judas and Jesus in the Garden of Gethsemane.

We can find several lessons in the story of Judas. Let's look at three of them.

First, I find that even when I commit the worst sin against Jesus I will ever commit, he still considers me a friend. "Friend," he said to Judas, "do what you came to do."

They were hollow words. Judas had been chosen by Jesus to walk closely with him. For three years they had lived together, eaten together, faced the wrath of the religious establishment together. Jesus had chosen Judas, even though he knew from the beginning that Judas would be his betrayer. Yet he treated Judas the same as the others for all those months.

He does the same with me. He knows I'll turn on him occasionally, but he treats me the same every day. He treats me as a friend, even when I don't deserve the term.

Second, the story teaches us that some wrongdoings cannot be easily undone. Even when Judas came to the late realization that he'd sinned in his betrayal of Jesus, it was too late to undo the harm he had done. Trying to give back the money had no effect.

We've all seen homes destroyed by adultery. Business executives sent to prison for fraud. People permanently injured by a single bad decision to drink and drive. And all the sorrow in the world can't undo the consequences.

Third, the story tells me that I will have a legacy, whether good or bad. The entire earthly fortune of Judas was scattered on the floor of the Temple. It amounted to about a month's worth of wages—just enough to buy a field to bury the unfortunate strangers who died traveling through Jerusalem, and presumably to bury Judas himself.

An entire life lived and a legacy as a traitor. Three years of following Jesus now amounted to nothing. Judas didn't finish the course. He let greed blind him to the evil that was tempting him.

His money is like that of the rich fool in the parable of Jesus who determined after a good crop that he would tear down his old barn and build a bigger one, keeping all his harvest to himself (Luke 12:13–21). That very night the man died, and his fortune, which he'd tried to hoard, went to others. Like the man in the parable, Judas died, and not a single piece of silver crossed into eternity with him.

THOUGHTS TO PONDER

What changed Judas' heart? What do you think he thought would be the fate of Jesus when he turned him over to the soldiers? Why did he change his mind?

PRAYER

God, we know that Judas made his choices and then suffered the consequences. We pray that we will consider our actions carefully so that our fate will be better. Amen.

The Most Important Question

LUKE 22:63—23:12

63The men who were guarding Jesus began making fun of him and beating him. 64They blindfolded him and said, "Prove that you are a prophet, and tell us who hit you." 65They said many cruel things to Jesus.

66When day came, the council of the elders of the people, both the leading priests and the teachers of the law, came together and led Jesus to their highest court. 67They said, "If you are the Christ, tell us."

Jesus said to them, "If I tell you, you will not believe me. 68And if I ask you, you will not answer. 69But from now on, the Son of Man will sit at the right hand of the powerful God."

70They all said, "Then are you the Son of God?"

Jesus said to them, "You say that I am."

71They said, "Why do we need witnesses now? We ourselves heard him say this."

23 Then the whole group stood up and led Jesus to Pilate. 2They began to accuse Jesus, saying, "We caught this man telling things that mislead our people. He says that we should not pay taxes to Caesar, and he calls himself the Christ, a king."

3Pilate asked Jesus, "Are you the king of the Jews?"

Jesus answered, "Those are your words."

4Pilate said to the leading priests and the people, "I find nothing against this man."

5They were insisting, saying, "But Jesus makes trouble with the people, teaching all around Judea. He began in Galilee, and now he is here."

6Pilate heard this and asked if Jesus was from Galilee. 7Since Jesus was under Herod's authority, Pilate sent Jesus to Herod, who was in Jerusalem at that time. 8When Herod saw Jesus, he was very glad, because he had heard about Jesus and had wanted to meet him for a long time. He was hoping to see Jesus work a miracle. 9Herod asked Jesus many questions, but Jesus said nothing. 10The leading priests and teachers of the law were standing there, strongly accusing Jesus. 11After Herod and his soldiers had made fun of Jesus, they dressed him in a kingly robe and sent him back to Pilate. 12In the past, Pilate and Herod had always been enemies, but on that day they became friends.

DEVOTION

WHO IS JESUS? The question is central to both the unofficial inquest by the crowd and the official inquiry by Pilate. *Who do you say you are? Are you who they say you are?*

Knowing the identity of Jesus is important, because once we know who he is, we know what we have to do in response. Jesus posed a question to his followers one day, asking them who the crowds thought he was. Scripture tells us that they answered, " 'Some say you are John the Baptist. Others say you are Elijah, and still others say you are Jeremiah or one of the prophets.' Then Jesus asked them, 'And who do you say I am?' Simon Peter answered, 'You are the Christ, the Son of the living God.' Jesus answered, 'You are blessed, Simon son of Jonah, because no person taught you that. My Father in heaven showed you who I am'" (Matthew 16:14–17).

So many claims and counter-claims were swirling around Jesus that most of the time spent in his "trials" consisted of trying to figure out who he was. It's an important question today. Each of us must decide who Jesus is. If Jesus is simply a troublemaker, then ignore his teaching. But if he is the Son of God, then everything changes.

In the passage above, Peter "got it." He understood that Jesus was no latter day prophet. He was the real thing: the Son of God that they had anticipated for so long. And because of that, nothing in Peter's life would ever be the same. But Pilate didn't get it. Herod didn't get it. And because of that, their fate was sealed.

Who do you think Jesus is? And what difference does your answer make to your life?

THOUGHTS TO PONDER

How many courts does Jesus appear before in the story above? What happens at each one? Why was Jesus passed from the Jews to Pilate and from Pilate to Herod?

PRAYER

God, we pray that we will know exactly who Jesus is and know exactly what is required of us because of who he is. Amen.

WASHING OUR HANDS

MATTHEW 27:11–31

¹¹Jesus stood before Pilate the governor, and Pilate asked him, "Are you the king of the Jews?"

Jesus answered, "Those are your words."

¹²When the leading priests and the elders accused Jesus, he said nothing.

¹³So Pilate said to Jesus, "Don't you hear them accusing you of all these things?"

¹⁴But Jesus said nothing in answer to Pilate, and Pilate was very surprised at this.

¹⁵Every year at the time of Passover the governor would free one prisoner whom the people chose. ¹⁶At that time there was a man in prison, named Barabbas, who was known to be very bad. ¹⁷When the people gathered at Pilate's house, Pilate said, "Whom do you want me to set free: Barabbas or Jesus who is called the Christ?" ¹⁸Pilate knew that they turned Jesus in to him because they were jealous.

¹⁹While Pilate was sitting there on the judge's seat, his wife sent this message to him: "Don't do anything to that man, because he is innocent. Today I had a dream about him, and it troubled me very much."

²⁰But the leading priests and elders convinced the crowd to ask for Barabbas to be freed and for Jesus to be killed.

²¹Pilate said, "I have Barabbas and Jesus. Which do you want me to set free for you?"

The people answered, "Barabbas."

²²Pilate asked, "So what should I do with Jesus, the one called the Christ?"

They all answered, "Crucify him!"

²³Pilate asked, "Why? What wrong has he done?"

But they shouted louder, "Crucify him!"

²⁴When Pilate saw that he could do nothing about this and that a riot was starting, he took some water and washed his hands in front of the crowd. Then he said, "I am not guilty of this man's death. You are the ones who are causing it!"

²⁵All the people answered, "We and our children will be responsible for his death."

²⁶Then he set Barabbas free. But Jesus was beaten with whips and handed over to the soldiers to be crucified.

²⁷The governor's soldiers took Jesus into the governor's palace, and they all gathered around him. ²⁸They took off his clothes and put a red robe on him. ²⁹Using thorny branches, they made a crown, put it on his head, and put a stick in his right hand. Then the soldiers bowed before Jesus and made fun of him,

saying, "Hail, King of the Jews!" [30]They spat on Jesus. Then they took his stick and began to beat him on the head. [31]After they finished, the soldiers took off the robe and put his own clothes on him again. Then they led him away to be crucified.

DEVOTION

PILATE HAD ALREADY TRIED once to rid himself of Jesus. Discovering that Jesus was a Galilean, Pilate sent him over to Herod, the political ruler of that province. Luke tells us that these two men were rivals but actually bonded after their common experience of disposing of Jesus.

But now Jesus was Pilate's problem again, having been sent back from Herod, and Jesus wasn't making Pilate's job any easier with his refusals to answer the accusatory questions. So Pilate saw Barabbas as his last chance to get rid of his problem. Given the choice to free one prisoner during the celebration of the Feast of Unleavened Bread, surely they would choose the teacher over the murderer. But the crowds didn't help Pilate with his dilemma either as they shouted, "Barabbas!"

I see myself in Pilate, knowing that Jesus has done nothing to deserve the way I treat him with my actions. I see myself in the crowds, preferring the company of the sinner to the company of the Son of God. I see myself in Barabbas, suddenly and unexpectedly made free because Jesus is going to pay the ultimate price for me.

When my oldest son was in grade school, he took some valuable baseball cards to school. Wanting to be popular with the older boys, he traded his valuable cards for less valuable ones. He never got those valuable cards back, and he never became friends with the boys who took them.

The leading priests convinced the people to make a bad trade. But Satan tries to do the same thing with me every day. He whispers in my ear, trying to get me to trade a heavenly home in eternity for the temporary pleasures and gains of today.

Pilate will forever be remembered for washing his hands of Jesus. My prayer is that we never do the same thing by our actions today.

THOUGHTS TO PONDER

Do we ever prefer something else over Jesus? When given a choice to stand up for Jesus or be popular, which do we choose?

PRAYER

Father, we pray that we will never wash our hands of you or your Son, whether by our words or by our actions. Amen.

DECISION TIME

MARK 15:16–24

¹⁶The soldiers took Jesus into the governor's palace (called the Praetorium) and called all the other soldiers together. ¹⁷They put a purple robe on Jesus and used thorny branches to make a crown for his head. ¹⁸They began to call out to him, "Hail, King of the Jews!" ¹⁹The soldiers beat Jesus on the head many times with a stick. They spit on him and made fun of him by bowing on their knees and worshiping him. ²⁰After they finished, the soldiers took off the purple robe and put his own clothes on him again. Then they led him out of the palace to be crucified.

²¹A man named Simon from Cyrene, the father of Alexander and Rufus, was coming from the fields to the city. The soldiers forced Simon to carry the cross for Jesus. ²²They led Jesus to the place called Golgotha, which means the Place of the Skull. ²³The soldiers tried to give Jesus wine mixed with myrrh to drink, but he refused. ²⁴The soldiers crucified Jesus and divided his clothes among themselves, throwing lots to decide what each soldier would get.

MATTHEW 27:50–54

⁵⁰But Jesus cried out again in a loud voice and died.

⁵¹Then the curtain in the Temple was torn into two pieces, from the top to the bottom. Also, the earth shook and rocks broke apart. ⁵²The graves opened, and many of God's people who had died were raised from the dead. ⁵³They came out of the graves after Jesus was raised from the dead and went into the holy city, where they appeared to many people.

⁵⁴When the army officer and the soldiers guarding Jesus saw this earthquake and everything else that happened, they were very frightened and said, "He really was the Son of God!"

DEVOTION

HERE'S A STATEMENT you might find startling: it's not possible to call Jesus a good man or a good teacher while denying his divinity. Do what you want with Jesus—accept him or reject him. But those options—merely a good man or teacher—are not available to us. Here are your options in deciding what to do with Jesus: reject him or believe in him. He doesn't want it any other way.

The very idea that Jesus is just another in a long line of good teachers from whom we can take the "good" and leave the "bad" is a very dangerous idea. The people putting him on the cross might have acknowledged that he was a good teacher, yet they crucified him anyway. Considering the claims that Jesus made, one must conclude that he was crazy, that he was intentionally deceiving people, or that he really was exactly who he claimed to be: the Son of God. And only one of those possibilities is worth his death and my life.

The soldiers who took Jesus to the cross demonstrated our options in stark contrast. On the one hand, there were the ones who took delight in their role in this drama. They mocked him, hit him, beat him, and spit on him. They even pretended to worship him, getting on their knees and bowing before him. They forced him to carry his cross until he could go no further. They squatted at the foot of the cross, gambling over his clothes, ignoring the fact that he was dying above them.

On the other hand were the ones who guarded the cross. They saw the sky turn dark as night in the middle of the day (Luke 23:44). They felt the earth shake and saw the rocks break. Perhaps they heard that the curtain in the Temple ripped in half. Perhaps they heard of the dead who came out of the graves. Whatever they saw and whatever they heard, they did the only logical thing to do in light of the evidence: they believed in Jesus.

Now the choice is ours. We can join the mockers or we can join the believers. But we can't ride some imaginary fence in the middle. If Jesus was a madman or a fraud, he can be ignored. But if he is God incarnate, then there are demands that must be met.

Jesus put our choices in terms of black and white. It's either the wide road or the narrow road (Matthew 7:13–14). You're either ready for the bridegroom or you are not (Matthew 25:1–13). You're either on the left hand or the right (Matthew 25:31–46) on the Judgment Day. Jesus doesn't give us the choice to mock his claims to be God but admire his ability to tell a story, and he doesn't give us the ability to bow to him on Sunday and spit on him during the week.

Scripture tells us that the soldiers were frightened when they said, "He really was the Son of God!" I think I know why. Because once we say it, we begin to see the terrifying truth of our sins against God, and we begin to see that we must change our lives. And only the Savior can help us with that.

THOUGHTS TO PONDER

What was it that caused you to believe that Jesus was the Son of God? How did it change your life?

PRAYER

God, we pray that in our lives and works we will be numbered among those bowed at the foot of the cross and not among the mockers. Amen.

Freed from Slavery

MARK 15:21–39

²¹A man named Simon from Cyrene, the father of Alexander and Rufus, was coming from the fields to the city. The soldiers forced Simon to carry the cross for Jesus. ²²They led Jesus to the place called Golgotha, which means the Place of the Skull. ²³The soldiers tried to give Jesus wine mixed with myrrh to drink, but he refused. ²⁴The soldiers crucified Jesus and divided his clothes among themselves, throwing lots to decide what each soldier would get.

²⁵It was nine o'clock in the morning when they crucified Jesus. ²⁶There was a sign with this charge against Jesus written on it: THE KING OF THE JEWS. ²⁷They also put two robbers on crosses beside Jesus, one on the right, and the other on the left. [²⁸And the Scripture came true that says, "They put him with criminals."] ²⁹People walked by and insulted Jesus and shook their heads, saying, "You said you could destroy the Temple and build it again in three days. ³⁰So save yourself! Come down from that cross!"

³¹The leading priests and the teachers of the law were also making fun of Jesus. They said to each other, "He saved other people, but he can't save himself. ³²If he is really the Christ, the king of Israel, let him come down now from the cross. When we see this, we will believe in him." The robbers who were being crucified beside Jesus also insulted him.

³³At noon the whole country became dark, and the darkness lasted for three hours. ³⁴At three o'clock Jesus cried in a loud voice, "Eloi, Eloi, lama sabachthani." This means, "My God, my God, why have you abandoned me?"

³⁵When some of the people standing there heard this, they said, "Listen! He is calling Elijah."

³⁶Someone there ran and got a sponge, filled it with vinegar, tied it to a stick, and gave it to Jesus to drink. He said, "We want to see if Elijah will come to take him down from the cross."

³⁷Then Jesus cried in a loud voice and died.

³⁸The curtain in the Temple was torn into two pieces, from the top to the bottom. ³⁹When the army officer who was standing in front of the cross saw what happened when Jesus died, he said, "This man really was the Son of God!"

Devotion

THE CIVIL WAR that has been waged between rival tribes in the African nation of Sudan for more than four decades has become ugly even by the brutal standards of war. The stronger tribes have a policy of killing the men and taking the women and children for slaves, mostly to fill a sexual role. The captives are doomed to a life of the cruelest form of slavery.

A group of American missionaries heard about the plight of the captives and went to the leaders of the dominant tribe with a question. "Could we buy the slaves from you?" they asked. The tribal leaders mulled the question, and, sensing a moneymaking opportunity, offered a deal. You can redeem the slaves for thirty-three American dollars each, they told the missionaries. So the exchange began, and the former captives got a second chance at life.

Because of our sins we became prisoners, and the price of our sins is death (Romans 5:12). The Good News is that we can be redeemed, but the cost is steep. No thirty-three dollar bargains here. The blood of bulls and goats won't do either. Our sins require a sacrifice that was as perfect as my life was imperfect. And that perfect sacrifice was found in Jesus, the Son of God, who was with the Father from the dawn of Creation. He was willing to come to earth, take on the body of a man, and die the cruelest death imaginable. And when the blood flowed, it was possible for me to be released from the slavery of sin.

It was all part of a plan, Paul told his readers in Rome—a plan that God enacted at precisely the right time: "When we were unable to help ourselves, at the right time, Christ died for us, although we were living against God . . . God shows his great love for us in this way: Christ died for us while we were still sinners. So through Christ we will surely be saved from God's anger, because we have been made right with God by the blood of Christ's death. While we were God's enemies, he made us his friends through the death of his Son. Surely, now that we are his friends, he will save us through his Son's life" (Romans 5:6, 8–10).

Because of Christ, I walk free today, redeemed from my sin. And, here's good news: so can you.

THOUGHTS TO PONDER

What is the best earthly gift you have ever been given? How did you respond? How can we possibly respond to a gift as great as this?

PRAYER

Father, we know that our sins required the death of Jesus on the cross, and we marvel at the sacrifice you made to reclaim us from our slavery to sin. Our words are inadequate to thank you for this unimaginable gift. Amen.

WAITING FOR THE KINGDOM

MARK 15:40-47

⁴⁰Some women were standing at a distance from the cross, watching; among them were Mary Magdalene, Salome, and Mary the mother of James and Joseph. (James was her youngest son.) ⁴¹These women had followed Jesus in Galilee and helped him. Many other women were also there who had come with Jesus to Jerusalem.

⁴²This was Preparation Day. (That means the day before the Sabbath day.) That evening, ⁴³Joseph from Arimathea was brave enough to go to Pilate and ask for Jesus' body. Joseph, an important member of the Jewish council, was one of the people who was waiting for the kingdom of God to come. ⁴⁴Pilate was amazed that Jesus would have already died, so he called the army officer who had guarded Jesus and asked him if Jesus had already died. ⁴⁵The officer told Pilate that he was dead, so Pilate told Joseph he could have the body. ⁴⁶Joseph bought some linen cloth, took the body down from the cross, and wrapped it in the linen. He put the body in a tomb that was cut out of a wall of rock. Then he rolled a very large stone to block the entrance of the tomb. ⁴⁷And Mary Magdalene and Mary the mother of Joseph saw the place where Jesus was laid.

MATTHEW 27:62-66

⁶²The next day, the day after Preparation Day, the leading priests and the Pharisees went to Pilate. ⁶³They said, "Sir, we remember that while that liar was still alive he said, 'After three days I will rise from the dead.' ⁶⁴So give the order for the tomb to be guarded closely till the third day. Otherwise, his followers might come and steal the body and tell people that he has risen from the dead. That lie would be even worse than the first one."

⁶⁵Pilate said, "Take some soldiers and go guard the tomb the best way you know." ⁶⁶So they all went to the tomb and made it safe from thieves by sealing the stone in the entrance and putting soldiers there to guard it.

DEVOTION

THE HERO OF THIS STORY is Joseph of Arimathea. As a member of the Jewish council, also known as the Sanhedrin, he risked the wrath of the Jews in order to ensure that Jesus received a proper burial.

Proper burial sites were not cheap. Because the tradition was to bury the dead in caves, good burial sites were expensive and usually held many members of the same family. Joseph was probably giving up his own burial site in order to honor Jesus. In addition, he was risking his place in the council if other members of that group found out what he did.

Why, then, would Joseph take such a risk? I think we find the key in a phrase in the story above when we read that he was "one of the people who was waiting for the kingdom of God to come." The statement is similar to what was later written about the "heroes of faith" (Hebrews 11) who were committed to remaining focused on their heavenly homes and their spiritual citizenship.

People like Joseph had "television." Not the receiver unit in your home that you watch programs on, but real *television*. It literally means "to see afar." Joseph had the long view. He was watching and waiting for the kingdom of God, and if it was to come from this man who claimed he would be raised in three days, then Joseph was going to do whatever he could to facilitate the coming of the kingdom, even if he didn't understand it perfectly.

Joseph undoubtedly took linens and some spices to prepare the body. But because the time was late and sundown—and therefore Sabbath—was coming, he possibly didn't do as thorough a job as the women would have preferred, which will lead to them coming back to the tomb early in the morning after the Sabbath. Meanwhile, Pilate sealed and guarded the tomb.

From an early point in his ministry, Jesus was aware that he would die and remain in the tomb for three days. He referred to it in an episode recorded by Matthew in which he refused to do a sign for his unbelieving critics. We read: "Jesus answered, 'Evil and sinful people are the ones who want to see a miracle for a sign. But no sign will be given to them, except the sign of the prophet Jonah. Jonah was in the stomach of the big fish for three days and three nights. In the same way, the Son of Man will be in the grave three days and three nights. On the Judgment Day the people from Nineveh will stand up with you people who live now, and they will show that you are guilty'" (Matthew 12:39–41).

This, Jesus says, is the sign you are asking for: the tomb will not hold me. Either believe it or be found guilty on the Judgment Day.

THOUGHTS TO PONDER

In what ways did the Jonah story serve as a precursor for the story of Jesus? Why would Joseph take the risk that he did in this story?

PRAYER

Father, we pray that we, like Joseph, will be among the people who are waiting for your coming. Amen.

THE ONLY EMPTY TOMB

JOHN 20:1–18

20Early on the first day of the week, Mary Magdalene went to the tomb while it was still dark. When she saw that the large stone had been moved away from the tomb, ²she ran to Simon Peter and the follower whom Jesus loved. Mary said, "They have taken the Lord out of the tomb, and we don't know where they have put him."

³So Peter and the other follower started for the tomb. ⁴They were both running, but the other follower ran faster than Peter and reached the tomb first. ⁵He bent down and looked in and saw the strips of linen cloth lying there, but he did not go in. ⁶Then following him, Simon Peter arrived and went into the tomb and saw the strips of linen lying there. ⁷He also saw the cloth that had been around Jesus' head, which was folded up and laid in a different place from the strips of linen. ⁸Then the other follower, who had reached the tomb first, also went in. He saw and believed. ⁹(They did not yet understand from the Scriptures that Jesus must rise from the dead.)

¹⁰Then the followers went back home. ¹¹But Mary stood outside the tomb, crying. As she was crying, she bent down and looked inside the tomb. ¹²She saw two angels dressed in white, sitting where Jesus' body had been, one at the head and one at the feet.

¹³They asked her, "Woman, why are you crying?"

She answered, "They have taken away my Lord, and I don't know where they have put him." ¹⁴When Mary said this, she turned around and saw Jesus standing there, but she did not know it was Jesus.

¹⁵Jesus asked her, "Woman, why are you crying? Whom are you looking for?"

Thinking he was the gardener, she said to him, "Did you take him away, sir? Tell me where you put him, and I will get him."

¹⁶Jesus said to her, "Mary."

Mary turned toward Jesus and said in the Hebrew language, "Rabboni." (This means "Teacher.")

¹⁷Jesus said to her, "Don't hold on to me, because I have not yet gone up to the Father. But go to my brothers and tell them, 'I am going back to my Father and your Father, to my God and your God.' "

¹⁸Mary Magdalene went and said to the followers, "I saw the Lord!" And she told them what Jesus had said to her.

DEVOTION

THERE'S A SMALL, nondescript monastery in Rome famous for one thing: on display in rows and rows of shelves are the dead bones of monks who have served at the monastery. For hundreds of years, deceased monks had been buried in a small cemetery behind the simple structure. But over the years, the space proved to be inadequate. So the monks decided to "recycle" the plots and bring the bones back into the monastery as a respectful reminder of the finiteness of life for the monks inside.

After a period of years, when all the flesh is gone, the coffins are dug up, opened, and the bones are taken out to be shelved inside the monastery. Hundreds of skulls are piled in one spot, torsos and limbs in another. The monastery is supported by the donations of curious tourists who want to see the bones, like my family and the college students we took over to Italy.

In the hundreds of years this tradition has been practiced, never once has the coffin been empty. There are always bones inside. Even among hundreds of men who lived lives devoted to the service of their Catholic faith, none escaped death. The only empty tomb is the one belonging to Jesus, and because it is empty, the grip of sin and the power of Satan have been broken once and for all time.

The triumph over death was the final victory for Jesus. He had already resisted the temptations of Satan in the desert when Satan tried three times to get Jesus to sin. He had already fulfilled all the prophecies written about the Messiah to come. Now only death remained, and Jesus conquered it as well. Paul would later tell his readers in Corinth that death was the "last enemy" (1 Corinthians 15:26) and that Jesus had taken away the "victory" of death (1 Corinthians 15:55).

Will there be bones in our graves years from now? Absolutely. But thanks to the work of Jesus on the cross, our souls will be with him.

THOUGHTS TO PONDER

What does the empty tomb mean to you? What does Jesus mean when he tells Mary, "Don't hold on to me because I have not yet gone up to the Father"?

PRAYER

Father, we thank you for the empty tomb that means you have defeated death once and for all. Help us to claim the victory for ourselves through your Son. Amen.

THE BEST ENDING

MARK 15:40—16:8

⁴⁰Some women were standing at a distance from the cross, watching; among them were Mary Magdalene, Salome, and Mary the mother of James and Joseph. (James was her youngest son.) ⁴¹These women had followed Jesus in Galilee and helped him. Many other women were also there who had come with Jesus to Jerusalem.

⁴²This was Preparation Day. (That means the day before the Sabbath day.) That evening, ⁴³Joseph from Arimathea was brave enough to go to Pilate and ask for Jesus' body. Joseph, an important member of the Jewish council, was one of the people who was waiting for the kingdom of God to come. ⁴⁴Pilate was amazed that Jesus would have already died, so he called the army officer who had guarded Jesus and asked him if Jesus had already died. ⁴⁵The officer told Pilate that he was dead, so Pilate told Joseph he could have the body. ⁴⁶Joseph bought some linen cloth, took the body down from the cross, and wrapped it in the linen. He put the body in a tomb that was cut out of a wall of rock. Then he rolled a very large stone to block the entrance of the tomb. ⁴⁷And Mary Magdalene and Mary the mother of Joseph saw the place where Jesus was laid.

16 The day after the Sabbath day, Mary Magdalene, Mary the mother of James, and Salome bought some sweet-smelling spices to put on Jesus' body. ²Very early on that day, the first day of the week, soon after sunrise, the women were on their way to the tomb. ³They said to each other, "Who will roll away for us the stone that covers the entrance of the tomb?"

⁴Then the women looked and saw that the stone had already been rolled away, even though it was very large. ⁵The women entered the tomb and saw a young man wearing a white robe and sitting on the right side, and they were afraid.

⁶But the man said, "Don't be afraid. You are looking for Jesus from Nazareth, who has been crucified. He has risen from the dead; he is not here. Look, here is the place they laid him. ⁷Now go and tell his followers and Peter, 'Jesus is going into Galilee ahead of you, and you will see him there as he told you before.'"

⁸The women were confused and shaking with fear, so they left the tomb and ran away. They did not tell anyone about what happened, because they were afraid.

DEVOTION

MARK'S ACCOUNT of the Resurrection—from which the passage above is taken—is unique. Your Bible may say something like this after verse eight: "Verses 9–20 are not included in some of the earliest surviving Greek copies of Mark." This means that there's a possibility the last thing Mark originally wrote in his account of the life, death, and resurrection of Jesus is this: the women fled—trembling, bewildered, afraid. End of story.

It is possible that an early, well-meaning scribe, borrowing from other Gospel accounts in circulation, brought closure to Mark's Gospel. Perhaps he felt he improved Mark's account. Most certainly he didn't think that he would be caught and that virtually every Bible sold a millennium and a half later would contain a footnote about his extracurricular activity.

My faith isn't shaken by this incident. Instead, my faith in the authenticity of the Scriptures is actually strengthened when I learn the extent to which modern detection methods have allowed us to know so much more about the proper canon of the Bible than earlier translators did.

As a writer, I can understand the urge of a scribe to do such a thing. Surely a manuscript page blew away. Surely Mark didn't just leave the women bewildered and looking for answers. Why not add the incredible, true ending of the story?

Truthfully, I don't always fully grasp the meaning of the Resurrection. Sometimes I feel like the women in this story, running away from the tomb and not sure what to make of the story. I don't know what to make of the fact that someone loved me so much he felt compelled to die for me. I don't know what to make of the fact that the tomb couldn't hold him, and he arose out of it. I can't wrap my mind around the concept of a dead body coming to life and joining the living again.

So perhaps verse 8 truly is the end of Mark's Gospel. And if so, then it's fitting, because some answers will only come after the trembling.

THOUGHTS TO PONDER

What caused the women to react as they did? What might they have been frightened of?

PRAYER

Father, the power of the Resurrection is awesome even today. Help us to be unafraid in telling others the Good News of the empty tomb. Amen.

THE EVIDENCE OF FAITH

MATTHEW 28:1–15

28 The day after the Sabbath day was the first day of the week. At dawn on the first day, Mary Magdalene and another woman named Mary went to look at the tomb.

²At that time there was a strong earthquake. An angel of the Lord came down from heaven, went to the tomb, and rolled the stone away from the entrance. Then he sat on the stone. ³He was shining as bright as lightning, and his clothes were white as snow. ⁴The soldiers guarding the tomb shook with fear because of the angel, and they became like dead men.

⁵The angel said to the women, "Don't be afraid. I know that you are looking for Jesus, who has been crucified. ⁶He is not here. He has risen from the dead as he said he would. Come and see the place where his body was. ⁷And go quickly and tell his followers, 'Jesus has risen from the dead. He is going into Galilee ahead of you, and you will see him there.' " Then the angel said, "Now I have told you."

⁸The women left the tomb quickly. They were afraid, but they were also very happy. They ran to tell Jesus' followers what had happened. ⁹Suddenly, Jesus met them and said, "Greetings." The women came up to him, took hold of his feet, and worshiped him. ¹⁰Then Jesus said to them, "Don't be afraid. Go and tell my followers to go on to Galilee, and they will see me there."

¹¹While the women went to tell Jesus' followers, some of the soldiers who had been guarding the tomb went into the city to tell the leading priests everything that had happened. ¹²Then the priests met with the elders and made a plan. They paid the soldiers a large amount of money ¹³and said to them, "Tell the people that Jesus' followers came during the night and stole the body while you were asleep. ¹⁴If the governor hears about this, we will satisfy him and save you from trouble." ¹⁵So the soldiers kept the money and did as they were told. And that story is still spread among the people even today.

DEVOTION

RECENTLY IN AUSTRIA, a man was prosecuted under a law in that country which declares it is a crime to deny that the Holocaust happened. The man had given a series of lectures denying that any Jew ever died in a gas chamber under the Nazi regime, despite evidence and eyewitness accounts to the contrary. For his defiance of the law, the man was transferred to the state penitentiary in Graz.

The debunking of the resurrection of Jesus began quite early. Faced with an empty tomb, a plausible story had to be concocted. It's interesting that the authorities didn't just kill the soldiers and claim they were derelict in their duty, allowing someone to steal the body. Instead, they bribed the soldiers. I think the reason they were spared was so they could become zealous advocates of the lie they were paid to perpetuate. And by the time Matthew wrote his account, the story still had a life of its own.

To the best of my knowledge, no country has a law prohibiting a denial of the resurrection of Jesus Christ. Not only are we not legally forced to believe the Resurrection story, we've been left with no physical evidence to verify that miracle beyond a reasonable doubt.

So why is the signal event for all of human history—the defeat of death and therefore the defeat of Satan by Jesus—left with no tangible evidence? I think it's because God wants us to come to him by faith or not at all.

The writer of Hebrews defines faith as "being sure of the things we hope for and knowing that something is real even if we do not see it" (Hebrews 11:1). The empty tomb is as real to me as if I had walked into its cold, damp interior and seen the empty burial shelf.

Why? Because I see the evidence every day. I see it in my classmate who faces cancer but never turns her back on God. I see it my friend who came to know Jesus only after his son died in combat and now waits to see his son in the resurrection. I read of it in the lives of the apostles who would all face martyrdom rather than deny what they knew to be true.

I hope my children will look at me and know that the only explanation for how I've lived my life is that I know there is a life to come. You see, we are the evidence of the Resurrection today. If the world is to see the risen Savior, they must see it in our lives.

THOUGHTS TO PONDER

How do you know the Bible to be true? Do you ever harbor doubts? What helps when doubts arise?

PRAYER

God, we pray that the evidence of our risen Savior will be written each day in the lives we lead—lives that demand an explanation by the rest of the world. Amen.

Believing without Seeing

JOHN 20:19–31

¹⁹When it was evening on the first day of the week, Jesus' followers were together. The doors were locked, because they were afraid of the elders. Then Jesus came and stood right in the middle of them and said, "Peace be with you." ²⁰After he said this, he showed them his hands and his side. His followers were thrilled when they saw the Lord.

²¹Then Jesus said again, "Peace be with you. As the Father sent me, I now send you." ²²After he said this, he breathed on them and said, "Receive the Holy Spirit. ²³If you forgive anyone his sins, they are forgiven. If you don't forgive them, they are not forgiven."

²⁴Thomas (called Didymus), who was one of the twelve, was not with them when Jesus came. ²⁵The other followers kept telling Thomas, "We saw the Lord."

But Thomas said, "I will not believe it until I see the nail marks in his hands and put my finger where the nails were and put my hand into his side."

²⁶A week later the followers were in the house again, and Thomas was with them. The doors were locked, but Jesus came in and stood right in the middle of them. He said, "Peace be with you." ²⁷Then he said to Thomas, "Put your finger here, and look at my hands. Put your hand here in my side. Stop being an unbeliever and believe."

²⁸Thomas said to him, "My Lord and my God!"

²⁹Then Jesus told him, "You believe because you see me. Those who believe without seeing me will be truly blessed."

³⁰Jesus did many other miracles in the presence of his followers that are not written in this book. ³¹But these are written so that you may believe that Jesus is the Christ, the Son of God. Then, by believing, you may have life through his name.

Devotion

THE WORLD CALLS HIM "Doubting Thomas." Perhaps it's fair; maybe it's harsh. Before we address that, the actions of Jesus are interesting here as well.

First, notice that Jesus came back in his crucified body. Surely the one who conquered death could have come back in any form he wanted. He could have had a perfect body, but he chose the body with the nail scarred hands. He came back in the body with the spear-pierced side. And this was the body he showed to his followers hiding behind closed doors on a Sunday—they were afraid that the authorities wouldn't be satisfied with killing Jesus and might come after them next.

Second, notice that Jesus didn't pass judgment on Thomas, he simply provided Thomas with the proof he needed in order to believe. I think Thomas wanted to believe, but was afraid that the buzz around the other followers couldn't possibly be true. Jesus wanted Thomas to believe, just as he wanted the others to believe and just as surely as he now wants me to believe, even though I haven't seen the scars.

Third, for the benefit of all the others, we're told that Jesus performed many other miracles that are not recorded in the gospels. But the ones recorded are written for the benefit of John's readers, including you and me. Even centuries later, Jesus wants believers. Jesus intentionally left evidence of his deity on the earth.

"Doubting Thomas," might also be called "Searching Thomas." Perhaps he strongly wanted to believe, but his sense of logic said that no one, not even the Teacher, could be raised from such a brutal death. But Jesus came back in a form that would aid Thomas and all the others in their quest to believe.

Jesus is still searching for believers today. He offers his blessings to those today who believe even though they haven't seen the holes in his hands. But I do see him. I see him in the lives of his people every day. That's how I know he still lives.

THOUGHTS TO PONDER

Is the popular term "Doubting Thomas" justified? How do we know, beyond doubt, that we serve a risen Savior today?

PRAYER

Father, we pray that we will be among those who are blessed for believing without seeing. Amen.

Seeing Jesus

LUKE 24:13–35

[13]That same day two of Jesus' followers were going to a town named Emmaus, about seven miles from Jerusalem. [14]They were talking about everything that had happened. [15]While they were talking and discussing, Jesus himself came near and began walking with them, [16]but they were kept from recognizing him. [17]Then he said, "What are these things you are talking about while you walk?"

The two followers stopped, looking very sad. [18]The one named Cleopas answered, "Are you the only visitor in Jerusalem who does not know what just happened there?"

[19]Jesus said to them, "What are you talking about?"

They said, "About Jesus of Nazareth. He was a prophet who said and did many powerful things before God and all the people. [20]Our leaders and the leading priests handed him over to be sentenced to death, and they crucified him. [21]But we were hoping that he would free Israel. Besides this, it is now the third day since this happened. [22]And today some women among us amazed us. Early this morning they went to the tomb, [23]but they did not find his body there. They came and told us that they had seen a vision of angels who said that Jesus was alive! [24]So some of our group went to the tomb, too. They found it just as the women said, but they did not see Jesus."

[25]Then Jesus said to them, "You are foolish and slow to believe everything the prophets said. [26]They said that the Christ must suffer these things before he enters his glory." [27]Then starting with what Moses and all the prophets had said about him, Jesus began to explain everything that had been written about himself in the Scriptures.

[28]They came near the town of Emmaus, and Jesus acted as if he were going farther. [29]But they begged him, "Stay with us, because it is late; it is almost night." So he went in to stay with them.

[30]When Jesus was at the table with them, he took some bread, gave thanks, divided it, and gave it to them. [31]And then, they were allowed to recognize Jesus. But when they saw who he was, he disappeared. [32]They said to each other, "It felt like a fire burning in us when Jesus talked to us on the road and explained the Scriptures to us."

[33]So the two followers got up at once and went back to Jerusalem. There they found the eleven apostles and others gathered. [34]They were saying, "The Lord really has risen from the dead! He showed himself to Simon."

[35]Then the two followers told what had happened on the road and how they recognized Jesus when he divided the bread.

DEVOTION

DISCUSSIONS LIKE THIS were probably happening all over Galilee. Jesus had impacted thousands of lives, and word of his death was spreading all over the area. The difference with this one was that Jesus happened to drop in.

What would it have been like to hear Jesus trace the predictions about himself, beginning with Moses and continuing through the prophets? I was once in the audience when a famous scholar addressed a huge group of scholars, all of whom had used his original thinking in their books and papers in the previous three decades. How much more thrilling to hear Jesus talking about the many writers who had prophesied his coming in their works?

There is a particularly interesting phrase in the men's report above: "It felt like a fire burning in us when Jesus talked to us," they said. Ever the teacher, the passion of Jesus had been transferred to his listeners.

How long has it been since you felt on fire because of the words of Jesus? From the sermons to the parables, there are thrilling pronouncements everywhere in the four Gospel accounts. Which passages burn inside you?

But there's another phrase above that's a bit haunting. Some of their group, they said, went to the tomb, found it, but did not see Jesus. I think that's still possible today. I think we can come close to Jesus without finding him. It wasn't until Jesus opened their eyes that they recognized they were in his presence.

If we are to catch the fire, we have to first see Jesus. And he told us where he would be found (Matthew 25:42–45). He would be found among the sick, the hungry, the imprisoned, and the unclothed. When we get on fire for the cause of showing love to these people, we will see Jesus.

THOUGHTS TO PONDER

Why might Jesus have chosen these men for one of his post-resurrection appearances? What might Jesus have been explaining to the men when he taught them from the Scriptures?

PRAYER

Father, we pray you will show yourself to us, not in person as you did to those on the road to Emmaus, but though your Word and through your people. Amen.

GONE FISHING

JOHN 20:26—21:14

²⁶A week later the followers were in the house again, and Thomas was with them. The doors were locked, but Jesus came in and stood right in the middle of them. He said, "Peace be with you." ²⁷Then he said to Thomas, "Put your finger here, and look at my hands. Put your hand here in my side. Stop being an unbeliever and believe."

²⁸Thomas said to him, "My Lord and my God!"

²⁹Then Jesus told him, "You believe because you see me. Those who believe without seeing me will be truly blessed."

³⁰Jesus did many other miracles in the presence of his followers that are not written in this book. ³¹But these are written so that you may believe that Jesus is the Christ, the Son of God. Then, by believing, you may have life through his name.

21 Later, Jesus showed himself to his followers again—this time at Lake Galilee. This is how he showed himself: ²Some of the followers were together: Simon Peter, Thomas (called Didymus), Nathanael from Cana in Galilee, the two sons of Zebedee, and two other followers. ³Simon Peter said, "I am going out to fish."

The others said, "We will go with you." So they went out and got into the boat. They fished that night but caught nothing.

⁴Early the next morning Jesus stood on the shore, but the followers did not know it was Jesus. ⁵Then he said to them, "Friends, did you catch any fish?"

They answered, "No."

⁶He said, "Throw your net on the right side of the boat, and you will find some." So they did, and they caught so many fish they could not pull the net back into the boat.

⁷The follower whom Jesus loved said to Peter, "It is the Lord!" When Peter heard him say this, he wrapped his coat around himself. (Peter had taken his clothes off.) Then he jumped into the water. ⁸The other followers went to shore in the boat, dragging the net full of fish. They were not very far from shore, only about a hundred yards. ⁹When the followers stepped out of the boat and onto the shore, they saw a fire of hot coals. There were fish on the fire, and there was bread.

¹⁰Then Jesus said, "Bring some of the fish you just caught."

¹¹Simon Peter went into the boat and pulled the net to the shore. It was full of big fish, one hundred fifty-three in all, but even though there were so many, the net did not tear. ¹²Jesus said to them, "Come and eat." None of the followers dared ask him, "Who are you?" because they knew it was the Lord. ¹³Jesus came and took the bread and gave it to them, along with the fish.

¹⁴This was now the third time Jesus showed himself to his followers after he was raised from the dead.

DEVOTION

PERHAPS THEY HAD GIVEN UP. Perhaps they were hungry. Perhaps they didn't know what else to do. But they returned to fishing—the thing they knew the best.

Did they understand they had been in the presence of the Son of God all these years? Did they grasp the significance of the fact that he had been raised from the dead? Didn't they remember all the miracles?

They had run away after Jesus was arrested. Later, they had heard the story from the women that the stone was rolled away and the tomb was empty. They had locked themselves in a room and Jesus had walked right through the walls. Yet they still didn't understand.

"I am going out to fish," Peter declared, and seven of the remaining eleven followers went with him.

Was it a concession to defeat? We're not told. But at the least it says something about our human nature. We can be in the presence of Jesus one moment and then decide to do it all on our own the next. Not only had they witnessed the signs that we read in the gospels, John tells us that Jesus did "many other miracles" in their presence.

So why were they fishing? For the same reason that I sometimes pray to God for healing and then worry myself sick about the outcome. For the same reason that I pray for my daily bread and then overwork to earn it. I go back to fishing even after I've been in the presence of Jesus. Luke tells us, "Then Jesus opened their minds so they could understand the Scriptures" after the episode of fishing (Luke 24:45). We should pray for the same.

THOUGHTS TO PONDER

What does it say about the apostles that they had returned to their previous vocation of fishing so soon after the Crucifixion of Jesus? Had they recognized his deity? Had they given up, or merely become hungry?

PRAYER

Father, we read that you have written all these things that we may believe. Help us to read and believe. Amen.

"FOLLOW ME"

JOHN 21:20–22

²⁰Peter turned and saw that the follower Jesus loved was walking behind them. (This was the follower who had leaned against Jesus at the supper and had said, "Lord, who will turn against you?") ²¹When Peter saw him behind them, he asked Jesus, "Lord, what about him?"

²²Jesus answered, "If I want him to live until I come back, that is not your business. You follow me."

DEVOTION

AFTER YEARS of not understanding this passage, I got a lesson in its application through four separate traumatic incidents in the space of a couple of weeks. Let me share this lesson with you.

In the Christian school association that I head, we often share prayer requests by e-mail when events happen that we need to lift to God. With schools all over the country, we've shared our problems: tornadoes, floods, hurricanes, illnesses, and accidents. In one month, we had two similar pairs of cases. In the first, a six-year-old girl and a five-year-old boy were in need of prayers for treatment of brain tumors. In the second pair, within the span of a few days, two teenaged girls from towns a couple of hours apart were involved in separate accidents.

Here's how the situations turned out. Within a few days, the young girl with the tumors got an excellent diagnosis; the young boy passed away from a particularly aggressive form of cancer pressing on his brain. One teenaged girl died instantly from her injuries in the wreck. She was her parents' only child. The other was comatose for days with little hope for recovery, and then took a turn for the better and made a miraculous recovery.

In my Christian school association, we wept with those who were weeping and we rejoiced with those who were rejoicing, even in our sadness. It was the father of the girl who recovered from the wreck—David Gushee, a college professor of Moral Philosophy and Christian Studies—who called our attention to this Bible passage in writing about his daughter:

> "In this tear-stained world, one must simultaneously celebrate the moments of deliverance and grace while grieving those who are not delivered, and grieving with their families. We groan for the complete and total redemption of our world, for the time when every tear is wiped away and there will be no more death or mourning or crying or pain, when the old order of things will pass away.

"I would be an ungrateful wretch if I did not conclude that God intervened and did a miracle here. Of course, this raises other questions and yearnings. One has to wonder why everyone's child is not spared. One has to yearn for a world in which no parent ever has to bury a child. I am sensitive to the fact that our celebration is matched by the pain of those parents who have not received their children back from the grip of death.

"After his reinstatement, Peter asked Jesus what was going to happen to the follower Jesus loved. Jesus essentially said that this was none of Peter's business. 'If I want him to live until I come back, that is not your business. You follow me.' I draw from this that none of us really can understand God's dealings with others, and it is not really our place to try to do so. I can't hide or deny my own amazed joy at what has happened with my daughter, Holly, because I am wondering why everyone does not get delivered from death like Holly has been. But I can 'follow Jesus' by remembering how much it hurt to see Holly suffer so much, and remembering how sad and grieved and scared we were, and then turning that painful set of memories into much deeper compassion for those who worry over and mourn for their children. I have discovered that such frightened and grieved parents are everywhere, if you know where, and how, to look."

"Peter," Jesus was saying, "Follow me without question. Even when you don't understand my ways, it's still your job to follow me."

I've come to realize that we may be looking for the wrong miracles when we ask God to heal. The real miracle might not be when the tumors shrink or the comatose awake. The real miracle might be when we accept a tragedy as deep as losing a child but refuse to lose our own faith. Keeping faith in God no matter what life hands you is a miracle in itself, regardless of the outcome of the illness or the accident.

So when life hands us a seemingly insurmountable challenge, we must obey these final words of Jesus: *follow me.*

THOUGHTS TO PONDER

What do you think Peter was wondering about when he asked Jesus about the fate of John? What is the significance of the answer that Jesus gave? What does it mean to follow Jesus on a daily basis?

PRAYER

God, we know we will never understand all your ways, but we pray that we will continue to walk by faith until that wonderful day when you reveal everything to us. Amen.

Taken up to Heaven

LUKE 24:45–53

[45]Then Jesus opened their minds so they could understand the Scriptures. [46]He said to them, "It is written that the Christ would suffer and rise from the dead on the third day [47]and that a change of hearts and lives and forgiveness of sins would be preached in his name to all nations, starting at Jerusalem. [48]You are witnesses of these things. [49]I will send you what my Father has promised, but you must stay in Jerusalem until you have received that power from heaven."

[50]Jesus led his followers as far as Bethany, and he raised his hands and blessed them. [51]While he was blessing them, he was separated from them and carried into heaven. [52]They worshiped him and returned to Jerusalem very happy. [53]They stayed in the Temple all the time, praising God.

ACTS 1:1–3, 6–11

[1]To Theophilus.

The first book I wrote was about everything Jesus began to do and teach [2]until the day he was taken up into heaven. Before this, with the help of the Holy Spirit, Jesus told the apostles he had chosen what they should do. [3]After his death, he showed himself to them and proved in many ways that he was alive. The apostles saw Jesus during the forty days after he was raised from the dead, and he spoke to them about the kingdom of God.

[6]When the apostles were all together, they asked Jesus, "Lord, are you now going to give the kingdom back to Israel?"

[7]Jesus said to them, "The Father is the only One who has the authority to decide dates and times. These things are not for you to know. [8]But when the Holy Spirit comes to you, you will receive power. You will be my witnesses—in Jerusalem, in all of Judea, in Samaria, and in every part of the world."

[9]After he said this, as they were watching, he was lifted up, and a cloud hid him from their sight. [10]As he was going, they were looking into the sky. Suddenly, two men wearing white clothes stood beside them. [11]They said, "Men of Galilee, why are you standing here looking into the sky? Jesus, whom you saw taken up from you into heaven, will come back in the same way you saw him go."

DEVOTION

THE NUMBER of people whom the Bible describes as ascending into heaven without experiencing death is very small. The first is Enoch, about whom little is known other than the fact that he walked with God in a way that pleased God so much that he took Enoch from the earth (Genesis 5:24). Better known is the account of the prophet Elijah who was taken into the heavens in a fiery chariot in the presence of Elisha (2 Kings 2:11). Moses was buried by God in a location unknown to any man (Deuteronomy 34:5–6). When he later appeared with Elijah and Jesus on the mountaintop (Mark 9:4), some later non-biblical writers assumed that Moses, too, had ascended into heaven.

Luke is the predominant source of information about the physical ascension of Jesus into heaven, ending his Gospel and beginning the Book of Acts with further information about the ascension. The ascension was taught as fact just days later during the first Good News sermon preached on Pentecost when Peter told the crowd, "Jesus is the One whom God raised from the dead. And we are all witnesses to this. Jesus was lifted up to heaven and is now at God's right side" (Acts 2:32–33).

Paul's writings are the principal source concerning the spiritual component of the ascension and Resurrection. In writing to the Philippians, Paul wrote, "God raised him to the highest place. God made his name greater than every other name so that every knee will bow to the name of Jesus—everyone in heaven, on earth, and under the earth. And everyone will confess that Jesus Christ is Lord and bring glory to God the Father" (Philippians 2:9–11). Paul told the Romans and the Ephesians that Christ is now at the right side of God (Romans 8:34; Ephesians 1:20).

Finally, Paul said that some believers will experience ascension when Jesus returns. To the Thessalonians he wrote: "The Lord himself will come down from heaven with a loud command, with the voice of the archangel, and with the trumpet call of God. And those who have died believing in Christ will rise first. After that, we who are still alive will be gathered up with them in the clouds to meet the Lord in the air. And we will be with the Lord forever" (1 Thessalonians 4:16–17).

THOUGHTS TO PONDER

Why do you think God took Jesus into heaven in the presence of the followers? What impression would that make on them?

PRAYER

Father, we know we serve a risen Savior, who is now in heaven seated at your right hand. We pray that you will come quickly to claim us as your own. Amen.

SHARING EVERYTHING

ACTS 2:43-47; 4:32-37; 6:1-7

⁴³The apostles were doing many miracles and signs, and everyone felt great respect for God. ⁴⁴All the believers were together and shared everything. ⁴⁵They would sell their land and the things they owned and then divide the money and give it to anyone who needed it. ⁴⁶The believers met together in the Temple every day. They ate together in their homes, happy to share their food with joyful hearts. ⁴⁷They praised God and were liked by all the people. Every day the Lord added those who were being saved to the group of believers.

³²The group of believers were united in their hearts and spirit. All those in the group acted as though their private property belonged to everyone in the group. In fact, they shared everything. ³³With great power the apostles were telling people that the Lord Jesus was truly raised from the dead. And God blessed all the believers very much. ³⁴There were no needy people among them. From time to time those who owned fields or houses sold them, brought the money, ³⁵and gave it to the apostles. Then the money was given to anyone who needed it.

³⁶One of the believers was named Joseph, a Levite born in Cyprus. The apostles called him Barnabas (which means "one who encourages"). ³⁷Joseph owned a field, sold it, brought the money, and gave it to the apostles.

6 The number of followers was growing. But during this same time, the Greek-speaking followers had an argument with the other followers. The Greek-speaking widows were not getting their share of the food that was given out every day. ²The twelve apostles called the whole group of followers together and said, "It is not right for us to stop our work of teaching God's word in order to serve tables. ³So, brothers and sisters, choose seven of your own men who are good, full of the Spirit and full of wisdom. We will put them in charge of this work. ⁴Then we can continue to pray and to teach the word of God."

⁵The whole group liked the idea, so they chose these seven men: Stephen (a man with great faith and full of the Holy Spirit), Philip, Procorus, Nicanor, Timon, Parmenas, and Nicolas (a man from Antioch who had become a follower of the Jewish religion). ⁶Then they put these men before the apostles, who prayed and laid their hands on them.

⁷The word of God was continuing to spread. The group of followers in Jerusalem increased, and a great number of the Jewish priests believed and obeyed.

DEVOTION

THESE THREE PASSAGES contain our best glimpse into the *koinonia* of the early church—a Greek term for brotherly love and fellowship that marked the early Christians. Repeatedly we're told that they shared everything.

I'm reminded of a story from February of 2003, when 305 people became ill in a Chinese province. Five died soon after becoming sick. Although the problem was respiratory, all tests came back negative for influenza. More outbreaks occurred in China and Hong Kong. News reports of this strange, new, deadly disease spread faster than the disease itself, disrupting economies and travel.

Soon the World Health Organization (WHO) contacted major laboratories across the world to see if they would work on the SARS virus simultaneously, sharing results via the Web and teleconferences. Eleven labs in all cooperated in the massive effort that literally reached around the world. By April 16, a blink of the eye in terms of scientific research, the cause of the illness, a "coronavirus" thought previously to affect only animals, was discovered.

But speed wasn't the most impressive part of the SARS story. More impressive is that no one was technically in charge of the project. There was no "SARS czar." Every lab worked independently, and every lab shared every bit of information they discovered. In short, they had all things in common, much like the early church.

When the church grew exponentially in Acts, we are told that everything, from property to meals, was considered common property. No one kept more than he or she needed and no one took more than was necessary. Even though we have grown a little more financially sophisticated today, it is still the offering—the sharing by those who have much to feed, clothe, and house those who have nothing—that is at the heart of our mission. Paul tells us that Jesus gave up equality with God to become a servant (Philippians 2:6–7). Sacrifice like that demands my respect and my response every chance I get.

THOUGHTS TO PONDER

Why do you think that the leaders of the early church practiced a form of communalism where everything was held in common? In what ways did that foster the early church? What outside conditions may have made this the best way? Would it work today?

PRAYER

God, you have always wanted your people to share. Help us to be generous with those in need. Amen.

NEWFOUND BOLDNESS

ACTS 3:1–16

3 One day Peter and John went to the Temple at three o'clock, the time set each day for the afternoon prayer service. [2]There, at the Temple gate called Beautiful Gate, was a man who had been crippled all his life. Every day he was carried to this gate to beg for money from the people going into the Temple. [3]The man saw Peter and John going into the Temple and asked them for money. [4]Peter and John looked straight at him and said, "Look at us!" [5]The man looked at them, thinking they were going to give him some money. [6]But Peter said, "I don't have any silver or gold, but I do have something else I can give you. By the power of Jesus Christ from Nazareth, stand up and walk!" [7]Then Peter took the man's right hand and lifted him up. Immediately the man's feet and ankles became strong. [8]He jumped up, stood on his feet, and began to walk. He went into the Temple with them, walking and jumping and praising God. [9-10]All the people recognized him as the crippled man who always sat by the Beautiful Gate begging for money. Now they saw this same man walking and praising God, and they were amazed. They wondered how this could happen.

[11]While the man was holding on to Peter and John, all the people were amazed and ran to them at Solomon's Porch. [12]When Peter saw this, he said to them, "People of Israel, why are you surprised? You are looking at us as if it were our own power or goodness that made this man walk. [13]The God of Abraham, Isaac, and Jacob, the God of our ancestors, gave glory to Jesus, his servant. But you handed him over to be killed. Pilate decided to let him go free, but you told Pilate you did not want Jesus. [14]You did not want the One who is holy and good but asked Pilate to give you a murderer instead. [15]And so you killed the One who gives life, but God raised him from the dead. We are witnesses to this. [16]It was faith in Jesus that made this crippled man well. You can see this man, and you know him. He was made completely well because of trust in Jesus, and you all saw it happen!

DEVOTION

THE ABILITY to heal the sick had passed from Jesus to his apostles. In the previous chapter, Luke, the author of Acts, tells us, "The apostles were doing many miracles and signs, and everyone felt great respect for God" (Acts 2:43).

The apostles had possessed the power before his death, and at one point Jesus had even sent them out into the countryside with instructions to take the ministry of healing to the people. But we have no accounts of particular healings by the apostles until this point.

663

Peter was quite specific as to where the power came from. In healing the man, he invoked the name of Jesus. When the people were amazed that the man they had passed by all those years at the gate of the Temple was now walking and even jumping, Peter again gave credit to God. But this time, he reminded the people that they were guilty of Jesus' murder. They had been among the crowd who had called out for Barabbas when Pilate had given them a chance to release Jesus. Now, less than two months later, Peter felt certain that some of the crowd from Pilate's porch were in the Temple worshiping God on that day.

How ironic that Peter would find them in the Temple. But Jesus' leading critics had always been the religious leadership of the day. His teachings, his claims, and his actions were an affront to their twisted religious sensibilities. In fact, the lame man outside the Temple gate called "Beautiful" would not have even been allowed inside, since disease was supposedly a sign of underlying sin.

When Peter led the lame man into the Temple, he was turning the prevailing thinking on its head. The real sinners were the ones inside the Temple at the three o'clock prayers, not the lame man who begged them for coins as they went in. In just a few short weeks, Peter's transformation had been completed—from the man once scared to admit that he knew Jesus to the man unafraid to call the same people he once feared the murderers of his Master.

THOUGHTS TO PONDER

How did the apostles use miracles to build the early church? Do we today have anything better than silver and gold to give to the needy of the world? How do we find the right proportion of benevolence and evangelism for those who are the neediest of the world?

PRAYER

Father, we pray that we will share hope with those who need it most. We pray that as we bring meals and medicine that we will also bring your Good News to a desperate world. Amen.

DAILY MIRACLES

ACTS 4:1-22

4 While Peter and John were speaking to the people, priests, the captain of the soldiers that guarded the Temple, and Sadducees came up to them. ²They were upset because the two apostles were teaching the people and were preaching that people will rise from the dead through the power of Jesus. ³The older leaders grabbed Peter and John and put them in jail. Since it was already night, they kept them in jail until the next day. ⁴But many of those who had heard Peter and John preach believed the things they said. There were now about five thousand in the group of believers.

⁵The next day the rulers, the elders, and the teachers of the law met in Jerusalem. ⁶Annas the high priest, Caiaphas, John, and Alexander were there, as well as everyone from the high priest's family. ⁷They made Peter and John stand before them and then asked them, "By what power or authority did you do this?"

⁸Then Peter, filled with the Holy Spirit, said to them, "Rulers of the people and you elders, ⁹are you questioning us about a good thing that was done to a crippled man? Are you asking us who made him well? ¹⁰We want all of you and all the people to know that this man was made well by the power of Jesus Christ from Nazareth. You crucified him, but God raised him from the dead. This man was crippled, but he is now well and able to stand here before you because of the power of Jesus. ¹¹Jesus is

'the stone that you builders rejected,
    which has become the cornerstone.'   *Psalm 118:22*

¹²Jesus is the only One who can save people. No one else in the world is able to save us."

¹³The leaders saw that Peter and John were not afraid to speak, and they understood that these men had no special training or education. So they were amazed. Then they realized that Peter and John had been with Jesus. ¹⁴Because they saw the healed man standing there beside the two apostles, they could say nothing against them. ¹⁵After the leaders ordered them to leave the meeting, they began to talk to each other. ¹⁶They said, "What shall we do with these men? Everyone in Jerusalem knows they have done a great miracle, and we cannot say it is not true. ¹⁷But to keep it from spreading among the people, we must warn them not to talk to people anymore using that name."

¹⁸So they called Peter and John in again and told them not to speak or to teach at all in the name of Jesus. ¹⁹But Peter and John answered them, "You decide what God would want. Should we obey you or God? ²⁰We cannot keep quiet. We must speak about what we have seen and heard." ²¹The leaders warned the apostles again and let them go free. They could not find a way to punish

them, because all the people were praising God for what had been done. [22]The man who received the miracle of healing was more than forty years old.

DEVOTION

HAS ANYONE ever observed you and your behavior and concluded, as the religious leaders in the Temple did about Peter and John, that you "had been with Jesus"? What a compliment to have others realize that there is no other explanation for your actions than the fact that you'd been in the presence of Jesus.

And while we aren't able to perform a healing today as these apostles did, we can nonetheless work small miracles wherever we are that will leave people looking for an explanation. We can carry more than our part of the load at work without complaining. We can allow others to take the credit for ideas we help to generate. We can give generously to all who ask, regardless of our own current financial circumstances. We can face the adversity of illness without wavering in our faith. There are many "daily miracles" we can perform that will leave others searching for the reason.

I run large conventions of Christian educators annually at hotels across the nation. One year, a hotel made a mistake in its bid and overpromised what they would be able to deliver. I caught the error five months before the conference—a very short time in an industry where it's common to work years ahead. We had a tough meeting scheduled and I had the option of voiding a very large contract. But we worked out the problem amicably in a short amount of time.

Repeatedly during the meeting, the sales staff said, "You're being so kind. That's so unusual." I could only answer that with the name "Christian" in the title of the association on the contract; it would be unusual to act any other way.

Can people see that you have been with Jesus?

THOUGHTS TO PONDER

Why would Peter and John reply that they could not keep quiet about Jesus? Wouldn't they be more valuable to the early church free than imprisoned? Alive, rather than dead? Why would they refuse to compromise? What does that tell us today?

PRAYER

God, help us to be bold in our faith, and help us to have the attitude that we must speak of you in every opportunity. Amen.

REAL GENEROSITY

ACTS 4:32—5:11

³²The group of believers were united in their hearts and spirit. All those in the group acted as though their private property belonged to everyone in the group. In fact, they shared everything. ³³With great power the apostles were telling people that the Lord Jesus was truly raised from the dead. And God blessed all the believers very much. ³⁴There were no needy people among them. From time to time those who owned fields or houses sold them, brought the money, ³⁵and gave it to the apostles. Then the money was given to anyone who needed it.

³⁶One of the believers was named Joseph, a Levite born in Cyprus. The apostles called him Barnabas (which means "one who encourages"). ³⁷Joseph owned a field, sold it, brought the money, and gave it to the apostles.

5 But a man named Ananias and his wife Sapphira sold some land. ²He kept back part of the money for himself; his wife knew about this and agreed to it. But he brought the rest of the money and gave it to the apostles. ³Peter said, "Ananias, why did you let Satan rule your thoughts to lie to the Holy Spirit and to keep for yourself part of the money you received for the land? ⁴Before you sold the land, it belonged to you. And even after you sold it, you could have used the money any way you wanted. Why did you think of doing this? You lied to God, not to us!" ⁵⁻⁶When Ananias heard this, he fell down and died. Some young men came in, wrapped up his body, carried it out, and buried it. And everyone who heard about this was filled with fear.

⁷About three hours later his wife came in, but she did not know what had happened. ⁸Peter said to her, "Tell me, was the money you got for your field this much?"

Sapphira answered, "Yes, that was the price."

⁹Peter said to her, "Why did you and your husband agree to test the Spirit of the Lord? Look! The men who buried your husband are at the door, and they will carry you out." ¹⁰At that moment Sapphira fell down by his feet and died. When the young men came in and saw that she was dead, they carried her out and buried her beside her husband. ¹¹The whole church and all the others who heard about these things were filled with fear.

DEVOTION

THE GREEK WORD for the phenomenon of the early church is *koinonia*, a word we translate "fellowship." In a day before insurance, welfare, and other forms of public and private safety nets, the church took care of its own. Luke

667

states flatly that there were no needy among them, thanks to the way God blessed them, and thanks to the generosity of those who had been blessed.

But Satan can work his way into our good intentions, and he found a way into the hearts of Ananias and Sapphira. They sold their land and kept back a part of the proceeds for themselves. Note that keeping part of the money was *not* the sin. The sin was the misrepresentation of the gift.

The history of giving to God runs very deep. In the fourth chapter of Genesis we see the story of Cain and Abel offering their gifts to God. Abel's was acceptable; Cain's was not. By the fourteenth chapter of Genesis, after Abram (later Abraham) had rescued Lot from the destruction of Sodom, we see him tithing to God's priest who came from a land called Salem. Later, Abraham would be asked by God to offer his only son to him, and Abraham stood ready to obey until an angel kept him from plunging the knife into his beloved child.

What we see from these stories is that God has always been pleased with gifts that represented a significant sacrifice. And why not? When God gave us a gift, it was his only Son.

So Ananias and Sapphira conspired to be selfish with God and lie to appear more generous than they were. God had already dealt with this problem before when he instructed Samuel that he had rejected Saul as king of Israel for bringing back the best of the spoils of war to sacrifice to God rather than destroying everything as he was told. Samuel asked him, "What pleases the LORD more: burnt offerings and sacrifices or obedience to his voice? It is better to obey than to sacrifice. It is better to listen to God than to offer the fat of sheep" (1 Samuel 15:22).

God didn't need all the proceeds from the sale of the field belonging to Ananias and Sapphira. But he did require their obedience.

THOUGHTS TO PONDER

Do we hold back from God? Do we enjoy fellowships where we are not doing our full part? Does God still expect a tithe of us today?

PRAYER

God, we pray that we will be generous in our giving, remaining mindful that you sent your Son for us. Help us to remember that when we give to the neediest of the world, we are giving to you. Amen.

Faith and Adversity

ACTS 5:12–30

¹²The apostles did many signs and miracles among the people. And they would all meet together on Solomon's Porch. ¹³None of the others dared to join them, but all the people respected them. ¹⁴More and more men and women believed in the Lord and were added to the group of believers. ¹⁵The people placed their sick on beds and mats in the streets, hoping that when Peter passed by at least his shadow might fall on them. ¹⁶Crowds came from all the towns around Jerusalem, bringing their sick and those who were bothered by evil spirits, and all of them were healed.

¹⁷The high priest and all his friends (a group called the Sadducees) became very jealous. ¹⁸They took the apostles and put them in jail. ¹⁹But during the night, an angel of the Lord opened the doors of the jail and led the apostles outside. The angel said, ²⁰"Go stand in the Temple and tell the people everything about this new life." ²¹When the apostles heard this, they obeyed and went into the Temple early in the morning and continued teaching.

When the high priest and his friends arrived, they called a meeting of the leaders and all the important elders. They sent some men to the jail to bring the apostles to them. ²²But, upon arriving, the officers could not find the apostles. So they went back and reported to the leaders. ²³They said, "The jail was closed and locked, and the guards were standing at the doors. But when we opened the doors, the jail was empty!" ²⁴Hearing this, the captain of the Temple guards and the leading priests were confused and wondered what was happening.

²⁵Then someone came and told them, "Listen! The men you put in jail are standing in the Temple teaching the people." ²⁶Then the captain and his men went out and brought the apostles back. But the soldiers did not use force, because they were afraid the people would stone them to death.

²⁷The soldiers brought the apostles to the meeting and made them stand before the leaders. The high priest questioned them, ²⁸saying, "We gave you strict orders not to continue teaching in that name. But look, you have filled Jerusalem with your teaching and are trying to make us responsible for this man's death."

²⁹Peter and the other apostles answered, "We must obey God, not human authority! ³⁰You killed Jesus by hanging him on a cross. But God, the God of our ancestors, raised Jesus up from the dead!"

DEVOTION

MANY OF US may never be in a position in which we're required to decide whether to obey God or a human authority, but untold numbers of men and women around the world must make such a decision every day. In much of the world, professing one's faith in Christ is ill-advised if not illegal.

When I spent a semester in Vienna with a group of college students, we met Christians from Muslim nations who would never return to see their families again. We met a Chinese student who didn't know how she would find other Christians when she returned to her native country since no one worshiped in public. Recently, I met an American couple who planned to enter communist China as teachers of English, fully aware that openly offering to study the Bible with their students would not be allowed and aware that even seemingly interested persons might actually be spies for the Communist Party.

But faith can grow, even in adversity. And all around the world, Christians worship in private where worshiping in public is not allowed.

But the question for us is this: can faith grow in a comfortable environment? Absent any adversity, how strong will my faith be? Lose a tooth in your upper gum and the opposing tooth in the lower gum will never be as healthy. Why? The lack of opposition is not the natural state for your tooth.

Perhaps the lack of opposition is not the natural state for growing faith either. What if Satan decides to tempt me with no opposition at all? What if his strategy for me is to soften my faith by making it easy to worship God on Sunday now, and then making it easy to ignore God on Sunday later? What if I begin to take my Christianity for granted because it scarcely costs me anything at all?

Adversity has its challenges; privilege has its challenges as well. And while few of us would pray for adversity to strengthen our faith, we can at least pray that the religious freedoms we enjoy don't weaken it.

THOUGHTS TO PONDER

What is the greatest adversity you have ever endured for your faith? How did you feel? Why do you think God allowed the critics of Jesus to turn their sights on the apostles?

PRAYER

Father, strengthen our faith in you, no matter what the circumstances. Please find us faithful no matter what the tests of life may be. Amen.

LIVING PROOF

ACTS 5:27–42

²⁷The soldiers brought the apostles to the meeting and made them stand before the leaders. The high priest questioned them, ²⁸saying, "We gave you strict orders not to continue teaching in that name. But look, you have filled Jerusalem with your teaching and are trying to make us responsible for this man's death."

²⁹Peter and the other apostles answered, "We must obey God, not human authority! ³⁰You killed Jesus by hanging him on a cross. But God, the God of our ancestors, raised Jesus up from the dead! ³¹Jesus is the One whom God raised to be on his right side, as Leader and Savior. Through him, all people could change their hearts and lives and have their sins forgiven. ³²We saw all these things happen. The Holy Spirit, whom God has given to all who obey him, also proves these things are true."

³³When the leaders heard this, they became angry and wanted to kill them. ³⁴But a Pharisee named Gamaliel stood up in the meeting. He was a teacher of the law, and all the people respected him. He ordered the apostles to leave the meeting for a little while. ³⁵Then he said, "People of Israel, be careful what you are planning to do to these men. ³⁶Remember when Theudas appeared? He said he was a great man, and about four hundred men joined him. But he was killed, and all his followers were scattered; they were able to do nothing. ³⁷Later, a man named Judas came from Galilee at the time of the registration. He also led a group of followers and was killed, and all his followers were scattered. ³⁸And so now I tell you: Stay away from these men, and leave them alone. If their plan comes from human authority, it will fail. ³⁹But if it is from God, you will not be able to stop them. You might even be fighting against God himself!"

The leaders agreed with what Gamaliel said. ⁴⁰They called the apostles in, beat them, and told them not to speak in the name of Jesus again. Then they let them go free. ⁴¹The apostles left the meeting full of joy because they were given the honor of suffering disgrace for Jesus. ⁴²Every day in the Temple and in people's homes they continued teaching the people and telling the Good News—that Jesus is the Christ.

DEVOTION

GAMALIEL HAD SEEN it all before. As one of the most respected teachers of the law, he had seen others pose as the Messiah. The coming of the Son of God had been prophesied for hundreds of years, so it made sense that a few opportunists would try to seduce the people with their claims of being divine. And Jesus was at least the third one that Gamaliel had seen in his time.

Now, like the first two, Jesus had also been killed. But the murder of Jesus hadn't been the end of the affair. Because unlike the followers of Theudas or Judas, these apostles of Jesus hadn't scattered. Oh, they had been scarce for a few weeks, but here they were back in the most public of places, performing signs that were stirring up the people, and giving the credit to this dead Messiah. There was even a rumor that he hadn't stayed dead—that the tomb of Joseph of Arimathea was empty.

Even beatings and imprisonment did not deter them, these dogged followers of the itinerant rabbi out of Galilee. To Gamaliel, they were the difference. They hadn't fled to the countryside. They hadn't dissolved into the population of Jerusalem. Instead they were still boldly preaching that Jesus was the one for whom they had been waiting.

Even today, when the people of the world need proof that Jesus is the Christ, raised from the dead to be seated on the right side of God, they need only to look at his followers. Followers who don't forsake Jesus when times are hard. Followers whose lives of service to him must be explained.

Just like the apostles before us, you and I are the living proof that Jesus lives. The cross on which he was crucified rotted long ago. The empty tomb is lost. But the changed lives continue. And if we draw our strength from God, the world will not be able to stop us.

Want proof that Jesus exists? Check out the lives of his followers today. And anyone who disputes that "might even be fighting against God himself."

THOUGHTS TO PONDER

How must Christians live in order for the world to see the risen Savior in us? Have you ever reached the spiritual maturity where you can rejoice in persecution? Why type of faith must that take?

PRAYER

God, we pray that we will be your witnesses today that you have risen and that you will come again to call your own to yourself. Amen.

MARTYR OR FRAUD?

ACTS 6:8—7:1, 51–60

[8]Stephen was richly blessed by God who gave him the power to do great miracles and signs among the people. [9]But some people were against him. They belonged to the synagogue of Free Men (as it was called), which included people from Cyrene, Alexandria, Cilicia, and Asia. They all came and argued with Stephen.

[10]But the Spirit was helping him to speak with wisdom, and his words were so strong that they could not argue with him. [11]So they secretly urged some men to say, "We heard Stephen speak against Moses and against God."

[12]This upset the people, the elders, and the teachers of the law. They came and grabbed Stephen and brought him to a meeting of the leaders. [13]They brought in some people to tell lies about Stephen, saying, "This man is always speaking against this holy place and the law of Moses. [14]We heard him say that Jesus from Nazareth will destroy this place and that Jesus will change the customs Moses gave us." [15]All the people in the meeting were watching Stephen closely and saw that his face looked like the face of an angel.

7 The high priest said to Stephen, "Are these things true?"

Editor's note: Stephen gives a speech here about the relationship of God with Moses and the descendants of Abraham. He continues by telling them that the Temple, which he is accused of conspiring to destroy, is not the dwelling place of God. He concludes below.

[51]Stephen continued speaking: "You stubborn people! You have not given your hearts to God, nor will you listen to him! You are always against what the Holy Spirit is trying to tell you, just as your ancestors were. [52]Your ancestors tried to hurt every prophet who ever lived. Those prophets said long ago that the One who is good would come, but your ancestors killed them. And now you have turned against and killed the One who is good. [53]You received the law of Moses, which God gave you through his angels, but you haven't obeyed it."

[54]When the leaders heard this, they became furious. They were so mad they were grinding their teeth at Stephen. [55]But Stephen was full of the Holy Spirit. He looked up to heaven and saw the glory of God and Jesus standing at God's right side. [56]He said, "Look! I see heaven open and the Son of Man standing at God's right side."

[57]Then they shouted loudly and covered their ears and all ran at Stephen. [58]They took him out of the city and began to throw stones at him to kill him. And those who told lies against Stephen left their coats with a young man named

Saul. [59]While they were throwing stones, Stephen prayed, "Lord Jesus, receive my spirit." [60]He fell on his knees and cried in a loud voice, "Lord, do not hold this sin against them." After Stephen said this, he died.

DEVOTION

IN THIS STORY, Stephen became the first martyr for the Christian faith. He had angered members of the synagogue of Free Men, former slaves or sons of slaves of all nationalities who worshiped together. This rough group spread lies about Stephen that landed him before the Sanhedrin, the highest court of the Jews.

When you think about it, all Stephen had to do to save himself from the wrath of the court was denounce or deny his previous statements. After all, Peter had denied Jesus and he had later been restored to the eleven remaining apostles by Jesus himself. Surely there would be a greater good in denying his statements today and living to preach again tomorrow.

But Stephen didn't see it that way. He was emboldened by the Holy Spirit even before he began to speak and he was ushered into heaven by the Spirit, getting a glimpse of his eternal reward even before the rocks began to rain down on him.

No greater good would have been served by denying Jesus even if it meant he lived a long time afterwards, and Stephen knew it. Once your message is compromised, it's very hard for anyone to hear you again. Cheat on the numbers at work, and you can forget about inviting any of your coworkers to visit your congregation. Swear like everyone else on the team or in the bleachers and your ability to witness is gone.

Stephen's ministry was over one way or the other. He would either go out a martyr or he would go out a fraud.

THOUGHTS TO PONDER

Have you ever witnessed Christians acting out of character? Have you ever done it yourself? What kind of message does it send to nonbelievers?

PRAYER

God, we might not be called to die for you, but we have most certainly been called to live for you. Help us be consistent in our walk. Amen.

Casual Christianity

ACTS 8:5–25

⁵Philip went to the city of Samaria and preached about the Christ. ⁶When the people there heard Philip and saw the miracles he was doing, they all listened carefully to what he said. ⁷Many of these people had evil spirits in them, but Philip made the evil spirits leave. The spirits made a loud noise when they came out. Philip also healed many weak and crippled people there. ⁸So the people in that city were very happy.

⁹But there was a man named Simon in that city. Before Philip came there, Simon had practiced magic and amazed all the people of Samaria. He bragged and called himself a great man. ¹⁰All the people—the least important and the most important—paid attention to Simon, saying, "This man has the power of God, called 'the Great Power'!" ¹¹Simon had amazed them with his magic so long that the people became his followers. ¹²But when Philip told them the Good News about the kingdom of God and the power of Jesus Christ, men and women believed Philip and were baptized. ¹³Simon himself believed, and after he was baptized, he stayed very close to Philip. When he saw the miracles and the powerful things Philip did, Simon was amazed.

¹⁴When the apostles who were still in Jerusalem heard that the people of Samaria had accepted the word of God, they sent Peter and John to them. ¹⁵When Peter and John arrived, they prayed that the Samaritan believers might receive the Holy Spirit. ¹⁶These people had been baptized in the name of the Lord Jesus, but the Holy Spirit had not yet come upon any of them. ¹⁷Then, when the two apostles began laying their hands on the people, they received the Holy Spirit.

¹⁸Simon saw that the Spirit was given to people when the apostles laid their hands on them. So he offered the apostles money, ¹⁹saying, "Give me also this power so that anyone on whom I lay my hands will receive the Holy Spirit."

²⁰Peter said to him, "You and your money should both be destroyed, because you thought you could buy God's gift with money. ²¹You cannot share with us in this work since your heart is not right before God. ²²Change your heart! Turn away from this evil thing you have done, and pray to the Lord. Maybe he will forgive you for thinking this. ²³I see that you are full of bitter jealousy and ruled by sin."

²⁴Simon answered, "Both of you pray for me to the Lord so the things you have said will not happen to me."

²⁵After Peter and John told the people what they had seen Jesus do and after they had spoken the message of the Lord, they went back to Jerusalem. On the way, they went through many Samaritan towns and preached the Good News to the people.

DEVOTION

WHEN THE FIRST SERVANTS of the church were chosen to ensure that the Greek-speaking widows were not overlooked in the daily distribution of the church's food, Philip was one of the seven chosen (Acts 6:5). He received the gift of healing and became one of the leading figures in the first-century church.

Several times in the Bible, we're confronted with phenomena we can't explain. For instance, we don't know how the Egyptian king's magicians were able to match the miraculous signs that God performed through Aaron to convince the king that Moses had been sent by God. Or why some men seemed to possess the ability to interpret dreams or read the stars. And in Samaria, we encounter a man whose magic was so compelling that he had gained followers from every economic class. He was undoubtedly making a good income off of his magic.

But when he saw the works that Philip could do, he was converted, but perhaps not for the most noble of reasons. He wanted to buy the power to bestow the Holy Spirit on the believers.

Peter's response was not casual. He told Simon that both he and his money "should be destroyed" and encouraged him to change his heart and pray for forgiveness. Strong words, but needed. Simon soon repented.

Can we be guilty of the same thing? Can people be in the Lord's church because it gives them respectability? A large pool of potential business clients? A gym to play a good game of pickup basketball without paying any dues? Extra "face time" with a religious boss?

Casual Christians are not unlike Simon. They take more than they give. They enjoy the benefits of fellowship without the sacrifices. But someday, all deeds and motives will be laid bare and the casual Christians will be revealed for who they are.

THOUGHTS TO PONDER

Is it possible for people to want to be in the Lord's church for the wrong reasons today? How can we guard our motives so that they are always pure?

PRAYER

God, help us to seek only your gain as we labor in your kingdom. Put away any selfish reasons we may have in wanting to be among your people. Amen.

IMMEDIATE RESPONSES

ACTS 8:26–40

²⁶An angel of the Lord said to Philip, "Get ready and go south to the road that leads down to Gaza from Jerusalem—the desert road." ²⁷So Philip got ready and went. On the road he saw a man from Ethiopia, a eunuch. He was an important officer in the service of Candace, the queen of the Ethiopians; he was responsible for taking care of all her money. He had gone to Jerusalem to worship. ²⁸Now, as he was on his way home, he was sitting in his chariot reading from the Book of Isaiah, the prophet. ²⁹The Spirit said to Philip, "Go to that chariot and stay near it."

³⁰So when Philip ran toward the chariot, he heard the man reading from Isaiah the prophet. Philip asked, "Do you understand what you are reading?"

³¹He answered, "How can I understand unless someone explains it to me?" Then he invited Philip to climb in and sit with him. ³²The portion of Scripture he was reading was this:

"He was like a sheep being led to be killed.

　　He was quiet, as a lamb is quiet while its wool is being cut;

he never opened his mouth.

³³　　He was shamed and was treated unfairly.

He died without children to continue his family.

　　His life on earth has ended."　　　　　　　　　　*Isaiah 53:7–8*

³⁴The officer said to Philip, "Please tell me, who is the prophet talking about—himself or someone else?" ³⁵Philip began to speak, and starting with this same Scripture, he told the man the Good News about Jesus.

³⁶While they were traveling down the road, they came to some water. The officer said, "Look, here is water. What is stopping me from being baptized?" ³⁷Philip answered, "If you believe with all your heart, you can." The officer said, "I believe that Jesus Christ is the Son of God." ³⁸Then the officer commanded the chariot to stop. Both Philip and the officer went down into the water, and Philip baptized him. ³⁹When they came up out of the water, the Spirit of the Lord took Philip away; the officer never saw him again. And the officer continued on his way home, full of joy. ⁴⁰But Philip appeared in a city called Azotus and preached the Good News in all the towns on the way from Azotus to Caesarea.

DEVOTION

SHE CAME TO ME on the next to the last day of church camp. "I think I need to be baptized, but my parents say I shouldn't until I know more," she said, tears in her eyes. She was a young teen, brought to the camp by a girlfriend who had attended church regularly all her life. But this was her first exposure to the Good

News and now she was confused. The parents who were counseling her to go slow had never taken her to church as a child.

We decided that the best thing to do was to study the Bible to determine what the Scriptures told her to do. She hadn't been banned by her parents from being baptized; they simply saw little need for it, and besides, they promised they would take her to church when she came home. But she didn't want to wait.

When we opened the Scriptures, we found that responses to the Good News in Acts were almost always instantaneous.

The people who heard Peter's sermon on the day of Pentecost.

Saul, later known as the apostle Paul.

The members of the house of Cornelius.

The Philippian jailer.

Throughout the Book of Acts, those who believed were baptized spontaneously like the eunuch in the story above.

So we studied the passages and then we went to the lake's edge just outside the gates of the camp. There, with all the girls of the cabin looking on, I baptized the girl. And with that, she joined untold numbers of Christians throughout the years who have entered the waters of baptism in response to the Good News. I heard from her a few more times after she returned home, but lost track of her after that. But I still remember her eagerness to do what was right.

But there's another story in Acts where the response wasn't spontaneous. Luke tells us that Paul had several meetings with a Roman official named Felix and his wife. Felix listened to Paul's witness about Jesus, but replied, "Go away now. When I have more time, I will call for you" (Acts 24:25). However, there is no record that he ever did.

Today is the only day we are guaranteed. All the conversions recorded in Acts include immediate responses to the message. Have you responded?

THOUGHTS TO PONDER

Based on the eunuch's response when he saw the water, what must Philip have taught him? What does that tell us about the nature of the Good News?

PRAYER

God, we pray that we will do what you want us to do to the best of our understanding, and that our actions will please you. Amen.

FINDING THE WILL OF GOD

ACTS 9:1–19

9 In Jerusalem Saul was still threatening the followers of the Lord by saying he would kill them. So he went to the high priest ²and asked him to write letters to the synagogues in the city of Damascus. Then if Saul found any followers of Christ's Way, men or women, he would arrest them and bring them back to Jerusalem.

³So Saul headed toward Damascus. As he came near the city, a bright light from heaven suddenly flashed around him. ⁴Saul fell to the ground and heard a voice saying to him, "Saul, Saul! Why are you persecuting me?"

⁵Saul said, "Who are you, Lord?"

The voice answered, "I am Jesus, whom you are persecuting. ⁶Get up now and go into the city. Someone there will tell you what you must do."

⁷The people traveling with Saul stood there but said nothing. They heard the voice, but they saw no one. ⁸Saul got up from the ground and opened his eyes, but he could not see. So those with Saul took his hand and led him into Damascus. ⁹For three days Saul could not see and did not eat or drink.

¹⁰There was a follower of Jesus in Damascus named Ananias. The Lord spoke to Ananias in a vision, "Ananias!"

Ananias answered, "Here I am, Lord."

¹¹The Lord said to him, "Get up and go to Straight Street. Find the house of Judas, and ask for a man named Saul from the city of Tarsus. He is there now, praying. ¹²Saul has seen a vision in which a man named Ananias comes to him and lays his hands on him. Then he is able to see again."

¹³But Ananias answered, "Lord, many people have told me about this man and the terrible things he did to your holy people in Jerusalem. ¹⁴Now he has come here to Damascus, and the leading priests have given him the power to arrest everyone who worships you."

¹⁵But the Lord said to Ananias, "Go! I have chosen Saul for an important work. He must tell about me to those who are not Jews, to kings, and to the people of Israel. ¹⁶I will show him how much he must suffer for my name."

¹⁷So Ananias went to the house of Judas. He laid his hands on Saul and said, "Brother Saul, the Lord Jesus sent me. He is the one you saw on the road on your way here. He sent me so that you can see again and be filled with the Holy Spirit." ¹⁸Immediately, something that looked like fish scales fell from Saul's eyes, and he was able to see again! Then Saul got up and was baptized. ¹⁹After he ate some food, his strength returned.

DEVOTION

I'VE NEVER HAD a "bright light" experience and I'm betting you haven't either. Our conversions weren't nearly as dramatic as Saul's, but luckily not as painful either.

But there's a part of Saul's conversion that we need to pay attention to in our own lives. God spoke to Ananias and said of Saul, "I will show him how much he must suffer for my name." How many of us know what God has planned for us? Even though we will probably never be called on to endure the beatings, arrests, and imprisonments of Saul, God does have a plan for us. But first, we must get in tune with his voice.

In his Letter to the Romans, Paul (formerly Saul) wrote of the prerequisite for knowing God's will in our lives: "So brothers and sisters, since God has shown us great mercy, I beg you to offer your lives as a living sacrifice to him. Your offering must be only for God and pleasing to him, which is the spiritual way for you to worship. Do not be shaped by this world; instead be changed within by a new way of thinking. Then you will be able to decide what God wants for you; you will know what is good and pleasing to him and what is perfect" (Romans 12:1–2).

Look carefully at the verse again. First, we must change the way we live and change the way we think. Then, and only then, will we be able to decide what God's will is for our lives.

God won't come shine a light in my eyes or yours. Instead, he'll wait for us to climb off the throne of our lives and on to the altar of sacrifice. Then, when our lives are no longer like the world's way of living, we'll hear his voice. Then, he'll reveal what he wants us to do for his name.

THOUGHTS TO PONDER

Why would Saul be chosen to be God's messenger based on his history as a persecutor of Christians? Why would God leave Saul in darkness for three days before sending Ananias to his side? How did you come to a knowledge of God's will for your life?

PRAYER

God, we pray that you will use us with all our flaws, just like you used Saul. We thank you for taking us, even with our imperfections, and using us in your kingdom. Amen.

FINDING ACCEPTANCE

ACTS 9:19–31

¹⁹Saul stayed with the followers of Jesus in Damascus for a few days. ²⁰Soon he began to preach about Jesus in the synagogues, saying, "Jesus is the Son of God."

²¹All the people who heard him were amazed. They said, "This is the man who was in Jerusalem trying to destroy those who trust in this name! He came here to arrest the followers of Jesus and take them back to the leading priests."

²²But Saul grew more powerful. His proofs that Jesus is the Christ were so strong that his own people in Damascus could not argue with him.

²³After many days, they made plans to kill Saul. ²⁴They were watching the city gates day and night, but Saul learned about their plan. ²⁵One night some followers of Saul helped him leave the city by lowering him in a basket through an opening in the city wall.

²⁶When Saul went to Jerusalem, he tried to join the group of followers, but they were all afraid of him. They did not believe he was really a follower. ²⁷But Barnabas accepted Saul and took him to the apostles. Barnabas explained to them that Saul had seen the Lord on the road and the Lord had spoken to Saul. Then he told them how boldly Saul had preached in the name of Jesus in Damascus.

²⁸And so Saul stayed with the followers, going everywhere in Jerusalem, preaching boldly in the name of the Lord. ²⁹He would often talk and argue with the Jewish people who spoke Greek, but they were trying to kill him. ³⁰When the followers learned about this, they took Saul to Caesarea and from there sent him to Tarsus.

³¹The church everywhere in Judea, Galilee, and Samaria had a time of peace and became stronger. Respecting the Lord by the way they lived, and being encouraged by the Holy Spirit, the group of believers continued to grow.

DEVOTION

SAUL MAY HAVE BEEN converted, but he could not escape his past—at least not immediately. In this passage, he found himself caught between two groups. On the one side were his former followers who had gone with him to Damascus with orders to bring back Christians to be persecuted in Jerusalem. On the other side were Christians who were suspicious that his preaching in the synagogues might be a ploy to arrest those who listened and take them back to the leading priests in Jerusalem.

Worse yet, one group wanted Saul killed while the other was wary about giving him refuge. So in a dramatic nighttime escape, Saul went over the wall of the city in a basket and headed back to an uncertain welcome in Jerusalem.

Imagine the plight. Imagine you've repented of your old ways, but you can't find acceptance in the church. I listened a couple of years ago as a young lady told her story of leaving her former life as an exotic dancer for a new life as a believer. I listened to her address a group of Christians about the difficulties of her exit out of that lifestyle and her attempts to live the life of a Christian.

And there were many difficulties. Her finances changed dramatically as she gave up the hundreds of dollars per night she had made stripping at a men's club and went back to school to learn a marketable skill. Few of her old clothes were suitable for her new life. She had to distance herself from virtually all her friends and their drug-addled lifestyles. She left her boyfriend with whom she was living.

But as hard as that was, the real difficulty was in gaining acceptance from the Lord's people. Women were suspicious of this beautiful single woman who was open about her past and her desire to leave it behind. Perhaps she was just looking for a higher-class man to latch on to. And the men were wary of showing any sympathy for her because of the suspicions it might stir up.

Compounding the problem, she told the crowd, was the fact that in several of the churches she visited, she recognized faces of her former customers—men who had tipped her on Saturday night and had tithed in church on Sunday morning. She didn't fit in her old world, and she didn't know if she would ever fit in this new one.

But thanks to God's providence, she found a "Barnabas" who vouched for her, who coached her and counseled her as she transitioned from her old life to the new walk with God.

But what happens to those who come to us who don't find their Barnabas? The addicts, the teenaged mothers, and the runaways who want the help of our churches but find only suspicious stares. Do you have it in you to be a Barnabas to them?

THOUGHTS TO PONDER

> What risks was Saul taking by being an outspoken voice for Christianity so soon after his former life? Why would he do that? What risks was Barnabas taking by accepting Saul? Why would he do that?

PRAYER

> God, we know that we are all sinners and that you see all sin the same. Help us to accept your children as you have accepted us. Amen.

CALLED TO BE DIFFERENT

ACTS 9:32–43

³²As Peter was traveling through all the area, he visited God's people who lived in Lydda. ³³There he met a man named Aeneas, who was paralyzed and had not been able to leave his bed for the past eight years. ³⁴Peter said to him, "Aeneas, Jesus Christ heals you. Stand up and make your bed." Aeneas stood up immediately. ³⁵All the people living in Lydda and on the Plain of Sharon saw him and turned to the Lord.

³⁶In the city of Joppa there was a follower named Tabitha (whose Greek name was Dorcas). She was always doing good deeds and kind acts. ³⁷While Peter was in Lydda, Tabitha became sick and died. Her body was washed and put in a room upstairs. ³⁸Since Lydda is near Joppa and the followers in Joppa heard that Peter was in Lydda, they sent two messengers to Peter. They begged him, "Hurry, please come to us!" ³⁹So Peter got ready and went with them. When he arrived, they took him to the upstairs room where all the widows stood around Peter, crying. They showed him the shirts and coats Tabitha had made when she was still alive. ⁴⁰Peter sent everyone out of the room and kneeled and prayed. Then he turned to the body and said, "Tabitha, stand up." She opened her eyes, and when she saw Peter, she sat up. ⁴¹He gave her his hand and helped her up. Then he called the saints and the widows into the room and showed them that Tabitha was alive. ⁴²People everywhere in Joppa learned about this, and many believed in the Lord. ⁴³Peter stayed in Joppa for many days with a man named Simon who was a tanner.

DEVOTION

THE FAITH of the saints in Joppa is reminiscent of the faith that Jesus was talking about when he claimed that if his followers had a faith that was even the size of a mustard seed—one of the smallest of all seeds—nothing would be impossible for them (Matthew 17:20). Tabitha, a faithful Christian woman, had died suddenly; when her friends heard that Peter was in Lydda, they never hesitated. "Hurry up," was their message to Peter. This was a woman dearly loved and already missed in the community, and they believed that Peter could do something about it.

Notice that Peter is not the source of the power, but the channel for it. When he healed Aeneas at the beginning of this story, he claimed: "Aeneas, Jesus Christ heals you." Before he raised Tabitha from the dead, he knelt to pray. What a far cry from the time the disciples failed to cast a demon out of a boy, and after Jesus had come to the boy's aid, he had admonished his followers: "This kind only comes out with prayer." Peter had learned the lesson, and now prayer was his first resort, not his last.

Luke calls the believers "saints" from the Greek word *hagios*. The word is often translated "holy" as well. Paul starts nearly all his letters with the same term, calling his readers "saints" in the various churches where he writes.

The Greek word carries the connotation of being "different" or "set apart for a God's purposes." A holy life is, quite simply, a different life. God's people have always been called to be different.

Peter would later write that Christians "are a chosen people, royal priests, a holy nation, a people for God's own possession" (1 Peter 2:9). In the next verse, Peter would remind them that "At one time you were not a people, but now you are God's people" (1 Peter 2:10).

The saints at Lydda (*hagios* is translated "God's people" in verse 32 above) and at Joppa (verse 41) were living different lives, and the death of even one of them, such as Tabitha, diminished them all.

This chapter and the next end Luke's focus on Peter. His ministry will eventually give way to Paul's. But Peter, one of the disciples closest to Jesus known for his brashness, had fully matured into a church leader.

THOUGHTS TO PONDER

> What was the effect of the miracle in Lydda on the surrounding people? What does this tell you about the role of miracles in building the early church?

PRAYER

> God, we know that all your saints are precious in your sight. Help us to live lives of service like Tabitha and look forward to joining you in heaven. Amen.

The Prayer of a Sinner

ACTS 10:1–23

10 At Caesarea there was a man named Cornelius, an officer in the Italian group of the Roman army. ²Cornelius was a religious man. He and all the other people who lived in his house worshiped the true God. He gave much of his money to the poor and prayed to God often. ³One afternoon about three o'clock, Cornelius clearly saw a vision. An angel of God came to him and said, "Cornelius!"

⁴Cornelius stared at the angel. He became afraid and said, "What do you want, Lord?"

The angel said, "God has heard your prayers. He has seen that you give to the poor, and he remembers you. ⁵Send some men now to Joppa to bring back a man named Simon who is also called Peter. ⁶He is staying with a man, also named Simon, who is a tanner and has a house beside the sea." ⁷When the angel who spoke to Cornelius left, Cornelius called two of his servants and a soldier, a religious man who worked for him. ⁸Cornelius explained everything to them and sent them to Joppa.

⁹About noon the next day as they came near Joppa, Peter was going up to the roof to pray. ¹⁰He was hungry and wanted to eat, but while the food was being prepared, he had a vision. ¹¹He saw heaven opened and something coming down that looked like a big sheet being lowered to earth by its four corners. ¹²In it were all kinds of animals, reptiles, and birds. ¹³Then a voice said to Peter, "Get up, Peter; kill and eat."

¹⁴But Peter said, "No, Lord! I have never eaten food that is unholy or unclean."

¹⁵But the voice said to him again, "God has made these things clean, so don't call them 'unholy'!" ¹⁶This happened three times, and at once the sheet was taken back to heaven.

¹⁷While Peter was wondering what this vision meant, the men Cornelius sent had found Simon's house and were standing at the gate. ¹⁸They asked, "Is Simon Peter staying here?"

¹⁹While Peter was still thinking about the vision, the Spirit said to him, "Listen, three men are looking for you. ²⁰Get up and go downstairs. Go with them without doubting, because I have sent them to you."

²¹So Peter went down to the men and said, "I am the one you are looking for. Why did you come here?"

²²They said, "A holy angel spoke to Cornelius, an army officer and a good man; he worships God. All the people respect him. The angel told Cornelius to ask you to come to his house so that he can hear what you have to say." ²³So Peter asked the men to come in and spend the night.

The next day Peter got ready and went with them, and some of the followers from Joppa joined him.

DEVOTION

PERHAPS THE MOST important lesson of this story is that God hears the prayers of anyone who seeks him. By the Jews reckoning, there were two reasons why Cornelius wouldn't be heard by God. First, he was a non-Jew and therefore unclean. Second, he was a sinner who had never offered an atonement sacrifice. But despite the common sentiment among the Jews that God didn't hear the prayers of sinners, God heard the prayer of Cornelius.

The vision that Peter received only made sense when he got the call to go to the house of Cornelius. Just as God had not created any animals inherently unclean, he had not created any inherently unclean races of people. In order for Peter to be the ambassador to the non-Jews that God needed him to be, Peter had to overcome his prejudice. Peter, the rough fisherman, still carried the attitude of many Jews that all other races were inferior.

Even today, you hear controversies about whose prayers God hears. I've heard that God doesn't hear the prayers of "unrepentant sinners." One prominent religious leader made headlines a while back when he said that God doesn't hear the prayers of Jews.

But reading the story of Cornelius, none of this seems to ring true. I think God is inclined to hear anyone who wants to talk with him. Scripture tells us we were all "far away" from God at one point (Ephesians 2:13). Even when I was in that condition, he heard my prayers, just like he heard the prayers of Cornelius and just like he hears the prayers of sinners today.

THOUGHTS TO PONDER

Why might God have picked Peter to be the messenger to the Jews? In what way was the vision getting Peter ready for taking the Good News to non-Jews?

PRAYER

God, we know you have no favored people and that you call all of us to be saved. Help us to set aside our prejudices and see all people as you do. Amen.

JESUS, THE LORD OF ALL PEOPLE

ACTS 10:24–36

²⁴On the following day they came to Caesarea. Cornelius was waiting for them and had called together his relatives and close friends. ²⁵When Peter entered, Cornelius met him, fell at his feet, and worshiped him. ²⁶But Peter helped him up, saying, "Stand up. I too am only a human." ²⁷As he talked with Cornelius, Peter went inside where he saw many people gathered. ²⁸He said, "You people understand that it is against our law for Jewish people to associate with or visit anyone who is not Jewish. But God has shown me that I should not call any person 'unholy' or 'unclean.' ²⁹That is why I did not argue when I was asked to come here. Now, please tell me why you sent for me."

³⁰Cornelius said, "Four days ago, I was praying in my house at this same time—three o'clock in the afternoon. Suddenly, there was a man standing before me wearing shining clothes. ³¹He said, 'Cornelius, God has heard your prayer and has seen that you give to the poor and remembers you. ³²So send some men to Joppa and ask Simon Peter to come. Peter is staying in the house of a man, also named Simon, who is a tanner and has a house beside the sea.' ³³So I sent for you immediately, and it was very good of you to come. Now we are all here before God to hear everything the Lord has commanded you to tell us."

³⁴Peter began to speak: "I really understand now that to God every person is the same. ³⁵In every country God accepts anyone who worships him and does what is right. ³⁶You know the message that God has sent to the people of Israel is the Good News that peace has come through Jesus Christ. Jesus is the Lord of all people!

DEVOTION

I STARED AT THE PHOTO at the exhibit in the Smithsonian Institution. Even though it predated my birth, it looked strangely familiar. The black and white photo showed an elderly, dignified gentleman seated at a wooden desk. He was wearing a suit and tie, and his hat was resting on one corner of the desk. His book was opened and he was in deep attention to the proceedings, oblivious to the photographer who was about to take a picture that would forever enshrine him in the archives of the Library of Congress as an example of racism in America.

You see, this was no ordinary classroom photo. The elderly man was African-American; the other students were white. They sat inside a university classroom in

1948 while he sat in the hall, just outside the door, looking in on the proceedings, but not fully a part of them. When he went to the library he sat at his own table. When he ate in the cafeteria, he ate alone in the section for "colored" students.

All George McLaurin wanted to do was pursue a doctorate degree in his retirement. He loved to learn and he wanted to use his free time to stretch his mind in directions that jobs and obligations hadn't allowed during his working years. But in order to pursue his dream, he first had to fight the Regents of the university for admission. And while he won the right to take classes, he didn't win the right to sit in them.

So there he sat in the photograph, on the outside looking in, like a child being punished in the hall. Then I realized why the photograph looked so familiar to me. Four decades later, I had pursued a doctorate from that same university in that same aging building. But for the luck of birth, I could have been George McLaurin, seated in the hall, ignored by my fellow students simply because of the color of my skin.

The same could be said for all us. So much of the good fortune we enjoy in our lives is not of our own making. I was not smarter than George McLaurin or more deserving than he. But my path to my doctorate was much easier than his. Today, the photograph of George McLaurin seated outside that classroom I was privileged to sit inside, is the screensaver on my computer. It reminds me of the lesson that Peter required a special vision to learn: we are all the same to God.

So look around you today at the homeless. Or those with AIDS. The downtrodden and rejected of society. May God open our eyes to see them as he sees them—one of his own.

THOUGHTS TO PONDER

Have you ever been looked down upon for who you are? Have you ever been tempted to look down on others based on insignificant factors like income or race? How do we overcome these tendencies?

PRAYER

God, we know you accepted us as we were, and we pray that we will do the same for those around us. Amen.

EVIDENCE OF CONVERSION

ACTS 11:1–18

11 The apostles and the believers in Judea heard that some who were not Jewish had accepted God's teaching too. ²But when Peter came to Jerusalem, some people argued with him. ³They said, "You went into the homes of people who are not circumcised and ate with them!"

⁴So Peter explained the whole story to them. ⁵He said, "I was in the city of Joppa, and while I was praying, I had a vision. I saw something that looked like a big sheet being lowered from heaven by its four corners. It came very close to me. ⁶I looked inside it and saw animals, wild beasts, reptiles, and birds. ⁷I heard a voice say to me, 'Get up, Peter. Kill and eat.' ⁸But I said, 'No, Lord! I have never eaten anything that is unholy or unclean.' ⁹But the voice from heaven spoke again, 'God has made these things clean, so don't call them unholy.' ¹⁰This happened three times. Then the whole thing was taken back to heaven. ¹¹Right then three men who were sent to me from Caesarea came to the house where I was staying. ¹²The Spirit told me to go with them without doubting. These six believers here also went with me, and we entered the house of Cornelius. ¹³He told us about the angel he saw standing in his house. The angel said to him, 'Send some men to Joppa and invite Simon Peter to come. ¹⁴By the words he will say to you, you and all your family will be saved.' ¹⁵When I began my speech, the Holy Spirit came on them just as he came on us at the beginning. ¹⁶Then I remembered the words of the Lord. He said, 'John baptized with water, but you will be baptized with the Holy Spirit.' ¹⁷Since God gave them the same gift he gave us who believed in the Lord Jesus Christ, how could I stop the work of God?"

¹⁸When the believers heard this, they stopped arguing. They praised God and said, "So God is allowing even other nations to turn to him and live."

DEVOTION

I KNOW THE FEELING of the brethren back in Jerusalem when they heard the news of Cornelius. Perhaps, like me, you've wondered about the motives of someone who claims to be converted.

My skepticism comes from a bad experience. Our congregation has a large prison ministry in a metropolitan area. Many prisoners—men and women—are converted each year.

William was one of those, and when he got out of prison he began worshiping in our congregation. We had him in our home for a meal. We gave him a Bible.

Then one Sunday we found out William was gone. He was back in jail—arrested for sexually molesting a child. We were crushed, then, inevitably we were wary.

Cornelius was not only an uncircumcised non-Jew—he was a Roman soldier, a commander of one hundred men in the Italian Regiment. Could he be trusted? Could he possibly be infiltrating the church to see if it was a threat to Rome?

Peter counters the questioning of the brethren in Jerusalem by recounting his experience in the house of Cornelius. He told them how the Holy Spirit had come on Cornelius and his family, and how they had been able to speak in tongues—just like the apostles on Pentecost Day. Once Peter had seen evidence of the Holy Spirit being visited on the non-Jews, he knew that to refuse to baptize them would be to oppose God.

Even today, this a good test to determine the truly converted—starting with me. Do I manifest the fruits of the Holy Spirit? Is the gift of the Holy Spirit, promised to me at the point of my conversion (Acts 2:38), evident in my life?

When I see the poor, the homeless, or the prisoner converted to Jesus or when I see thousands on the mission fields obeying the Great Commission, I can either be like the skeptical brethren in Jerusalem or I can be like Peter and look for the Spirit in their lives.

The story here has a good ending. Those who had questioned the conversion of Cornelius heard the story of Peter and realized that God had granted the non-Jews an opportunity for eternal life.

That's good news for us. It means that God has brought his salvation to you and me.

THOUGHTS TO PONDER

Where did the prejudice of the early church members against the non-Jews come from? What was the role of the six believers who went with Peter? What does the readiness of the church leaders to believe the conversion story tell you about them?

PRAYER

God, we pray that we will be as accepting of your people as the leaders of the church in Jerusalem were of the first non-Jew converts. Thank you for accepting us. Amen.

PRAYING HARD

ACTS 12:1–23

12During that same time King Herod began to mistreat some who belonged to the church. ²He ordered James, the brother of John, to be killed by the sword. ³Herod saw that some of the people liked this, so he decided to arrest Peter, too. (This happened during the time of the Feast of Unleavened Bread.)

⁴After Herod arrested Peter, he put him in jail and handed him over to be guarded by sixteen soldiers. Herod planned to bring Peter before the people for trial after the Passover Feast. ⁵So Peter was kept in jail, but the church prayed earnestly to God for him.

⁶The night before Herod was to bring him to trial, Peter was sleeping between two soldiers, bound with two chains. Other soldiers were guarding the door of the jail. ⁷Suddenly, an angel of the Lord stood there, and a light shined in the cell. The angel struck Peter on the side and woke him up. "Hurry! Get up!" the angel said. And the chains fell off Peter's hands. ⁸Then the angel told him, "Get dressed and put on your sandals." And Peter did. Then the angel said, "Put on your coat and follow me." ⁹So Peter followed him out, but he did not know if what the angel was doing was real; he thought he might be seeing a vision. ¹⁰They went past the first and second guards and came to the iron gate that separated them from the city. The gate opened by itself for them, and they went through it. When they had walked down one street, the angel suddenly left him.

¹¹Then Peter realized what had happened. He thought, "Now I know that the Lord really sent his angel to me. He rescued me from Herod and from all the things the people thought would happen."

¹²When he considered this, he went to the home of Mary, the mother of John Mark. Many people were gathered there, praying. ¹³Peter knocked on the outside door, and a servant girl named Rhoda came to answer it. ¹⁴When she recognized Peter's voice, she was so happy she forgot to open the door. Instead, she ran inside and told the group, "Peter is at the door!"

¹⁵They said to her, "You are crazy!" But she kept on saying it was true, so they said, "It must be Peter's angel."

¹⁶Peter continued to knock, and when they opened the door, they saw him and were amazed. ¹⁷Peter made a sign with his hand to tell them to be quiet. He explained how the Lord led him out of the jail, and he said, "Tell James and the other believers what happened." Then he left to go to another place.

¹⁸The next day the soldiers were very upset and wondered what had happened to Peter. ¹⁹Herod looked everywhere for him but could not find him. So he questioned the guards and ordered that they be killed.

Later Herod moved from Judea and went to the city of Caesarea, where he stayed. [20]Herod was very angry with the people of Tyre and Sidon, but the people of those cities all came in a group to him. After convincing Blastus, the king's personal servant, to be on their side, they asked Herod for peace, because their country got its food from his country.

[21]On a chosen day Herod put on his royal robes, sat on his throne, and made a speech to the people. [22]They shouted, "This is the voice of a god, not a human!" [23]Because Herod did not give the glory to God, an angel of the Lord immediately caused him to become sick, and he was eaten by worms and died.

DEVOTION

THERE'S A BIT OF HUMOR in this story and some insight into human nature as well. Rhoda was so excited by the appearance of Peter that she shut the door in his face. The believers gathered inside, no doubt fervently praying for the release of Peter, were unable to believe that their prayers had been heard. All the while, Peter stood outside, no doubt wondering if he'd come all this way only to be caught again by the guards who would soon realize he was missing.

Perhaps you've experienced the feeling: praying so hard for something to come true that you refuse to believe it when your prayers are actually answered. But God always hears our prayers. Sometimes the answer is yes, other times we have to wait for eternity to know why God was silent.

God had a plan for Peter just like he has a plan for you and me. Like Peter, we all have a role in the kingdom and he preserves our lives so we can fulfill those roles.

THOUGHTS TO PONDER

Why did God rescue Peter when Herod was allowed to kill James? Do you think God intervenes directly in the lives of his followers today? Do angels have the power today that they did when Peter was rescued from prison?

PRAYER

God, we pray that you will protect us as we seek to do your will. Amen.

SUFFERING WITH CHRIST

ACTS 14:8–28

[8]In Lystra there sat a man who had been born crippled; he had never walked. [9]As this man was listening to Paul speak, Paul looked straight at him and saw that he believed God could heal him. [10]So he cried out, "Stand up on your feet!" The man jumped up and began walking around. [11]When the crowds saw what Paul did, they shouted in the Lycaonian language, "The gods have become like humans and have come down to us!" [12]Then the people began to call Barnabas "Zeus" and Paul "Hermes," because he was the main speaker. [13]The priest in the temple of Zeus, which was near the city, brought some bulls and flowers to the city gates. He and the people wanted to offer a sacrifice to Paul and Barnabas. [14]But when the apostles, Barnabas and Paul, heard about it, they tore their clothes. They ran in among the people, shouting, [15]"Friends, why are you doing these things? We are only human beings like you. We are bringing you the Good News and are telling you to turn away from these worthless things and turn to the living God. He is the One who made the sky, the earth, the sea, and everything in them. [16]In the past, God let all the nations do what they wanted. [17]Yet he proved he is real by showing kindness, by giving you rain from heaven and crops at the right times, by giving you food and filling your hearts with joy." [18]Even with these words, they were barely able to keep the crowd from offering sacrifices to them.

[19]Then some evil people came from Antioch and Iconium and persuaded the people to turn against Paul. So they threw stones at him and dragged him out of town, thinking they had killed him. [20]But the followers gathered around him, and he got up and went back into the town. The next day he and Barnabas left and went to the city of Derbe.

[21]Paul and Barnabas told the Good News in Derbe, and many became followers. Paul and Barnabas returned to Lystra, Iconium, and Antioch, [22]making the followers of Jesus stronger and helping them stay in the faith. They said, "We must suffer many things to enter God's kingdom." [23]They chose elders for each church, by praying and fasting for a certain time. These elders had trusted the Lord, so Paul and Barnabas put them in the Lord's care.

[24]Then they went through Pisidia and came to Pamphylia. [25]When they had preached the message in Perga, they went down to Attalia. [26]And from there they sailed away to Antioch where the believers had put them into God's care and had sent them out to do this work. Now they had finished.

[27]When they arrived in Antioch, Paul and Barnabas gathered the church together. They told the church all about what God had done with them and how God had made it possible for those who were not Jewish to believe. [28]And they stayed there a long time with the followers.

DEVOTION

JUST HOW FICKLE the crowds could be is seen in how the people of Lystra treated Paul and Barnabas. One moment they were calling them gods and trying to offer sacrifices to them, and the next moment they were stoning Paul, dragging him out of town and leaving him for dead.

But notice what Paul did next. He picked himself up and went right back into the town where he had been stoned. And in the days to come, Paul and Barnabas would return to both Antioch and Iconium, the towns where the tormentors came from. Paul lived the words he preached: "We must suffer many things to enter God's kingdom."

There is never a guarantee that Christians are going to be popular. Jesus called his way the narrow road and said that not many would take it (Matthew 7:14). And because it is the road less taken, it is the road most misunderstood. It took only a few words from the evil men who had followed Paul to Lystra to turn the crowds from adoring to vengeful.

Persecution can come in all forms. Perhaps it's happened to you or someone you know. Losing a client who went somewhere a kickback was offered. Missing a promotion that went to someone who cheated on the numbers. The same world that can praise us one moment for our ethics can overlook us the next as being hopelessly outdated. To which Paul would say, "We must suffer many things to enter God's kingdom."

THOUGHTS TO PONDER

What will we be asked to endure in order to enter God's kingdom? How can we discern between the normal problems of life and discouragement that Satan might throw at us?

PRAYER

God, we pray that when the time to suffer comes, we will be found faithful. Amen.

INSIGNIFICANT
DISTINCTIONS

ACTS 15:1–11, 30–31; 16:1–5

15 Then some people came to Antioch from Judea and began teaching the non-Jewish believers: "You cannot be saved if you are not circumcised as Moses taught us." ²Paul and Barnabas were against this teaching and argued with them about it. So the church decided to send Paul, Barnabas, and some others to Jerusalem where they could talk more about this with the apostles and elders.

³The church helped them leave on the trip, and they went through the countries of Phoenicia and Samaria, telling all about how the other nations had turned to God. This made all the believers very happy. ⁴When they arrived in Jerusalem, they were welcomed by the apostles, the elders, and the church. Paul, Barnabas, and the others told about everything God had done with them. ⁵But some of the believers who belonged to the Pharisee group came forward and said, "The non-Jewish believers must be circumcised. They must be told to obey the law of Moses."

⁶The apostles and the elders gathered to consider this problem. ⁷After a long debate, Peter stood up and said to them, "Brothers, you know that in the early days God chose me from among you to preach the Good News to the nations. They heard the Good News from me, and they believed. ⁸God, who knows the thoughts of everyone, accepted them. He showed this to us by giving them the Holy Spirit, just as he did to us. ⁹To God, those people are not different from us. When they believed, he made their hearts pure. ¹⁰So now why are you testing God by putting a heavy load around the necks of the non-Jewish believers? It is a load that neither we nor our ancestors were able to carry. ¹¹But we believe that we and they too will be saved by the grace of the Lord Jesus."

Editor's note: The text of the letter of the Jerusalem elders is here.

³⁰So they left Jerusalem and went to Antioch where they gathered the church and gave them the letter. ³¹When they read it, they were very happy because of the encouraging message.

16 Paul came to Derbe and Lystra, where a follower named Timothy lived. Timothy's mother was Jewish and a believer, but his father was a Greek.

²The believers in Lystra and Iconium respected Timothy and said good things about him. ³Paul wanted Timothy to travel with him, but all the people living in that area knew that Timothy's father was Greek. So Paul circumcised Timothy to please his mother's people. ⁴Paul and those with him traveled from town to town and gave the decisions made by the apostles and elders in Jerusalem for the people to obey. ⁵So the churches became stronger in the faith and grew larger every day.

DEVOTION

ONE OF THE FIRST CRISES in the church came early on. What was to be done about the law of circumcision when non-Jews became believers? For that matter, what was to be done with all of the Law of Moses?

The first converts to Christianity had been Jews, beginning with those pricked in their hearts when they heard Peter accuse them of the death of Jesus during his Pentecost sermon (Acts 2). But God had made it clear through the vision he sent to Peter and through bestowing the gift of the Holy Spirit on Cornelius, the Roman centurion, that the Good News was for all nations.

Were these Greek non-Jewish converts to be accepted into the kingdom of God without first performing the ritual that every male who claimed to follow the one true God had performed for hundreds of years?

Peter's statement was profound: "To God, those people are not different from us." From that starting point, the leaders in the church were able to draft a letter outlining some ways for the Jewish Christians and Greek Christians to live in harmony, and Paul and Barnabas departed with the news that was met with enthusiasm on the receiving end.

Peter's statement is valid today. God sees everyone the same. Paul will go on to write that in Christ there is no Jew or Greek, slave or free—not even male or female (Galatians 3:28). All of the distinctions that seem to matter to the rest of the world mean nothing at the foot of the cross.

However, Paul knew he lived in a real world, and when he picked a new helper—the young man Timothy who was highly respected in his home region—he circumcised Timothy to please the Jews they would be working with.

THOUGHTS TO PONDER

How can you reconcile the decision of the elders in Jerusalem to not command circumcision for the Greek believers with Paul's decision to circumcise Timothy before taking him on as a helper? Do we impose standards of "orthodoxy" today on those who want to believe where God has put no standards? What might some be?

PRAYER

God, we know you see all of us in the same way. Help us to look at the less fortunate of the world through your eyes and not our own. Amen.

The Source of All Joy

ACTS 16:16–39

¹⁶Once, while we were going to the place for prayer, a servant girl met us. She had a special spirit in her, and she earned a lot of money for her owners by telling fortunes. ¹⁷This girl followed Paul and us, shouting, "These men are servants of the Most High God. They are telling you how you can be saved."

¹⁸She kept this up for many days. This bothered Paul, so he turned and said to the spirit, "By the power of Jesus Christ, I command you to come out of her!" Immediately, the spirit came out.

¹⁹When the owners of the servant girl saw this, they knew that now they could not use her to make money. So they grabbed Paul and Silas and dragged them before the city rulers in the marketplace. ²⁰They brought Paul and Silas to the Roman rulers and said, "These men are Jews and are making trouble in our city. ²¹They are teaching things that are not right for us as Romans to do."

²²The crowd joined the attack against them. The Roman officers tore the clothes of Paul and Silas and had them beaten with rods. ²³Then Paul and Silas were thrown into jail, and the jailer was ordered to guard them carefully. ²⁴When he heard this order, he put them far inside the jail and pinned their feet down between large blocks of wood.

²⁵About midnight Paul and Silas were praying and singing songs to God as the other prisoners listened. ²⁶Suddenly, there was a strong earthquake that shook the foundation of the jail. Then all the doors of the jail broke open, and all the prisoners were freed from their chains. ²⁷The jailer woke up and saw that the jail doors were open. Thinking that the prisoners had already escaped, he got his sword and was about to kill himself. ²⁸But Paul shouted, "Don't hurt yourself! We are all here."

²⁹The jailer told someone to bring a light. Then he ran inside and, shaking with fear, fell down before Paul and Silas. ³⁰He brought them outside and said, "Men, what must I do to be saved?"

³¹They said to him, "Believe in the Lord Jesus and you will be saved—you and all the people in your house." ³²So Paul and Silas told the message of the Lord to the jailer and all the people in his house. ³³At that hour of the night the jailer took Paul and Silas and washed their wounds. Then he and all his people were baptized immediately. ³⁴After this the jailer took Paul and Silas home and gave them food. He and his family were very happy because they now believed in God.

³⁵The next morning, the Roman officers sent the police to tell the jailer, "Let these men go free."

³⁶The jailer said to Paul, "The officers have sent an order to let you go free. You can leave now. Go in peace."

[37]But Paul said to the police, "They beat us in public without a trial, even though we are Roman citizens. And they threw us in jail. Now they want to make us go away quietly. No! Let them come themselves and bring us out."

[38]The police told the Roman officers what Paul said. When the officers heard that Paul and Silas were Roman citizens, they were afraid. [39]So they came and told Paul and Silas they were sorry and took them out of jail and asked them to leave the city.

DEVOTION

THIS IS THE FIRST TIME that Paul invoked his Roman citizenship and it struck fear in the Roman officers who knew that he hadn't been given due process before his beating and imprisonment. The owners of the slave girl had perjured themselves when they claimed that the men were speaking against Rome.

Keen readers of the text will notice that this is one of the "we" passages in Acts, meaning that when Paul decided to go preach in Macedonia, Luke, the physician who wrote this book (in addition to the Gospel of Luke), was a part of the entourage. That makes this story a firsthand account.

Even after being beaten and placed in stocks inside of the jail, Paul and Silas were praying and singing songs. Because of their witness, they were able to lead their jailer to God.

Joy in adversity. It's one of the hardest attitudes a Christian will ever be asked to witness to the world. Can we be treated unfairly and still praise God? Can we be in pain and still sing? If we can, others will notice, and like the Philippian jailer, some will come to know God who is the source of all joy.

THOUGHTS TO PONDER

Why did Paul not invoke his Roman citizenship before the beating? Why wouldn't he want to avoid the pain? Might God's plan for the jailer have been part of the reason?

PRAYER

God, we pray that when life is not fair that we will never lose faith. We pray that we will find a way in any situation to give praise to you. Amen.

THE UNKNOWN GOD

ACTS 17:16–34

¹⁶While Paul was waiting for Silas and Timothy in Athens, he was troubled because he saw that the city was full of idols. ¹⁷In the synagogue, he talked with the Jews and the Greeks who worshiped God. He also talked every day with people in the marketplace.

¹⁸Some of the Epicurean and Stoic philosophers argued with him, saying, "This man doesn't know what he is talking about. What is he trying to say?" Others said, "He seems to be telling us about some other gods," because Paul was telling them about Jesus and his rising from the dead. ¹⁹They got Paul and took him to a meeting of the Areopagus, where they said, "Please explain to us this new idea you have been teaching. ²⁰The things you are saying are new to us, and we want to know what this teaching means." ²¹(All the people of Athens and those from other countries who lived there always used their time to talk about the newest ideas.)

²²Then Paul stood before the meeting of the Areopagus and said, "People of Athens, I can see you are very religious in all things. ²³As I was going through your city, I saw the objects you worship. I found an altar that had these words written on it: TO A GOD WHO IS NOT KNOWN. You worship a god that you don't know, and this is the God I am telling you about! ²⁴The God who made the whole world and everything in it is the Lord of the land and the sky. He does not live in temples built by human hands. ²⁵This God is the One who gives life, breath, and everything else to people. He does not need any help from them; he has everything he needs. ²⁶God began by making one person, and from him came all the different people who live everywhere in the world. God decided exactly when and where they must live. ²⁷God wanted them to look for him and perhaps search all around for him and find him, though he is not far from any of us: ²⁸'By his power we live and move and exist.' Some of your own poets have said: 'For we are his children.' ²⁹Since we are God's children, you must not think that God is like something that people imagine or make from gold, silver, or rock. ³⁰In the past, people did not understand God, and he ignored this. But now, God tells all people in the world to change their hearts and lives. ³¹God has set a day that he will judge all the world with fairness, by the man he chose long ago. And God has proved this to everyone by raising that man from the dead!"

³²When the people heard about Jesus being raised from the dead, some of them laughed. But others said, "We will hear more about this from you later." ³³So Paul went away from them. ³⁴But some of the people believed Paul and joined him. Among those who believed was Dionysius, a member of the Areopagus, a woman named Damaris, and some others.

DEVOTION

GREEK CULTURE was pervasive at the time of Paul. In fact, the writers of the New Testament wrote their works in *koine* or "common" Greek, as that language would be recognized throughout the known world.

Part of the Greek culture was an insatiable hunger for any new ideas. And while every boy whose parents could afford it was sent to school at the age of seven, adults were also engaged in a form of continuing education as well. The system was called the Areopagus and was a form of an adult education committee. Interested adults could also sit in on the classes in literature, philosophy, and politics that were the standard for boys over the age of sixteen. It was a crowd of eager learners, based on hundreds of years of tradition dating back to the ancient Greek philosophers.

Paul commended them for being religious, but soon became forceful with them. The God you seek, he said, is the God I serve. And while God had overlooked it in the past when people did not understand him, those days were over. God now stood ready to judge the world he had created. And even though the group scoffed at the idea of a bodily resurrection from the dead, in true Athenian style they said they would listen to Paul some more at a later time.

Do you know God? The Athenians worshiped many gods in the hopes of appeasing them all. Christians believe in one God. What have you done to get acquainted with him? Is he still "a god who is not known" to you?

THOUGHTS TO PONDER

Is tolerance of every idea a virtue or is it a sign of weakness? Do we sometimes follow "fads" in our Christian walk today, chasing the latest ideas like the Athenians? Do we still worship an unknown God?

PRAYER

God, we know that you give to us life and breath and everything else we need each day. Help us to draw closer to you so that others may know you through us. Amen.

Bad for Business

ACTS 19:23–41

²³And during that time, there was some serious trouble in Ephesus about the Way of Jesus. ²⁴A man named Demetrius, who worked with silver, made little silver models that looked like the temple of the goddess Artemis. Those who did this work made much money. ²⁵Demetrius had a meeting with them and some others who did the same kind of work. He told them, "Men, you know that we make a lot of money from our business. ²⁶But look at what this man Paul is doing. He has convinced and turned away many people in Ephesus and in almost all of Asia! He says the gods made by human hands are not real. ²⁷There is a danger that our business will lose its good name, but there is also another danger: People will begin to think that the temple of the great goddess Artemis is not important. Her greatness will be destroyed, and Artemis is the goddess that everyone in Asia and the whole world worships."

²⁸When the others heard this, they became very angry and shouted, "Artemis, the goddess of Ephesus, is great!" ²⁹The whole city became confused. The people grabbed Gaius and Aristarchus, who were from Macedonia and were traveling with Paul, and ran to the theater. ³⁰Paul wanted to go in and talk to the crowd, but the followers did not let him. ³¹Also, some leaders of Asia who were friends of Paul sent him a message, begging him not to go into the theater. ³²Some people were shouting one thing, and some were shouting another. The meeting was completely confused; most of them did not know why they had come together. ³³They put a man named Alexander in front of the people, and some of them told him what to do. Alexander waved his hand so he could explain things to the people. ³⁴But when they saw that Alexander was a Jew, they all shouted the same thing for two hours: "Great is Artemis of Ephesus!"

³⁵Then the city clerk made the crowd be quiet. He said, "People of Ephesus, everyone knows that Ephesus is the city that keeps the temple of the great goddess Artemis and her holy stone that fell from heaven. ³⁶Since no one can say this is not true, you should be quiet. Stop and think before you do anything. ³⁷You brought these men here, but they have not said anything evil against our goddess or stolen anything from her temple. ³⁸If Demetrius and those who work with him have a charge against anyone they should go to the courts and judges where they can argue with each other. ³⁹If there is something else you want to talk about, it can be decided at the regular town meeting of the people. ⁴⁰I say this because some people might see this trouble today and say that we are rioting. We could not explain this, because there is no real reason for this meeting." ⁴¹After the city clerk said these things, he told the people to go home.

DEVOTION

EPHESUS WAS A PEACEFUL PROVINCE of Rome, and as a non-threatening subject of the Roman Empire, it was governed by two local proconsuls who dispensed justice from a court in the center of the city. Keeping this peace was a major concern since other less stable provinces felt the heavy hand of Roman soldiers and governors in their midst.

So Demetrius was shrewd in making public trouble for Paul. The silversmith guild in Ephesus was known throughout the world, and some of the most popular trinkets were those associated with the temple of the goddess Artemis. Some were crude and obscene in keeping with the worship practices that went on inside the temple.

The guild was established to control the number of silversmiths in the city and to keep prices high. When Paul's teaching threatened their livelihood, the guild created a riot that lasted for hours. Only when the city clerk intervened did the people quiet down. He reminded them of the prohibition against rioting and sent them home.

The lustful nature of the people of Ephesus and their temple worship of Artemis was still on the mind of Paul years later when he wrote to the church now established in Ephesus. Knowing the culture that surrounded these new Christians, Paul wrote, "But there must be no sexual sin among you, or any kind of evil or greed. Those things are not right for God's holy people. Also, there must be no evil talk among you, and you must not speak foolishly or tell evil jokes. These things are not right for you. Instead, you should be giving thanks to God. You can be sure of this: No one will have a place in the kingdom of Christ and of God who sins sexually, or does evil things, or is greedy" (Ephesians 5:3–5).

THOUGHTS TO PONDER

Why did Paul speak in a way that was guaranteed to upset the Ephesians? Can you think of any instances today where the practices of Christianity are bad for someone's business?

PRAYER

Father, we pray that we will always be about your business and that we will never seek personal gain over seeking you. Amen.

CAREFULLY EXAMINE
THE TRUTH

ACTS 20:1–12

20 When the trouble stopped, Paul sent for the followers to come to him. After he encouraged them and then told them good-bye, he left and went to the country of Macedonia. ²He said many things to strengthen the followers in the different places on his way through Macedonia. Then he went to Greece, ³where he stayed for three months. He was ready to sail for Syria, but some evil people were planning something against him. So Paul decided to go back through Macedonia to Syria. ⁴The men who went with him were Sopater son of Pyrrhus, from the city of Berea; Aristarchus and Secundus, from the city of Thessalonica; Gaius, from Derbe; Timothy; and Tychicus and Trophimus, two men from Asia. ⁵These men went on ahead and waited for us at Troas. ⁶We sailed from Philippi after the Feast of Unleavened Bread. Five days later we met them in Troas, where we stayed for seven days.

⁷On the first day of the week, we all met together to break bread, and Paul spoke to the group. Because he was planning to leave the next day, he kept on talking until midnight. ⁸We were all together in a room upstairs, and there were many lamps in the room. ⁹A young man named Eutychus was sitting in the window. As Paul continued talking, Eutychus was falling into a deep sleep. Finally, he went sound asleep and fell to the ground from the third floor. When they picked him up, he was dead. ¹⁰Paul went down to Eutychus, knelt down, and put his arms around him. He said, "Don't worry. He is alive now." ¹¹Then Paul went upstairs again, broke bread, and ate. He spoke to them a long time, until it was early morning, and then he left. ¹²They took the young man home alive and were greatly comforted.

DEVOTION

LEAVING THE TURMOIL in Ephesus, Paul wished the believers well and headed to Macedonia, a destination that had been revealed to him in a vision. Perhaps because of yet another threat on his life, Paul's entourage began to grow with Jews and Greeks alike.

The events in Troas occurred either on a Saturday night or a Sunday night, depending on whether the Jewish or Asian reckoning of time is used. To the Jews, a day began at sundown. Therefore most Christian traditions believe that the three "days" that Jesus was in the tomb began Friday afternoon and ended Sunday morning. The preaching service above probably started after sundown on Saturday and continued late into the evening.

We also see that one of the main reasons for meeting on the first day was to "break bread," a term usually used to describe the Lord's Supper, instituted by Christ in the upper room shortly before his death (Luke 22:14–20).

As Paul described the Lord's Supper in his first Letter to the Corinthians, it was a symbolic meal that consisted of the bread and the wine (called the "cup") that Jesus offered his followers on that evening. Paul wrote: "On the night when the Lord Jesus was handed over to be killed, he took bread and gave thanks for it. Then he broke the bread and said, 'This is my body; it is for you. Do this to remember me.' In the same way, after they ate, Jesus took the cup. He said, 'This cup is the new agreement that is sealed with the blood of my death. When you drink this, do it to remember me.' Every time you eat this bread and drink this cup you are telling others about the Lord's death until he comes" (1 Corinthians 11:23–26).

We also see that preaching had become a part of the reason the believers met together. Perhaps Eutychus would argue that it was too large a part . . . he fell asleep during the sermon. I can certainly relate. The point is that these were believers who had already heard and responded to the Good News, but were now anxious to be taught even more. If the movement was to ever mature and grow, the believers would need to know more than the bare essentials, and Paul's teachings and letters became a big part of that process.

Interestingly, Paul did not ask to be believed blindly. In Acts 17:11, Luke comments on how the Christians in Berea not only listened to Paul, but studied the Scriptures for themselves to see if Paul's teachings were true.

I think if Paul were here today, he'd undoubtedly say, "Wake up!" and encourage us to discover these truths for ourselves.

THOUGHTS TO PONDER

Have you examined for yourself the beliefs of your church? Have you critically analyzed the faith you inherited from your parents? If you are a relatively new convert, have you continued to grow?

PRAYER

God, help us to be eager to hear your Word and to examine it closely so that we will be pleasing to you in our worship and in our lives. Amen.

UNDETERRED BY CONSEQUENCES

ACTS 20:13–17; 21:1–16

¹³We went on ahead of Paul and sailed for the city of Assos, where he wanted to join us on the ship. Paul planned it this way because he wanted to go to Assos by land. ¹⁴When he met us there, we took him aboard and went to Mitylene. ¹⁵We sailed from Mitylene and the next day came to a place near Kios. The following day we sailed to Samos, and the next day we reached Miletus. ¹⁶Paul had already decided not to stop at Ephesus, because he did not want to stay too long in Asia. He was hurrying to be in Jerusalem on the day of Pentecost, if that were possible.

¹⁷Now from Miletus Paul sent to Ephesus and called for the elders of the church.

Editor's note: Paul's address to the Ephesian elders is contained in Acts 20:18–38.

21 After we all said good-bye to them, we sailed straight to the island of Cos. The next day we reached Rhodes, and from there we went to Patara. ²There we found a ship going to Phoenicia, so we went aboard and sailed away. ³We sailed near the island of Cyprus, seeing it to the north, but we sailed on to Syria. We stopped at Tyre because the ship needed to unload its cargo there. ⁴We found some followers in Tyre and stayed with them for seven days. Through the Holy Spirit they warned Paul not to go to Jerusalem. ⁵When we finished our visit, we left and continued our trip. All the followers, even the women and children, came outside the city with us. After we all knelt on the beach and prayed, ⁶we said good-bye and got on the ship, and the followers went back home.

⁷We continued our trip from Tyre and arrived at Ptolemais, where we greeted the believers and stayed with them for a day. ⁸The next day we left Ptolemais and went to the city of Caesarea. There we went into the home of Philip the preacher, one of the seven helpers, and stayed with him. ⁹He had four unmarried daughters who had the gift of prophesying. ¹⁰After we had been there for some time, a prophet named Agabus arrived from Judea. ¹¹He came to us and borrowed Paul's belt and used it to tie his own hands and feet. He said, "The Holy Spirit says, 'This is how evil people in Jerusalem will tie up the man who wears this belt. Then they will give him to the older leaders.' "

¹²When we all heard this, we and the people there begged Paul not to go to Jerusalem. ¹³But he said, "Why are you crying and making me so sad? I am not only ready to be tied up in Jerusalem, I am ready to die for the Lord Jesus!"

¹⁴We could not persuade him to stay away from Jerusalem. So we stopped begging him and said, "We pray that what the Lord wants will be done."

[15]After this, we got ready and started on our way to Jerusalem. [16]Some of the followers from Caesarea went with us and took us to the home of Mnason, where we would stay. He was from Cyprus and was one of the first followers.

DEVOTION

BY THIS POINT, Paul was sensing the imminent conclusion of his ministry. He informed the Ephesian elders that he would never see them again (Acts 20:25). He told them that he feared what would happen to him in Jerusalem and that the same Holy Spirit that was instructing him to go to Jerusalem was telling him that trouble and even imprisonment awaited him there (Acts 20:23).

Then came the prophecy of Agabus. Any message from a prophet was to be taken seriously. But when a prophet combined a visual lesson with his oral utterances it was a sign that words alone couldn't convey how deeply the Spirit was instructing him to deliver the message. The prophesy of Agabus was like the message of the prophet Ahijah in 1 Kings 11 where he tore his new coat into twelve pieces to signify that the twelve tribes of Israel will soon be torn apart into two nations. Agabus, in the most visual way possible, reinforced what Paul already knew—in a short while he would no longer be free.

Have you ever had a bittersweet feeling that you were doing the right thing, but knew it was going to come at a great personal cost? Have you been frank with a friend, knowing it could cost the friendship? Admitted a mistake, knowing there would be a penalty? Done what was right, knowing others would take a shortcut and be rewarded for it? Then you know to a small degree how Paul must have felt. He headed toward Jerusalem and the final chapter of his ministry, undeterred by the consequences.

THOUGHTS TO PONDER

Why were Paul's companions so insistent that Paul avoid going to Jerusalem? How was Paul's view of life different from their view? What does that tell us about our lives?

PRAYER

God, we pray that when we face adversity we will never shrink back, but that we will follow your will no matter what the consequences. Amen.

GIVING UP FREEDOM

ACTS 21:27–40; 22:22–29

Editor's note: In the preceding verses, Paul took four men into the Temple for a seven-day Jewish purification rite.

[27]When the seven days were almost over, some of his people from Asia saw Paul at the Temple. They caused all the people to be upset and grabbed Paul. [28]They shouted, "People of Israel, help us! This is the man who goes everywhere teaching against the law of Moses, against our people, and against this Temple. Now he has brought some Greeks into the Temple and has made this holy place unclean!" [29](They said this because they had seen Trophimus, a man from Ephesus, with Paul in Jerusalem. They thought that Paul had brought him into the Temple.)

[30]All the people in Jerusalem became upset. Together they ran, took Paul, and dragged him out of the Temple. The Temple doors were closed immediately. [31]While they were trying to kill Paul, the commander of the Roman army in Jerusalem learned that there was trouble in the whole city. [32]Immediately he took some officers and soldiers and ran to the place where the crowd was gathered. When the people saw them, they stopped beating Paul. [33]The commander went to Paul and arrested him. He told his soldiers to tie Paul with two chains. Then he asked who he was and what he had done wrong. [34]Some in the crowd were yelling one thing, and some were yelling another. Because of all this confusion and shouting, the commander could not learn what had happened. So he ordered the soldiers to take Paul to the army building. [35]When Paul came to the steps, the soldiers had to carry him because the people were ready to hurt him. [36]The whole mob was following them, shouting, "Kill him!"

[37]As the soldiers were about to take Paul into the army building, he spoke to the commander, "May I say something to you?"

The commander said, "Do you speak Greek? [38]I thought you were the Egyptian who started some trouble against the government not long ago and led four thousand killers out to the desert."

[39]Paul said, "No, I am a Jew from Tarsus in the country of Cilicia. I am a citizen of that important city. Please, let me speak to the people."

[40]The commander gave permission, so Paul stood on the steps and waved his hand to quiet the people. When there was silence, he spoke to them in the Hebrew language.

Editor's note: The crowd listened to Paul's account of his conversion until he talked about taking the Good News to the nations.

[22]The crowd listened to Paul until he said this. Then they began shouting, "Get rid of him! He doesn't deserve to live!" [23]They shouted, threw off their coats, and threw dust into the air.

²⁴Then the commander ordered the soldiers to take Paul into the army building and beat him. He wanted to make Paul tell why the people were shouting against him like this. ²⁵But as the soldiers were tying him up, preparing to beat him, Paul said to an officer nearby, "Do you have the right to beat a Roman citizen who has not been proven guilty?"

²⁶When the officer heard this, he went to the commander and reported it. The officer said, "Do you know what you are doing? This man is a Roman citizen."

²⁷The commander came to Paul and said, "Tell me, are you really a Roman citizen?"

He answered, "Yes."

²⁸The commander said, "I paid a lot of money to become a Roman citizen." But Paul said, "I was born a citizen."

²⁹The men who were preparing to question Paul moved away from him immediately. The commander was frightened because he had already tied Paul, and Paul was a Roman citizen.

DEVOTION

MUCH HAS BEEN WRITTEN about whether Paul belonged in the Temple helping these men fulfill their Nazirite vows, a purification ritual that lasted up to thirty days. But Paul's behavior is consistent with his attempts to be respectful to Jewish customs while at the same time promoting the Good News. As Paul would tell the Corinthians, "To the Jews I became like a Jew to win the Jews" (1 Corinthians 9:20). Paul was obeying a request of James by taking the men to the Temple. And it was at this time that he was falsely accused of admitting a non-Jew into the Temple.

Paul had seen freedom for the last time. He was in the custody of Rome for the rest of his days. And although the Roman judges found no merit to the claims of the Jews, his insistence on his full rights as a Roman citizen eventually propelled Paul to Rome where he wrote letters to believers and lived out the rest of his days awaiting his appointment with Caesar.

THOUGHTS TO PONDER

Why would Paul agree to be part of a ritual that he knew was not essential for salvation? Did his vision of being imprisoned in Jerusalem play a part in his decision to go to the Temple?

PRAYER

Father, we know you have made us citizens of your kingdom, and because of that, no earthly harm is to be feared. May we bravely face the future as citizens of an eternal kingdom. Amen.

The Right Man for the Job

ACTS 23:12–35

¹²In the morning some evil people made a plan to kill Paul, and they took an oath not to eat or drink anything until they had killed him. ¹³There were more than forty men who made this plan. ¹⁴They went to the leading priests and the elders and said, "We have taken an oath not to eat or drink until we have killed Paul. ¹⁵So this is what we want you to do: Send a message to the commander to bring Paul out to you as though you want to ask him more questions. We will be waiting to kill him while he is on the way here."

¹⁶But Paul's nephew heard about this plan and went to the army building and told Paul. ¹⁷Then Paul called one of the officers and said, "Take this young man to the commander. He has a message for him."

¹⁸So the officer brought Paul's nephew to the commander and said, "The prisoner, Paul, asked me to bring this young man to you. He wants to tell you something."

¹⁹The commander took the young man's hand and led him to a place where they could be alone. He asked, "What do you want to tell me?"

²⁰The young man said, "The Jews have decided to ask you to bring Paul down to their council meeting tomorrow. They want you to think they are going to ask him more questions. ²¹But don't believe them! More than forty men are hiding and waiting to kill Paul. They have all taken an oath not to eat or drink until they have killed him. Now they are waiting for you to agree."

²²The commander sent the young man away, ordering him, "Don't tell anyone that you have told me about their plan."

²³Then the commander called two officers and said, "I need some men to go to Caesarea. Get two hundred soldiers, seventy horsemen, and two hundred men with spears ready to leave at nine o'clock tonight. ²⁴Get some horses for Paul to ride so he can be taken to Governor Felix safely." ²⁵And he wrote a letter that said:

²⁶From Claudius Lysias.

To the Most Excellent Governor Felix:

Greetings.

²⁷Some of the Jews had taken this man and planned to kill him. But I learned that he is a Roman citizen, so I went with my soldiers and saved him. ²⁸I wanted to know why they were accusing him, so I brought him before their council meeting. ²⁹I learned that these people said Paul did some things that were wrong by their own laws, but no charge was worthy of jail or death. ³⁰When I was told that some of them

were planning to kill Paul, I sent him to you at once. I also told them
to tell you what they have against him.

[31]So the soldiers did what they were told and took Paul and brought him to
the city of Antipatris that night. [32]The next day the horsemen went with Paul to
Caesarea, but the other soldiers went back to the army building in Jerusalem.
[33]When the horsemen came to Caesarea and gave the letter to the governor, they
turned Paul over to him. [34]The governor read the letter and asked Paul, "What
area are you from?" When he learned that Paul was from Cilicia, [35]he said, "I will
hear your case when those who are against you come here, too."

DEVOTION

WHEN YOU LOOK at all the credentials of Paul, you can tell why he was handpicked by God to be the chief evangelist of the early church. When it came to arguing with Jews about the law, Paul had sat at the feet of the great Gamaliel and
learned the law inside and out. When he rose to speak, he could start at any point
in the Scriptures and lead the audience to the predictions of the Messiah, whom
he knew to be the man Jesus.

But perhaps Paul's Roman citizenship was just as important. On more than
one occasion (including this one), that fact alone saved his life, allowing him to
reach his ultimate goal of taking the Good News to Rome. In addition, he spoke
Greek, the universal language of the day, and that allowed him to communicate
wherever the Holy Spirit led him.

But the intangibles of Paul's character were what made him so valuable. He
was resilient, never letting the momentary circumstances get him down. He was
flexible, willing to change plans due to circumstances or the commands of God.
And finally, he was obedient, always willing to submit his own desires to God's will.

When God picks a person for his work, he empowers them with the characteristics and abilities to get the job done.

THOUGHTS TO PONDER

What has God equipped you to do? What skills do you have that are
best explained as God-given abilities for accomplishing his purposes?

PRAYER

God, we pray that we will find our abilities and use them for building your kingdom in this world. Amen.

No Time for the Truth

ACTS 24:1-16, 22-25

24 Five days later Ananias, the high priest, went to the city of Caesarea with some of the elders and a lawyer named Tertullus. They had come to make charges against Paul before the governor. ²Paul was called into the meeting, and Tertullus began to accuse him, saying, "Most Excellent Felix! Our people enjoy much peace because of you, and many wrong things in our country are being made right through your wise help. ³We accept these things always and in every place, and we are thankful for them. ⁴But not wanting to take any more of your time, I beg you to be kind and listen to our few words. ⁵We have found this man to be a troublemaker, stirring up his people everywhere in the world. He is a leader of the Nazarene group. ⁶Also, he was trying to make the Temple unclean, but we stopped him. [And we wanted to judge him by our own law. ⁷But the officer Lysias came and used much force to take him from us. ⁸And Lysias commanded those who wanted to accuse Paul to come to you.] By asking him questions yourself, you can decide if all these things are true." ⁹The others agreed and said that all of this was true.

¹⁰When the governor made a sign for Paul to speak, Paul said, "Governor Felix, I know you have been a judge over this nation for a long time. So I am happy to defend myself before you. ¹¹You can learn for yourself that I went to worship in Jerusalem only twelve days ago. ¹²Those who are accusing me did not find me arguing with anyone in the Temple or stirring up the people in the synagogues or in the city. ¹³They cannot prove the things they are saying against me now. ¹⁴But I will tell you this: I worship the God of our ancestors as a follower of the Way of Jesus. The others say that the Way of Jesus is not the right way. But I believe everything that is taught in the law of Moses and that is written in the books of the Prophets. ¹⁵I have the same hope in God that they have—the hope that all people, good and bad, will surely be raised from the dead. ¹⁶This is why I always try to do what I believe is right before God and people.

²²Felix already understood much about the Way of Jesus. He stopped the trial and said, "When commander Lysias comes here, I will decide your case." ²³Felix told the officer to keep Paul guarded but to give him some freedom and to let his friends bring what he needed.

²⁴After some days Felix came with his wife, Drusilla, who was Jewish, and asked for Paul to be brought to him. He listened to Paul talk about believing in Christ Jesus. ²⁵But Felix became afraid when Paul spoke about living right, self-control, and the time when God will judge the world. He said, "Go away now. When I have more time, I will call for you."

DEVOTION

FOLLOWING THE UNREST in Jerusalem caused by the Jews, Paul invoked his Roman citizenship moments before he was to receive a beating from soldiers who wanted to know why his words had stirred up the people. The soldiers quickly prepared him for a trip to Caesarea to be questioned by the governor. In the meantime, Paul saw a vision telling him that his appeal would eventually take him to Rome, so he went into this hearing knowing that his fate would ultimately be decided by Caesar.

The story of Felix is one of the saddest in the New Testament. Luke tells us that Felix already understood much about Christianity, and as the husband of a Jewess, he undoubtedly had heard about the great works of God. In this passage he seemed to be curious to hear more about the Way of Jesus.

But after listening, he decided that the price was too high. When Paul began to talk about the Christian lifestyle—righteous living and self-control—he became afraid. "When I have more time, I will call for you."

How many people have uttered those words, thought those words and, sadly, lived out those words? "I'll get back to you later, Jesus," they say.

I'm starting my career; come back later Jesus.

I've just been married; can you please call on me again?

I've got children to raise; perhaps I will have more time later.

I've got pressing health issues; can I get back with you?

The excuses can last a lifetime. And sooner or later, time runs out. We've kept Jesus waiting for a lifetime, and now we face the judgment.

Felix had every opportunity to believe, but didn't. Does he sound like anyone close to you?

THOUGHTS TO PONDER

Why would Felix not believe in Jesus? What are some of the reasons people give today for not believing in Jesus?

PRAYER

Father, we have heard your message and believed. Help us to reach those who have not yet believed. Amen.

EVERY CIRCUMSTANCE IS USEFUL

ACTS 24:27—25:12

²⁷But after two years, Felix was replaced by Porcius Festus as governor. But Felix had left Paul in prison to please the Jews.

25 Three days after Festus became governor, he went from Caesarea to Jerusalem. ²There the leading priests and the important leaders made charges against Paul before Festus. ³They asked Festus to do them a favor. They wanted him to send Paul back to Jerusalem, because they had a plan to kill him on the way. ⁴But Festus answered that Paul would be kept in Caesarea and that he himself was returning there soon. ⁵He said, "Some of your leaders should go with me. They can accuse the man there in Caesarea, if he has really done something wrong."

⁶Festus stayed in Jerusalem another eight or ten days and then went back to Caesarea. The next day he told the soldiers to bring Paul before him. Festus was seated on the judge's seat ⁷when Paul came into the room. The people who had come from Jerusalem stood around him, making serious charges against him, which they could not prove. ⁸This is what Paul said to defend himself: "I have done nothing wrong against the law, against the Temple, or against Caesar."

⁹But Festus wanted to please the people. So he asked Paul, "Do you want to go to Jerusalem for me to judge you there on these charges?"

¹⁰Paul said, "I am standing at Caesar's judgment seat now, where I should be judged. I have done nothing wrong to them; you know this is true. ¹¹If I have done something wrong and the law says I must die, I do not ask to be saved from death. But if these charges are not true, then no one can give me to them. I want Caesar to hear my case!"

¹²Festus talked about this with his advisers. Then he said, "You have asked to see Caesar, so you will go to Caesar!"

DEVOTION

THERE ARE CERTAIN parallels between the way Paul was treated in Caesarea and the way Jesus was treated in Jerusalem just before he was crucified. As you may recall, Jesus was passed between Pilate and Herod and back again before Pilate finally washed his hands of the matter and allowed Jesus to be crucified. Throughout the night, neither Pilate nor Herod can see any merit in the charges, but neither had the fortitude to stand up against the will of the people who had been whipped into a frenzied state by the leading priests and teachers of the law whose authority was threatened by the teachings of Jesus.

Paul had already been before Felix, the Roman-appointed governor of the region, regarding charges that he had defiled the Temple in Jerusalem. Felix had been interested in the case, and even somewhat interested in the movement Paul represented. But when Paul failed to produce a bribe to Felix, he had been left in jail for two years.

Felix was replaced by Festus, who began his tenure with a tour of the region. Jerusalem was an important but potentially troublesome part of his domain because of this strange sect known as the Jews whose heritage allegedly went back hundreds of years and whose people claimed they worshiped the one and only true God. The people would remain peaceful only if they were allowed to live their lives according to their religious traditions, and Festus, like any other Roman official, wanted only peace within his region.

So three days after his appointment, Festus spent several days in Jerusalem. There he learned of this prisoner, Paul, and he determined that he would hear this man when he returned to Caesarea.

There's another parallel between the treatment of Jesus and the treatment of Paul. Just as the fate of Jesus was in the hands of petty officials who wanted to please the people while at the same time pleasing their Roman bosses, the fate of Paul was now in the hands of a man who wanted to please the Jews (verse 9) and preserve his standing with Rome (verse 12). God used the weakness of Festus and his inability to make a decision, even though there is no merit to the charges, to get Paul to Rome and to take his message all the way to Caesar.

Just as Paul's invocation of his Roman citizenship had stopped a potential beating in Jerusalem and earned him safety in Caesarea, his appeal to Caesar ended any judgment that Festus could render and propelled him on to Rome. God's purposes are always at work and his timing is perfect, even if the process seems slow to us.

THOUGHTS TO PONDER

Why do you think the Jews were still angry at Paul after two years? What do we learn about Paul from the way he handles his appearances with Felix and Festus? Why was he determined to receive a trial?

PRAYER

God, we know that things work in your time. And we know that you use all circumstances for your good purposes. Help us to see in our circumstances the possibilities for carrying out your will. Amen.

ALWAYS READY

ACTS 25:13—26:8

¹³A few days later King Agrippa and Bernice came to Caesarea to visit Festus. ¹⁴They stayed there for some time, and Festus told the king about Paul's case. Festus said, "There is a man that Felix left in prison. ¹⁵When I went to Jerusalem, the leading priests and the elders there made charges against him, asking me to sentence him to death. ¹⁶But I answered, 'When a man is accused of a crime, Romans do not hand him over until he has been allowed to face his accusers and defend himself against their charges.' ¹⁷So when these people came here to Caesarea for the trial, I did not waste time. The next day I sat on the judge's seat and commanded that the man be brought in. ¹⁸They stood up and accused him, but not of any serious crime as I thought they would. ¹⁹The things they said were about their own religion and about a man named Jesus who died. But Paul said that he is still alive. ²⁰Not knowing how to find out about these questions, I asked Paul, 'Do you want to go to Jerusalem and be judged there?' ²¹But he asked to be kept in Caesarea. He wants a decision from the emperor. So I ordered that he be held until I could send him to Caesar."

²²Agrippa said to Festus, "I would also like to hear this man myself."

Festus said, "Tomorrow you will hear him."

²³The next day Agrippa and Bernice appeared with great show, acting like very important people. They went into the judgment room with the army leaders and the important men of Caesarea. Then Festus ordered the soldiers to bring Paul in. ²⁴Festus said, "King Agrippa and all who are gathered here with us, you see this man. All the people, here and in Jerusalem, have complained to me about him, shouting that he should not live any longer. ²⁵When I judged him, I found no reason to order his death. But since he asked to be judged by Caesar, I decided to send him. ²⁶But I have nothing definite to write the emperor about him. So I have brought him before all of you—especially you, King Agrippa. I hope you can question him and give me something to write. ²⁷I think it is foolish to send a prisoner to Caesar without telling what charges are against him."

26 Agrippa said to Paul, "You may now speak to defend yourself."

Then Paul raised his hand and began to speak. ²He said, "King Agrippa, I am very blessed to stand before you and will answer all the charges the evil people make against me. ³You know so much about all the customs and the things they argue about, so please listen to me patiently.

⁴"All my people know about my whole life, how I lived from the beginning in my own country and later in Jerusalem. ⁵They have known me for a long time. If they want to, they can tell you that I was a good Pharisee. And the Pharisees

obey the laws of my tradition more carefully than any other group. [6]Now I am on trial because I hope for the promise that God made to our ancestors. [7]This is the promise that the twelve tribes of our people hope to receive as they serve God day and night. My king, they have accused me because I hope for this same promise! [8]Why do any of you people think it is impossible for God to raise people from the dead?

DEVOTION

KING AGRIPPA II was the son of Herod Agrippa I, who is mentioned in Acts 12, the man who put James to death and imprisoned Peter. There is an interesting story about his death at the end of that chapter—his manner of death seemed to be symbolic of his bloated ego. Agrippa II was also the great-grandson of Herod the Great, who executed all the baby boys in Bethlehem in at attempt to kill the baby Jesus (Matthew 2:16–18). Also with Agrippa II was Bernice, who was actually his sister and acting wife; she would later have an illustrious career as the mistress of two emperors—Titus and Vespasian.

Both Herod the Great and Herod Agrippa I had been named vassal kings under Roman rule. This granted each of them the title "king of the Jews." Herod Agrippa II did not have the same relationship with Rome as his father, so during his time as Tetrarch of the northern territories, two procurators, Felix and Festus, ruled the remainder of the country for Rome. His sister, Drusilla, was the wife of Felix.

These were the personalities who would hear Paul's defense against the false charges of the Jews. Their main concern was not justice, but rather the appeasement of the Jews whose favor they needed in order to keep their status with Rome as leaders of a peaceful province.

THOUGHTS TO PONDER

Why would Paul bother speaking on this occasion when he had already appealed to be heard by Caesar? What could he hope to accomplish?

PRAYER

Father, help us to be ready with an answer at any point we are called on to defend our faith. Thank you for the examples of faith you have given us such as Paul. Amen.

Stop Resisting

ACTS 26:9-32

⁹"I, too, thought I ought to do many things against Jesus from Nazareth. ¹⁰And that is what I did in Jerusalem. The leading priests gave me the power to put many of God's people in jail, and when they were being killed, I agreed it was a good thing. ¹¹In every synagogue, I often punished them and tried to make them speak against Jesus. I was so angry against them I even went to other cities to find them and punish them.

¹²"One time the leading priests gave me permission and the power to go to Damascus. ¹³On the way there, at noon, I saw a light from heaven. It was brighter than the sun and flashed all around me and those who were traveling with me. ¹⁴We all fell to the ground. Then I heard a voice speaking to me in the Hebrew language, saying, 'Saul, Saul, why are you persecuting me? You are only hurting yourself by fighting me.' ¹⁵I said, 'Who are you, Lord?' The Lord said, 'I am Jesus, the one you are persecuting. ¹⁶Stand up! I have chosen you to be my servant and my witness—you will tell people the things that you have seen and the things that I will show you. This is why I have come to you today. ¹⁷I will keep you safe from your own people and also from the others. I am sending you to them ¹⁸to open their eyes so that they may turn away from darkness to the light, away from the power of Satan and to God. Then their sins can be forgiven, and they can have a place with those people who have been made holy by believing in me.'

¹⁹"King Agrippa, after I had this vision from heaven, I obeyed it. ²⁰I began telling people that they should change their hearts and lives and turn to God and do things to show they really had changed. I told this first to those in Damascus, then in Jerusalem, and in every part of Judea, and also to the other people. ²¹This is why the Jews took me and were trying to kill me in the Temple. ²²But God has helped me, and so I stand here today, telling all people, small and great, what I have seen. But I am saying only what Moses and the prophets said would happen— ²³that the Christ would die, and as the first to rise from the dead, he would bring light to all people."

²⁴While Paul was saying these things to defend himself, Festus said loudly, "Paul, you are out of your mind! Too much study has driven you crazy!"

²⁵Paul said, "Most excellent Festus, I am not crazy. My words are true and sensible. ²⁶King Agrippa knows about these things, and I can speak freely to him. I know he has heard about all of these things, because they did not happen off in a corner. ²⁷King Agrippa, do you believe what the prophets wrote? I know you believe."

²⁸King Agrippa said to Paul, "Do you think you can persuade me to become a Christian in such a short time?"

²⁹Paul said, "Whether it is a short or a long time, I pray to God that not only you but every person listening to me today would be saved and be like me—except for these chains I have."

³⁰Then King Agrippa, Governor Festus, Bernice, and all the people sitting with them stood up ³¹and left the room. Talking to each other, they said, "There is no reason why this man should die or be put in jail." ³²And Agrippa said to Festus, "We could let this man go free, but he has asked Caesar to hear his case."

DEVOTION

THERE'S AN INTERESTING COMMENT by God in the revelation to Saul above. When Saul was told that he was only hurting himself by fighting God, he used a term taken from the training of oxen. As oxen are being trained to not kick out of the yoke, the yeoman will attach a board studded with spikes to the front of the wagon so that the stubborn ox will only hurt himself if he continues to kick and flail. It was called "kicking against the pricks," a literal phrase which is retained in some other translations of Scripture.

It's not that uncommon to see people today "kicking against the pricks." They overeat, overwork, or get into bad relationships. They battle addictions. They try everything possible except submitting their will to God's will.

Saul (later called Paul) saw the light, literally, and went on to become a valuable messenger for the Good News of Christ, whose followers he once persecuted. The good news for us today is that we serve a God who gives second chances, and who waits patiently for us to stop resisting his offers.

THOUGHTS TO PONDER

How does God get our attention today? Why is it that people who are "kicking against the pricks" rarely realize it until something bad happens?

PRAYER

God, we pray that we will follow your will and not be guilty of struggling against it. Amen.

STORMS OF LIFE

ACTS 27:1, 4–26

27 It was decided that we would sail for Italy. An officer named Julius, who served in the emperor's army, guarded Paul and some other prisoners.

⁴We left Sidon and sailed close to the island of Cyprus, because the wind was blowing against us. ⁵We went across the sea by Cilicia and Pamphylia and landed at the city of Myra, in Lycia. ⁶There the officer found a ship from Alexandria that was going to Italy, so he put us on it.

⁷We sailed slowly for many days. We had a hard time reaching Cnidus because the wind was blowing against us, and we could not go any farther. So we sailed by the south side of the island of Crete near Salmone. ⁸Sailing past it was hard. Then we came to a place called Fair Havens, near the city of Lasea.

⁹We had lost much time, and it was now dangerous to sail, because it was already after the Day of Cleansing. So Paul warned them, ¹⁰"Men, I can see there will be a lot of trouble on this trip. The ship, the cargo, and even our lives may be lost." ¹¹But the captain and the owner of the ship did not agree with Paul, and the officer believed what the captain and owner of the ship said. ¹²Since that harbor was not a good place for the ship to stay for the winter, most of the men decided that the ship should leave. They hoped we could go to Phoenix and stay there for the winter. Phoenix, a city on the island of Crete, had a harbor which faced southwest and northwest.

¹³When a good wind began to blow from the south, the men on the ship thought, "This is the wind we wanted, and now we have it." So they pulled up the anchor, and we sailed very close to the island of Crete. ¹⁴But then a very strong wind named the "northeaster" came from the island. ¹⁵The ship was caught in it and could not sail against it. So we stopped trying and let the wind carry us. ¹⁶When we went below a small island named Cauda, we were barely able to bring in the lifeboat. ¹⁷After the men took the lifeboat in, they tied ropes around the ship to hold it together. The men were afraid that the ship would hit the sandbanks of Syrtis, so they lowered the sail and let the wind carry the ship. ¹⁸The next day the storm was blowing us so hard that the men threw out some of the cargo. ¹⁹A day later with their own hands they threw out the ship's equipment. ²⁰When we could not see the sun or the stars for many days, and the storm was very bad, we lost all hope of being saved.

²¹After the men had gone without food for a long time, Paul stood up before them and said, "Men, you should have listened to me. You should not have sailed from Crete. Then you would not have all this trouble and loss. ²²But now I tell you to cheer up because none of you will die. Only the ship will be lost. ²³Last

night an angel came to me from the God I belong to and worship. [24]The angel said, 'Paul, do not be afraid. You must stand before Caesar. And God has promised you that he will save the lives of everyone sailing with you.' [25]So men, have courage. I trust in God that everything will happen as his angel told me. [26]But we will crash on an island."

DEVOTION

HAVE YOU EVER FELT like these sailors? Have you ever felt blown around by the winds of life—forces stronger than you are and forces out of your control? How hopeless they must have felt. They were at the mercy of the captain and ship owner and at the mercy of the winds, which looked favorable one moment and unfavorable the next.

But Paul reminded them that this was no ordinary voyage. The real captain of this voyage was God. And though the earthly captain was making ill-advised choices, God was ultimately in control. Paul knew that on two levels. First, he knew that he served a God who had already demonstrated through Jesus that he controlled the winds and the waves. Second, his faith had been reinforced by the appearance of an angel who told Paul that he would ultimately reach Rome with no loss of life on the ship.

I battle the storms of life daily. And while I have never received an angelic vision, I get the assurances of God through his Word that there is a safe harbor that awaits me in heaven. And meeting me at the harbor will be his Son, who conquered death once and for all.

THOUGHTS TO PONDER

How can we ignore the fickle winds of life and fix our eyes on the safe harbor? Why does this seem so hard?

PRAYER

Father, we know that you control our paths and we pray that we will seek your path and stay on it. Amen.

WORKING WITHIN GOD'S PROVIDENCE

ACTS 27:27–44

²⁷On the fourteenth night we were still being carried around in the Adriatic Sea. About midnight the sailors thought we were close to land, ²⁸so they lowered a rope with a weight on the end of it into the water. They found that the water was one hundred twenty feet deep. They went a little farther and lowered the rope again. It was ninety feet deep. ²⁹The sailors were afraid that we would hit the rocks, so they threw four anchors into the water and prayed for daylight to come. ³⁰Some of the sailors wanted to leave the ship, and they lowered the lifeboat, pretending they were throwing more anchors from the front of the ship. ³¹But Paul told the officer and the other soldiers, "If these men do not stay in the ship, your lives cannot be saved." ³²So the soldiers cut the ropes and let the lifeboat fall into the water.

³³Just before dawn Paul began persuading all the people to eat something. He said, "For the past fourteen days you have been waiting and watching and not eating. ³⁴Now I beg you to eat something. You need it to stay alive. None of you will lose even one hair off your heads." ³⁵After he said this, Paul took some bread and thanked God for it before all of them. He broke off a piece and began eating. ³⁶They all felt better and started eating, too. ³⁷There were two hundred seventy-six people on the ship. ³⁸When they had eaten all they wanted, they began making the ship lighter by throwing the grain into the sea.

³⁹When daylight came, the sailors saw land. They did not know what land it was, but they saw a bay with a beach and wanted to sail the ship to the beach if they could. ⁴⁰So they cut the ropes to the anchors and left the anchors in the sea. At the same time, they untied the ropes that were holding the rudders. Then they raised the front sail into the wind and sailed toward the beach. ⁴¹But the ship hit a sandbank. The front of the ship stuck there and could not move, but the back of the ship began to break up from the big waves.

⁴²The soldiers decided to kill the prisoners so none of them could swim away and escape. ⁴³But Julius, the officer, wanted to let Paul live and did not allow the soldiers to kill the prisoners. Instead he ordered everyone who could swim to jump into the water first and swim to land. ⁴⁴The rest were to follow using wooden boards or pieces of the ship. And this is how all the people made it safely to land.

DEVOTION

IMAGINE FOURTEEN DAYS without food. Imagine fourteen days of being rocked about aimlessly by the ocean's waves. Add to that the cutting loose of the lifeboats and the throwing of the food into the sea, and you can see the desperate situation that the 276 passengers on the boat faced.

The ship that Paul had been placed on was an Alexandrian grain ship bound for Rome. Grain ships were among the largest seagoing vessels, measuring two hundred feet long with a displacement of twelve hundred tons. The process of emptying the cargo into the sea would have been an arduous one, probably requiring all night.

Only because the officers listened to Paul were they saved. He alone had the assurances of the angel. He alone knew what God expected of them in order that they might be saved from drowning.

One of the themes throughout the Book of Acts is the individual's role in the providence of God. As the book begins, Jesus is ascending into the heavens, leaving the Good News in the hands of the apostles with the instruction of carrying the message to the world. Gradually, the apostles learned the full will of God. They learned that the Good News is for the non-Jews as well as the Jews. They discovered that Paul, a former persecutor of Christians, would be the chief mouthpiece for the new movement. And finally they found out that obedience to the old ways of Judaism were not to be demanded of the new non-Jewish converts. Over time, and with much prayer, the converted learned the will of God.

Paul had seen the providence of God repeatedly during his time as a Christian and now he was determined to follow his instructions to the letter in order to save all on the ship.

There's a lesson in this for us today. We must cast off all the baggage of life that keeps us from the safe haven that God offers each of us.

THOUGHTS TO PONDER

What qualities must Paul have had that would cause the Romans to listen to him? Why do you think God allowed the ship to be broken up by the waves?

PRAYER

God, we know you have revealed your will to each of us, and that the words of life are in it. We pray that we will discover your will and follow it to the end. Amen.

The Purpose behind Our Trials

ACTS 28:1–16, 30–31

28 When we were safe on land, we learned that the island was called Malta. [2]The people who lived there were very good to us. Because it was raining and very cold, they made a fire and welcomed all of us. [3]Paul gathered a pile of sticks and was putting them on the fire when a poisonous snake came out because of the heat and bit him on the hand. [4]The people living on the island saw the snake hanging from Paul's hand and said to each other, "This man must be a murderer! He did not die in the sea, but Justice does not want him to live." [5]But Paul shook the snake off into the fire and was not hurt. [6]The people thought that Paul would swell up or fall down dead. They waited and watched him for a long time, but nothing bad happened to him. So they changed their minds and said, "He is a god!"

[7]There were some fields around there owned by Publius, an important man on the island. He welcomed us into his home and was very good to us for three days. [8]Publius' father was sick with a fever and dysentery. Paul went to him, prayed, and put his hands on the man and healed him. [9]After this, all the other sick people on the island came to Paul, and he healed them, too. [10-11]The people on the island gave us many honors. When we were ready to leave, three months later, they gave us the things we needed.

We got on a ship from Alexandria that had stayed on the island during the winter. On the front of the ship was the sign of the twin gods. [12]We stopped at Syracuse for three days. [13]From there we sailed to Rhegium. The next day a wind began to blow from the south, and a day later we came to Puteoli. [14]We found some believers there who asked us to stay with them for a week. Finally, we came to Rome. [15]The believers in Rome heard that we were there and came out as far as the Market of Appius and the Three Inns to meet us. When Paul saw them, he was encouraged and thanked God.

[16]When we arrived at Rome, Paul was allowed to live alone, with the soldier who guarded him.

[30]Paul stayed two full years in his own rented house and welcomed all people who came to visit him. [31]He boldly preached about the kingdom of God and taught about the Lord Jesus Christ, and no one stopped him.

DEVOTION

WHEN I WRITE, I have a few favorite places. A coffee shop not too far from my campus. My cabin in the mountains. My favorite chair at home. I've tried airplanes, hotel rooms, and offices with interruptions, and the results just aren't the same.

One of the outcomes of Paul's time in Rome is that he had time to write to the churches and believers he loved so dearly. Sometimes called the Prison Letters, the list includes the Letter to Philemon and the letters to the churches at Ephesus, Philippi, and Colossae. He also wrote two Pastoral Letters to Timothy. The letters written during those two years are among of the richest source material we have today for how the church should operate and how individual Christians should live.

Whatever Paul's original goal may have been for wanting to take his message to Rome, he became the leading scholar and apologist for the Christian faith while there. He referred to himself commonly as a prisoner for Christ in these letters and was never ashamed of that circumstance (Ephesians 3:1; Philippians1:7; 2 Timothy 1:8). When you read the salutations of letters where Paul wrote of his longing to go places we know he would never again visit, you feel that his life had a greater good than simply traveling to the churches of his day. Through his letters, Paul traveled across time and oceans, and the words God gave to him speak to us today.

Perhaps there's a lesson for us today. Can I find a way to turn my unpleasant circumstances into something positive? Can I channel my disappointments into a way to serve others? Perhaps an apparent detour in life is actually a bridge to a new destination.

Paul endured beatings, imprisonment, shipwrecks, and more, yet found a way to turn his immediate situations into eternal good for others. He even found a way to live with a nagging physical problem after praying repeatedly to be healed, figuring that his weakness worked out to God's glory. Imagine having the power of healing yet having to live with a handicap and doing it without grumbling. All too often, my first reaction to an infinitely smaller problem is to blame God and pout like Jonah did when his vine wilted (Jonah 4).

Trials have a purpose. Our task is to follow the example of Paul in Rome and find that purpose.

THOUGHTS TO PONDER

What circumstances do you have in your life that can be turned into opportunity? How do we get the attitude of Paul in this passage?

PRAYER

God, we pray that our weaknesses will lead to opportunities. Open our eyes so we can see. Amen.

SPIRITUAL ANCESTORS

COLOSSIANS 4:5–18

⁵Be wise in the way you act with people who are not believers, making the most of every opportunity. ⁶When you talk, you should always be kind and pleasant so you will be able to answer everyone in the way you should.

⁷Tychicus is my dear brother in Christ and a faithful minister and servant with me in the Lord. He will tell you all the things that are happening to me. ⁸This is why I am sending him: so you may know how we are and he may encourage you. ⁹I send him with Onesimus, a faithful and dear brother in Christ, and one of your group. They will tell you all that has happened here.

¹⁰Aristarchus, a prisoner with me, and Mark, the cousin of Barnabas, greet you. (I have already told you what to do about Mark. If he comes, welcome him.) ¹¹Jesus, who is called Justus, also greets you. These are the only Jewish believers who work with me for the kingdom of God, and they have been a comfort to me.

¹²Epaphras, a servant of Jesus Christ, from your group, also greets you. He always prays for you that you will grow to be spiritually mature and have everything God wants for you. ¹³I know he has worked hard for you and the people in Laodicea and in Hierapolis. ¹⁴Demas and our dear friend Luke, the doctor, greet you.

¹⁵Greet the brothers and sisters in Laodicea. And greet Nympha and the church that meets in her house. ¹⁶After this letter is read to you, be sure it is also read to the church in Laodicea. And you read the letter that I wrote to Laodicea. ¹⁷Tell Archippus, "Be sure to finish the work the Lord gave you."

¹⁸I, Paul, greet you and write this with my own hand. Remember me in prison. Grace be with you.

DEVOTION

WHAT DO YOU SAY to a child or friend about to go off to college or walk down the aisle in marriage? What do you say to your aging parents or grandparents if you don't know when or if you will see them again? What do you say to your younger siblings, children, or grandchildren if you're the one in failing health?

Final words are important. They tell us what is important to the speaker. I've sent off more than twenty-five years worth of senior students from the Christian university where I teach the capstone course in our department, and I struggle over the words every year.

This is Paul's valedictory address. He's a prisoner in Rome; he'll never get out. The young churches he planted are now maturing and, like adolescents, some of them are pleasing him as a parent in Christ and some of them are disappointing him. Either way, Paul never fails to encourage.

So what was important to Paul? First, Paul knew that time is fleeting. He encouraged believers in both Colossae and Ephesus to not miss any opportunities to do good. Paul knew that an opportunity missed might never present itself again, and he wanted his children in the faith to know that it was their duty to make the most of every chance to serve God (Ephesians 5:15–16).

Second, even though the days were fleeting, people mattered more than appointments, and Paul mentioned many fellow believers in his last letters. There was Tychicus, the faithful minister now gladly willing to be Paul's postman to the churches in Ephesus, Colossae, and Laodicea (Ephesians 6:21). He was accompanied by Onesimus, the former runaway slave, now going home to his master Philemon, whom Paul urged to accept his former slave as a brother in Christ.

The story of John Mark, the cousin of Barnabas is perhaps one of the most touching in Scripture. As a young man, Mark had left Paul and Barnabas on their first missionary journey to return home (Acts 13:13). When Mark wanted to rejoin the two missionaries on their next journey, Paul and Barnabas disagreed so sharply that they decided to go separate ways (Acts 15:37–40). Paul took Silas as his traveling companion; Barnabas took Mark. But now Mark was a part of Paul's trusted inner circle. He'd been given a second chance and proven himself valuable.

There was Luke, the personal physician to Paul. There was Nympha, who was welcoming the church into her home, perhaps at some danger to herself. There was Epaphras, who was from the area of Colossae, but was now content to stay with Paul.

Their names and others are preserved for us. They're our spiritual ancestors, carrying the faith forward to generations ahead, including ours, and reminding us of our responsibility to carry the Good News forward one more generation.

They also remind me that while I might not be a Paul, perhaps I can be an Archippus, faithful in finishing the work given to me.

THOUGHTS TO PONDER

Who has given you a second chance in your life? Have you given a second chance to anyone? Who are your loyal friends? To whom are you loyal?

PRAYER

God, we pray that we will find our roles in your kingdom and fulfill them to the best of our ability for all of the days you give us. Amen.

From Slavery to Freedom

PHILEMON 1–21

[1]From Paul, a prisoner of Christ Jesus, and from Timothy, our brother.

To Philemon, our dear friend and worker with us; [2]to Apphia, our sister; to Archippus, a worker with us; and to the church that meets in your home:

[3]Grace and peace to you from God our Father and the Lord Jesus Christ.

[4]I always thank my God when I mention you in my prayers, [5]because I hear about the love you have for all God's holy people and the faith you have in the Lord Jesus. [6]I pray that the faith you share may make you understand every blessing we have in Christ. [7]I have great joy and comfort, my brother, because the love you have shown to God's people has refreshed them.

[8]So, in Christ, I could be bold and order you to do what is right. [9]But because I love you, I am pleading with you instead. I, Paul, an old man now and also a prisoner for Christ Jesus, [10]am pleading with you for my child Onesimus, who became my child while I was in prison. [11]In the past he was useless to you, but now he has become useful for both you and me.

[12]I am sending him back to you, and with him I am sending my own heart. [13]I wanted to keep him with me so that in your place he might help me while I am in prison for the Good News. [14]But I did not want to do anything without asking you first so that any good you do for me will be because you want to do it, not because I forced you. [15]Maybe Onesimus was separated from you for a short time so you could have him back forever— [16]no longer as a slave, but better than a slave, as a loved brother. I love him very much, but you will love him even more, both as a person and as a believer in the Lord.

[17]So if you consider me your partner, welcome Onesimus as you would welcome me. [18]If he has done anything wrong to you or if he owes you anything, charge that to me. [19]I, Paul, am writing this with my own hand. I will pay it back, and I will say nothing about what you owe me for your own life. [20]So, my brother, I ask that you do this for me in the Lord: Refresh my heart in Christ. [21]I write this letter, knowing that you will do what I ask you and even more.

DEVOTION

THE CONVERSION of the runaway slave Onesimus presented a problem for Paul. How could he convince the master of Onesimus to take back his errant slave, not as a troublemaker but as a brother in Christ?

The plea was necessary because Roman law did not limit how masters could treat their slaves. They could punish them and even kill them if they had been offended by them. History has accounts of miscreant slaves being used as human torches in the gardens of their masters, their burning bodies a message for any other would-be troublemakers.

The body of Christ was a delicate balance of Jews and Greeks, men and women, slaves and free. All were supposed to be equal in the Lord's church. It's a message Paul sent in his Letter to the Colossians: "In the new life there is no difference between Greeks and Jews, those who are circumcised and those who are not circumcised, or people who are foreigners, or Scythians. There is no difference between slaves and free people. But Christ is in all believers, and Christ is all that is important" (Colossians 3:11).

And Paul had addressed the problem of slaves and masters in his Letter to the Ephesians where he wrote, "Slaves, obey your masters here on earth with fear and respect and from a sincere heart, just as you obey Christ . . . Work as if you were serving the Lord, not as if you were serving only men and women. Remember that the Lord will give a reward to everyone, slave or free, for doing good. Masters, in the same way, be good to your slaves. Do not threaten them. Remember that the One who is your Master and their Master is in heaven, and he treats everyone alike" (Ephesians 6:5, 7–9).

Paul valued Onesimus as a man. He was given dignity in Christ. And any of us who have been slaves to sin know the value of being accepted as a brother or sister rather than a slave. The blood of Christ has loosed us from the shackles of our sin.

THOUGHTS TO PONDER

What do you think was the result of Paul's letter? Why would this personal letter of Paul's be preserved for us today? What is the universal theme taught by the story of Philemon and Onesimus?

PRAYER

God, we're thankful that you take us back even when we've been slaves to sin and allowed ourselves to be captured by the wiles of Satan. Please help us to live as your children, not as slaves of evil. Amen.

No More Tears

REVELATION 20:11—21:5

[11]Then I saw a great white throne and the One who was sitting on it. Earth and sky ran away from him and disappeared. [12]And I saw the dead, great and small, standing before the throne. Then books were opened, and the book of life was opened. The dead were judged by what they had done, which was written in the books. [13]The sea gave up the dead who were in it, and Death and Hades gave up the dead who were in them. Each person was judged by what he had done. [14]And Death and Hades were thrown into the lake of fire. The lake of fire is the second death. [15]And anyone whose name was not found written in the book of life was thrown into the lake of fire.

21 Then I saw a new heaven and a new earth. The first heaven and the first earth had disappeared, and there was no sea anymore. [2]And I saw the holy city, the new Jerusalem, coming down out of heaven from God. It was prepared like a bride dressed for her husband. [3]And I heard a loud voice from the throne, saying, "Now God's presence is with people, and he will live with them, and they will be his people. God himself will be with them and will be their God. [4]He will wipe away every tear from their eyes, and there will be no more death, sadness, crying, or pain, because all the old ways are gone."

[5]The One who was sitting on the throne said, "Look! I am making everything new!" Then he said, "Write this, because these words are true and can be trusted."

Devotion

I CRY MORE than I once did. Sad movies will do the trick. So will old photographs. Or hearing about the illness of a childhood friend. And perhaps the hardest of all, visiting an aging teacher or neighbor or relative who was so important to my upbringing with the knowledge deep down that our parting will be final this time.

And it's been a good year for crying, as I suppose every year in history has been. A tsunami of unprecedented strength. A record number of hurricanes, some the fiercest in history. Floods in one corner of the country and brushfires in another. Terrorists bombing or threatening to bomb. Conflict with no end in sight. And that's just a single year. Regardless of when you read this, I'm sure you'll be able to relate.

Perhaps it's my age, perhaps its events around me, but I take more and more comfort from this passage with each passing year, especially the part about no more crying. I was introduced to it in high school choir when one of the songs in our repertoire included a song about heaven that had a reading of Revelation 21:3–4 while the chorus hummed in the background. I was chosen to be the narrator. Let it be noted that my only solo in high school chorus was a speaking, not singing, role.

But the words stuck. There's a certain symmetry to the words: God will live with his people; they will be his people and he will be their God. No tears. No death. No sadness. No crying. No pain. I don't know if it sounded like paradise to an eighteen-year-old boy hoping to remember all the clauses in time to finish at the same time as the humming, but it sure sounds like paradise three decades later.

This brings us full circle in this book. In the introduction we talked about how the heart of any classic story is a central question. And the really classic stories have a happy ending. Dorothy *does* get home to Kansas. Alice *does* escape Wonderland. The burning question of the Bible—*Can the sons and daughters of Adam make it back to Eden?*—is now answered. Yes, they can.

But the story is still being written for this generation and yet to be written for generations to come. Each of us must write our own ending to the story. Will *you* make it back to the New Jerusalem described by John as a continual relationship with God? It's an important question because Scripture is clear that there are only two possible endings, and they stand in stark contrast in the passages above. Will your story end at Revelation 20—the lake of fire—or Revelation 21—the holy city? It's a choice you must make.

THOUGHTS TO PONDER

> In what ways is heaven like a "bride"? What image comes to mind for you? Why do you think that heaven is described as the absence of bad things—tears, sadness, etc.—rather than the presence of pleasant things—for instance, pleasure, harmony, etc.?

PRAYER

> God, we've read the great stories of your people in your Word. Let us add our own story to these many stories of faith as we prepare to join you for all eternity. Amen.

To experience more of God's life-changing Word, consider these titles by Thomas Nelson.

Life Connecting™ Bible:

The Life Connecting™ Bible—providing answers for today's generation!

Have you ever picked up a Bible, only to put it down moments later in frustration? Perhaps you were tripped up by all the "Thees" and "thous" and "whatsoevers." Or, if you were finally able to read a few lines, you wondered how it could possibly apply to your life, here in the 21st century.

Tackling tough issues that face modern readers—including career, family, money, and government—more than 1,100 supplemental sidebars demonstrate how God is still speaking to us through his Word, offering wisdom and guidance that apply to whatever life throws at us.

Special Features Include:
- Easy to read and understand, meaning-for-meaning translation—New Century Version®
- Introductions to the Old and New Testaments
- More than 1,100 enlightening Life Point notes on subjects such as work, money, integrity, relationships, and stress, demonstrating how the Bible is relevant to modern readers
- Introductions to each book, offering readers significant background information and main themes within the text
- A helpful index to topics in this Bible's Life Point notes referenced by page numbers

The Scriptures

Ever thought the Bible could read like a novel? Now that the easy-to-read New Century Version translation is available in a single column text setting, don't be surprised if you find yourself reading page after page of the stories in the Bible—stories of grace & hope, love & war, and mystery & redemption. Available in both hardcover and unique alligator-like bonded leather, this is a wonderfully fresh approach to reading the Bible! *The Scriptures* offers these great features:

- The complete Old and New Testaments in easy-to-understand vocabulary
- An introduction to the Bible, which shares how to get the most out of your reading
- A six-week reading plan, which spotlights some of the Bible's most important passages
- Helpful footnotes to enhance your understanding of people, places, terms, and ideas in the Bible
- Bible dictionary with concordance

The Last Eyewitness

The Voice, featuring writings from Chris Seay, Brian McLaren, Lauren Winner and others, is the product of the best minds in this emerging generation of Christian leaders. Together they are helping young people fall in love with the Scriptures. Instead of confining God's Word in the framework of biblical criticism, *The Voice* highlights the beauty of God's communication to us. This is a work by the most highly skilled voices of our time. In *The Voice* we hear the voice of God as clearly as when He first revealed His truth.

A beautiful retelling of the last week in the life of Jesus Christ (from John 13–21), this unique work captures the urgency of the last living disciple telling his students about the most significant event in history. The compelling story gives the reader the sense of being around a campfire with first century believers, hearing the story directly from John. So come into the story, smell the mixture of the salty air and billows of smoke floating from the bonfire and hear the Last Eyewitness.

About the Author

Dr. Philip Patterson is a Distinguished Professor of mass communication at Oklahoma Christian University where he has trained future journalists since 1981. He is also the president of the National Christian School Association, a position he has held since 1997.

The author of several books for the religious market, such as *Living Stones: Bedrock Truths for Quicksand Times,* Philip has specialized in writing on the effects of media and culture on children and lecturing to parent groups across the United States and in foreign countries including Canada, Australia and Austria. He is also the co-author of the nation's leading college textbook in media ethics entitled *Media Ethics: Issues and Cases,* now in its sixth edition. As a journalist, Dr. Patterson has recognized the effectiveness of storytelling in today's culture, and has brought this understanding to his work on the applications and devotional writings in *The Greatest Stories of the Bible.*

Philip and his wife, Linda, share a love of their three children—Amy, Andrew, and Joshua—the Christian school movement, and their cabin nestled in God's beautiful creation in the mountains of northern New Mexico where much of this writing was done.